UNBUILT AMERICA

UNBUILT

Forgotten Architecture in the United States from Thomas Jefferson to the Space Age

AMERICA

A Book by Alison Sky and Michelle Stone

Introduction by George R. Collins

McGraw-Hill Book Company
New York St. Louis San Francisco Auckland Bogotá Düsseldorf
Johannesburg London Madrid Mexico Montreal New Delhi
Panama Paris São Paulo Singapore Sydney Tokyo Toronto

The research and development of UNBUILT AMERICA has been made possible through grants from the **Graham Foundation for Advanced Studies in the Fine Arts**, the **Samuel H. Kress Foundation**, the **National Endowment for the Arts**, and the **Rockefeller Family Fund.**

Library of Congress Cataloging in Publication Data

Sky, Alison.
Unbuilt America.

Bibliography: p.
Includes index.
1. Architecture—United States—Designs and plans. 2. Architecture—United States—Sketch-books. I. Stone, Michelle, joint author. II. Title.
NA705.S55 720'.973 76-21735
ISBN 0-07-057760-9

234567890 HDBP 785432109876

Additional credit information may be found on page 302.

The editors for this book were Jeremy Robinson and Virginia Fechtmann, and the production supervisor was Frank P. Bellantoni. UNBUILT AMERICA was designed by Alison Sky and Michelle Stone. It was set in Optima by University Graphics, Inc.
It was printed by Halliday Lithograph Corporation and bound by The Book Press.

UNBUILT AMERICA is the seventh in an ongoing series of publications entitled ON SITE. This series deals with architecture and the environmental arts and is prepared by SITE, Inc., a certified public, non-profit arts and educational organization.

In the center of Fedora, that gray stone metropolis, stands a metal building with a crystal globe in every room. Looking into each globe, you see a blue city, the model of a different Fedora. These are the forms the city could have taken if, for one reason or another, it had not become what we see today. In every age someone, looking at Fedora as it was, imagined a way of making it the ideal city, but while he constructed his miniature model, Fedora was already no longer the same as before, and what had been until yesterday a possible future became only a toy in a glass globe.

The building with the globes is now Fedora's museum: every inhabitant visits it, chooses the city that corresponds to his desires, contemplates it, imagining his reflection in the medusa pond that would have collected the waters of the canal (if it had not been dried up), the view from the high canopied box along the avenue reserved for elephants (now banished from the city), the fun of sliding down the spiral, twisting minaret (which never found a pedestal from which to rise).

On the map of your empire, O Great Kahn, there must be room both for the big, stone Fedora and the little Fedoras in glass globes. Not because they are all equally real, but because all are only assumptions. The one contains what is accepted as necessary when it is not yet so; the others, what is imagined as possible and, a moment later, is possible no longer.

Italo Calvino, Invisible Cities.

PREFACE

There are very few who are not inspired by the poetic implications of forgotten dreams—the unknown quantity, the nostalgic significance of ideas, thoughts, circumstances which "might have been."

Through firsthand experience with frustrated ventures, lost competitions, unrealized commissions, a new world has materialized consisting of the unbuilt and subsequently overlooked or forgotten. A history of the United States in terms of what did not physically occur, UNBUILT AMERICA is a collection of unusual architectural proposals which, in most cases, were intended to be realized, were technically possible to realize when conceived, and yet, for a variety of reasons, remained unbuilt.

In the period of time spent developing this book, the most prevalent response concerning its contents has been—why hasn't a publication of this nature ever been done before? A whole subject area seems to have been rediscovered, or perhaps just a few prejudices swept away. The definition of architect is one who designs, draws up plans, and supervises the construction of buildings. A pioneer mentality mixed with functionalism and pragmatism has edited this definition to be: An architect is a builder. Following the logic of this progression: A builder (architect) who does not build is not an architect. In the intention to disregard or discredit that which did not "happen," a whole history has been passed over and ignored. The emphasis in the United States is shifting, by necessity, from construction to reconsideration, reclamation, recycling and redevelopment. The projects in UNBUILT AMERICA and the people who conceived them constitute this whole new wave of introspection.

The research for this book took us across the United States to meet with individuals and work in collections containing original documentation. For the most part architects were tremendously enthusiastic, and grateful for the interest expressed in projects which may have consumed years of work before being locked away in dusty file drawers. In certain cases, however, we were viewed with distrust and a fear that our attention would condemn a pending project forever to the ranks of the unbuildable. Several attempted to ward us off by insisting that they were far too busy with "real" projects to be concerned with dreams, and could not be bothered with preservation of the unrealized. The first half of this statement speaks for itself, and we hope was more defensive rationale than anything else; the second half, unfortunately represents a truth which is predominately evident.

Architectural drawings, it seems, have fared little better than unbuilt projects in the United States. We were pained to discover in many instances that the material had been destroyed—accidentally or purposefully one year, six months, or sometimes only several weeks prior to our arrival. Many firms systematically clean out their files, or, burdened with an unwanted historical collection, resent the very space it occupies. As a result the architectural legacy of the United States has all but been demolished. Those documents and drawings which have managed to survive have done so through the vision and valiant effort of a steadily growing group of individuals across the country.

Most gratifying was the time devoted to our project and access to original material afforded us by many generous and prominent historians, librarians, architects, artists, and their heirs. In only one or two instances were we refused access to this information. This was on both occasions in the case of an historical figure where the successor firm, perhaps envious of the attention paid to its eminent founder, has attempted to condemn this material to darkness wherever possible. We were able to circumnavigate this obstacle through other channels in all but one particular instance and as a result an unusual and previously unpublished project by Frederick Law Olmsted was unfortunately sacrificed.

In attempting to coordinate this highly visual collection of projects, ranging in date from the eighteenth through the twentieth centuries, we decided upon an alphabetical arrangement, according to the name of the designer. The collection begins with Thomas Jefferson and ends with Gerard O'Neill in the Space Age, the only two exceptions to the alphabetical order. Brief biographical notes accompany each section. These are provided merely to establish a point of reference in a juxtaposition of historical and contemporary figures, and are far too brief to be considered major additions to the body of information already known. The descriptions accompanying the projects are, wherever possible, quoted from the architect or artist, or from an authority on this person's work. We have always felt that the words of the person who conceived the idea are the most reliable documentation of the concept expressed.

Within this collection are many familiar historical and contemporary figures. In some cases the project included may fall into a classic category, such as the *Mile-High Skyscraper* by Frank Lloyd Wright, which was almost a unanimous choice in response to our request for suggestions of a favorite unbuilt work. In other instances, the projects included offer a complete surprise and new insight into the creative development of an individual, such as the *Flag Building* by William Adams Delano, which seems to be completely unfamiliar to even his own professional associates. Many of the designers represented will not be found in other architectural books, historical or contemporary. Rejected because they did not build, they were labeled as eccentrics or incompetent because they were involved with philosophical statements which either fell out of favor or never caught on. These were serious people and proposals such as Robert Stacy-Judd's search for an "All American Architecture" based on the ancient Mayan culture, Franklin Smith's plan for the "Aggrandisement of Washington, D.C.," Francisco Mujica's "Neo American Style," and the ideal "Hexagonal City Plan" developed by Charles Lamb. Their ideas were presented and published in Congressional journals, their models were in many instances displayed prominently in institutions such as the Patent Office and White House in Washington, D.C. Their ideas were debated and forgotten and are now included to be reconsidered as part of the fabric which has formed the creative development of the United States.

In addition to projects by individuals there are some major categories, also arranged alphabetically, dealing with: The Century of Progress Exposition (Chicago's second world's fair), Chicago Tribune Tower Competition, Crystal Palace Competition for New York, Cathedral of St. John the Divine Competition, Washington Monument Proposals and Competition. Aside from the fact that many people are not aware that these were initially competitions, several are important delineators of the development of our country and focal turning points in its architectural history. In addition, UNBUILT AMERICA contains the only published documentation of the United States Centennial Competition, and the only comprehensive documentation of planned United States Bicentennial Proposals.

In attempting to assemble a collection of this nature, we initially faced several major decisions. The material represented encompasses a highly subjective selection, drawn from enough documentation to easily fill several volumes. In many instances it would have been feasible to do an entire book on the projects of one or several of the individuals included.

Our conviction, however, from its inception, was that the first book broaching this vast area should function merely as an introduction. To do this effectively, we felt it necessary to present as many individuals and projects as clearly as possible. Through only a hint of what exists, serious attention could be focused on a reconsideration of the entire subject of unbuiltism.

Sky and Stone.

ACKNOWLEDGMENTS

The authors are deeply grateful to the many people who have assisted in the preparation of UNBUILT AMERICA.

None of this would have been possible without the foundations which have continuously supported our endeavors through the years, permitting us to bring our ideas to fruition. For their continued financial and moral support, we would like to express our gratitude to Mary Davis and the Samuel H. Kress Foundation; Bill N. Lacy and the National Endowment for the Arts; Carter Manny and the Graham Foundation for Advanced Studies in the Fine Arts; and Harold Snedcof and the Rockefeller Family Fund.

For their constant encouragement and innumerable suggestions that contributed towards developing and refining the central thesis of this book, our deepest appreciation goes to James Wines and to George R. Collins.

We are indebted to all the artists, architects, and their heirs, offices and archives who gave painstakingly of their time, and provided the material which made this book possible.

For their valuable insights at the onset of this project we would like to express our thanks to: John Coolidge, John D. Entenza, W. R. Hasbrouck, Henry-Russell Hitchcock, Richard Longstreth, Esther McCoy, Lewis Mumford, William Seale, and George Tatum.

We owe a debt of gratitude to Avery Library at Columbia University and Adolf K. Placzek, without whose cooperation this book might never have become a reality. We would like to thank the directors and staff of two additional archives with outstanding collections for permitting us access to their wealth of material: David Gebhard, Director, University Art Galleries, University of California at Santa Barbara and Warren A. Seamans, Director, The Historical Collections, Massachusetts Institute of Technology.

For sharing their collections of original material with us we are also indebted to: Anthony Barnard; Joan Capelin, Haines Lundberg and Waehler; Theresa Cederholm, Boston Public Library; Robert Judson Clark, Princeton University; Robert Clements; Jane B. Davies, Columbia University; Arthur Drexler, The Museum of Modern Art; Ferdinand Eiseman, Walker O. Cain Associates; Bob Ennis; Ludwig Glaeser, The Museum of Modern Art; Karl Gruppe; John F. Harbeson; Sinclair H. Hitchings, Boston Public Library; Lillian Kiesler; Alan K. Lathrop, University of Minnesota; John Maass; Randell L. Makinson, The Gamble House; Dion Neutra; George Pettengill; Ruth Shoneman, Burnham Library, The Art Institute of Chicago; George E. Thomas; Nathalia Wright, The University of Tennessee.

Among individuals and institutions who are gratefully remembered for providing suggestions, photographs and information are: Bill Alex; Sonja Bay, Art Library, Yale University; John Beach; David P. Becker, Houghton Library, Harvard University; Edith Lutyens Bel Geddes; Anthony M. Bond, The Historical Collections, MIT; Phyllis Braff, Nassau County Museum; Kenneth Cardwell, University of California at Berkeley; Jane A. Combs, The University of Texas at Austin; Joyce Cooper, Pennsylvania Hospital; Annette Fern, Burnham Library, The Art Institute of Chicago; James Goode, Smithsonian Institution; Sidney Katz; David H. Katzive, Philadelphia Museum of Art; Jean F. Leich; Mary Jane Lightbown, The Museum of Modern Art; Felicia Marsh; Ellwood C. Parry III, Columbia University; John Pflueger; John Poppeliers, The Park Service; Tom Slade, The National Trust; Richard L. Tooke, The Museum of Modern Art; Rafael Villamil; Robert M. Vogel, Smithsonian Institution; Barbara Wriston, The Art Institute of Chicago.

Additionally deserving of our thanks are our painstaking research and production team: Margaret Betz; Dennis Doordan; Juanita Ellias; Richard Hopkins; Susan McDonough; Carol Willis. Also to Fay Brugger and Pamela Wenzel for tackling the typing of our manuscript. A special thanks goes to Michael McDonough for assistance well beyond the call of duty. We are especially grateful to Jeremy Robinson and Virginia Fechtmann, our editors at McGraw-Hill, for making what could otherwise be a harrowing experience, a pleasant one. Also, to Marvin Kantor, Jeff Barrie, Mike Post and University Graphics for their patient co-operation in preparing this book for press.

And a final thanks to Richard Mauro, Suzan Wines and Emilio Sousa for keeping the faith.

CONTENTS

INTRODUCTION

America, the Land of Promise, has inspired countless persons to delineate their dreams. Artists, architects, planners, engineers, utopians, and a miscellany of inventors have, among them originated a panorama of an America that might have been but, for one reason or another, is not.

In the back offices of architects, in the depths of landscape paintings, in museum storage, in Patent Office files, and in the pages of magazines—old and new—linger the projects that have been brought together in this book. This has been done not only to create a vision of unbuilt America but also to explore in a general way what it means to be unbuilt.

The French author and critic Michel Ragon observed in his "Retrospective de la prospective architecturale": "It can be asked if the real history of architecture is not that of schemes which were never built; . . . and if there are not, in fact, two architectures, one of research and projects, the other of completed buildings—the second being but a weak echo of the first."

Ragon was speaking as a protagonist of the visionary in architecture. Actually, few of the projects assembled here are visionary or utopian. Most simply never came about; they were practical enough and seemed to be so certain to be built that it has been difficult to determine why they were not. Some, on the other hand, were hardly intended to be architecture in the usual sense. Nor would America necessarily have been the better if all of these projects had been carried out.

Shakespeare said in *The Tempest:* "These our actors . . . were all spirits and are melted into air, into thin air: . . . The cloud-capp'd towers, the gorgeous palaces, the solemn temples, the great globe itself . . . shall dissolve and . . . leave not a rack behind: We are such stuff as dreams are made of. . . ."

But the history of America is bound up with imperishable dreams and aspirations, with personal and social utopias, and until lately with a faith in infinite progress. One of the major groups of projects illustrated is precisely representative of this traditional faith: The Chicago Fair of 1933 was called "A Century of Progress" when things scarcely looked optimistic, and the designs stressing progress afforded a glimpse of a golden future. *"Oh beautiful for patriot dream that sees beyond the years. Thine alabaster cities gleam. . . ."*

* * *

For what reason have these projects collected here remained unfulfilled? There are almost an infinite number of explanations—many of which are so complex to determine and interpret that they can be only hinted at by terms such as "unbuilt," "unsuccessful entry," or "prototype" that have been used to characterize the project's status in the descriptions.

The term "unbuilt," where it has been used, means that it is certain that the design was never carried out although the reason for this is not precisely known. When queried, some living designers have been evasive about this information. Projects which are historically removed may simply be too sparsely documented or remain quite unresearched at the present time. Consider, for instance, one specific category of the unbuilt: the unsuccessful entries in a long-past competition. Information regarding these is often elusive. Any recognition at the time was usually reserved for the winning design or for the several leaders, even though the winner itself may never have been taken seriously by the authorities who may have subsequently erected a different structure entirely, ignoring their own competition. Unless the competition was famous—and many are very local examples of civic boosterism—the entries were probably not published in the kind of professional magazine that would provide the necessary data. Any extended description would perhaps have been printed in a local newspaper, but to find it would be seeking the needle in the haystack. So this is called "unsuccessful competition entry" which it patently is, but really does not tell much more than just "unbuilt."

The various reasons for unbuiltness range from positive to negative, albeit the terms positive and negative become ambiguous when one is speaking of the state of being unbuilt (which is here considered to be a "positive" situation). Something built would have lost its magic, and here would be considered to be "negative."

The major categories of unbuiltness would appear to be (1) not carried out as planned; (2) not really intended by its instigator to be "done"; and (3) begun but never completed. The first would be considered to be a negative situation (although the intention was positive), the second to be a positive situation (although the intention would appear quite negative), and the third to be half-and-half. The whole matter is, then, a bit like the mathematics of imaginary numbers, and it may be that our subject is quite appropriate for these times when complexity and contradiction are popular terms in architectural dialogue.

Perhaps it would be useful to categorize methodically the various explanations that have been isolated to describe why the designs presented have been left unbuilt, and to cite one or more examples of each class of explanation.

Simply not carried out

An obvious group of this category is the unsuccessful competition entry. Nearly a quarter of the projects illustrated were entries in various kinds of competitions. In nine cases the competition has been considered to be of sufficient historical importance to include the entries under the name of the competition. In other instances the fact that the designer was a contestant seemed of secondary interest, and the proposal is therefore listed under the name of its designer. For instance, Thomas Jefferson's 1792 design for the *President's House;* Horatio Greenough's design for the *Bunker Hill Monument* of 1825; Henry Hobson Richardson's *Town Hall* for Brookline, Massachusetts, in 1870; and Venturi & Rauch's *Bill-Ding-Board* for the National Football Hall of Fame in 1967, are all listed by the creator. It may be noted that Jefferson's house design lost, but he himself eventually *won*—moving into a White House designed by someone else. (His entry had been anonymous because he had actually organized the competition.)

The schemes that did not have a patron at their conception or never obtained one belong to a second distinct class. Characteristic examples would be the one thousand foot high *Centennial Tower* suggested by the engineering firm of Clarke Reeves & Company in 1874 for the coming Centennial Exhibition in Philadelphia, and the *Survival Dome* proposed by Doloris Holmes in 1970 to provide city dwellers a place to breathe uncontaminated air. Another instance is the *Underground House* designed by Malcolm Wells in 1964 that has inspired interest, but not a client at that time.

The projects that were not realizable due to circumstances with regard to scale, complexity, or cost create another class of the unbuilt. Many of the designs for towers included are examples of excessive scale, as was also the case of the art acropolis that sculptor George Grey Barnard proposed for northern Manhattan and for which he modeled his hundred foot high *Rainbow Arch.* Perhaps the scale was thought simply inappropriate, as President Wilson deemed the *Summer Capitol* that Jacques Benedict designed for him in the mountains of Colorado. With regard to over-complexity, the 1971 Bicentennial proposal of the architects Davis Brody & Associates for a *World Environmental Laboratory,* consisting of an inflated structure 40 stories in height and a mile-and-a-half across can be cited. It was said that the special materials involved could not be produced for a 1976 deadline. Excessive cost is often given as the reason for a project's languishing; this was the case with the building designed by William G. Preston for the abortive World's Fair in New York City in the 1880s, and also with the elaborate artificial environment for living things that Edward Barnes devised in 1974 for the Bronx Botanical Gardens.

Finally, and most commonly, the project—and the designer—may simply have been *frustrated.* The term "frustrated" is used here in its broadest sense, to describe situations ranging from petty material annoyance to the kind of devastating trauma that led Edgar Chambless to commit suicide in despair. Often frustration arises from difficulties concerning patrons. The patron may simply be lost, as in Lawrence Halprin's *Flushing Meadows Sports Park* which fell through when project advocate Thomas Hoving left his post as Parks Commissioner for the city. The patron's ideas about economics are an important factor: the project illustrated by Alice Aycock (1975), an intricate maze, was too much for the pocketbook of a Far Hills, New Jersey patron, whereas the penthouse barrio *Sky Alleys/Townhouses* that the Alley Friends of Philadelphia proposed to erect on top of the Academy House was rejected because it threatened to be so financially successful that the sale of the lower floors of the building would suffer. Often the patron may have had a change of heart, which was definitely the case in a number of proposals for the U.S. Bicentennial celebration—

especially those designs for the city of Philadelphia where both the city and the Federal government wavered back and forth for nearly a decade. Or again, there may have been a drastic change in the patron's financial circumstances before construction began. Such funding may have been expected from a public authority, as in the case of Konrad Wachsmann's *Air Force Hangar* of the early 1950s; or it may have been private as with the Carrère & Hastings cooperative housing *New Versailles* on Long Island in 1916. This was a gargantuan project which dropped so completely out of sight that neither the official Nassau County historian, the town clerk of Manhasset, nor a recent doctoral researcher has been able to find out anything further about it, although at the time it was considered to be "the biggest thing" undertaken by one of our most influential architectural firms. This is truly an example of Forgotten Architecture.

Another case of changing economic circumstances of the patron involves William Randolph Hearst who, believe it or not, had trouble with bank overdrafts—and with his project for Wyntoon, a Hearst castle in the mountains of California that was to incorporate a whole Castilian monastery looted stone by stone from Spain in the critical years of 1930–1931. The designer in this case, Julia Morgan, perhaps our most outstanding woman architect, became the innocent accomplice in one of the most heinous crimes against historic architecture.

The *frustration* may be bureaucratic. Architects and engineers are often engulfed with bureaucracy, and many of our projects were smothered by this in one way or another: for instance, the *Niagara Ship Canal.* Present members of the New York State Legislature tell us that they have never heard of this issue, but the fact is that the legislatures of all states bordering on the Great Lakes as well as our Federal government were beset from the 1790s until the early twentieth century with groups pressuring for and against the construction of a canal through United States territory that could handle ships as well as barges and circumvent the Falls. The print of the Niagara Gorge presented gives a bizarre view of ships in the proposed locks and was perhaps made in connection with the incorporation of a company set up in New York State in the mid-nineteenth-century on the basis of a survey done some twenty years earlier by the army engineer Capt. William G. Williams who apparently commissioned the print. Neither the State nor Congress ever came through on this project. A classic example of bureaucratic opacity is the case of the proposed extension for the *National Headquarters* of the American Institute of Architects in Washington, D.C., as designed by the architectural firm of Mitchell/Giurgola. Turned down repeatedly by the Washington Fine Arts Commission, in the end Mitchell/Giurgola simply threw in the towel. This is an instance of the *winning* design in a competition remaining unbuilt.

On the other hand, frustration may come in the form of resistance from the local community. One thinks of such aroused community consciousness as part of the urban scene of the 1960s, but in 1921 Ralph Adams Cram and his associate Arthur Shurcliff suffered a setback at the hands of local residents when they proposed that an island be made in the Charles River as a monument to the Armed Forces. Like the Philadelphia Schuylkill, the broad Charles River has long attracted oarsmen, designers, and developers as witnessed by the building up of Back Bay itself, which met no such resistance. Nor would it be supposed that the community would object to Athena Tacha's sensitive and topographically arranged riverbank steps of 1974—although they also remain unbuilt.

Another source of frustration for the designer may have come from the project being too radical aesthetically, technically, socially, or even politically. We are not surprised to find Bruce Goff's works considered aesthetically extreme, which is apparently why his design for *Giacomo's Motor Lodge* in Oklahoma was frustrated in 1964. Louis Christian Mullgardt's *Commercial Center* for Honolulu in 1917 was not carried out for similar reasons. Many of the projects illustrated may remain unfulfilled because of the radical technology required. Two recent examples of this are Oscar Newman's underground cities to be created by controlled nuclear explosion (1969), and Gerard O'Neill's system of building habitable environments in outer space, constructed in part from materials mined and ejected from the moon's surface—although O'Neill is quite sanguine about his scheme, and there have been large conferences devoted to it. As examples of projects unexecuted for reason of their social or political radicalism, we include utopian ideas such as Robert Owen's *New Harmony* of the 1820s and Paul Laffoley's *Atlantis Project* of 1973—although the latter would appear to be more radical technologically than politically.

Perhaps a project was frustrated for reason of changing physical circumstance, either human or material. The death of the patron or of the designer prevented execution of some plans. For instance, Lloyd Wright's grandiose *Twentieth Century Metropolitan Cathedral* for Los Angeles in 1931 was aborted by the death of the bishop of the diocese; the death of his patron in 1968 halted the *Dinsha House* that John Barrington Bayley was to construct. The death of an architect would presumably thwart any project that had been planned but was not yet underway. This circumstance explains the abandonment of John Wellborn Root's *Fine Arts Museum* designed in 1890 in anticipation of the World's Columbian Exposition of 1893, and Donn Barber's unusual multi-purpose *Broadway Temple* projected the year he died, 1925.

The change in use of the site intended for the structure has also frustrated many designs. Perhaps it was decided not to build and instead to modify or recycle an existing structure, as with the Howe & Lescaze proposal for New York's Museum of Modern Art in 1930. This is a circumstance that will probably become increasingly common in response to both the growing power of our Preservation/Restoration movement on the one hand, and the ascendancy of the No Growth (Club of Rome) mood on the other. The latter, a sort of neo-Malthusian pessimism whose statistics are challenged by optimists like Buckminster Fuller, might be said to be more Millenial than Bicentennial. The motto of its prophet, E. F. Schumacher, "Small is Beautiful," could conceivably be paraphrased as "Unbuilt is Beautiful," and we would then agree. But even proposals involving recycling can be frustrated: both of Jasper Ward's schemes to reuse an abandoned railroad bridge and a group of 24 grain silos miscarried when the structures that he had planned to convert were demolished, all or in part. Zion & Breen's planned adaptation of New York's Pennsylvania Station as a museum and galleria, developed to focus attention on the plight of historic landmarks met a similar fate when the station was torn down.

Perhaps something else was constructed on the site to serve the same purpose but with a less interesting or more conventional character, as was the case with Alan Lapidus's proposed *Olympic Tower* on Fifth Avenue in New York, designed, among other things, to preserve and reuse certain existing buildings by exercising "air rights." Or the property was put to other use, as presumably occurred when the land intended for A. J. Davis' 1834 Hudson River *Villa in the English Collegiate Style* was sold. These circumstances tend to be for economic rather than philosophical reasons. It was the simple change in the exposition site from Washington Park to Jackson Park which eliminated John Root's extravagant towering project dubbed the "Kremlin" for the Chicago Columbia Exposition.

Not really intended

Another category of unbuilt projects consists of those which the designer never intended to be executed. These are no less serious, just more abstract or ideal and not planned for specific circumstances, places, or people. Their unbuilt state is part of the original designer's intent and not due to the fact the particular design did not "win," or was out-scaled, under-patronized, un-sited, or frustrated by some historical occurrence. Many city or regional planning schemes, especially ideal ones, belong to this category. They are generalized or diagrammatic designs presumably applicable to a wide range of circumstances, but they would have to be particularized and detailed to be applied to any specific situation if they could be at all. An architect's design for a house or commercial building or even a monument is usually specific, with its details corresponding to a particular program of needs or uses. Architects solve problems: planners often play games (Knight's pawn to Queen 4 is the urban renewal game). Practicing architects may gamble with circumstances: planning students in some schools are taught by "game planning" to take the gamble out of gaming. Buckminster Fuller stages big public "World Games"; is he therefore a planner, architect, or engineer?

A great many of the unbuilt schemes that are illustrated have been called "prototypes." These are presumably perfected but generalized models designed to fulfill a certain purpose or purposes, and are not related to a specific place, patron, or time. An example of this would be patents, e.g., Buffington's *Skyscraper* that he did patent, inadvisably, in 1887. Similar, but more concerned with *system,* would be the Eggers Partnership's 1969 *Stratasystem* method for achieving humane urban renewal. An example of a very schematic design that was heavily loaded with meaning, intentions, and *Zeitgeist:* Frank Lloyd Wright's *Broadacre City* spanning the 1930s through the 1950s.

Related to the "prototype" are several other classes of projects which have been labeled "theoretical proposal," "hypothetical proposal," "feasibility study," and "study sketch." It should be noted that in most instances whatever term the designer used has been applied and that the designer may not have been aware of the fine semantic distinctions between the different labels. Assuming a "prototype" is a successful original on which duplicates might be patterned, the "theoretical proposal" is more in the nature of an experimental or exploratory model following up some theory: for instance, Siah Armajani's various towers, or the geometrical systems of Robert Le Ricolais and Anne Tyng—both of the latter having served as Louis Kahn's experimental geometers. Wright's *Broadacre City* would fall into this class had it not been enlarged upon in such detail during three decades of its designer's writings and rhetoric. A "hypothetical study" additionally borders on the visionary or improbable. Of course what is improbable to one person may not be to another, and semantic and semeiological problems arise. As examples: if Philip Johnson says that his *Third City Scheme* of 1961 for remodeling an existing city center was not a realistic proposal, perhaps it is correctly referred to as hypothetical, and certainly Raymond Hood's *Manhattan Bridge Lined with Apartment Houses* and Hugh Ferriss' *Apartments on Bridges* are of this same class (they assisted each other with these designs in 1929). A "feasibility study" is an effort to determine if a process works; an example being found in General Electric's *Bottom Fix* of 1969, an interconnected set of modular bathyspheres for underwater oceanic living. Perhaps if it were now available for installation it might better be called "prototype." John Johansen's *Leapfrog Housing* of 1967–1968 would also appear to have a tentative "feasibility" character as compared with the Eggers *Stratasystem* of the following year, packaged and on the market (although no buyers as yet). "Study sketches" are, for the most part, drawings of a spontaneous quality, for example, Frederick Kiesler's *Tooth House* series.

Several of these "not intended" unbuilts can be called visionary. A visionary scheme is new or radically different and deals with prime concerns or problems of its day, attempting to resolve them by means of a prototype, or model, or even possibly by extrapolating them into a hypothetical future. There are different types of visionary schemes. They may be utopian, i.e., social, as exemplified in the proposals of Robert Owen and Frank Lloyd Wright. They may be technological as several just discussed, a particular genre being science fiction, illustrated in the designs of Chesley Bonestell. They may be futuristic—either projecting decidedly into the future or deriving in part from Italian Futurism of the teens: both definitions of this are exemplified in the projects of Norman Bel Geddes and Hugh Ferriss. Or they are pure fantasy, either of retreat or of projection. Some of the "study sketches" such as Kiesler's, Oldenburg's, or Halprin's might be so denominated; William Beard's *American Museum* of 1873 and the Helmle/Corbett *King Solomon's Temple* of 1925 both have a quality of fantasy about them but could actually have been constructed. Generally speaking, pure fantasy in the unbuilt has been avoided in this collection. There is little or nothing among the projects that resembles that "retreat" into fantasy observed in the Expressionist architectural projects of the post-World War I years in Germany.

Another category of the non-intended is conceptual or idea architecture. Being an art, architecture naturally has a role in today's conceptual art movement, a movement which is perhaps most simply characterized as a tendency to eliminate the art object itself. As conceptual means unbuilt, almost by definition, some of the unbuilts we have here are inevitably conceptual architecture. Examples would include Ed Kienholz' enigmatic engraved plaques with their elaborate (and finger-printed) programs, and Superstudio, who state in their *Model for Total Urbanization,* "our projects and our actions leave ever further behind them the physical nature of architecture and design, and thus (through a circular form of logic) come ever nearer to architecture and design. . . ." The architectural philosopher Colin Rowe has suggested that conceptual architecture is "the presence of absence . . . something that quite simply *is not there.* Its specifications are there, but nothing more." (*NET Magazine,* 1975.)

The last situation of "not intended to be built" is an obvious one: the student project. Several of these have been included, and in addition a substantial group, spanning more than a half-century, drawn from the archives of the Massachusetts Institute of Technology, the first school of architecture in the U.S.A. Joseph Wythe's *Eagle Nest* was actually done immediately after his graduation from the University of Oklahoma in 1948 on the basis of a sketch he had made a few weeks earlier while daydreaming in a lecture course. William Turnbull's refurbishing of Ellis Island was developed as his master's thesis at Princeton University in 1959 as a monument to nineteenth-century emigration; students often elect idealizing and commemorative projects such as this. (Ellis Island, incidentally, has been surrounded by controversy for some time—witness Philip Johnson's proposal of 1966 when he was commissioned to resolve this situation in New York Harbor.)

None of the student projects mentioned here are particularly well known, but oddly enough some student designs, usually diploma or thesis projects, have been more influential in modern times than virtually any built structure which can be brought to mind. Tony Garnier's project for a *Cité Industrielle,* prepared in 1901–1904 while he was a *pensionnaire* at the French Academy in Rome, was enormously influential on both architecture and planning for the duration of the century. Ivan Leonidov's designs for the Lenin Institute in Moscow in 1927 are so universally considered the prototypical expression of Russian avant garde architecture of the 1920s that many are not aware that this was merely the diploma project of a graduating student.

Pending or unfinished

A number of the projects included can be considered unbuilt although construction had actually begun. Others, although not realized, can be considered to be "pending." Certainly nothing could be more frustrating than a commission partly underway and then modified beyond recognition, such as William Thornton's design for the *U.S. Capitol* and Robert Mills' for the *Washington Monument.* Alan Sonfist's *Time Landscape* for Finch College in New York City, in which he intended to turn back the clock by planting vegetation representative of various historical periods of Manhattan's development is another case in point; ironically, the College itself "withered" suddenly and went out of operation before he could get much past the planning stage. The term "pending" seems obvious as regards current (1975/1976) projects; however, there are also those of some years back that, while still presumably viable, seem to be indefinitely suspended, examples being Mario Ciampi's table-like *Executive Office Development* at San Mateo, California (1973), and *Myriad Gardens* with its exposed underground river in Oklahoma City by Conklin & Rossant (1972).

* * *

Although it has been noted that some of the projects in UNBUILT AMERICA were not intended to be part of that high—and formerly elitist—art which is called Architecture and that others are too schematic or too urbanistic to be termed "buildings," nearly all of them are physical in intent and structured in form and were to become part of the built environment. With few exceptions, it was the hope of the designers that these projects or something like them be "built" physically, i.e., they are architecture in the general sense that we assume that term to mean today.

And architecture is a recalcitrant art. There is a long process, fraught with many obstacles, before an architectural idea becomes a built reality—and sometimes the final product is actually a sorry distortion of the original intention. The difference between an architectural project and the end product—if indeed it ends up in other than a wastebasket—is of another order than, for instance, an unperformed piece of music or a painter's sketch and his finished canvas. Ragon, we see, has suggested that there are, in this sense, actually two distinct architectures and histories of architecture—the Built and the Unbuilt—and that, for reasons suggested, the history of the Unbuilt is as valid a history of the art of building. Plato and others might have agreed. As great a reality resides in that which a people believes, as in what they actually do or did. "The history of architecture," Ragon wrote, "closely resembles an absurd history of lost chances."

Certainly, unbuilt architecture can be as influential in history as that which has been built. An unbuilt design, if published and widely circulated, can be viewed by millions, while relatively few individuals other than the owner and users may ever visit an existing building, and photographs of it, although frequently published, may not really do justice to it. Tony Garnier's industrial city has been mentioned in this connection; some of his designs were actually constructed, but only scholars know which, and few of the scholars have ever visited them. So unbuilt architecture, like paper money, circulates widely and can give the impression that it is the real thing.

In fact, certain influential architectural moments in this century, such as Mies van der Rohe's "work" of the years 1919–1923, are characterized by an absence of built structures. And some leaders of the profession today such as the Smithsons in Britain and the Venturis in the United States received few commissions. Others—artists, planners, utopians, inventors mentioned previously—are not really interested in *building.* Progress, i.e., pathbreaking, is for some not achieved by experimenting as much as by theorizing; the experiment (the building) is merely to check the adequacy of the theories.

The present book could be said, then, to be an accurate sampling of the history of American architecture. As such it would seem to approach the level of better American poetry and fiction that plumbs our intrinsic character by suggesting our frustrations and fantasies in the struggle against the societal bonds into which our spirits are locked.

The complete history of architecture is therefore the history of both built and unbuilt, although no one ever seems to have thought of piecing together a thorough chronicle of the latter. The history of architecture is a weaving together of the variously textured strands of both these elements. Our capital city is a case in point: for a long time Washington, D. C., was just an idea—and a mess. It then became a physical reality without an underlying plan (or with frustrated plans like Downing's for the Mall). Then by chance someone found again the idea that lay behind it all (L'Enfant's Plan) and succeeded in unbuilding some of the wrongly built. When in the early 1960s they tried once again to straighten things out—this time on a regional scale—they called it the "Year 2000 Plan," which probably means never to be built. And so on . . .

* * *

Lest one think that Unbuiltism is strictly an American phenomenon—that the state of being "undone" can be associated exclusively with our new continent, a word should be said about the Unbuilt in world history.

Little study seems to have been made of the history of the unbuilt as such. Architectural projects and projections are generally scattered in with those constructed when an architect is written about or when an architectural history of a region, period, or style is published. Historians of city planning have, perforce, concentrated more on theoretical or unbuilt designs, and there are numerous studies of ideal and utopian projects of a physical kind for communities, cities, and regions. There have also been various serial publications dealing with architectural sketches, projects, competitions, and student designs. Michel Ragon wrote the short piece that we have mentioned in *Architecture: formes; fonctions* in 1968 at the height of the fad for visionary "research architecture." But the only book-length publication preceding this one that deals exclusively with the unbuilt as a phenomenon is Josef Ponten's *Architektur, die nicht gebaut wurde (Architecture that was not Built),* assembled with the aid of two colleagues in Berlin in 1925. It is a period piece and collector's item and was clearly influenced by the recent Expressionist fascination with vision and fantasy in architecture in Germany. It is mainly a picture book with a brief general text. While Ponten's illustrations included a number of visionary and ideal projects—Filarete, Leonardo da Vinci, Piranesi, Schinkel, etc.—many are simply façades, palaces, and parts of churches that were never carried out. Virtually all twentieth-century examples were drawn from Germany and not one American project was included.

Thus neither the history of worldwide Unbuilt nor of Unbuilt America has really ever been written, and we can make only tentative suggestions here with regard to the worldwide context. Our overview will be somewhat sketchy because it cannot deal with the entire history of the unbuilt but can only suggest those periods or moments in the history of architecture that are notable for the production of unbuilt designs.

We begin in ancient times with a rather curious category. These are structures that may or may not have once been built but have somehow passed into mythology or Biblical legend and then became the inspiration for later designs, which in turn usually remained unbuilt. They are hardy perennials, surviving in some cases into our own century.

The Tower of Babel: man's aspirations to build high—and broadly—striving up to heaven along an *axis mundi* (as the Romans called it) that would unite the two realms of heaven and earth. This desire has never totally disappeared, not merely because of man's technological ambitions with regard to construction, but also because of the need of man on earth to orient himself and relate his immediate daily built environment to his eternal cosmos by some type of cosmic pole or structure. More than two dozen of the designs illustrated here—from Jefferson to the present—are for towers or skyscrapers.

Noah's Ark: the idea of a completely self-sufficient and contained environment, floating and protective. At least a dozen of the contemporary examples are floating buildings, cities, or islands, and a number involve totally or partially artificial environments.

Solomon's Temple: a holy of holies whose architecture is omnipotent by virtue of its method of construction and the geometrical proportions of its units and members. Refer to the design by Helmle & Corbett in 1925 for the Philadelphia Sesquicentennial Exposition.

Atlantis: the prototypical utopia as described by Plato in his *Timaeus* and *Critias* and the inspiration for many utopian colonies and novels throughout history. See the *Atlantis Project,* a floating city, of 1973 by Paul Laffoley.

During the medieval period illuminated manuscripts were often illustrated with buildings, arches, canopies, and domes which were not copied from actual structures but were, so far as can be determined, unbuilt fantasies, although totally functional in the context in which they appear. Two such representations are holdovers from the ancient world (or Old Testament) and are especially meaningful. One is Babylon (a term derived from both the heathen city and the Tower of Babel) which represents the City of Man and human activity with its multiplicity of tongues and evils; the City of Rome after its fall came to be interchangeable with Babylon. The other is the City of God (of St. Augustine), identified with the Holy Jerusalem as described by John in the *Book of Revelations* and thus depicted four-square. This is perhaps what Will Insley is dealing with in his *One City* of 1975. No one wished to construct Babylon, naturally, although the Tower of Babel is sometimes illustrated being constructed; no one *could* build the City of God, of course, but it was presumed to exist in the mystical atmosphere of great urban cathedrals of the Gothic period. In the later Middle Ages, with occasional east-west travel, fantasies circulated about great buildings and cities in the other exotic earthly realm, a sense of which is evoked by Italo Calvino's recent fictional *Invisible Cities* (A Helen and Kurt Wolff Book, 1974).

In the Renaissance many books appeared on architecture modeled after that of the Roman Vitruvius and illustrated with buildings that we would refer to as "prototypes," some of which were, of course, much copied—that is, built. But also sketches appeared which we would call "hypothetical" or "theoretical," specifically in the notebooks of Leonardo and others. This proliferates in the Baroque period, particularly with the development of architectural competitions such as that for the façade of the Cathedral of Milan.

A triumphant moment for unbuilt architecture came in the late eighteenth century with the emergence of Romantic Classicism and the visionary designs of Ledoux, Boullée, Lequeu, Desprez, Piranesi, and the famous *Grand Prix* renderings. British architects and the Germans around Schinkel also produced countless project designs that make the early, contemporary, proposals in this book seem quite provincial by comparison.

During the nineteenth century many handbooks (like Durand's which was filled with unbuilt designs) were printed, and the École des Beaux Arts regularly turned out the extravagant proposals that have recently received much attention in the United States. Tony Garnier's *Cité Industrielle* which has been mentioned previously represents a very special instance of this tradition. Many of the late nineteenth-century designs in this book reflect their authors' training in Paris—which is noted in their biographical descriptions.

With regard to the development of innovative architecture in the twentieth century, certain special moments of Unbuiltism should be mentioned. Just after the turn of the century in Vienna the lavish *Wagnerschule* publications of the circle of Otto Wagner, containing many projects, appeared. The famous renderings of Antonio Sant'Elia were produced just before World War I, during which he was killed; his work was left unbuilt but nevertheless his legacy remains as the foundation of architectural Futurism. The next episode was the outburst of colorful sketches and ideas in Germany during the period of Architectural Expressionism, roughly 1918–1923. There are presently numerous publications dealing with this period—the one that comes closest to being a survey of Unbuilts (although many constructed buildings are also included) is *Architecture of Fantasy,* by Conrads, Sperlich, & Collins (Praeger, 1962). The decade 1920–1930 in Soviet Russia was another productive period when several competing radical groups of designers, generally designated as "Constructivists," developed many striking projects ranging from small art objects to regional plans, almost all of which—for reasons of resources, time, and political change—were never built. Some of them have, however, been extremely influential as prototypes, albeit outside the USSR.

During the late 1950s and early 1960s, there was an outburst of projects of a visionary nature on an international scale that is partly documented in this book. These have, in turn, been succeeded by the emergence of conceptual architecture already discussed.

We have, then, in a way come full circle. With contemporary conceptual art and architecture we are again at a point when the idea of a Tower of Babel, a Noah's Ark, or a Holy Jerusalem could mean more to us as idea than as built form. And, architecturally at least, we may gain a richer appreciation of the meaning of mythology.

* * *

Now let us shift our attention to the chronological history of unbuilt projects in the U.S.A. The projects illustrated in this book are drawn from almost every decade since the founding of the Republic. The fact that there are far fewer examples from before the late nineteenth century than from after that period does not mean that they were not assiduously sought. The fact is that during our country's first century the traces of unbuilt structures which remain are not on the whole terribly interesting. Except for occasional large competitions, it would seem that the unbuilt scheme was actually of less interest than a realized structure—which would explain why that which was built was built. Additionally, utopianism on this continent was largely social, not architectural, as evidenced when Robert Owen transported his own scale model for New Harmony with him from the old country and left it with President Adams as a gift and reminder.

From the mid-1890s on almost every year is represented by some design and occasionally by quantities of projects resulting from several large competitions—especially during the last decade with its plethora of U.S. Bicentennial proposals. If certain years are slim in quantity, it is because ruthless cutting was necessary to keep the anthology balanced in character and of manageable size. For reasons that are not entirely clear, since shortly before 1900 an enormous number of paper or visionary projects have been produced, emanating from all directions and certainly not just from architects. In American architecture, this may be in response to the establishment of professional architectural schools and the popularity of the Beaux Arts method of instruction, with the *esquisse,* etc. Architectural rendering as a calling burgeoned, as did architectural magazines with pages to fill, in which drawings by renderers such as Hugh Ferriss appeared also in advertisements. With the increase in licensed architects and their aspirations as professionals, American architects naturally became locked into their noble art, and when a recession hit the building trades, *projects* would be ground out instead of working drawings; if it had been possible to obtain *all* unbuilt projects there would probably be an increased number during economic depression.

The first half of this century, with its automobiles, airplanes, atom bombs, and the like, produced a technological optimism and a corresponding increase in physical schemes that are, perhaps, a counterpart to the quantities of social utopias in nineteenth-century America. This expansionist fervor early incorporated civic virtue, civic art, and progressive politics, and even cartoonists turned out images. (There were originally several humorous schemes including a vision of Newark, New Jersey, in 1984 in this book.) All sorts of people produced designs which were found not only in architectural magazines but also in general periodicals such as *Century Magazine.*

Visionary schemes that were couched in terms of advanced technology and science fiction seem to have peaked in the late 1960s. Today we find, on the one hand, a return to the vernacular: Roger Welch's proposal involving recall attempts to recreate a house that most people would probably want to forget—as a celebration for the Bicentennial. On the other hand, the technocrats have shifted from hardware to software, the artistic parallel to which is presumably the conceptual art previously mentioned. If the Idea, the program, is the most important thing, then why build at all? One can even, as Richard Haas does, make an unconstructed image of a once-built structure (Furness' bank) that was "unbuilded" (by demolition) appear on a remaining wall at the site where the disaster occurred. Looking ahead, then, in America, if we now value the Idea as much or more than the Thing, then the unbuilt will continue to flourish and before long a supplement to the present book will be called for.

* * *

"Oh, say, can you see . . ."? What would America look like, if all these dreams *had* been realized? What types of projects have been selected?

As the only efficient arrangement of these designs and their descriptions seemed to be alphabetical, it would be useful, perhaps, to make some general statements about what they represent and to cite particular examples of each type. A complete listing of each category described here can be consulted, of course, in the Index.

A great many of the schemes are suggestions for living quarters, either private or collective, although rather more of the latter. In the nineteenth century, houses tended generally to look like houses, so that the selection has been of designs by better known architects like Alexander Jackson Davis and Benjamin Henry Latrobe in unguarded moments, when the result was something especially sculptural or picturesque.

In the twentieth century, and especially in recent years, the house designs changed radically in character. They have been alluvial (Fiorenzoli), dental (Kiesler), translucent (Schindler), miniature (Simonds), troglodytic (Abraham), suspended (Wythe), to mention only a few additions to the repertoire of American types. Most of those depicted are of modest scale. Others were intended to be more palatial: Thomas Jefferson's *President's House* of 1792, Jacques Benedict's *Summer Capitol* of 1913, and the *Estate on an Island* by Louis Rosenburg, an MIT student, also 1913. A considerable variety of housing schemes has been suggested, ranging from Marion Mahoney's *Town of Hill Crystals* of 1943 in which she attempts to integrate structures into the rolling terrain of Texas, to Gerard O'Neill's slowly spinning sphere out at Point Lagrange 5 between Earth and Moon (1975) within which he hopes to create an artificial landscape that resembles some portion of the earth. Collective housing that is perhaps as technologically advanced as the latter but planned for *terra firma* would include Edgar Chambless' continuous self-building concrete house *Roadtown* of 1910, James Lambeth's *Solar Village* for the Ozarks of 1975, Paolo Soleri's mechanistically intricate city *3-D Jersey* of 1968–1970, and Richard Snibbe's *Handloser Project* of 1973 for a community suspended by cable and utilizing space age technology for construction.

The matter of relocation within large cities has been studied by a number of the designers. Both John Johansen and the Eggers Partnership tried to perfect painless relocation systems in the late 1960s when it had become obvious that current techniques were inhumane and were provoking protest. In the search for unoccupied urban sites, Hugh Ferriss and Raymond Hood in 1929 suggested building apartments on the bridges in Manhattan, as Louis Christian Mullgardt had proposed in 1924 for San Francisco and Jasper Ward was to advise for Louisville in 1968. The New York City problem is critical; for instance, for several decades there have been plans to convert former Welfare Island in the East River between Queens and Manhattan from institutional buildings into a residential New-Town-in-Town. In the early 1960s a major proposal, included here, was developed by Victor Gruen for what he would have renamed *East Island.* Gruen is a sensitive planner of the Viennese school, but his towering buildings and multilevel ground facilities are characteristic of the futuristic scaling that was then in vogue—as witnessed by the new city centers of Philadelphia and Montreal. Subsequently the site was remanded to the State Urban Development Corporation, renamed Roosevelt Island, and put under the general planning of Philip Johnson, with housing designed by José Luis Sert and John Johansen. Finally in 1974 an international competition was announced to develop a mixed income site, and some 250 entries were received embracing all the up-to-date housing technologies. In May 1976 an aerial tramway opened to the island. Juan Downey's visionary entry in the housing competition is illustrated here; four winners were selected, with 50 runners-up, but none of these will be constructed. Roosevelt Island is becoming another case of building, unbuilding, rebuilding, and the unbuilt.

Another popular unrealized structure is the public building: the town hall (Richardson, 1870), civic centers (Burnham, 1909, F. L. Wright, 1947, Wachsmann 1966–1967). In addition several entries for the competition for the U.S. Capitol in 1792 have been included.

Religious buildings include a number of projects from MIT, the Cathedral of St. John the Divine Competition in 1889, Lloyd Wright's cathedral of 1931, and Louis Kahn's synagogue of the 1960s. An interesting circumstance was the controversy that arose over the efforts by Barber (1925) and Hood (1927) to design churches into mixed-usage, income-producing urban complexes.

Other classic programs were for theaters, auditoria, and museums. Of these perhaps the most unusual are the bizarre entrance to an *American Museum of Art* in New York City proposed by William Beard in 1873, the gargantuan domed structure suggested as a museum by Rafael Guastavino in 1909, Eric Gugler's *Hall of American History* of 1953, and Reginald Malcolmson's *Natural Science Museum* of 1957–1958. Also related would be the unsuccessful entry by Bruce Goff for a *Cowboy Hall of Fame* in 1960 and the Venturi & Rauch design for the *Football Hall of Fame* in 1967 in New Brunswick, New Jersey, where the first intercollegiate game was played in 1869.

Another rather conventional class of project is the monument. Designs for monuments illustrated here include a number of famous competitions: the Bunker Hill Monument (Greenough, 1825); the different Washington Monument proposals; the competition for General Grant's Tomb in 1885; the Indianapolis Soldiers and Sailors Monument (Buffington, 1888). The Washington Monument designs, spanning several decades, are good indicators of changing style; the Romantic Classicism of Peter Force and Robert Mills confronts the almost contemporaneous Gothic Revival of Calvin Pollard, while the later ones are wildly Victorian. A number of other monuments seem to have been largely the initiative of their designers: Bruce Price, 1898; Cass Gilbert, 1919; Ralph Adams Cram, 1921; and William LeBaron Jenney. Unrealized designs for sculpture that could be considered monuments in a general sense are the *Surf Sculpture* of Herbert Bayer, the work of Isamu Noguchi, and the stepped forms of Hollein, Saret, and Tacha. Noguchi's are interesting in that they anticipate contemporary earth sculpture and one, that of 1947, was designed to be visible from the planet Mars.

As has been pointed out, a major source of unbuilt designs is the competition. Entries in some two dozen American competitions are presented in this book, of which the major ones are that in 1792 for the U.S. Capitol, 1852 for the New York City Crystal Palace, those for the Washington Monuments, 1873 for the Philadelphia Centennial Exhibition of 1876, 1885 for the General Grant Monument, 1889 for the Cathedral of St. John the Divine, 1922 for the Chicago Tribune Tower, 1928–1931 for the Century of Progress Exposition in Chicago, and a myriad for the U.S. Bicentennial. Nearly twenty other designs illustrated were submitted to competitions that have not been dealt with as such.

About a dozen expositions are represented by designs, including the Philadelphia Centennial of 1876, the World Columbian Exposition of 1893, and the Century of Progress Exposition of 1933. Nineteenth-century expositions were always associated with technical prowess, and a number of the extravaganzas that they provoked have already been noted.

As might be expected from what has been discussed previously, quite a few of the designs illustrated are concerned with cities, towns, and communities and their planning; a number of these tend to be highly schematic and regional in scope. This is particularly true of the linear plans which are of that form because of the special attention that they pay to transportation and the transmission of utilities and services. Examples include Edgar Chambless' *Roadtown* of 1910/1930 which is based on public rapid transit; Richard Neutra's *Rush City Reformed* of the 1920s, demonstrating sophisticated handling of the motor car; Reginald Malcolmson's *Metrolinear* of 1956 that makes downtown into a linear core; and the Michael Graves, Peter Eiseman team project of the 1960s, *New Jersey Corridor,* which adapts a number of these principles to the New Jersey section of the New York–Washington continuum. The *Polis* project developed by Cambridge Seven for the U.S. Bicentennial might also be considered a linear network following the same route.

An in-city plan of diagrammatic character is Charles R. Lamb's *Hexagonal Plan* for a large metropolis; this design, developed along the lines of the then current City Beautiful aesthetic, stresses the advantages of this particular geometric form for property values, local and express traffic, and the sectoring of the city into various uses.

Other city plans are of a smaller scale and more in the nature of city building—a concern with particular physical urban elements such as plazas, parks, city centers, and ornamental features: Jack Cosner's *Piazza d'Italia* of 1975 is a typical example, in this case combining tradition with ingenious hydraulic machinery.

A great number of the projects dealing with inner city specifics are as concerned with transportation as were the large linear plans. Highways, bridges, tunnels, terminals, multilevel traffic ways, moving sidewalks, and airports, as well as skyscrapers (which are essentially vertical transportation) frequently appear among the designs illustrated. Other proposals deal with the humanization of interstate highways, specifically the U.S. Bicentennial Nebraska projects of Saret, SITE, and Vandeberg.

Several of the bridges are designed to carry shops and dwellings—in two instances (Jasper Ward's *Big Four Bridge* and St. Florian's U.S. Bicentennial Project) in the tradition of Florence's Ponte Vecchio. Two others (Ferriss and Hood) anticipate recent ideas concerning megastructures—large support systems that have places within them like shelves on which full-scale urban structures can be built. The megastructure is popular; it has figured in Philadelphia Bicentennial proposals, in Paul Rudolph's *Graphic Arts Center* of 1967 for Lower Manhattan, and in Yona Friedman's *Slung City* for Park Avenue of 1969. Although Friedman's proposal may seem overwhelming and mechanistic, he, along with Hans Hollein and Paolo Soleri, is concerned with what Soleri defines as "miniaturization"—providing small-scale options for the individual.

Many projects are for new towns, and these take a variety of futuristic guises: containers with artificial atmospheres, underground structures, underwater habitats, floating cities and islands, and cities in the air.

Finally, as regards the typology of the projects that are illustrated, there is one additional factor to take into account, and that is the hand of the actual renderer of the design. Some of the projects are almost shorthand sketches or *bozzetti* by talented artists and architects: Oldenburg, Kiesler, Marsh, and Smithson. Others are paintings in which architectural elements have been included: Thomas Cole and Erastus Salisbury Field. Several are by individuals who were themselves famous renderers, as exemplified by Jules Guerin in the earlier City Beautiful period and Hugh Ferriss in the modernistic phase in American architecture that followed World War I. Ferriss additionally illustrated a number of projects included in this book that were not his own: for Barber, Hood, Gugler, Helmle, and Walker.

* * *

One can hardly draw a simple conclusion from such a large quantity of visual material. This essay has attempted several things: To analyze somewhat the phenomenon of "unbuiltism" and suggest the various circumstances that give rise to it in the American context. To make a few assertions concerning unbuiltism in world history. To discuss the chronology of American unbuiltism as documented in this volume and the categories of projects that are illustrated—i.e., what our country might look like if the unbuilt had been built.

Little has been said here about the matter of *style*—either of the objects illustrated in the projects or of the drawings and designs themselves. As regards the latter, the style of architectural drawings, not very much has ever been written. Just as architectural history has tended to concentrate on the built rather than the unbuilt, so architectural drawings have usually been studied for what they evidence about the built structures which they represent or which they, as studies, lead to, rather than for the intrinsic value of the drawings and renderings themselves as works of art.

Although the projects in this book are of a fairly representative chronological distribution from the time of Jefferson to the Space Age, they can hardly be expected to give us a very complete documentation of the economic and social history of the U.S.A. From the competitions and expositions that we have discussed one can see that the projects do touch on many high points in the history of our country. Also some of the low points are detectable; certain of the projects remained unrealized due to major historic crises. Jefferson's projects were apparently affected in two cases by the Revolutionary War, William Price and Carrère & Hastings by World War I, Bel Geddes and Larkin due to the Great Depression, and Maybeck's owing to the outbreak of World War II. These are, however, only the roughest of indicators because the reason for a design not being carried out even in times of economic crisis may be other than economic.

There are curious paradoxes to be found in this material as social documentation. For instance regarding the "Land of Promise," one would presume that, as America was the immigrating land par excellence, a considerable number of the unrealized designs would be by ambitious immigrants. The crews that laid the railways, the labor that built the commercial edifices, those workers whom we see in old photographs in their derbies (the nineteenth century construction helmets) were largely immigrants. Only experienced Italian masons could have turned out the lavish ornament that daily erodes and falls off our remarkable urban structures. Is New York, after all, not in fact the largest Italian city in the world?

However, less than one tenth of the designers of the projects that were found for this book are either immigrants or foreign born—although they do come from more than twenty different countries. Is unbuilt America, therefore, largely native American? Certainly unrealized designs do not seem to have been produced by members of the immigrant laboring class: this would indeed hardly have been expected for a variety of sociological and economic reasons. The data suggests that the designing of the unbuilt environment has actually been something of an elite activity. An immigrant architect like Leopold Eidlitz had received substantial technical education before leaving Europe, as did the master builder (not an architect by title) Rafael Guastavino. Most of those not born in America are from Austria, France, Germany, Italy, and the United Kingdom, precisely the locus of the dominant "Modern Movement" in architecture. Not one comes from farther east than western Russia and only three from below the equator—and these from Latin America. Also, many of the projects illustrated were produced by Americans who had acquired considerable training at the École des Beaux Arts in France; in fact, the increase in projects that has been mentioned previously would seem to be contemporaneous with the influx into the American architectural profession of individuals educated in Paris and other European cities.

One conclusion from this material might be, then, that while the vision of UNBUILT AMERICA has been sketched out largely by native Americans, these dreams and unfulfilled ideas are as much a part of general international Western culture as is the Republic itself, established as it was by revolutionary impulses like so many of our Unbuilts but fully in keeping with that humanistic tradition which traces its ancestry back at least to Plato—who in a certain sense produced one of the first great Unbuilts, itself a republic.

George R. Collins.

UNBUILT AMERICA

You see I am an enthusiast on the subjects of the arts. But it is an enthusiasm of which I am not ashamed, as its object is to improve the taste of my countrymen, to increase their reputation, to reconcile to them the respect of the world and procure them its praise.

Thomas Jefferson, Papers, VIII.

1. Monticello Observation Tower. Elevation.

Thomas Jefferson (Virginia 1743—Virginia 1826)
Education: William and Mary College.
Among Major Architectural Works: 1768–1809, the construction of his own home Monticello, Virginia; 1784–1786, Virginia State Capitol, Richmond (designed with French architect C. L. A. Clérisseau, based on the Maison Carrée at Nîmes); 1817–1825, planning and design of the University of Virginia, Charlottesville (which he called an "academical village"); 1821, Buckingham County Courthouse, Virginia; 1823, Charlotte County Courthouse, Virginia.

1776, drafted the Declaration of Independence; 1784–1789, U.S. Minister and Ambassador to France; 1801–1809, third President of the United States.

Observatory Towers—ca. 1770

Location: Monticello, Virginia.
Status: Unbuilt.

Studies for a "Georgian Steeple"

The towers, as the notes on the back indicate, were to have their columns and entablatures of "planks with only the projections cut" and the front windows "so much lower than those in the back" as to "direct the line of sight to Monticello." They were then to form objects in the landscape seen primarily from a given point of view, and, as intended to be seen from below, must have been for some nearby mountain.

The first would seem to be the earlier of the two, having the inadmissible overlapping of the pediment and columns, as well as columns coming down over voids. The expense of the second, even though it lacked the composite order, induced a suggestion for the omission of the Tuscan order. Finally there was added this note: "a Column will be preferable to anything else, it should be 200 f. high, & have a hollow of 5 f. in the center for stairs to run up on the top of the capitel a ballustrading."

Abridged from Fiske Kimball, **Thomas Jefferson Architect**, 1968.

2. Monticello Observation Tower. Elevation.

The Montalto Observatory—ca. 1776 –1778
Location: Montalto or High Mountain, known today as Patterson Mountain, Virginia.
Status: Interrupted by the Revolutionary War (?).
During the early stages of the Revolutionary War, Jefferson was deeply involved not only in Philadelphia with Continental Congress, but also in Williamsburg where, with a few others, he was rewriting the repressive colonial laws of Virginia and, at the same time, simplifying the Georgian "verbosity (and) their endless tautologies." In the midst of this creative legislative activity, he designed the most imaginative structure of his architectural career; an observatory tower 120′ high, composed of four setback cubes, the lower three serving as filled-in-foundation, solidly supporting the lofty observation room.

Jefferson's functional design began at the top with a minimal brick cube, 18′ × 18′ × 18′. Between 18″-thick walls he squeezed the 10′ × 15′, barrel-vaulted instrument and workroom; 3′ × 6′ windows opened in three directions; a fireplace was centered on the other wall, which enclosed his standard 30″-wide stairway, also vaulted.

According to Jefferson's written notation, the tower was intended for the summit of "Montalto" or High Mountain which he purchased 14 October 1777. This taller sister to "Monticello" is a rounded cone, now partially draped in woods, whose uniformly sloping sides are less tillable than those of Monticello. Montalto's promontory was less than a mile from the west portico of Monticello and rose more than 400′ higher, dominating the view toward the southwest. Obviously the crenellated, setback tower of cubes was designed to be seen from the house against the dramatic skyline, [and was to] serve primarily a practical, scientific purpose.

Abridged from Buford Pickens, *Journal of the Society of Architectural Historians*, XXXIV, December 1975.

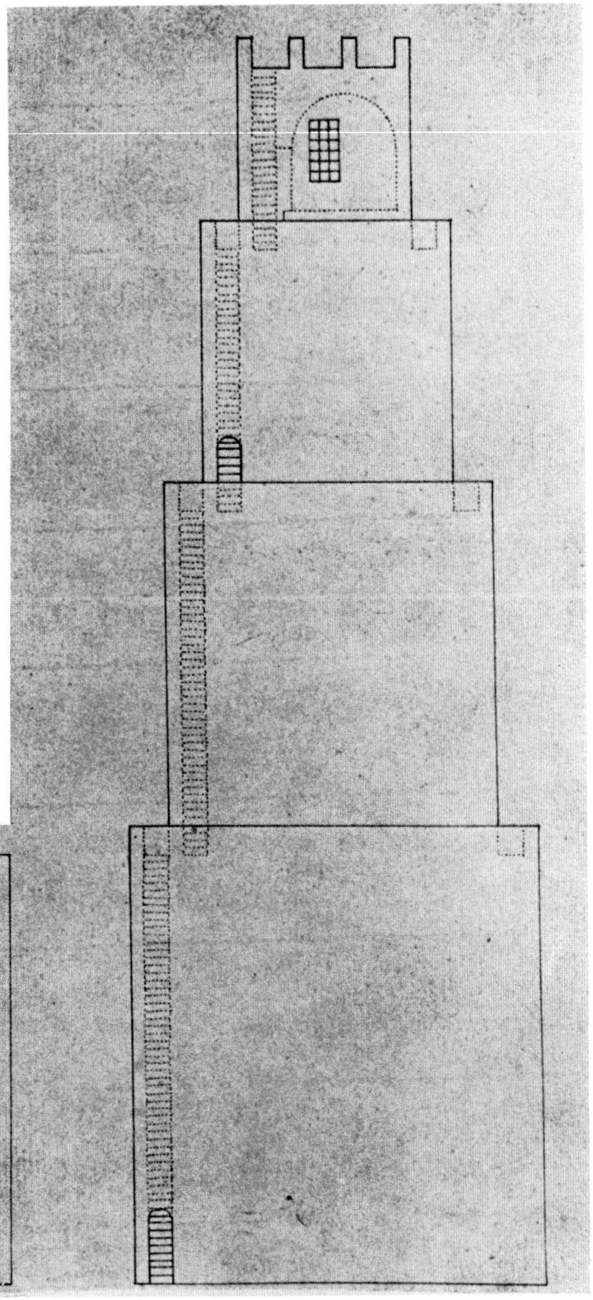
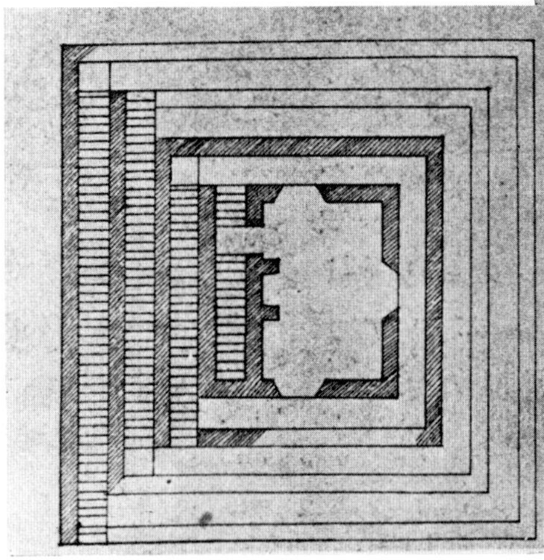

3. The Montalto Observatory. Plan and Elevation.

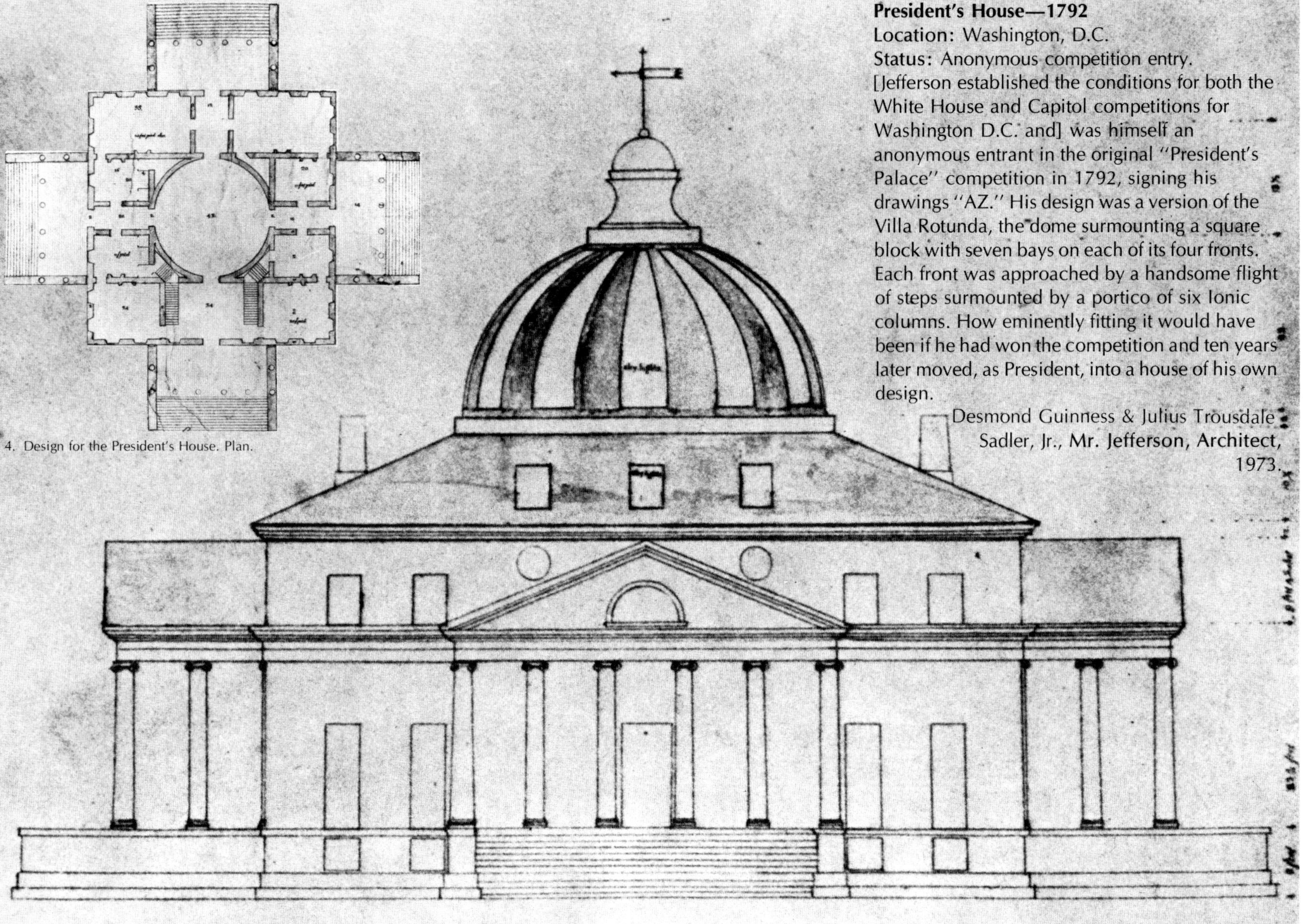

4. Design for the President's House. Plan.

President's House—1792
Location: Washington, D.C.
Status: Anonymous competition entry.

[Jefferson established the conditions for both the White House and Capitol competitions for Washington D.C. and] was himself an anonymous entrant in the original "President's Palace" competition in 1792, signing his drawings "AZ." His design was a version of the Villa Rotunda, the dome surmounting a square block with seven bays on each of its four fronts. Each front was approached by a handsome flight of steps surmounted by a portico of six Ionic columns. How eminently fitting it would have been if he had won the competition and ten years later moved, as President, into a house of his own design.

—Desmond Guinness & Julius Trousdale Sadler, Jr., **Mr. Jefferson, Architect,** 1973.

5. Design for the President's House. Elevation.

To the Space Age

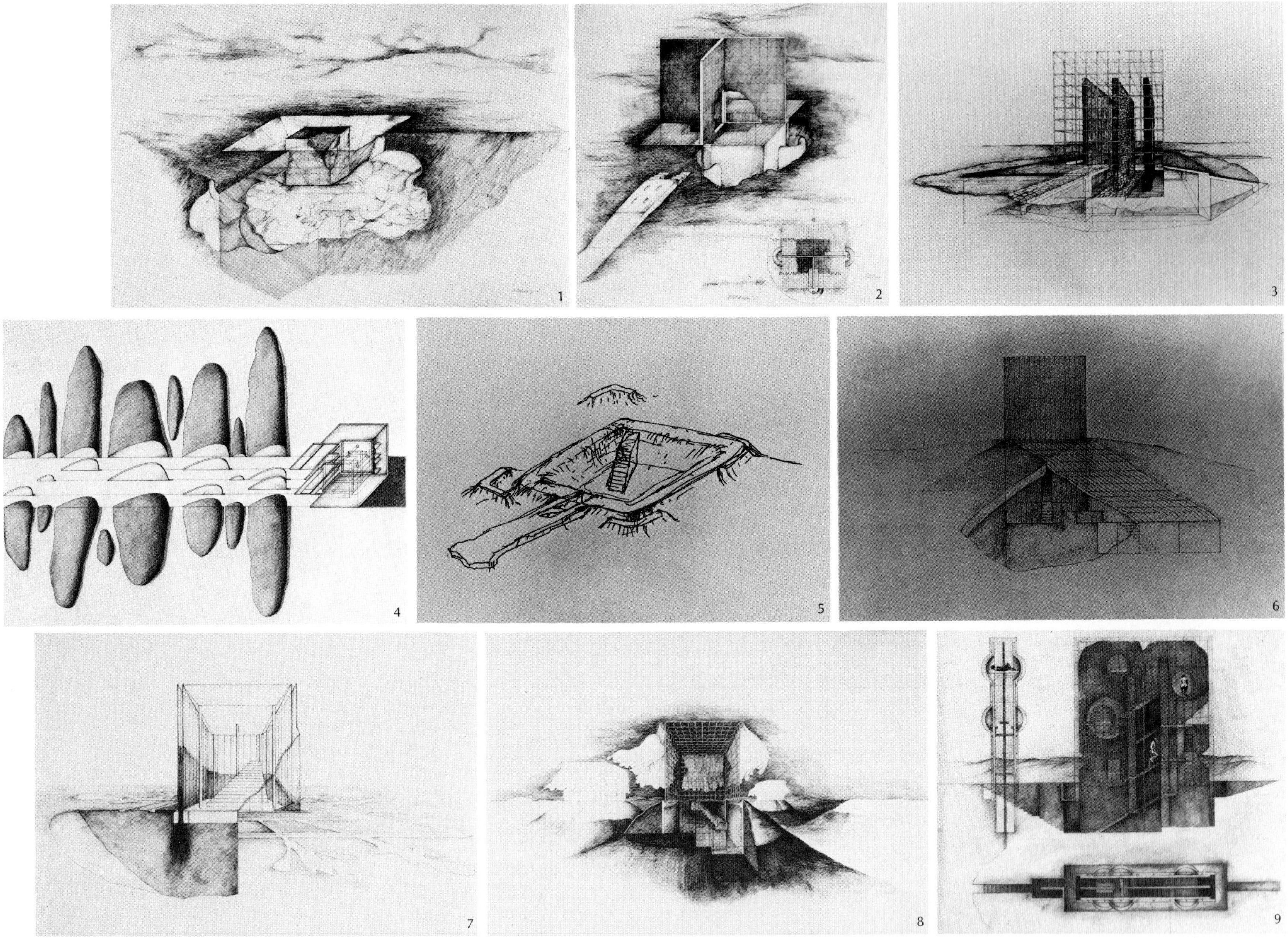

6–14 Nine Themes: 1. Earth-Cloud House 1970. 2. House with Three Rooms 1972. 3. House with Three Walls 1972. 4. House with Path 1972. 5. House with Permanent Shadow 1972. 6. House with Two Horizons 1973. 7. House with Flower Walls 1973. 8. House with Curtains 1971–1972. 9. House without Rooms 1974.

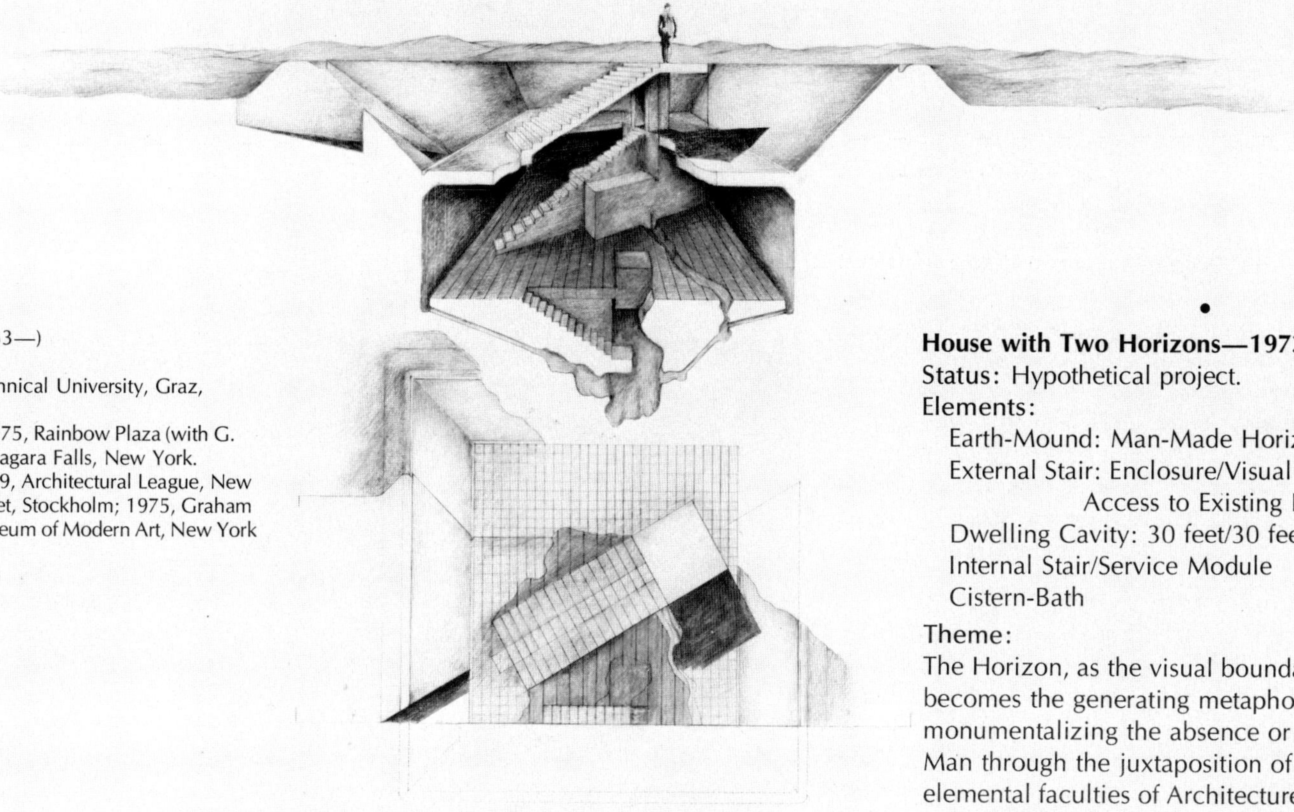

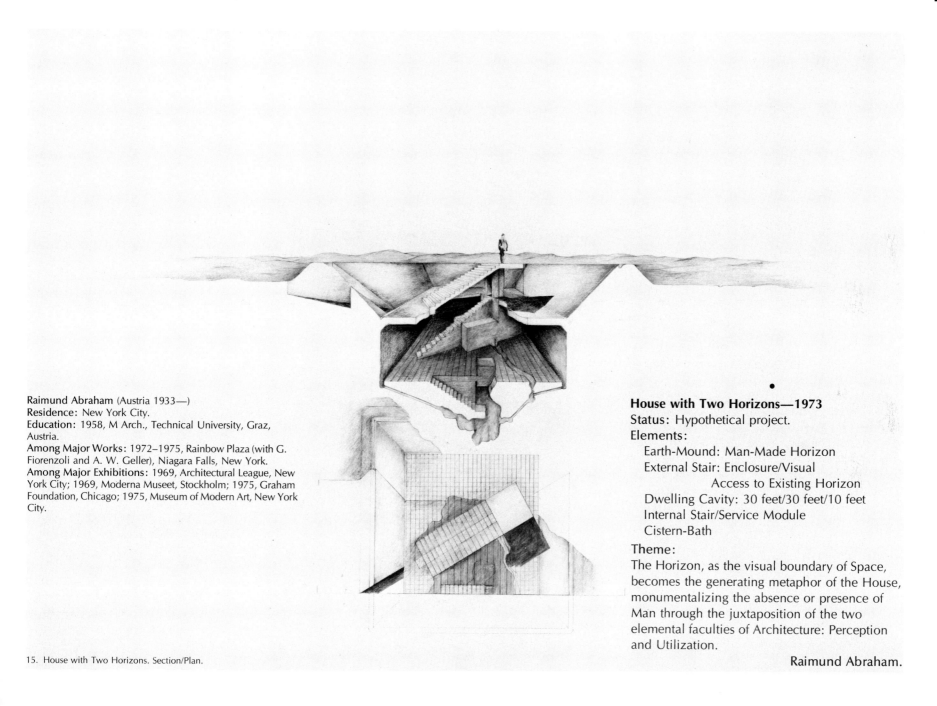

Raimund Abraham (Austria 1933—)
Residence: New York City.
Education: 1958, M Arch., Technical University, Graz, Austria.
Among Major Works: 1972–1975, Rainbow Plaza (with G. Fiorenzoli and A. W. Geller), Niagara Falls, New York.
Among Major Exhibitions: 1969, Architectural League, New York City; 1969, Moderna Museet, Stockholm; 1975, Graham Foundation, Chicago; 1975, Museum of Modern Art, New York City.

15. House with Two Horizons. Section/Plan.

House with Two Horizons—1973
Status: Hypothetical project.
Elements:
Earth-Mound: Man-Made Horizon
External Stair: Enclosure/Visual Access to Existing Horizon
Dwelling Cavity: 30 feet/30 feet/10 feet
Internal Stair/Service Module
Cistern-Bath
Theme:
The Horizon, as the visual boundary of Space, becomes the generating metaphor of the House, monumentalizing the absence or presence of Man through the juxtaposition of the two elemental faculties of Architecture: Perception and Utilization.

Raimund Abraham.

Alley Friends (established Philadelphia 1971—)
Principals: Richard Carl Stange and Alan Charles Johnson.
Among Major Works: Piedmont Virginia Community College, Charlottesville, Va.; planning of and participation in a four-site Minneapolis urban festival; design of several inflatable sculptures and buildings, including the Crystal Ball (greater Philadelphia Cultural Alliance's "Magic City") on JFK Plaza; 360-unit solar community, under construction.

Alley Friends was formed as a multidisciplinary design group practicing in the fields of architecture, city planning, interior and set design, and graphic and product design. Their work focuses on experimental solutions and recycled materials.

Sky Alleys/Townhouses—1973
Location: Philadelphia, on top of Academy House Building.
Status: Project was cancelled because there was more sales interest in the rooftop townhouses than in the luxury units on lower floors.
Though the Academy House itself is under construction, these last three floors have been deleted from the plans. In fact, they are not floors as such, but a pedestrian street faced with two-story and three-story townhouses. The tradition of residential alleys is very strong in Philadelphia and is as old as the city itself. In this case the units not only enjoy the intimacy of an alley but also a large-scale panorama of the city. As in any other street, circulation is open to the elements; all units therefore have exposure on at least two sides. User design of units was to be encouraged.
Alley Friends.

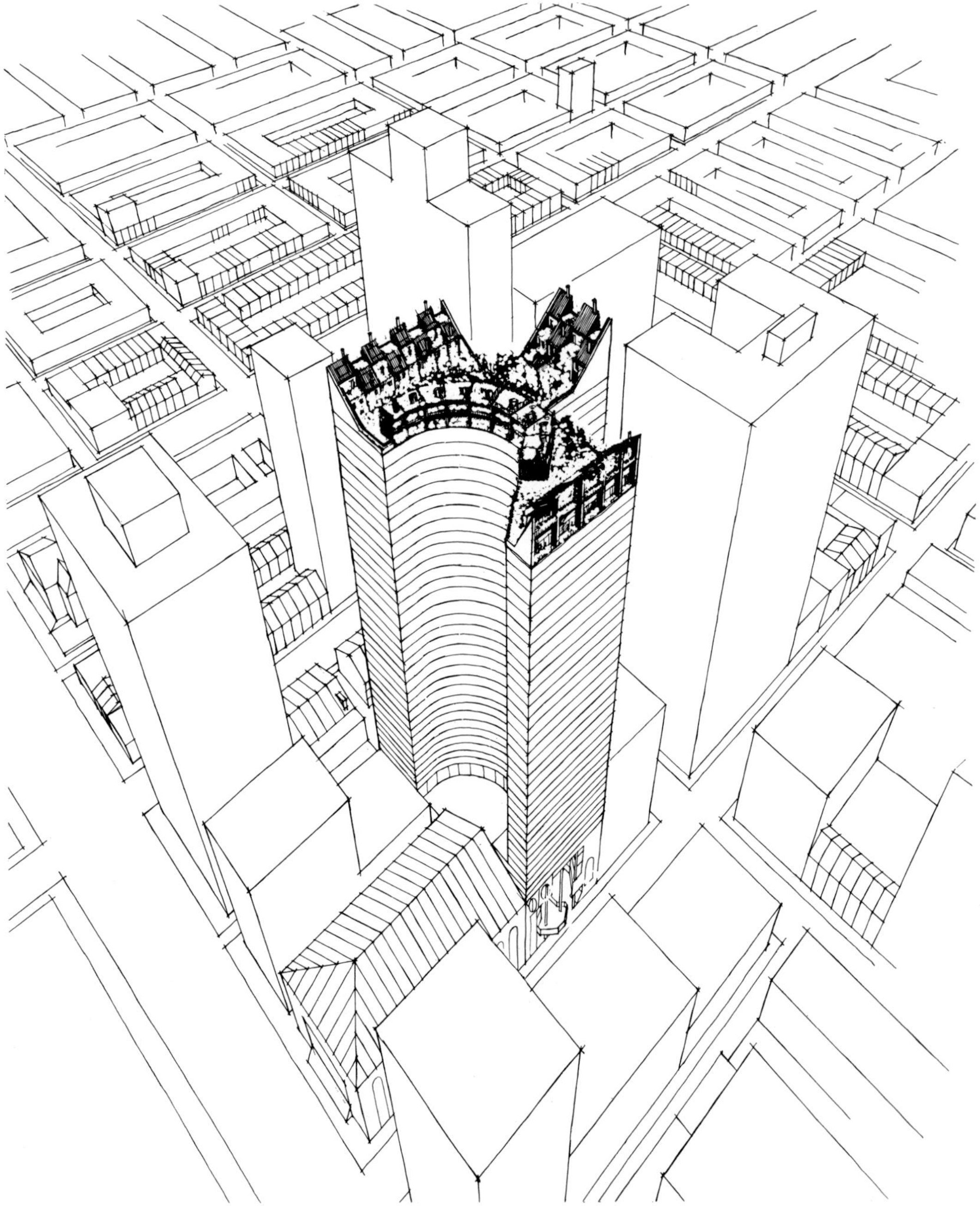

16. Sky Alleys/Townhouses. Aerial View.

17. First National Bank of Minneapolis. Hologram Tower.

Siah Armajani (United States 1939—)
Residence: Minneapolis, Minnesota.

The Ghost Tower—1969
Location: Minneapolis, Minnesota.
Status: Theoretical study.
Proposal to top an existing 382 foot tower (First Minneapolis Bank) by a 382 foot inverted holographic image of the same (First Minneapolis Bank) which will appear and disappear according to lighting conditions.

Description of the existing First Minneapolis Bank building: Site of the building occupies about half of the entire block bounded by Fifth and Sixth Streets and Marquette and Second Avenues in Minneapolis.

Architects and engineers—Holabird & Root, Chicago; Thorshov & Cerny, Inc., Minneapolis.

A total 50,000 cubic yards of dirt and rock were excavated for the basement and sub-basement. Fossils 400 to 500 million years old were found during the excavation. A historic capsule placed behind the cornerstone at Second Avenue and Sixth Street contains, among other things excerpts from President Eisenhower's 1956 speech on Centennial Plaza, site of the building; a U.S. half-dime minted in 1857, the year the Bank was founded; and a microfilmed copy of *The Falls Evening News* which was published in 1857.

Height of building is 382 feet. Length of building from Sixth Street towards Fifth Street, excluding Plaza, is 204 feet. Width of building is 198 feet (Second Avenue to Rand Tower). The building contains more than 5,100 tons of structural steel. More than 19,000 cubic yards of concrete were used.

Siah Armajani.

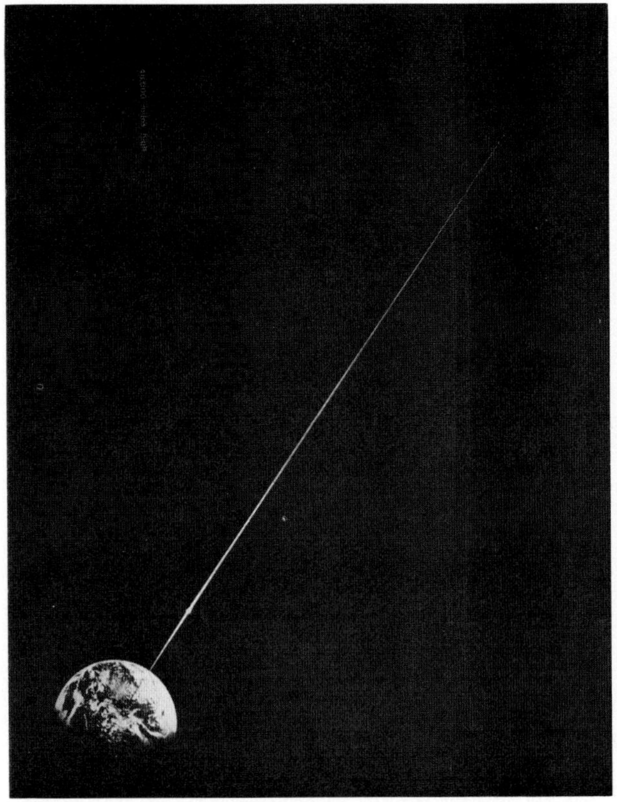

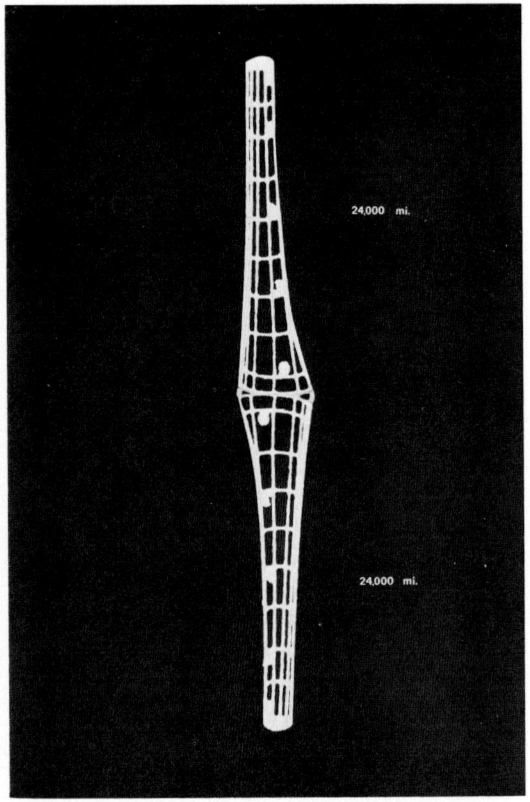

Left: 18. A Fairly Tall Tower—48,000 Miles High.
Right: 19. A Fairly Tall Tower. Detail.

A Fairly Tall Tower, 48,000 Miles High—1969
Location: Outer Space.
Status: Theoretical study.
Proposal to build a self-supporting tower suspended in space but anchored at one point to the earth (U.S.).

All synchronous satellites of the earth are located at the synchronous altitude. This altitude is about 24,000 miles above the earth's surface. It is the height above the surface of the earth at which the gravitational force of the earth just equals the centrifugal force tending to move an object away from the earth. Thus an object placed in orbit at this altitude tends to remain stationary over the earth's surface.

A cable suspended from the satellite toward the earth would tend to pull the satellite out of synchronous orbit since between the earth and the satellite the force of gravity exceeds the centrifugal force. If a cable of equal length and weight were hung from the satellite away from the earth it tends to pull the satellite out of synchronous orbit, away from the earth. The latter force is away from the earth since at altitudes above the synchronous orbit centrifugal force exceeds gravitational force. Using both cables causes equal and opposite forces.

The tower required could be composed of two structures joined at the synchronous orbit altitude . . . one reaching to the ground and the other out into space. To design such a tower certain assumptions are made:

Synchronous orbit altitude is 24,000 miles.
Tower cross section is circular.
Tower should be 48,000 miles high.
Tensile stress (force per unit area) should be constant along entire length of tower.

To keep tensile stress constant throughout the cable it is necessary that the cable be tapered with maximum cross-sectional area of the "top." Thus in the tower problem a tapered tower is anticipated with maximum radius at the synchronous orbital altitude.

Siah Armajani.

Alice Aycock (Pennsylvania 1946—)
Residence: New York City.
Education: 1964–1968 BA, Douglass College; 1968–1971 MA, Hunter College.
Among Exhibitions: 1971, the Aldrich Museum of Contemporary Art, Ridgefield, Conn.; 1972, the Museum of Modern Art, N.Y.C.; 1975, Biennale de Paris, Museum of Modern Art, Paris; 1975, "Projects, in Nature," Far Hills, N.J.; 1975, "Labyrinth," Philadelphia College of Art.

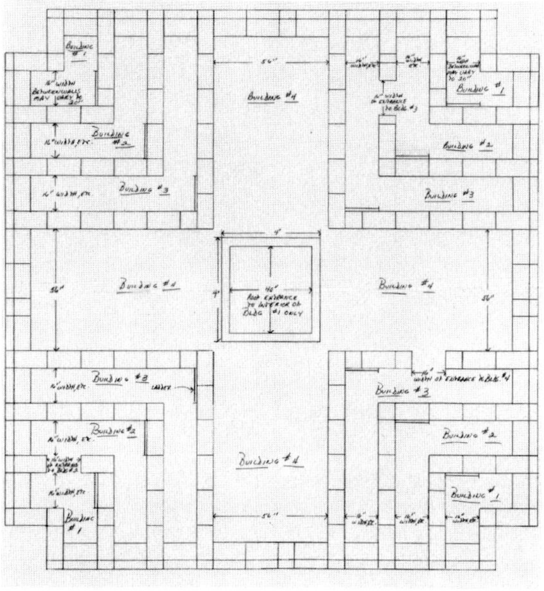

20. Project for a Vertical Maze. Plan.

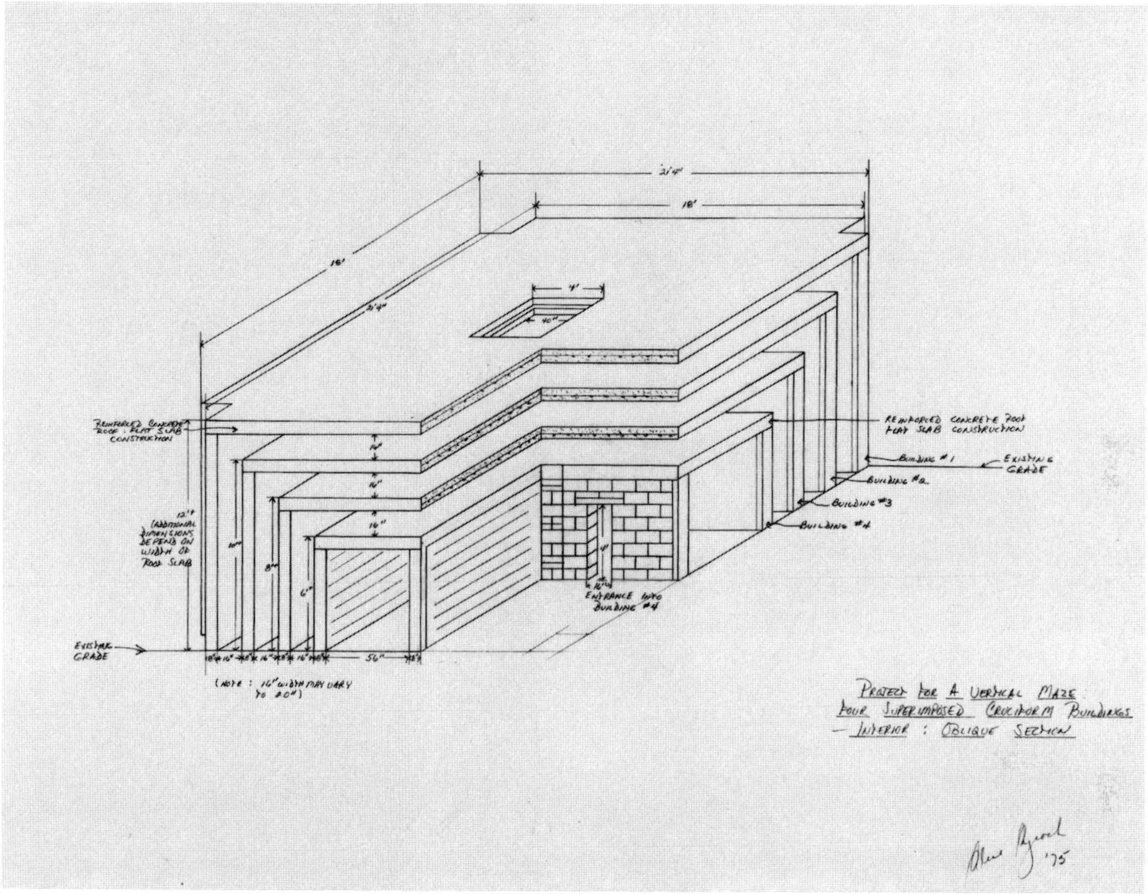

21. Project for a Vertical Maze. Oblique Section.

Project for a Vertical Maze—1975
Location: Far Hills, New Jersey.
Status: Exceeded available resources.
Four Superimposed Cruciform Buildings: Construct four concrete buildings one inside the other so that the floor of building no. 1 is the roof of building no. 2, and so on. All four buildings share a common wall on four sides. They diminish in height and in width at the corners from a maximum of 12 feet high and 18 feet wide to a minimum of 6 feet high and 56 inches wide. The crawl space between floors and corner walls is 16 inches on the plans but may be widened to 20 inches. Small openings in the walls will let in light from the outside. The structure is entered through an opening in the roof of building no. 1. One then crawls across the roof of building no. 2, and climbs down the four corners searching for the entrance to building no. 2. This procedure of climbing down the corners of each building and across the roofs is repeated until the innermost building has been reached.

Alice Aycock.

Donn Barber (Washington, D.C. 1871–New York City 1925)
Education: 1893, Yale University; 1893–1894, special course in architecture at Columbia University; 1898, École des Beaux Arts, Paris.
Among Major Works: New York Cotton Exchange; Randall's Island Hospital Group, N.Y.C.; Central Branch Y.W.C.A., N.Y.C.; Department of Justice Building, Washington, D.C.; Connecticut State Supreme Court Building, Hartford.

Donn Barber, one of the originators of the atelier concept in the United States, was head of the Atelier Donn Barber. He was president of the Society of Beaux Arts from 1909 to 1910, and editor of *The New York Architect* for four years.

Broadway Temple—ca.1925
Location: New York City.
Status: Unbuilt due to death of architect.

The Broadway Temple marks the beginning of the practice of building accommodations for religious purposes into structures that have a large part of the space devoted to uses which make the church self-supporting, and perhaps even profit-producing. Figures prepared by a real estate expert show that this building can yield a profit through the rentals received from apartments, hotel rooms and stores in the building, and it was intended to devote the profit earned in this way to the advancement of religious causes and to philanthropy.

The architect's solution places the church auditorium and its related rooms in the lower part of a great central tower, the upper part of which is occupied by a complete modern hotel. The stories between the auditorium and the bottom of the hotel provide the gymnasium with its swimming pool, placed where it is convenient for use in connection with both the church and the hotel. Flanking the central tower are two complete and independent apartment houses. Barber had hoped to make the Broadway Temple, one of his last great architectural dreams, his crowning achievement.

Abridged from *Pencil Points,* VI, December 1925.

22. Proposed Broadway Temple. Perspective. Rendering by Hugh Ferriss.

23. The Rainbow Arch. A One Hundred Foot Arch to Peace. Model with Painted Rainbow.

George Grey Barnard (Pennsylvania 1863—New York 1938)
Education: Art Institute of Chicago; 1880s, École des Beaux Arts, Paris.
Among Major Sculptures: 1894, "Struggle of the Two Natures in Man"; ca. 1900, "Pan"; 1911, "Love and Labor," "The Burden of Life."

Rainbow Arch—ca. 1920
Location: New York City.
Status: Unbuilt due to lack of funds.
Through his declining years the increasingly visionary Barnard's great repute dwindled in an art world in which change was rampant and most of it, as he viewed it, deplorable. Moreover, he channeled his creative efforts and resources into the accomplishment of one overriding desire—to give to the world a vast and noble monument to Peace. The grand scheme that he first proposed, one that would have enlisted for a decade the services of a host of artists—estimated at a half a hundred each of sculptors, painters, architects and other craftsmen—was the transformation of "God's Thumb," the rugged northern promontory of Manhattan Island, into an "art acropolis" crowned with a splendidly enriched monumental ensemble. Eventually it was Barnard alone who toiled through ten years on one of its elements, the hundred-foot high "Rainbow Arch," to be dedicated to the mothers of those sacrificed in war. The full scale model of the arch, with its flanking multi-figured groups in plaster, for a while drew crowds to the abandoned powerhouse where it was set up for viewing; but Barnard's death mercifully prevented his seeing what he had hoped would be his crowning work end, like peace itself, as a shattered dream, the model dismantled and the plasters in time allowed to disintegrate.

Excerpted from Harold E. Dickson, George Grey Barnard, Centenary Exhibition, 1964.

Edward Larrabee Barnes (Chicago 1915—)
Residence: New York City.
Education: 1938, BS, Harvard University; 1942, M Arch., Harvard Graduate School of Design.
Among Major Works: Neiman-Marcus Shopping Center, Fort Worth, Texas; U.S. Consulate, Tabriz, Iran; Underground Cross Campus Library, Yale University, New Haven, Conn.; Walker Art Center, Minneapolis, Minn.; IBM Office Tower, N.Y.C.

Plants and Man Building—1974
Location: Botanical Garden, Bronx, New York.
Status: Unbuilt due to lack of funds.
Additional Credit: Marcia Previti, hexagonal concept; Alistair Bevington, associate.
The Plants and Man building is composed of hexagonal modules, roughly forty-five feet across, that may be grouped together to house the biomes [''a complex of communities characterized by a distinctive type of vegetation and maintained under the climatic conditions of the region''—Random House Dictionary, 1967] in chambers of any desired size. Unlike the traditional dome or shed-roof greenhouse where plant growth is often confined, the walls of these chambers rise vertically to whatever height is required for plants. Thus, the alpine biome would have one hexagonal module twenty feet high, and the veldt module would have three modules fifty feet high. The rain forest biome, with its many tiered woodland life, would be housed in a chamber of seven modules rising to ninety feet. Each biome would have its own indigenous climate.

The asymmetrical, apparently informal grouping of these biomes reflects subtle internal and external requirements. Biomes that require shade hide behind those that need full sun. The total cluster is set in a grove of sweetgum and oak trees. The undulating glass structure is not a closed prismatic form. It interlocks with nature and the surrounding landscape.

The supporting structure is a system of slender pipe columns, tubular beams, and diagonal tension rods. The frame is of Cor-ten steel, and the large sheets of glass are tempered to avoid breakage. The hexagonal roof of each module slopes to a central gutter and internal downspout. Roof water will be stored in a cistern for use in the building. The climate for each biome is provided first of all by the greenhouse effect of the building itself. Photosynthesis, essential to all plant growth, is accomplished naturally by sunlight through the glass, not artificially by electric light. Some biomes, such as the desert southwest, need little mechanical assistance since the plants tolerate heat in daytime and near freezing temperatures at night. Because the biomes cluster together, it is possible to transfer unneeded heat from cold climates to hot climates. The tundra, darkened in winter months, will have its soil frozen (from below) to simulate permafrost, while at the same time the tropical rain forest will require constant warm temperature. The requirements of one biome will be balanced against the other. Ample outside ventilation will be provided through hopper vents located in the vertical glass walls. Necessary seasonal screening will be provided by synthetic fiber net ''sails'' inside the glass.

Edward Larrabee Barnes.

Above: 24. Plants and Man Building. Site Plan.
Below: 25. Plants and Man Building. Model.

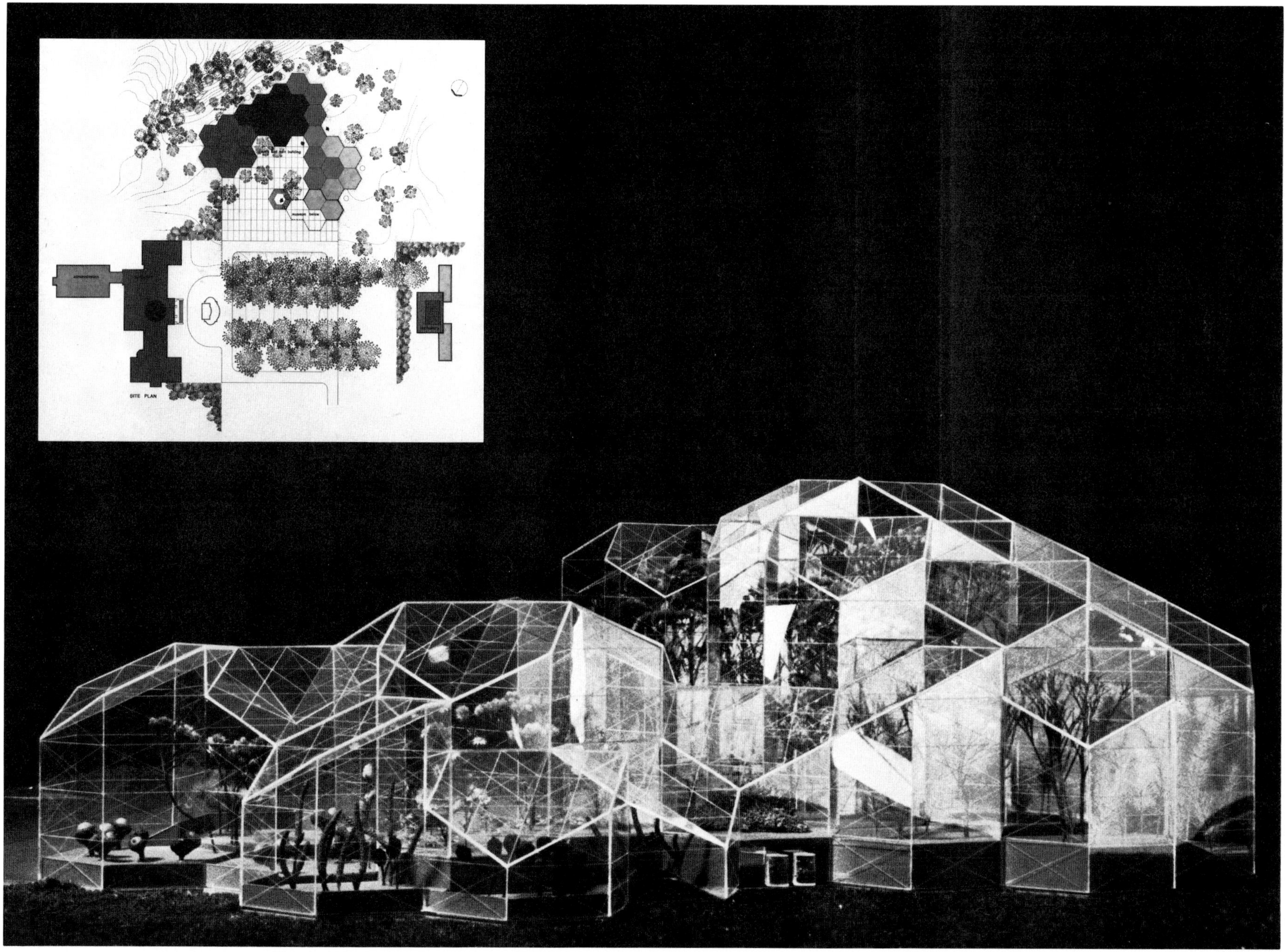
SITE PLAN

Herbert Bayer (Austria 1900—)
Residence: Aspen, Colorado.
Education: 1921–1923, student at the Weimar Bauhaus in typography and in the mural workshop of Wassily Kandinsky.
Among Published Works: 1938, *Bauhaus 1919–1928* (co-editor); 1953, *World Geo-Graphic Atlas* (editor); 1961, *Herbert Bayer Book of Drawings.*

From 1925 to 1928, master of graphic design and printing workshop at the Dessau Bauhaus; 1956–1965, Chairman, design department of the Container Corporation of America; since 1964, consultant and architect, Aspen Institute for Humanistic Studies; since 1966, art and design consultant, Atlantic Richfield Company.

Herbert Bayer believes in a totality of art and design integrated with the life of our time. He has collaborated extensively with industry and other institutions toward the visual improvements in life.

Surf Sculpture I—1972

Status: Prototype.

Surf sculpture utilizes the force and motion of the waves breaking against a massive concrete barrier. The various forms are designed to make the water conform to their curved surfaces and thereby produce a kinetic design, rhythmically changing with the oncoming breakers. The power of the waves under the overhang of the sculpture forces the water through the channels appearing on the platform as jets, their size changing with the strength of the surf. All water forced onto the surface runs off over the steps on the opposite side, dripping down to the calmer water area.

The piece will be active during high tide, and static during low. The T-shaped structure is a quay from which one can view the action of the surf fountain.

Herbert Bayer.

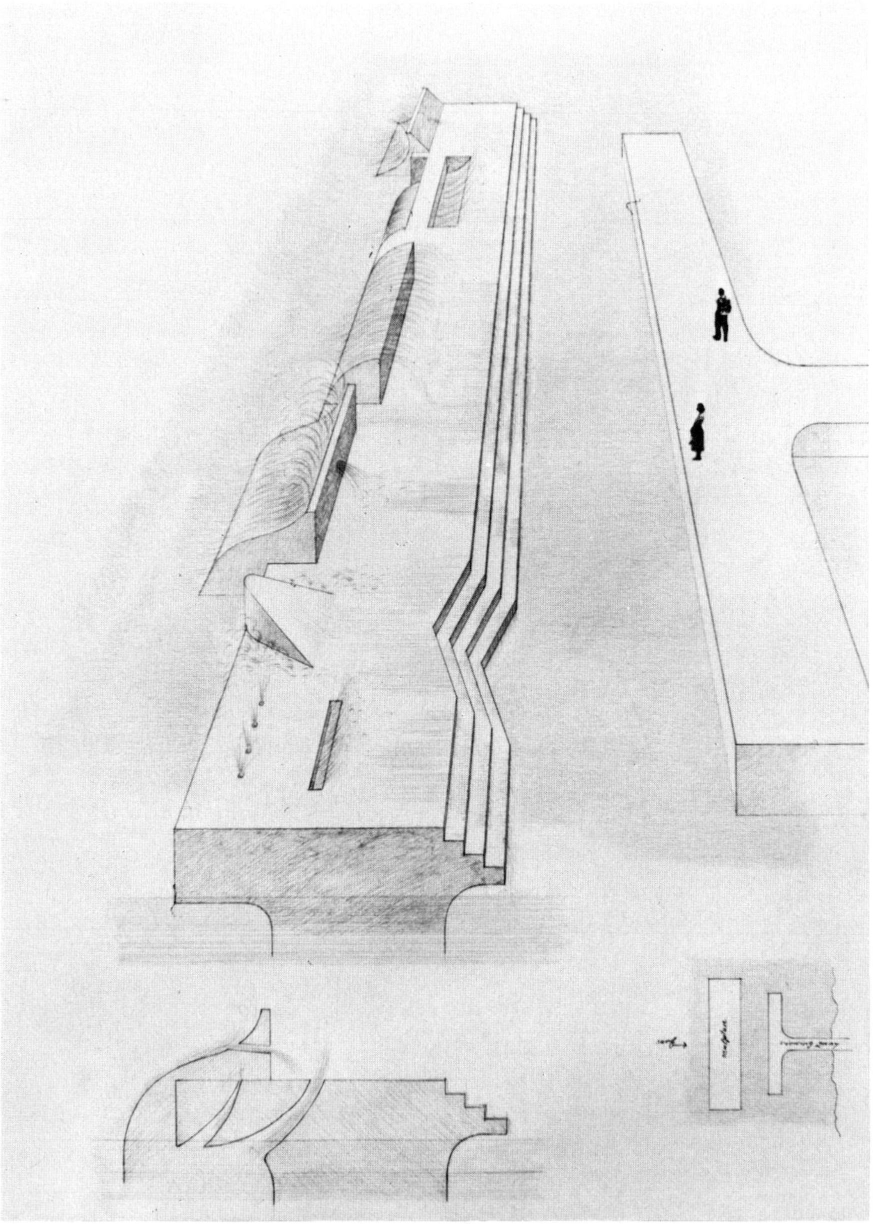

26. Surf Sculpture I. Aerial View.

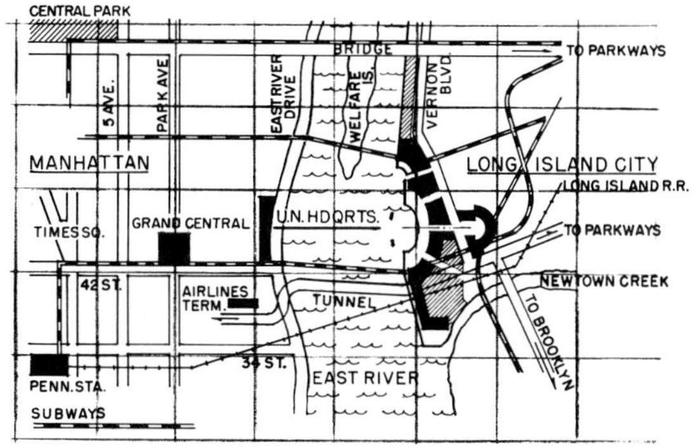

27. Long Island City. Site Plan.

28. Long Island City. Perspective.

John Barrington Bayley (California 1914—)
Residence: New York City.
Education: 1933–1937, BA, Harvard College; 1939–1942, B Arch., Harvard Graduate School of Design; 1970, M Arch., Harvard Graduate School of Design; 1947–1950, American Academy in Rome.
Among Major Works: 1959–1961, General Services Administration Building, N.Y.C., in collaboration with Eggers and Higgins, Kahn and Jacobs, and Alfred Easton Poor; 1963–1967, drawings for Gracie Mansion addition, N.Y.C.; 1967, renovation of Fraunces Tavern Block, N.Y.C., with H. H. Goldstone; 1973–1975, addition to the Frick Collection, N.Y.C., with Harry van Dyke.

Long Island City—1957

Location: Long Island City, New York City.
Status: Hypothetical study.

When classical architecture was adapted to modern times—the steel frame—great openings framed with columns and arches, etc., were produced very commonly for banks. The scale was completely revolutionary. There had never been any window openings so large before, and they were filled with steel and glass. The very grandest "American Bays," as at Grand Central or the Cunard Building, have gangways through them so you can see people walking back and forth. The human figure gives instant scale.

The east bank of the East River has a superb view. The inhabitants there see the towers of Manhattan in the morning flooded with light, and in the evening they are silhouetted by the setting sun. The dwellings in the picture face this view, and there is an esplanade on the water. The buildings themselves are based on the "American Bay," and behind them are the loft–like apartments. The giant scale of the "Bays" makes possible a composition of vast size without its being a cellular grid. A grid can be used for a skyscraper or a radio or air conditioner face. It has no scale. When scale is lost people are lost, and cosmic *Angst* takes over.

John Barrington Bayley.

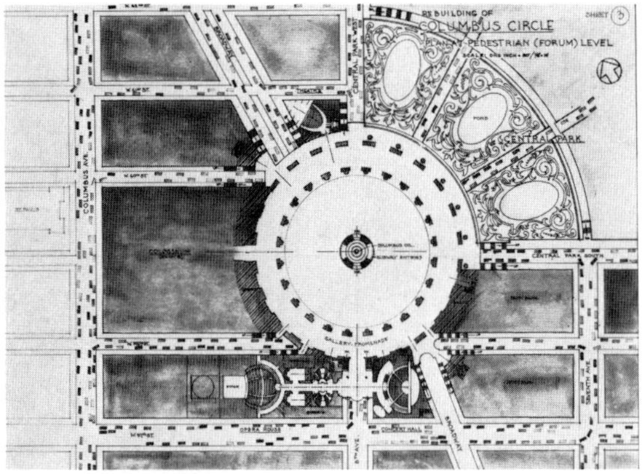

29. Lincoln Square. Plan.

30. Lincoln Square. Hall of Mirrors. Interior Detail.

Lincoln Square—1959
Location: New York City.
Status: Hypothetical study.
Roman architecture is façade architecture. Interior and exterior stand apart; structure and finish are independent. In modern building, structure is of course the master, and is free to abolish the visible envelope in favor of metal panels or glass, which often cost more than masonry. The best structure is that which supports a building most economically.

There is also the matter of aging. Roman architectural surfaces improve with age; the more they are used the better their modelling reads. They gain patina, high places are polished, and low ones are darkened. The modern building does not improve with age. Unbroken surfaces of glass and steel are at their best when brand-new. This newness can be maintained for a time by constant washing, but even the most devoted maintenance cannot preserve the pristine glitter of newness against time and the elements. In sum, modern buildings are like automobiles or contemporary furniture; the initial cost is high, depreciation is swift, and there is no re-sale value. Basically the argument for impermanence confuses change with progress; it was when the idea of material progress really got going in the 19th Century that it was applied to everything, including art. Art does not progress, it endures; and a building which exemplifies art should, ideally, last forever. The theory of impermanence is the negation of art in architecture; it is the apotheosis of a technocratic romanticism which makes architecture a vehicle for mechanical contrivances.

John Barrington Bayley.

31. Lincoln Square. Aerial View.

32. Dinsha House. Elevation.

Dinsha House—1968

Location: Upstate New York.

Status: Unbuilt due to death of client.

My purpose in designing the Dinsha house was to achieve the charm of historical allusion while avoiding the absurdities of overprecision. The property, located some 45 minutes northeast of Manhattan, is completely isolated, with the surrounding landscape very small in scale. The actual site for the house is a rocky eminence rising sharply above a smallish lake in a heavily glaciated region of rocky outcroppings, brooks, and ponds—a setting which bears a general resemblance to the terrain behind the Petit Trianon where the ground rises to the belvedere. It is an ideal spot for a small, self-contained estate. No balanced landscape compositions or perspectives are possible or necessary; the *jardin a l'anglaise* is built right in.

The owner's requirements for his home were simplicity itself; bed, bath, sitting and dining rooms, and services. The house is small enough to allow one room to open directly into another, without the necessity of a parallel corridor. Accordingly, my design proposed an enfilade, or train-of-cars plan, centered upon a mirrored oval room which seemed absolutely indispensable to both Mr. Dinsha and myself.

Abridged from John Barrington Bayley in *Classical America,* I, no. 1, 1971.

33. Dinsha House. Plan.

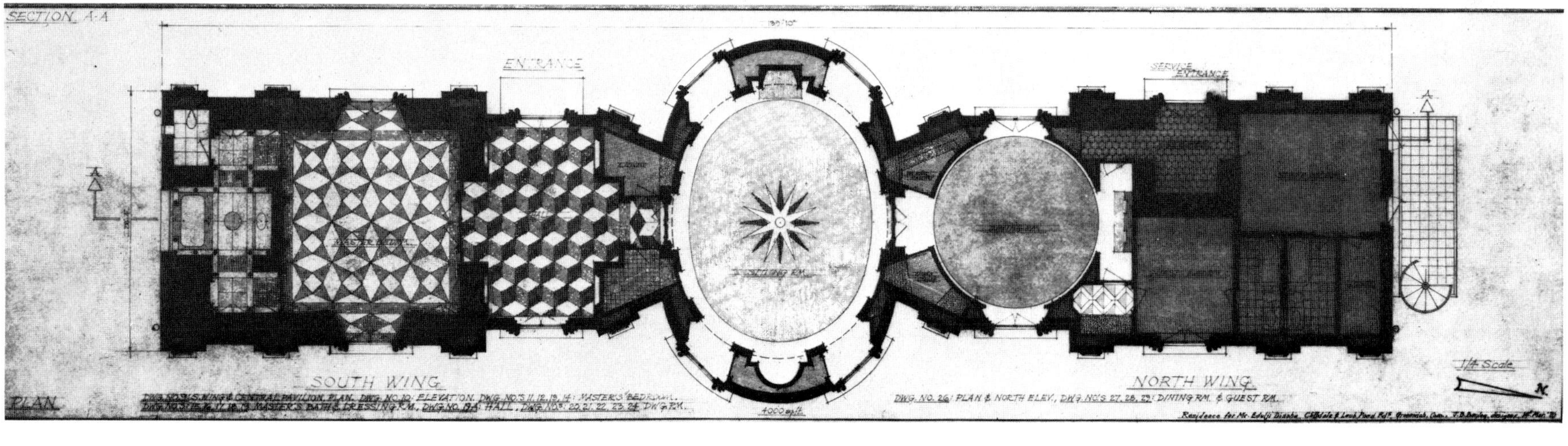

William Holbrook Beard (Ohio 1824—New York City 1900)
Among Major Paintings: "Grimalkin's Dream"; "Bears and a Bender"; "The Bear's Temperance"; "Kittens and Guinea Pig"; "Power of Death"; "Flaw in the Title."

An American Museum of Art—1873
Location: New York City.
Status: Unbuilt.

It was proposed to found in New York City a great Museum of Art that would be the best example of architectural art which America was capable of producing. The essential feature of Mr. Beard's design is the underground approach. In one of the views the elevation of a building is seen in the background, but this is a mere fancy sketch added by the artist to show the relation of the gallery and its approaches and is not intended as an architectural plan.

Entering the Museum from the Park we find, somewhere near the Eighth Avenue wall, the opening of a wide and well-ventilated tunnel. Vines and shrubbery hang over the arched entrance. On either side stands a colossal stone figure: Ignorance, with the threatening aspect, and Superstition, with repulsive mien, barring the avenue to aesthetic culture. Passing these grim giants, we find ourselves in an irregular and slightly tortuous subterranean roadway with rough-hewn sides. In the obscurity of this passage, symbolical of the rude origin of art, huge carven forms of beasts glare upon us from the shelving rock. The whole way is lined with figures, typical of the difficulties to be overcome before the student enters into the real enjoyment and comprehension of the beautiful. In the distance is seen a light antechamber where another colossal figure, a benign old man who may represent perhaps the guardian genius of the place, sits by a suitcase surrounded with fragments of ancient armor. The recumbent image of a naked youth looks upon him from above, and strange animals crouch upon the rocks by his side. Here the visitor finds himself at the portals of Art. The winding steps at the back of the old man lead to an elevated gallery of statues, effigies possibly of the famous characters of recent times. A tablet of stone bears the names of the founders of the Museum, and beneath it Time lies sleeping—a delicate intimation of the immortality of fame which will reward the gift of a thousand dollars or so to the Museum. Various passage-ways branch off from the room. One, guarded by grotesque antediluvian animals of immense size, leads out to the open air, and through it there gleams a vista of trim lawns and waving trees. Another mounts by broken flights of steps to galleries of sculpture, and so into the Museum proper.

Abridged from J. R. G. Hassard in *Scribner's Journal,* August 1871.

35. An American Museum of Art. Inner Grotto or Approach to the Museum.

36. An American Museum of Art. Second Entrance.

Left: 34. An American Museum of Art. Main Entrance and Building.

Norman Bel Geddes (Michigan 1893—New York City 1958)
Education: 1910, formal education ended when he was expelled from the ninth grade for drawing a caricature on the blackboard; briefly attended Cleveland School of Art and Chicago Institute of Art.
Among Published Works: 1932, *Horizons* (one of the first books to explore the potential of industrial design applied to most objects of modern life); 1940, *Magic Motorways* (visions of the future).

Norman Bel Geddes designed everything from theatrical productions to industrial objects, airplanes to kitchen stoves, and though not an architect, he designed several buildings. His styling of streamlined and "tear-drop" forms combined a modernistic aesthetic and the idea of functionalism. Through Bel Geddes' influence, streamlining became the dominant modernistic style of the 1930s.

Norman Bel Geddes worked from 1929–1933 as consultant to the architectural committee for the 1933 Chicago Century of Progress Exposition.

Island Dance Restaurant—1929
Location: 1933 Chicago Century of Progress Exposition.
Status: Abandoned due to the financial crisis of the time.

I have indicated that restaurant architecture should comprise features which in themselves are capable of furnishing amusement.

This restaurant is a group of four islands. Three small canals radiate from the inner lagoon that encircles the dance floor, joining it with the main outer lagoon. These entrance canals divide the dining terraces into three sections. It is possible for canoes to enter from the main lagoon and circle the dance floor without disturbing dancers or diners. The restaurant has space for an orchestra of thirty pieces in the center. The dance floor comfortably accommodates two hundred couples. It completely surrounds the orchestra and is separated from the dining terraces by a canal fourteen feet wide. Six bridges span this canal. Thirty-six slender neon tubes spring from the orchestra floor and unite in a series of interlacing arches, which are the main source of illumination. These tubes not only light the restaurant and the central area of the Exposition grounds but would be the largest beacon in the world and visible for a great distance.

Abridged from **Norman Bel Geddes, Horizons**, 1932.

37. Island Dance Restaurant. Aerial View.

38. Aquarium Restaurant. Aerial View.

At the moment . . . we are still thinking in grooves. We are too much inclined to believe, because things have long been done a certain way, that *that* is the best way to do them. Following old grooves of thought is one method of playing safe. But it deprives one of initiative and takes too long. It sacrifices the value of the element of surprise. At times, the only thing to do is to cut loose and *do the unexpected!* It takes more even than imagination to be progressive. It takes vision and courage.

Norman Bel Geddes, Horizons, 1932.

Aquarium Restaurant—1929

Location: 1933 Chicago Century of Progress Exposition.

Status: Abandoned due to the financial crisis of the time.

The Aquarium Restaurant is an underwater eating place suitable only for Fair or amusement grounds where expense is no particular object, providing a unique result is obtained. It was designed to be built across a lagoon where it forms a dam, for the water to flow over. The building consists of a triangular shaped aquarium in the center with a restaurant to each side of the aquarium and joining it with the shores.

The entrance to the aquarium is by a dock at the lower water level. This entrance dock is reached by boats from either shore. A trip through the aquarium is planned to give the visitor the feeling of having made a journey to the bottom of the sea. The interior walls, floor and ceiling are glass tanks containing underwater plant and animal life. Thus the tanks are above, below, and on all sides. The arrangement creates the illusion that any one passing through the building, instead of looking at tanks containing fish, is himself *within* the tank with the fish on the outside all around him.

The exterior walls of the building, over which falls a curtain of water, are illuminated by invisible lights underneath the water. On the roof of the aquarium is an open-air terrace with a seating capacity for one hundred and twenty persons. Water flows underneath its glass floor and in a curtain over the walls of the terrace.

Abridged from Norman Bel Geddes, Horizons, 1932.

39. Aerial Restaurant. Model.

Aerial Restaurant—1929
Location: 1933 Chicago Century of Progress Exposition.
Status: Abandoned due to the financial crisis of the time.

A casual observer inspecting this design might assume that in its engineering and structural features, it is impractical. The facts are otherwise. While the shaft is thin in proportion to the whole mass, it is actually thirty-two feet wide. Though the upper structure appears to have more weight on one side than the other, the segments of the three cantilevered levels are actually so arranged that they balance on each side of the center with sufficient leeway to take care of all live loads.

The Aerial Restaurant offers an observation platform with clear vision for miles around. It looks out over the lake and the city. The building's greatest novelty is that the entire structure slowly revolves, so that during a meal restaurant patrons get two complete panoramic views of the Fair Grounds, the City of Chicago, and Lake Michigan from an elevation of twenty-seven stories. There are three restaurants on three different levels, with a seating capacity of fifteen hundred persons.

In the not too distant future I anticipate restaurants of this type in our larger cities attracting generous patronage. Up to the present moment, architects and public alike have shown no initiative or imagination in utilizing their roofs. Utilization of roof area will be one of the leading architectural developments of the next few years.

Abridged from Norman Bel Geddes, Horizons, 1932.

40. Rotary Airport. Detail.

41. Rotary Airport. Aerial View.

Rotary Airport—1930
Location: New York City.
Status: Prototype.
Merely to suggest the idea of locating a floating airport anywhere in the navigable portions of New York Harbor, with its tugs, lighters, barges, ferries and sightseeing boats, brings endless protest from the owners and operators of these harbor craft. Nevertheless this location, southwest of Battery Park, between the Aquarium and the Staten Island Ferry slips, is ideal for such an airport in terms of proximity to the financial center, unobstructed landing area, relatively stable and uniform winds, excellent land transportation facilities, and lack of interference with vessels of deep draft.

As a possible solution to the airport problem New York City will ultimately face, I have designed this floating airport for the accommodation of land planes. It is a large deck fifteen hundred feet long by seven hundred and fifty feet wide. The traffic through these strips is one of continuous motion. One strip is for landing, the middle one is a taxi strip, and the third is a take-off strip.

Passengers arriving by plane debark into a waiting room located beneath the deck. A shuttle tunnel, fifteen feet below the bottom of the harbor and eight hundred feet long, has a moving walk to take passengers ashore. The weight of this floating airport is supported by columns upon ballasted buoyancy tanks. These tanks, located below the portion of the water disturbed by surface waves, keep the deck level in all weather, the waves passing easily around the columns and under the bottom of the deck structure. The landing deck rotates with the wind to give the ideal landing and take-off facilities. This rotation is accomplished by motor-driven marine propellers located at the extremities of the long axis of the deck below the water surface. Inasmuch as the starting switches of these propeller-motors are controlled by a remote wind-indicator, they are fully automatic. The deck with its definite traffic lanes is constantly held in the best position and there is no confusion to landing planes. To facilitate the easy rotation of the deck, the float tanks are streamlined.

Abridged from Norman Bel Geddes, *Horizons*, 1932.

Jacques J. B. Benedict (Chicago 1879—Denver 1948)
Education: Graduate, École des Beaux Arts, Paris.
Among Major Works: St. Thomas Seminary; Central Savings Bank, City Hall, Flatiron Building, St. Malo Chapel, all in Denver, Colorado.

From 1906 to 1909, worked for Carrère and Hastings Architects, N.Y.C. Adept at story telling, Mr. Benedict was the life of the many parties he attended. He was an immaculate dresser and went through Beaux Arts with a valet, an unusual thing for an art student. *Rocky Mountain News,* January 18, 1948.

Summer Capitol for President Woodrow Wilson—1915
Location: Mount Falcon, Colorado.
Status: After viewing the actual design of the building it is believed that President Wilson decided that it was too extravagant a venture for him.

A Mountain Palace for Our Presidents

The announcement that President Wilson has consented to lay the cornerstone of a proposed castle of granite upon Mount Falcon, in Colorado, places an official stamp upon the plan to dedicate the structure as the "Summer Capitol" of the United States—as the residence of the President and his staff during the intolerably hot months which afflict the city of Washington.

This plan would, for a part of each year, effect a transfer of the seat of the national executive power from the Potomac, in the East, to the foothills of the Rocky Mountains, in the heart of the West. Presidents have hitherto had to shift for themselves in the matter of summer homes. John Wanamaker gave Harrison a house at Cape May. Cleveland owned his own summer residence at Buzzard's Bay, as did Roosevelt at Oyster Bay. McKinley went back to his home at Canton, Ohio. Taft rented a house at Beverly, Mass. Wilson rents a house in Cornish, N.H., and at Washington has taken refuge from the heat in a tent, which is pitched on the White House lawn.

The site is upon land donated by John Brisben Walker. The castle is to cost fifty thousand dollars and its approaches two hundred thousand dollars more. It is promised that the main part of the building will be completed in time for President Wilson to spend there the summer of nineteen hundred and fifteen.

According to the architect's plans, the castle's north terrace, upon which the drawing room and library will open, will look down over a precipice which has a sheer fall of two thousand feet. To the south looms Pike's Peak and to the northeast lies Denver, fifteen miles away as the crow flies, but forty miles distant by a winding road.

The finest view from Mount Falcon, however, lies to the west. Granite cliffs drop perpendicularly into a wooded valley, of green mountain ledges, rising gradually higher until they reach a climax in the snow-covered peaks of the distant Rockies. Mount Falcon is not one of the high peaks of the Rockies, but is some hundreds of feet higher than Denver. It lies about midway between the extreme foothills on the east and the Continental Divide. Within sight on clear days is Mount Evans, fourteen thousand, three hundred and twenty-one feet high, or more than two hundred feet loftier than Pike's Peak.

To make the project national, or at least Western, its promoters plan to raise by popular subscription the funds necessary to erect the castle and construct its approaches. The building, according to present plans, is to be held in trust by the Governors of the twenty-two States west of the Mississippi River, all of whom have enlisted as official sponsors of the undertaking.

Abridged from Robert H. Moulton in *The Craftsman,* XXVII, February 1915.

42. A Mountain Palace for Our Presidents. Perspective.

Chesley Bonestell (San Francisco 1888—)
Residence: Carmel, California.
Education: 1911, graduated from Columbia University School of Architecture.
Among Published Works: 1949, *The Conquest of Space* (with Willy Ley); 1953, *Conquest of the Moon* (edited by Cornelius Ryan); 1972, *Beyond Jupiter* (with Arthur C. Clarke); 1974, *The Golden Era of the Missions: 1769–1834* (with Paul Johnson).

Chief designer in the office of Willis Polk, San Francisco, for seven years. Designer in the New York firms of Warren and Wetmore; Thomas Hastings; McKim, Mead and White; Cass Gilbert, and William Van Alan. Worked with Joseph Strauss on the design of the Golden Gate Bridge.

Bonestell is a renowned space artist with major works in the collections of planetariums and museums including: a 10- by 20-foot mural of Milky Way Galaxy in the Museum of Science, Boston; the Adler Planetarium, Chicago; Smithsonian Institution National Air and Space Museum.

A Colony on Mars Under Plastic Domes—1964
Status: Science fiction.
Plastic domes inflated with an atmosphere of such composition and pressure as to make human beings comfortable would be the beginning of establishing a colony on Mars. Energy will be furnished by nuclear reactors and the inflated domes will house plant life, hydroponic gardens, air and water-regenerating plants, living quarters, storage, etc.

Chesley Bonestell.

44. A Colony on Mars Under Plastic Domes. Painting.

Space Station Over New York City—1949
Status: Science fiction.
Rocket planes have shot up to a point 500 miles above the earth, where they will be practically weightless. The globular asteroid is being built around one of the rocket planes. Everything—planes, sphere, and men in oxygen-supplied suits—would move eastward in an orbit around the parent body, the earth, at five miles a second. The path of this space headquarters would be a great circle hinged on our equator. The course of the man-made "moon" would provide observation of all civilized portions of our globe during its travels around the earth. Artificial gravity, to keep the men from floating too far away in their chemically-made air, could be produced by spinning the space station on power obtained from the sun's rays, according to the British rocket expert, Harry E. Ross.

Abridged from *New York Sunday Mirror Magazine,* June 19, 1949.

43. Constructing a Space Station Over New York City. Painting.

45. Skyscraper. Perspective for U.S. Patent No. 383,170. May 22, 1888.

Leroy S. Buffington (Ohio 1847—Minnesota 1931)
Education: College of Cincinnati, where he received training as a mechanical and civil engineer.
Among Major Works: 1880, Boston Block; 1883, Pillsbury Mill; 1883, Sidle Block; 1883, Eastman Block; 1884, West Hotel, all in Minneapolis, Minnesota.

Buffington's career was not without controversy. In 1887, he applied for and subsequently received (1888) a patent for the steel skeleton method of construction, the basis upon which modern skyscrapers were and still are built. Despite ridicule from fellow architects, he proceeded to defend his patent by initiating a series of lawsuits aimed at collecting royalties for patent infringement. These suits dragged on through the courts, in the end winning Buffington nothing, but instead costing him $30,000 in legal fees.

Harvey Ellis (see General Grant's Tomb Competition, for biographical information) was a draftsperson in the office of Leroy S. Buffington and figured prominently in many of the firm's projects.

Skyscraper—1887

Status: Prototype.

This skyscraper of twenty-eight stories was intended to illustrate Buffington's claimed "invention" of steel skeleton construction, and, by his own admission, was never intended for fabrication as it appeared in the perspective.

Buffington claimed the invention of the steel skeleton method of building construction as early as 1882. In the 1940s, however, two independent researchers concluded from documentary evidence that Buffington had been stimulated by William LeBaron Jenney's Home Insurance Building, and that the concept of the steel skeleton system was not originally his as he had steadfastly maintained. Ellis is credited with bringing the Richardsonian Romanesque style to Buffington, who used it in this design. No traces of it appear in his work before Ellis arrived in the office in 1886, nor, according to a draftsman who preceded Ellis, did Buffington demonstrate any knowledge of skyscraper construction in the early 1880s as he claimed.

Alan Lathrop, University of Minnesota.

46. Soldiers and Sailors Monument. Elevation.

Soldiers and Sailors Monument—1888
Location: Indianapolis, Indiana.
Status: Unsuccessful competition entry.
This drawing was one of several prepared for an international competition to design a state war monument for a city square in Indianapolis. The ship and banner labelled "Yorel" are Buffington's devices to identify the design while preserving anonymity in the competition. The drawing was made by Harvey Ellis. The competition was won by Bruno Schmitz of Berlin, whose design was carried out by Frederick Baumann of Chicago.

The monument was to be built of Indiana limestone. The surrounding terrace was floored with encaustic tile, laid in a pattern depicting corps badges of U.S. troops in the Civil War. The only ornaments which appeared on the four faces of the monument were carved palms. The base was to be surrounded by statuary.

Inside, the monument's chamber featured bronze tablets bearing the names of all the Indiana soldiers who had served in the nation's wars, and would contain space for storage of the records of the Adjutant General's office. Allegorical mosaics on the vaults were intended to be executed by the mural painter Elihu Vedder, famous for his illustrations for the *Rubaiyat of Omar Khayyam*.

Alan Lathrop, University of Minnesota.

Steel Tent—1889
Location: Chicago.
Status: Unbuilt proposal for the Columbian Exposition.
The steel tent, Buffington's design for a huge exposition hall, was created as a design suggestion for the Columbian Exposition in Chicago in 1893. It was an enormous building, elliptical in plan, surmounted by a cone-shaped roof terminating in a world globe. An electric railway spiraled to the top of the roof and became an observation tower. Pretentious and awesome in size and construction, it was probably not accepted because of its potentially high construction cost.

Buffington revived this plan again in 1929 for presentation to the designers of the 1933 Chicago Century of Progress Exposition. Once again, it failed to be accepted. It is obvious that this time Buffington retraced Harvey Ellis' original drawing which is reproduced here.

Alan Lathrop, University of Minnesota.

47. Steel Tent. Perspective.

48. Plan of Chicago. Elevation of Central Administration Building. Drawing by F. Janin.

Daniel Hudson Burnham (New York 1846—Germany 1912)
Education: No college or architectural school training.
Among Major Works: *see* Root, John Wellborn.

In 1901 Burnham was called to Washington, D.C., to become chairman of a commission to plan the enlargement and extension of the L'Enfant layout of the District of Columbia. With this project Burnham embarked on a new phase of his career—city planning—which became national in scope and occupied much of his time throughout the rest of his life (John Garraty and Edward James, *Dictionary of American Biography*, 1974). Cities he drew plans for include: San Francisco, Cleveland, Detroit, Chicago, and the rebuilding and modernization of the old city of Manila.

Plan of Chicago, Civic Center—1909
Status: Unbuilt.

As it is proposed to group in Grant Park the buildings pertaining to art, literature, and science, so it is planned to create on the axis of Congress Street a composition representing the dignity and importance of the city from the administrative point of view. Where Congress Street intersects Halsted Street, a civic center should be established.

The buildings comprised in the civic center naturally fall into three divisions, represented by the City of Chicago, by Cook County, and by the Federal Government; and inasmuch as a single building would be insufficient to accommodate the offices either of the city or of the general government, there should eventually be three groups. Of these three the city group would predominate.

The central administrative building, as shown in the illustrations, is surmounted by a dome of impressive height, to be seen and felt by the people, to whom it should stand as the symbol of civic order and unity. Rising from the plain upon which Chicago rests, its effect may be compared to that of the dome of St. Peter's at Rome. The buildings are shown raised on terraces one story in height. These terraces would give great dignity

49. Plan of Chicago. View, Looking West, of the Proposed Civic Center Plaza and Buildings, Showing It as the Center of the System of Arteries of Circulation of the Surrounding Country. Painting by Jules Guerin.

to the structures, and would mark the transition from them to the great open space on which they front.

The civic center will be dependent for its effectiveness on the character of the architecture displayed in the buildings themselves, in their harmonious relations one with another, and in the amount of the space in which they are placed. The attainment of harmony, good order, and beauty is not a question of money cost, for in the end good buildings are far cheaper than bad buildings. What is required is enlightened understanding and competent planning; the great buildings of the world are simple and inexpensive when compared with many of the over elaborate structures of the present day; but for centuries they have served their important purposes and the people will not give them up, because they have become part and parcel of their life. They typify the permanence of the city, they record its history, and express its aspirations. Such a group of buildings as Chicago should and may possess would be for all time to come a distinction to the city. It would be what the Acropolis was to Athens, or the Forum to Rome, and what St. Mark's Square is to Venice—the very embodiment of civic life.

Abridged from **Daniel Burnham** and **Edward Bennett, Plan of Chicago,** 1909.

Carrère and Hastings

John Merven Carrère (Rio de Jañeiro 1858—New York City 1911)
Education: 1872–1873, Institute Breitenstein, Switzerland; 1878, École des Beaux Arts, Paris; 1883–1884, apprenticed as draftsman in the office of McKim, Mead and White.

Thomas Hastings (New York City 1860—New York City 1929)
Education: Columbia University; 1880, École des Beaux Arts, Paris; 1883–1884, apprenticed as draftsman in the office of McKim, Mead and White.

Among Major Works of Firm: 1889–1911, New York Public Library, Main branch at 42 Street and Fifth Avenue, N.Y.C.; 1903, country house for Murray Guggenheim, in New Jersey; 1905, Senate Office Building, Washington, D.C.; 1912, residence of Henry Clay Frick, N.Y.C.

New Versailles
Manhasset Cooperative Housing Project—1916
Location: Manhasset Bay, Long Island, New York.
Status: Unbuilt due to financial difficulties during First World War.

Versailles is the biggest thing I have ever undertaken. When anything like this has been done before it has been for royalty. This is a home—a combination of individual homes. It is like the *Prix de Rome,* with the added interest that it is going to be executed. If the Chateau of this American Versailles is not the biggest building in the world, it will be the biggest architectural feature or mass in America. To answer its splendid purpose it must be something between a great building and a small town.

Thomas Hastings.

50. A New Versailles. Chateau-on-the Hill. Painting by Jules Guerin.

51. A New Versailles. Bird's-Eye View. Painting by Jules Guerin.

New Versailles offers the art-lovers of America an opportunity, during the rehabilitation of Europe which will follow the war, to make America a center of large modern artistic expression in a way that will have an immeasurable effect upon our national life. It is to be an expression of the highest in art, the most exclusive in human environment and the most reasonable in cost.

It is difficult to speak moderately of New Versailles in its relation to art from a national standpoint. Egypt has its Luxor and Karnak, Athens its Acropolis, Rome its Forum, Spain its Alhambra and France its Versailles. The last of these achievements dates back more than a century, and meanwhile America has produced a sky line of office buildings and a few local architectural successes. Through New Versailles, America may take its rightful and high place in the world of art, and offer to its artists the added inspiration afforded by the knowledge that their work is to endure.

The land selected on Manhasset Bay (approximately 180 acres) lends itself naturally to the purposes of the architect and artist, sloping gradually downward from a height of 150 feet to the shore, to a harbor nearly one-quarter of a mile wide. The gardens, some two hundred acres in extent, will contain two groups of residences which will be called Chateaus, one to be on the hill and one near the bay. The bird's-eye view shows the general layout of the proposed development. The Chateau-on-the-Hill is located about a quarter mile from the water's edge and will vary in height from eight to sixteen stories. These will contain about 2500 units of space, each approximately 10,000 cubic feet. These units or apartments are to be the homes of the several owners or stockholders to the scheme and in addition, reception halls, restaurants, tea rooms, and ballrooms. The residents of the Chateau-by-the-Sea will find similar accommodations provided in the Clubhouse, to be erected close to the bay.

Near the Chateau-on-the-Hill there will be erected school and theatre buildings, and not far away there will be an outdoor school and an outdoor theatre. Commodious quarters will be provided for the servants, and a well-appointed employees' club will be an important part in the plan for providing service. Ample buildings will be provided for garage and stables. There will be a casino, a yacht club house, an aviation field near by, a golf course closely accessible, tennis courts, archery course, baseball field, running track, athletic field, and gymnasium. All privileges of the grounds will be open to purchasers of apartments and members of the club.

The entire running expenses of this American Versailles will be met by the income derived from club and other features, and the cost of space for residences will compare most favorably with the cost of corresponding space in a high-class city apartment or country house. No part of the chateau will be rented. It will be accessible as a living space solely for the stockholders. The secret of the advantages of life in New Versailles is Co-operation; co-operation in building apartments, in creating beautiful gardens, in maintaining schools, in pursuing sports, co-operation in buying and hiring, all of which benefits both the community and the individual.

Walter Russell [probably the New York illustrator] first conceived the idea of New Versailles and with Penrhyn Stanlaws developed it until sketches were taken to Thomas Hastings, of Carrère & Hastings, architects, who designed the buildings and grounds. Owen Brainard, of the same firm, worked out the engineering problems. The embellishments of the grounds and buildings are to be in the hands of the most noted sculptors and painters. Frederick MacMonnies, Paul Bartlett, and Robert Aitken will create the three largest fountains and act as a committee in control of all sculptural features, while the mural and interior decorations will be in the hands of J. Alden Weir, Edwin Blashfield, Jules Guerin and Frank V. DuMond.

Abridged from **Exhibition Catalogue of the National Academy of Design,** 1916, and *The American Architect,* CIX, June 1916.

James L. Aspinwall (New York City 1854—1936)
In 1880, James Aspinwall became a partner of James Renwick, and William Russell, and with them submitted the entry to the competition for the Cathedral of St. John the Divine.

Carrère and Hastings (see Carrère for biographical information).

Edward Pearce Casey (Maine 1864—New York City 1940)
Education: Studied at Columbia University School of Mines; studied at the École des Beaux Arts, Paris.

Robert W. Gibson (England 1854—New York City 1927)
Education: In England.

Bertram Grosvenor Goodhue (Conn. 1869—New York City 1924)
At age 15, Goodhue entered the office of James Renwick. In 1891, he joined the office of Ralph Adams Cram, and later became a partner in the firm Cram, Goodhue, and Ferguson.

James Renwick (New York City 1818—New York City 1895)
Education: 1836, Columbia University.
Among Major Works: 1858–1879, St. Patrick's Cathedral, N.Y.C.
Submitted the entry to the competition for the Cathedral of St. John the Divine with James Aspinwall and William Hamilton Russell.

William Hamilton Russell (New York City 1854—1907)
Russell was a partner in the firm Aspinwall, Renwick, and Russell; jointly they submitted the entry to the competition for the Cathedral of St. John the Divine.

William Halsey Wood (1855—1897)
Wood spent his whole life and practice in Newark, New Jersey.

Cathedral of St. John the Divine Competition—1889
Location: New York City.
Status: Unsuccessful competition entries.
In the year 1873 it was decided, at the instigation of the Bishop, Horatio Potter, that the Diocese of New York should have a Cathedral and a Charter was then obtained. In 1887 the present site was

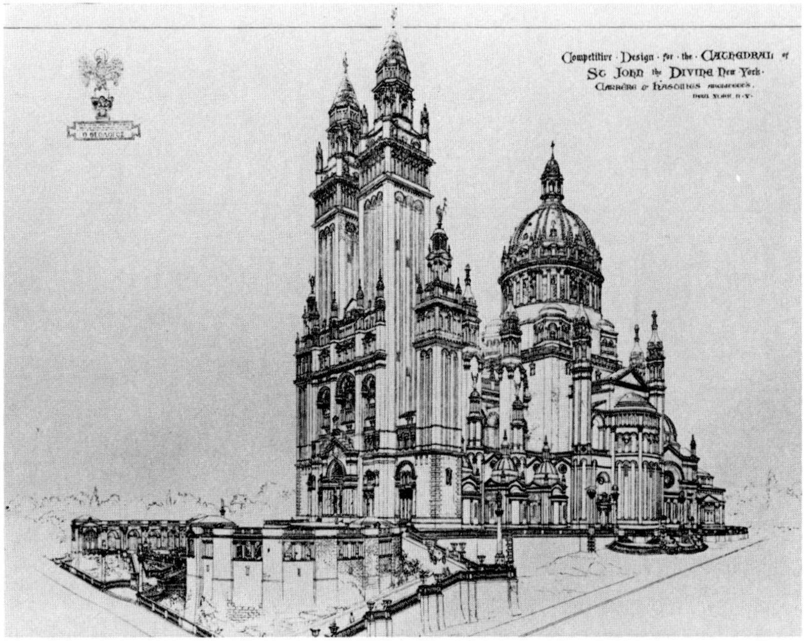

52. Entry by Carrère and Hastings. Perspective.

53. Entry by James Renwick, James L. Aspinwall and William H. Russell. Perspective.

54. Entry by Bertram Grosvenor Goodhue. Perspective.

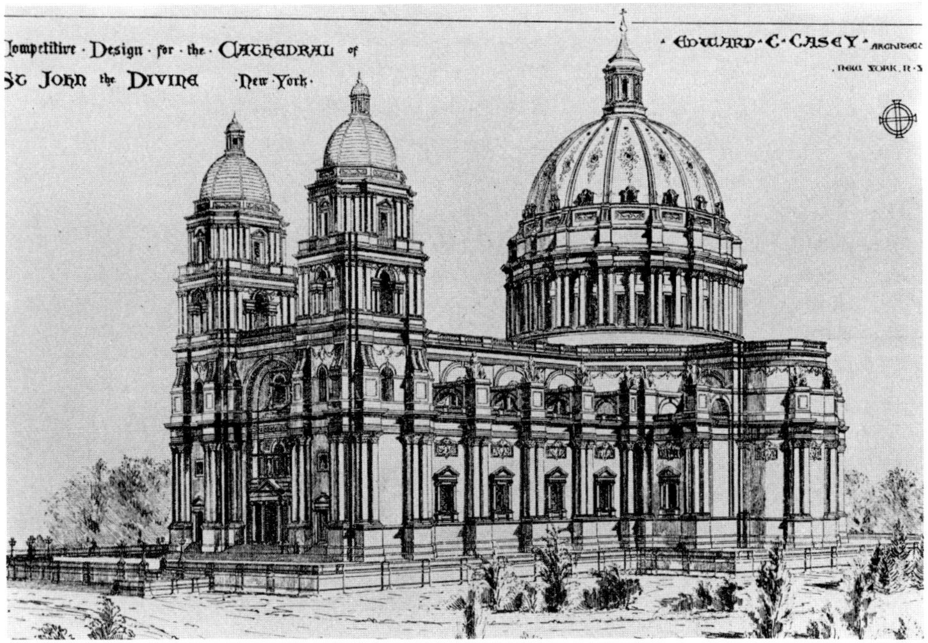

55. Entry by Edward C. Casey. Perspective.

acquired by Bishop Henry C. Potter and one of those open competitions, then unhappily in vogue, was instituted. This meant that anyone might submit designs—architects, draughtsmen, amateur artists, anyone, in fact, without regard to race, colour or previous condition of servitude. If I remember correctly, sixty or seventy schemes were turned in.

At that time the art of church-building in the United States was in a somewhat indeterminate condition. A great but baffling opportunity confronted American architects, and they met it variously. Every phase of English Gothic was represented in the competitive designs, from the thirteenth to the sixteenth century.

There were a few Renaissance adaptations, of which that by Carrère and Hastings was naturally the most distinguished, together with a large block of curious inventions the provenance of which could not possibly be determined. All the Gothic schemes (including my own alternate) were conscientiously archaeological. Two designs alone (as I now remember) escaped this, at the time, almost inevitable antiquarianism—the one measurably, the other completely. The first was that submitted by Heins & La Farge, the second that of Halsey Wood. It was this first-named scheme that received the award.

The second design, that by Halsey Wood, was simply astounding, not only in view of the time when it was produced, but in itself. Had it been built it would, I am persuaded, have marked an era in the development of American architectural style, so anticipating by some years the significant trend towards vital design that ultimately was initiated by that equally great genius Louis Sullivan, carried forward by that active but less responsible genius, Frank Lloyd Wright, and brought to its climax in Goodhue's Nebraska State Capitol. Visionary,—impractical and fantastic if you like,—wholly original and

56. Entry by Robert W. Gibson. Perspective.

instinct with tremendous vitality, it represented an emotional impulse that, I believe, could easily have been given a rational practicality if only the ecclesiastical authorities of the time had had the imagination and the courage to see their opportunity and to avail themselves of it. I admit this would have been asking beyond reason. Nothing like Halsey Wood's project had ever been seen before. While it diverged completely from every Anglican tradition, both architectural and doctrinal, all the same it was the most original and creative piece of architectural design thus far produced in America. For my own part I think Halsey Wood was potentially one of the greatest architects of modern times. I have been told that his failure to win the award broke his heart (I think this highly probable); in any case he died very soon afterwards.

As I already have indicated, I tried to get the thing both coming and going, for I sent in two designs, one most conscientiously, even slavishly, Richardsonian, the other in a Gothic approximation of what was to be our accepted mode. Fortunately neither commended itself to the authorities. I am not wholly ashamed of them as the product of a draughtsman of only five years' office experience, with no office of his own and the minimum of professional education and familiarity with the monuments of the past. I remember with some clarity my feelings when, on the train to Hampton Falls for a visit, I read the result of the competition. I hardly anticipated then that exactly twenty-five years later I should be asked to take over the work and carry it on, as far as possible, to completion.

Ralph Adams Cram, My Life in Architecture, 1936.

57. Entry by William Halsey Wood. Perspective.

A Century of Progress—1933
Chicago's Second World's Fair
Location: Chicago.
Status: Unsuccessful exposition entries.
Raymond Hood was asked to advise the Board of Directors of a proposed World's Fair (to commemorate a Century of the existence of Chicago as a city) about the formation of a design group. He asked Harvey Wiley Corbett, who later became Chairman, Paul Cret, Arthur Brown, Edward Bennett, Hubert Burnham, John Wellborn Root and myself [Ralph Walker] to join him in creating a design board [The Architectural Commission]. This group entered into a series of competitions with each other—without too much basic understanding of the economics of exposition building.

Ralph T. Walker, Ralph Walker, Architect, 1957.

Frank Lloyd Wright had been excluded from the plans for the Century of Progress Exposition because it was feared that he would not cooperate with the other architects involved.

In 1931 a Town Hall meeting was held in protest of this situation. Several ideas subsequently suggested by Wright at this meeting included a vast woven steel canopy which would have encompassed the entire exposition; a fair composed of floating elements inclusive of buildings, gardens and bridges; and a half-mile-high skyscraper that would have risen above the lake shore site.

Hubert Burnham (Chicago 1882—Chicago 1968)
Education: 1912, Diplôme, École des Beaux Arts, Paris.
Among Major Works of His Firm: Burnham Building; Bankers Building; Carbide and Carbon Building; Presbyterian Hospital; St. Luke's Nursing Home; all in Chicago.

Hubert Burnham was the son of Daniel Burnham, and in 1912 joined his father's firm, D. H. Burnham and Company.

Harvey Wiley Corbett, New York City (see Corbett for biographical information).

Paul Philippe Cret (France 1876—Philadelphia 1945)
Education: 1896–1903 École des Beaux Arts, Paris, where he studied in the Atelier of Pascal.
Among Major Works: 1922, Detroit Institute of Arts; 1928, Rodin Museum, Philadelphia; 1929, Folger Shakespeare Library, Washington, D.C.; 1937, Federal Reserve Building, Washington, D.C.

Paul Cret was Professor of Design at the University of Pennsylvania from 1903 to 1937. There he established his own Atelier, and strictly followed the Beaux Arts tradition in his teaching.

Holabird and Root, Chicago

John A. Holabird (Illinois 1886—Chicago 1945)
Education: 1907, Graduate, U.S. Military Academy, West Point; ca. 1913, Diplôme, École des Beaux Arts, Paris.

John Holabird was the son of William Holabird and joined his father's firm, Holabird and Roche. Upon the death of the senior Holabird (1923) and Roche (1927) the partnership was terminated and the new firm of Holabird and Root (John Holabird, John Root) was established. Holabird found "modernism" distasteful, and felt it essential that a firm should include a full organization of engineers and architects to enable it to handle all aspects of major complex building projects. He was the first to be consulted on the selection of the Architectural Commission for the Chicago World's Fair of 1933; he suggested that Raymond Hood be appointed chairman and that the decision concerning committee members be left to Hood.

John Root (1887—Massachusetts 1963)
Education: 1909, B Arch., Cornell University; ca.1915, Diplôme, École des Beaux Arts, Paris.

John Root was the son of John Wellborn Root; he joined the firm of Holabird and Roche ca.1916, which became Holabird and Root.

Among Major Works of Firm: 1927, Palmer House, Chicago; 1928, Daily News Building, Chicago; Illinois Bell Telephone Building; Ramsey County Court House and City Hall, St. Paul, Minn.; Statler Hotel, Washington, D.C.

Raymond M. Hood, New York City (see Hood for biographical information).

Ralph T. Walker (Connecticut 1889—New York City 1973)
Education: 1911, B Arch., Massachusetts Institute of Technology.
Among Major Works of Firm (Voorhees, Gmelin and Walker): New York Telephone Company building, N.Y.C.; Irving Trust Company, N.Y.C.; Bell Telephone Laboratories, Murray Hill, N.J.; A.F.L.-C.I.O. Building, Washington, D.C.; I.B.M. Research Center, Poughkeepsie, N.Y.

In 1957 Ralph T. Walker was hailed by the American Institute of Architects as "the architect of the century." Earlier he had won an accolade from late Frank Lloyd Wright, no great admirer of his professional colleagues, as "the only other architect in America." *New York Times*, Jan. 8, 1973.

Preliminary Schemes, December, 1928
[The Architectural Commission] after preliminary meetings during which the ideas of each were made known to all, prepared [these] suggested designs, independent of each other.

The fair is to be held along the lake front, partly on the mainland and partly on a group of man-made islands which will extend north and south for a distance of about 50 city blocks.

To avoid the fatigue which has been experienced in the past by visitors to other expositions, the architects decided to adopt a system of moving sidewalks extending throughout the scheme. Also, since the land is practically at water level, they decided upon a network of canals passing through and between the buildings so that noiseless electric launches can be added to the transportation facilities designed to reduce foot-weariness.

To lower congestion at entrances of buildings visitors will be transported by escalators to the upper levels immediately on their arrival. Principal entrances to buildings will therefore be on the roofs and the crowds entering a building will circulate through it from the top down. It was agreed that, in order to eliminate any shut-in feeling which might be experienced by visitors to floors below the roof level, each story should project out beyond the story above it, forming a system of terraces in each building.

58. John A. Holabird. Preliminary Scheme. January 1928.

Proposal by John A. Holabird
A Hall of Science as a dominant feature, located at the north end of the lagoon. Light will be used freely in achieving more spectacular effects than have ever been attained before in expositions. The architectural forms are, of course, simply suggestions to be worked out in detail later.
Pencil Points, X, April 1929.

Proposal by Hubert Burnham
Elevated roadways, bridges and viaducts developed around a central tower structure.

59. Hubert Burnham. Preliminary Scheme. January 1928.

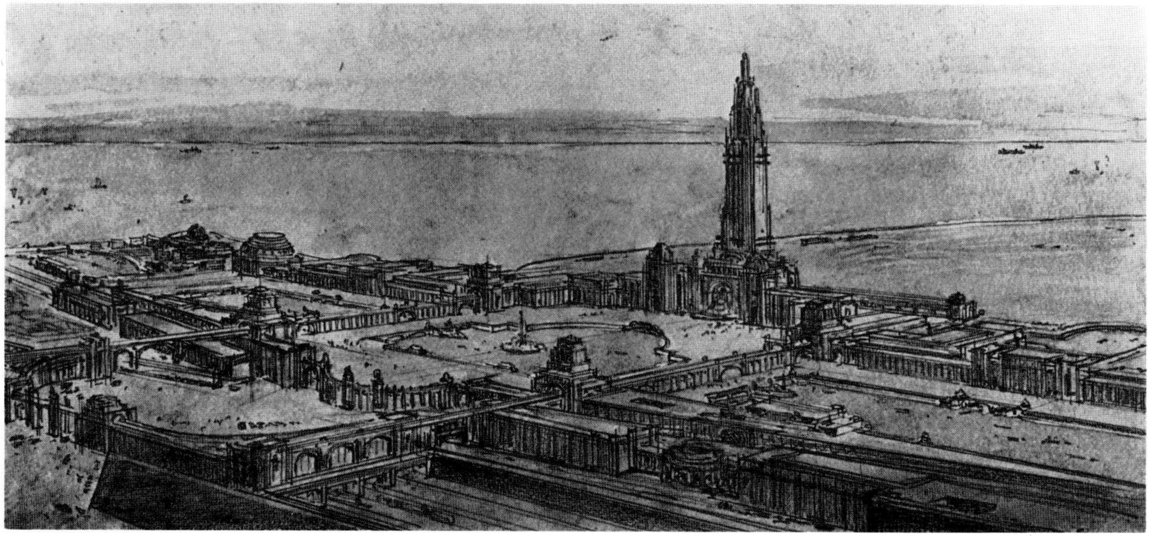

The arrangements for lighting the exposition are being provided for from the beginning. The tremendous progress of the art of using artificial light for floor-lighting made in recent years will undoubtedly be taken advantage of to the fullest possible extent so that the exposition at night will be one huge system of "permanent fireworks" controlled so as to achieve a tremendous dynamic effect. The fact that many thousands of people will view the fair from the air is influencing the designers to consider the purely aesthetic aspect of the plan to a larger degree than heretofore. It will have to be composed as a giant piece of jewelry.
Excerpted from *Pencil Points,* X, April 1929.

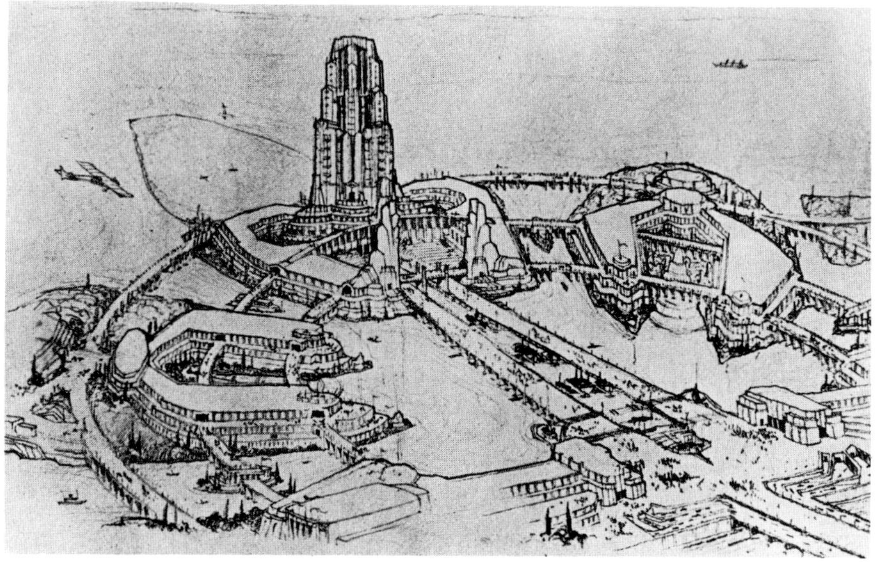

60. Ralph T. Walker. Preliminary Scheme. January 1928.

Proposal by Ralph T. Walker
A study of terraces and moving sidewalks in an amphitheatre plan.

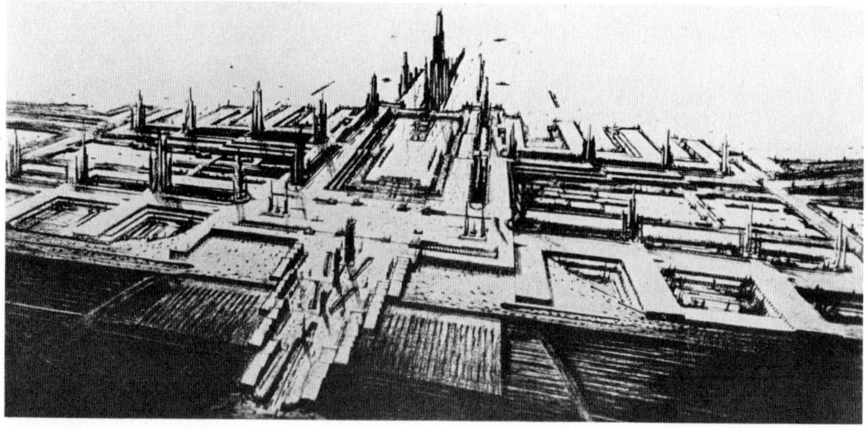

62. Harvey W. Corbett. Preliminary Scheme. January 1928.

Proposal by Harvey W. Corbett
Terraces and roof plaza with vertical ornamentation, clearly show how the exposition will be made up of multi-storied buildings.

Pencil Points, X, April 1929.

61. Raymond M. Hood. Preliminary Scheme. January 1928.

Proposal by Raymond M. Hood
Suggested arrangement of buildings in block-plan with moving sidewalks, providing for indefinite expansion.

Pencil Points, X, April 1929.

Schemes, January 1929
It is assumed the purpose of the meeting at which these drawings were presented was to develop the shape of the Fair in relation to the three-mile-long site area. Light was an important element, and these are all night views illustrating how it would work with architectural form.

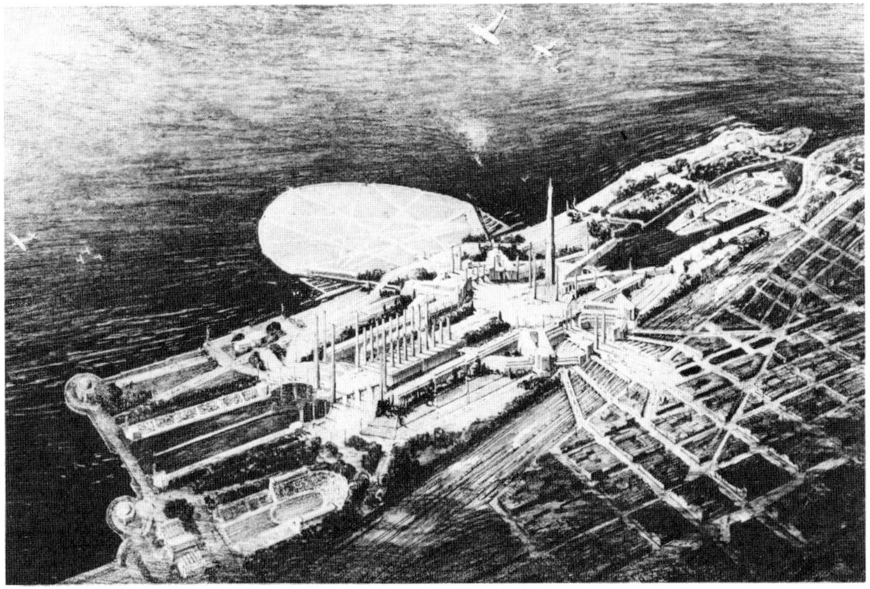

63. Ralph T. Walker. January 1929.

64. Ralph T. Walker. Elevation of Central Tower. January 1929.

Proposal by Ralph T. Walker

A centralized plan (north-south axis) opened by a water allée to the north and including an airport with an unusual landing strip pattern. The amphitheater of the first scheme is further developed, and the central tower has increased drastically in scale and taken on a crystallized form. Also incorporated are the moving sidewalks and Holabird's Hall of Science Building.

Proposal by Paul P. Cret

A series of terraced buildings opening to a central garden or court and focusing upon a great tower. The structures are crystalline cascading forms suffused with light (north-south axis).

Proposal by Raymond M. Hood

A concentric plan (east-west axis) encompassing a double circle of buildings around the central "power plant" and "volcano of light." The circles are bridged by buildings and gardens. Other elements included: water aerial display and moving sidewalks.

65. Paul P. Cret. January 1929. Aerial View.

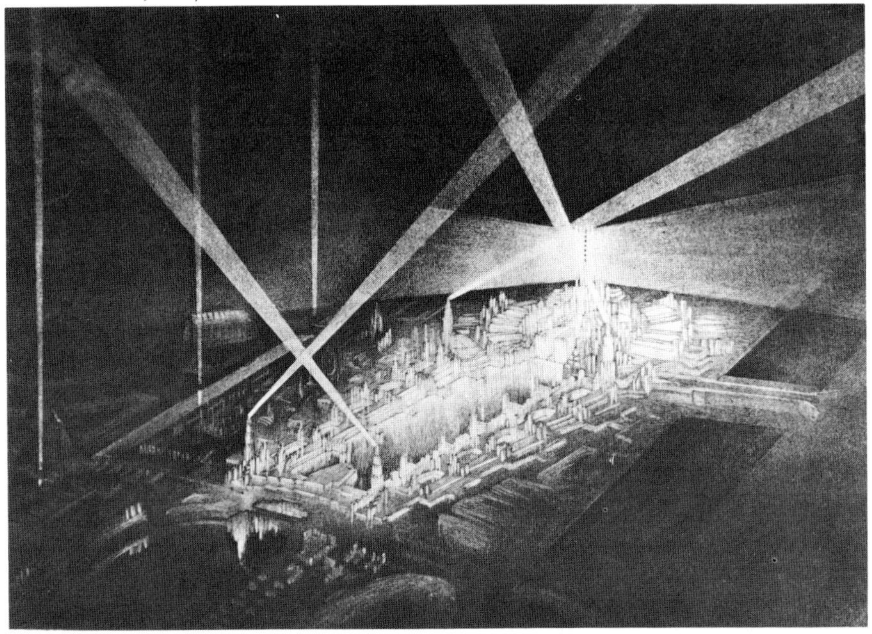

66. Raymond M. Hood. January 1929. Plan.

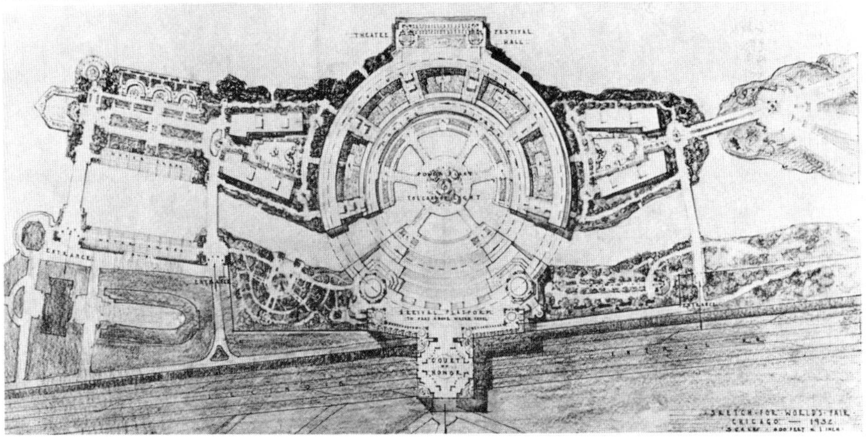

67. Raymond M. Hood. May 1929. Aerial View Based on Asymetric Plan.

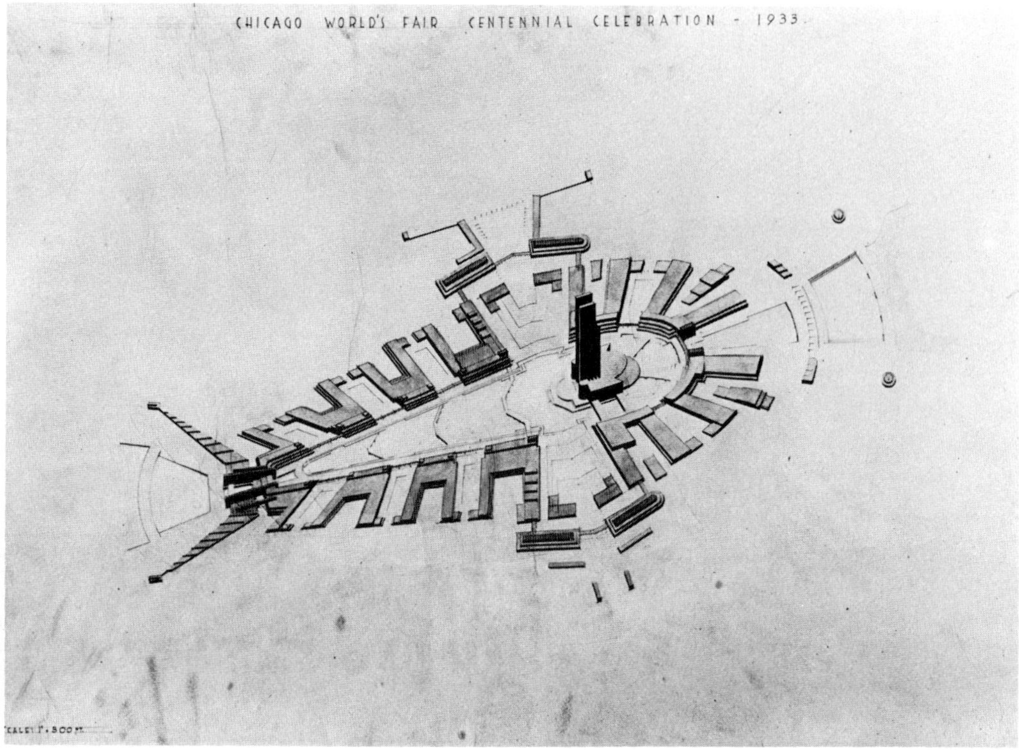

68. Holabird and Root. May 1929. Model. Detail.

Schemes, May 1929

The Fair was to occupy a portion (approximately three miles) of an extensive landfill area to have been created on the lakefront site. The cost of this endeavor (approximately $25,000 per acre) resulted in only about ¾ of a mile being completed by the time the Architectural Commission began drawing their plans in 1928. By April 1929 the site had still not been settled upon, continuing the indeterminate nature of the plans. In the January 1929 meeting the moving sidewalk concept had been abandoned as prohibitive in cost, as would have been Holabird's Hall of Science and Walker's Volcano of Light and Water.

In the end, according to Walker, it was Hood who came up with an idea acceptable to all. Unusual in that it was an asymmetrical scheme, it was a departure in itself from the classic pattern of World's Fairs. The idea came to Hood while on vacation in Amalfi. Hurrying back to Paris, he collected together all of his "boys" he could find, which included Louis Skidmore, Carl Landerfelt, and Frank Roorda. In the manner of the old student "charette" they batted out the scheme in ten days and got it off on the boat to Chicago.

Walter H. Kilham, Jr., Raymond Hood, Architect, 1973.

Proposal by Raymond M. Hood

The asymmetrical plan (north-south axis) incorporating lagoons, an airport and huge tower which Hood described as the "Apotheosis of Chicago." Although the final plan executed for the Fair was also asymmetrical, this version was not carried out.

Proposal by Holabird and Root

Incorporates lagoons and airport, on north-south axis.

Finally, however, Hood developed a simple scheme and from that point it was my task to bring together all the others into an agreement in principle. The idea that finally evolved was to have the plan divided into eight parts and to have the designer of each section confer closer with his immediate neighbors, and this was thought desirable and everybody was satisfied. We drew lots and the high point of the scheme became the part I was to design.

Ralph T. Walker, Ralph Walker, Architect, 1957.

70. Ralph T. Walker. Volcano of Light and Water. Rendering by John Wenrich.

Proposal by Ralph T. Walker—1930
Volcano of Light and Water

After considerable study with the engineers from the Aluminum Company of America and from the Carrier Corporation, an aluminum tower was designed to have three sheltered sides to baffle the spray. The tower was to be placed in a lagoon and be reached by cantilever bridges. The surrounding buildings contrary to all the other groups being designed, were to be made largely of glass.

The inside was designed like a great dirigible with the fins strutting out like enormous buttresses to give strength to the whole structure. The Board of Directors of the Century of Progress made several attempts to sell the tower to the Aluminum Company, but the Great Depression was a deterrent as well as the fact that the project was a huge experiment, so it was never built.

Ralph T. Walker, Ralph Walker, Architect, 1957.

69. Ralph T. Walker. Volcano of Light and Water. Rendering by Hugh Ferriss.

Edgar Chambless (1871—1936)
Education: Unknown.
Major Writing: *Roadtown,* N.Y., 1910.

A writer, sociologist, and inventor, Edgar Chambless is known for his promotion of the linear city in terms of a continuous house, as first described in his book of 1910. His scheme was promoted in the 'teens by *Sunset* magazine as a means of establishing market gardens in California. He apparently came closest to success during the New Deal when the proposal illustrated here was discussed in Washington. When the project was not carried out, Chambless took his own life, as described below by Clarence Pickett, Executive Secretary of the American Friends Service Committee, who was serving as consultant to the Farm Security administration at that time.

One day a tall gaunt man came into my office in Washington, slumped down in the chair before my desk, and laid a beautiful drawing on the table. His name I cannot remember, but his story was a vivid one. He wanted to reorganize American life around what he called the "road town idea." His proposal was to build all the housing for people living on farms or subsistence homesteads along a beautifully developed road. This road would make possible all kinds of modern services: adequate shopping centers, telephone, mail, and other public facilities; and from their homes on this road people could move out to their farms of larger or smaller size, thus having the advantages of both town and country. I remember introducing him to Dr. Wilson, and insisting that he also hear the story. Encouraged by our listening ear, this man persisted for weeks, getting his story told to government officials and to other groups in Washington, all interested, but nobody ready to commit himself to the plan, for varying reasons. Perhaps greater frankness on the part of those of us who listened to him might have been a kindness; for in the end this man could not accept the fact that nothing much was going to come of all his labors. One morning the newspapers reported that he had jumped out of the window of his hotel in New York.

Clarence Pickett *For More than Bread,* 1953.

Roadtown—1910
Location: In the country.
Status: Theoretical proposal.

I became a patent investigator, and in my business was acquainted with numerous inventions that would never be realized. So I began to dream of new conditions in which some of these shelved inventions might be utilized to ease the burden of life for mankind. One plan after another was abandoned until the idea occurred to me to lay the modern skyscraper on its side and run the elevators, pipes, and wires horizontally instead of vertically. Such a house would not be limited by the stresses and strains of steel; it could be built not only a hundred stories, but a thousand stores or a thousand miles—in short, I had found a workable way of coupling housing and transportation into one mechanism, and a human way for land-moving man to live—I would not cure the evils of congestion by perfecting congestion as in the case with the skyscraper—I would build my city out into the country. I would take the apartment house and all its conveniences and comforts out among the farms by the aid of wires, pipes and of rapid and noiseless transportation. I would extend the blotch of human habitations called cities out in radiating lines. I would surround the city worker with the trees and grass and woods and meadows and the farmer with all the advantages of city life—I had invented Roadtown.

The Roadtown will start at the end of the present subways or other rapid transportation systems of present cities or tap these lines far enough out to get comparatively cheap land and build out in the direction of other cities, passing near enough to the smaller cities, towns and villages to summarily attract much of their renting population. This movement will surely mark the "Beginning of the end" of such wasteful loafing centers for the few, and the stagnant pools of wasted energy for the many. It will be a line of city through the country.

Edgar Chambless, Roadtown, 1910.

71. Roadtown 1910. Aerial View. Even the Splendid Isolation of Wealth May Take Advantage of the Roadtown Idea.

72. Roadtown ca. 1910. Public Buildings, Surrounded by Parks Instead of Farms, will Depend Upon the Service Through the Endless Basement.

PROPOSED FIRST TEN MILES BETWEEN BALTIMORE AND WASHINGTON SCHEME NO ONE
ROADTOWN
LINES OF CITIES THROUGH THE COUNTRY
ROADTOWN FOUNDATION
BUREAU NAT'L SURVEY
POTENTIAL PROD CAP'Y
EDGAR CHAMBLESS

73. Roadtown 1931. Scheme No. 1. Lines of Cities Thru the Country. Proposed First Ten Miles Between Washington and Baltimore.

Roadtown—1931
Location: Between Washington, D.C., and Baltimore.
Status: Theoretical proposal.
The Empire State Building, the world's largest and most modern skyscraper and the last word in scientific and mechanical thought, best illustrates Roadtown. This giant building furnishes everything needed to take care of thousands of people. Roadtown is the Empire State Building *laid flat on its side on the ground!*

Roadtown comprises one row of houses with the passageway *within*. It is a series of villages linked together. It proposes to decentralize urban population by substituting for present communities of congested city blocks, new communities built in lines, projected out through the country and so arranged that all business, industrial, dwelling and other houses will be within one continuous structure. Private lawns, gardens and farms thus will lie on two sides of every house. There may even be lawn spaces between homes so long as the ground story constitutes a continuous structure. Where lawns do not so divide the upper part of the community structure into detached homes or where such lawns are narrow enough to be bridged over the roofway which may thus be made continuous, they will be used as a sidewalk and for light vehicles, to supplement the other transportation facilities.

Edgar Chambless, Roundtown to Roadtown, 1931.

Chicago Tribune Tower Competition—1922
Location: Chicago.
Status: Unsuccessful competition entries.
The Chicago Tribune's Architectural Competition announced on June 10, 1922, attained a threefold objective: It coincided with the seventy-fifth anniversary of The Chicago Tribune, coming as a fitting commemoration of three-fourths of a century of amazing growth and brilliant achievement. It had for its prime motive the enhancement of civic beauty. It aimed to provide for the world's greatest newspaper a worthy structure, a home that would be an inspiration to its own workers as well as a model for generations of newspaper publishers.

The Tribune proposes to erect an office building upon its North Michigan Avenue property for the housing of its executive and business departments, the project to include enlarged quarters for the steadily expanding departments now operating in the Plant Building. The new structure will be erected directly in front of the Plant with a frontage of 100 feet along Michigan Boulevard, and will become the headquarters of this great city newspaper. In addition to ample facilities for present operations, the building will be adaptable to the future expansion of all departments.

To erect the most beautiful and distinctive office building in the world is the desire of The Tribune, and in order to obtain the design for such an edifice, this competition has been instituted.

The Competition will be of international scope, qualified Architects of established reputation in all parts of the world being eligible, and not more than ten (10) Architects or firms of Architects of repute in the United States will be specially invited to submit designs.

The Tribune Tower Competition, 1923.

Alfred Fellheimer (Chicago—New York City)
Education: 1895, BS, University of Illinois.
Among Major Works: Union Station, Cincinnati; Turnpike Buildings, New Jersey; Queens College Science Building, N.Y.C.; Allied Chemical Company Lab, Morristown, New Jersey.

Walter Burley Griffin (Illinois 1876—India 1937)
Education: 1899, BS, U. of Illinois.
Among Major Works: 1912, won the international competition for the plan of the new capital city Canberra, Australia; 1921, began work on the Castlecrag development in Sydney; 1935, began supervision of the construction of the U. of Lucknow Library, India.

From 1902–1906, Griffin was a member of the Frank Lloyd Wright Oak Park studio.

Walter Gropius (Berlin 1883—Massachusetts 1963)
Education: 1903–1907, student of architecture, Berlin Hochschule and Munich Hochschule.
Among Major Works: 1925–1926, Bauhaus buildings, Dessau; 1936, Impington College, Cambridgeshire (with Maxwell Fry); 1937, Gropius house (with Marcel Breuer), Lincoln, Mass.; 1949, Graduate Center (with TAC), Harvard University; 1963, Pan Am Building (with Pietro Belluschi, and Emory Roth and Sons), New York City.

In 1918 as Director of the School of Arts and Crafts and the Academy of Arts in Weimar, Gropius amalgamated those institutions into the famous Staatliche Bauhaus which was forced to move to Dessau in 1925, and to close in Berlin in 1933; in 1946, he founded The Architects' Collaborative (TAC), when he was professor of Architecture and Chairman of the Department of Architecture at Harvard University.

Adolf Loos (Austria 1870—Austria 1933)
Education: University of Dresden; Technische Hochschule, Dresden.
Among Major Works: 1899, Cafe Museum, Vienna; 1904, Villa Karma, Switzerland; 1911, Steiner house, Vienna; 1912, Scheu house, Vienna; 1926, Tzara house, Paris.

Adolf Meyer (1881—1929)
Meyer became Gropius' first partner ca. 1910, and in 1919 Meyer joined the Bauhaus staff in Weimar. He did a number of Berlin houses on his own as well as industrial buildings.

Claes Oldenburg (1929—) (see Oldenburg for biographical information).

Eliel Saarinen (Helsinki 1873—Michigan 1950)
Education: Helsinki Institute Polytechnic.
Among Major Works: 1900, Finnish pavilion, Paris Expo; 1902, National Museum, Helsinki; 1904, Helsinki Railway Station; 1905, Molchow (country house), Germany; 1939, Cranbrook Academy, Bloomfield Hills, Mich.; 1940, Tabernacle Church, Columbus, Indiana.

James Salmon (Glasgow 1873—?)
Education: Glasgow School of Art and Technical College.
Among Major Works: Mercantile Chambers; St. Vincent Chambers; British Linen Bank (extensions); Queen Street, all in Glasgow.

Bruno Taut (Königsberg 1880—Istanbul 1938)
Education: 1897–1901, Baugewerkschule, Königsberg; 1904–1908, apprenticeship with Theodore Fischer, Stuttgart; 1908–1909, studied city-planning at Technische Hochschule, Berlin.
Among Major Works: 1912–1913, Falkenberg garden suburb; 1914, Glashaus, Werkbund Exposition, Cologne; 1921–1923, city planner of Magdenburg; 1924–1931, large-scale housing in Berlin.

Taut was a prime mover of German Expressionist architecture; he helped found the Arbeitsrat für Kunst in Berlin in 1918 and sparked the Utopian Correspondence of these architects and artists during 1919–1920.

Steward Wagner (Texas 1886—New York City 1958)
Education: 1907–1909, special drawing and design course, Columbia University; 1907–1910, Beaux Arts Institute, Atelier Hornbostel, N.Y.C.

Eric Fisher Wood (?—Pennsylvania 1962)
Education: 1911, graduate, Yale University; Columbia University; École des Beaux Arts, Paris.

Eric Wood, a Major General in the U.S. Army, was a founder of the American Legion.

Proposal by Adolf Loos

No pictorial representation is capable of rendering the effect of this column; the smooth burnished surfaces of the cube and the fluting of the column overwhelm the observer. It would create a surprise, a sensation, even in our modern and blasé times.

The large Greek Doric column will be built. If not in Chicago then in another city. If not for the *Chicago Tribune* perhaps for someone else. If not by myself, then by another architect.

Adolf Loos.

74. Adolf Loos. France.

75. Saverio Dioguardi. Italy.

76. Alfred Fellheimer and Steward Wagner. New York City.

77. Walter Gropius and Adolf Meyer. Germany.

78. Walter Burley Griffin. Australia.

79. Ludwig Koloch. Germany.

80. Frank Fort. New York City.

C CHICAGO TRIBUNE TOWER COMPETITION 1922

81. Heinrich Mossdorf, Hans Hahn and Bruno Busch. Germany.

82. Einar Sjostrom and Jarl Eklund. Finland.

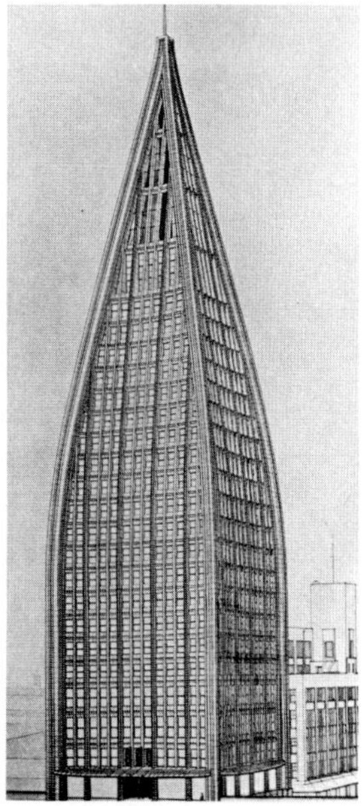

83. Bruno Taut, Walter Gunther and Kurz Schutz. Germany.

84. Eliel Saarinen. Finland. Dwight Wallace and Bertell Grenman. Chicago.

85. James Salmon. Scotland.

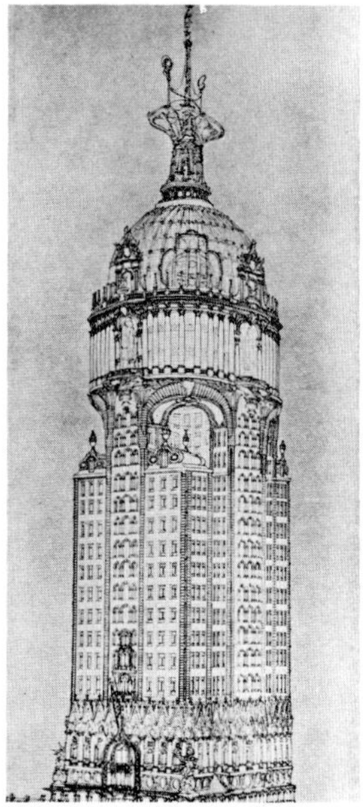

86. Anonymous Entry.

87. Late Submission by Claes Oldenburg. New York City.

Proposal by Claes Oldenburg
Late Submission to the Chicago Tribune
Architectural Competition of 1922—1967
Location: Chicago.
Status: Late submission.
When I flew to Chicago in October, 1967, I took along an old-fashioned wooden clothespin because I liked its shape. Later back in New York, I worked the pin up as a skyscraper, inspired by recollections of the *Chicago Tribune* Competition of 1922. Among the designs submitted were several versions of a skyscraper in the form of a column, including one by Adolf Loos: a building in the form of an Indian with raised tomahawk, another in the form of Skeezix, the comic-strip character. My clothespin seemed to belong in this company, especially since it had a gothic look—like the winner, still standing, the Tribune Tower.

The "spring" of the Colossal Clothespin is a tunnel through which the wind can sound. The area between the "legs" would also be a huge wind tunnel, with blue glass facing the inside. The rod of the spring along the side of the building would be glassed in and contain a restaurant.

Claes Oldenburg, Object into Monument, 1971.

Christo (Bulgaria 1935—)
Residence: New York City.
Education: 1952–1956, Fine Arts Academy, Sofia, Bulgaria.
Among Major Works: 1958, first "Packages" and "Wrapped Objects," Paris; 1968, first packaging of a public building "Packed Kunsthalle Berne," Documenta 4, Kassel, Germany; 1969, "Wrapped Coast-Little Bay-One Million Square Feet," Sydney, Australia; 1971–1972, "Valley Curtain," Grand Hogback, Rifle, Colo. (200,000 square feet of Nylon Polyamide); 1974, "Ocean Front," Newport, R.I. (150,000 square feet of floating polypropylene).

Wrapped Building No. 1—1968

Location: Times Square, New York City.
Status: Hypothetical proposal.

88. Wrapped Building No. 1. Times Square. Collaged Photograph.

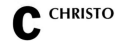

Closed Highway—1969
Location: Across the U.S.A.
Status: Hypothetical proposal.
Project for closing 5,000 miles, 6 lanes, East-West Highways across the U.S.A. At all entrances there will be glass walls, 36 to 48 feet high and 36 inches thick.

Christo.

89. Closed Highway. Aerial View.

Mario J. Ciampi (California 1907—)
Residence: San Francisco, California.
Education: 1927–1929, San Francisco Architectural Club; 1930–1932, Harvard University Graduate School of Architecture; 1932–1933, Beaux Arts Institute of Design, Paris.
Among Major Works: 1954, Westmoor High School, Master Plan, Daley, Calif.; 1962, Downtown San Francisco Master Plan; 1970, University Art Museum, University of California, Berkeley; 1966, Panhandle and Golden Gate Freeway study, San Francisco, in association with John Carl Warnecke; 1971, Embarcadero Plaza, San Francisco, in association with Lawrence Halprin, and John Bolles.

Callan Executive Office Development—1973

Location: San Mateo, California.
Status: Pending.

The site is a wooded, hilly landscape. The intention is to create a dynamic synthesis of building and site in one organic sculpture. There has been criticism by the developers that it does not have the appearance of conventional towers. Further development of the project has been deferred until the economic climate improves.

Mario Ciampi.

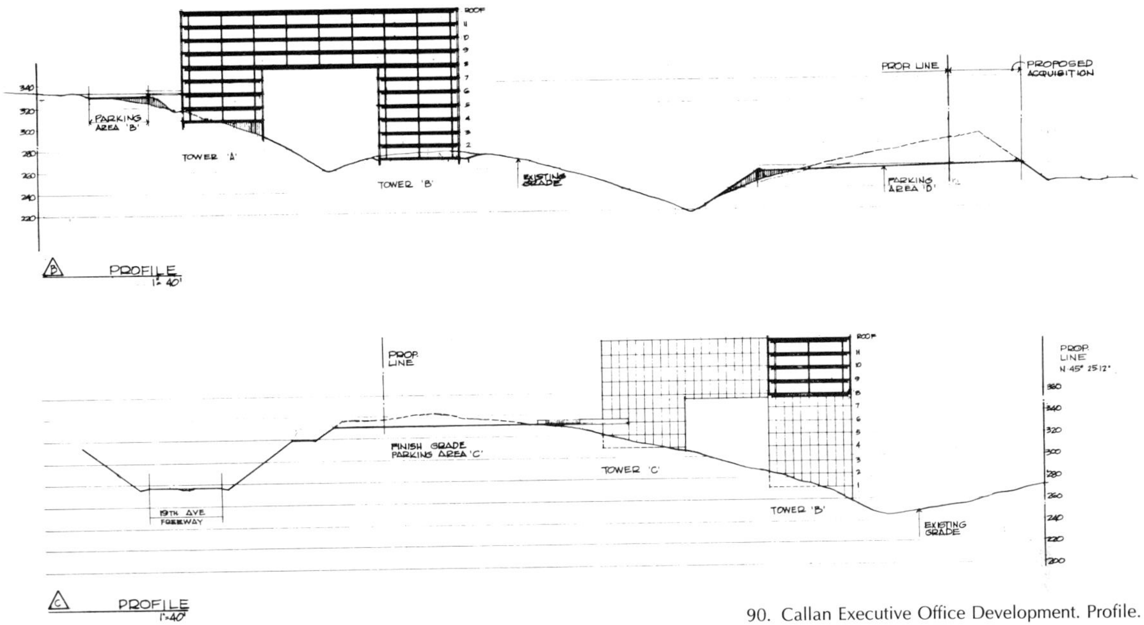

90. Callan Executive Office Development. Profile.

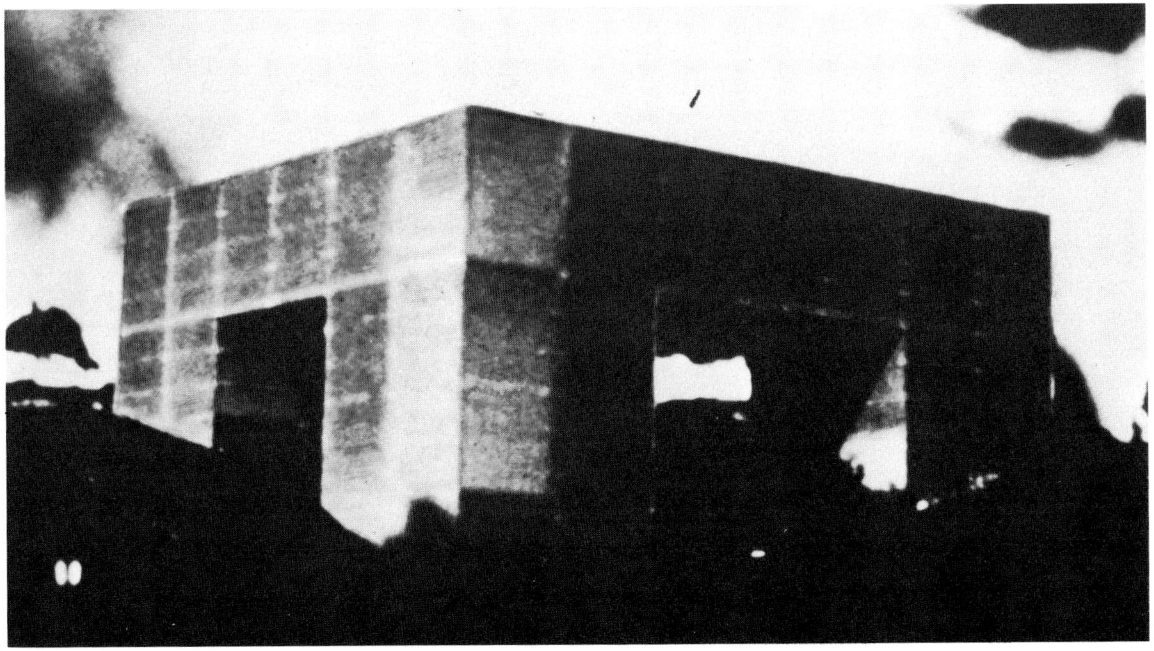

91. Callan Executive Office Development. Photo Montage.

Thomas Cole (England 1801—New York 1848)
Education: As a boy of fourteen, Cole worked as an apprentice to a designer of calico prints, a year later he was an engraver's assistant; 1823–1825, studied painting formally at the Pennsylvania Academy of Fine Arts, Philadelphia.
Among Major Paintings: 1828, "Expulsion from the Garden of Eden"; 1833, "The Titan's Goblet"; 1837, "In the Catskills"; 1838, "Dream of Arcadia."

The Voyage of Life—Youth—1840
Status: An allegorical series of paintings.
The series is comprised in Four Pictures. The first represents the period of Childhood; the second, Youth; the third, Manhood; the fourth, Old Age.

YOUTH—The stream now pursues its course through a landscape of wider scope, and more diversified beauty. Trees of rich growth overshadow its banks, and verdant hills form the base of lofty mountains. The Infant of the former scene is become a Youth, on the verge of Manhood. He is now alone in the Boat, and takes the helm himself, and in an attitude of confidence and eager expectation, gazes on a cloudy pile of Architecture, an air-built Castle, that rises dome above dome in the far-off blue sky. The Guardian Spirit stands upon the bank of the stream, and, with serious, yet benignant countenance, seems to be bidding the impetuous Voyager Godspeed. The beautiful stream flows for a distance, directly toward the aeriel palace; but at length makes a sudden turn, and is seen in glimpses beneath the trees, until it at last descends with rapid current into a rocky ravine, where the Voyager will be found in the next picture. Over the remote hills, which seem to intercept the stream, and turn in from its hitherto direct course, a path is dimly seen, tending directly toward that cloudy Fabric, which is the object and desire of the Voyager.

The scenery of the picture—its clear stream, its lofty trees, its towering mountains, its unbounded distance, and transparent atmosphere—figure forth the romantic beauty of youthful imaginings, when the mind elevates the Mean and Common into the Magnificent, before experience teaches what is the Real. The gorgeous cloud-built palace whose glorious domes seem yet but half revealed to the eye, growing more and more lofty as we gaze, is emblematic of the daydreams of Youth, its aspirations after glory and fame; and the dimly-seen path would intimate that Youth, in its impetuous career, is forgetful that it is embarked on the Stream of Life, and that its current sweeps along with resistless force, and increases in swiftness, as it descends toward the great ocean of Eternity.

Thomas Cole in Louis Legrand Noble's
The Life and Works of Thomas Cole,
1856.

92. Voyage of Life—Youth. Painting.

Conklin and Rossant (established New York City 1963—)
Principals: William Conklin, James Rossant.
Among Major Works of Firm: 1966, First Village and Heron House, Reston, Virginia; 1968, Two Charles Center, Baltimore, Md.; 1968, Usdan Day Camp for Music and Arts, New York; 1969, Wilton State School for Mentally Retarded, New York; 1969, State University of New York Upstate Medical Center.

Myriad Gardens—1971
Location: Oklahoma City.
Status: Pending.
Additional Credit: Giuliano Fiorenzoli, Peter Mahony, Hammer, Greene, Siler Associates, Victor Tabaka and Associates.

In a unique, intentional and planned manner, Myriad Gardens will consolidate a series of parks and gardens, along with facilities for shopping, civic activities, exhibition, commerce and entertainment to become the new focus for downtown Oklahoma City. It will bring together separated pieces and functions of downtown to define a new relationship between urban man and the natural world where the environment will be exclusively oriented to the pedestrian.

On the edge of the central business district of Oklahoma City, a 25-ft.-deep underground stratum of clear stream water will be tapped and revealed to create a canyon where, in four levels along its walls, all new functions will have their access and frontage. As the center and symbol for the new urban ecology, the glass enclosed Botanical Garden will span the canyon walls over a newly created lake to provide a daily travel link between peripheral parking and the downtown core.

Conklin and Rossant.

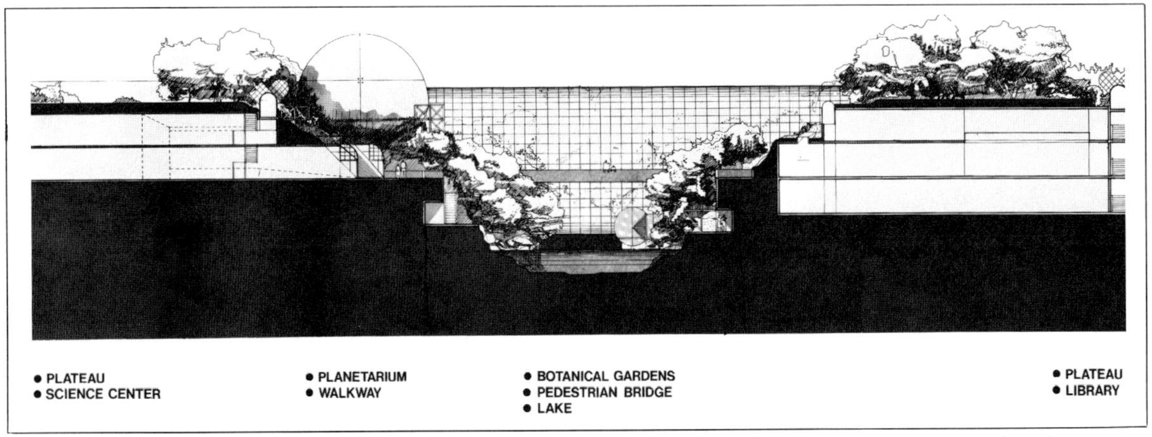

93. Myriad Gardens. Section.

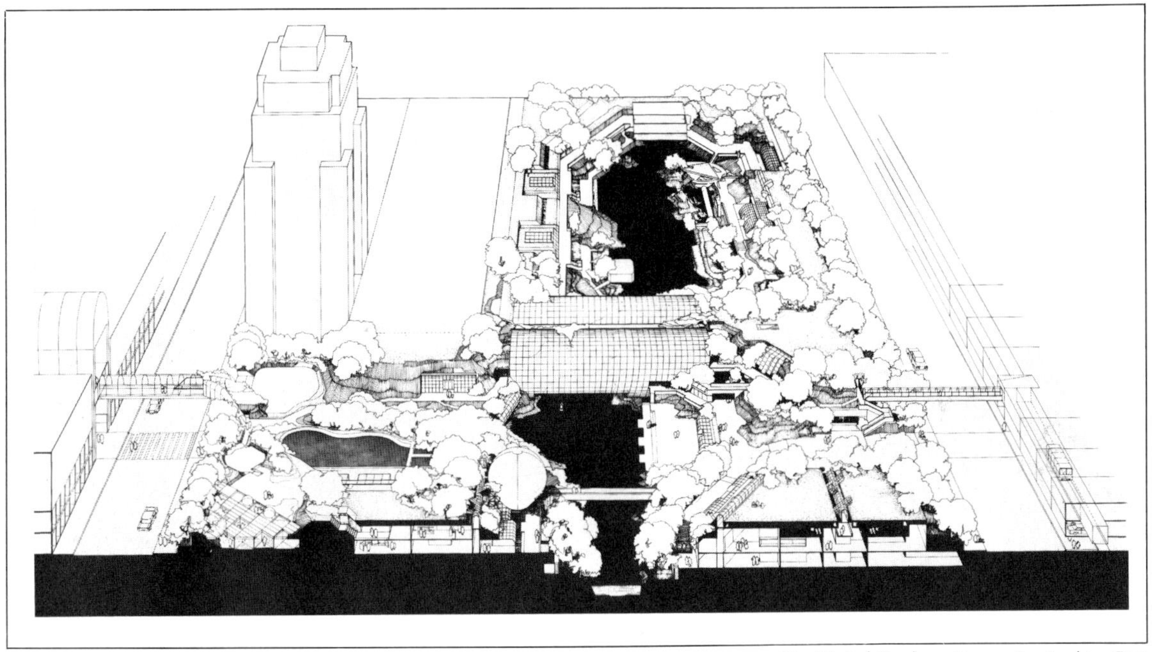

94. Myriad Gardens. Perspective Looking East.

Future City—1973
Status: Study sketch.
A city developed around communication, service and circulatory systems. The outer surface of this network is utilized for living.

James Rossant.

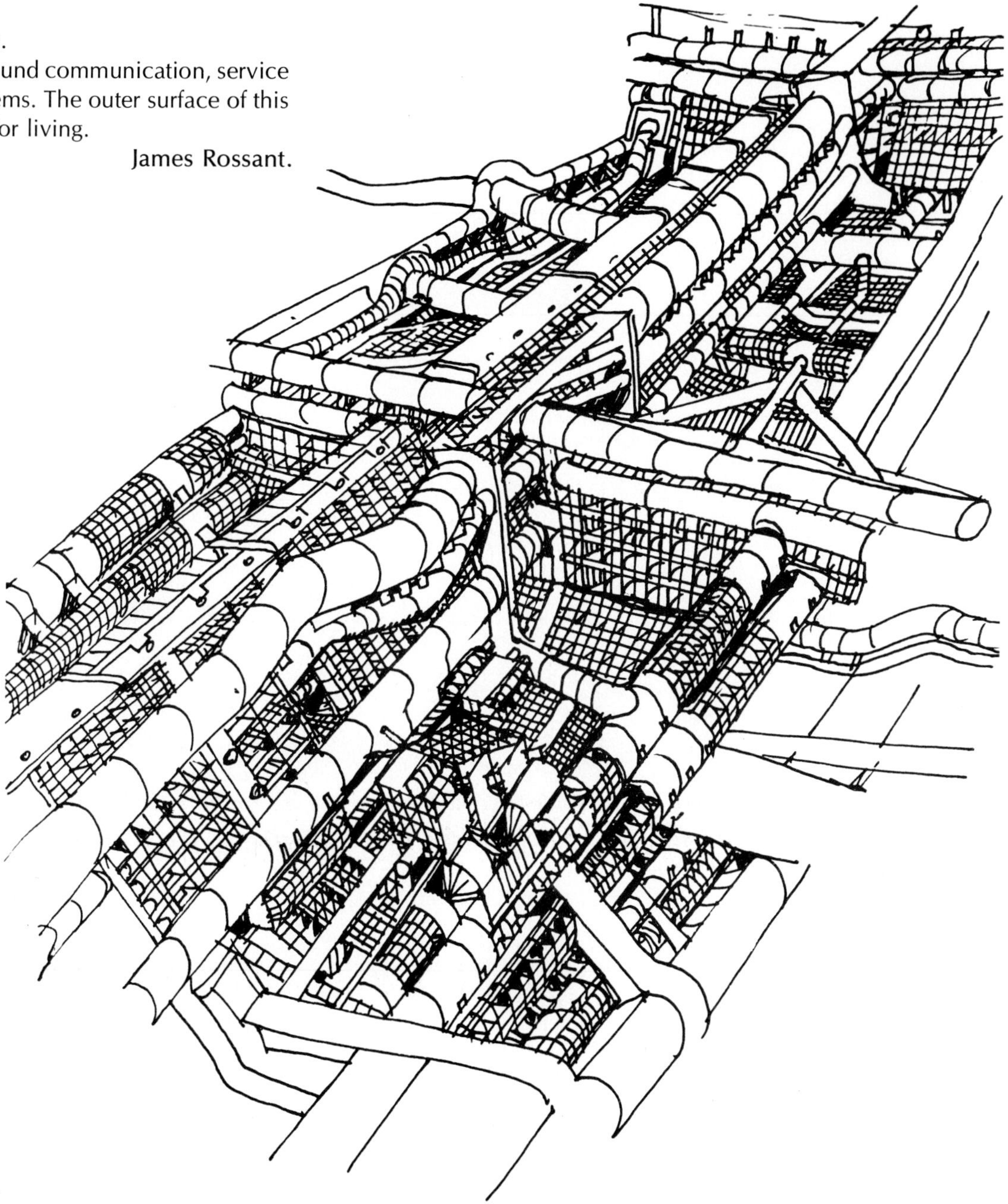

95. Future City. Aerial View. Drawing by James Rossant.

Harvey Wiley Corbett (San Francisco 1873—New York 1954)
Education: Engineering degree, University of California; 1900, Diplôme, École des Beaux Arts, Paris.
Among Major Works: 1923, Roerich Museum; 1923, Criminal Courts Building, N.Y.C.; 1930–1932, Rockefeller Center (Corbett was the senior architect in the firm of Corbett, Harrison and MacMurray, which was one of the three firms in the design of the center).
In 1922, Corbett prepared zoning envelope studies in collaboration with Hugh Ferriss. He was the chairman of the architectural committee for the Chicago Century of Progress Exposition of 1933, and chairman of the advisory committee for the 1939 New York World's Fair theme.

The Problem of Traffic Congestion—1927
Location: New York City.
Status: Prototype.

My belief is based upon the fact that a city is composed of human elements which may constantly present changing equations. The city may be likened to a living body, with arteries, veins, and capillaries. As the corpuscles of the blood carry the nutriment through the arteries, slow down to deposit it in the capillaries, take up the waste and carry it away through the veins—so, metaphorically speaking, do the various forms of conveyance in the city carry the people and freight, which are the food of the city, through the avenues, slow down in the side streets, stop and deposit their loads in the buildings, take up new loads, and again continue the cycle. This movement of traffic is just as essential to the life of the city as the movement of the blood is to the life of the body.

To retain existing property lines, in principle, even though the city increases the restrictions over what may be done within those lines, is always simpler than any attempt to change those lines. I therefore question the desirability of a wholesale cutting of new streets or a widening of present streets, but since the city must grow, the streets must be increased in capacity, and since they can't be widened or increased in number, some form of double decking of streets is not a new idea. Leonardo da Vinci proposed it in a scheme to replan Milan.

It seems rational in any scheme proposing to divide traffic into divisions through a process of double or triple decking the streets, that we start by placing the wheel traffic, the largest and most rapidly growing, on the present street level, which is already there and requires neither to be dug out nor built up; that all rail traffic be placed underground, as subways; and that foot traffic be raised one story above the street level, carrying bridges across at all corners, and at one or two points in the long blocks as well, so that people can move uninterruptedly throughout as large a district as is covered by the expansion of the double decking idea. Double decking, while difficult, is not impossible. Supposing even this to become crowded it could continue until the entire surface under the buildings is available for traffic, if ever such a condition should demand it.

Visualizing the result we see a city with sidewalks arcaded and with solid railings. We see the smaller parks of the city, of which we trust there will be many more than at present, raised to this same sidewalk-arcade level, public parking space for autos being provided underneath, and the whole aspect has become that of a very modernized Venice, a city of arcades, piazzas and bridges, with canals for streets, only the canals will not be filled with water but with freely flowing motor traffic, the sun glittering on the black tops of the cars and the buildings reflected in this waving flood of rapidly rolling vehicles.

Abridged from **Harvey Wiley Corbett** in *Architectural Forum,* XLVI, March 1927.

96. Present Condition of an Average Street.

97. First Step Toward Improvement.

98. Parking Space Provided Beneath Buildings.

99. Arcaded Sidewalks Within Buildings.

100. Early Proposal for the Elevated Sidewalk: How it will solve City Transportation Problems. If the real capacity of power-propelled machinery is to be gained in city transportation, foot and vehicular traffic must be segregated. Each type of transport will be free to develop itself along its own lines. *Scientific American,* Cover, 1913.

Jack R. Cosner (Louisiana 1935—)
Residence: New Orleans, Louisiana.
Education: BS, University of Houston; B Arch., Tulane University; MS Urban Design, Columbia University.
Among Major Works: Hilton Hotel on the Mississippi Gulf Coast; renovation and design for the Lamar County (Mississippi) Courthouse; restoration of his own home originally constructed in 1840, for which he received an award from the Vieux Carré Commission; revitalization of the (1834) Old U.S. Mint Building in New Orleans.

Piazza d'Italia—1975
Location: New Orleans, Louisiana.
Status: Unsuccessful competition entry.
Additional Credit: Charles Colbert.

New Orleans exists primarily because of the Mississippi River, yet few present-day residents recognize the river's historic significance. The most magnificent flora resulting from the river are the Live Oak and Bald Cypress trees. The New Orleans Italian community could make a lasting contribution to their city if they would acknowledge in a new and dynamic way these symbols of the lower Mississippi Valley and its historic ecology.

A piazza is by definition an open public square. The proposed site for the Piazza d'Italia in New Orleans is, as it currently exists, a series of alleys with no opportunity for "an open public square." Consequently, it is proposed that certain buildings that have been rated "historically significant" be relocated to adjacent properties, the Tchoupitoulas Street façade be retained intact, and be treated as a "veil" or "screen" for the piazza beyond. By extending the piazza paving pattern to building lines of the surrounding streets, the effective area of the piazza is doubled.

In this proposal, the force of the river activates the rising and falling of a fully grown Lousiana Live Oak Tree, with a system of hydraulics based upon the principal of the barometer. This fluctuation can vary up to nineteen feet in any given year. The Water Court would seat 500 people for outdoor performances, and always be sheltered from the elements by the gigantic transparent space frame forty feet above.

Jack Cosner and Charles Colbert.

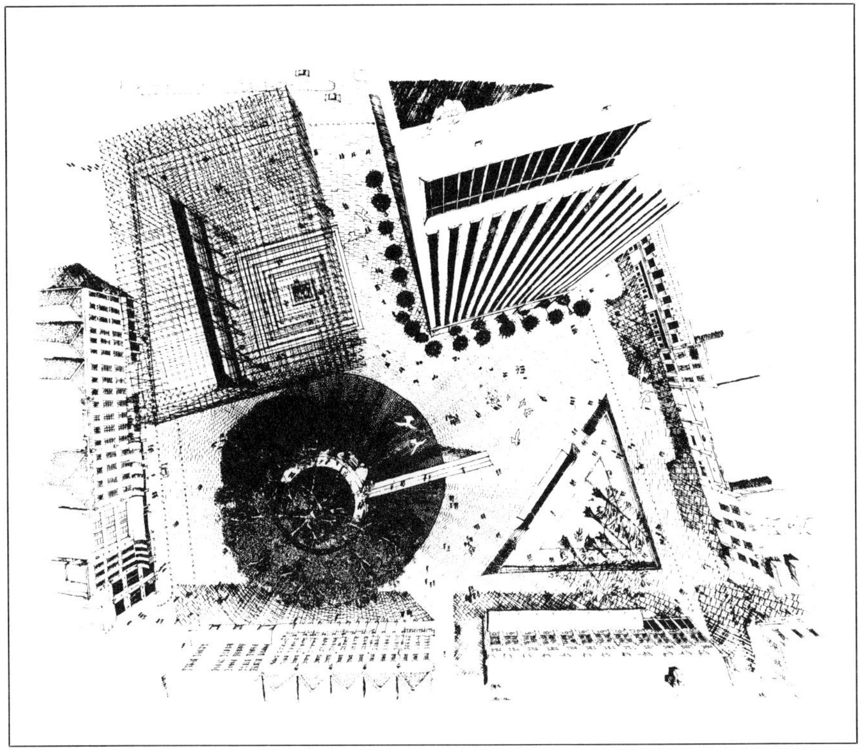

101. Piazza d'Italia. Aerial View.

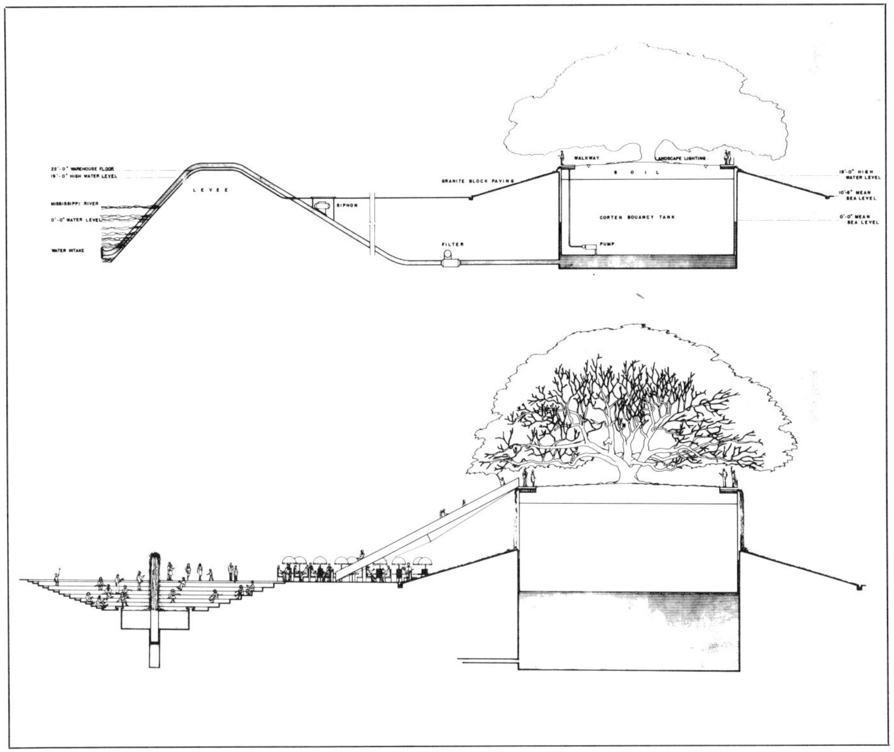

102. Piazza d'Italia. Section at River, High Water.

Ralph Adams Cram (New Hampshire 1863—Boston 1942)
Education: 1881–1886, apprenticed in Boston in the firm of Rotch and Tilden, both of whom had been trained at the École des Beaux Arts, Paris.
Among Major Works: 1903–1910, won the competition for the rebuilding of West Point and designed the Cadet Chapel; 1906, St. Thomas Church, N.Y.C.; 1915–1925, academic and dormitory buildings, Exeter Academy, New Hampshire; 1909–1931, supervising architect for Princeton University, N.J.; 1911–1942, consulting architect for the redesign of the Cathedral of St. John the Divine, N.Y.C.

Arthur Asabel Shurcliff (Boston 1870—Boston 1957)
Education: 1894, Graduate, Massachusetts Institute of Technology; 1896, Graduate, Lawrence Scientific School of Harvard University.
Among Major Works: Landscape architect for restoration of Williamsburg, Virginia; redesigned the Boston Common; laid out the Storrow Memorial Embankment along the Charles River, Boston.

Mr. Shurcliff worked with the firm of Olmsted and Olmsted from 1896 to 1905. In 1900, he helped to establish the Harvard School of Landscape Architecture.

Samuel Chamberlain (Iowa 1895—Massachusetts 1975)
Education: Graduate, Arch., Massachusetts Institute of Technology.
Among Major Publications: *Sketches of Northern Spanish Architecture, Domestic Architecture in Rural France, Tudor Homes in England, Cape Cod in the Sun.*

Although an architect, Samuel Chamberlain devoted most of his energy to drawing, photography, writing, and book illustration.

Memorial to Soldiers, Sailors and Marines—1921

Location: Boston.
Status: Unbuilt due to resistance of local residents.

The plan proposes that an island of perhaps ten acres be built in the Charles River contiguous to the western side of Harvard Bridge. There would be practically no cost for the land for the island, only for reclamation, as it would presumably be made out of land dredged from the Basin.

Upon this island the plan proposes a high tower rising from a colonnade and containing a great carillon or chime of bells. The tower would have somewhat the same uplifting spiritual dominion over its environment that a cathedral has over a countryside, or that a New England church spire has over its village. The plan proposes two utilities both important yet both incidental and subordinate to the memorial:

1. The erection of an open air auditorium west of the tower capable of holding a very large number of people.

2. The development of the residue of the island with trees and shrubs and grass, making

103. Ralph Adams Cram. Proposed Island in the Charles River. Aerial View.

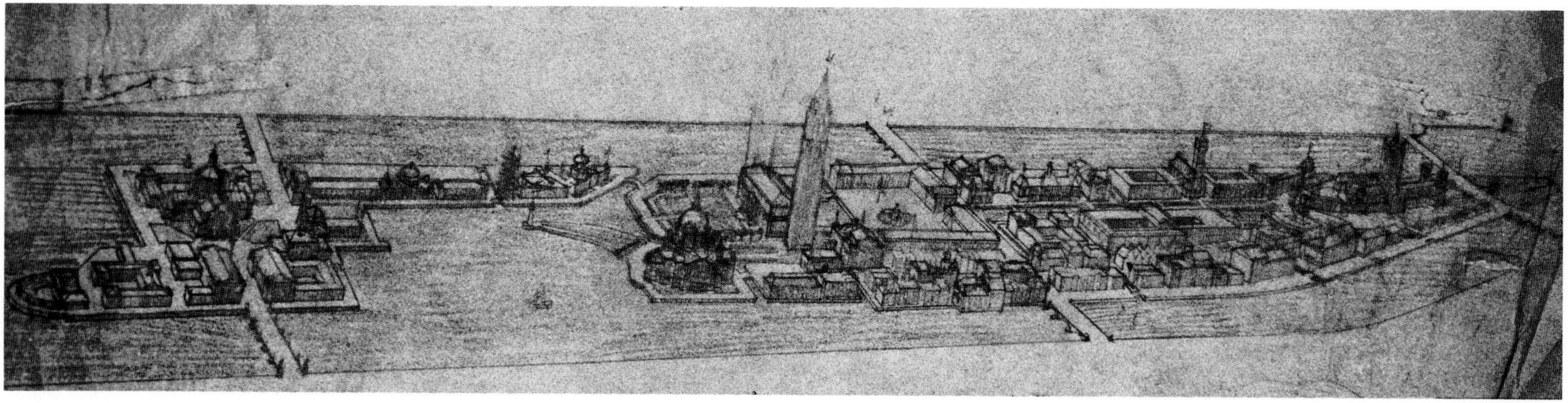

with its presumably indented shore line a beautiful water park open to all the public.

From **A Report of the Sub-Committee** appointed by the Mayor of Boston in 1921, to submit plans for a soldiers', sailors', and marines' memorial. **Ralph A. Cram and Arthur Shurcliff** were both members of the committee.

I suppose the particular invention of mine which aroused the greatest indignation was that for an island in the Charles River Basin, across the axis of the old Harvard Bridge. Simultaneously and without collusion, Arthur Shurcliff and I evolved the same idea, though the configuration and placing of the island were different in the two cases. As for my own device, it was to be of practically the size and shape as the *Île de la Cité* in Paris, and was to provide settings for, amongst other structures, a new City Hall, Cathedral, and open-air theatre. It was a grand scheme, I am persuaded; but, again through lack of imagination, citizens, particularly those resident on the water side of Beacon Street, could not endure even the mention of such a thing.

Ralph A. Cram, My Life in Architecture, 1936.

104. Sub-Committee Proposal. Island in the Charles River. Detail of Tower. Painting by Samuel Chamberlain.

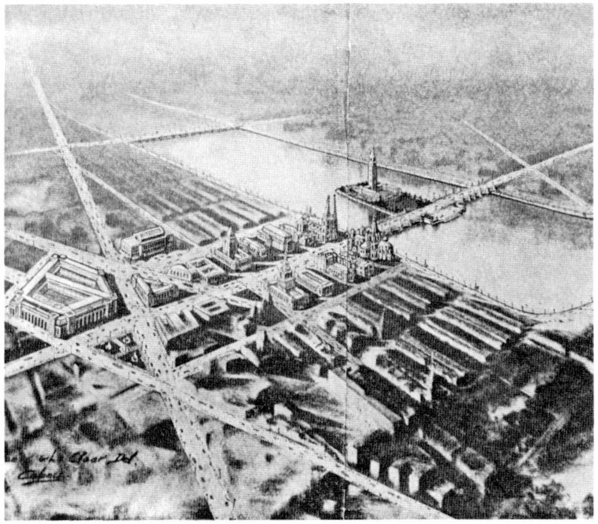

105. Sub-Committee Proposal. Island in the Charles River. Aerial View.

Crystal Palace Competition—1852
Location: New York City.
Status: Unsuccessful competition entries.
This was to be America's first World's Fair. The idea grew out of the Crystal Palace in London, which Joseph Paxton designed and built the previous year.

It was the desire to afford the masses in America an opportunity to see the grand total of the world's industry, and manifold productions and applications of the arts of design brought in one comparative view. New York was selected as the locality of the Exhibition, because of its great advantages as a commercial centre, and as the chief entrepôt of European goods.

The New York palace constructed, was designed by Georg Carstensen and Karl Gildenmeister, German architects. Presumably fireproof, the contents of the building caught fire, and it burned down in 1858.

Professor B. Silliman, Jr., and C. R. Goodrich, Esq., editors, The World of Art and Industry, 1854.

James Bogardus (New York State 1800—1874)
Education: Attended school irregularly until the age of fourteen; apprenticed to a watchmaker.
Among Major Works: 1854, Harper and Brothers printing plant, New York City; 1855, shot tower for the McCullough Shot and Lead, Co., New York City; Baltimore Sun Building; Adams Express Building, Washington, D.C.; Public Ledger Building, Philadelphia.

Bogardus was an inventor, and in 1849 patented his system of cast-iron construction. He introduced the universal I-beam to the United States, and in 1850 erected his own five-story factory building which is said to have been the first complete cast-iron building in the world.

Andrew Jackson Downing (New York 1815—New York 1852)
Education: Completed formal schooling at age sixteen; self-taught through reading, correspondence with professionals, and travel.
Among Major Writings: 1841, *Treatise on the Theory and Practice of Landscape Gardening, Adapted to North America;* 1842, *Cottage Residences;* 1846, became editor of *The Horticulturalist;* 1853, *Rural Essays.*

Downing was America's first great landscape gardener, adapting the principles of informal English garden planning to the North American environment. His books created a national interest in landscaping country homes and estates, and his ideas influenced Frederick Law Olmsted.

Leopold Eidlitz (Prague 1823—New York 1908)
Education: Studied at the Polytechnic, Vienna.
Among Major Works: 1853, Holy Trinity Church, New York City; 1859, Broadway Tabernacle, New York City; Emanuel Synagogue, New York City; American Exchange Bank, New York City; 1860, Brooklyn Academy of Music.

Entry by James Bogardus
Its form is circular, forming an amphitheatre 1200 feet in circumference, and designed to cover the whole ground. The entire structure is a multiple of three or four principal parts, any one of which could afterwards be employed in constructing ordinary iron warehouses. The plan was recommended by its economy, the parties offering to put up the whole building for the sum of two hundred thousand dollars. The tower in the centre was to serve the double purpose of a support for the hanging roof of sheet-iron suspended from it by rods in a catenary curve, and also as a grand observatory. For this end it was to be 300 feet high, and provided with a mechanism for hoisting observers to the top by steam power.

Professor B. Silliman, Jr., and C. R. Goodrich, Esq.

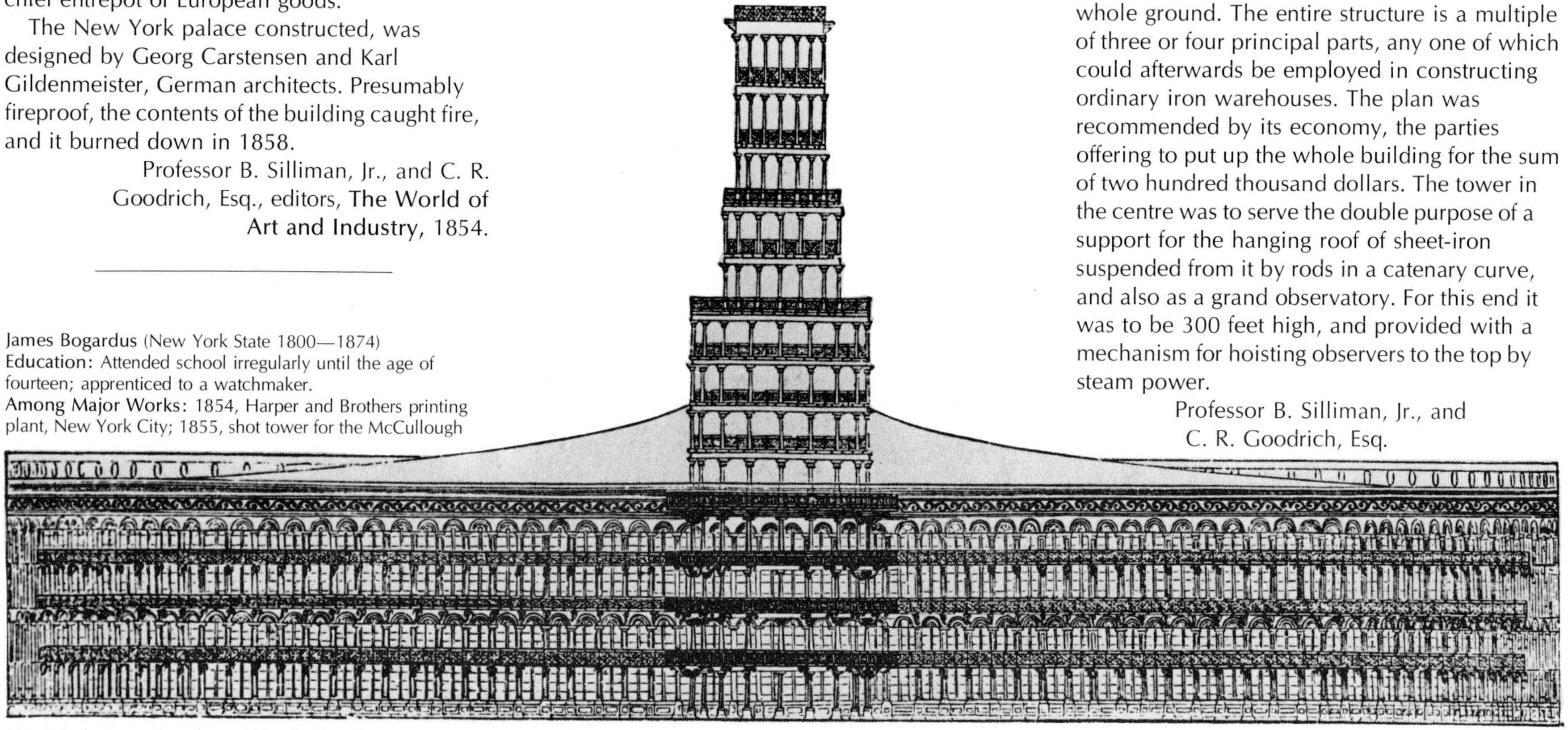

106. Entry by James Bogardus and Hoppin. Elevation.

Entry by Andrew Jackson Downing
The ground plan is a circle intended to occupy the whole of the site, and to be surmounted by a colossal dome, built of wood and canvas, with supporting columns of iron. The canvas, lining the interior, is designed to be of pearl-gray color at the springing line, gradually deepening into an intense blue at the crown. The external ribs, being covered with tin and glass tiles, would produce an effect similar to that of silvering. The general plan has been to make the interior light and airy, and to give unity of character to the design, by avoiding smallness of parts, and arranging in such a manner that it may be conspicuous at a distance.

Professor B. Silliman, Jr., and C. R. Goodrich, Esq., editors, *The World of Art and Industry*, 1854.

Entry by Leopold Eidlitz
This proposal involved an extensive use of iron. The progenitor of the design was Joseph Paxton's London Crystal Palace, except that the rectangular panels of glass and iron are square headed instead of arched. The use by Eidlitz of an external, frankly expressed, system of iron buttressing on the first level and ties on upper levels was unique.

H. Allen Brooks, Jr., *Leopold Eidlitz, 1823–1908*, 1955.

107. Entry by Andrew Jackson Downing. Elevation. Rendering by Calvert Vaux.

108. Entry by Leopold Eidlitz. Detail.

109. Entry by Sir Joseph Paxton. Interior Detail.

110. Entry by Sir Joseph Paxton. Perspective.

Joseph Paxton (England 1803—England 1865)
Education: Woburn Free School, England.
Among Major Works: 1836–1840, Great Conservatory, Chatsworth; 1839–1841, laid out the estate village of Edensor, Derbys; 1845, layout and planning at Buxton, Derbys; 1849, Barbrook House, Edensor, Derbys; 1850–1851, the Crystal Palace, London.

Paxton designed a Great Victorian Way, a continuous arcade of glass and iron which was intended to encircle London and thus avoid congestion in the City, but was never realized.

Entry by Joseph Paxton

The ground plan of the building is a parallelogram; its total area, including the terrace, 24 feet wide, which surrounds it, is about three acres. Its extreme length is 653 feet, and its width 199 feet. The framework is composed of cast-iron columns, connected together by wrought and cast-iron arches and girders, on which rest the wooden arches of the roofs.

Great skill has been shown in constructing the galleries, so as not to interfere with the long perspective of the interior. The galleries were not designed for the display of goods, but for promenades. Its noble nave, lofty and free, with its crowning clerestory, combines with the general simplicity of the plan to give a degree of grandeur to the whole structure, which is conducive to the best architectural effect.

Professor B. Sillman, Jr., and C. R. Goodrich, Esq., editors, *The World of Art and Industry*, 1854.

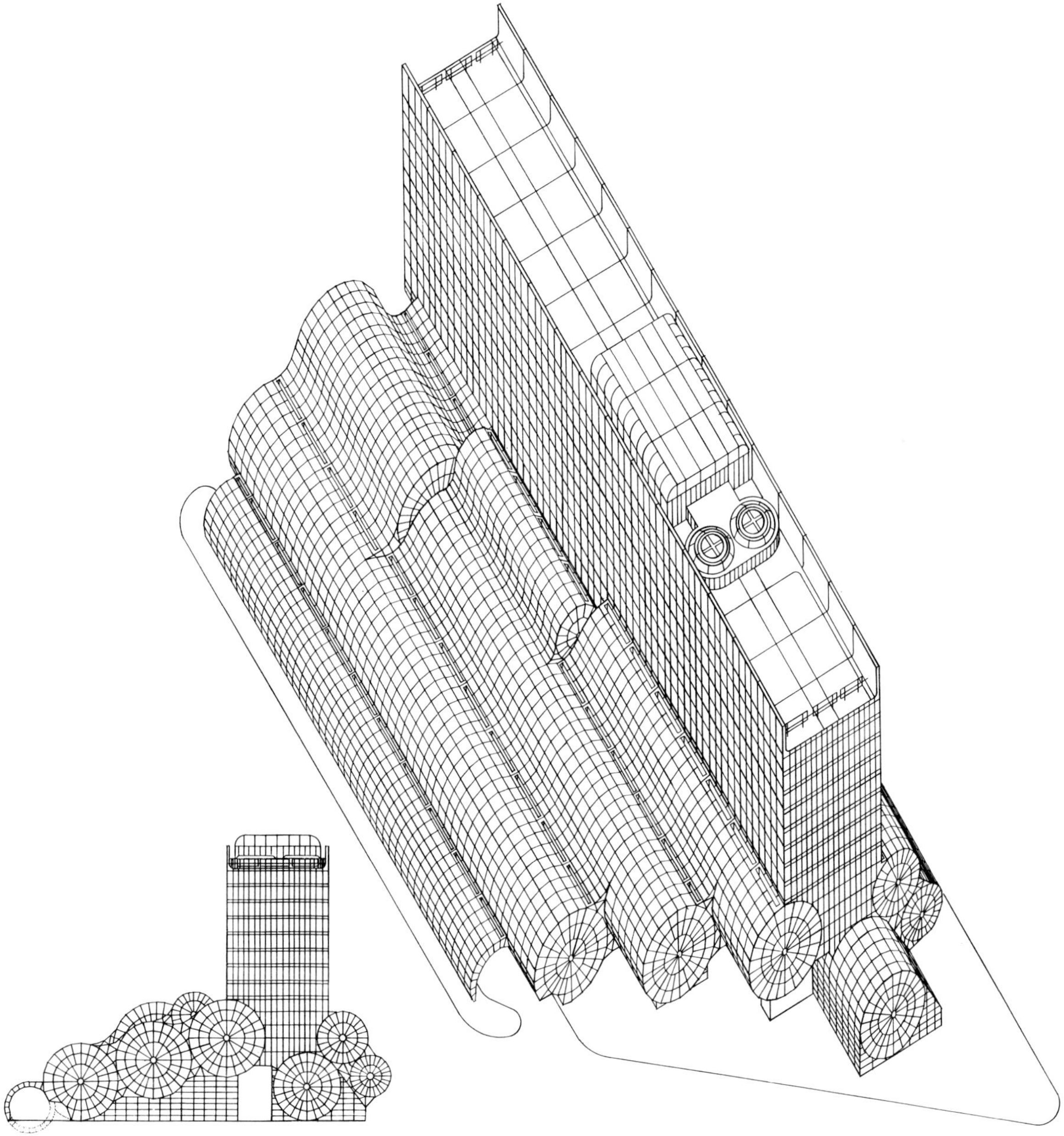
111. North East Elevation.

112. Beverly Hills Plaza Hotel. Axonometric from East.

DMJM (Daniel, Mann, Johnson, and Mendenhall)

Anthony J. Lumsden (England 1928—)
Residence: Los Angeles, California.
Education: B Arch., University of Sydney, Australia.
Among Major Works: Century Bank Building, Federal Aviation Building, One Park Plaza (DMJM Headquarters Building), Kukui Gardens; designer of projected rapid transit system for the Southern California Rapid Transit District.

Anthony Lumsden was associated with the late Eero Saarinen for a period of ten years. He joined DMJM in 1964, and is responsible for the direction of all architectural design.

Beverly Hills Plaza—1973
Location: Beverly Hills, California, on Santa Monica Boulevard.
Status: Promoters were unable to raise investment capital.
The ground floor consists of the automobile entrance and delivery, access to parking, and street-related commercial shops. Retail shops are located at grade in relation to the commercial streets and established pedestrian patterns. Lobby space, public areas, restaurants, and recreation deck are positioned above the garage. The two upper levels are connected by a series of landscaped terraces. The organization of the garage, commercial, and public space elevates the hotel rooms for views of the Santa Monica Mountains, Century City, and the adjacent golf course.

The structural system of the tower is concrete bearing walls extending from basement to the top of the hotel. The roof varies with changes in volume relating to functions of the public area. Exterior walls are lightweight membrane enclosures of glass and aluminum panels. Roofs over the public areas are glass and aluminum with aluminum mullions supported on steel trusses and frames.

Anthony Lumsden.

Alexander J. Davis (New York City 1803—New Jersey 1892)
Education: Attended the "Antique School" of the National Academy of Design; studied under John Trumbull.
Among Major Works: 1831–1835, State Capitol, Indiana; 1833, U.S. Custom House, N.Y.C.; 1833–1834, State Capitol, North Carolina (all with Ithiel Town); 1838–1841, and 1864–1867, Lyndhurst (for William and Philip B. Paulding and George Merritt), Tarrytown, N.Y.; 1849–1860, Virginia Military Institute buildings, Lexington, Va.
Among Major Publications: 1837 *Rural Residences,* a design handbook for cottage and villa architecture; 1841–1850, architectural illustrations for the publications of Andrew Jackson Downing.

Davis began his career as an artist, drawing views of buildings, and his approach to architecture remained essentially that of an artist and designer, fascinated by problems of composition and massing and by the relationship of buildings to their site and landscape.

The first professional American architect, [Davis] was naturally widely copied by many whose ability was not sufficient to originate or create. *The American Architect and Building News,* XXXV, February 1892.

113. Villa in the English Collegiate Style. Perspective.

Villa in the English Collegiate Style—1834

Location: Fishkill Landing (now Beacon), New York.
Status: The property was sold before the building was executed.

This plan was designed for Robert Donaldson, Esq., of Blithewood, on the Hudson River. The design is irregular, and suited to scenery of a picturesque character, and to an eminence commanding an extensive prospect. The dimensions are 60 feet in front by 30 feet in depth; and the side 50 feet by 20 feet, forming an L like figure, as in the plan. The octagon tower is 50 feet high; the turrets, one on each angle of the front, 37 feet, and the battlement 32 feet. On the right is shown a wing building, intended for a library; and on the left, the kitchen offices, wood, and coach-house. The floors are divided, as shown by plan. A picture gallery might be formed over the entrance hall, and receive its light from the oriel window above the porch; or the same might serve for a library, in which case the wing building would accommodate a collection of pictures.

Alexander Jackson Davis, Rural Residences, 1827.

Although this design previously has been described as built, it was definitely noted by Davis in his office journal that the plans were "not executed." Donaldson sold the property at Fishkill Landing before building, and bought another estate farther up the Hudson at Barrytown; this new estate was called Blithewood, for which Davis made a number of designs, but this design (Villa in the English Collegiate Style) was not carried out there.

Jane B. Davies, Columbia University.

United States Post Office—1867

Location: New York City.
Status: Unsuccessful competition entry.

Davis' exuberant imagination, was always that of an architect. It made of this eclectic work an exciting course in variety of effect—but effects always controlled by a single, personal, architectural imagination. The "Davisean window," for instance (the combining of two windows one above the other into a single vertical motif, with a recessed spandrel), which had appeared in his drawings as early as the late 1820s, was a characteristically liberating form. It became a common feature of many eclectic designs, but in itself it was not eclectic but a new creation. To Davis eclecticism was no mere copying of styles, and his later drawings—chiefly for buildings never erected—are often amazingly prophetic. Take for example his design of 1867 for the United States Post Office in New York; does it not look more like a design of 1916? The scheme reveals, too, his delight in glass, the superb new nineteenth-century building material that was to revolutionize architecture.

Talbot Hamlin, *Journal of the Society of Architectural Historians,* XI, May 1952.

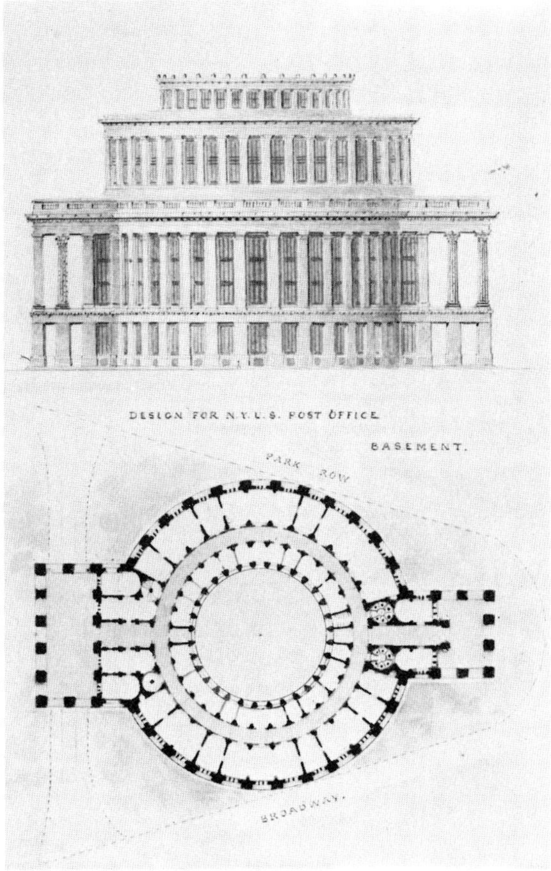

114. Design for United States Post Office. Plan and Elevation.

Forest Lodge No. 1—ca. 1855
Status: Study.
This is possibly one of several studies which Davis made for his own summer "lodge" on Orange Mountain, West Orange, New Jersey.
Jane B. Davies, Columbia University.

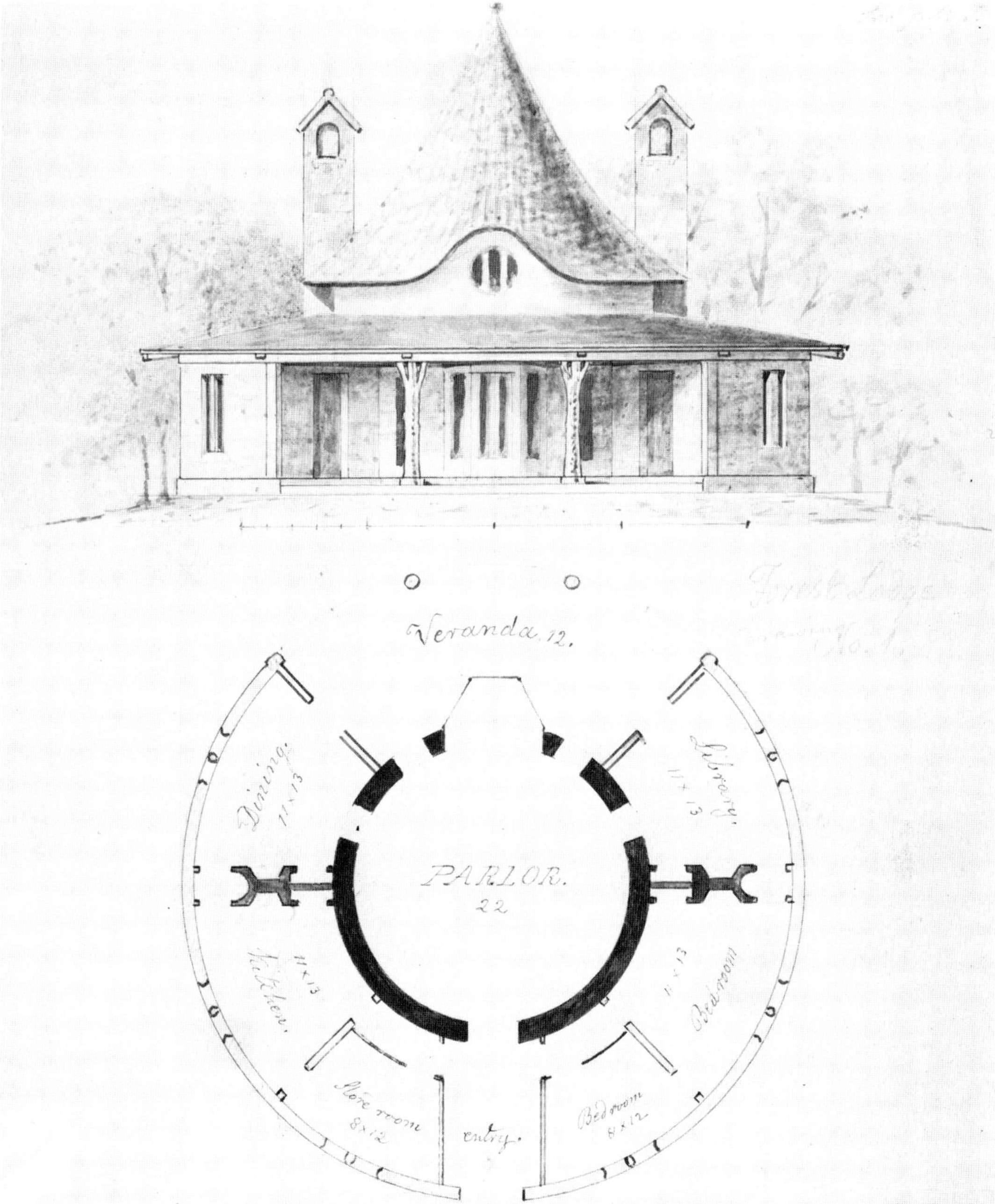

115. Forest Lodge No. 1. Plan and Elevation.

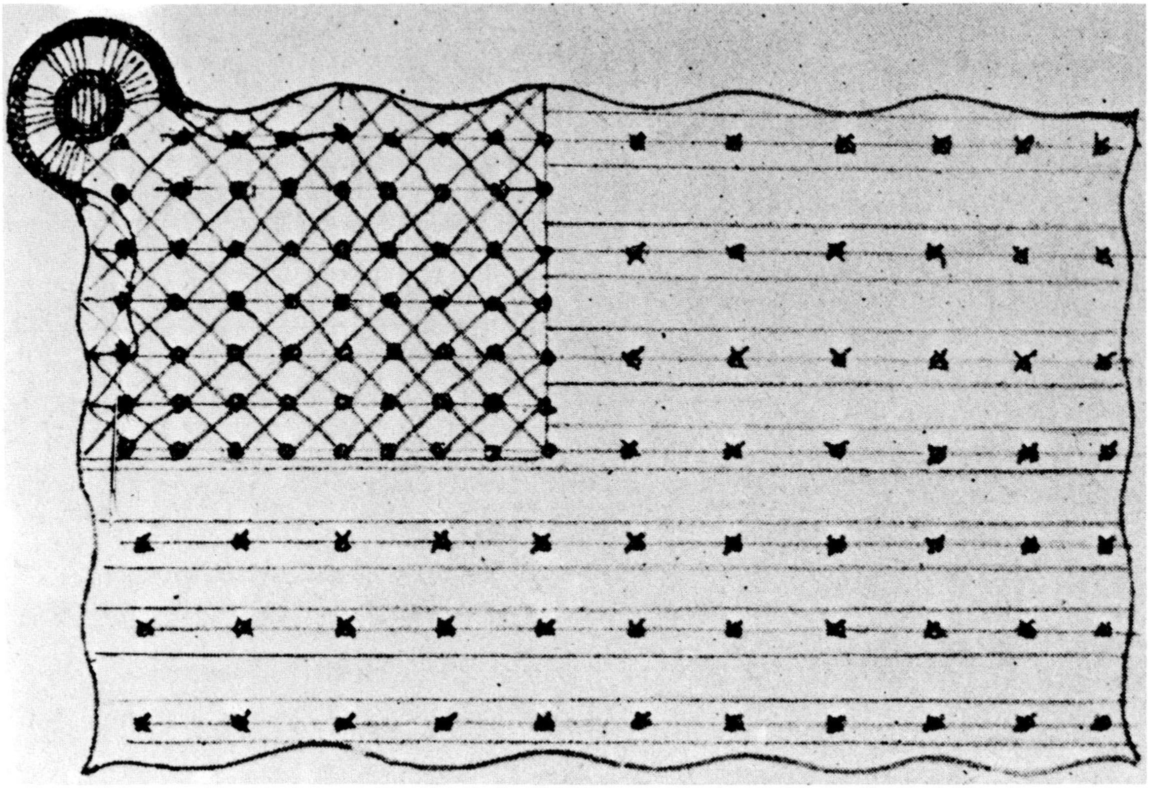

116. A Government Office Building for a Metropolis. Plan.

William Adams Delano (New York City 1874—New York City 1960)
Education: 1895, BA, Yale University; 1903, Diplôme, École des Beaux Arts, Paris; 1908, BFA, Yale University.
Among Major Works: American Embassy, Paris; Japanese Embassy, Washington, D.C.; Post Office Building in Washington's Triangle; La Guardia Airport Terminal building, N.Y.; the Knickerbocker, Colony, India House, Brook and Union Clubs, N.Y.C.

William Adams Delano was Professor of Design at Columbia University, from 1903 to 1910. In the late 1890s he had worked in the firm of Carrère and Hastings where he met Chester Holmes Aldrich. From 1902 to 1950 they formed the partnership of Delano and Aldrich. As a firm they continued the Beaux Arts tradition in New York.

A Government Office Building for a Metropolis—ca. 1932
Status: Theoretical study.

I feel that it contains all the elements of great architecture. It shows freedom from restraint; it displays none of the narrow provincialism which characterizes the work of the architects of Greece, Italy, France, and even our own Colonial Period. It is free from all prejudices, inhibitions, fallacies, and traditions which throughout the ages have done so much to cramp architecture and bring it into disrepute. It has form, mass, and movement. The plan expresses the elevation and the elevation the plan. Both are simple and straightforward and display those qualities of Nationalism, Fundamentalism, Functionalism, and Space-enclosurism so rarely found and so much to be desired in the best architecture.

William Adams Delano in *Pencil Points,* XIII, July 1932.

117. A Government Office Building for a Metropolis. Elevation.

118. Beacon of Progress. Perspective.

Constant Desiré Despradelle (France 1862—Boston 1912)
Education: 1887, Diplôme, École des Beaux Arts, Paris, where he studied in the atelier of Pascal.

Despradelle held a chair at MIT from 1893 to 1912. During this time he briefly engaged in private practice with the architect Stephen Codman. Despradelle also served as the consulting architect for the new buildings of the Boston Museum of Fine Arts, with Guy Lowell.

Beacon of Progress—1900
Location: Chicago.
Status: Unbuilt.

When visiting the United States for the first time in 1893, I proceeded directly to Chicago, where I was struck by the splendor of the Exposition as well as by the marvellous energy of a people capable not only of developing material things to a superlative degree, but of an artistic manifestation of such a high order.

The impression of the happy effect of the White City so boldly erected on the shores of Lake Michigan haunted me. It seemed that such a manifestation should not pass without leaving some trace, and the idea of commemorating this noble initiative was born. I immediately began the study of a monument as a memorial of the Chicago Exposition. This, after some months, resolved itself into the expression of a still more comprehensive thought, one of a national character, both to fix the memory of the vanished White City and to glorify a great people. All the forces which have shaped the American nation marshalled themselves in the form of a glorious monument, the symbol of progress and grandeur. The history of Rome was inscribed upon Trajan's column: that of America should be written at the base of a column fifteen hundred feet in height, of a "Beacon of Progress," a monument typifying the apotheosis of American civilization, to be erected on the site of the World's Fair at Chicago. The studies for this gigantic undertaking, covering a period of six years, were developed in Boston and Paris.

The monument is supposed to be placed in Jackson Park, the site of the World's Fair, facing Lake Michigan. It is to be connected with the principal roads and avenues of the park, the chief access being from the lakeside by a maritime boulevard. A sort of esplanade precedes the access to the principal terraces and platforms, from which can be read the different facts in American history, represented by sculptures in groups of statuary, bas-relief, etching, lettering, names of eminent men who have made the nation strong and great, a triumphal *cortège* of industries, science, arts, commerce, etc.,—in short, sculptured trophies of all descriptions. The States and Territories are represented by female figures hand in hand, symbolizing the indissoluble chain of union. Constellations of stars indicate their number.

In the place of honor, in the axis of the monument, are written the names of the thirteen original colonies; and upon the "Stela," guarded by the eagle, is the goddess of the twentieth century, the modern Minerva, flanked by ranks of lions roaring the glory of America. At the base is a great amphitheatre, forming a sort of sanctuary where orators, philanthropists, and *savants* may deliver inspiring words before the altar of their country. In the interior, elevators conduct to different stories and balconies, as well as to the powerful beacon placed fifteen hundred feet above the ground.

Abridged from **Desiré Despradelle** in *The Technology Review,* II, October 1900.

119. Comparison of Beacon of Progress with Great Monuments of the World.

Juan Downey (Chile 1940—)
Residence: New York City.
Education: 1957–1961, School of Architecture, Catholic University of Chile; 1963–1965, studied printmaking at the Atelier 17, Paris.
Among Video Performances: 1968, Smithsonian Institution, Washington, D.C.: 1970, Howard Wise Gallery, N.Y.C.; 1972, Central Michigan University; 1973, Everson Museum of Art, Syracuse, N.Y.; 1975, Richmond College, Staten Island, N.Y.

Roosevelt Island Housing Competition—1975
Location: New York City.
Status: Unsuccessful competition entry.

It was a requirement to keep a visual axis from East 73 Street in Manhattan to the bridge, connecting Queens to Roosevelt Island. This invisible chunk of space is designed to become a heat collector when sided by two 20-story-high concave mirrors. The heat will purify some of the East River water, and will work the furnaces in the sunken factories. On the surface, 10,000 square feet of terrace is allowed per family to build their lightweight home.

Housing is provided on exterior terracing under which the neighbors meet and exercise in large steam baths, with natural light entering from the glass façade of the riverside. The members of this community work at postindustrial disassembly lines—in sunken factories—where mass produced gadgets are melted back to their pure chemical elements and stored in their original form.

Juan Downey.

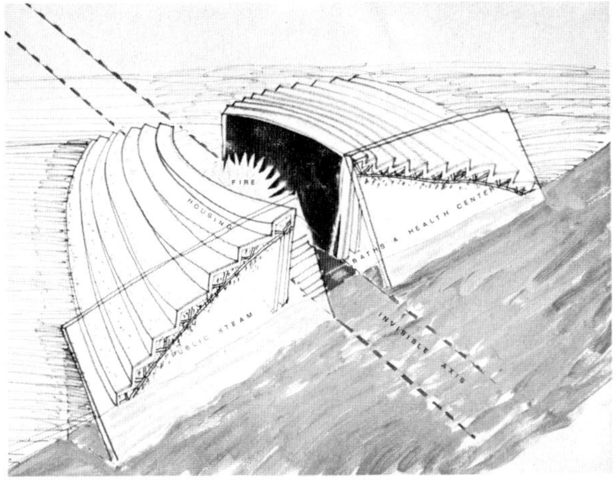

120. Roosevelt Island Proposal. Aerial View of Community.

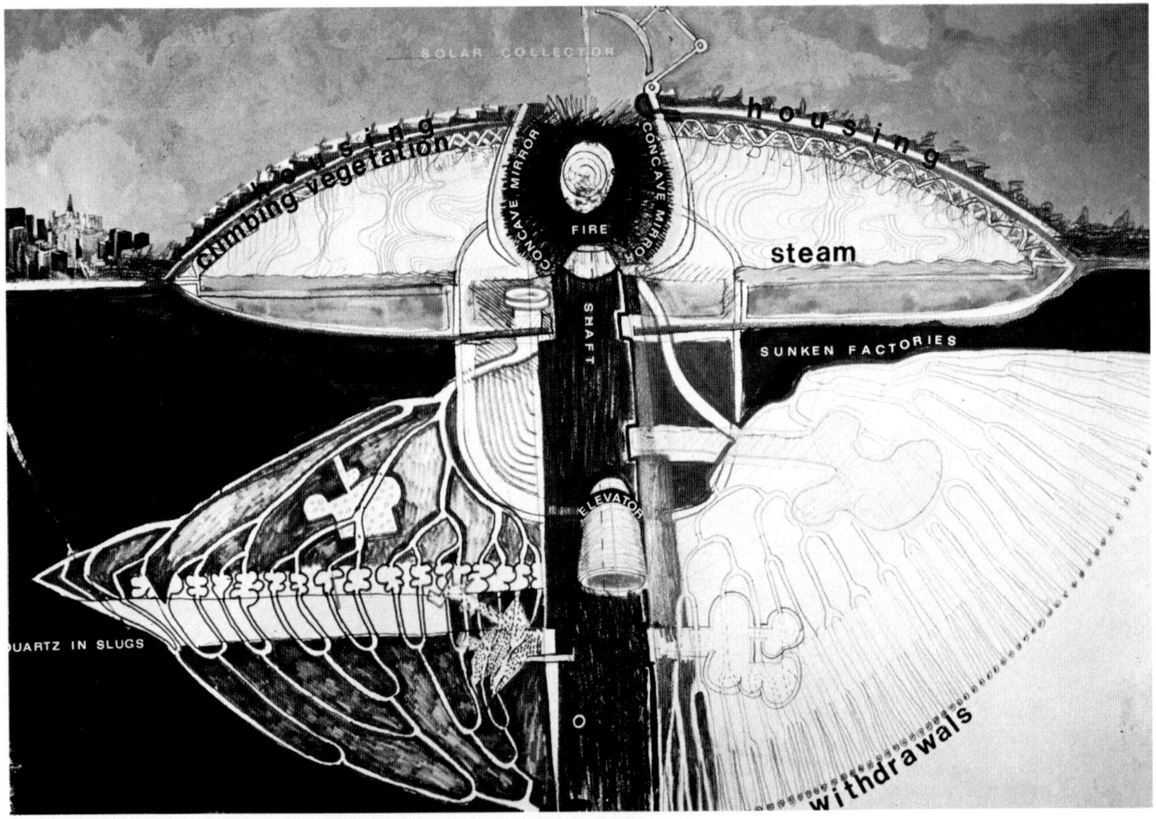

121. Roosevelt Island. Section of Proposed Community.

The Eggers Partnership (established New York City 1937—)
Principals: David L. Eggers, R. Jackson Smith, C. Gates Beckwith, Frank W. Munzer, Robert L. Bien, Bernward U. Kurtz, Thomas H. Price, Jr., Robert H. Welz, Richard F. Eggers.
Among Major Works: 1966, V.A. Hospital, Gainesville, Fla.; 1968, U.S. Customs Court and Federal Office Building, N.Y.C.; 1971, Ford Motor Company Building, N.Y.C.; 1971, Uniroyal Headquarters, Conn.; 1971, Pace University, N.Y.C.

Syska and Hennessy (established New York City 1928—)
Principals: John F. Hennessy, Arnold L. Windman, Sital Daryanani, K. Steve Rasiej, Charles E. Schaffner, Alfred C. Zuck.
Among Major Engineering Works: 1952, The United Nations, N.Y.C.; 1962–1966, Lincoln Center for the Performing Arts, N.Y.C.; 1975–1979, New Jersey College of Medicine and Dentistry, Newark; 1968, Madison Square Garden, N.Y.C.; 1972, McGraw-Hill Building, N.Y.C.

Systemodule—1973

Location: New York Metropolitan Area.
Status: Prototype.
Planning Team: The Eggers Partnership—David L. Eggers, Frederic A. Davidson, Bernward U. Kurtz, Bryant P. Gould; Syska and Hennessy—John F. Hennessy, Jr., Alfred C. Zuck, Charles E. Schaffner.

Systemodule is an artificial island constructed by the methods used for centuries by the people of the Netherlands. The perimeter of the island is a dike holding back the sea from the interior portion (or "polder") which will be at the approximate level of the ocean bed. The polder will provide a site for a major jetport, a waste processing and landfill area, nuclear power plants and a harbor and pumping station for superships. The Systemodule designed for this study will be located three to four miles off Long Island and connected to the mainland by a tunnel.

The much needed new jetport will be provided without usurping open area on the mainland. The polder will be far enough from populated districts to prevent sonic disturbance or damage caused by jet takeoffs and landings, to prevent contamination from the nuclear power plant, and will allow control of oil spills from even the largest supertankers.

The Eggers Partnership, Syska and Hennessy.

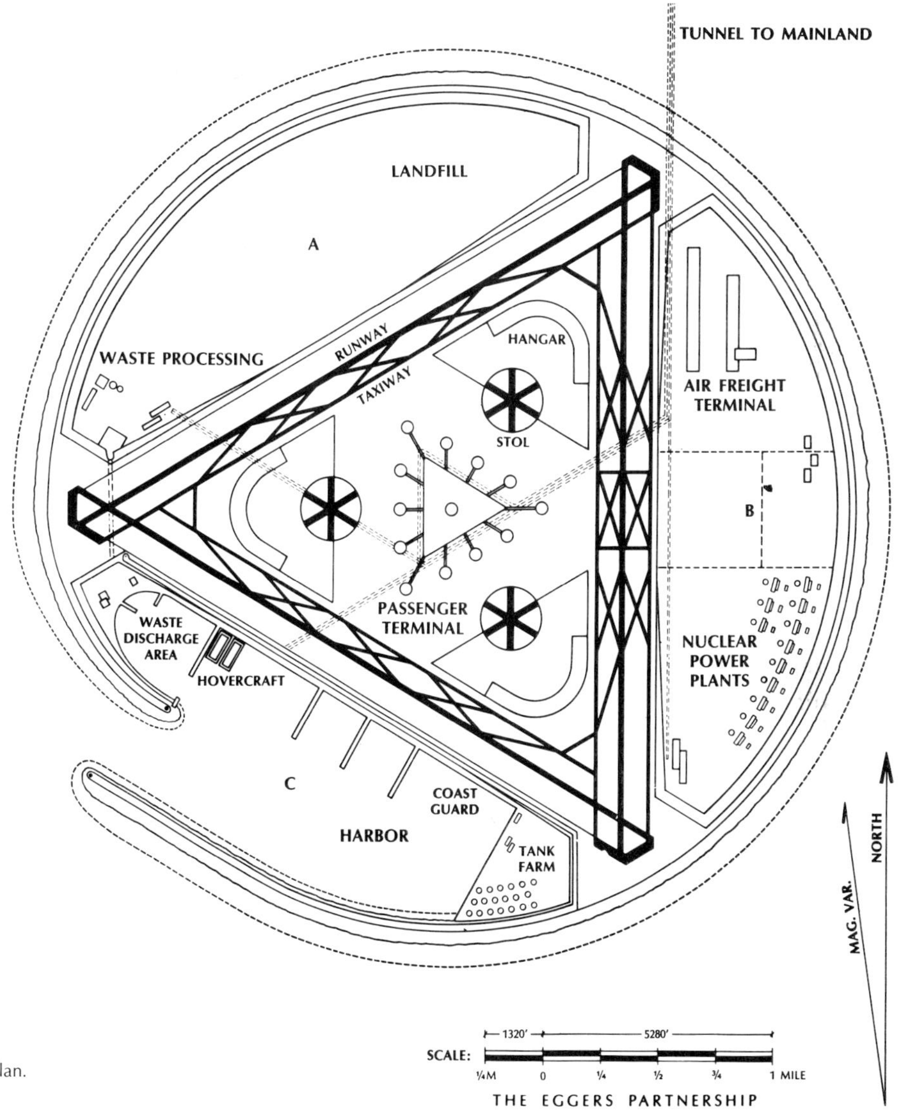

122. Systemodule. Plan.

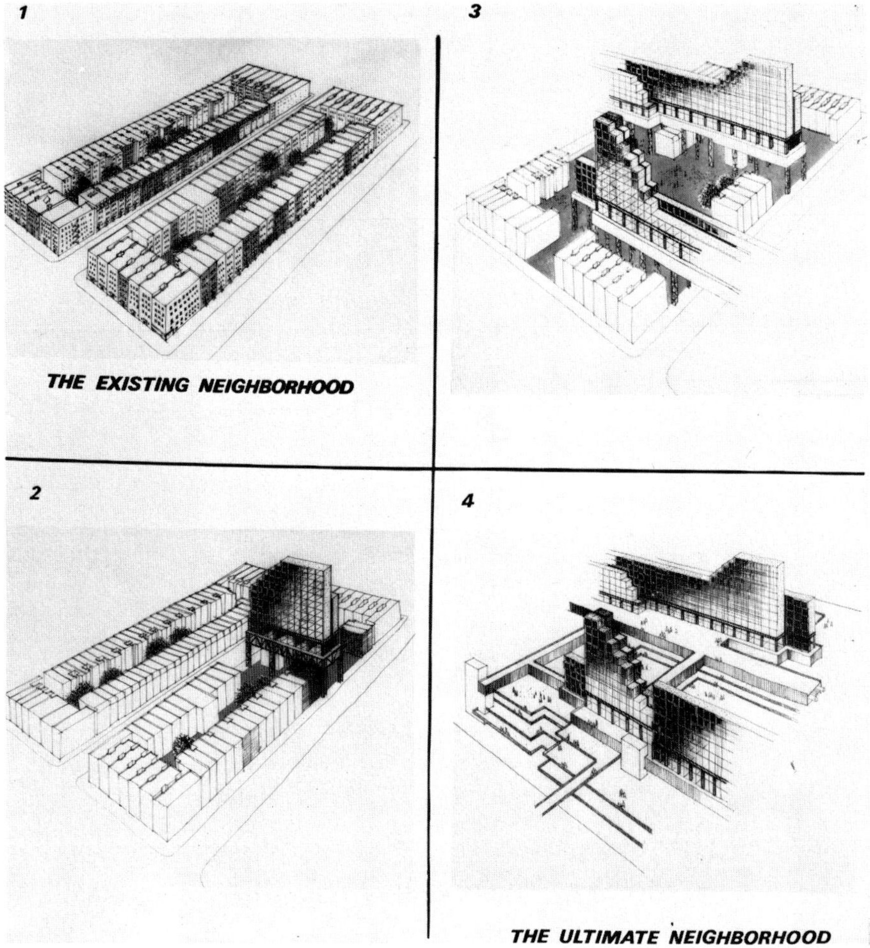

123. Stratasystem Construction Sequence. 1.A two block, 11 acre, residential neighborhood with low rise housing. 2. The construction of the first housing increment. 3. Sequence of construction and demolition. 4. The completed Stratasystem neighborhood.

124. Stratasystem Community. Section.

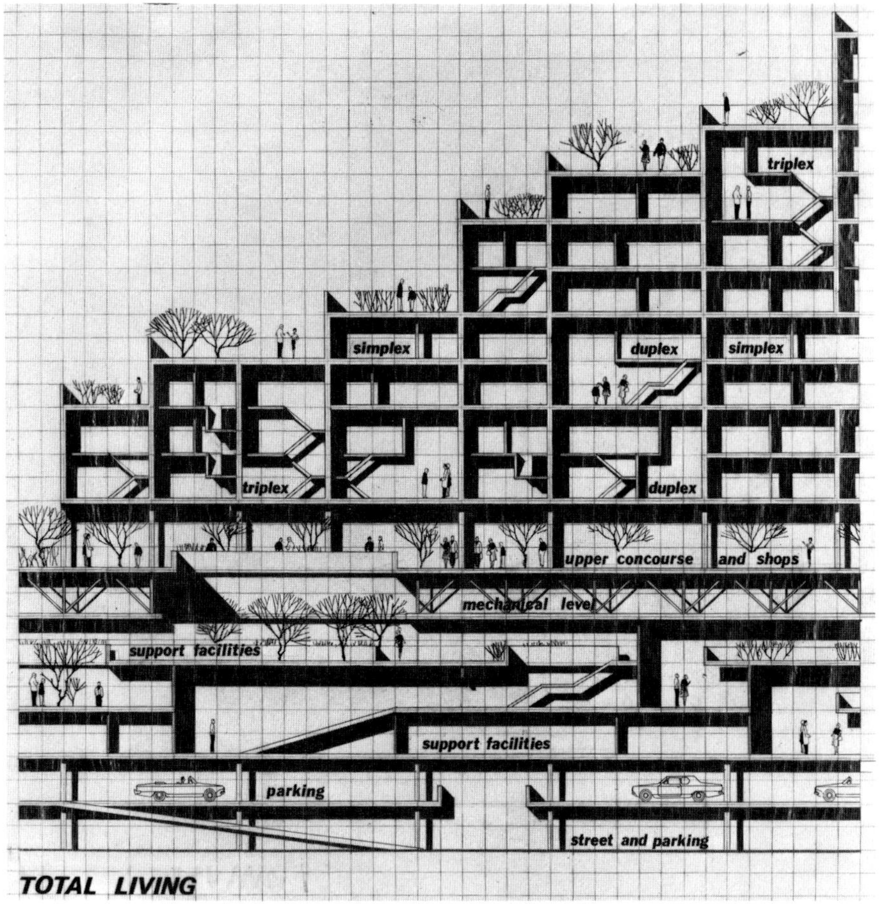

Stratasystem—1969
Location: A large U.S. City.
Status: Prototype.
Developed by: C. Gates Beckwith, Partner-in-Charge; Paul Lampl, Associate Design Coordinator; David Finci, Project Designer; Bryant Putnam Gould, Project Planner.

The Stratasystem is a new concept for the rebuilding of America's cities that creates vertically structured, self-contained neighborhoods and eliminates the need for mass relocation during large scale renewal projects. The vertical land use concept of Stratasystem, envisions each neighborhood as a distinct entity providing all essential services for its residents with traffic and parking functionally separated from living and working space.

The basic minimum area for application of the Stratasystem is an eleven acre neighborhood. The neighborhood area would contain up to 5,500 residents as compared to many existing ghetto densities of less than 2,000 residents. Six to eight neighborhoods linked by pedestrian malls on the concourse or housing level and service levels beneath would form a Stratasystem community. The largest planning unit presently envisioned would be a district of up to 200,000 population. It would contain a series of communities.

The drawings and model suggest a new form of housing neither "high nor low-rise." They propose instead small modular town houses which rise in varying increments to higher levels. The apartments and buildings are based on a flexible four-foot module which can be expanded or contracted to suit the individual needs of the community. Illustrated are rectangularly planned apartment buildings with dwelling units flanking a longitudinal corridor. This arrangement was chosen for its suitability to conventional construction methods or to such innovations as "plug in" or "clip on" modules, prefabricated boxes or component assemblies.

Stratasystem offers a matrix within which it will be possible to solve a growing number of critical urban problems. It involves no new usage or materials and is not predicated on any predetermined architectural expression or style. Complete freedom of planning and design is possible within the framework of the basic concept.

The Eggers Partnership.

125. Stratasystem. Aerial View of Model.

126. Overhead Traffic-Ways.

Hugh Ferriss (St. Louis 1889—New York City 1962)
Education: 1911, BS Arch., Washington University.
Among Published Works: 1929, *The Metropolis of Tomorrow;* 1953, *Power in Buildings.*

From 1912 to 1915, draftsman for Cass Gilbert during that firm's design of the Woolworth Building, N.Y.C.; 1936–1939, design consultant for New York World's Fair; 1947–1949, special consultant and official renderer to the committee designing the United Nations, N.Y.C.

In the 1920s, Hugh Ferriss became one of the most popular renderers in the country, delineating most of the great Art Deco skyscrapers. His work was influential not only in selling new concepts to clients and in advertising buildings, but also in influencing public acceptance of the modernistic skyscraper style. Though Ferriss was trained as an architect, he never had a building of his own design constructed.

Overhead Traffic-Ways—1929
Location: New York City.
Status: Study of future city development.
To the skyscraping heights of the Future City, the popular fancy usually adds something remarkable in the way of overhead traffic avenues. Scores of drawings have been produced, showing viaducts at the twentieth floor! Indeed, in some sketches, architectural values have been so completely neglected as to show the taller towers connected at their very pinnacles by a network of aerial traffic bridges which would infallibly cast their gloomy shadow permanently on the city beneath.

Following such leads, one might easily imagine, as in the accompanying drawing, that all "set-backs" of buildings have been aligned and made into automobile highways. One could drive at will across the façades of buildings, at the fifth, tenth, fifteenth or twentieth story. Automobiles below one, automobiles above one! Furthermore, there will be the aeroplanes. The drawing suggests tower-hangars in whose shelves they will—why not?—land neatly!

Abridged from **Hugh Ferriss, The Metropolis of Tomorrow**, 1929.

Apartments On Bridges—1929
Location: New York City.
Status: Study of future city development.
Not only upward, in skyscrapers, does the city appear forced to move, but also outward—over its bridges. At a recent meeting Architect Raymond Hood outlined the plausible possibility of utilizing the framework of bridges for apartments or offices. The idea could, of course, be visualized in various forms—in the accompanying sketch, the suspension type of bridge is assumed; the towers rise up into fifty or sixty story buildings; the serried structure between is suspended—the buildings literally hung—from cables.

At first glance it would appear that such a location for office or residence is unusually desirable as to exposure, light and air. We may naturally assume landing stages, at the bases of the towers, for launch, yacht and hydroplane—whence it would be only a minute by elevator, to one's private door.

Facetious minds have suggested that the placing of apartments in such a fashion would introduce a bizarre—not to say dangerous—element into domestic life! On the other hand, serious minds have claimed that the project is not only structurally sound but possesses unusual advantages, financially.

Hugh Ferriss, The Metropolis of Tomorrow, 1929.

127. Apartments on Bridges. Perspective.

Vista in an Imaginary Metropolis—1929
Status: Prototype city.
It is dawn, with an early mist completely enveloping the scene. There lies beneath us, curtained by the mist, a Metropolis—and the curtain is about to rise. But, in this case, let us have it rise, not on the existing city, but on a city of the imagination.

As the mist begin to disperse, there come into view, one by one, the summits of what must be quite lofty tower-buildings; in every direction the vistas are marked by these pinnacles as far as the eye can reach. It is apparent that this city, like those with which we had been previously familiar, contains very tall buildings and very many of them; indeed, we may assume, from their dimensions and their disposition over so wide an area, that here is an even greater center of population than anything we had hitherto known.

Looking off to the right, we distinguish a group of these centers which seem larger than the rest. They stand together about a large open space; they seem to constitute a sort of nucleus of the city—perhaps they are its primary centers.

At this point, there stands a tower [the Philosophy Center] about which are gathered the colleges of Arts and Sciences. Since this tower seems to stand somewhat apart, let us give a moment to examining the particular elements of its design.

In plan, it seems to show, at all levels, variations of a nine-pointed star—in other words of three superimposed triangles. Being planned, basically, on the equilateral triangle, the shaft rises—or, so to speak, grows—in what seem definite stages.

Abridged from Hugh Ferriss, The Metropolis of Tomorrow, 1929.

128. Vista in an Imaginary Metropolis. Philosophy Tower.

129. Historical Monument of the American Republic. Painting.

Erastus Salisbury Field (Massachusetts 1805—Massachusetts 1900)
Education: Self-taught except for three months under Samuel F. B. Morse in 1824. Mr. Field is remembered for scenes of classical mythology and Biblical history.

Historical Monument of the American Republic—ca. 1875
Status: A painting.
Towers in different architectural styles spring high in the air from a long base that almost fills the fourteen-foot width of the canvas. Every level of every tower is keyed to an incident in American history, and illustrated in *grisaille* as bas-relief or as sculpture. In the highest rooms Field envisioned exhibitions illustrating everyday life. His crowning imagery is the aerial railway with balloon-stack engines connecting the exhibition rooms of seven of the eight towers.

Mary Black in *Art in America,* January–February, 1966.

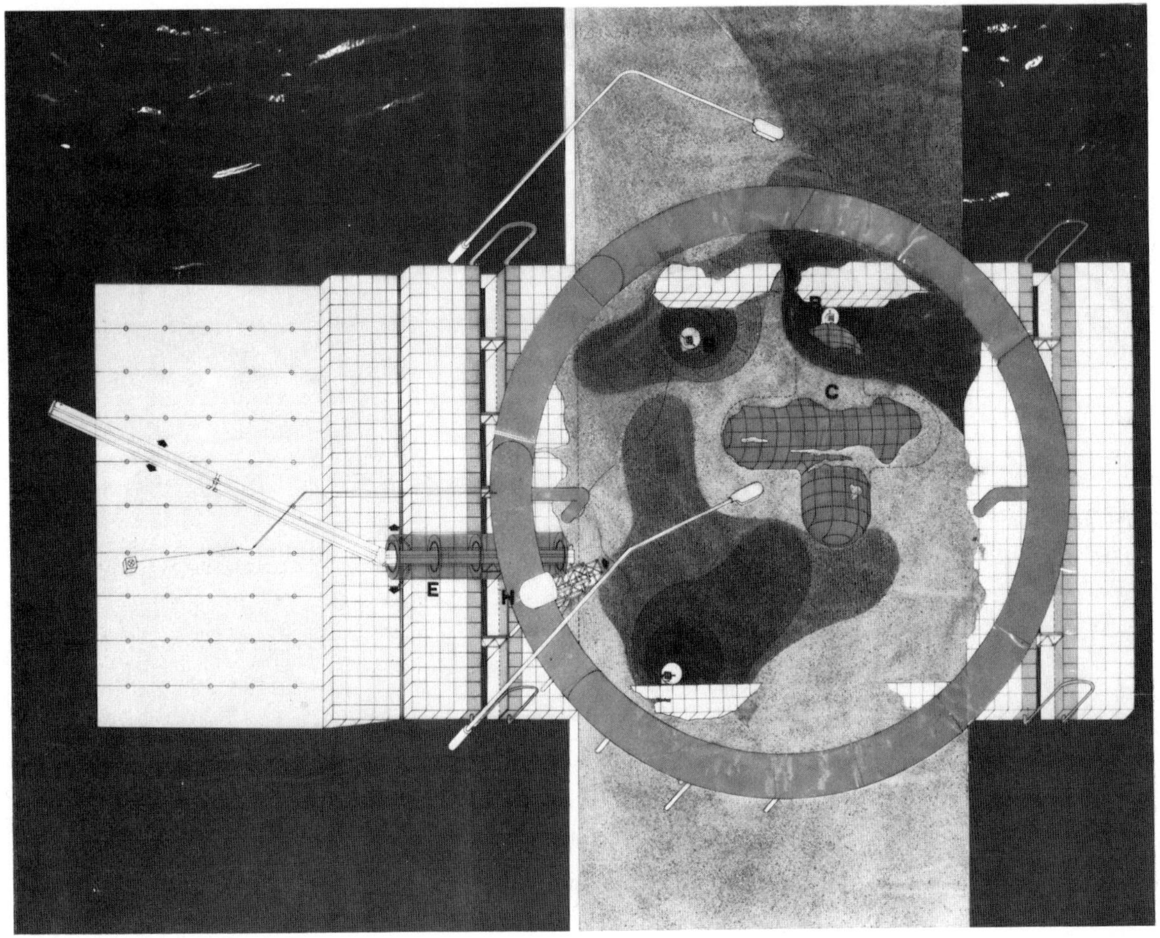

130. Sand House. Axonometric.

Giuliano Fiorenzoli (Italy 1943—)
Residence: New York City.
Education: 1963–1964, Diploma in Fine Arts, Florence, Italy; 1968–1969, M Arch., University of Florence; 1969–1971, M Arch., Massachusetts Institute of Technology.
Among Major Works: 1963, teamwork with Leonardo Ricci, on the project "New Habitat"; 1968, urban design renewal plan for the historical center of Florence; 1971–1972 planning of a new town, Shanahon, with Llewelyn Davies Assoc.; 1972, design of "Myriad Gardens," while at the firm of Conklin & Rossant, N.Y.C.; 1973–1974, implementation and construction of Rainbow Center Plaza, Niagara, N.Y., in collaboration with R. Abraham and W. Geller.

Sand House—1973

Status: Theoretical study.

The Sand House represents the intersection of a linear strip of sand with a house. The sand trapped by the bridging house, becomes an animated part of it—its landscape, or even better, its central core. The play room, a circular corridor, represents not only an elevated connection between the two points of the house, but also a tool needed to move (by means of a small crane) objects to be placed in it. Funnels will be created in the sand to change the landscape if so desired. An elevated room is visible, which will be a special place floating in the sand—a changeable landscape.

Giuliano Fiorenzoli.

131. Slung City. Section. Illustration by Roger Hane.

Yona Friedman (Budapest 1923—)
Residence: Paris.
Education: Budapest Institute of Technology; Haifa University, Israel.
Among Major Works: 1958, City in the Air;
1959, Paris in the Air; 1963, Bridge City over the English Channel; 1964, Business Center over Paris Station.

Slung City—1969
Location: Park Avenue, New York City.
Status: Hypothetical study.
The idea is to take an existing city, one which is no longer capable of adapting to our needs, and build within it a self-contained grid with all the services—plumbing, electricity, transportation system—needed for an independent existence. Ideally, a slung city would be built for maximum pedestrian use, with moving sidewalks and elevators; vehicles for transportation and movement of cargo would continue to use the streets of the old city below. The slung city would be highly flexible. It could be changed and expanded as necessary, since its units would be moved around and plugged into the central power source as needed. Eventually this city would absorb all the activity of the old city, but it would do this at its own pace, taking its own shape. In the final phase of the life of the old city, such of the original buildings as the inhabitants want to preserve could be kept as monuments or museums, the rest torn down.

Oscar Newman, *Esquire*, LXXIII, December 1969.

132. Floating Geodesic Spheres.

Quite clearly, a man, free to enjoy all of his planets . . . will also be swiftly outward bound to occupy ever greater ranges of the universe.
R. Buckminster Fuller.

R. Buckminster Fuller (Massachusetts 1895—)
Residence: Massachusetts.
Education: Milton Academy, Massachusetts; Harvard University.
Among Major Works: Author, inventor, engineer, architect, philosopher, he has pioneered: the geodesic dome, the Dymaxion world map, the Dymaxion 4-D house, the Dymaxion 4-D automobile.
Among Published Works: 1938, *Nine Chains to the Moon;* 1962, *Education Automation;* 1963, *No More Secondhand God;* 1975, *Synergetics.*

Floating Geodesic Spheres—1967
Status: Prototype.
When the sun shines on an open frame aluminum geodesic sphere of one-half mile diameter, the sun penetrating through the frame and reflected from the concave far side bounces back into the sphere and gradually heats the interior atmosphere. When the interior temperature of the sphere rises only one degree Fahrenheit, the weight of air pushed out of the sphere is greater than the weight of the spherical frame geodesic structure, and the total weight of the interior air, plus the weight of the structure, is much less than the surrounding atmosphere. This means that the total assemblage of the geodesic sphere and its contained air will have to float outwardly, into the sky, being displaced by the

heavy atmosphere around it. When a great bank of mist lies in a valley in the morning and the sun shines upon it, the sun heats the air inside the bank of mist. The heated air expands and therefore pushes some of itself outside the mist bank. The total assembly of the mist bank weighs less than the atmosphere surrounding it and the mist bank floats aloft into the sky. Thus are clouds manufactured. As geodesic spheres get larger than one-half mile in diameter they become floatable cloud structures. Such sky-floating geodesic spheres may be designed to float at preferred altitudes of thousands of feet. The weight of human beings added to such prefabricated "cloud nines" would be relatively negligible.

R. Buckminster Fuller.

Dome Over Midtown Manhattan—1968
Location: New York City.
Status: Prototype.
Those who have had the pleasure of walking through the great skylighted arcades, such as the Galleria in Milan, Italy, are familiar with the delights of covered city streets. They can envision the effect of a domed-over city, where windows may be open the year round and gardens bloom in the dust-free atmosphere. From below, the dome would appear as a translucent film through which the sky, clouds and stars would be visible.

There is no method more effective in wasting heating and cooling energy than the system employed by New York and other skyscraper cities of the world. A dome over mid-Manhattan would reduce its energy losses approximately 50-fold. Such a dome would reach from the East River to the Hudson at 42nd Street on its east-west axis, from 64th to 22nd Street on its north-south axis, and would consist of a hemisphere two miles in diameter and one mile high at its center. When such large domes are made, the captive atmosphere in itself is enough to support the structural shell, as in a large pneumatic tire. The cost of snow removal in the city would pay for the dome in 10 years.

Electric resistance wires imbedded in the skin of the surface of the dome, would maintain a temperature sufficient to melt snow and ice. Both the melted snow water and rain would run neatly to a guttering, clear of the pollution of the streets, down into a canal around the dome's lower rim from whence it would flow to great collection reservoirs. The dome would be high enough to cause the water to flow gravitationally back to the storage reservoirs in Westchester County.

The dome's skins, consisting of wire-reinforced, one-way-vision, shatter-proof glass, mist-plated with aluminum, would have the exterior appearance of a mirrored dome, while the viewer inside would see out without conscious impairment. This will cut down the interior sunlight to non-glare level. Such domes would also provide a prime shielding against atomic radiation fallout.

Abridged from **R. Buckminster Fuller** in *Think,* XXXIV, January–February, 1968.

133. Dome Over Midtown Manhattan.

General Electric

Bottom-Fix—1969
Location: Ocean bottom.
Status: Pending.
Additional Credit: E. T. Myskowski, inventor; Corning Glass Works.
Bottom-Fix is the name of the General Electric Company's focal project for the development of deep ocean system capabilities. The objective of this project is to develop the technologies, systems, subsystems, and hardware required to permit manned occupation of the ocean bottom at depths up to 20,000 feet. The spherical structural module, jointly developed by General Electric and Corning Glass Works, is the basic building block for the Ocean Bottom Station. Each module is made up of pentagonal segments of Pyroceramglass ceramic contained in a lattice of titanium alloy. External shells of fiberglass and titanium provide protection against impact and corrosion. Designed for a depth of 12,000 feet, the modules have a diameter of 12 feet and a weight/displacement ratio of 0.5. The design depth can be increased to 20,000 feet. The Bottom-Fix modular concept would also permit on-site construction of various size stations. Modules could be added, removed or exchanged as the need arises.

General Electric.

134. Bottom Fix Deep Submergence Modules. Units May be Added, Removed or Exchanged Using the Deep Ocean Service Vehicle Illustrated.

Harlan H. Georgesco (Romania 1918—)
Residence: Los Angeles.
Education: Graduate, Academy of Architecture, Bucharest, Romania.

Harlan Georgesco taught for seven years at the Academy of Architecture, Bucharest, and for three years at the School of Architecture, University of Nebraska.

Relocation of Los Angeles—1965–1967
Status: Hypothetical proposal.

In the early 'fifties, Los Angeles seemed to be emerging as the ideal twentieth century city. In the early sixties, aided by the gasoline-tax-generated new freeway system, speed and consumerism became the trend. For the land developed, the ONE CITY from San Francisco to Los Angeles was in the making.

The smog, pollution, freeway boredom, and skyrocketing land prices which soon occurred presented questions concerning the destruction of land and nature. Energy had become the way of life. Commuting between the deserted suburb and the overcrowded urban center had caused the family unit and traditional neighborhood to be destroyed.

In continuing to develop horizontally, all of southern California will be flattened, paved, and subdivided from San Francisco to San Diego. An alternative proposal involves vertical land development.

Land subdivided into 300 × 300 foot plots by the "horizontal tract" can house 12 families. The same land utilized as a vertical tract can house 200 families, offices, shops, schools, parks, and recreation areas.

Ninety acres can be subdivided into 385 horizontal lots on the average. The same land can be developed into 5 vertical villages, each containing 1,000 homes. As a result, one square mile can absorb 20,000 homes, offices, shops, etc., and adequate land for manufacturing.

These villages could be constructed through the use of steel in tension. The most extraordinary example of this system is the Golden Gate Bridge. An average house (1,600 square feet) can be built on a 40 × 40-foot slab that can easily be lifted and suspended by cables at the four corners. Slabs can be spaced vertically, every 20 feet, to provide areas for two-story dwellings.

In conclusion, the "vertical villages" can be built for a one-mile distance on both sides of the existing San Diego Freeway, from Beverly Hills to Long Beach. This would amount to a fraction of what has already been spent in the Los Angeles area. At least five million people would occupy these villages which would reestablish the neighborhood and family unit, and eliminate traffic, smog, and waste.

Harlan Georgesco.

135. Deserted Suburb.

136. Overcrowded Urban Center.

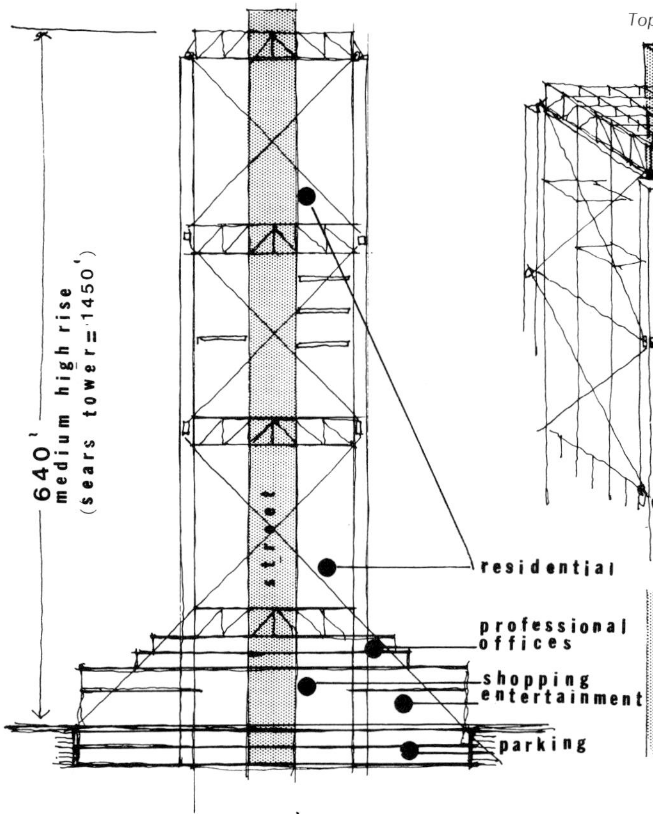

Top Left, Center, Right: 137. Development of Vertical Tract.

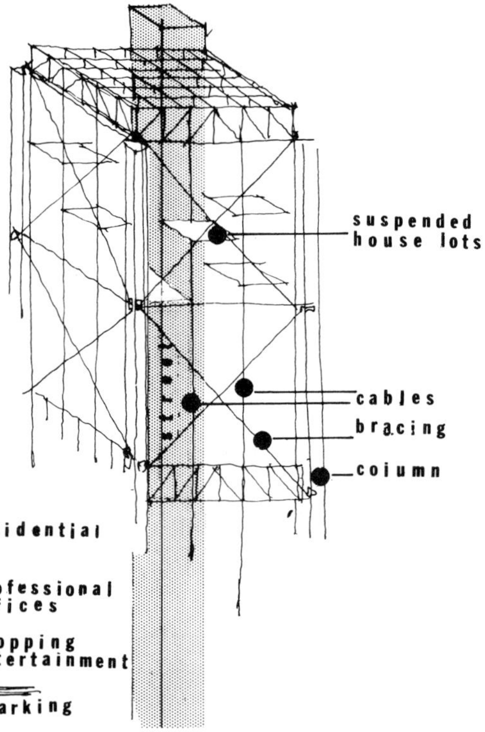

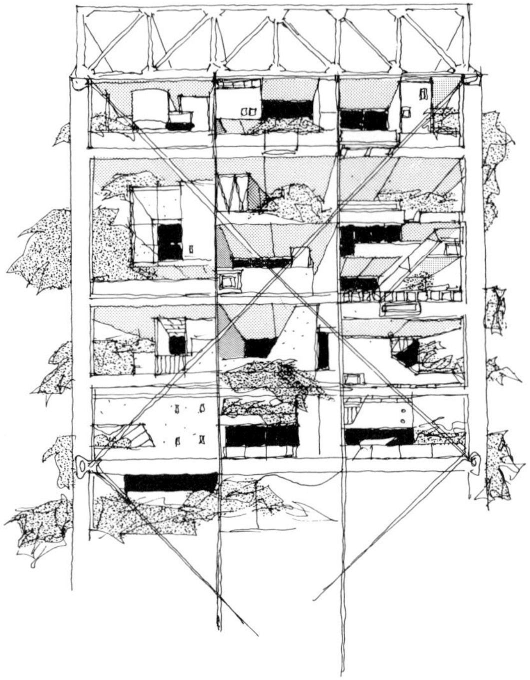

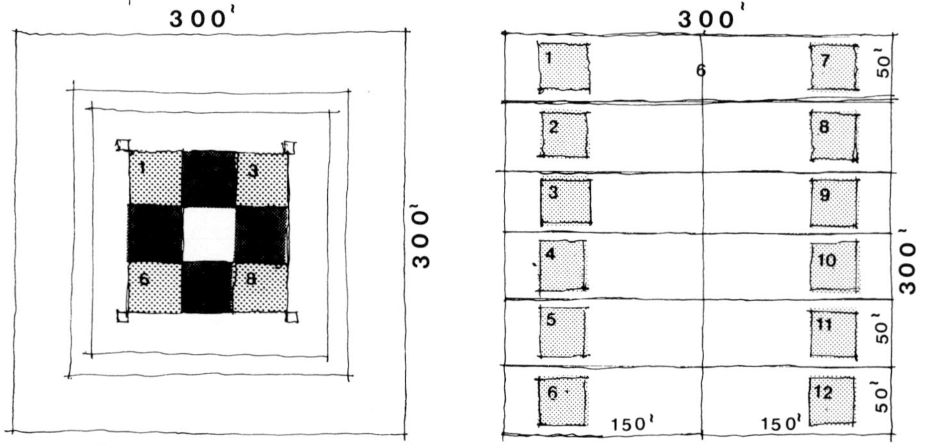

138. Comparison of Vertical Versus Horizontal Subdivision of Land Area.

139. Location of Vertical Villages.

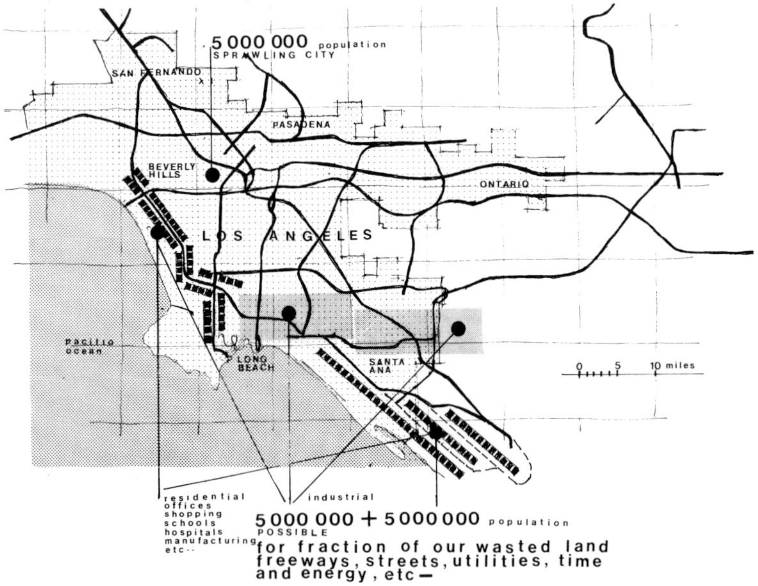

Cass Gilbert (Ohio 1859—England 1934)
Education: 1879, Massachusetts Institute of Technology.
Among Major Works: 1903, Minnesota State Capitol; 1907, New York Custom House, N.Y.C.; 1913, Woolworth Building, N.Y.C.; 1925, U.S. Chamber of Commerce, Washington, D.C.; 1935, U.S. Supreme Court Building, Washington, D.C.

Cass Gilbert worked in the firm of McKim, Mead and White from 1880–1882, before joining to form the firm of Gilbert & Taylor with James Knox Taylor in St. Paul, Minn. Gilbert was a founder and president of the Architectural League of New York. The Woolworth Building, completed in 1913, remained the tallest building in the world until 1931. "The mounting chords of the Stabat Mater kept sounding in my mind while I was piling up that building [Woolworth Building]." Cass Gilbert.

Peace and War Memorial—1919

Location: New York City (?).
Status: Unbuilt.

A war memorial should be so designed and executed that it gives one the impression only, and that the impression should be one of sheer beauty, strongly suggestive of the ideals for which the memorial stands; namely, Courage, Bravery, Liberty, and Victory. It should be thought of only in relation to those who were most actively and intimately engaged in the war. I am speaking of those who not only gave their lives on the field of battle, but of the men and women alike who gave themselves entirely to the aid of the Government in helping the men on the battle line.

Cass Gilbert in *The American Architect,* CXIX, January 1921.

140. Peace and War Memorial. Rendering by Frederick G. Stickel.

Bruce Goff (Kansas 1904—)
Residence: Tyler, Texas.
Education: Architectural training as an apprentice from age 12.
Among Major Works: 1949, Ford House, Illinois; 1950, Bavinger House, Oklahoma; 1957, Price House, Oklahoma; 1958, Durst House, Texas; 1965, Duncan House, Illinois.

Bruce Goff was Chairman of the School of Architecture at the University of Oklahoma from 1947 to 1956.

Dewlen Aparture—1956
Location: Texas.
Status: Unbuilt due to death in family of client.

The Dewlen Aparture was designed for Al Dewlen, well-known writer of early Texas historical novels, his wife and son.

The site was situated in a semi-desert area overlooking an extensive barren valley with low hills backing up the property, several miles from Amarillo, Texas. No other structures were in the vicinity, nor were there apt to be any.

The clients required that the interior be a large continuous open space containing a swimming pool, an oasis garden, cooking, dining, bathing, dressing, and sleeping accommodations for the family and their guests. The father needed a private "Sanctum" in which to write, and the mother required a studio and gallery for her paintings. The son needed a third of the area for his hobbies and guests. There was to be a minimum of "loose" furniture. Most of it was to be built as an integral part of the house. The plan developed into a triangular pool with three surrounding living areas for the three occupants. A ramp beginning at the entry divided, into a Y shape above the pool. These two ramps became galleries for showing the paintings. They extended upwards through the suspended room and terminated in two studios with large plastic windows looking out over the valley below. The mobile feather sculptures outside these windows turned with the wind. The three identical serpent-like exterior walls of the principal space were to be constructed of hard coal masonry with running veins of pyrite (fools-gold), and lit from above with continuous skylights. The large tent-like roof, suspended from the central frame, would be composed of cables covered with metal fabric, the exterior sprayed with aluminum pellets in plastic binder, and interior with styrofoam pellets, also in plastic binder, for insulation and acoustic treatment. The ramp tubes would be constructed of welded steel mesh. A large plastic skylight in the center lit the pool and provided interior views of the sky and roof structure. The earth was to have been bermed around the exterior walls, merging the revetments for the carport and two terraces with the site.

The owner intended to build it himself with the help of his family and some skilled labor. He preferred to think of it as more than a house and coined the word "aparture" for its name from such words as departure, aperture, apart, and apartment. About the time it was scheduled to begin, their son, who had joined the military service, lost his life for his country. This tragedy destroyed all incentive to build the aparture.

Bruce Goff.

141. Dewlan Aparture. Aerial View.

Giacomo's Motor Lodge—1964
Location: Oklahoma.
Status: The design proved too adventuresome for the client and remains unbuilt.
The client wished to build an "eye-catcher" motor lodge on a scenic highway near McAlester, Oklahoma. The gently sloping site rose up from the highway and commanded beautiful views of the valley.

The entrance office and restaurant had a tower topped with a cocktail lounge. The pairs of three story circular rooms were entered at the second level from the drive and parking areas behind, resulting in only one flight up or down for the other two floors. This arrangement provided quiet in the rooms from the motel traffic and enabled their balconies to view the large central area of terraced gardens with sweeping sculptural "waves" of local red sandstone and glass cullet masonry, with water gardens, swimming pool, etc., as well as the valley view beyond.

The architect's intention was to create a new harmony of structures, gardens, and site which would draw a clientele interested in an imaginative and beautiful stopping place as an oasis on their travels.

Bruce Goff.

142. Giacomo's Motor Lodge. Perspective.

Cowboy Hall of Fame—1960
Location: Oklahoma City.
Status: Unsuccessful competition entry.
When the competition for the Cowboy Hall of Fame was announced, the architect, who had always taken a jaundiced-view of competitions in general, was intrigued enough by the challenge of the problem to enter a design for it.

The site was an impressive one on a hillside near Oklahoma City along one of the main highways leading to and from the city. It was to be a large project and site plan, general perspective, plans, elevations, and other explanatory drawings plus detailed cubage computations, all of which had to be crowded onto one sheet of drawings. Despite this difficulty, the scheme was drawn very beautifully by Herb Greene for the presentation.

Although the architect had never been an avid "Wild West" fan, his Oklahoma background helped him to take the program seriously and he tried to solve it as a worthy and dignified monument and museum to this vanishing pioneer race. Inasmuch as the cowboy had never been identified with any particular style of building or architecture, it seemed appropriate to use characteristic design motifs of things he associated with in his daily life as elements from which a suitable grammar of architectural character could be realized. Hence forms, materials, colors and textures of saddles, spurs, leather stitching, ranch brands, horseshoes, all of robust ruggedness and with much feeling for the great outdoors played their parts as inspiration for the design which would have been an honest tribute to the cowboys' healthy and honest life.

Because of its "unusual" (?!) nature it was one of the first designs to be discarded by the jury who chose a noncommittal design instead, sufficiently familiar to make no one mad . . . or glad. It is there now in body, if not in spirit.

Bruce Goff.

143. Cowboy Hall of Fame. Rendering by Herb Greene.

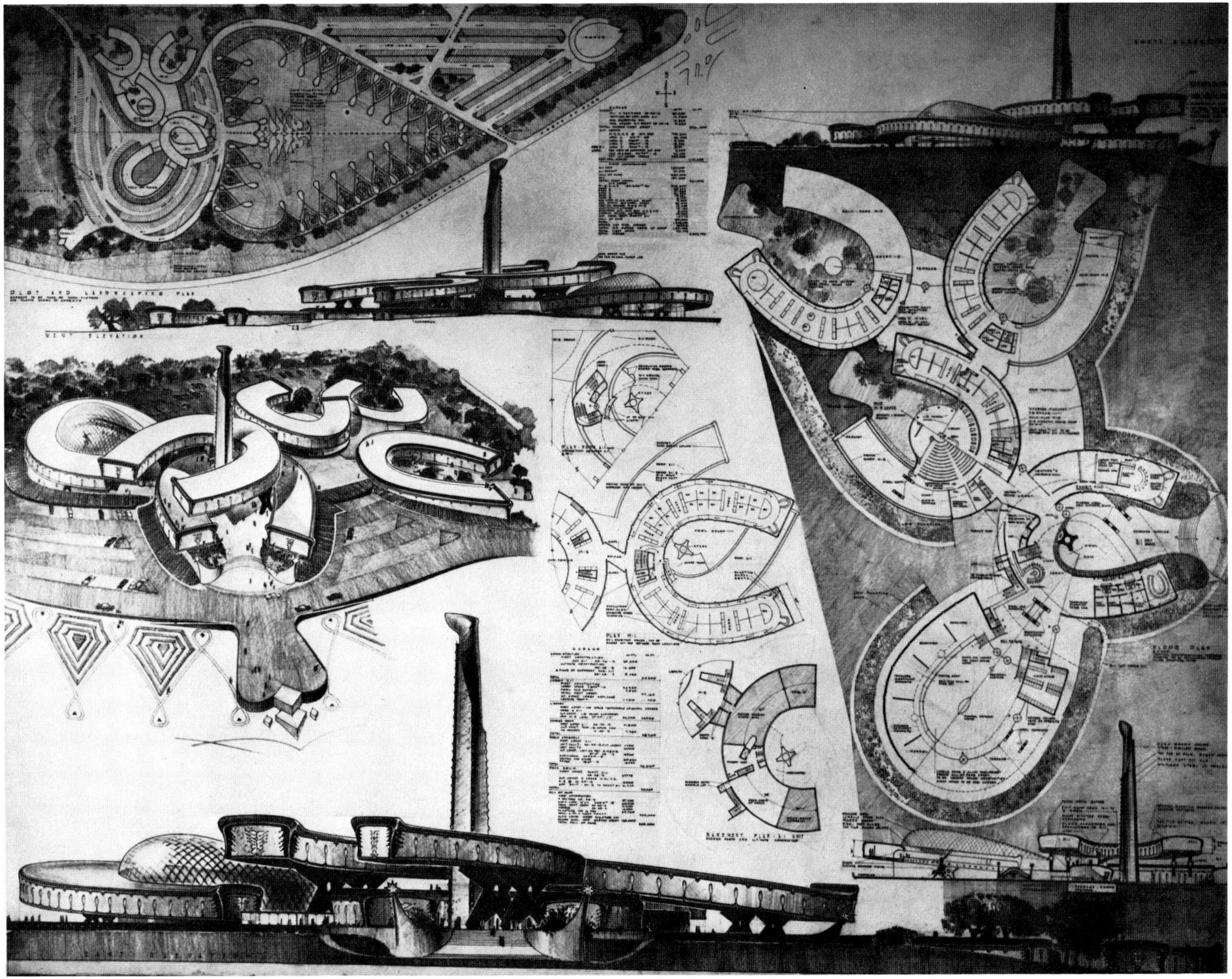

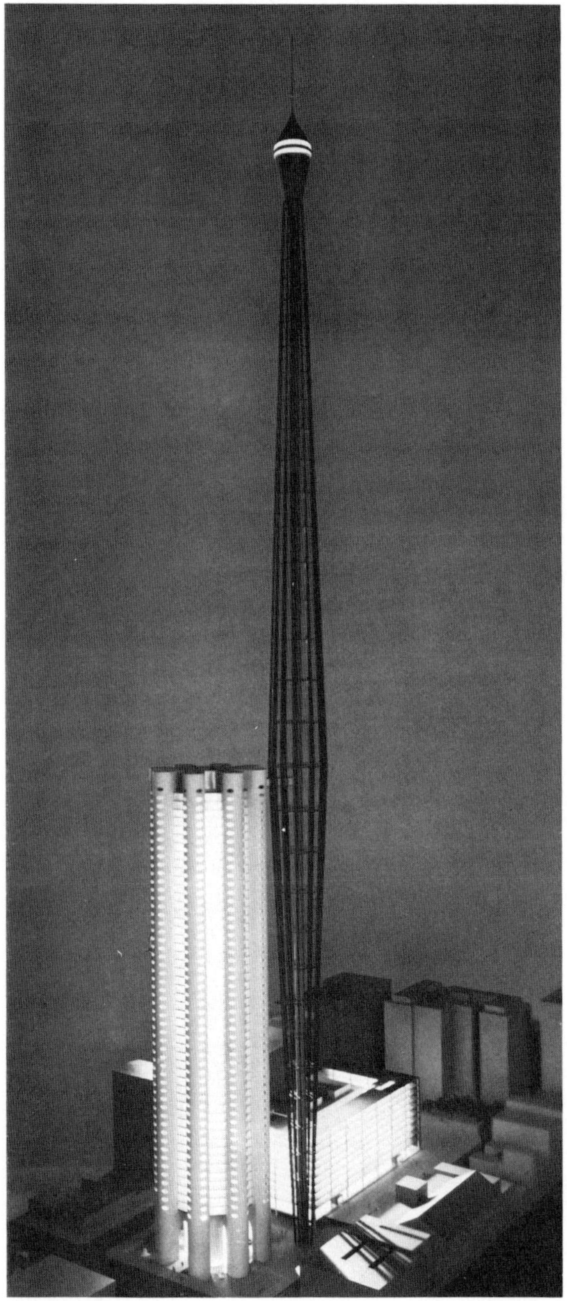

144. ABC Building. Aerial View of Model.

Bertrand Goldberg (Chicago 1913—)
Residence: Chicago, Illinois.
Education: 1930–1932, Harvard University; 1932–1933, Berlin Bauhaus under Ludwig Mies van der Rohe; Armour Institute of Technology.
Among Major Works: 1937–1944, designed and constructed the town of Suitland, Maryland; 1945–1948, developed a prefabricated unit bathroom, marketed as Stanfab Unit Bathroom; 1960 Marina City, Chicago; 1963, Raymond Hilliard Center, Chicago; 1968, St. Joseph Hospital, Tacoma, Washington.

ABC Building—1963
Location: New York City.
Status: The board of directors was afraid that the unusual space, quite suitable for ABC, would not be commercially rentable if ABC were ever to abandon it.

145. ABC Building. Floor Plan Section.

The ABC (American Broadcasting Company) Building is a structure developed for corporate identity in New York City in the midst of all the Miesian boxes packaging a corporate world.

Its location was to be Columbus (9th) Avenue and 67th Street, and it would have incorporated a broadcasting tower higher than the Empire State Building, as well as an environment which would induce closer working communications between the 80 divisions and 1,200 employees housed there.

The building rises from below street level at Columbus Avenue. The structure has been shifted from the central core to the exterior walls where concrete can do more work, particularly in a high-rise situation. Vertical concrete enclosures creating contained administrative spaces are counterpointed against vertical shafts defining open service support spaces.

The floor areas are divided into two kinds of activity: administrative and supportive. My general observation of administrative people who occupy floor-to-ceiling glass environments in urban centers, is that they frequently close themselves off from any view of the exterior so as to partially protect themselves. Very few decision makers who are active in business dilute their work environment by permitting the external world to intrude; particularly if this 'external world' is a neighboring skyscraper as in New York. People in supportive capacities, on the other hand, seem to like the distraction of an exterior community. Our structure was woven between these two activities, and at the same time maintained close proximity between the different work divisions, facilitating communication. To interrelate these departments, it seemed to me, was a very important achievement for an office building.

Bertrand Goldberg.

146. San Diego Theater. Model.

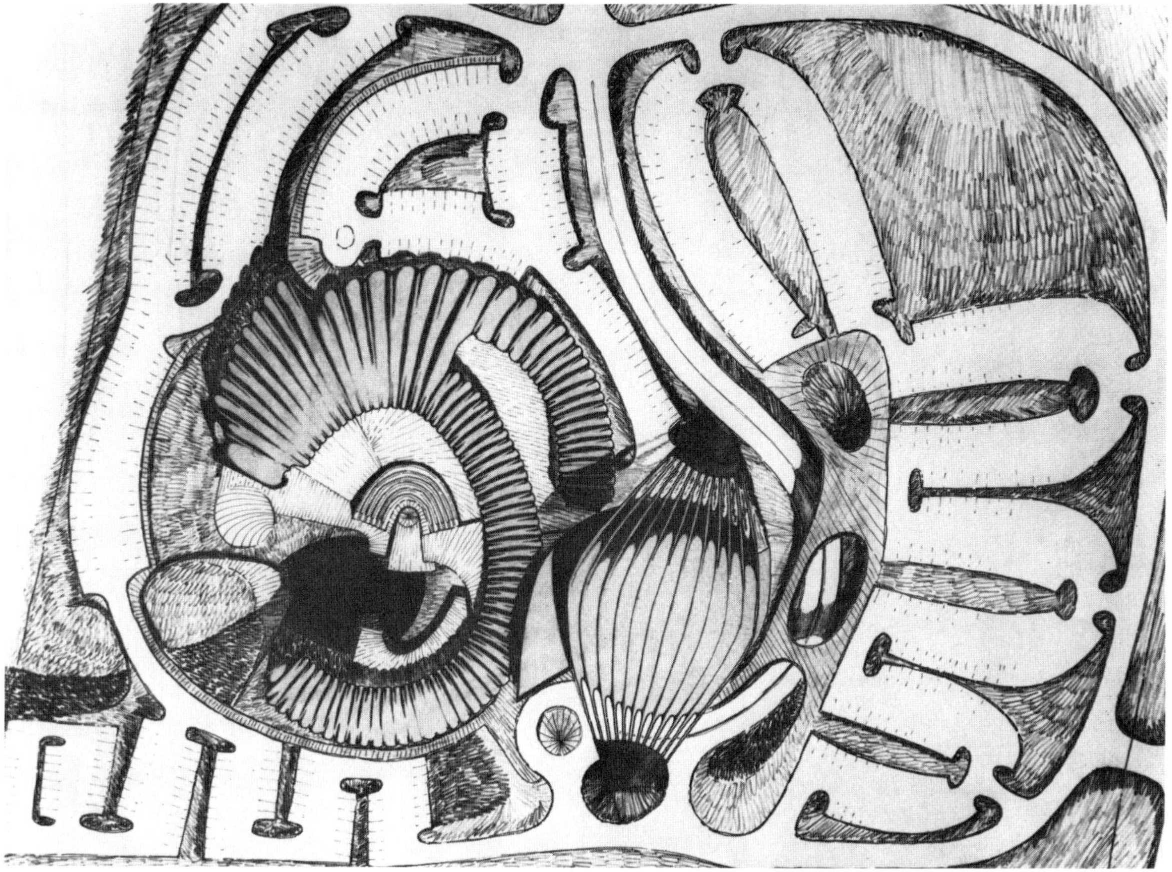

147. San Diego Theater. Aerial View.

San Diego Theater—1965
Location: San Diego, California.
Status: Unbuilt due to financial considerations.
The forms of the San Diego Theatre being subjective needed the flexibility available in a "biological shell system." The spatial development follows the land, in several stages: a large enclosed space for 1,200 seats (created by scooping out earth and pouring in seats); a rehearsal stage; a small "art" theater (room with a span of about 60 feet that can be set up in many different ways for experimental theater); and an outdoor theater (open-bowl form in the middle). The building broadens and then narrows in order to shape spaces appropriately for all kinds of shops and administration.

Design flexibility is achieved by the capacity of these forms to be extended in two dimensions: the span between the points of support can be widened by deepening the convolution, and the supports can be changed in height. The spaces are biological to the extent that they can respond to their environment, to their function, and to the movement of people within them.

Bertrand Goldberg.

General Grant Monument Competition—1885
Location: New York City.
Status: Unsuccessful competition entries.

To the Chairman of the Committee for the Erection of a Monument to General Grant:
Sir,—It being manifest that the design for the monument to the late illustrious General, Ulysses S. Grant, should represent the best architectural talent the country can produce, we the undersigned architects do respectfully suggest:

1. That there should be a competition for the same.
2. That the American Institute of Architects be invited by the Chairman of the Committee to send to him the names of ten members of the profession in this country, whom it considers best qualified to make an appropriate design for the monument.
3. That the ten architects, so selected, be invited to enter into a competition for the monument with the understanding that the programme for the competition shall be prepared by a Committee of not less than three of their number, and that each of the ten be paid a certain sum of money, say $1,000.
4. That the competition shall be open to every architect desirous of sending in a study.
5. That the order of merit of the whole number of designs submitted, be voted on by each member of a Committee of twenty, composed of ten to be nominated by the Monument Committee, and of the ten selected architects, and that the design receiving the largest number of votes, shall be accounted first, and its author employed to carry out the work.
6. That prizes of the value of say $1,000 and $500 be awarded to the best designs prepared by architects not specially invited to compete.

The American Architect and Building News, XVIII, September 1885.

148. Entry by Henry O. Avery, New York City. Elevation of Granite Tower 150 Feet High.

149. Entry by Henry O. Avery. Sketch.

151. Entry by Harvey Ellis. Utica, New York. Perspective.

Henry Ogden Avery (New York 1852—New York City 1890)
Education: Cooper Union Art School, N.Y.C.; 1870–1872, apprenticed in the office of Russell Sturgis, N.Y.C.; 1872–1879, École des Beaux Arts, Paris.
Among Major Works: House for General Stuart Woodford, N.Y.C.; Fire Monument, Milwaukee; art galleries for the Art Institute of Chicago.

Henry O. Avery was a founder of the Architectural League of New York. The Avery Architectural Library was founded in his memory at Columbia University in 1890 by his parents, who later donated Avery Hall, which houses Columbia University's School of Architecture.

150. Entry by Arthur Bohn, Indianapolis, Indiana. Elevation.

Harvey Ellis (New York 1852—New York 1904)
Education: 1871, West Point, New York.
Among Major Works: 1886, twenty-eight story skyscraper, Minneapolis, Minn.; 1887, Charles Pillsbury residence, Minneapolis; 1889, competition drawing for the Cathedral of St. John the Divine, N.Y.C.; 1891, Security Bank, Minneapolis—all are renderings done in the firm of Leroy Buffington; 1903–1904, renderings for the *Craftsman* magazine, N.Y.C.

Harvey Ellis worked in the firms of H. H. Richardson, and Leroy Buffington. Most of his life, however, is cloaked with mystery, and much of it must remain speculation. It is believed by some that many of the renderings done for Leroy Buffington were actually the designs of Ellis himself, and not Buffington's.

Arthur Bohn (Kentucky 1862—Indiana 1948)
Education: 1883–1888, 1902–1904, studied in France, Germany, and Italy.
Among Major Works: Second Trust and Savings Bank; Herron Art Institute; Methodist Hospital; State Plaza and Library, all in Indianapolis, Indiana.

152. Entry by "Hermit." Perspective Sketch.

Henry A. Nisbet (Scotland—Colorado 1885)
Education: Scotland.
After immigrating to Rhode Island, he worked in several architectural offices as an assistant.

153. Entry by Henry A. Nisbet. Denver, Colorado. Plan, Perspective and Interior View.

154. Entry by C. C. Yost. Columbus, Ohio. Elevation.

Joseph Warren Yost (Ohio 1847—Pittsburgh 1923)
Education: 1868, Mt. Union College, Ohio, studied architectural mechanics and civil engineering.
Among Major Works: Guardian Life Insurance Building, Tilden Building, addition to R. M. Hunt's Tribune Building, all in New York City.

155.

156.

Michael Graves (Indiana 1934—)
Residence: Princeton, New Jersey.
Education: 1958, BS Arch., University of Cincinnati; 1959, M. Arch., Harvard University.
Among Major Works: 1968–1970, Hanselmann residence, Fort Wayne, Indiana; 1969, Rockefeller residence, Tarrytown, N.Y.; 1971–1972, Snyderman residence, Fort Wayne, Indiana; 1974, Wageman residence, Princeton, N.J.; 1975, Newark Museum Carriage House renovation, New Jersey.

Peter Eisenman (Newark, New Jersey 1932—)
Residence: New York City.
Education: 1955, B Arch., Cornell University; 1960, MS Arch., Columbia University; 1962, MA, University of Cambridge, England; 1963, PhD, University of Cambridge, England.
Among Major Works: 1966, Manhattan Waterfront Project (with Michael Graves), N.Y.C.; 1967–1976, Houses I–X; 1973, Low-rise/High-rise Density Housing, Staten Island, N.Y.; 1975, Roosevelt Island Competition, N.Y.C.

Jersey Corridor Project—1964–1966
Location: Northeast corridor or coast of the United States.
Status: Theoretical study.
Additional Credit: Anthony Eardley.

The Linear City: An Idea

THERE ARE NO TWENTIETH
CENTURY CITIES

our cities of today have evolved from eighteenth and nineteenth century foundations

the twentieth century expansion and development of these cities were based on twentieth century technologies and systems, but imposed on nineteenth century organizations

the expansion of nineteenth century patterns destroyed the integrity of these organizations

the imposition of twentieth century technologies did not create a better city for a better life

the spiralling effect: the more the city disintegrates: the more people leave the less good the city becomes: the less people want to live in less good cities

today do we know what a good city can be?

157.

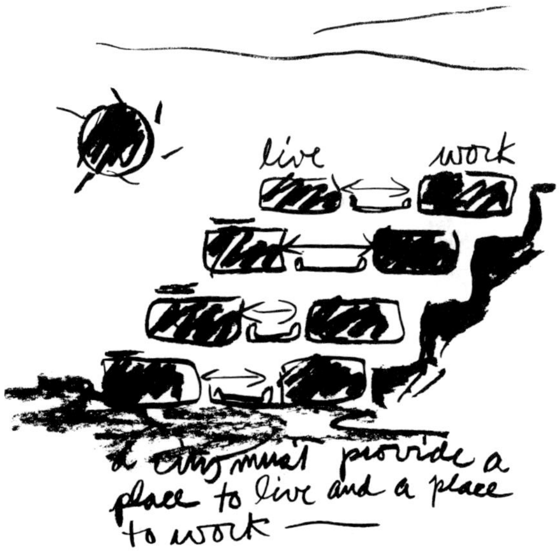

158.

A LINEAR CITY IS A TWENTIETH CENTURY CITY

a linear city is a twentieth century city

a linear city is not a series of point cities in a line

a linear city is not a connection between point cities

a linear city does not need end points

a linear city is not a new suburb or a series of suburbs

a linear city is not a dormitory on a highway

a linear city is not the glorification of an efficient transportation system

a linear city is a nineteenth century concept

this linear city is an attempt to overcome the deficiencies of the nineteenth century concept

it is a twentieth century city.

THE JERSEY CORRIDOR PROJECT: NEW BRUNSWICK–TRENTON

this is a case study to realize the ideal: to particularize the general

it is an attempt to produce a physicial urban environment

a sense of place
a sense of relationship
a sense of choice

qualitative and quantitative

the good life in the great society

the linear city will combine the valid aspects of city and suburb

it will provide for the pastoral ideal:

man in relation to nature—his own ground
private ownership of land—his own ground
sun, space and green—his own ground

159.

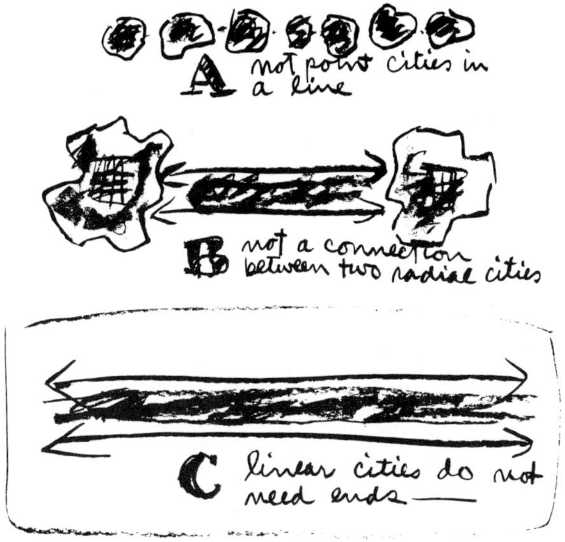

160.

the linear city is based on the distance man walks: the human side

man will have a sense of choice:

he may walk in all directions
he may walk to all his daily functions

school
shops
work
play

he will live at a density to provide for this choice at a walking distance

the linear city will provide different densities of experience

it will not be homogenous

it will provide a change in scale from walking to vehicular scale;

from daily experience to sense of occasion

these changes will occur rationally within the system

this rational order will provide a sense of place a sense of relationship

from house—to street—to vehicle—to occasion a complete experience

man always in relation to his physical environment

the linear city will provide a separation between pedestrian and vehicular circulation

the linear city will begin a continuous system of linear ground transportation in the length of megalopolis

this system will minimize the need for and number of point interchanges

the linear city will have a sense of place

it will have linear centers: in series rather than in point clusters man can move to linear centers today in the same time he moved to radial centers of the past

the linear city will prevent sprawl

it will provide a contrast: a tension between what is rural and what is urban

it will provide more contiguous, accessible open space for more people with more leisure time

it is the most rational and efficient organization to do this

the linear city will provide for change and growth

new systems of transportation

new industry

the consequent new patterns of life

new leisure

the linear city is the acknowledgement; the response to these new patterns

the linear city will provide the understandable physical environment that is the framework for a better way of life

that will make ultimate use of the qualitative and quantitative potential in twentieth century technologies.

our society can send a rocket safely to the moon

our society now will have a city that will send a person in dignity to the opera

a glorification of our society

not for posterity . . . but for now

Michael Graves, Peter Eisenman.

161. Linear City. Aerial Perspective.

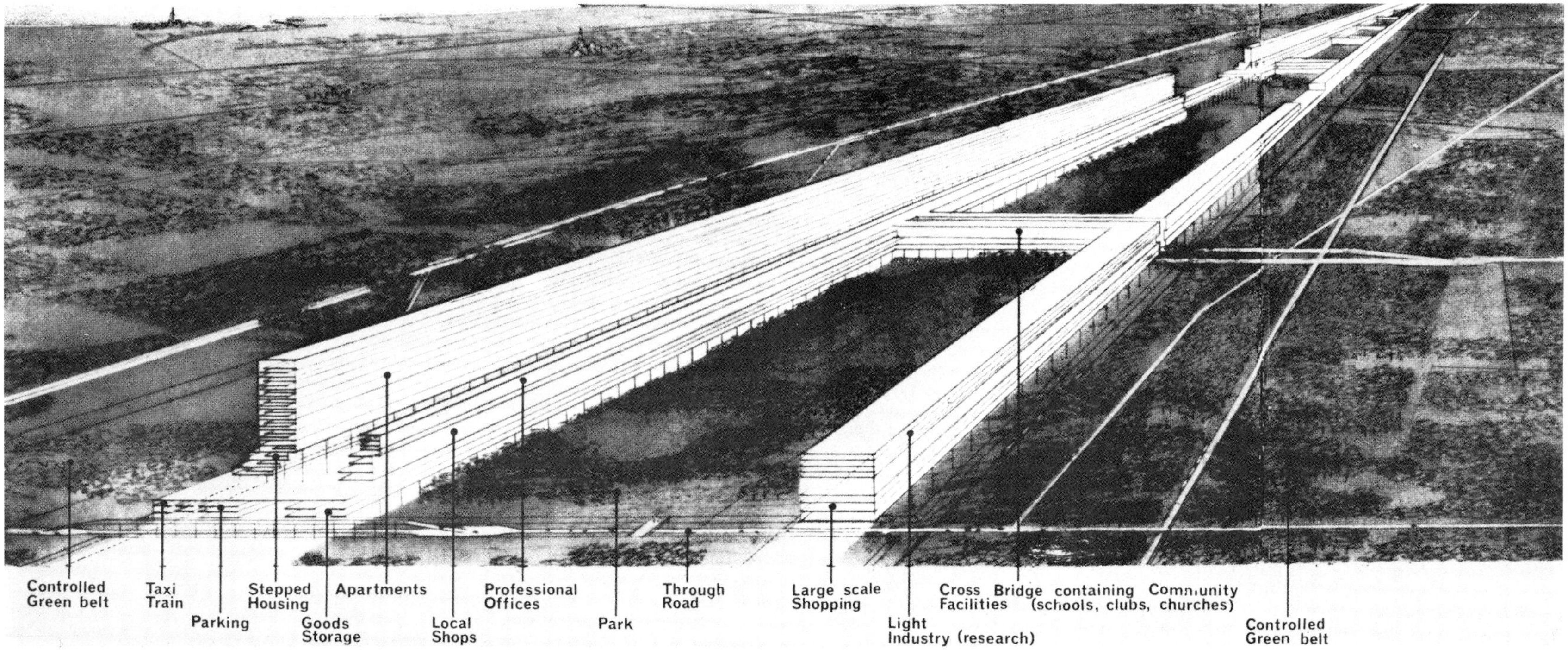

Horatio Greenough (Boston 1805—Massachusetts 1852)
Education: 1825, Harvard University.
Among Major Works: 1833–1843, George Washington sculpture now in the Smithsonian.

Greenough's importance in the history of American sculpture is due to the influence of his career rather than to the intrinsic merit of his work. Dedicating himself to his art with the utmost earnestness, he did much to dignify it [art] in the minds of his countrymen. The first American sculptor to go to Italy to live, he set a fashion that lasted for half a century.
John Garraty and Edward James, *Dictionary of American Biography,* 1974.

Bunker Hill Monument—1825
Location: Boston, Massachusetts.
Status: Competition entry, chosen and then rejected by the committee (Daniel Webster, Gilbert Stuart, Washington Allston, Loammi Baldwin, George Ticknor).
[While a college senior, at the age of nineteen, Greenough learned of the competition for the Bunker Hill Monument. The model he submitted was his first important project.]

To the Committee of the Bunker Hill Monument Association:

GENTLEMEN,—Having designed an obelisk instead of a column, and presented a model rather than a perspective drawing for the purpose of illustration, it has seemed to me proper to explain what might be interpreted a wilful or negligent disregard to the published proposals of your committee.

I have given you my design in a model, because, as it may be examined from every quarter, it may be said to *contain* in itself a perspective of the object, as seen from *every point* instead of *one only,* and is on that account more easily and perfectly understood.

I have made choice of the obelisk as the most purely *monumental* form of structure. The column, grand and beautiful as it is *in its place* (where it stands beneath the weight of a pediment, and supports a long line of heavy entablature), considered as a monument, seems liable to unanswerable objections. It steps forth from that *body,* of which it has been made a harmonious *part,* to take a situation which, of all others, requires *unity* of form: hence the more completely it has been fitted to a situation so different, the greater must be the number of *useless* appendages and *unmeaning* parts when it assumes its new place and office.

The proportions of this obelisk are taken from one at ancient Thebes. The height from the ground to the top of the plinth is twenty feet; from the plinth to the apex of the shaft, one hundred feet.

The entrance would be reached by ascending a flight of twenty steps, which are to be seen on each side of the lower base in the model. The four blocks at the angles are designed to receive four groups of monumental or allegorical sculpture.

Horatio Greenough in C. W. Warren's History of the Bunker Hill Monument, 1877.

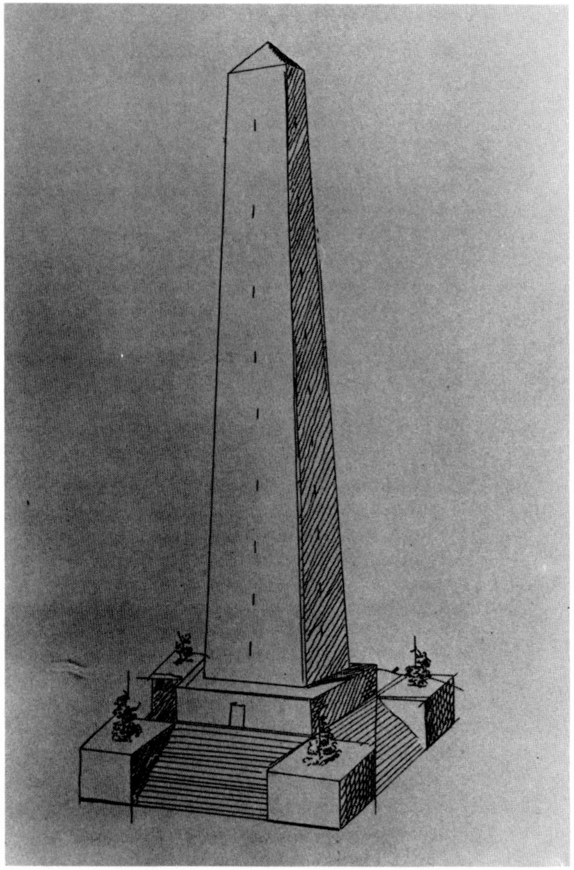

162. Bunker Hill Monument Proposal. Sketch of the Obelisk.

163. Sketches of Statuary to Surround Obelisk.

Robert Grosvenor (New York City 1937—)
Residence: New York City.
Education: 1956, École des Beaux Arts, Dijon, France; 1957–1959, École Supérieure des Arts Decoratifs, Paris; 1958, Università di Perugia, Italy.
Among Exhibitions: Grosvenor has exhibited extensively since 1962, with shows at the Paula Copper Gallery, N.Y.C.; Institute of Contemporary Art, Boston; Philadelphia Museum of Art; Los Angeles County Museum of Art; and Walker Art Gallery, Minneapolis, Minn.

Removal of Manhattan Island—1975
Location: New York City.
Status: Theoretical proposal.
The first of a series of projects dealing with:

1. The removal of Manhattan.
2. Trials to test the seaworthiness of the island.
3. The reclamation of the island.

Robert Grosvenor.

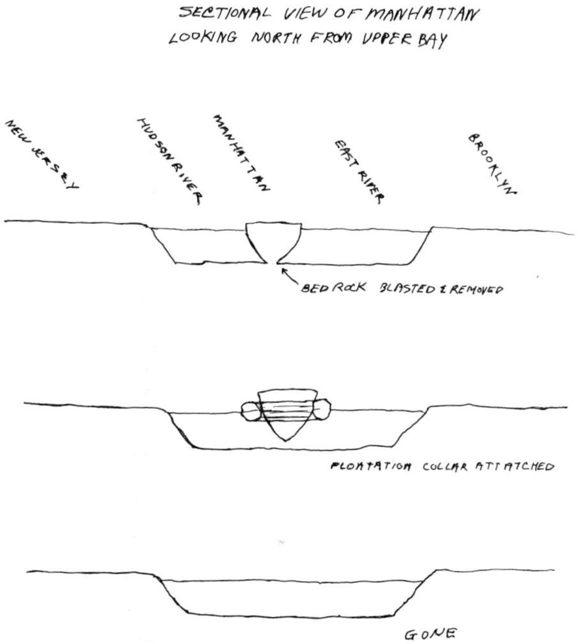

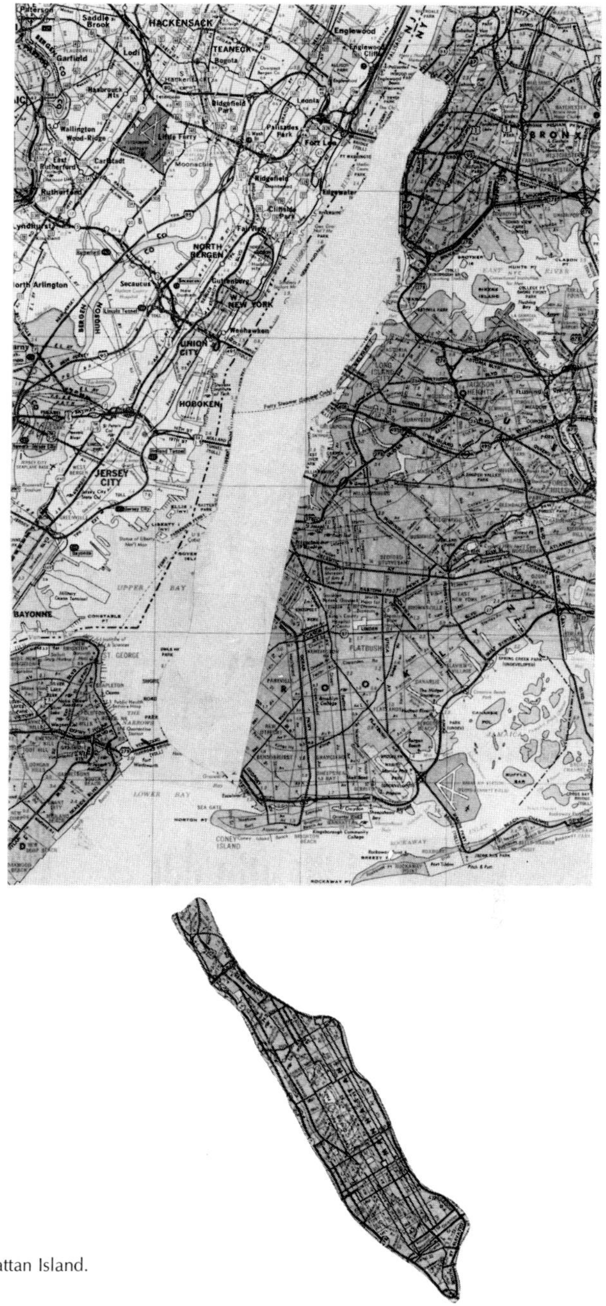

164. Removal of Manhattan Island.

Victor Gruen (Vienna 1903—)
Residence: Austria.
Education: 1924, Vienna Technical Institute; 1925, *Baumeister,* Academy of Fine Arts, Vienna.
Among Major Works: 1956, Southdale Center, Minneapolis; 1958, Wilshire Terrace, Los Angeles; 1962, Midtown Plaza, Rochester, N.Y.; 1963 Fulton Street Mall, Fresno, Ca.

East Island—ca. 1963
Location: Welfare Island, New York.
Status: Feasibility study.
[Welfare Island in New York City's East River has a long and checkered history, before the City acquired title in 1828 and made it into an institutional enclave. The Regional Plan Association in the 1930's had recommended its conversion to housing and recreation but nothing happened until one evening in the 1960's when, according to architect John Belle, then Gruen's assistant, "the idea of building a total community on the two-mile strip of land came about over dinner, in a Sutton Place apartment which overlooks the island. Purely out of speculation, Gruen put together a comprehensive plan for the development of the island as a high-density community—a plan backed by Frederick Richmond, a financier and investor. When Gruen and Richmond, a staunch Democratic supporter and benefactor, presented their plan to the newly elected Republican Mayor, John Lindsay, they were denied the commission." Instead, Mayor Lindsay authorized a competition for the residential development of the Island under the auspices of the A.I.A. Specifications for the competition were drawn up by John Belle, but it was never held, and the island's development was, during 1968–1969, turned over to the New York State Urban Development Corporation.]

"If the cities are to recapture their economic health, they must offer better opportunities for these commercial, industrial and residential developments for which their central position is a distinct advantage." John F. Kennedy, Special Message to Congress on Housing and Community Development, March 9, 1961.

The concept of East Island is visualized as being a middle income community developed within the framework of federally-assisted urban renewal. A concrete platform would be constructed covering most of the land area, and raised about 22 feet above the existing ground. The space below this platform would be utilized for those purposes which usually are placed into basement areas. Along the perimeter of the space below the platform would be placed schools, with windows directed toward the East River.

In the central location and running the entire length of the community area would be a wide and airy concourse connecting all building lobbies with each other. On the balcony level of this concourse would operate the internal transportation system. This is a "Carveyor" continuous transportation system with stations set approximately 900 feet apart. The system consists of individual platforms carrying seats, designed to move speedily between stations and to slow down near stations. The stops would be reached by speed ramps leading from the lower level of the concourse to the balcony level. The ramps continue as moving sidewalks along the station platform, moving at the same speed as the "Carveyor" system at the stations. Thus, an easy and safe transfer is achieved from ramps and moving belts to the individual seats mounted on the platforms. From the top of the platform would rise the residential structures. The scheme contemplates buildings of various heights, shapes and sizes.

Victor Gruen.

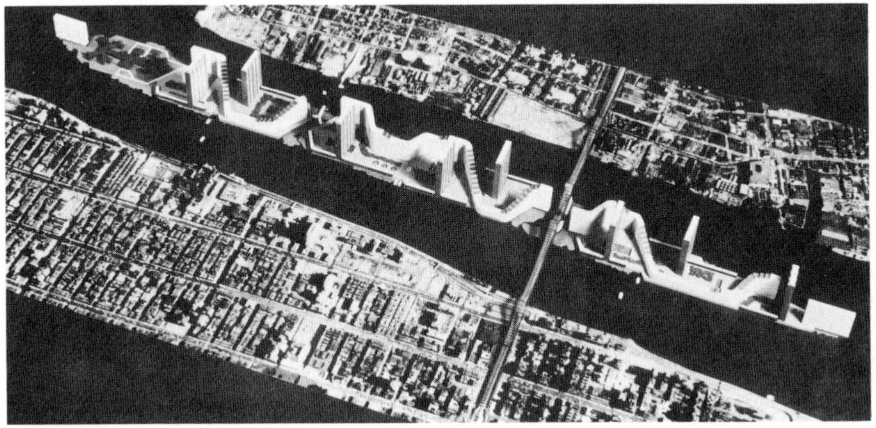
165. East Island. Aerial View.

166. East Island. Carveyor Continuous Transportation System. Detail.

Rafael Guastavino (Spain 1842—North Carolina 1908)
Education: 1871, School of Industrial Engineering, Barcelona; 1871–1875, *maestro de obras,* School of Architecture, Barcelona.
Among Major Works: Thin-shell tile vaulting was installed in numerous buildings in Catalonia and, by him and his son, in over 1000 buildings in the United States—in virtually every state and territory. These include: 1889–1895, Boston Public Library; 1908–1939, Cathedral of St. John the Divine, New York City; 1907–1910, Pennsylvania Railroad Station, New York City; 1912, Grand Central Terminal, New York City; 1922–1932, Nebraska State Capitol, Lincoln.

The Guastavino (Fireproof) System is a modern refinement by means of high-grade Portland cement mortar of an old Mediterranean tradition of laminated tile vaults, domes, and stairway shells. Called "surface resistant structures," these shells achieve their strength through their double-curvature, and they use little if any of the usual metal frames or reinforcement common in their day.

Century Record Building
Structure of Masonry and Steel—1905
Status: U.S. Patent.

My invention relates to structures of masonry and steel and is particularly adapted to act as a receptacle for century records, or other records, museums, libraries, offices, storage, safe deposit, etc., and for similar purposes and permits of the arrangement of these libraries, exhibits, records, etc., along one of more continuous floorings or halls arranged-spirally within the structure and extending a considerable distance while the said structure itself may cover a limited ground space.

The drawings illustrate a building structure of considerable dimensions and adapted to cover a square or more of ground space and is composed of a series of buildings or walls of any desired height and containing halls, rooms or compartments. I have shown a rectangular or square arrangement of these buildings or walls, the corner structures being square, of several stories and surmounted by a dome, but it is obvious that they may terminate in any other desired manner of construction.

In one of the central structures a library may be arranged on one or more of the floors while the various rooms and halls may be used as art galleries and lecture halls or contain cases for the display of various objects. Within the inner walls of these buildings as above described is a dome rising above them and composed of two shells, the distance between their facing sides being of any desired or suitable distance and the whole surmounted by a lantern which is a circular room with windows to give light to the interior of the dome, having a vaulted ceiling, and the whole being topped by a globe or structure of ornamental design which may be used as an observatory.

Excerpted from Rafael Guastavino, United States Patent No. 915,026, March 9, 1909.

167. Century Record Building. Structure of Masonry and Steel. Section. United States Patent No. 915,026. March 9, 1909.

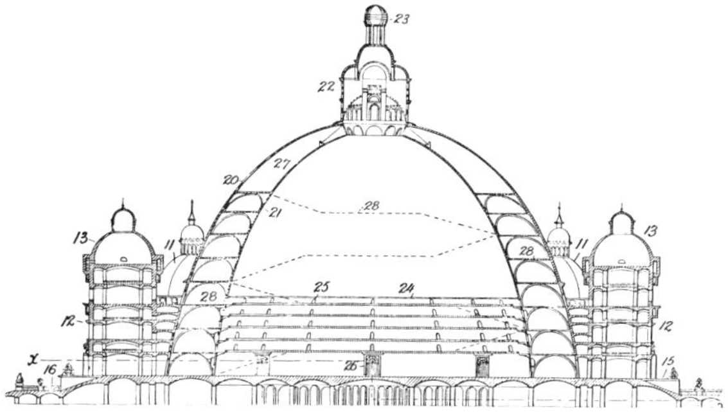

168. Century Record Building. Elevation.

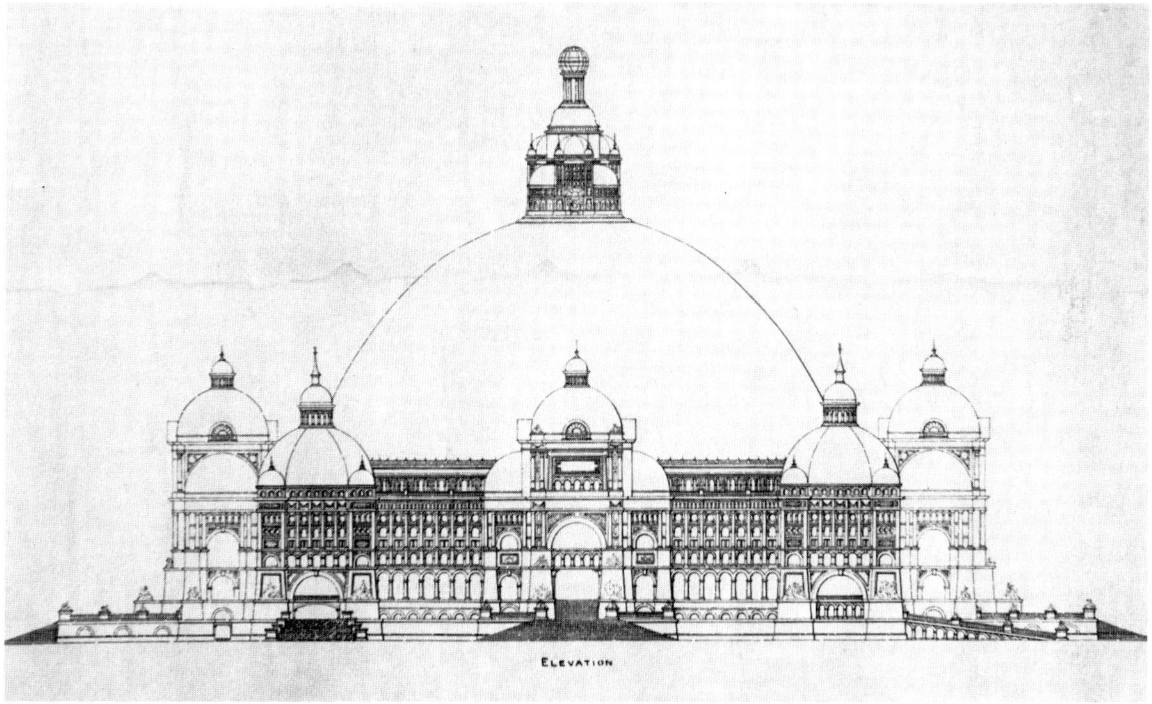

Eric Gugler (Wisconsin 1889—New York State 1974)
Education: Armour Institute of Technology; Art Institute of Chicago; 1911, BA, Columbia University.
Among Major Works: Enlargement and reconstruction of the Executive Office wing of the White House, Washington, D.C.; rehabilitation of the Subtreasury Building, New York City; Business Administration Building, New York World's Fair of 1939–1940; Chicago War Memorial (with Roger Bailey); Statue of Theodore Roosevelt on an island in the Potomac River, Washington, D.C.

The Hall of Our History—1953
Location: Pine Mountain, Georgia.
Status: Were unable to raise sufficient funds.
The monument, to be known as the Hall of Our History, will be erected over the next ten years at an estimated cost of $25,000,000 on the high plateau of Pine Mountain, Georgia, approximately seventy miles south of Atlanta. Groundbreaking will begin within the next two years.

169. Hall of Our History. Site Elevation. Pine Mountain, Georgia.

The Hall of Our History is conceived as a vast court of granite measuring 247 feet wide, 418 feet long and 90 feet high, to be set in a grove of towering pines and open to the sky. Sculptors of today will complete on all four walls the story of our country from the Age of the Discoverers through World War I. It is the decision of the project's historians that events subsequent to 1920 must be left to the perspective of time for evaluation and recording.

The carved history will begin with a panel depicting the Era of Discovery. Among other subjects planned are Daniel Webster delivering his "Union Forever" address to the United States Senate, the Lewis and Clark explorations, and the long train of covered wagons that followed westward. There will be only two free-standing sculptures in the shrine—one a seated Lincoln before the section of carved wall including the period preceding and following the Civil War, and a heroic Washington standing before a temple enshrining the Declaration of Independence, the Constitution, the Bill of Rights and the Northwest Ordinance.

According to Charles F. Palmer, chairman of the Hall of Our History, Incorporated, funds for the shrine will be raised by public subscription, with special emphasis placed on small and numerous contributions, so that as many Americans as possible may participate in its building.

Sculptors and historians who assisted in the creation of the initial models with Mr. Gugler or who will work on the project in the immediate future are: James Earle Fraser, Paul Manship, Donald De Lue and Cecil Howard, sculptors; and John A. Krout, Ronald F. Lee, Roy F. Nichols and Francis S. Ronalds, historians.

"The Hall of Our History," *National Sculpture Review,* II, no. 4, 1953.

170, 171. Hall of Our History. Detail. Rendering by Roger Bailey.

172. Hall of Our History. Detail. Rendering by Hugh Ferriss.

Richard Haas (Wisconsin 1936—)
Residence: New York City.
Education: 1959, BS Art, University of Wisconsin; 1964, MFA Painting, University of Minnesota.
Among One-Man Exhibitions: 1974, Whitney Museum of American Art, N.Y.C.; 1972, 1973, 1974, Hundred Acres Gallery, N.Y.C.; 1973, 1974, Brooke Alexander Gallery, N.Y.C.; 1975, Harkus Krakow Gallery, Boston, Mass.; 1976, Delahunty Gallery, Dallas, Texas.

The Provident Life and Trust Company—1976
Location: Chestnut Street, Philadelphia, Pennsylvania.
Status: Prototype.
Replica of Frank Furness' Provident Life and Trust Company to be painted in its original scale on the wall adjacent to the site where it once stood in Philadelphia, near the corner of 4th and Chestnut Streets.

This is one of a series of proposals returning facades of demolished structures to the locations where they once stood. Since it is generally impossible to reconstruct a necessary and important building removed by callous indifference, it should at least be possible to repaint the facade on or near the original site, as a memorial of its former existence.

Richard Haas.

173. The Provident Life and Trust Company. Facade.

World Trade Center Towers—1976
Location: New York City.
Status: Theoretical proposal.
Paint the shadows of the Empire State and the Chrysler Buildings on the World Trade Center. Ratio: one to one. (Actual shadows should face north.)

Richard Haas.

174. Proposal for the World Trade Center Towers.

Lawrence Halprin and Associates (established San Francisco 1949—)
Location: San Francisco/New York City.
Principals: Lawrence Halprin, Dean Abbott, Harold Baxter, Jim Burns, Donald Ray Carter, William R. Hull, Thomas R. Koenig, Byron McCulley, Satoru Nishita, Angela Danadjieva, Barry L. Wasserman, Timothy Wilson.
Among Major Works: Portland Open Space Sequence including: Lovejoy Plaza and Fountain, Auditorium Forecourt Fountain and Plaza, and Pettigrove Park, Portland, Oregon; Sea Ranch, Sonoma County, Calif.; Ghirardelli Square, San Francisco; Ida Crown Plaza, Jerusalem; Sproul Plaza, University of California, Berkeley.

"Our approach is synergistic, which is to say that we view the environment as a totality—as the result of a process of interaction between man and all the other inhabitants of the earth and where and how he lives." Lawrence Halprin and Associates.

Marcel Breuer and Associates (established New York City 1947—)
Location: New York City, Paris, Iran, Bahrain.
Principals: Marcel Breuer, Herbert Beckhard, Tician Papachristou, Mario Jossa.
Among Major Works: 1958, UNESCO Headquarters, Paris; 1961, Flaine ski town, France; 1966, The Whitney Museum of American Art, N.Y.C.; 1968, Department of Housing and Urban Development Headquarters, Washington, D.C.; 1968, Department of Health, Education and Welfare Headquarters, Washington, D.C.

Kenzo Tange (Imbari, Japan 1913—)
Residence: Japan.
Education: 1938, Graduate, University of Tokyo; 1941, Graduate work, University of Tokyo.
Among Major Works: 1957, Tokyo City Hall; 1946–1956, Peace Center, Hiroshima; 1948–1952, Master Plan for Hiroshima; 1955–1958, Sogetsu Art Center, Tokyo; 1961–1964, Olympic Arenas, Tokyo.

Urtec—Urbanists and Architects Team (established Japan 1961—)
Location: Japan.
Among Major Works: 1964, National Indoor Stadium for Tokyo Olympics; 1960, Plan for the Tokyo Tsukiji area; 1965, Plan for Skopje, Yugoslavia; 1966, Yamanaski Communications Center.

The Urtec group consists of twenty members. They work as a team and will deal with any aspect of the urban or architectural human scale. Urtec was founded by Kenzo Tange.

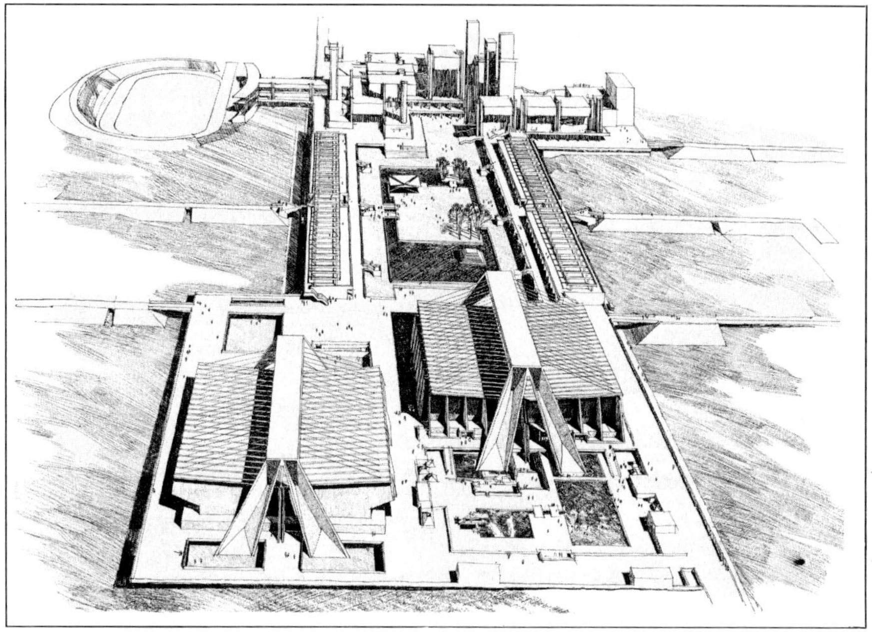

175. Flushing Meadows Sports Park. View from the South. Arena (left foreground); Swimming Pavilion (right); Central Mall (beyond) flanked by "Spines" and Tange's buildings with a link to the Stadium.

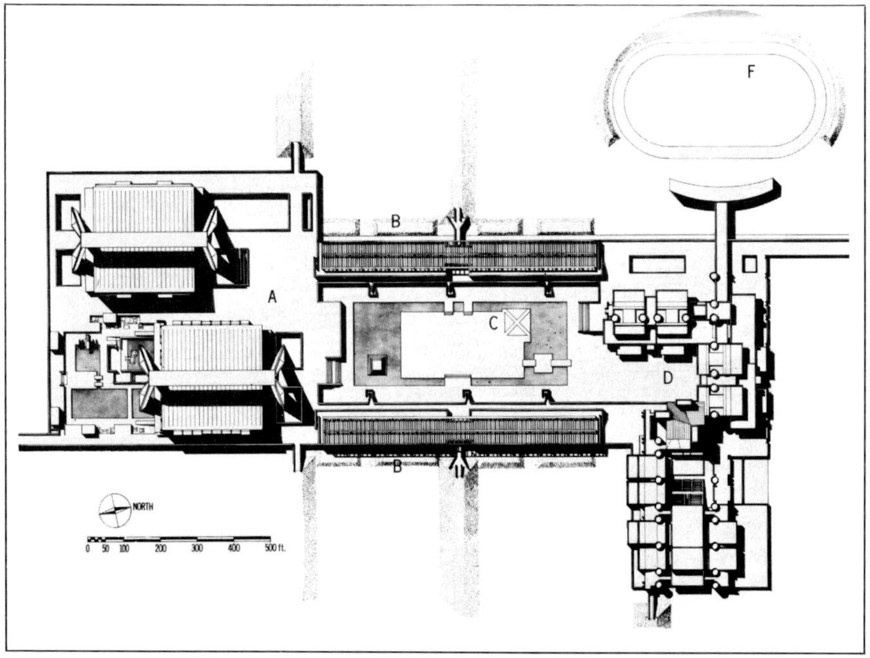

176. Flushing Meadows Sports Park Proposal. A. South Complex; B. Spines; C. Central Mall; D. Field Areas; F. Stadium. Development: Marcel Breuer and Herbert Beckhard (South Complex, Spines, N-S Approach); Lawrence Halprin and Associates (Central Mall, Field Areas); Kenzo Tange and Urtec (North Complex, Garden Restaurant, Stadium).

Flushing Meadows Sports Park—1968
Location: Queens, New York.
Status: Thomas Hoving, the moving force for the project, left the Parks Department, and with this the project died.
Additional Credit: Marcel Breuer, Kenzo Tange, Urtec.
This is quite possibly the first concept of a truly twentieth century public park. In the last century, the park ideal as enunciated by Frederick Law Olmsted was the creation of a rural landscape in an urban setting. Flushing Meadow Sports Park, on the site of two World's Fairs, is a specifically urban statement based on active recreation and sports rather than passive use. As a 600-acre urban/regional park serving the entire metropolitan New York-New Jersey-Southern Connecticut area, it would provide complete sports, recreational, and cultural facilities so that families could spend whole days or even weekends enjoying its advantages and opportunities.

Lawrence Halprin and Associates.

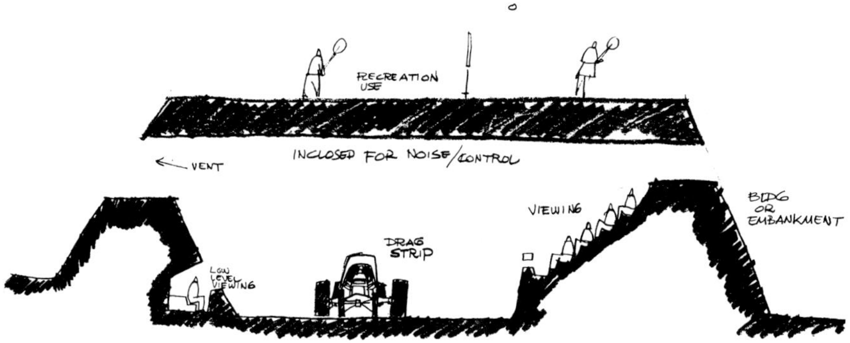

177. Flushing Meadows Sports Park. Indoor Drag Strip.

178. Flushing Meadows Sports Park. Scuba Diving Aquarium.

179. Flushing Meadows Sports Park. The Bath House.

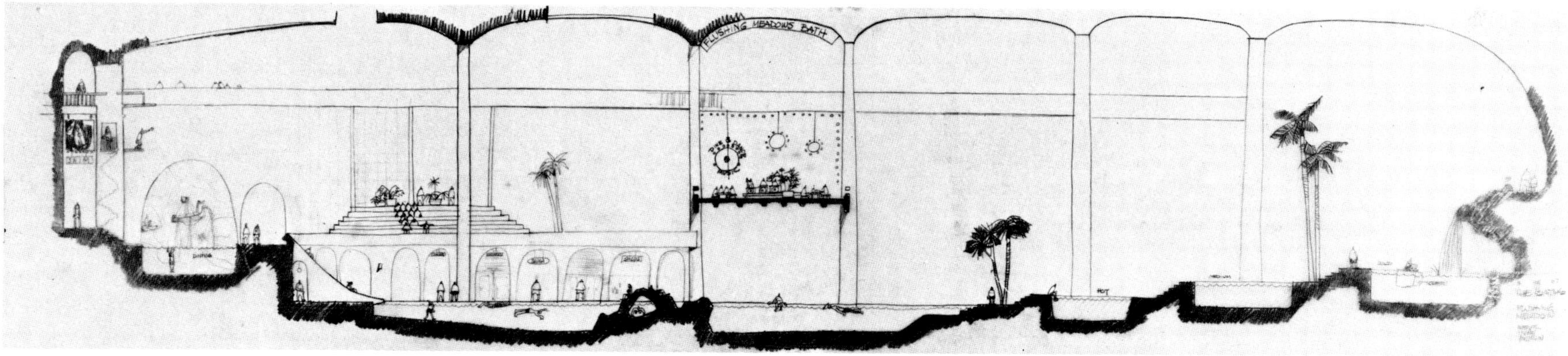

Grand Coulee Dam—1972
Location: State of Washington.
Status: Study proposals.
The study was prepared at the request of the U.S. Bureau of Reclamation, Department of the Interior. The spectacular overspill at Grand Coulee will cease in a few years when a new power station will phase it out. This will markedly alter its attraction for visitors since no water will be pouring over the dam. To create alternative ideas of what might happen in this powerful environment and allow it to continue as a point of interest, the Bureau asked us to generate design proposals for possible new and future attractions at the dam. After survey, reconnaissance and movie-making by a member of the firm, the entire office pitched in at a high energy level and developed almost 50 alternative proposals for what might happen at Grand Coulee. These proposals ranged from plans involving the entire region and its history as a multifaceted experience, to floating islands beneath the dam and special multimedia exhibitions on the dam face itself. The Bureau reviewed the work with enthusiasm and hopes to implement a number of the proposals that we created.

Lawrence Halprin and Associates.

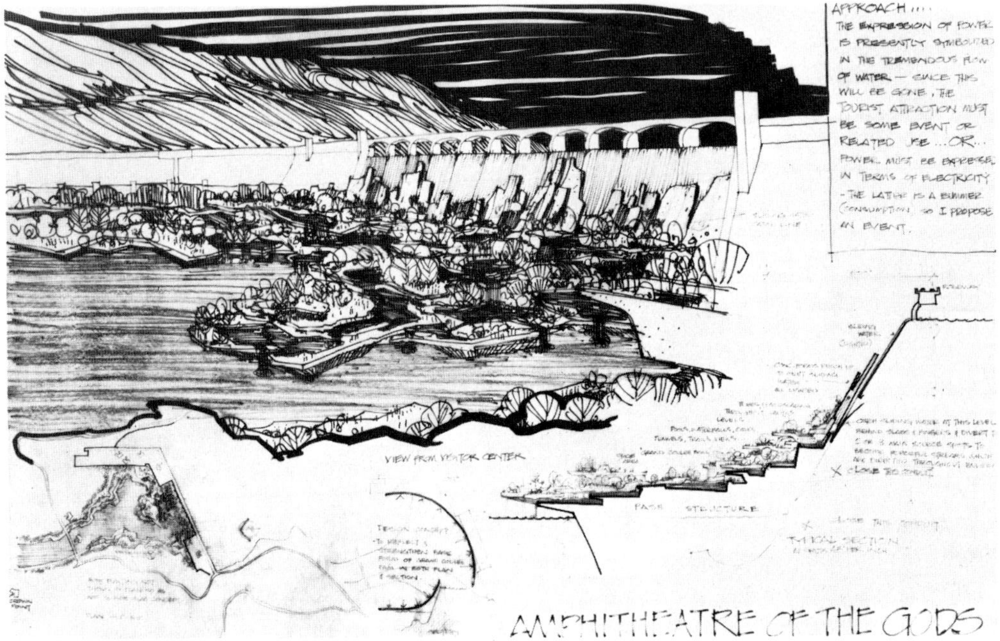

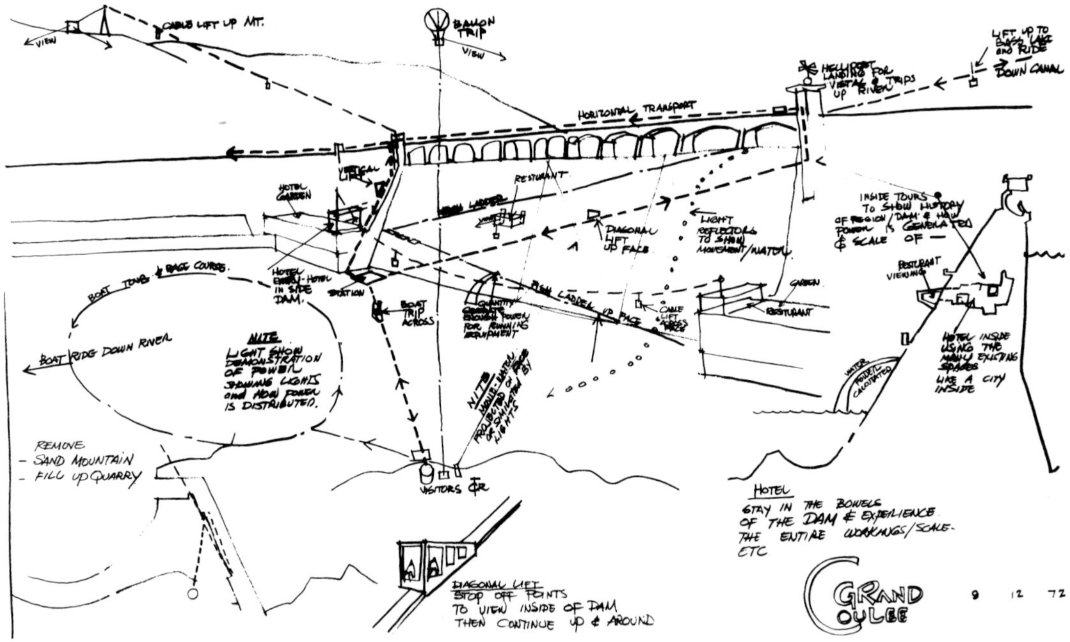

Above: 180. Grand Coulee Dam. Amphitheatre of the Gods.
Below: 181. Grand Coulee Dam. Proposal.

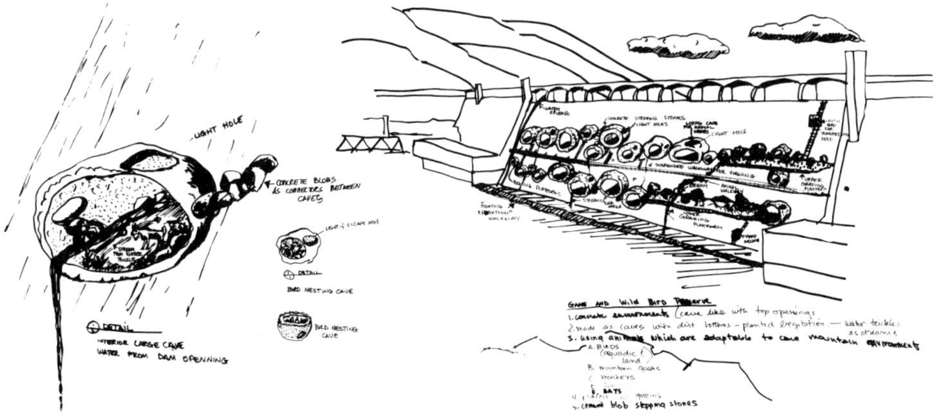

182. Grand Coulee Dam. Game and Wild Bird Preserve.

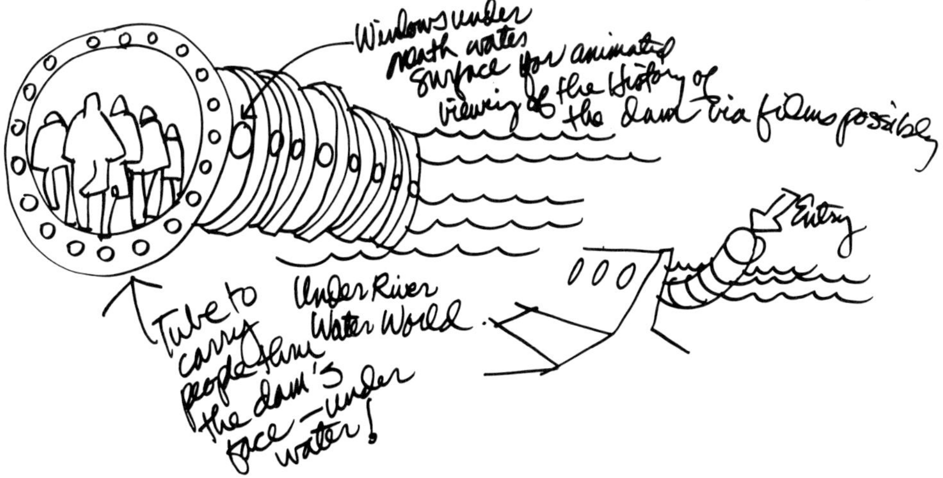

183. Grand Coulee Dam. Under River Water World.

184. Grand Coulee Dam. Pedestrian Promenade. Space Frame and Plexiglass.

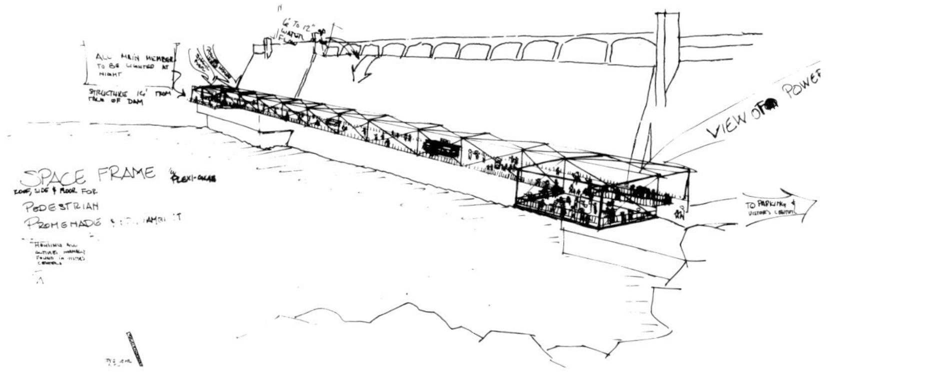

Helmle and Corbett

Frank Helmle (Ohio 1869—New York 1939)
Education: Studied at Cooper Union, N.Y.C.; School of Fine Arts of the Brooklyn Museum, N.Y.C.

Harvey Wiley Corbett (for biographical material, see Harvey Wiley Corbett).

Among Major Works of Firm: The Bush Terminal, N.Y.C.; Pennsylvania Power and Light Co., Allentown, Pa.; Guarantee Trust, New Jersey; No. 1 Fifth Avenue, N.Y.C.

Restoration of King Solomon's Temple and Citadel—1925
Location: Philadelphia.
Status: Unsuccessful exposition proposal.
A restoration of King Solomon's Temple that bears evidence of authority has at last been made. Helmle and Corbett, Architects, have carried out the idea of John Wesley Kelchner, who, inspired by religious zeal has made the reconstruction of the Temple his chief object in life for over thirty years.

As a result of the research and design work carried on by Helmle and Corbett during the past four years this restoration is now splendidly shown in a large group of interesting drawings made by Birch Burdette Long, Hugh Ferriss, Taber Sears and others. Soon this restoration will be actually built as a part of the Sesquicentennial International Exposition to be held in Philadelphia in commemoration of the one hundred and fiftieth anniversary of the signing of the Declaration of Independence. The opening date of the Exposition is June 1, 1926.

Visitors will be able to walk about the courts and to experience the sensation of having been carried back to King Solomon's time, for it is understood that life is to be given to this picture by pageantry illustrating the customs, dress and activities of that time. The Temple will be completely fitted and will have replicas of the great branched candlesticks, shewbread, the heavily jewelled priestly breast plates and of the vestments and other accessories. In the Most Holy Place, back of a mystic veil of blue, scarlet and purple, will rest a reproduction of the Ark of the Covenant, guarded by gigantic golden cherubim.

It is intended to incorporate a system of pipes through which, when the building is empty of visitors, it will be possible to force volumes of gas which will envelope the structure to its full height presenting, in conjunction with other means, an impressive spectacle of the destruction of the Temple. When the clouds of gas drift away the structure will be found unharmed.

As we know, Solomon's Temple was built during the period of peace and prosperity which followed the turbulent days of war under King David and it is fitting that the reconstruction of the Temple at Philadelphia is to stand as a symbol of world peace to all who come to this International Exposition.

Mr. Corbett at the outset laid down clearly two basic principles: first, that in making this restoration the architects must proceed as the architect, or architects, of the Temple necessarily did, assuming the use of only such methods of construction, materials and architectural forms as were employed, or might have been employed, at that time. The second principle was that the site must be assumed to be in the condition which existed at the time the Temple was built, not in its present condition.

In the matter of design character Solomon's Temple showed a co-mingling of styles current at the time of its building and previous to that time, for Jerusalem was the gateway through which much of the traffic of the then-known world passed. The Egyptian design influence was also particularly strong because of Solomon's alliance with the court of Egypt through his marriage with a princess of the Egyptians. It may be mentioned in passing that one of the most interesting features of the reconstruction at Philadelphia will be the rebuilding of the palace, adjoining the temple grounds, which the King built for his wife.

The entire Citadel of Jerusalem will be reconstructed at Philadelphia embracing, besides the Temple, King Solomon's Palace, "The House of the Forest of Lebanon," "The Queen's Palace," "Porch of the Pillars," and other structures. The Citadel was enclosed within military walls which began at the bottom of the mount. The large court will be 400 ft. by 200 ft. beyond which, within its terraced court on a higher level, will be the impressive pile formed by The Holy Place, The Most Holy Place, and The Great Porch. The latter will rise 300 ft. in white and gold against the sky as a step back tower of majestic effectiveness.

Abridged from Eugene Clute in *Pencil Points,* VI, November 1925.

---

185. Restoration of King Solomon's Temple and Citadel. The Plaza. "Solomon's Pool" (left center). Palace in Background.

186. King Solomon's Temple and Citadel. View From the North East Corner. Rendering by Birch Burdette Long.

187. The Restoration of King Solomon's Temple. Scene at Night. Rendering by Hugh Ferriss.

Right: 188. Restoration of King Solomon's Temple. Porch of Judgement. Rendering by Hugh Ferriss.

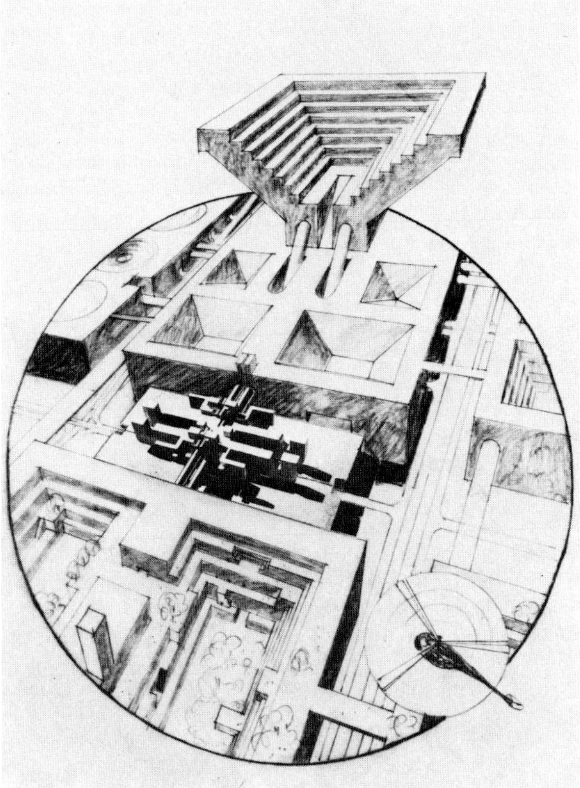
189. Walk-on City. Detail.

190. Walk-on City. Aerial View.

Hans Hollein (Vienna, Austria 1934—)
Residence: Vienna, Austria.
Education: 1956, Diploma, Academy of Fine Arts, Vienna School of Architecture, Austria; 1958–1959, Illinois Institute of Technology; 1960, M Arch., College of Environmental Design, University of California, Berkeley.
Among Major Works: 1969, Richard L. Feigen Gallery, N.Y.C.; 1972–1975, Siemens AG Headquarters, Munich, West Germany; 1972, Media-Lines Olympic Village, Munich; 1976, Municipal Museum, Mochengladbach, Germany; 1976, Museum of Modern Art, Florence, Italy.

"Walk-on" City—1963
Location: New York City.
Status: Prototype.
A city is formed with the concept of buildings as integrated structural units, usable in all dimensions. Building surfaces are at the disposal of the inhabitants, and the system allows for integration of all elements necessary for city life: transportation, recreation, sport, ritual—accommodated at appropriate areas on surface and subsurface levels. The basic grid structure of New York has been retained to facilitate transformation of existing conditions into future needs.

Hans Hollein.

City for South-Western USA—1959
Location: Southwestern USA.
Status: Prototype.
The experience of the Arizona and New Mexico landscape and thoughts about living together in large communal structures or "cities," are the basis for this project. A variety of spatial options, rather than flexibility in terms of rearranging walls, furniture, etc., facilitate discovery of living situations. The objective is integration with nature, resulting in forms responsive to the shape of the environment.

Hans Hollein.

191. City for South-Western United States. Model.

Doloris Holmes (Connecticut 1929—)
Residence: New York City.
Education: 1957, MS Social Science, Boston University.
Among Major Works: Exhibitions—1962, St. Mark's Church, N.Y.C.; 1964, Long Island University, Brooklyn, N.Y.; 1974, Second Story Gallery, N.Y.C.; 1975, Metropolitan Museum, Group Show, N.Y.C. Performances—1970, Mixed Media, Guild Hall, Long Island; FISH-JOY, a play presented at the Soho 20 Gallery, N.Y.C.

Survival Dome—1970
Location: New York City.
Status: Unbuilt due to lack of funding.
The basic feature of the Oxygen Utility Dome, proposed here for construction in New York, is its controlled atmosphere, which will use the appropriate amounts of nitrogen, oxygen, helium, water vapor and possibly inert trace elements that constitute clean air.

The Oxygen Dome will be a utility along the lines of Con Edison. Home units for controlled air would be made available to the public at reasonable prices. A major purpose of this Dome would be educational, and in addition, reduce the anxiety over the loss of the prehistoric and inalienable right to breathe. The building itself would be large enough for three hundred individual units and a large communal room.

The customer would go through the following actions:

1. Enter the main door, which would lead to a store. Here he could buy a book, art supplies, or a headphone for listening to music, all for use in the individual rooms.
2. After leaving the store, he will either walk up a ramp or ascend in an elevator to his own Clean Air Room.
3. The customer will put a coin into a meter at the door of the room. Prices vary according to the amount of time: from a very brief reprieve from filthy air; to a long internal respiratory cleansing. (Japan already has public meters into which you can put a coin and get clean air.) Additional meters will be available for music, scents, or TV.
4. The customer could also enter the Communal Room. A section of this room would house a small botanical garden with emphasis on those plants which are becoming extinct. Bird calls of vanishing species might be heard in this section. In addition, there would be a children's zoo especially planned for allergic children. As all the inhabitants would have to be hairless and featherless, the exhibits would consist of such animals as the elephant, rhinoceros, fish and shellfish.

Doloris Holmes.

192. Oxygen Utility Dome. Section.

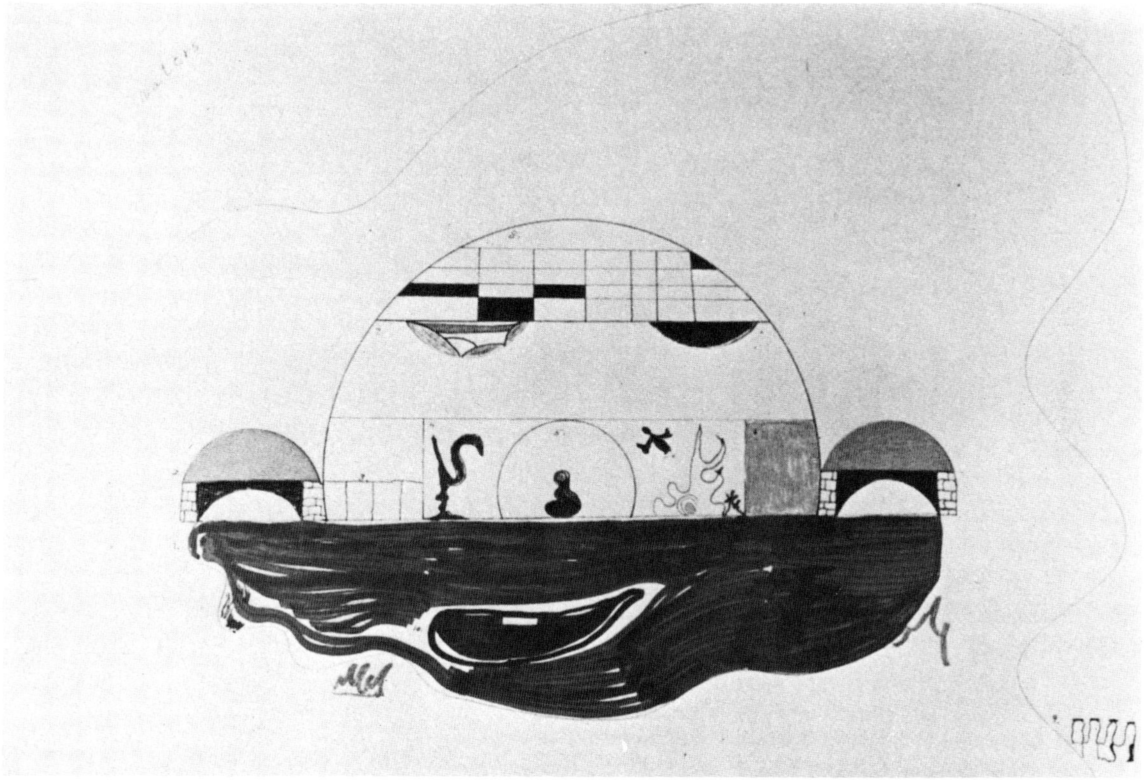

Raymond Hood (Rhode Island 1881—Connecticut 1934)
Education: 1903, BS Arch., Massachusetts Institute of Technology; 1911, Diplôme, École des Beaux Arts, Paris.
Among Major Works: 1924, the American Radiator Building, N.Y.C.; 1930, the Daily News Building, N.Y.C.; 1931, the McGraw-Hill Building, N.Y.C.; 1930, the Beaux Arts Apartments, N.Y.C.; 1930–1932, Rockefeller Center, N.Y.C.

Raymond Hood's skyscrapers were among the most influential buildings of the Art Deco period, aiding in the transition to the streamlined International Style designs of the 1930s.

Central Methodist Episcopal Church—1927
Location: Columbus, Ohio.
Status: Unbuilt.

A Methodist Episcopal parish in Columbus, Ohio, had acquired a block of land in the business center, and upon it the congregation wanted to build the greatest church in the world. As the name of Ralph Adams Cram was associated with the design of the finest Gothic cathedrals of the day, the Pastor had been sent to Boston to interview him.

Mr. Cram was delighted to see the Pastor, who explained the plan they had in mind to build this church. However, the congregation was one of businessmen and the site was an extremely valuable one. Therefore, they wished not only to build the greatest church in the world, but to combine it with revenue producing enterprises including a hotel, a YMCA, an apartment house with a swimming pool, and so on. On the street level would be shops to bring in high rentals, and in the basement, the largest garage in Columbus, Ohio. The garage was very important, because, in giving his congregation a place to park their cars on coming to work weekdays the Pastor would indeed make the church the center of their lives.

Mr. Cram was deeply distressed by the idea. He hastened to explain to the Pastor that if it was the congregation's intent to build the "greatest church in the world" it should be a cathedral of solid stone, built to last through the ages to the greater glory of God. It was unthinkable that it be combined with hotels, apartments and retail stores. As for the basement, there would be no room for cars because this noble structure would be constructed on tremendous granite piers, thirty feet across, that would support the structure through all time as a monument to their faith.

The Pastor, though impressed by all this, didn't feel he could return to his building committee and tell them their basement would be full of huge stone piers instead of automobiles. So he came to New York to see Raymond Hood, related the problem and the reaction of Mr. Cram. When he had finished, Mr. Hood said, "The trouble with Mr. Cram is that he has no faith in God. I will design a church for you that will be the greatest church in the world. It will include all the hotels, swimming tanks and candy stores you desire. Furthermore, in the basement will be the largest garage in Christendom because," he continued, "I will build your church on toothpicks and have faith enough in God to believe it will stand up!"

But like many another architect's dream, this one also ended with the model.

Walter H. Kilham, Jr., Raymond Hood: Architect, 1973.

193. Central Methodist Episcopal Church. Perspective.

Manhattan Bridge with Apartments—1929
Location: New York City.
Status: Hypothetical proposal.
New York was already densely built up as far as the location of apartments near business centers was concerned. To alleviate this situation Hood came up with the idea of great bridges of skyscraper apartments across the rivers. He carried the idea further to combining offices, apartments, stores, hotels and theaters in one great building covering three blocks, so that all activities of daily life could take place within one building.

Walter H. Kilham, Jr., Raymond Hood:Architect, 1973.

194. Proposed Manhattan Bridge Lined with Apartment Houses.

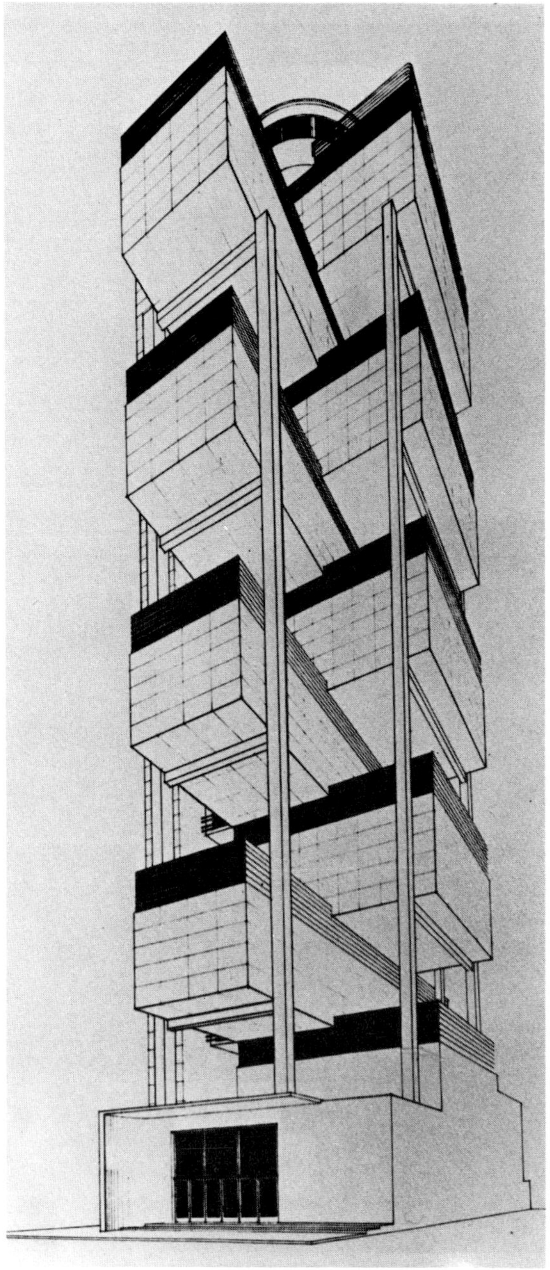

195. Museum of Modern Art. Second Variation of Scheme Four.

Howe and Lescaze

George Howe (Massachusetts 1886—New York City 1955)
Education: 1904–1907, Harvard University; 1908–1913, studied at the École des Beaux Arts, Paris.

William Lescaze (Switzerland 1896—New York City 1969)
Education: 1911–1914, studied painting at College de Genève; 1919–1920, studied architecture under Karl Moser, a pioneer modernist, at the Zurich Technische Hochschule.

Among Major Works of Firm: 1932, Philadelphia Savings Fund Society Building; 1929, the Oak Lane County Day School, Philadelphia; 1931, the Hessian Hills School, Philadelphia; 1931–1932, the Chrystie Forsyth Housing Development, N.Y.C.

Museum of Modern Art—1930
Location: New York City.
Status: Unbuilt due to change of circumstance; John D. Rockefeller donated an existing house for the Museum's use.
In May 1930, the trustees of the newly organized Museum of Modern Art asked Howe and Lescaze to prepare preliminary schemes for a new building, [initially, they prepared three].

In June, Howe and Lescaze were asked to develop a more complete scheme. The trustees had in mind two possible sites, both similar to that hypothesized in the preparation of the earlier schemes. In scheme four the architects imaginatively explored possibilities for lighting. By ingeniously combining artificial lighting with skylighting in a multifaceted light-mixing chamber, they made it possible for each gallery to be illuminated from many directions. The unique functional and spatial organization is derived from the limitations of the site and from the system of natural lighting. Each gallery is a self-contained spatial unit with its own entrance and exit. Nine boxes of space—Howe called them "horizontal blocks"—are placed one above another and at right angles to each other. The structural system was a simple and dramatic

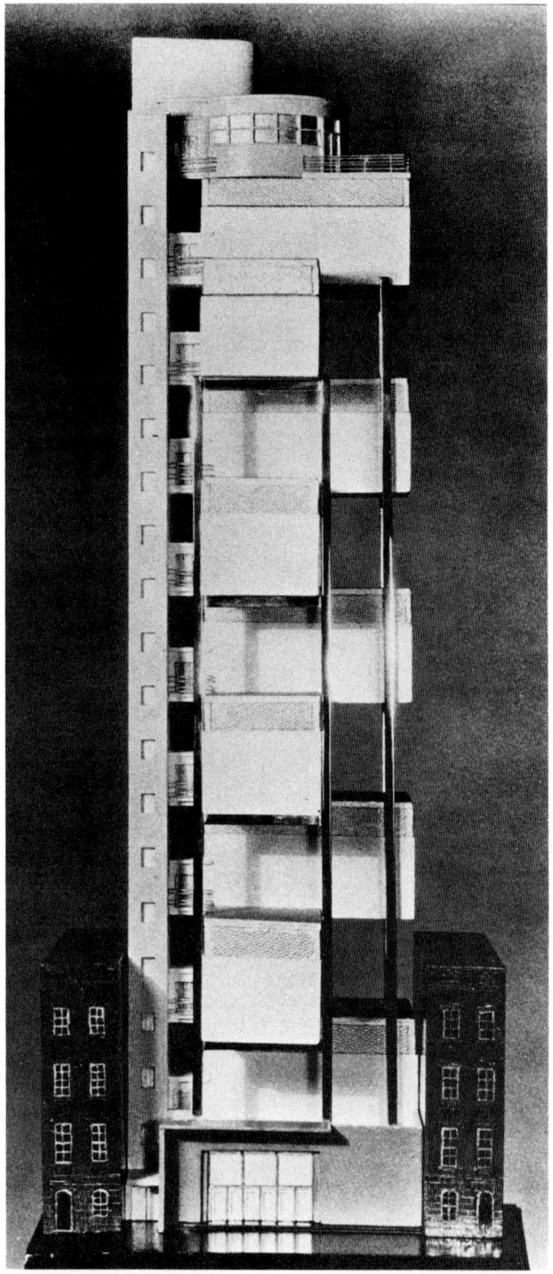

196. Museum of Modern Art. Variation of Scheme Four. Model.

197. Museum of Modern Art. Perspective of Scheme Five.

one of support and supported. Two sets of columns, tied by beams at each gallery level, rise uninterrupted for the height of the building. Slid in between the columns are the gallery boxes, which rest on the beams and not on the gallery below.

In the autumn of 1931, the museum's trustees renewed their interest in building a permanent home. Howe and Lescaze prepared two new schemes. In scheme five they adopted a system of staggered light chambers that received light from two sides only; this loss of lighting flexibility was compensated for by an increase in gallery space. Scheme six is in a sense a return to scheme two with its all-glass front of alternating clear and opaque glass. It is probably the most handsome of the sequence. Formally, it is an elegant solution in its clear separation of structure from bounding walls, the simple entrance symmetrically disposed, and the treatment of the round concrete columns at the penthouse level (predicting Le Corbusier's Visual Arts Center at Harvard in 1963). The clear separation of service tower from gallery space is sacrificed to what the architects regarded as a "novel solution of the traffic problem: visitors would be taken up to the uppermost floor and would go down through the galleries by means of a quarter of a flight of stairs at every exhibition room."

Abridged from Robert Stern, **George Howe: Toward a Modern American Architecture**, 1975.

198. Museum of Modern Art. Perspective of Scheme Six.

INSLEY, WILL

Will Insley (Indiana 1929—)
Residence: New York City.
Education: 1951, BA Amherst College; 1955, MA Arch. Harvard Graduate School of Design.
Among One-Artist Exhibitions: 1965, Stable Gallery, N.Y.C.; 1968, Walker Art Center, Minneapolis, Minn.; 1971, Museum of Modern Art, N.Y.C.; 1972, Paul Maenz, Cologne.

ONECITY—1975
Location: Central United States.
Status: Theoretical proposal.

Introduction

This brief report concerns information of a future civilization • Much has been written of its practical focus ONECITY in the book "Fragments from the Interior Building"—evidence purely diagrammatic and descriptive and offering sometimes contradictory facts and impressions • Isolated wall fragments have indeed been found but the structure and appearance of ONECITY spaces is at this time in conjecture • Certain clues now hopefully point to possibly soon discovering some actual visual evidence • Accurate visual information has been found however of some 35 religious/buildings/to date (the first of these uncovered in 1967) and a few of them are presented here as they in fact do future appear •

ONECITY
•
In central plains of United States
lies buried myth of ONECITY
horizontal dwelling of future
the poetry of city
theater of learning
the great plateau of future civilization
•
ONECITY is 400 × 400 mile spiral square
wave mounds rising falling within ratio limits
a dialogue with dominant topography
various slants and levels roofed with grass and trees
the horizon line of separate function layers
housing nation 400 million
•
Center is the Inner Field and Inner City
the "Opaque Library"
silent seed of waiting empty spaces
and ringing this the Outer Field and Outer City

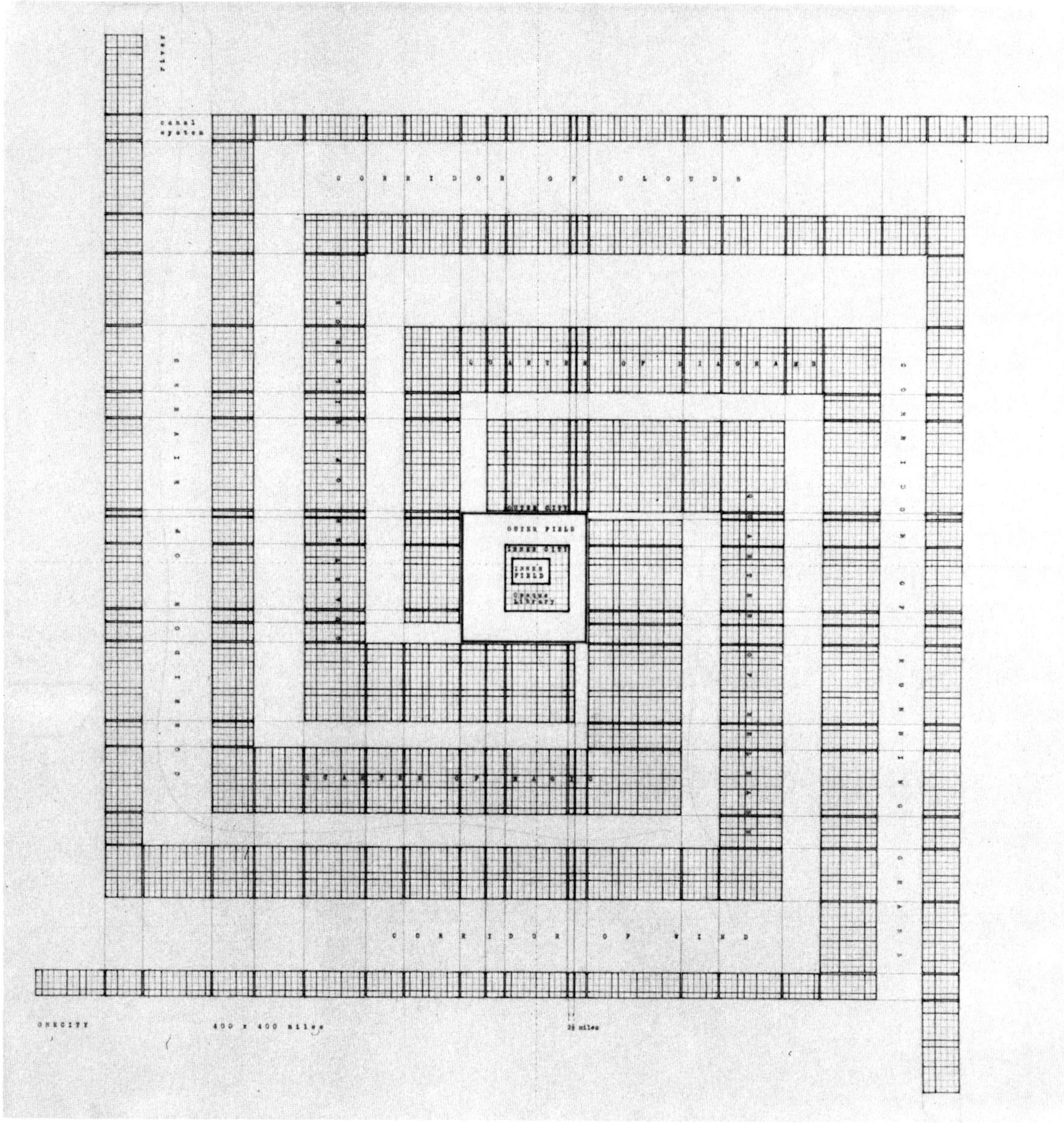

199. Plan of ONECITY / 400 miles x 400 miles.

\+ = above ground

− = below ground

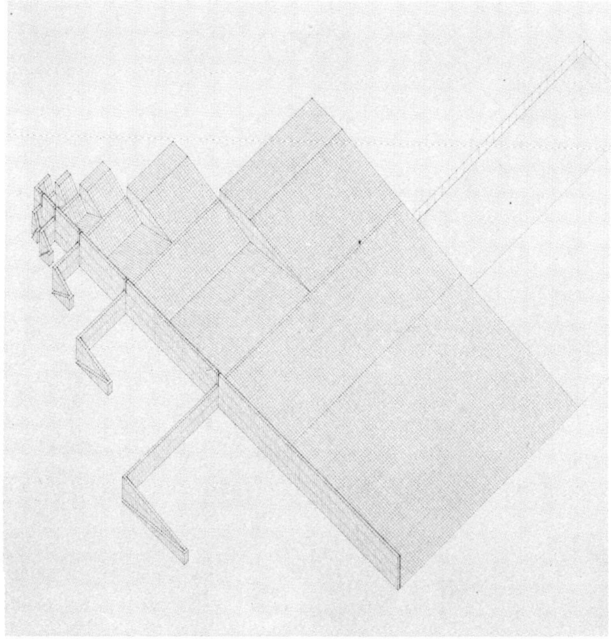

200. Stage Space Reduce /
+36′ x 585′ x 582′
−12′

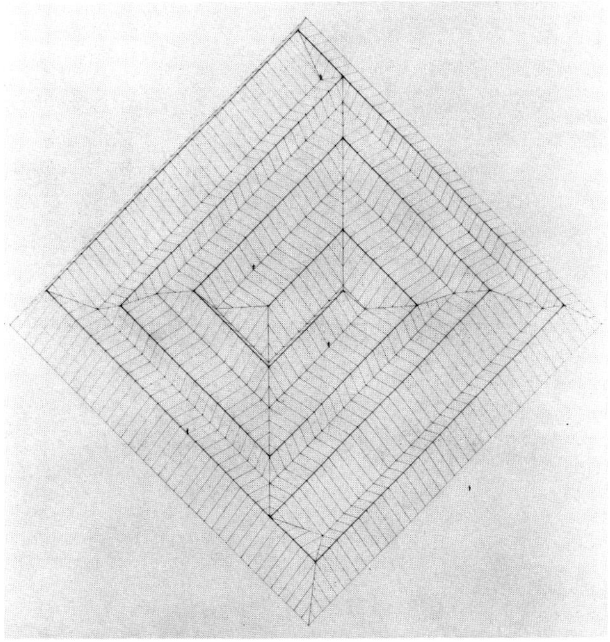

201. Channel Space Snake /
+12′ x 480′ x 480′

4 active city sections spiraling out in 4 leg moves
divided by 4 country corridors weaving in

•

ONECITY is organized in 4 layers
each lower one slipping out from under those above
walls angled towards the sun
plant leaves turned to light

•

Layers with separate function transportubes between
Layer 1 – *living*–each roof a garden
angle skywells pull sunair through under spaces
Layer 2 – *theater*–public performance
lightcell walls transfer sky information
illusion and reality–a walk through movie
Layer 3 – *control*–intellect contact and decision
plotting control of city life
Layer 4 – *supply*–receive process produce
and jetubes streaming underground to country

•

RELIGIOUS/BUILDINGS/

•

Related to "Opaque Library" core of ONECITY
but removed in distant wilderness
Extended Spaces are hidden
religious /buildings/ of the civilization

•

As people go into "Opaque Library" from the Outer City
to observe formal essence of their practical world
they also go out from ONECITY to seek structures
devoted to civilization myth of "The Interior Building"
based on passage present to future
and return in lifetime with future information
and ultimate passage through stages of death
to shell enclosing all possible human concepts of reality

•

4 /building/ categories echo nature forms
such as mountain valley cave and river bed
in various combinations

1–STAGE SPACE
first/buildings/built before realization of ONECITY
religious focus of temporary worker villages
during long development of the city
–"Stage Space Reduce"
player climbs to series of diminishing horizons
or descends again to more difficult terrain
or exits through the wall
five strange stairways of release

2–CHANNEL SPACE
primitive in concept
derived from continuous surface of slanted planes
between limits of raised horizon and earth
–"Channel Space Snake"
traveler climbs seeking slopes of least resistance
according to ratio progress of the structure
to view sea of rim and shadow shifting channels
•
3–PASSAGE SPACE
refinement of earlier /buildings/
introducing narrow passages
marking ratio measure
cutting through the structure
–"Passage Space Drift"
one descends from outer ground into /building/
into valley of passages open to the sky
shadow halls slice between closed denied areas
then open to run along and cross lowered spaces
and one looks down from passages become walls
into rooms once again denied
and one climbs hill of trenchant passages
discovering at last a low central court
and from the /building/ root passages extend
seeking potential continuation of the spaces
according to predetermined unrelenting ratio
•
4–VOLUME SPACE
ultimate development of the /buildings/
never rising above the ground
no outside profile evidence
only inside
a mental /building/
–"Volume Passage Space Interior Swing"
a swing-slip space complex and elusive
a central well sinks into the earth at angle
slipping from sky to roughwet rock floor deep below
and counteracting this space force
secondary spaces appear
motivated by a swing plane force
one channel space above open to the sky
one reverse cavern space below enclosed
and between these three volume spaces
a network of passages buried in the earth
4 horizontal layers deep
with descending angle connections
and from the /building/ root passages extend
•

Will Insley.

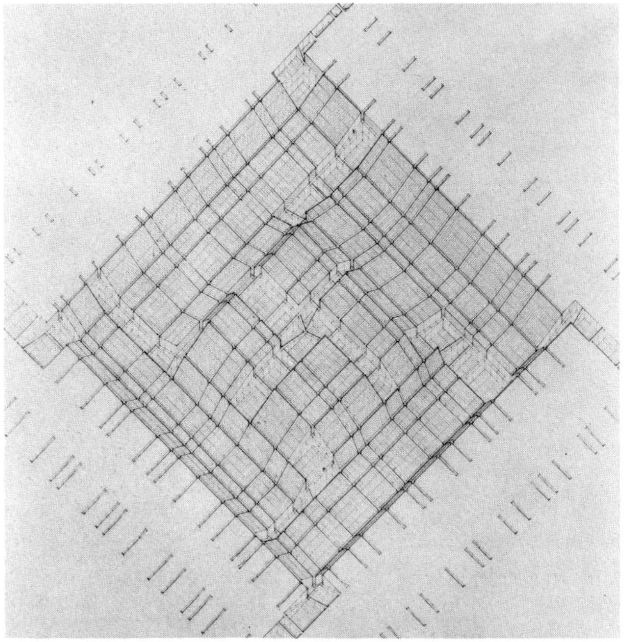

202. Passage Space Drift / +12′ x 789′ x 789′ −36′

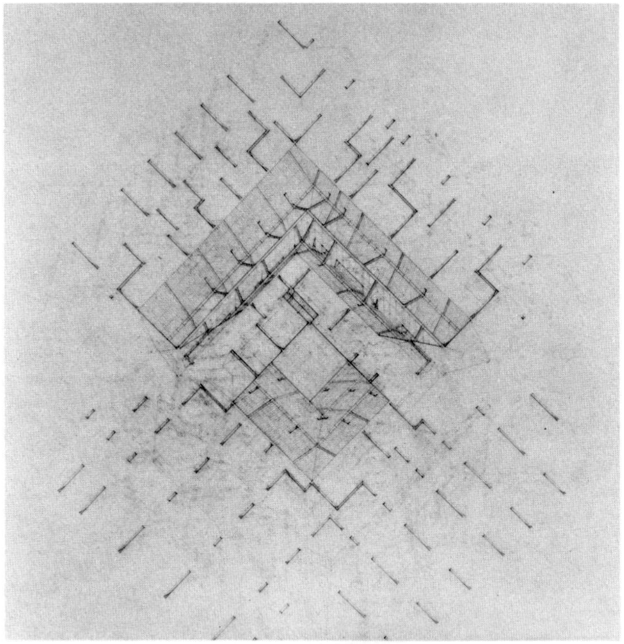

203. Volume Passage Space Interior Swing / −120′ x 789′ x 789′

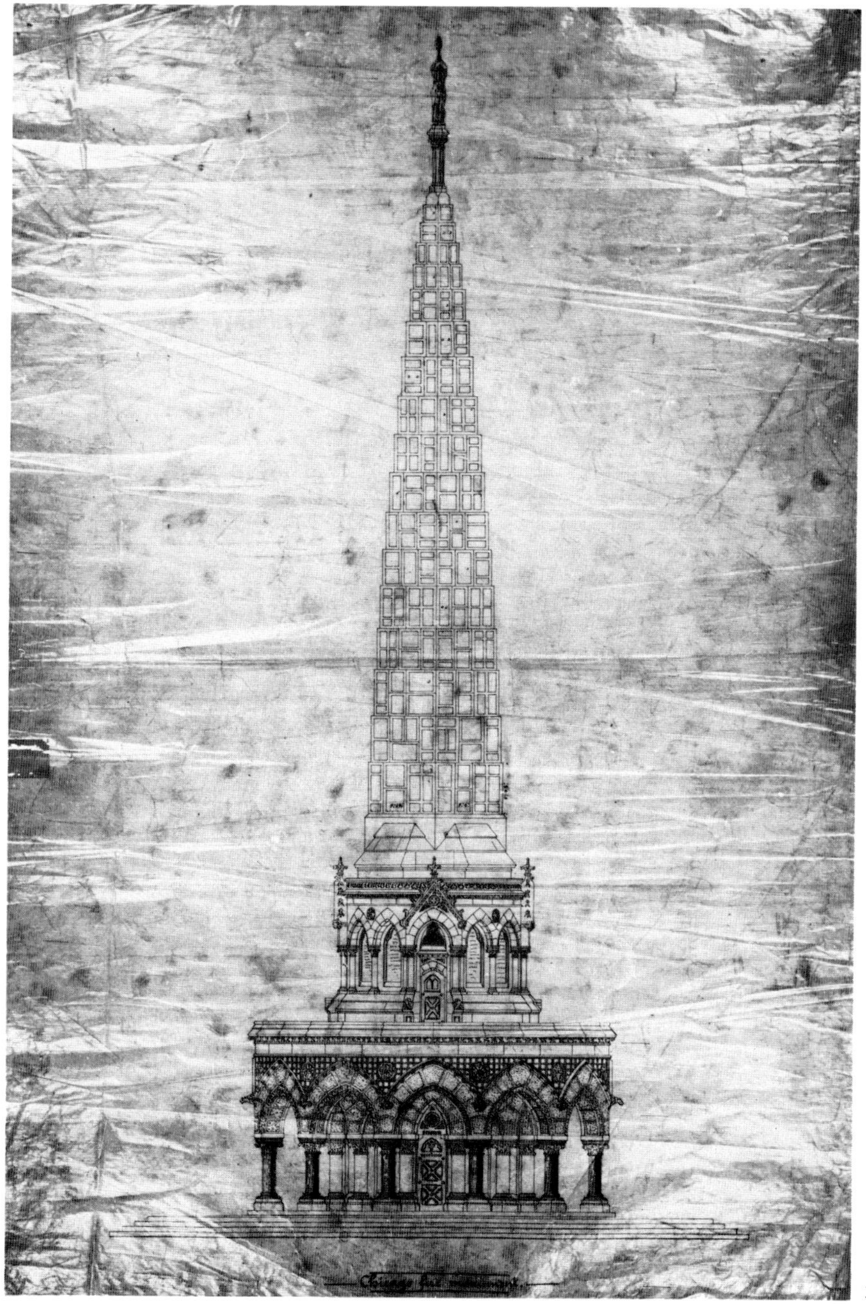

204. Chicago Fire Monument. Elevation.

Jenney and Mundie

William LeBaron Jenney (Massachusetts 1832—Los Angeles 1907)
Education: 1856, Diplôme, École Centrales des Arts et Manufactures.
Among Major Works: 1879, Leiter Building, Chicago; 1884–1885, Home Insurance Building, Chicago, which employed the first extensive use of the internal skeleton and curtain wall in a multistory building, and is often called "the true father of the skyscraper."

William B. Mundie (Ontario 1863—Illinois 1939)
Education: Graduate, Hamilton Collegiate Institute.

Among Major Firm Works: 1891, Manhattan Building, N.Y.C.; 1891, New York Life Insurance Building, N.Y.C.; 1893, Horticultural Building, Chicago Exposition of 1893.

Chicago Fire Monument—(?)
Status: Unbuilt.
Memorial to those killed in the Great Chicago Fire of 1871.

205. Typical Existing Conditions.

206. First Phase.

207. Second Phase.

208. Third Phase.

209. Completed Neighborhood.

John Johansen (New York City 1916—)
Residence: New York City.
Education: Harvard University; Harvard Graduate School of Design.
Among Major Works: 1963, Clowes Memorial Hall and Opera House, Indianapolis, Ind.; 1964, U.S. Embassy, Dublin, Ireland; 1967, Morris Mechanic Theater, Baltimore, Md.; 1970, Mummers Theater, Oklahoma City; 1970, Comprehensive Master Plan for the new campus of Western Connecticut State College, Danbury.

Leapfrog Housing—1967–1968
Location: East Harlem Triangle, New York City.
Status: Feasibility study.
The concept is that of building new housing structures above the roofs of existing inhabited tenements. If areas could be immediately and continually renewed, decaying parts replaced by new construction with no displacement of tenants within but simply moved upstairs, we would be respecting existing living patterns as well as the natural processes of the city as a living organism.

Although applicable to numerous areas in many cities, for the basis of this study it is intended that this concept of construction be applied to a particular existing area in New York City: that of the East Harlem Triangle. Typical tenements here are three, four, or five story walkups, old law, new law, and brownstone, usually row on row, block after block. In the common rear open yards of these buildings it is proposed to erect towers, probably two per block, to a height of about ten, twelve, or more stories. Mechanical services would be brought from the street, and the housing units would be attached to these towers—starting at the sixth story and continuing to the twelfth or fourteenth, cantilevered out or spanning between towers, but not interfering with existing, presently occupied tenements which would serve until the superstructure is completed above. New superstructure in housing might be built over light industry, commerce, institutions, or highways, thus making full use of air-rights and stratified zoning. This concept releases the planner and architect from the confining aspects of horizontal zoning and two-dimensional definitions of ownership, to deal with a truly three-dimensional concept accommodating freely disposed and changing elements of urban life.

John Johansen.

Philip Johnson (Cleveland 1906—)
Residence: Connecticut.
Education: 1930, BA, Harvard University; 1943, B Arch., Harvard Graduate School of Design.
Among Major Works: 1949, Glass House, New Canaan, Conn.; 1964, New York State Theater, Lincoln Center, N.Y.C.; 1973, I.D.S. Center, Minneapolis, Minn.; 1975, Penzoil Place, Houston, Texas.
Among Major Publications: 1932, *The International Style,* with Henry-Russell Hitchcock; 1947, *Mies van der Rohe.*

Ellis Island—1966
Location: New York City.
Status: Unbuilt.
The theme of the Ellis Island design was the photographic reproduction of the names of *all* the immigrants that passed through the control point. These were to be mounted on the ramps that encircle the monument.

Philip Johnson.

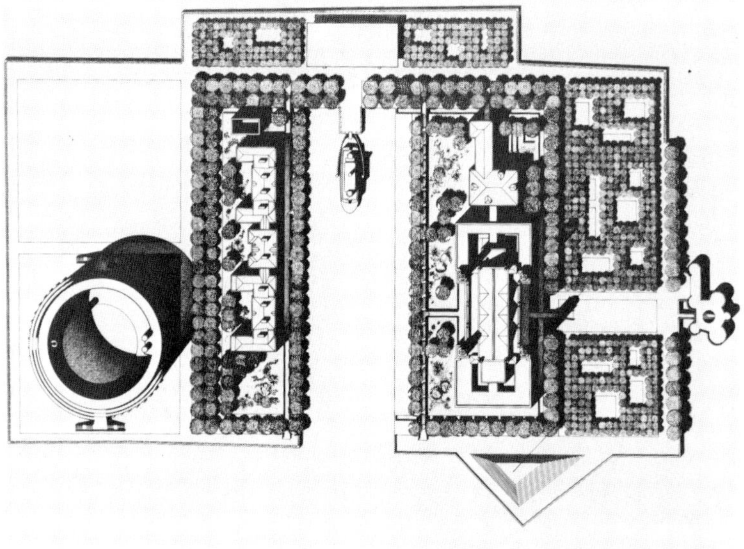
210. Ellis Island National Park. Plan.

211. Detail of Monument.

212. Ellis Island National Park. Model.

J JOHNSON, PHILIP

Third City—1966
Location: New York City.
Status: Hypothetical proposal.
The purpose of the Third City exercise was to investigate the effect of super skyscrapers constructed over an existing public transportation node surrounded by low- and medium-rise blocks built on existing street grids. In other words, how to recondition a city center in a grand way. It was not a realistic exercise.

Philip Johnson.

213. Third City. Aerial Perspective.

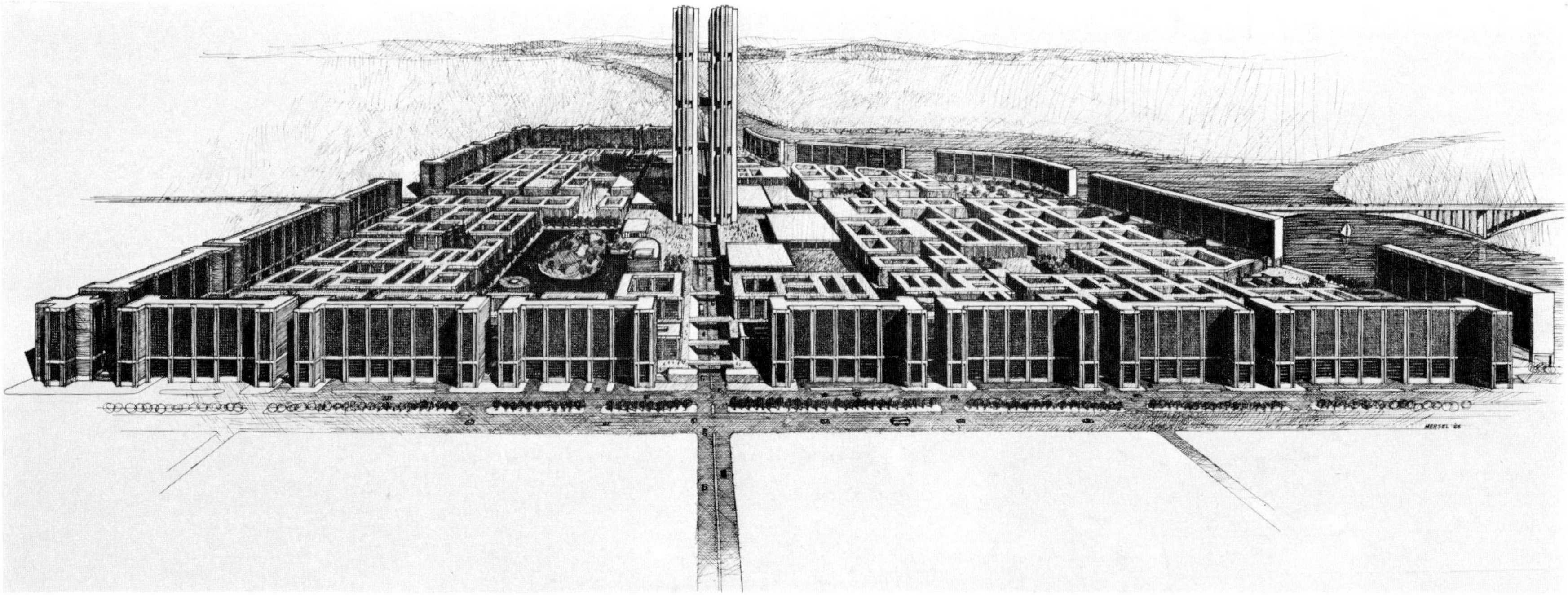

Louis I. Kahn (Russia 1901—New York City 1974)
Education: 1924, B Arch., University of Pennsylvania.
Among Major Works: 1952–1954, Yale University Art Gallery; 1957–1961, Richards Medical Center, Philadelphia; 1959–1965, Salk Institute for Biological Studies, San Diego; 1962–1979, Capital of Dacca, E. Pakistan.

Kahn did not emerge as a major figure until the 1950's; soon after this time, however, he was recognized as one of the most important architects, theorists, and teachers of the last quarter century. The expression of his concepts of "served and servant spaces," and what a building or material "wants to be," offered an alternative to the dominant Miesian and International Style, and influenced the development of the New Brutalist aesthetic.

Mikveh Israel—1961–1970
Location: Philadelphia.
Status: Unbuilt.
The synagogue is situated in the historic section of Philadelphia. The plan is structured with a series of cylindrical "rooms" surrounding the sanctuary and chapel. Light penetrates through these cylinders and is diffused. Thus, light is given a volumetric form. In the school building these volumes of light are reversed. The primary materials are brick and concrete.

Romaldo Giurgola and Jaimini Mehta,
Louis I. Kahn, 1975.

A space can never reach its place in architecture without natural light. Artificial light is the light of night expressed in positioned chandeliers, not to be compared with the unpredictable play of natural light . . . Architecture deals with spaces, the thoughtful and meaningful making of spaces. The architectural space is one where the structure is apparent in the space itself. A long span is a great effort that should not be dissipated by division within it. The art of architecture has wonderful examples of spaces within spaces, but without deception. A wall dividing a domed space would negate the entire spirit of the dome. The structure is a design in light. The vault, the dome, the arch, the column are structures related to the character of light. Natural light gives mood by space, by the nuances of light in the time of day and the seasons of the year as it enters and modifies the space. . . .

Louis I. Kahn.

214. Mikveh Israel Synagogue. Perspective Sketch.

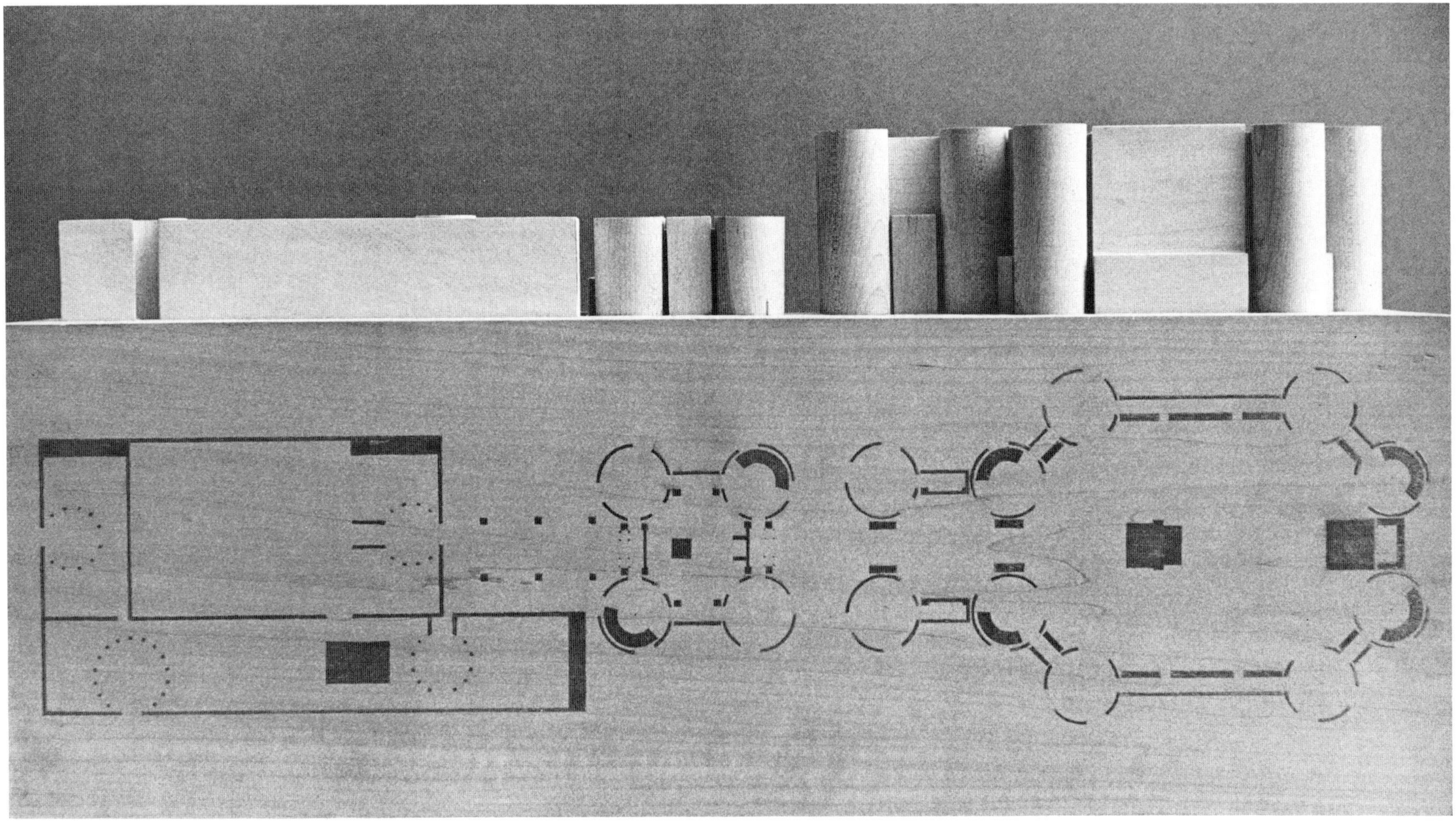

215. Mikveh Israel Synagogue. Model.

William Katavolos (New York City 1924—)
Residence: New York City.
Education: 1949, graduated in Industrial Design, Pratt Institute; 1964–1965, physics course, New York University.
Among Major Works: 1962–1963, Hawaii State Pavilion, New York World's Fair, in collaboration with R. Aarnio; 1965, Education Tower, experimental school building; 1965, Time & Life office partition systems, in collaboration with J. Luss; 1968, designed a playground made entirely of paper for mentally retarded children; 1969 to present, designer of new products for hospital and surgical field.

Chemical City—1959

Status: Theoretical study.

A new architecture is possible through the matrix of chemistry. Man must stop making and manipulating, and instead allow architecture to happen. There is a way beyond building just as the principles of waves, parabolas, and plummet lines exist beyond the mediums in which they form. So must architecture free itself from traditional patterns and become organic. New discoveries in chemistry have led to the production of powdered and liquid materials which, when suitably treated with certain activating agents, expand to great size and then catalyze and become rigid. We are rapidly gaining the necessary knowledge of the molecular structure of these chemicals, together with the necessary techniques that will lead to the production of materials which will have a specific program of behavior built into them while still in the sub-microscopic stage. Accordingly it will be possible to take minute quantities of powder and make them expand into predetermined shapes such as spheres, tubes and toruses. Houses such as this would grow to certain sizes, subdivide or fuse for larger functions. Great vaults would be produced with parabolic jets that catalyze on contact with the air. Exploding patterns of an instantaneous architecture of transformations, into desired densities, into known directions, for calculated durations.

William Katavolos, Organics, 1961.

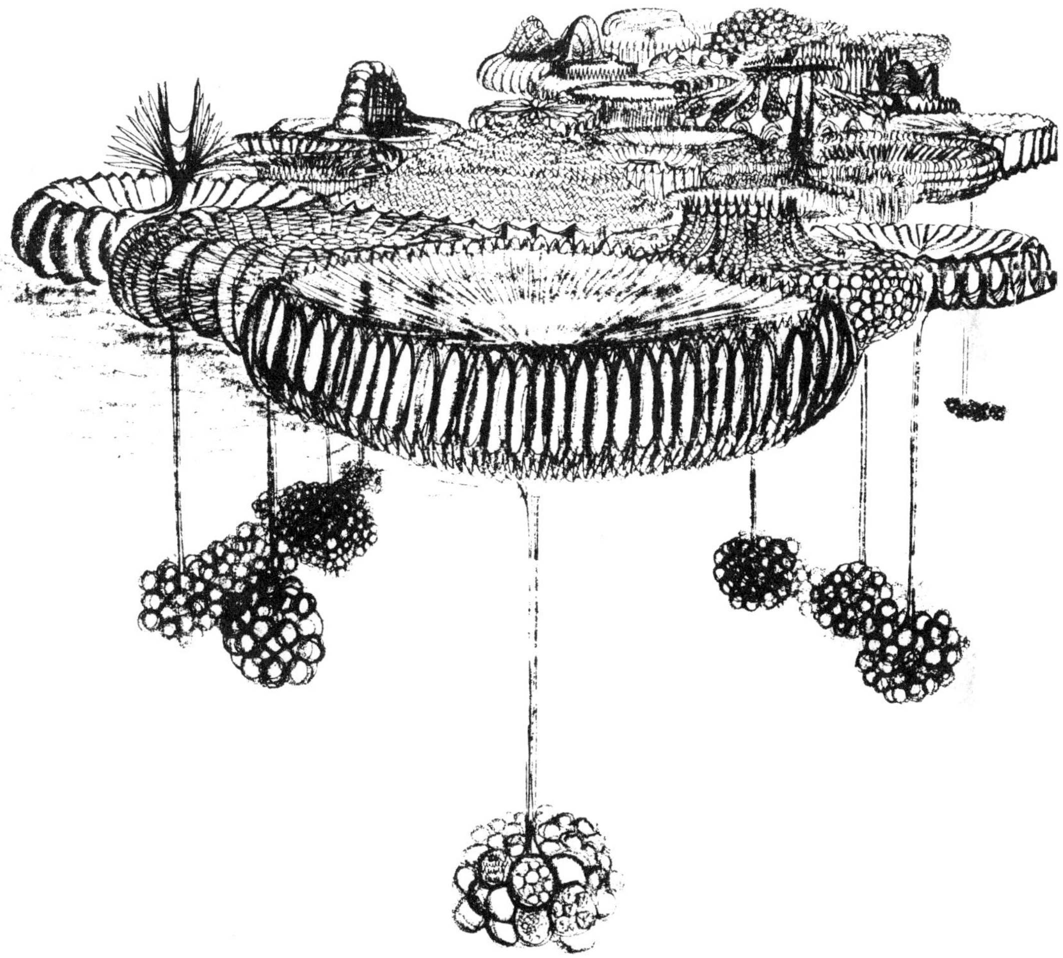

216. Chemical City. Perspective.

217.

Ed Kienholz (Fairfield, Washington 1927—)
Residence: Hope, Idaho.
Among Most Recent One-Artist Exhibitions: 1971, Institute of Contemporary Arts, London; 1972, Documenta 5, Kassel; 1973, Onnasch Gallery, Cologne; 1973, Städtische Kunsthalle, Berlin; 1974, Gallery Bocchi, Milan.

The World—1964
Status: Theoretical.

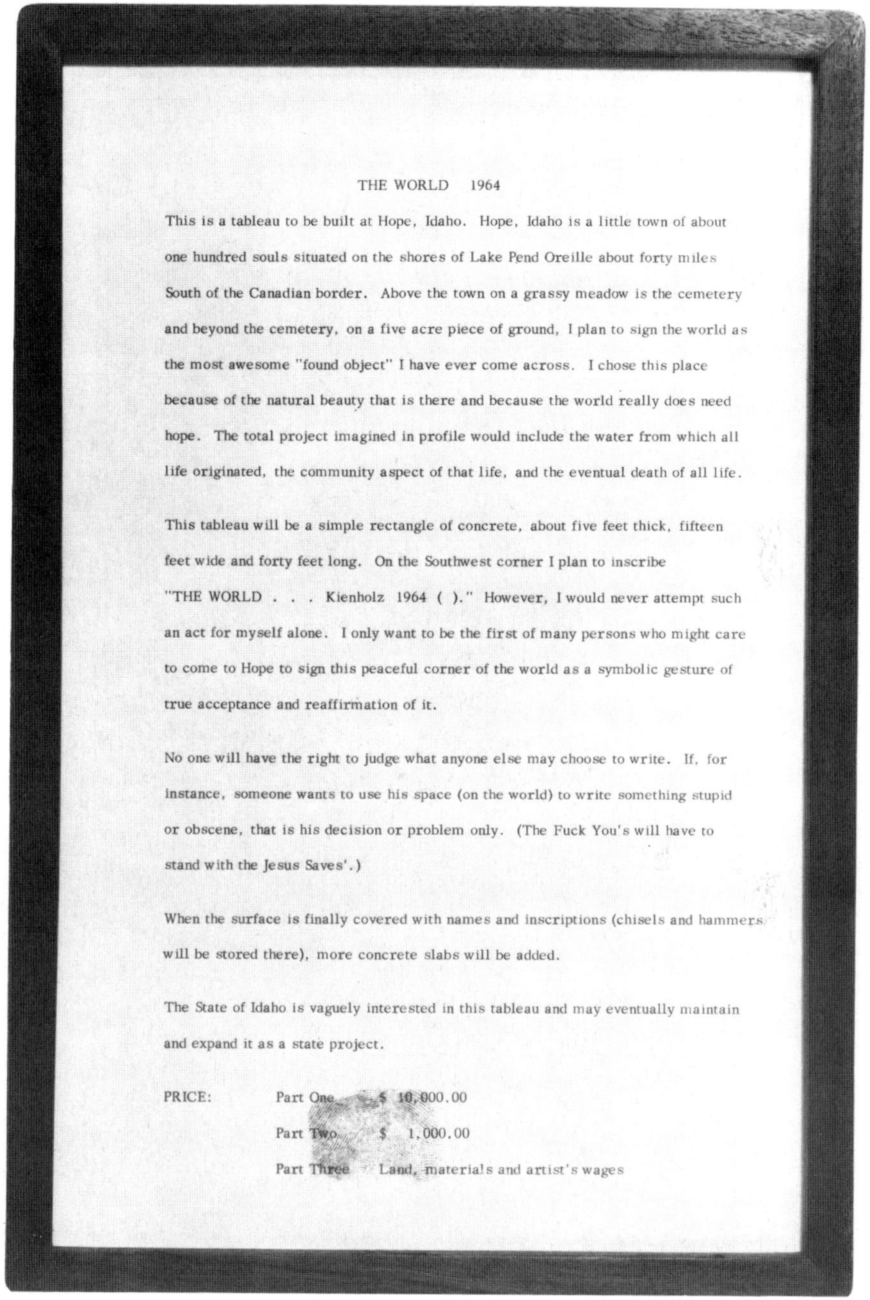

THE WORLD 1964

This is a tableau to be built at Hope, Idaho. Hope, Idaho is a little town of about one hundred souls situated on the shores of Lake Pend Oreille about forty miles South of the Canadian border. Above the town on a grassy meadow is the cemetery and beyond the cemetery, on a five acre piece of ground, I plan to sign the world as the most awesome "found object" I have ever come across. I chose this place because of the natural beauty that is there and because the world really does need hope. The total project imagined in profile would include the water from which all life originated, the community aspect of that life, and the eventual death of all life.

This tableau will be a simple rectangle of concrete, about five feet thick, fifteen feet wide and forty feet long. On the Southwest corner I plan to inscribe "THE WORLD . . . Kienholz 1964 ( )." However, I would never attempt such an act for myself alone. I only want to be the first of many persons who might care to come to Hope to sign this peaceful corner of the world as a symbolic gesture of true acceptance and reaffirmation of it.

No one will have the right to judge what anyone else may choose to write. If, for instance, someone wants to use his space (on the world) to write something stupid or obscene, that is his decision or problem only. (The Fuck You's will have to stand with the Jesus Saves'.)

When the surface is finally covered with names and inscriptions (chisels and hammers will be stored there), more concrete slabs will be added.

The State of Idaho is vaguely interested in this tableau and may eventually maintain and expand it as a state project.

PRICE: Part One $ 10,000.00
Part Two $ 1,000.00
Part Three Land, materials and artist's wages

218.

Frederick J. Kiesler (Vienna 1890—New York City 1965)
Education: Diploma, Akademie der Bildenden Kunste, Vienna; Technische Hochschule, Vienna; Academy of Fine Arts, Vienna.
Among Major Works: 1923, first Space Theatre in the Round, Vienna Theatre Festival; 1925, City in Space (a "constellation without boundaries"—floating dwellings, the habitat for man in the future), International Exposition of Decorative Arts, Paris; 1934–1937, stage sets for Juilliard School, Metropolitan Opera, and Martha Graham, N.Y.C.; 1959, Shrine of the Book, a sanctuary for the Dead Sea Scrolls, Hebrew University, Jerusalem (in association with Armand Bartos).
Among Major Publications: 1930, *Contemporary Art Applied to the Store and Its Display;* 1966, *Inside the Endless House.*

In the 1920s, Kiesler met Otto Wagner, Josef Hoffman, and Adolf Loos, whom he considered the major influences in architecture, and on himself. He began experiments in form with Mondrian, but instead of hard-edged rectangles Kiesler sought "the curve that warms." He was a member of the de Stijl, and in 1957, formed the firm of Kiesler and Bartos with Armand Bartos. In his 76 years, Kiesler had tried to integrate the arts with each other and in their environment.

Kiesler was, Philip Johnson once said, "the greatest nonbuilding architect of our time."
Lotus, III, 1966-1967.

Chestnut

[This is an undated manuscript, recently discovered by Mrs. Frederick Kiesler.]

From my earliest childhood on, one picture pursued me constantly. And I can still see it today very clearly before my eyes. This vision was an obsession with me, and why it happened to me, I cannot even explain today. Perhaps that it had something to do with the big chestnut trees that stood in our backyard and under whose shadows I played all summer long. I was very much attached to them, and often I would pick up the big fallen leaves, sit down quietly and take their structural affiliations apart and be delighted by the mystery of their intricacies.

But the main event came one day when the gardener drove a nail into the big trunk of the chestnut tree, because it was very convenient for him to hang his straw hat there. When he went away, I lifted the straw hat off and looked at the spot where the nail was driven in the trunk. I saw that the body of the tree was hurt, that light fluid had gathered around the hole, but that that clash of forces was not considered as something abnormal or prohibited, but rather as a matter of routine. If, so I said to myself, such a thing happened to the body of a human being, there would be violent reactions taking place, both audible and visible; but no one paid any attention to the clash of dead wood and dead steel. It was commonplace.

Constantly after this event I wanted to design pictures where I had brought my beloved chestnut tree to life and had enlarged the very minute particles of the wood of its trunk to rebel against the intrusion of that steel bar. The steel bar, still as I remember, figures as an inanimate chunk of form, the very villain in that drama. The composition in my vision was no less complicated than something such as the "Last Judgement" by Michelangelo, where the molecules of wood would be represented by human bodies that were engaged in the battle against the intruder. Again and again that vision appeared in my dreams. It constantly crowded itself, during my days behavior into my consciousness. That was around 1900. And it pursued me through the following high school years, the years at the Institute of Technology, and the Akademie.

The relationship between animate and inanimate matter absorbed me, and the studies of the old masters at the museums in Vienna, and the hand drawings at the Albertina, did a great deal to deepen that interest. How could the master paint a tree or a jar as if it were alive? What did he do to it that the legendary dead matter became living? Was it art that made it alive? Was it superimposed upon the dead model, or was it extracted from its invisible hiding place in that natural form?

In 1917, I conceived a woodcut to which I gave the name "Raumseele." It was rather a large woodcut, something like fourteen by ten inches. In the middle of the picture was a man seated, with closed eyes, his hands and feet immovable, as though in a state of petrification. From him into the background of this picture extended a landscape and the extension continued into the sky, and the sky bent above his head, then backwards into the foreground, into the earth again, and forward toward his seat. It was evident from this picture and from the title given to it, that the man was conscious of his interrelationship with his environment, although not seeing it or actually touching it.

Frederick Kiesler.

Tooth House—(?)
Status: Studies.
These are a series of undated drawings, recently discovered by Mrs. Frederick Kiesler among her husband's papers, in which houses evolve from tooth forms.

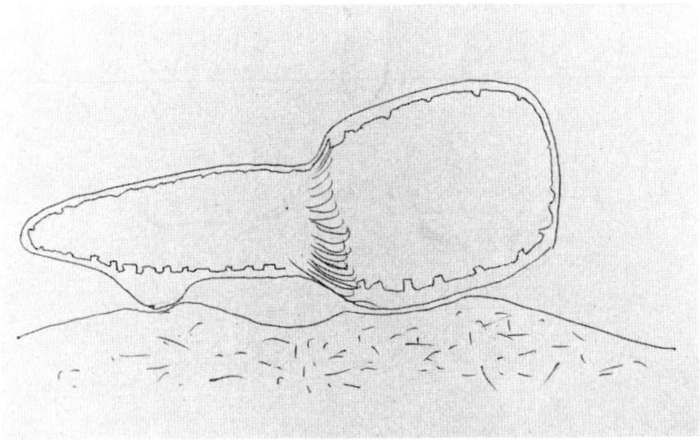

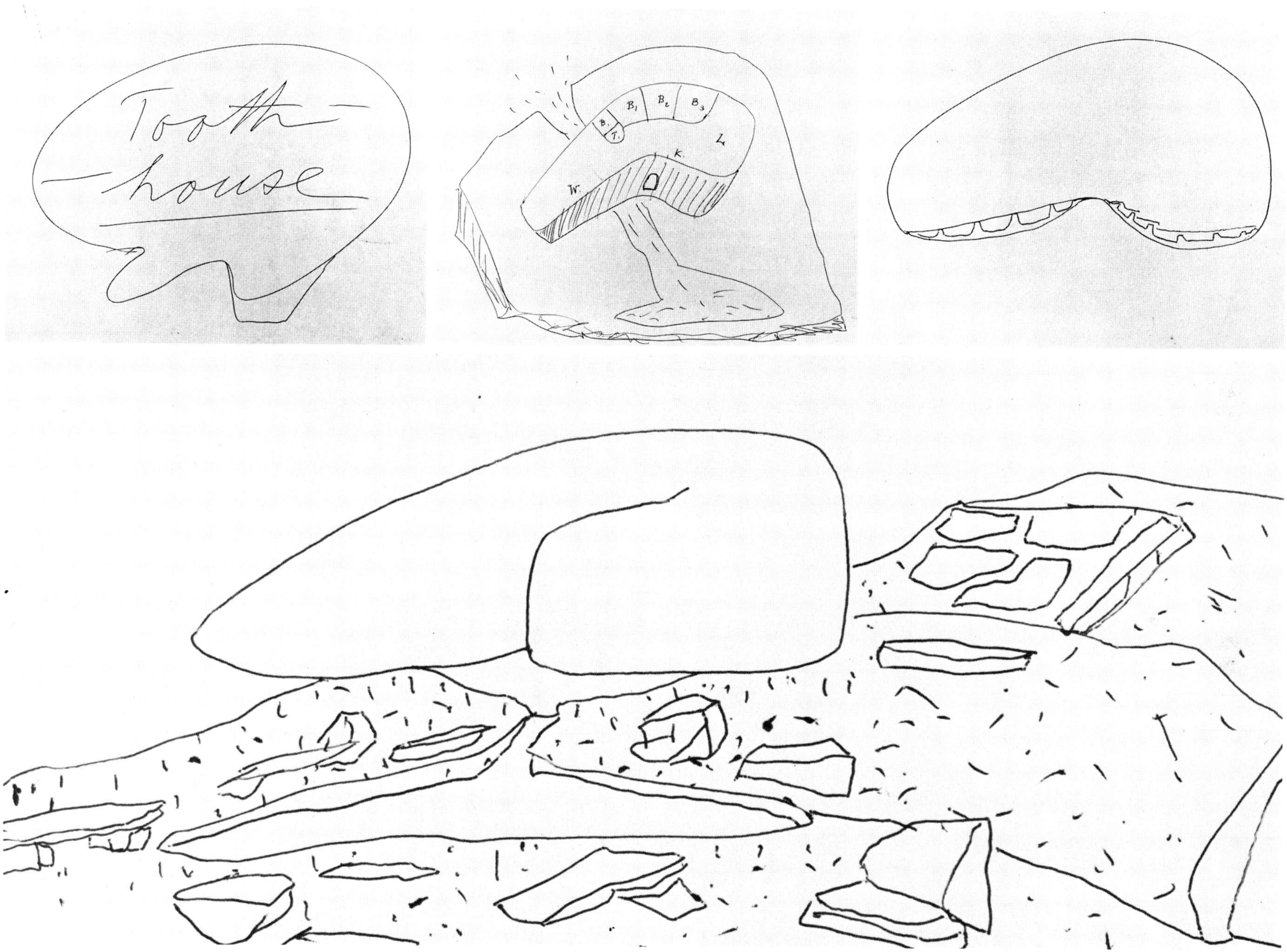

219–223. Tooth House. Series.

Endless House—1958–1960
Status: Prototype.
[The Endless House which] had no beginning and no end, like the human body.

The Endless House is not amorphous, not a free-for-all form. On the contrary, its construction has strict boundaries according to the scale of our living. Its shape and form are determined by inherent life forces, not by building code standards or the vagaries of decor fads.

Space in the Endless House is continuous. All living areas can be unified into a single continuum. But do not fear that one cannot find seclusion in the "Endless." Each and every one of the space-nuclei can be separated from the totality of the dwelling, can be secluded, and re-unified to meet various needs. The "Endless" can be not only a home for a family, but must definitely make room and comfort for the "visitors" from one's own inner world. Communion with oneself. The ritual of meditation.

Everybody is worried about windows, closets, computing kitchens, baths and bathtubs. The House is not a Machine for living. It is a living organism with a very sensitive nervous system. This we have not yet realized. The Endless House has.

Another general concern is the fear that the continuous construction might enclose the inhabitants in a deadly shell; but as the various plans show, each area has vast openings in different shapes and forms, according to the orbit of the sun and prevailing winds; these are filled not with glass, but with molded reliefs in colored plastics of various thicknesses, so that the heat of the sun is refracted. In each of these larger or smaller openings to the daylight (which during the evening, by the way, receive the same light from outside artificially) are certain sections which are clear and translucent, affording a free view and visual connection to the outside environment.

Excerpted from Frederick Kiesler, *Art in America,* LIV, May–June 1966.

224. The Endless House. Model.

225. The Grotto for Meditation. New Harmony, Indiana.

The Grotto for Meditation—1963
Location: New Harmony, Indiana.
Status: Building was postponed with no plans to proceed.
New Harmony has risen from the harmony of self-exiled German settlers of 1850. Resurrected, reconstructed by Jane Owen in the year 1950.

In 1963 Frederick Kiesler was commissioned by Mrs. Jane Owen to design a "Grotto for the New Being" for the Mid-western community of New Harmony, Indiana. To be built on a one-acre park dedicated to the memory of theologian Paul Tillich, the project reached completion on the drawing board in early 1964 and was scheduled for construction that summer. At the last moment, however, the building of the Grotto was postponed, and there are no specific plans to proceed.

Plans for the Grotto call for it to be constructed of reinforced thin-shell concrete, in the "continuous tension" principle of structure which Kiesler developed. The Grotto is designed to cover an area of approximately 1,200 square feet, with a maximum height of twenty. The interior is to be of smoothly finished concrete and the walking surfaces of local flagstone in random patterns. Kiesler specified that the pool areas be lined with blue glass mosaic tile.

Craft Horizons, XXVI, July/August, 1966.

Although a building may be a complete, protective structure, there are many ways to give the impression that the outer and inner worlds meet there, and that the inhabitant is part of a cosmic world—not only part of a street or a plaza or a community. In this respect, the Grotto was a very welcome project for me.

The Grotto for Meditation is a continuous tension construction with not a single structural joint. There are two main shells. The seashell form of the Grotto is surrounded, and protected, by a large dolphin, the symbol of Christ. By this, I hoped to point out our connection not only with human beings, but with the animal world, with vegetation, and with water and fire—the whole cosmic array of infinity.

The water which surrounds the fish, the water which derives from the interior of the cave and flows out and runs around and comes back to its source, should, by its sound, give back the memory which we always had in solitude, help find ourselves; and in finding ourselves, connect with the universe. It's impossible to find oneself and not connect with the universe.

Frederick Kiesler, *Craft Horizons,* XXVI, July/August 1966.

Alison Knowles (New York City 1933—)
Residence: New York City.
Education: 1952–1954, Middlebury College, Vermont; 1954–1957, BA, Pratt Institute.
Among Major Works: 1963, "Bean Rolls", a canned book of information about beans; 1967, "The Big Book", a portable environment; 1969–1970, "The House of Dust", a computer poem and built environment, California Institute of the Arts, Valencia; 1974, "Sumtime", an audience activated environment, Everson Museum, Syracuse, N.Y.; 1975, "Gentle Surprises" (with Bill Fontana), an audience activated environment with sound and objects touring Denmark.

227. The Bean Garden. Bean Soup.

The Bean Garden—1975

Status: Prototype.

Saihoji is a garden made of mosses. Ryoanji, another garden in Kyoto, has fifteen stones surrounded by white pebbles. In this garden there is also a large temple bell outdoors overlooking the garden. These gardens were created in 6th century Japan and essentially have not changed since. I had not studied them before my visit and I was very impressed being in their presence. I would like to build a bean garden—and environment in the spirit of Ryoanji—Instead of pebbles—white navy beans, for moss—split peas. For the bell sound, the amplification of bare feet walking on the beans in the garden. The bean garden would exist on a wooden floor, which would be covered with the white beans so they could roll fully and resonate. It feels good to walk on beans. The fifteen stones would be real rocks, with some select found objects placed here and there. An attendant would constantly rake the beans in circles back around the rocks. As I say, one walks in the garden and chimes sound— the result of transposing the foot resonances through a microphone and into bell jars. The source of the sound is the contact between foot and bean. The whole situation is as if in moonlight.

If you are in a room with a wooden floor and the normal activities that happen on floors occur while one of your ears is tightly against the wood, you will hear those activities travel through the wood as sound. If you rest a sensitive microphone on this floor and place a bell jar or other glass form over the microphone which is plugged into a simple amplifier/loudspeaker system you will hear the sounds that travel through the wooden floor become translated into the resonance spectrum of the bell jar. The ringing floor would have two bell jar listening centers at spatial extremities from each other compatible with a normal stereo system.

The disassembling of the garden would involve its transfiguration into food. Several days of bean banquets would include such delicacies as: white beans lamb shank, bean soup with sage, curried beans, bean cake and white beans milanese with sausage.

Alison Knowles.

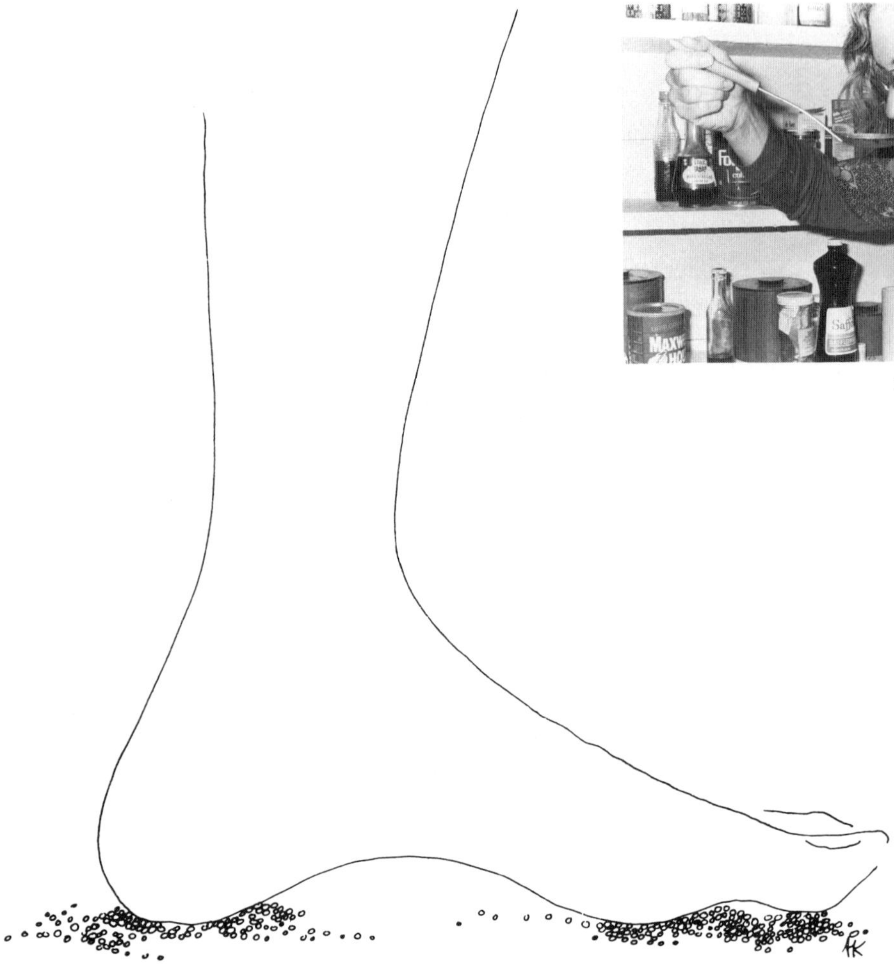

226. The Bean Garden.

Paul Laffoley (Massachusetts 1940—)
Residence: Boston.
Education: 1962, BA, Brown University; 1963, Harvard School of Design; 1963, Art Students League; 1965, Massachusetts Institute of Technology.
Among Major Exhibitions: 1970, The Institute of Contemporary Art, Boston; 1971–1972, The Boston Common; 1972, 1973, 1974, The Boston Center for the Arts; 1973, The Hayden Gallery, Cambridge.

Paul Laffoley is president of the Boston Visionary Cell, an association of Neo-Platonic artists, and others from disciplines which act as supporters and consultants, for the purpose of fostering visionary art, considered as an eternal genre—otherwise known as cosmic, cosmological, magical, mystical, or occult art—in the Boston and New England Area.

The Atlantis Project—1973
Location: Floating in the ocean.
Status: Theoretical proposal.

The problem I am concerned with in *The Atlantis Project* and *The New England Center for Comparative Utopias* is the architectural expression of an idea that has appeared to be without cultural or historical resolution. What I mean by this can be sensed by comparing the problem of utopia with the problem of housing regardless of the reassessment of the nature of housing over time, there are very few who would not consider housing a desirable goal of architectural effort. This is not the case with the concept of utopia.

Regardless of what attitude may be held concerning the existence of utopia, it can be described, I believe, as the resolution of the individual and collective aspects of human consciousness. This is beyond any technological, artistic, religious, or political manifestation of a particular utopia. In this sense utopia can be regarded as the spirit of many secular philosophies of histories of both the eastern and western traditions.

To implement the idea of study centers for the concept of utopia, I felt that there must be a network of centers acting in communication unison, but separated physically to accommodate local use. The location of the utopia centers are to be on neutral ground. Geomantic methods will be used to find land that is completely free of "power" points and "energy" lines.

For the physical form of this primary center I have adapted Plato's description of Atlantis, which is presented in the *Timaeus* and the *Critias*. From the dimensions given by Plato, the original Atlantis must have been about 387 miles long by 260 miles wide. I have reduced the dimensions of the island to approximately 1 mile wide by a little less than 2 miles long. These are the smallest dimensions possible by which you can zone the island as originally planned and still have portioned and usable spaces. Also I have turned it from an island attached to the ocean floor to a floating island or ferro-concrete ship.

228. The Island of Atlantis According to Plato. Model.

Upon a base of modular floating units, with a water draft of about 180 feet, is constructed another 180 foot thick platform covered with arable land. Above that are the various building and land forms which make up Atlantis. The volcanic mountains that rise to a height of 1,300 feet are hollow and contain sea water distilleries yielding water for the mountain streams. Giant heat pumps, also in the mountains, produce jets of warm air over the island, forming an air "roof." Around the entire periphery of the island-ship are huge air compressors, providing the motive power by creating underwater air jet streams. Since the ship is quite large, it might be possible to utilize the floating deposits of oil which now exist on the surfaces of all the oceans as fuel for its engines, thereby cutting down on the amount of in board fuel.

Paul Laffoley.

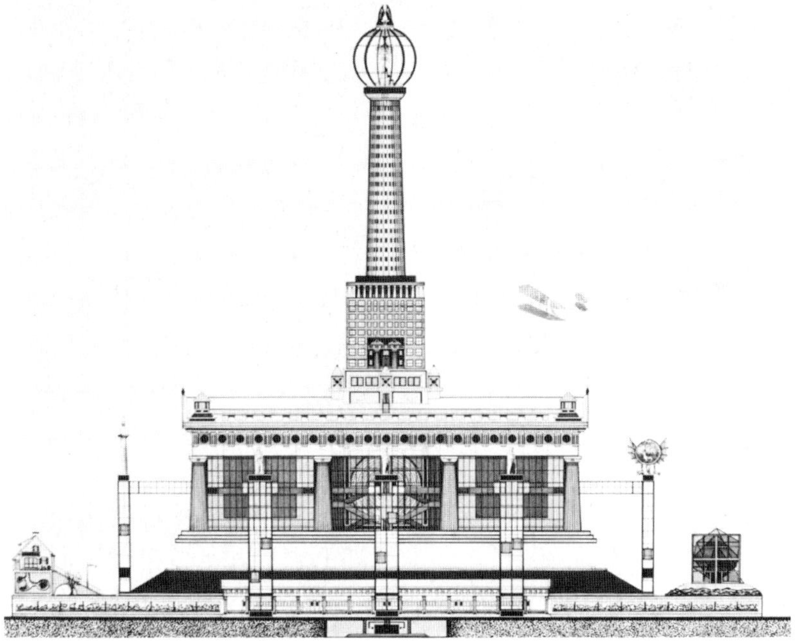

229. The New England Center for Comparative Utopias. Levitated Center.

230. The Apollo Sky-Walk.

The New England Center for Comparative Utopias—1973

Location: Revere Beach, Massachusetts.
Status: Theoretical proposal.

On a site discovered to be free of telluric energy systems, I proposed in 1973 that there be a *New England Center for Comparative Utopias*. This site was directly behind and also included the area on which existed the famous roller-coaster [*The Cyclone*] at Revere Beach in Massachusetts. The roller-coaster has now, unfortunately been destroyed.

In plan, *The New England Center for Comparative Utopias* appears to exist as two areas: (1) the restored roller-coaster area on Revere Beach Parkway, and (2) the main building on Ocean Avenue. But looking at the elevation, the center is revealed as three parts. The main building is actually levitated, by electro-mechanical means 16 feet off a prepared platform which is two stories high. When fully levitated the tip of the tower column on the main building reaches a height of 480 feet 6 inches.

The idea of floating or airborne architecture has always been associated in the popular imagination with the personal and collective freedom utopia may bring. The levitation is accomplished by electro-mechanical means, which consists of four interconnected systems. To provide actual lift-off, two small rocket motors are employed, which are backed up by a set of radio-frequency generators. The heat and flame will be controlled by the pool in the base. Once the building is in the air, sets of repelling electro-magnets control minor movements and provide the continuous life. In order to stabilize the building in space, a set of concentric nested gyroscopes are provided.

Centered in the pool is a model of the Atlantis-ship with an indication of where it is at any given time on the Earth. Directly in front of the levitated building is what I call *The Apollo Sky-Walk*. It is an accurate reconstruction of *The Cyclone* roller-coaster, only now, instead of it being used for coaster cars, it is made into a walk-way. By being a walk-way, the kinesthetic variations of the roller-coaster could be enjoyed by a greater age range of people than would normally go on a roller-coaster. The basic function of the sky-walk area is to provide the utopia center with a link to the immediate surroundings, which would be a replica of the beach area at the end of the nineteenth century.

Paul Laffoley.

Charles R. Lamb (New York City 1860—New Jersey 1942)
Education: City College of New York; while at college studied life drawing at the Art Students League in the evenings, under William Sartain. Apprenticed under father in family-run stained-glass ecclesiastical firm (the first in the country).
Among Major Works: Dewey Arch, N.Y.C.; Sage Memorial Chapel, Cornell University, Ithaca, N.Y.; Lakewood Memorial Chapel, Minneapolis; Park Chapel, Honolulu; various structures and decorations, in the Cathedral of St. John the Divine, N.Y.C.

City Plan—1904
Status: Hypothetical proposal.
It is a geometric axiom that the length of two sides of a right angle triangle is greater than the third, and that, therefore, any system of transit through streets of right-angled plan, north or south, east or west, must necessarily increase the distance to be traveled, as against the diagonal streets leading from one quarter of the city to another. Broadway, the one great diagonal through New York, proves how essential such diagonals are, and it is but recently that a serious attempt has been made to suggest modifications and improvements in the present plan of New York, so as to rectify many of the difficulties and adjust the changes to the inevitably increasing congestion of the growing metropolis.

It might be suggested as a wise measure to discuss the ideal city and assume for the moment, as Dowie did in Zion City, the designing of a city entirely from the commencement and arranging in the plan the possible developments of the future. This has frequently been done in an academical way, but never, to the writer's knowledge, with a full reference to the problems embodied in such a scheme. Indefinite statements about an "Ideal City," the "City Beautiful," or a "City of the Future," mean little, unless they embody the practical ideas which inevitably dictate the development of the schemes.

To the writer's mind, all forms of rectilinear designs must be discarded. The cutting of these with diagonals is, after all, but a make-shift. If not an oblong or a square, what form would be the basic one upon which to found the city? After the fullest consideration of all the possibilities that geometric figures give, the writer is tempted to suggest the scheme shown in the accompanying diagram, the hexagon. This permits the development of the city to the utmost that might be possible within many decades, because with the hexagon, the great advantage of the diagonal already discussed is secured; at the same time intervening spaces which can be secured for playgrounds and park areas, between the large central areas which, in turn, can be used for groups of civic buildings in certain parts of the city, and, in other parts of the city, seats of learning, recreation, business in all its forms (banking, publishing, the newspaper industries), and the thousand and one trades which, in their turn, seem to be desirous of grouping themselves around a common center.

Abridged from **Charles Lamb** in *The Craftsman,* VI, April 1904.

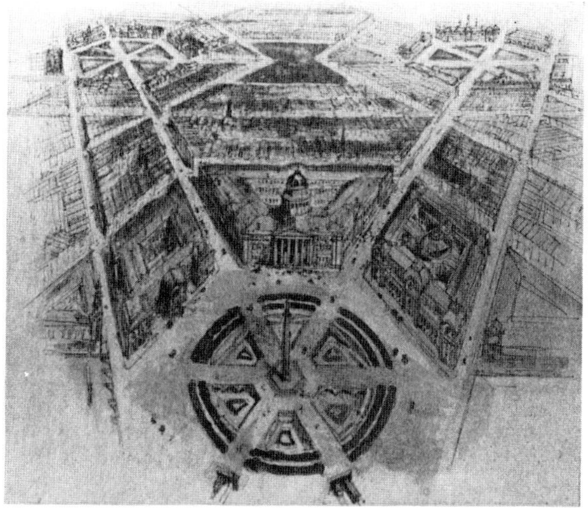
231. City Plan. Aerial Perspective of Model City.

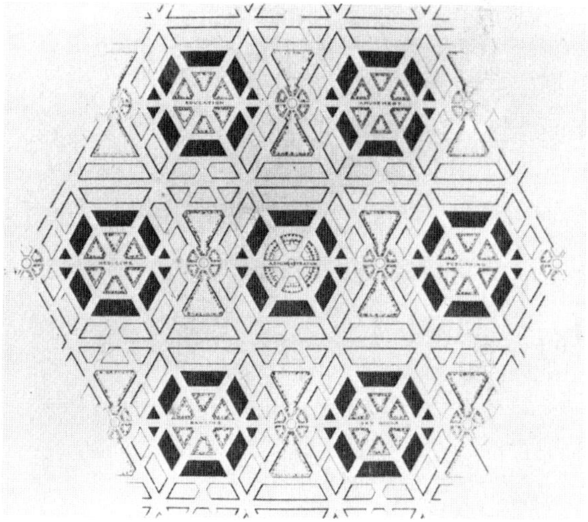
232. The Hexagon as a City. Plan.

James Lambeth (Missouri 1942—)
Residence: Fayetteville, Arkansas.
Education: 1964, BS Arch., Washington University; 1966, B Arch., Rice University; 1968, M Arch., Rice University.
Among Major Projects: 1969, Lambeth Residence, Fayetteville, Ark.; 1970, Yocum Lodge, Aspen, Colo. (utilizes the country's first reflective solar lens for snow melting); 1974, Ozark Mountain Solar Cabin, Newton County, Ark.; 1975, solar lens heated swimming pool, Strawberry Fields Apartments, Springfield, Missouri.

Solar Village—1975
Location: Lake of the Ozarks, Missouri.
Status: Prototype.
The recreational community design was the result of studies in solar efficient forms. A unit module was developed that supplied 75% of its internal climate control without any mechanical devices (passive solar system). A combination of large amounts of insulated glass and limited interior volume produced the form. Additional protection from summer sun is provided by large overhangs. The solar module was then studied in terms of different geometric groupings, always following strict rules concerning southern glass exposure.

The best grouping cascading down the southern slope to the lake provides each unit with a view of the mountain from private decks and a clear view over the module in front. In this way low winter sun penetration through the large glass wall of each structure is unobstructed. Parking, access, and service are from below. The plug-in, leave-out modular grid permits trees and light to permeate the village texture.

James Lambeth.

233. Solar Village. Superimposed on Site.

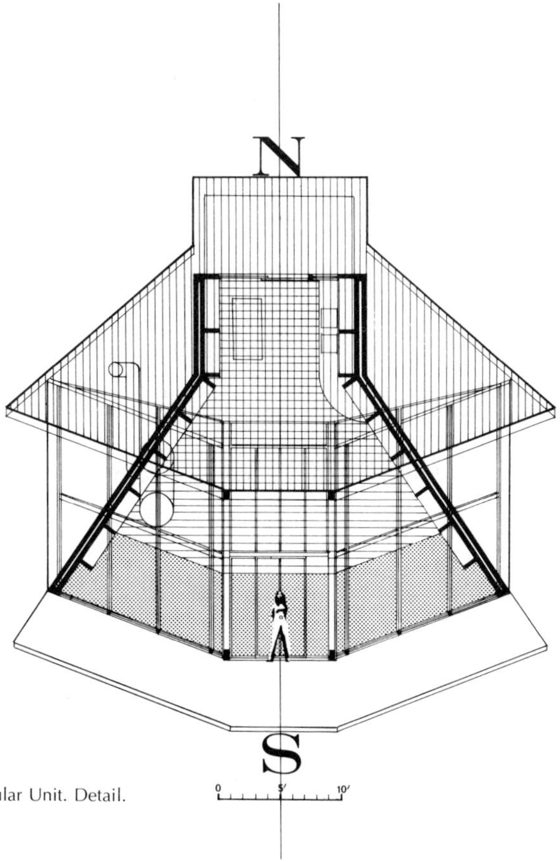

234. Solar Village. Modular Unit. Detail.

Morris Lapidus Associates (Miami/New York City)

Morris Lapidus (Russia 1902—)
Residence: Miami, Florida.
Education: 1927, Graduate, School of Architecture, Columbia University.

Alan Lapidus (New York City 1936—)
Residence: New York City.
Education: Trinity College; 1963, Graduate, School of Architecture, Columbia University.

Among Major Works of Firm: The Fontainebleau Hotel, Miami, Fla.; the Eden Roc Hotel, Miami; the Americana Hotels, Miami and N.Y.C.; "The Peoples Park," Bedford-Stuyvesant, N.Y.; Concert Hall and Music School, University of Miami.

Olympic Tower—1970
Location: New York City.
Status: Unbuilt due to change in site considerations.
Concept: Alan Lapidus.
The project was started as a joint venture between Arlen Properties, Meshulum Riklis of Rapid American Corporation, and Aristotle Onassis representing Victory Carriers. The object was to build an "Air Rights" building between 51st and 52nd Streets, fronting on Fifth Avenue. The term "Air Rights" is, in itself, a misnomer. What is involved is taking advantage of a provision in the law that states that if an existing building does not use up its allotted Floor Area Ratio (F.A.R.), this unused buildable space can be given to another building contiguous to it, provided that all such buildings are put in the same tax lot and, therefore, can never be subdivided in the future.

The basic logic behind the structure was, that rather than tearing down old structures (one of which, Cartier's, could not be torn since it is designated a landmark and the other, Best, which was a mercantile establishment still showing a profit) you could utilize their unbuilt space without destroying what was already there. The theory was that the additional costs of very expensive engineering and construction would be offset by comparatively small land costs for the project itself.

Our scheme was in preliminary working drawings and had already been engineered and costed out when the decision was made to tear Best and Company down and close the chain. It was made primarily because Best was simply not showing the profit that had been anticipated when the scheme was first conceived. It was decided that it would be more economical in light of Best's deficit operation to simply raze the building and go ahead with a conventional office tower.

Alan Lapidus.

235. Olympic Tower. Model.

Edward Larkin (ca. 1887—New Jersey 1959)
Among Major Works: Printing Crafts Building, N.Y.C.; a number of New York City apartment houses.

Larkin Building—1926
Location: New York City.
Status: Abandoned due to financial crisis of the time.

In December 1926 this building was announced as going to be the highest structure erected by man. The construction of it has been indefinitely postponed. Its principal features, in case it is built, would be the following: 1,208 feet high (curb to roof); area of plot: 47,077 square feet; cubic contents: 18,600,000 cubic feet; concrete foundations: 30,000 cubic yards; structural steel: 56,000 tons; concrete floors: 35,000 cubic yards; 1,300,000 terra cotta blocks; 3,400,000 front brick; 2,800,000 common brick; 4,800 windows; 4,200 doors; rentable area: 1,020,000 square feet; gross area first floor: 47,077 square feet; gross area nineteenth floor: 11,770 square feet; gross area 108th floor: 1,000 square feet; 59 elevators—single deck cars—which are planned to be changed later into double deck cars; heating is produced in ten separate sections, each section being independently controlled from the basement.

Francisco Mujica, History of the Skyscraper, 1929.

236. Larkin Building. Aerial Perspective.

Paul Laszlo (Hungary 1900—)
Residence: Beverly Hills, California.
Education: Studied in Vienna and Stuttgart.
Among Major Works: Ohrbach's department stores in New York and California; Century Towers Apartments, Century City, Calif.; Desert Inn, Las Vegas; other clients have included Gloria Vanderbilt, Norma Shearer, Sonja Henie.

Atomville U.S.A.—1950
Location: Underground.
Status: Prototype.

The Atomic Age, with its high technology of electronics, engineering, communications and transportations, has placed a new burden on us to upgrade our cities and installations which have been, and still are being planned on last-century concepts. The construction of the future, which means the planning of the present, indicates that these homes and factories will, for many reasons (including that of national survival), have to be built underground. The good earth will afford us advantages which seem irresistible when it comes to protecting, modernizing, and making our way of living and working more efficient. Primarily, Atomville gives our people and our production facilities protection from atomic attack. Aside from survival, Atomville is one of our best hopes for unclogging the already choking American community.

Paul Laszlo.

238. Atomville, U.S.A. Detail.

237. Atomville, U.S.A. Cross Section.

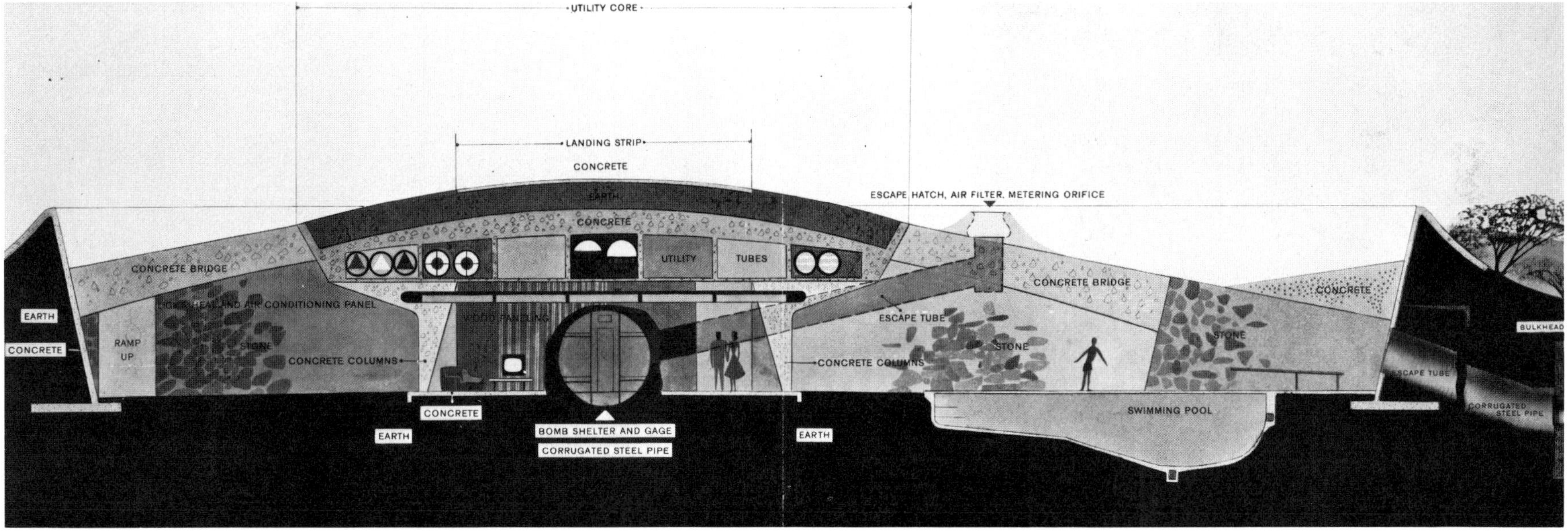

Benjamin Henry Latrobe, more than any other one man, was the creator in America of the architectural profession, as well as the instigator of a new kind of architecture [Greek Revival].

Talbot Hamlin, **Benjamin Henry Latrobe**, 1955.

Benjamin Henry Latrobe (England 1764—New Orleans 1820)
Education: University of Leipzig, Germany; studied briefly with John Smeaton, the British engineer.
Among Major Works: 1804–1821, the Baltimore Cathedral, the first Catholic cathedral in the United States; 1803, chosen by Thomas Jefferson to complete the Capitol Building in Washington, D.C.; 1807–1808, Bank of Philadelphia; 1820, State Bank of Louisiana; 1798–1801, devised a water system for Philadelphia, which was the earliest major waterworks in the country.

239. Design for a Theater Memorial in Richmond, Virginia. Watercolor.

Design for a Theater Memorial—1812
Location: Richmond, Virginia.
Status: Unbuilt.
It was suggested that a monument be built in remembrance of seventy-two persons that perished in a theater fire, in 1798.

Latrobe learned that it was planned to build both an Episcopal church and a commemorative monument on the old theater lot. But he disapproved of the idea; the money collected for the church could only build "a plain brick building such as we see everywhere." Instead, Latrobe proposed that only the monument should be erected; this should consist of a block 32 feet square, on which a pyramid 48 feet high should rise, and within there should be a chamber 20 or 24 feet square. On the inner walls should be carved the names of the victims and the appropriate inscriptions; in the center there would be a memorial statue, "a kneeling figure, representing the city . . . mourning over an urn."

Talbot Hamlin, **Benjamin Henry Latrobe**, 1955.

Designs of Buildings—1795 –1799
Status: Prototypes.
Location: Virginia.

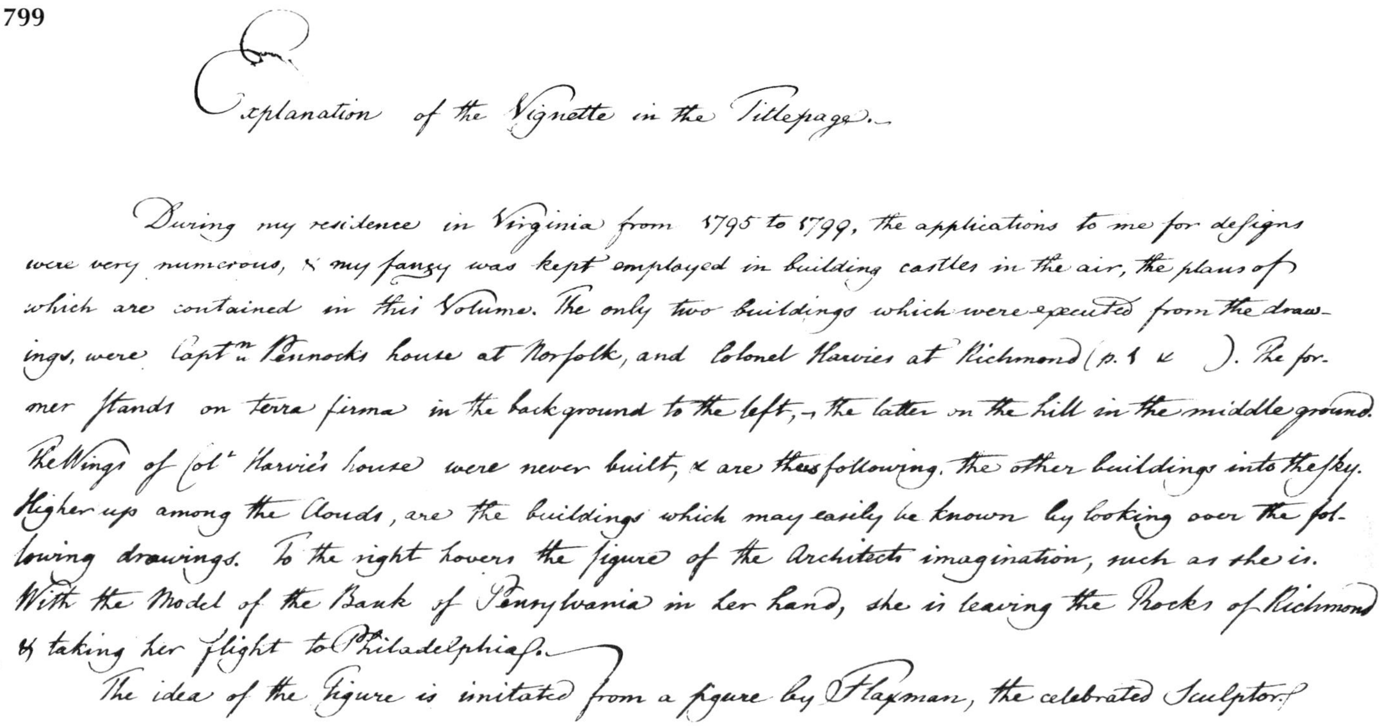

Explanation of the Vignette in the Titlepage.—

During my residence in Virginia from 1795 to 1799, the applications to me for designs were very numerous, & my fancy was kept employed in building castles in the air, the plans of which are contained in this Volume. The only two buildings which were executed from the drawings, were Captn Pennocks house at Norfolk, and Colonel Harvies at Richmond (p. 1 &). The former stands on terra firma in the background to the left, — the latter on the hill in the middle ground. The Wings of Colt Harvie's house were never built, & are thus following the other buildings into the sky. Higher up among the Clouds, are the buildings which may easily be known by looking over the following drawings. To the right hovers the figure of the Architects imagination, such as she is. With the Model of the Bank of Pennsylvania in her hand, she is leaving the Rocks of Richmond & taking her flight to Philadelphia.

The idea of the Figure is imitated from a figure by Flaxman, the celebrated Sculptor.

240. Designs of Buildings Erected or Proposed to Be Built in Virginia. Verso of Title Page.

241. Designs of Buildings Erected or Proposed to Be Built in Virginia. Title Page.

242. Designs of Buildings Erected or Proposed to Be Built in Virginia. Temple-type House. Elevation.

John Lautner (1911 Michigan—)
Residence: Los Angeles.
Education: 1933, AB, Northern Michigan University.
Among Major Works: Harpel House, Alaska; Stevens House, Malibu, Calif.; Elrod House, Palm Springs; Wolff House, Los Angeles.

John Lautner was a member of the Taliesin Fellowship in Wisconsin and Arizona, under Frank Lloyd Wright, from 1933 to 1939.

Alto Capistrano Apartments—1960
Location: San Juan Capistrano, California.
Status: Elevator companies would not build and maintain inclined elevators in this area.
The Alto Capistrano Apartments were designed as terraces on a mountainside, facing south and viewing the Pacific Ocean. Parking and recreational facilities would be at the top of the mountain, with inclined electric cars provided to transport people down to the apartment levels and shopping center below.

John Lautner.

Above and Below: 243, 244. Alto Capistrano Apartments. Pre-Cast Units to Suit Hill Site.

Robert Le Ricolais (France 1894—)
Residence: Philadelphia and Paris.
Education: Trained as a mathematician at the Sorbonne, Paris.

A mathematician, poet, painter, and artist, Robert Le Ricolais became interested in structure by the "beauty he found in corrugated metal." A senior fellow at the Graduate School of Fine Arts of the University of Pennsylvania for the past 17 years, he has dedicated himself to the search of pure and simple structures as found in nature.

Le Ricolais in his work is inspired by the growth of structures in nature. His work is unique in that he finds his motivations from the realizations of the nature of structure and not primarily from the desire to solve engineering problems. His structures therefore are full of wonder standing in their right as though they are nature itself, belonging thereby to everyone for personal stimulation.

Louis I. Kahn.

Alexander Messinger (Russia 1942—)
Residence: Philadelphia.
Education: 1968, B Arch. and Town Planning, Technion Israel Institute of Technology; 1970, M Arch. and Master of City Planning, Graduate School of Fine Arts of the University of Pennsylvania.

Alexander Messinger is currently teaching at the University of Pennsylvania, with an interest in housing and cities from the growth and change point of view. He feels that the house is an extension of the human body and is searching for new configurations, that do not deal with the engineering aspects alone.

The following studies deal with research conducted by Robert Le Ricolais, with the cooperation of Alexander Messinger over the past decade.

The focus is primarily on the organization of a city towards more flexible movement systems, the division of spaces within those systems, and the development of structures that utilize the nature of their materials in the most economical manner.

Although these projects are theoretical studies, they remain unbuilt due to the technical innovations involved and the emphasis of Robert Le Ricolais on the development of the idea rather than its implementation.

Alexander Messinger.

Suspended Structures—1960–1962
Status: Theoretical studies.
The floor system provides for a maximum area, with a minimum of support. It utilizes a minimum of material, by the exploration of its inherent properties, and its ability to be coordinated with other materials.

Robert Le Ricolais.

245. Suspended High Rise Office Building. Model.

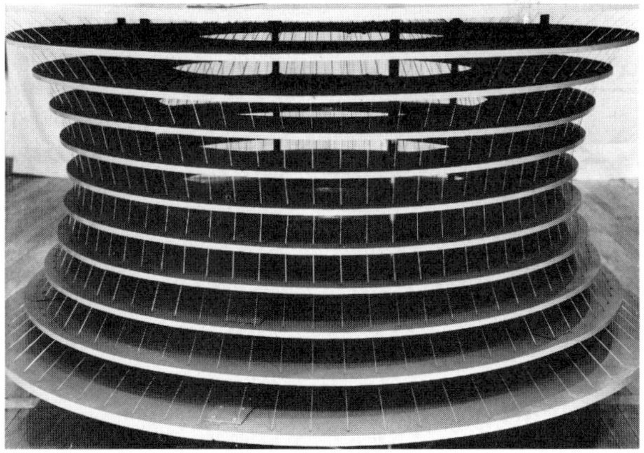
246. Suspended Parking Garage. Model.

The Trihex Network—1962–1972
Status: Theoretical study.
The Trihex system is concerned with the continuous flow of traffic and freedom of the pedestrian. It provides for better arrangement of potential routes, with a minimum number of intersections, by superimposing a hexagonal and a triangular grid pattern.

Robert Le Ricolais.

The Skyrail System—1962–1968
Status: Theoretical study.
The Skyrail system could consist of a Trihex network of aerial bridges spanning about 1,600 feet between interchange stations. These stations would be incorporated into buildings 30 to 40 stories high, and each one would connect two lines with banks of elevators and escalators leading to 300-foot platforms, where trains would arrive every 90 seconds.

With a system of elevated transit, we could perhaps open up a new, or lost, dimension—the aerial view of the city, the city being seen as a whole without losing the feeling or orientation. The form of a city is too important to be lost in subterranean traffic or even seen from the limited vistas of corridor streets.

Robert Le Ricolais.

248. Trihex Networks. Superimposition at Different Scales.

247. Skyrail Structural System. Model. Detail.

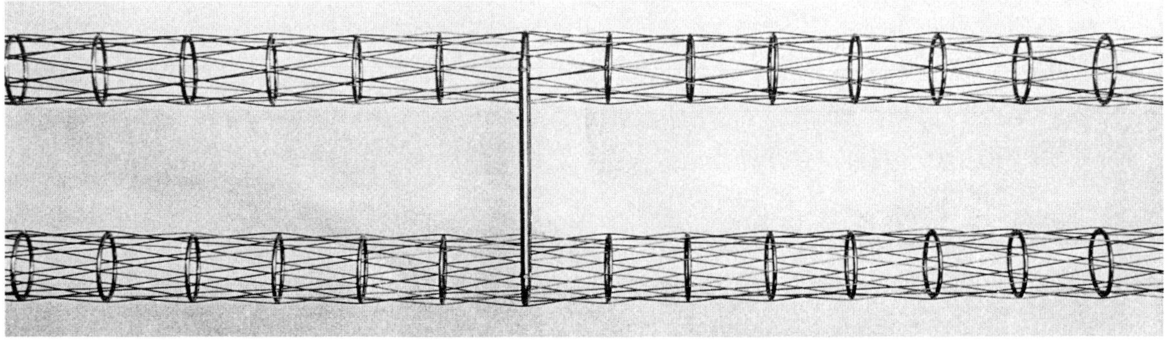

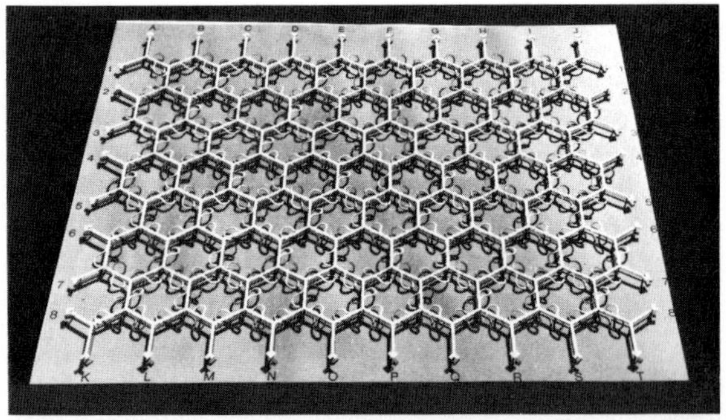

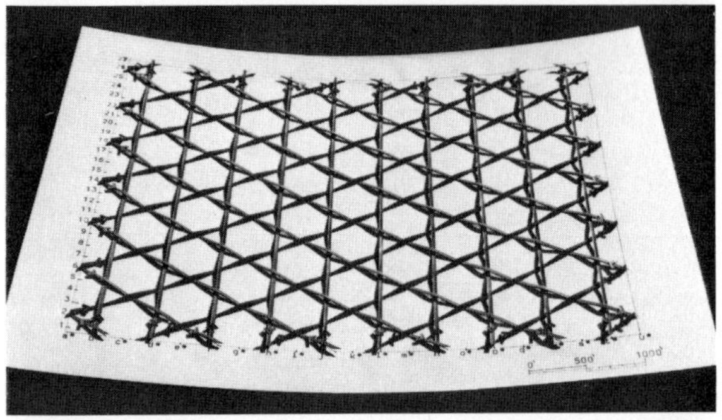

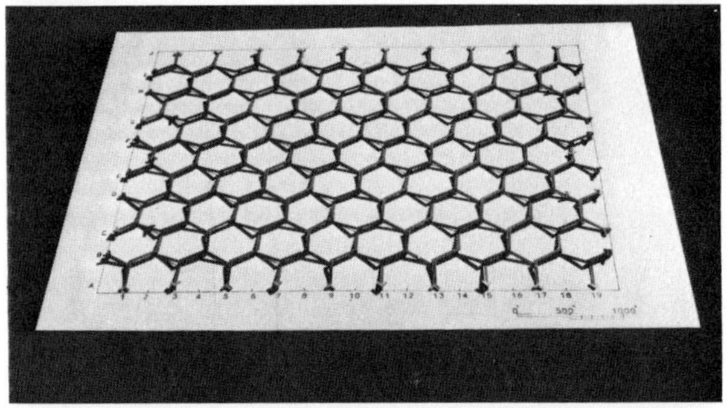

Above: 249–252. Continuous Flow Transportation Systems.

Mimi Lobell (Illinois 1942—)
Residence: New York City.
Education: 1963, BA, University of Pennsylvania; 1966, B Arch., University of Pennsylvania.
After several years of experience in conventional practice, Mimi Lobell is now researching, designing, teaching (Pratt Institute, Brooklyn, N.Y.), writing, and lecturing on integrative metaphysical architecture.

The Goddess-Temple—1975
Location: Colorado.
Status: Pending.
The Goddess-Temple defines and celebrates the feminine principle as a vital psychological and cultural force in the world today. Rather than housing an orthodox religious ceremony, the temple itself gives each woman or man who journeys through it an experience of being awakened to the feminine nature in her or his self.

In designing the temple, dialectic and meditative methods were combined to penetrate the mysteries of the feminine in a way that no amount of verbal analysis and conventional programming could have done. Thus the highly symbolic, archetypal nature of the design process in architecture was brought to life again.

The labyrinth became the place of the dark, physical, sensual, and primordial feminine (Tiamat, Gaia, Kali, Hecate, Persephone, gorgons, sirens, maenads, and serpent-goddesses). It is also the place of the unconscious with its creative prelogical wisdom that is tapped through meditation, dream analysis, and artistic expression. The labyrinth is a mandala of the continuity between the individual and the cosmos, between matter and spirit, and between the moment and eternity. It follows the serpentine path of telluric currents and feminine energy. At its heart is the grail-pool, the life source through which one must wade, be baptized, purified, and reborn to ascend the helical ladder to the upper temple.

Entering the upper temple through a glass hatch in the altar-eye of feminine consciousness, one arrives at a state of meditative rest surrounded and warmed by the fire of candles beyond which one sees a clear 360 degree vision of the real world beyond. The upper temple is the place of the light, wise, spiritual, benign, prophetic feminine (Prajnaparamita, Sophia, Athena, muses, sibyls, fates, and the Mothers of the Gods). It is the place of consciousness in perfect communication with the unconscious which energizes it from below; of transcendance of dualities and of ego, of oneness with the eternal feminine, the Tao, the unnameable before the World of God, and the natural order before the Laws of Men.

Mimi Lobell.

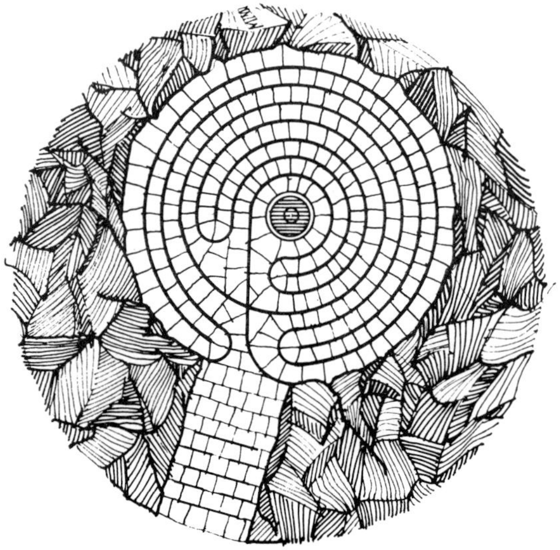
253. The Goddess-Temple. Plan of Labyrinth.

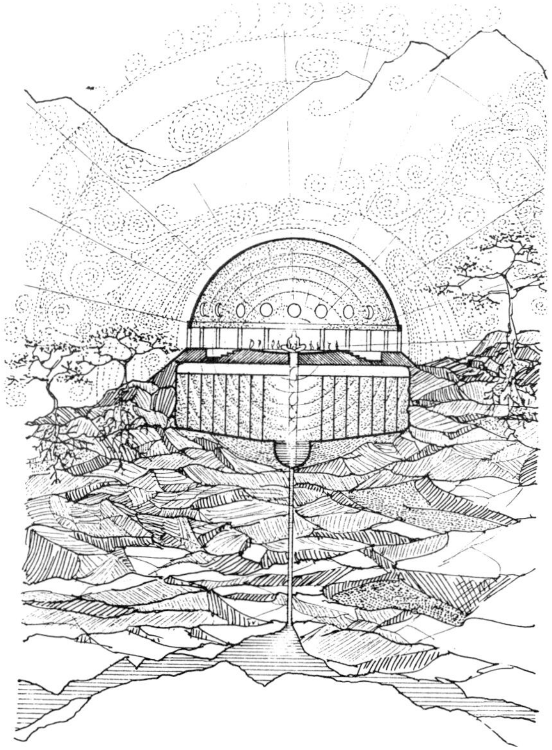
254. The Goddess-Temple. Section.

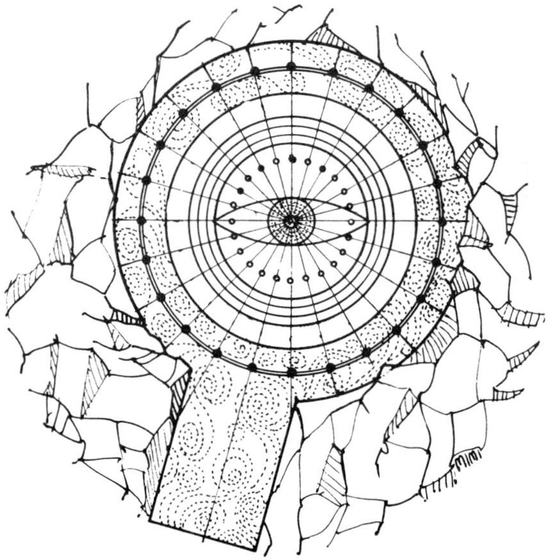
255. The Goddess-Temple. Plan of Upper Temple.

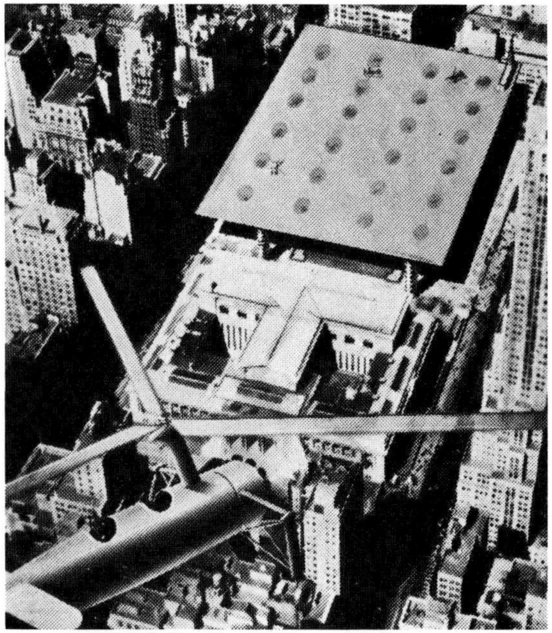

256. Mid-Town Airport. Aerial View.

257. Mid-Town Airport. Aerial View of Site.

Raymond Loewy (Paris, France 1893—)
Residence: New York City; California; Paris; London.
Education: 1910, Paris University, France; 1918, Graduate Engineering, École de Lanneau, France.
Among Major Designs: the Coca-Cola dispenser; the streamlined locomotive; the Greyhound scenicruiser; the postwar Studebaker; the interior of the Skylab; emblem of the U.S. Postal Service.

Founder, American Society of Industrial Design and Compagnie de l'Esthétique Industrielle, Paris; consultant to 200 worldwide corporations; since 1967, Habitability Consultant to NASA's Saturn-Apollo applications program, SKYLAB, and Shuttle Orbiter projects.

Midtown Airport—1941

Location: New York City.
Status: Unbuilt.

To meet New York's need for more rapid and convenient air transport, Designer Raymond Loewy proposes a helicopter landing field, built high up on steel pylons over the park behind the Public Library. The helicopters would act as air taxis between the city and the main field outside. The designer claims a dual value for his scheme: it could be used over an air raid shelter, the landing surface serving to break the impact of large bombs.

Architectural Forum, November 1941.

258. Mid-Town Airport. Perspective.

Marion Mahoney (Griffin) (Illinois 1871—1962)
Education: 1894, BS, Massachusetts Institute of Technology (first woman to receive a BS from MIT, where she had been a student of Desiré Despradelle).

Marion Mahoney was employed at drafting from 1895 to 1909 in the firm of Dwight Perkins under Frank Lloyd Wright, and continued doing presentations for her husband Walter Burley Griffin after their marriage in 1911.

The Town of Hill Crystals—1943
Location: Boerne, Texas.
Status: Unbuilt.

The general formation of the land hereabouts in Texas gives a unique problem to the occupancy designer. It forms a series of almost flat terraces, with quite sudden drops below. Hence the form of the layout is the reverse of rectangular, but adjusted to the succession of hilltops, and the series of terraces encircling them down to the river flats.

The present thoroughfare from San Antonio to Boerne establishes the location of the business center. The details are laid out only for the property unified under a single ownership. For the most part, park reserves follow the rivers. The school group and encircling grounds however are practically flat.

Marion Mahoney (Griffin), The Magic of America, New York Historical Society.

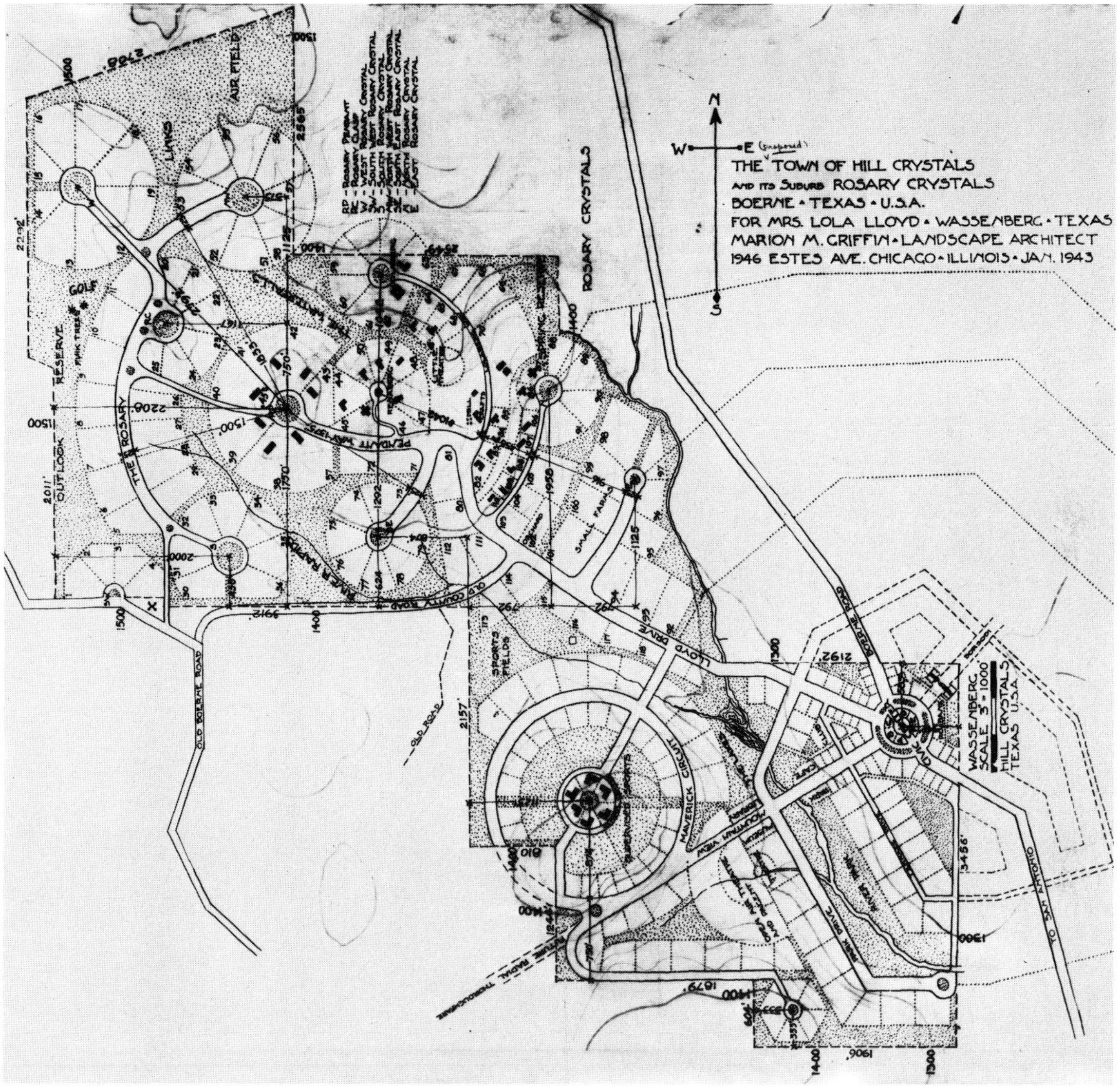

259. The Town of Hill Crystals and Its Suburb Rosary Crystals. Plan.

260. The Linear Metropolis. The main transportation axis.

Reginald Malcolmson (Ireland 1912—)
Residence: Ann Arbor, Michigan.
Education: 1947–1949, MS Arch., studied with Ludwig Mies van der Rohe, Illinois Institute of Technology.
Among Major Works: In the 1950s and 1960s many of his projects were published and exhibited in Chicago, New York, Los Angeles, Paris, London, Tokyo, Lima, Santiago, and Buenos Aires.

Mr. Malcolmson was a member of the faculty of the Illinois Institute of Technology in the architecture and city planning department from 1949 to 1964, and acting director for the year 1958 to 1959. He was administrative assistant to Mies van der Rohe from 1953 to 1958, and Dean of the College of Architecture and Design at the University of Michigan from 1964 to 1974.

Reginald Malcolmson is a visionary architect and proponent of the linear city.

The Linear Metropolis—1956

Status: Prototype.

Two parallel transportation routes run east and west and are over six miles apart. One is the backbone of the administration, commercial, civic and cultural centers, and light industries, with parallel residential units on either side. The other serves heavy industry and agriculture.

Basically there are two types of housing: vertical apartment buildings and horizontal multiunit structures. Each has its own parking facilities, schools, shops and stores, clubs, halls, and clinics. Service roads connect the residential

261. Panorama of the Linear City.

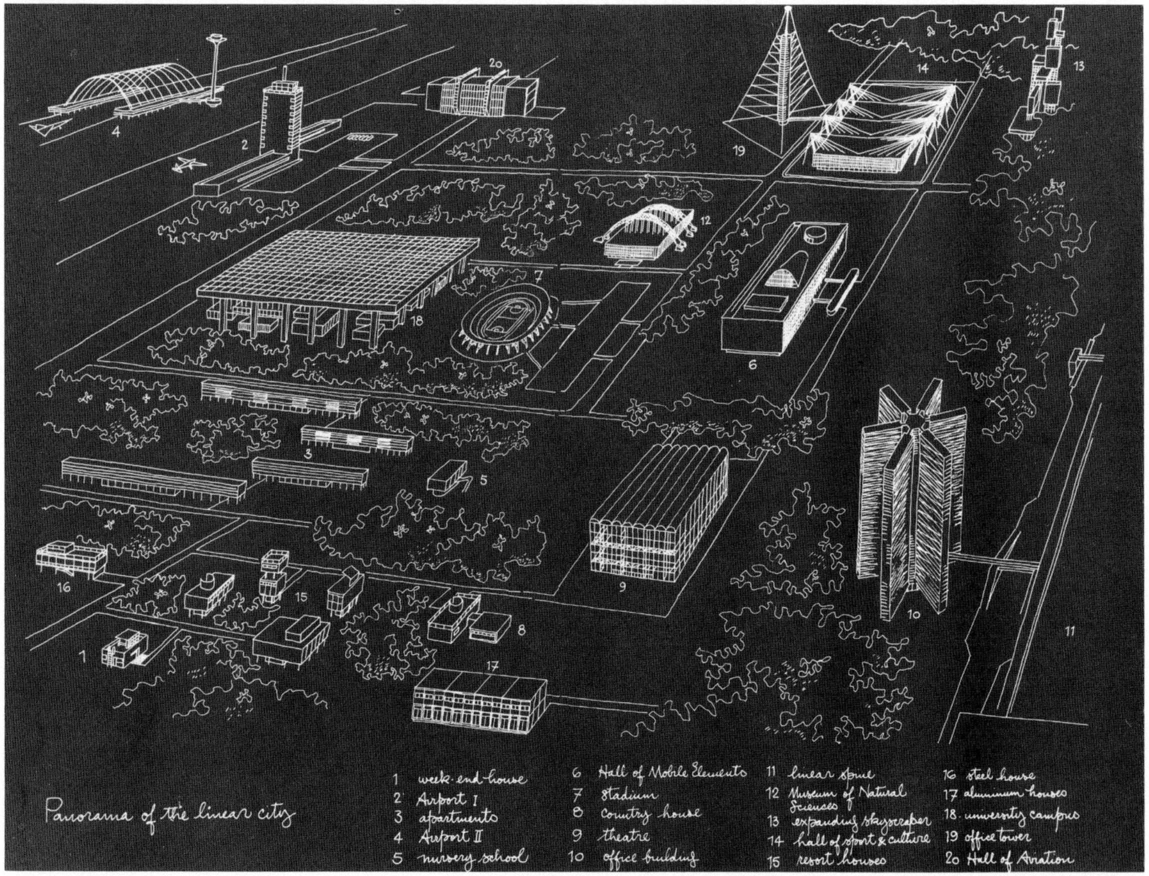

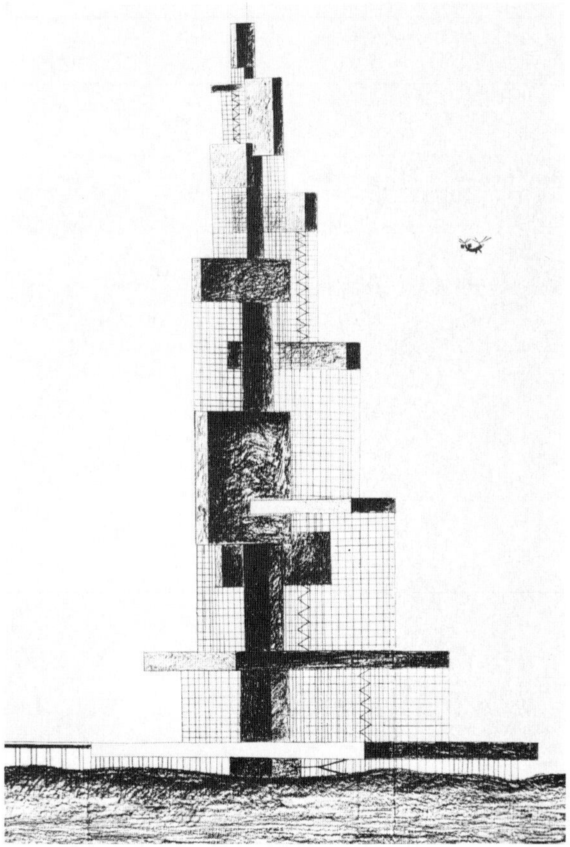

262. View of the Expanding Skyscraper.

areas to the main axis of transportation, at half-mile intervals.

The parallel transportation complex to the north consists of a waterway, highway, and railroad serving heavy industry and a farm belt; also a lake, resort center, and forest for recreation. Connecting links by road and rail join the parallel routes and occur at eight-mile intervals.

Enclosed volumes within the framework may be extended and expanded as necessity demands; in this way, different parts of the whole may grow independently, but all are related to one another by transportation and services. An entire community may be contained in such a tower to form a Vertical City.

Reginald Malcolmson, Visionary Projects for Buildings and Cities, 1974.

Museum of Natural Sciences—1957–1958
Status: Prototype.
In this proposal, a three-dimensional space-frame roof structure of tubular members is suspended by cables from steel crescent arches. The necessity for interior structural supports which might occupy considerable space is avoided.

The main floor area of the museum enclosed by the glass walls measures 504 feet by 780 feet. The only fixed elements in this vast interior are stairs at each corner giving access to utilities and storage on a lower level and to two auditoriums, one large and one small, connected by a common core unit.

263. Museum of Natural Sciences. Plan.

264. Museum of Natural Sciences. Interior View of Museum.

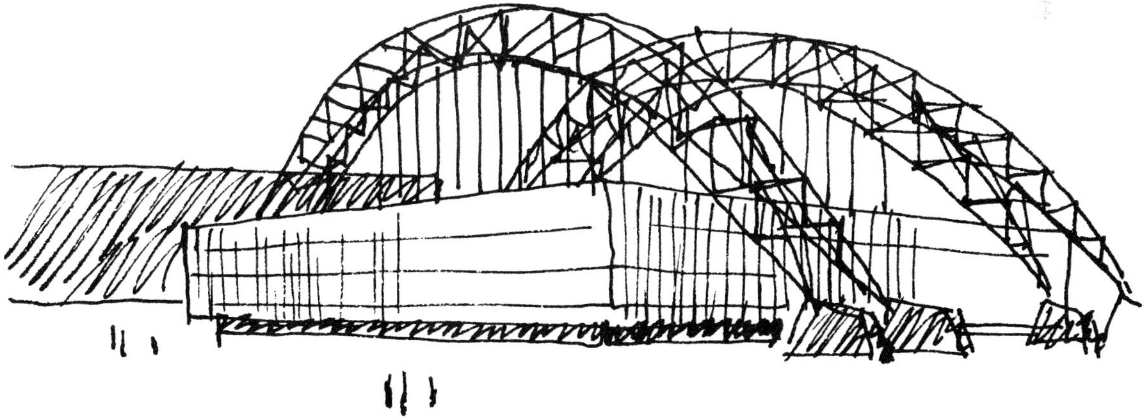
265. Museum of Natural Sciences. Exterior View.

The Expanding Skyscraper—1961
Status: Prototype.
This building is a complex of many buildings that are formed by enclosing parts of the main structural skeleton which is virtually a vertical megastructure. The main vertical axis of the megastructure is enclosed and contains high-speed and local elevators, as well as services.

Reginald Marsh (Paris ca. 1898—Vermont 1954)
Education: 1920, Yale University.
Among Major Works: Illustrator for the *Yale Record* and *New York Daily News;* murals for the U.S. Customs House, N.Y.C.; his works hang in the Metropolitan Museum of Art, and the Whitney Museum, N.Y.C., in numerous museums in Chicago and Philadelphia, and in the Library of Congress, Washington, D.C.

Mr. Marsh was noted for his portrayals of life in Greenwich Village, the Bowery, and Coney Island, New York City.

West Side Highway as a Grandstand—1938
Location: New York City.
Status: Prototype.

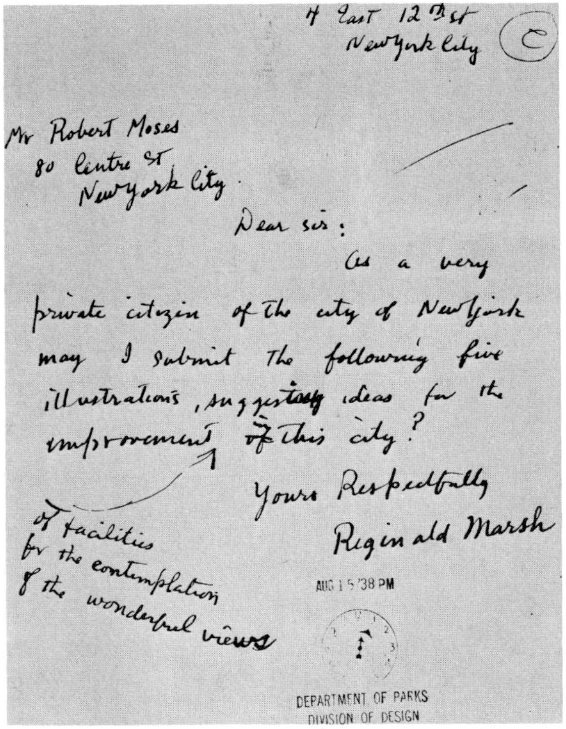
4 East 12th st
New York city

Mr Robert Moses
80 Centre st
New York city

Dear sir:
As a very private citizen of the city of New York may I submit the following five illustrations, suggesting ideas for the improvement of facilities for the contemplation of the wonderful views of this city?

Yours Respectfully
Reginald Marsh

AUG 15 '38 PM
DEPARTMENT OF PARKS
DIVISION OF DESIGN

266. Letter to Robert Moses.

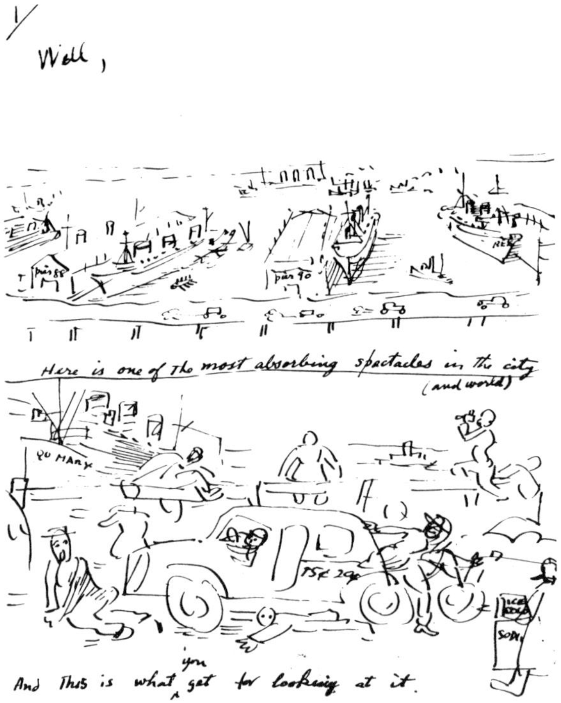

267. West Side Highway. Existing Conditions.

268. West Side Highway. Solution.

MIT Student Drawings

The Massachusetts Institute of Technology was the first architectural school in the United States. The Historical Collections at MIT began during the summer of 1971 as a modest effort by Richard M. Douglas of the Department of Humanities and by E. Neal Hartley, Institute Archivist, to assemble photographic and other visual material to commemorate the first fifty-five years of the Institute's history. In 1973, Warren A. Seamans became Director, and it was he together with Walt Taylor, James R. Killian and Howard W. Johnson who made most of the major discoveries and retrievals. The Collection quickly expanded and now includes: a Portrait Collection; a Photographic Collection; Architectural Theses and Student Drawings; Drawings, Plans and Models of MIT Buildings; Instruments, Inventions, and Patent Models; Memorabilia.

The projects shown below are from the collection of Architectural Theses and Student Drawings, of which there are over 6,000. The entire corpus of drawings has now been painstakingly restored. Since MIT is the oldest school of architecture in the country, the recovery of these drawings has yielded an incomparable resource for the history of design and city planning, covering a period of 100 years.

The descriptions accompanying these drawings were provided by Anthony M. Bond, MIT Historical Collections.

269. Henry A. Phillips. A Design for Water Works. First Degree Thesis Project Completed at MIT.

Henry A. Phillips (1852—1926)
Education: 1873, BS, MIT.

A Design for Water Works—1873

Status: First thesis project completed at MIT. Phillips' drawing was the first degree thesis project completed at MIT, the oldest school of architecture in the United States. Fountains help to underscore the structure's function, which, because of the park-like setting, is not readily apparent. The line quality and the facile use of watercolor washes, stressed by the École des Beaux Arts trained Professor of Design, Eugene Létang (1871–1892), illustrate the importance of the pictorial element in architectural presentation then, and for the next fifty odd years.

270. Henry W. Rowe. A Cathedral.

271. Louis C. Rosenburg. An Estate on an Island.

Henry W. Rowe (1880–1927)
Education: 1905, MS, MIT.

A Cathedral—1904
Status: Student drawing.
This great domed church can readily be said to look to St. Peter's in Rome for its inspiration. Yet the extremely large, blind (closed) lantern surmounted by a tall cross, the abundance of sculpture on the dome drum, and the classical portico lend the structure its individuality. Although the structural elements are clearly delineated, the sculptural elements are handled in a more sketch-like fashion colored with grey washes.

Louis C. Rosenburg (1894—)
Residence: Oregon.
Education: 1912–1914, attended MIT; studied with Malcolm Osborne at the Royal College of Art, London, due to the urging of Sir Francis Short.
In 1937, Rosenburg was second vice-president of the Society of American Etchers.

An Estate on an Island—1913
Status: Student drawing.
In an indication of his artistic talent, for which he later became known, Louis Rosenburg has created an elegant villa complete with terraced gardens, fountains, and glazed conservatory–green house. The Burnt Sienna (burnt orange) tones give the drawing an understated quality, while the bridge leading from this grand island estate to nowhere, and the tacked and curling sheets of drawing paper incorporated to act as a border, create a rather theatrical effect.

272. Frank S. Whearty. Isle of Spice. Plan.

Frank S. Whearty (1889—1966)
Education: 1912–1915, attended MIT.

Isle of Spice
An Amusement Group on an Island—1914

Status: Student drawing.
Befitting the nature and the function of the isle, the buildings have a festive quality, complemented by the fountains, gardens, and stairways to the beach, done in burnt orange washes. The precedents for this type of building group might well have been set by the Chicago World's Columbian Exposition of 1893 and by Frank Lloyd Wright's Midway Gardens.

273. Frank S. Whearty. Isle of Spice. An Amusement Group on an Island. Elevation.

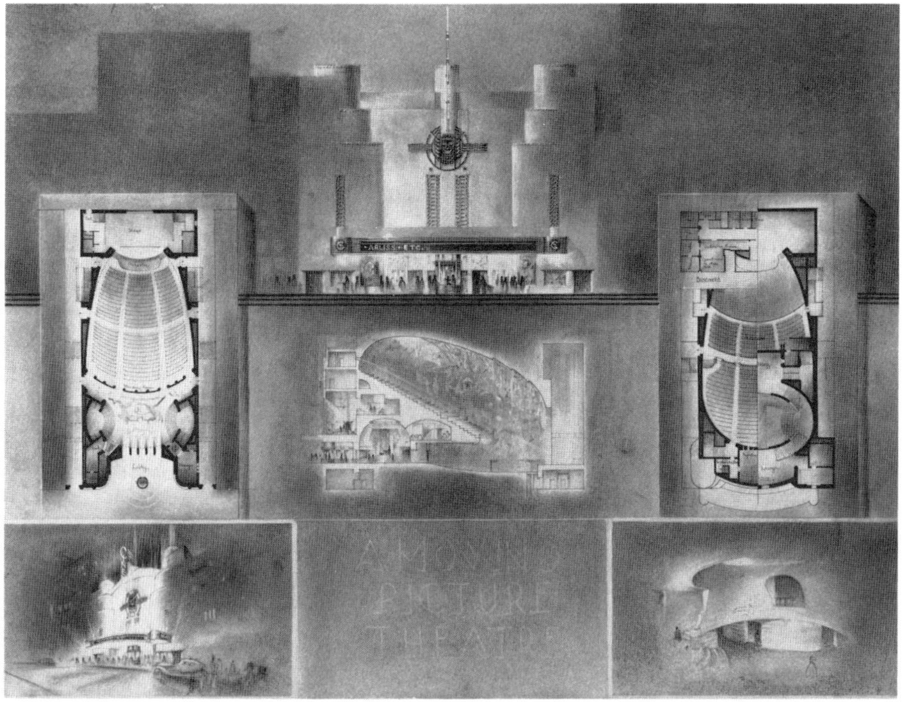

274. Stephen H. Richardson. A Moving Picture Theatre.

Stephen H. Richardson (1910—)
Education: 1934–1935, attended MIT.

A Moving Picture Theater—1934–1935

Status: Competition drawing for a Special Student Scholarship.
This was a winning design in the competition for a Special Student Scholarship. Set in a lot between two existing structures the theater derives its individuality through curvilinear tower forms, incised pattern designs on the plane wall surfaces, and through a visually arresting comic mask, the focal point of the façade. The curvilinear aspects of the exterior are expressed on the interior in the flowing surfaces of the grand foyer. A charcoal-like technique helps to create the play of light on curved and flat surfaces at night.

275. Thomas H. Dreihs. An Airport Terminal.

Henry K. Crowell, Jr. (1905—)
Residence: Philadelphia.
Education: 1928, M Arch., MIT.

Thomas H. Dreihs (1904—)
Education: 1925–1928, attended MIT.

An Airport Terminal—1927–1928

Status: Competition Drawings for the Beaux Arts Institute of Design.

This was a [design] competition sponsored by the Beaux Arts Institute of Design in which an air transportation terminal would occupy one out of twelve square blocks. The remaining area was to consist of commercial buildings with uniform roof levels to accommodate the three block wide, four block deep landing platform, which covered the streets.

276. Henry K. Crowell, Jr. An Airport Terminal.

277. Joseph D. Murphy. A Restaurant in the Air.

Joseph D. Murphy (1907—)
Residence: St. Louis.
Education: 1927–1929, attended MIT.
Joseph Murphy was professor of architecture at Washington University from 1935 to 1952, and dean from 1950 to 1952.

A Restaurant in the Air—1929

Status: Competition drawing for the Beaux Arts Institute of Design.

This drawing received a second prize in a competition for the Beaux Arts Institute of Design, where the problem was to develop a restaurant in a park with an elevation, from which one could get a view of the surrounding landscape. The restaurant was to be on two levels, the lower of which was to be fifty feet above the ground to clear the trees. Students were admonished to remember that the unusual developments of steel and reinforced concrete made possible this type of structure. Murphy's design, done in pastels, reflects somewhat a Wrightian influence in its massings and an Art Deco influence in its detailing.

Bernard Maybeck (New York City 1862—California 1957)
Education: 1882–1886, studied architecture at the École des Beaux Arts, Paris, in the atelier of Jules Louis André (same H. Richardson).
Among Major Works: 1899, Hearst Hall, University of California at Berkeley; 1910, First Church of Christ Scientist, Berkeley, Calif.; 1915, Palace of Fine Arts, Panama-Pacific Exposition, San Francisco; 1927, Hearst Memorial Gymnasium for Women (with Julia Morgan), University of California at Berkeley.

Maybeck was one of the pioneers in what is today called the First Bay Tradition of architects.

Merchant, William (California 1893—?)
Education: 1909, Graduate, Wilmerding School of Industrial Arts.
Among Major Works: 1932–1948, architect for 28 recreational areas, banks, office, commercial, and residential buildings, World Trade Center, San Francisco.

Music Temple—1939
Location: Golden Gate Exposition, San Francisco.
Status: Unbuilt owing to restricted funds and World War II.

This was an early sketch proposal for the exposition—a theme building set in a lagoon. The commission was presented to William G. Merchant, in whose office Maybeck was working at that time. (As Maybeck withdrew from practice during 1932–1938, Merchant established his own office at the same address and hired Maybeck to make preliminary sketches for many of his commissions, of which this was one.)

Kenneth Cardwell, University of California at Berkeley.

278. Music Temple. Elevation.

Ludwig Mies van der Rohe (Germany 1886—Chicago 1969)
Education: 1897–1900, Domschule Aachen, Germany; 1900–1902, Aachen Trade School, Germany.
Among Major Works: 1907, Riehl House, Germany, Mies's first house of his own design; 1940–1941, Master Plan, Illinois Institute of Technology, Chicago; 1945–1950, Farnsworth House, Illinois; 1948–1951, 860–880 Lake Shore Drive Apartments, Chicago; 1958, Seagram Building (with Philip Johnson), New York City.

Mies van der Rohe worked in the office of Peter Behrens in Berlin, from 1908–1911, along with Walter Gropius and Le Corbusier. Behren's work, combining elements of industrial design and neoclassicism, was an important influence on Mies. In 1912, he traveled to Holland where he came into contact with the work and philosophy of Berlage, which influenced his belief in honest expression of structure and materials. During the years 1930 to 1933 Mies was the director of the Bauhaus, until its closing in 1933.

Cantor Hiway Diner—1946
Location: Indiana.
Status: Unbuilt.
Additional Credit: Reginald Malcolmson.

The building provides a single, column-free space where optimum flexibility in the placing of functional elements was possible—it was, in fact, a form of universal space.

In clear span buildings the subsidiary functions for which enclosure is essential are accommodated either in free-standing cores on the main floor or on a separate level directly below.

Unlike the column-free spaces of the past (which generally accommodated the needs of one function and were spatially singular in character), those of Mies van der Rohe's clear span buildings have been given an entirely different meaning through his introduction of freely disposed elements of a non-structural nature. In these buildings the primary structure (the enclosing shell) is clearly expressed and separated from the secondary structure (the space-defining elements). We experience, at one and the same time, the relationship between the plurality of the particular spaces and the singularity of the total space—with all the rich variations of scale and space that this engenders.

Abridged from Peter Carter, *Mies van der Rohe at Work*, 1974.

---

279. Cantor Hiway Diner. Drive-in Restaurant for Joseph Cantor. Model.

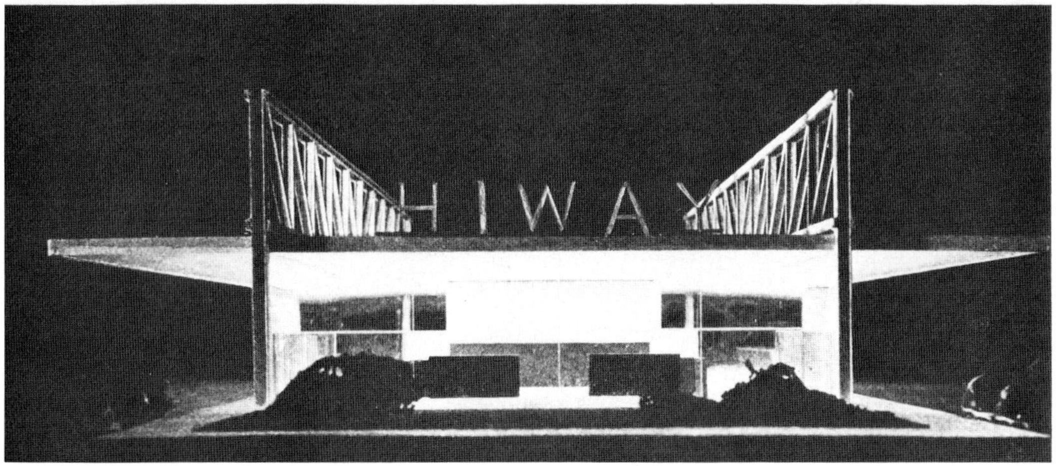

Convention Hall—1953–1954
Location: Chicago.
Status: Unbuilt.
The project for a Convention Hall was made at the request of the South Side Planning Board in Chicago. As it had to provide space for fifty thousand people, its location was partly determined by mass transportation facilities. The site chosen provides these facilities, being close to the railroad and elevated and connected with the highway system. Ample parking space is provided and it is also close to the Loop, the city's center, with its large hotels. Since conventions alone could not financially support such a hall, it was planned as a multi-purpose hall that could be used for political and cultural meetings, large musical and theatrical performances, as well as for industrial or cultural exhibits. At two sides and at a distance from it, are a group of smaller buildings. They contain restaurants, meeting and conference rooms and space for smaller exhibits. Some of the rooms could also be used for smaller conventions.

One other very important requirement for the development of the Convention Hall was that it should provide an area of five hundred thousand square feet free of interior obstructions. The hall is seven hundred and twenty feet square and one hundred and twelve feet in height. A square plan was chosen, because it has great advantages over other shapes and is visually and accoustically better fitted for the purpose. The structural problem was to span this vast space in such a way that the same conditions could be maintained throughout. This excluded arched and domed structures, which require a greater height at the center and cannot, therefore, sustain uniform conditions. A structure was chosen which retains a uniform ceiling height, which could be controlled and could become an object of proportion. The structure is based on a thirty foot module which determines the disposition of the structural elements, gives the structure unity and provides for an architectural harmony. The roof truss system is two-directional. The spacing of the roof trusses, as well as their height, is in accordance with the basic module. Twenty-four columns at the periphery, six at each side, support the roof. The distance between these columns is four modules. The first columns are two modules from the corners and rest on reinforced concrete piers which transmit the load to the foundation.

The basic idea of the Convention Hall is that it can be assembled from prefabricated parts, from the structural elements themselves to the enclosing panels and doors. We see here an artistic manifestation of our technological age in an objective architecture, free from the many misconceptions of individualism.

Quoted from L. Hilberseimer, Mies van der Rohe, 1956.

280. Convention Hall, Chicago. Aerial View.

281. Convention Hall, Chicago. Initial Structural Solution. Exterior View of Model.

Mitchell/Giurgola Associates (established Philadelphia 1962—)
Location: New York City and Philadelphia.
Among Major Works of Firm: 1973, Columbus High School, Indiana; 1975, Project, East Penn Mutual Life Insurance Co., Philadelphia; 1975, School of Law, University of Washington, Seattle; 1975, Indian Point Simulator and Visitor Center, Consolidated Edison Company, Buchanan, N.Y.; 1975, William Penn High School, Philadelphia.

National Headquarters of the AIA—1965
Location: Washington, D.C.
Status: Won the competition, but was rejected by the Washington Fine Arts Commission.

In sponsoring a national competition for its new headquarters building on the historic Octagon site, the American Institute of Architects sought a project of special significance, yet one that would complement and preserve a cherished symbol of another era. The surrounding environment is defined by eight-story private and governmental office buildings which adjoin the quiet Georgian house built in 1800 and its walled garden.

The scheme provides a means to complete the urban fabric and creates a physical context in which the Octagon is allowed to enrich and become a part of the present. The new building is an event that links the small scale of the Octagon to the larger buildings around it.

The headquarters is placed at the back portion of the property in order to preserve the existing garden. A semicircular glass screen dissembles the mass of the building. Its transparent curved facade is concave in vertical section, acting as a natural sun-controlling device. The building is oriented toward the Octagon, focuses on it, involves it, completes it while retaining its own independence and integrity. The new describes the context of the old: the old is the genesis of the new.

Subsequent to awarding the commission in 1965, the AIA obtained more land and expanded the program to include a 300-seat auditorium, lecture hall, and 60,000 square feet of additional office space. The initial concept was followed and developed. This scheme was rejected by the Washington Fine Arts Commission. A third proposal was then submitted in an effort to answer the Commission's objections to the second project. When this too was turned down, the firm resigned the commission.

Mitchell/Giurgola.

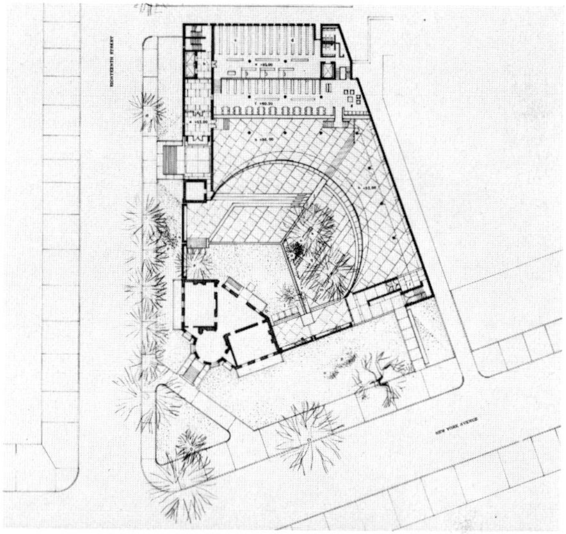

283. National AIA Headquarters. Scheme I. First Floor Plan.

282. National AIA Headquarters. Scheme I. Model.

Julia Morgan (San Francisco 1872—San Francisco 1957)
Education: 1894, University of California, first woman to graduate in the field of mechanical engineering; 1898–1900, first woman student at the École des Beaux Arts, Paris.
Among Major Works: 1904–1906, Mills College, Oakland, Calif.; 1910, St. John's Presbyterian Church, Berkeley, Calif.; 1915, appointed official architect for the National YWCA in the Western United States; 1919, began work on the Hearst estate at San Simeon; 1927, Hearst Memorial Gymnasium for Women, U. of California, Berkeley (with Bernard Maybeck).

Julia Morgan was the first woman licensed as an architect in the State of California.

Wyntoon—1930
Location: Northern California.
Status: Unbuilt due to lack of funds.

Arthur Byne, a representative of the Hispanic Society of America, had been selling European bric-a-brac to Americans for years. In 1930, he discovered a decaying thirteenth century Cistercian monastery, Santa Maria de Ovila, near Burgos, Spain.

Byne did some perspective sketches of the monastery, which for some reason he called Mountolive, and in late 1930 he sent them off to William Randolph Hearst. Hearst was delighted and wanted to buy the entire monastery and have it transported to California.

His mother had built a large hunting lodge called Wyntoon in the forests of northern California. Wyntoon had burned down, but Hearst planned to replace it with something truly stupendous— a medieval castle. It was to front on the McCloud River and rise in commanding towers and bastions to eight stories of pure fairy-tale splendor. It would have sixty-one bedrooms on six floors, and the eighth floor, at the top of the tallest tower, would contain only a solitary, round study for "the Chief," who could gaze upon his domain and the thousands of acres of virgin forest surrounding it.

When Arthur Byne found Santa Maria de Ovila Hearst seized the opportunity and instructed his architect, Julia Morgan, to incorporate pieces of the monastery into the main floor of the new Wyntoon Castle.

Ms. Morgan had no idea what it looked like, however, so she sent her associate Walter Steilberg to Spain to measure and survey the buildings, to design a packing method, and to help Byne oversee the removal. The problems they faced were formidable. Spanish politics in 1931 were unsettled; the monastery was remote; the work had to be done largely by hand; and the problems with packing and transportation were complex.

In addition, there were financial difficulties. There was no doubt that sooner or later Hearst would pay his enormous bills, but Byne's problem was cash flow. As he wrote in May, "Apart from the monastery I have laid out so much for you that I am stripped of all capital and must, perforce, carry along in hand to mouth fashion." Oddly enough, Byne's problem was exactly like his client's, for "hand to mouth" is the very phrase that Hearst's biographer, W. A. Swanberg, uses to describe Hearst's own existence. Although his income was enormous—estimates run as high as $15 million a year—he spent everything and was perpetually broke.

As the letters, photos and drawings from Walter Steilberg came into her San Francisco

284. Wyntoon. Plan of Santa Maria de Ovila's Chapel Transformed into a Swimming Pool.

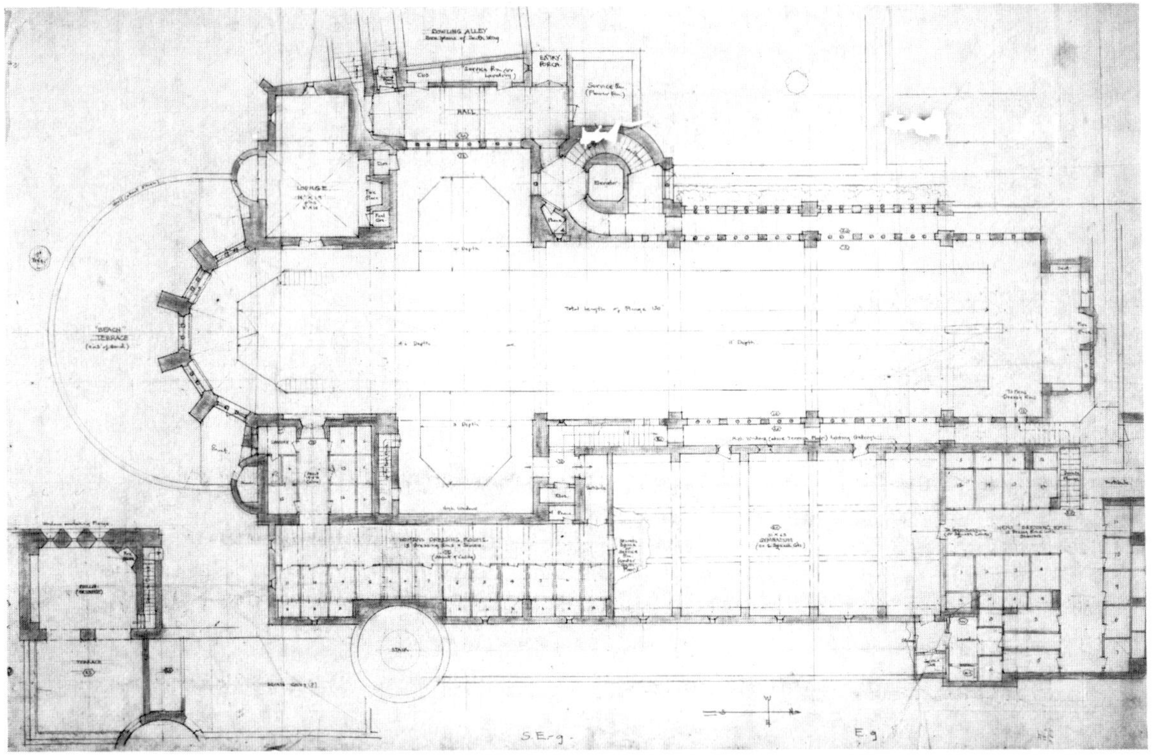

285. Wyntoon. Elevation. Rendering Believed to Be by Bernard Maybeck.

office, Julia Morgan began to fit all the pieces into her design. Practical considerations were not forgotten: Steilberg asked Byne to go out to the monastery's still-standing *bodega* and sing or talk loudly to test the echoes, as they were considering this large wine-storage barn for a movie theater.

The main problem was the chapel itself. This was the major building of the original monastery, that Saint Martin had waited to consecrate in September of 1213. In an early scheme, it was used as a living room, but the long, narrow dimensions of the space seem to have been disturbing. Even with several fireplaces it looked too much like a bowling alley. The final solution was breathtaking—the chapel was to become an enormous swimming pool. It was to be 150 feet long with the diving board where the altar had been, and the two side chapels converted into a lounge and a women's toilet. Around the apse there was to be a very wide deck with a southern exposure, filled to a depth of two or three feet with sand, so that one could sunbathe on "the beach" and proceed into the chapel for a swim.

Most of the monastery was to be used on the first floor of the castle, but not as a weight-bearing structure. for Wyntoon was of course much bigger than the original Santa Maria de Ovila. The medieval masonry would merely have been applied to the downstairs walls, like very thick wallpaper. From the outside, Wyntoon would look more like a fantasy of Maxfield Parrish than anything related to Spanish monasticism. From its lower gate on the river, it was to rise eight or nine stories in an irregular and utterly fantastic aggregation of arches, peaked roofs, towers and ramparts.

When the monastery finally arrived in eleven ships at San Francisco, the cost of construction, estimated at over $50 million dollars, was at this point well beyond Hearst's means. The current financial crisis of the country had finally caught up with his extravagant spending. The monastery was eventually put into storage. Over the years the packaged materials have undergone several devastating fires, until now all that remains of this dream is a decaying pile of rubble that has been dumped into San Francisco's Golden Gate Park.

Excerpted from Robert Clements, forthcoming article in *American Heritage.*

286. Wyntoon. The Remains of Santa Maria de Ovila in San Francisco's Golden Gate Park.

Francisco Mujica (Mexico—)
Residence: Mexico.
Education: Architectural degree, University of Chile; Architectural degree, University of Mexico; studied city planning at the Sorbonne in Paris.

Francisco Mujica spent years of research among the ruins of Mexico and Central America. He presents the interesting suggestion that we apply the work of the primitive peoples on the American continent to this product which is purely American. He seeks to re-create an architectural style truly American in spirit and distinguishable from those native to other lands. Happily the bold, rugged, and virile beauty of these ancient monuments is strikingly adaptable. The Temples and palaces are rich in archaeological material. The ancient "setbacked" and terraced monuments are by coincidence strangely appropriate to the zoning restrictions which so control the bulk and mass in our American cities.

John Sloan, Foreword to Mujica's *The History of the Skyscraper*, 1929.

287. The City of the Future. Hundred Story City in Neo-American Style.

The City of the Future—1917
Hundred Story City in Neo-American Style
Location: Somewhere in the American Continent.
Status: Theoretical proposal.

The conditions which have prevailed since the Conquest have caused to spring up within the architecture of America a great number of buildings that respond to modern needs completely alien to primitive times.

After a profound study of the ruins it is possible to conceive a *new* line in which only the sentiment of the American forms subsists. It appears to me correct to call this new type of architecture Neo-American.

The difference between the Renaissance and the Neo-American architecture is fundamental. The Renaissance works with a model before it. The Neo-American architecture is a new creative work which requires profound study of the primitive American architecture and of the geometrical and mechanical elements of the regional nature.

When all the forms peculiar to us have germinated in our minds and can follow the summons of our imagination we will be prepared to create this new architecture and to produce designs and plans embodying reminiscences of their primitive origin, but at the same time revealing their modern character clearly and powerfully.

Francisco Mujica, History of the Skyscraper, 1929.

Louis Christian Mullgardt (Missouri 1866—California 1942)
Among Major Works: 1908–1909, Henry W. Taylor Residence, Berkeley, California; 1912–1915, Court of the Ages, Panama-Pacific International Exposition, San Francisco; 1914–1916, Juvenile Court and Detention Home, San Francisco; 1916–1921, M. H. de Young Memorial Museum, San Francisco; 1917–1921, Theo. H. Davies and Co., Ltd. Building, Honolulu.

Louis Christian Mullgardt worked in the firms of: 1887, Shepley, Rutan and Coolidge, Boston; 1891, Henry Ives Cobb, Chicago; 1905, George Alexander Wright and Willis Polk, San Francisco; ca. 1903, received patent for reinforced concrete floor construction method, London; 1931, resigned from the American Institute of Architects; 1935, abandoned the architectural profession.

I don't ever believe I chose my profession, in fact, when the suggestion was made to me, I had never heard of the word architect. But it seems I fit rather contentedly into the plan. . . . Expositions are phantom kingdoms . . . similar to the mushroom and the moonflower, they vanish like setting suns in their own radiance.

Louis Christian Mullgardt.

La Parra Grande—1906–1907
Location: Montecito, California.
Status: Unbuilt.
A complex comprising the Montecito Hot Springs Company Hotel and series of wooden and stuccoed bungalows.

---

288. La Parra Grande. Montecito Hot Springs Company Hotel and Bungalows. Aerial View.

Commercial Center—1917
Location: Honolulu, Hawaii.
Status: All but one client chose less eccentric solutions.
Of all the opportunities that came to Louis Mullgardt as a result of his exposition fame, none was potentially greater than his commission for a commercial center in Honolulu. Seven firms planned to participate. When he presented the remarkable perspectives in June 1917, Mullgardt spoke of a new "architecture of the Mid-Pacific, the Hawaiian Renaissance style . . . the spirit of the Far West." Actually, the ideas were more sober than this quotation would suggest. Finding little architectural tradition in the Islands, he drew precedent from his own work of recent years, garnishing it with vague allusions to Venice—that exotic city closely associated with the sea and therefore analogous, somewhat, to Honolulu. For the complex of business houses radiating from the intersection of Bishop and Merchant Streets, so near the waterfront, Mullgardt sketched a series of lavish buildings, each harmonious in its use of street-level arcades and robust Italianate detail, but different in height, setback and fenestration.

Despite its anachronous character, the Honolulu commercial center would have been one of America's finest architectural groups. But only the Theo. H. Davies & Co., Ltd. Building was executed according to Mullgardt's design.

Mullgardt's "Hawaiian Renaissance" was spectacularly brief. When the restrictions of World War I had passed, the remaining Honolulu clients went to other architects for less eccentric solutions. Returning to San Francisco, Mullgardt was chagrined to find no work. Disillusioned by the failure of the Honolulu projects and weary of the professional compromises faced in recent years, he closed his office and embarked on a long-awaited world tour in 1922–1923. He never fully resumed an architectural practice.

Robert Judson Clark, **Louis Christian Mullgardt** [exhibition catalogue], The Art Gallery, University of California, Santa Barbara, 1966.

289. Commercial Center, Honolulu. Street View.

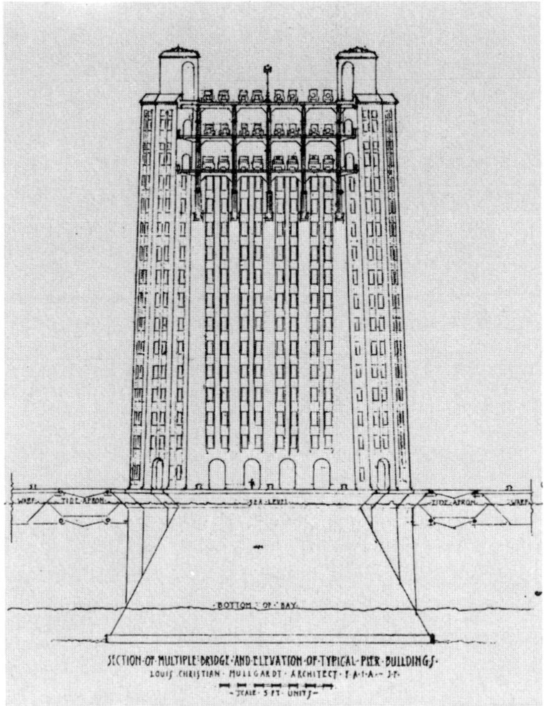

290. San Francisco Bay Bridge. Section of Multiple Bridge and Elevation of Typical Pier Buildings.

291. San Francisco Bay Bridge. Perspective.

San Francisco Bay Bridge—1924–1925
Location: San Francisco, California.
Status: Unbuilt.

Back in San Francisco by May 1923 [after a world tour begun in 1922], Mullgardt found the city alive with controversy about bridging the Bay. It was a thoroughfare to Oakland that caught his imagination, and in December 1924, Mullgardt unveiled this unsolicited proposal for a Bay Bridge. His drawings featured a sequence of giant piers stretching across the water, joined by steel trusses supporting a three-tiered roadway with twenty-four lanes of traffic. The pier forms were dotted with vertical patterns of dark rectangles which, Mullgardt explained, were windows for the apartments, offices and factories that would fill the towering supports. At midpoint in the twenties, Mullgardt simply combined two obsessions of that decade—the skyscraper and the bridge—resulting in a phantasm that had all the dynamic equipment of Piranesi or Sant'Elia, yet fit comfortably into no epoch at all.

Robert Judson Clark, **Louis Christian Mullgardt** [exhibition catalogue], The Art Gallery, University of California, Santa Barbara, 1966.

This material will be published by Robert Judson Clark in a forthcoming monograph on Louis Christian Mullgardt.

C. F. Murphy Associates (established Chicago 1937—)
Among Major Works: 1963, Chicago-O'Hare International Airport; 1971, McCormick Place, Chicago; 1975, Kemper Arena, Kansas City, Missouri.

C. F. Murphy Associates traces its lineage back to Daniel Burnham and the so-called Chicago School of Architecture, which was known for the development of the high-rise office building in the nineteenth century. The firm is recognized today as a leader of what is frequently referred to as the second Chicago School in which structure and building technology tend to be the principal rationale for architectural design.

Summer Music Shell for Grant Park—1972
Location: Chicago.
Status: Unanimous approval of property owners was not obtained.

Partner in Charge of Design: Gene Summers.
For several years the Chicago Park District has sought to replace an obsolete music shell at the south end of Grant Park. When the Park District Commissioners decided to proceed with a large (3,800 car) underground parking facility, they proposed incorporation of a new music shell into the project.

The music shell as developed was to be a two-way space truss combining arch and cantilever action, spanning 300 feet at the widest point and rising to a maximum of 60 feet. The open lattice work of the truss was to have transparent acrylic plaster infilling. Supporting facilities were to have been integrated into the underground parking structure immediately below the shell. Three thousand people were to have been accommodated under cover of the shell with another 12,000 on the continuation of the park beyond the shell.

There was a court ruling known as the Montgomery Ward decision dating from the turn of the century which makes it mandatory for the Park District to obtain the unanimous approval of all owners of property along Michigan Avenue—which faces Grant Park—before any structures can be built. Although the proposed music shell received endorsement from several music organizations and the press, the citizens group opposed it and prevailed upon three Michigan Avenue property owners to vote against it.

C. F. Murphy Associates.

292. Summer Music Shell for Grant Park. Model.

293. Summer Music Shell for Grant Park. Model.

Richard Neutra (Vienna 1892—West Germany 1970)
Education: 1917, Graduate, Technische Hochschule, Vienna.
Among Major Works: 1927–1929, Lovell House, Los Angeles; 1935, Corona Avenue School, Los Angeles; 1942, Channel Heights Housing, California; 1946, Kaufmann Desert House, Palm Springs; 1960, U.S. Embassy, Pakistan.

Richard Neutra met Adolf Loos in 1919, and was influenced by Loos' development of structures without ornamentation. In 1923, Neutra arrived in the U.S., where he was one of 1,328 draftpersons in the firm of Hinchman and Grillis, Chicago, and the same year worked for Holabird and Roche, also in Chicago. In 1925, Neutra moved to California, and shortly thereafter worked for R. M. Schindler.

Rush City Reformed—1923
Status: Theoretical proposal.

In its essential ideas, "Rush City Reformed" by Richard J. Neutra is based on the surveys Neutra made of the most congested metropolises of Europe more than a dozen years ago. The studies of "Rush City Reformed" have since been supplemented further with Neutra's surveys of such American cities as Philadelphia, New York, Chicago, Cleveland, Detroit, San Francisco and Los Angeles during the last decade together with similar surveys of Japanese centers and others on the Asiatic and African continent.

"Rush City Reformed" then does not base itself on an abstract and theoretically rigid scheme. It is rather a series of efforts to unroll urban problematics in a scientific manner, expressing a belief in the flexibility of city planning, even though our unstable social-economic order has not yet permitted valid methods of construction, financing and usage of land to exfoliate in accordance with existing technological advance.

For the planning of "Rush City Reformed," Neutra formulated the following rules: "Thinned habitation density, a consequence of motorcar use, calls for increased traffic area in the central district and in a number of auxiliary decentralized business districts. Thinned habitation density on the outskirts means decrease, by necessity, of over-built downtown area, size-reduction of downtown city blocks and multiplication of free spaces in the center of traffic gravitation." . . .

In dwelling zones the outlying housing blocks will grow in specific size and only a minimum of through-traffic streets will remain, that is, feeder arteries and radial avenues. The traffic area is diminished in proportion to its distance from the center. Local lanes and parking bays serve local business blocks and accompanying non-intersected sunken speedways form radial avenues and cross through habitation areas.

In order to overcome the handicap of inaccessibility to the center areas by congestion of traffic, Neutra developed the following proposals: Re-cutting of downtown city blocks to a long and narrow shape for optimum sun exposure, with the height of buildings limited to eleven stories; elimination of all interior courts with the full ground-floor area under skeleton building devoted to parking and rolling traffic; street width dimensioned in proportion to an amount of traffic carefully computed as to the daily use of this district.

As an alternative, Neutra also suggested

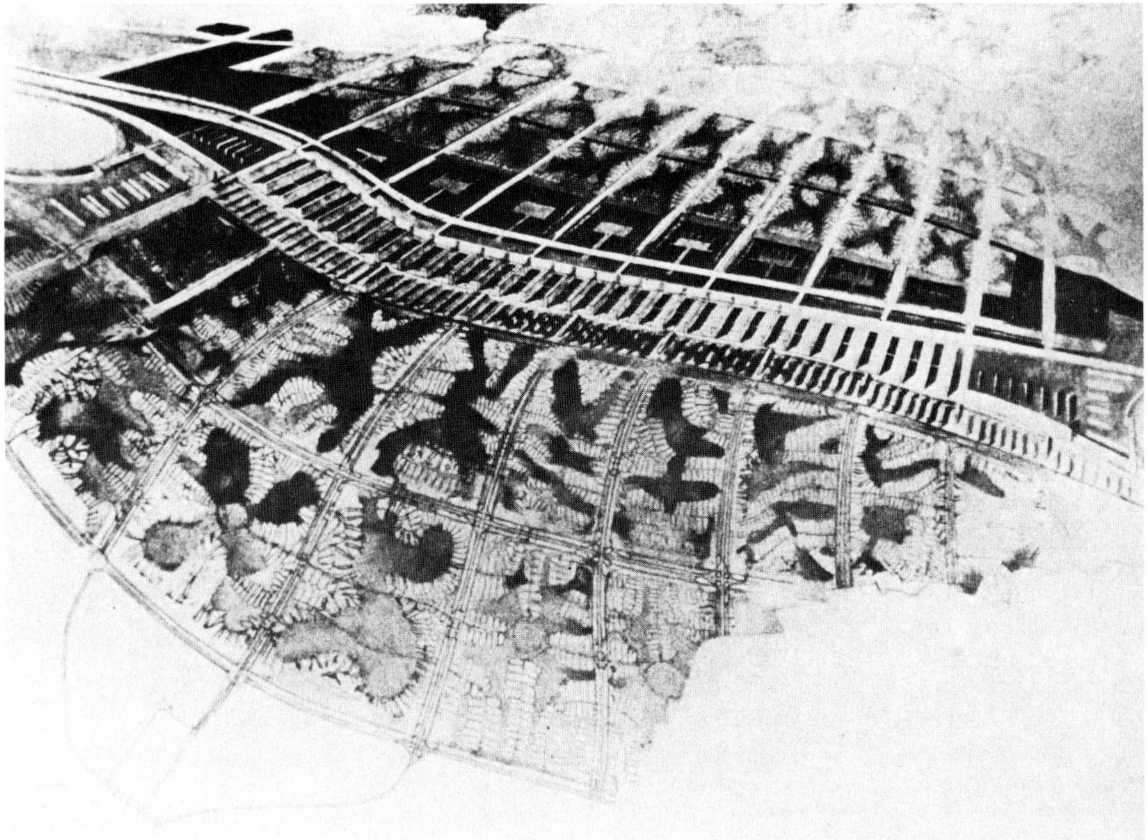

294. Rush City Reformed. Aerial View.

exclusion of all tire-traffic from the center district for public carriers on tracks and rolling sidewalks. This would result in reduction of wasteful street occupancy caused by both parked and moving vehicles, as for instance, six-passenger vehicles carrying one passenger. In both cases the pedestrian and store levels are raised to second and third stories and served by public elevators at street intersections. Tempered with an ingredient of elasticity and of extrapolation "Rush City Reformed" will define problems and serve concretely useful data.

"Rush City Reformed," *Shelter,* III, March 1938.

295. Rush City Reformed. Typical radial or cross town avenue with sunken speedway, connected by ramps with local lanes and parking bays in front of business buildings. Double deck bridges for cross traffic of pedestrians and rolling traffic on a level separate from crossings.

296. Rush City Reformed. Detail showing connection of radial avenue with boulevard between distributional zone and transient apartments.

Oscar Newman (Montreal 1935—)
Residence: New York City.
Education: 1959, B Arch., McGill University.
Among Major Works: 1959, *CIAM '59 in Otterlo,* published 1961, Hilversum, Holland; 1972, *Defensible Space.*

An Underground City—1969
Location: Any highly congested city.
Status: Hypothetical proposal.
In Nevada last spring, an underground atomic test produced a perfect hollow sphere, a half-mile in diameter, five hundred feet below the surface of the earth. When some places on earth, such as Manhattan, London, and Tokyo, become so highly-prized (and congested) that building must go somewhere, the suggestion is to move not only up, but down, into a sphere. Manhattan could have half-a-dozen such atomic cities strung under the city proper, each with adequate room for manufacturing and storage in the lower hemisphere, living and working quarters above that, and full use of the overhead sphere, perhaps, for Cinerama. The real problem in an underground city would be lack of view and fresh air, but consider its easy access to the surface and the fact that, even as things are, our air should be filtered and what most of us see from our windows is somebody else's wall.

Oscar Newman, *Esquire,* LXXIII, December 1969.

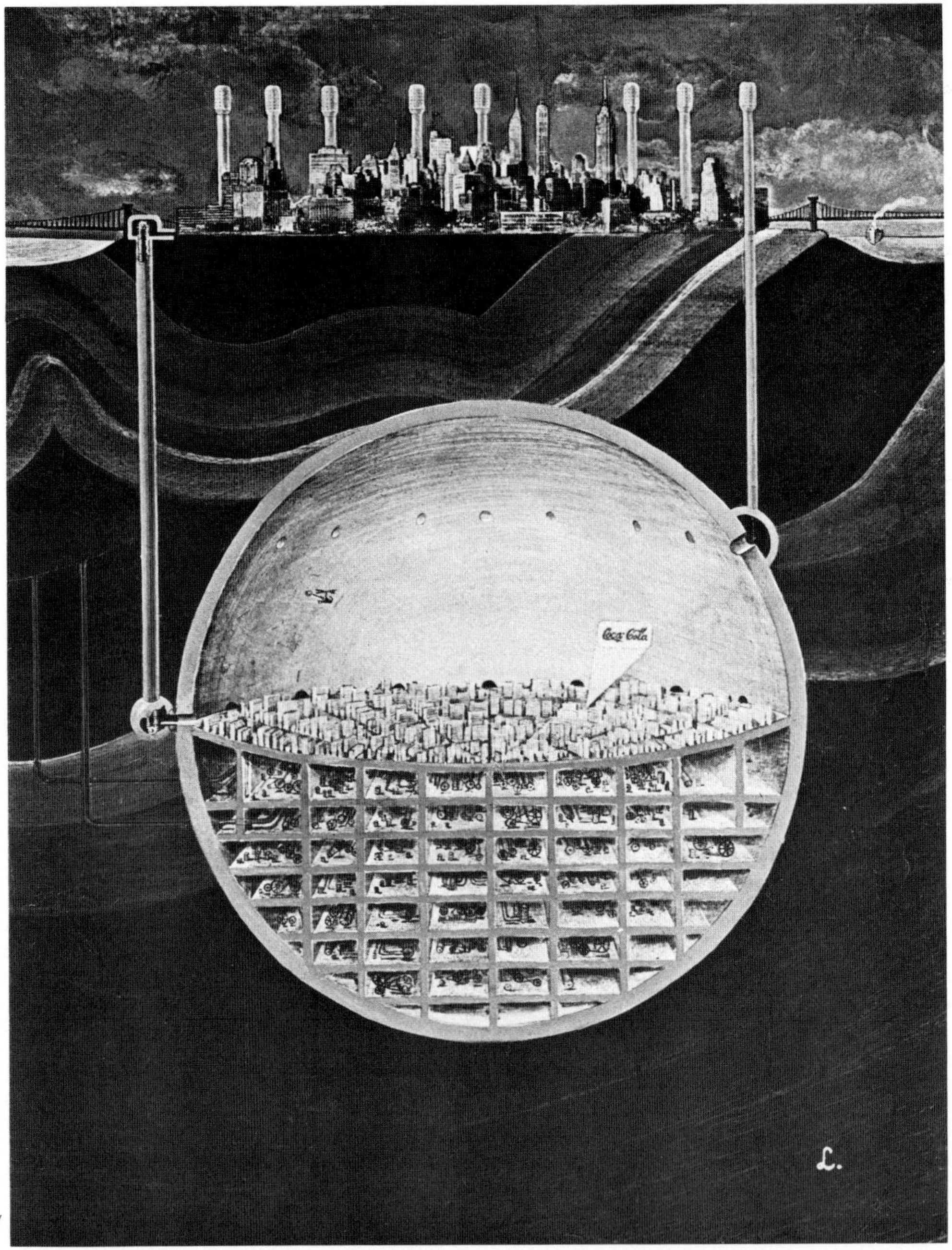

297. An Underground City. Section. Illustration by Jean Lagarrique.

The Niagara Ship Canal—1835–1836
Location: New York State, between Lake Erie and Lake Ontario.
Status: Unbuilt.
[The purpose of this project was to provide navigation around Niagara Falls on other than Canadian territory (the Welland Canal). Projects had been explored since the founding of the Republic and the controversy went on for over a century.]

The proposed Ship Canal is the only link wanting to give free communication through and between all the great Lakes and River St. Lawrence, for vessels of the largest size navigating the Lakes. This great enterprise has claimed the attention of the General Government for many years, and numerous Committees of Congress have recommended it as a work truly National in its character, and demanded by the highest considerations of public interest.

The area involved, includes a shore line within our territory of more than three thousand miles, and forms a navigable water boundary for eight of the most important States of the Union, with an aggregate population, in 1860, of over nine millions.

From those cities, and through these Lakes and Rivers, more than one hundred millions of bushels of grain, are already distributed annually to New York, New England and the Atlantic cities North of and including Baltimore.

While the Westward-bound commerce is highly important to the comfort and convenience of our Western fellow-citizens, their agricultural products are indispensable to the East. The arrest of this commerce, even for a brief period, would create a state of suffering and destitution to the inhabitants of New York and New England unparalleled in the history of our country.

The best interests of the country demand the cheapest possible transportation between the interior and the Atlantic coast. This would be obtained between the Lake country and tide water by the Niagara Ship Canal. It would relieve us from all apprehension of the diversion of any considerable portion of this trade from our own commercial cities. It would create a new bond of union between the East and West, and forever secure the military and commercial ascendancy on the great Lakes, to the Governments and citizens of the United States.

The Niagara Ship Canal: Its Military and Commercial Necessity, 1863.

298. Niagara Ship Canal. Caption on Print: This View of the Ship Canal Around the Falls of the Niagara is Dedicated with the utmost Respect and esteem to Lieut. Col. John J. Abert, Chief of the Corps of U.S. Top Engineers, by his obedient Servant, W. G. Williams, Capt. U.S. Top Engineers. Entered According to Act of Congress by Lewis P. Clover in the Clerks Office of the Southern District of New York.

Isamu Noguchi (Los Angeles 1904—)
Residence: New York City and Japan.
Education: 1922, Columbia University; 1924, Leonardo da Vinci School (New York City), worked with the Director Onorio Ruotolo; 1927, worked with Brancusi (mornings), and studied drawing at Academy Grande Chaumière, and the Collarosi School (Paris), in the evenings.
Among Major Works: 1930's–1960's, stage sets for Martha Graham, New York City; 1956, gardens for UNESCO Building, Paris; 1960–1964, marble garden for Beinecke Rare Book and Manuscript Library, Yale University; 1960–1965, Billy Rose Sculpture Garden for Israeli Museum, Jerusalem; 1960–1965, garden for Chase Manhattan Bank Plaza, New York City; 1967, sculpture for 140 Broadway, New York City.

My interest is the stage where it is possible to realize in a hypothetical way those projections of the imagination into environmental space which are denied us in actuality. There is joy in seeing sculpture come to life on the stage in its own world of timeless time. Then the very air becomes charged with meaning and emotion, and form plays its integral part in the re-enactment of a ritual. Theater is a ceremonial; the performance is a rite. Sculpture in daily life should or could be like this.

Isamu Noguchi, A Sculptor's World, 1968.

Play Mountain—1933
Location: New York City.
Status: Rejected by Park Commissioner Robert Moses.
Play Mountain was the kernal out of which have grown all my ideas relating sculpture to the earth. It is also the progenitor of playgrounds as sculptural landscapes. This was an original concept to expand playable space in a given city lot by tilting the surface into varidimensional steps of a pyramid, or of a roof, whose interior could also be used. In the shape of a spiral; the ridge is a slide for sleds in winter. There is another steeper slide with water flowing into a shallow pool. Along one side of *Play Mountain* is a swimming pool and on the other side a bandstand. The music would be heard by people sitting on the steps from across the water. This was presented to the New York Park Commissioner, Robert Moses, in 1934, to be met with something less than enthusiasm.

I wanted other means of communication—to find a way of sculpture that was humanly meaningful without being realistic, at once abstract and socially relevant. I was not conscious of the terms "applied design" or "industrial design". My thoughts were born in despair, seeking stars in the night. Such wishful thinking produced a Monument to the Plow, and Play Mountain.

Isamu Noguchi, A Sculptor's World, 1968.

299. Play Mountain. Model.

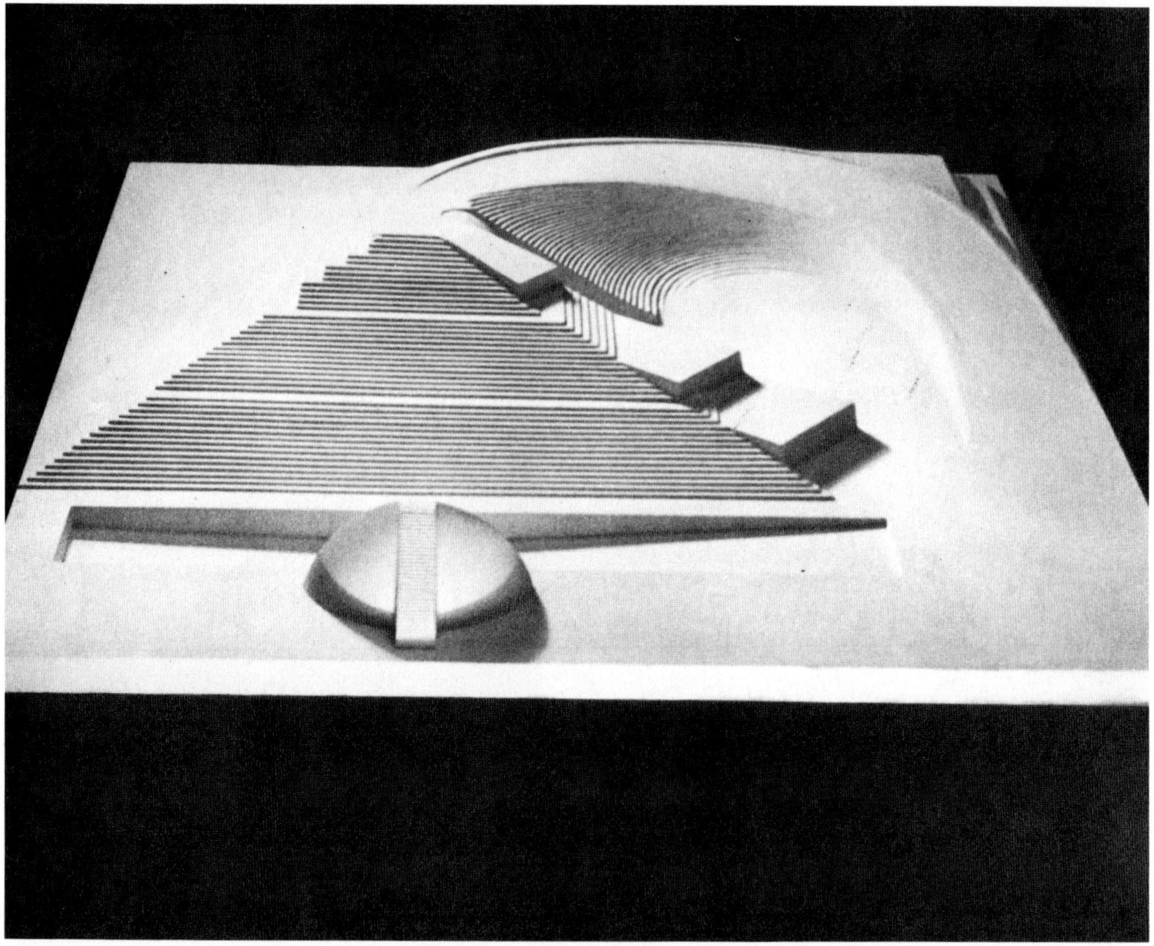

Monument to the Plow—1934
Location: Middle West, preferably at the geographical center of the United States.
Status: Unbuilt.
The steel plow, (I was told), had been devised through correspondence between Benjamin Franklin and Thomas Jefferson, which had then made possible the opening up of the western plains. My model indicated my wish to belong to America, to its vast horizons of earth. [The Monument to the Plow would be a] triangular pyramid, 12,000 feet wide at base, made of earth on one side tilled in furrows, one side planted with wheat, and topped with a huge block of concrete and a large stainless steel plow.

Isamu Noguchi, A Sculptor's World, 1968.

Pyramidal Memorial to Man to Be Visible from Mars—1947
Location: Unspecified.
Status: Unbuilt.

Proposed size of nose—one mile.

300. Pyramidal Memorial to Man to Be Visible from Mars. Model.

301. Monument to the Plow. Perspective.

Claes Oldenburg (Stockholm 1929—)
Residence: New York City.
Education: 1950, Yale University.
Among Major Works: 1963, "Soft Pay Telephone", first piece in vinyl; 1969, "Bedroom Ensemble, Replica I", London and Darmstadt; 1969, "Giant Lipstick", Yale University; 1970, "Ice Bag", Expo '70, Osaka; 1971, "Trowel", the Netherlands.

302. Diner in the Form of a Knee. Sketch.

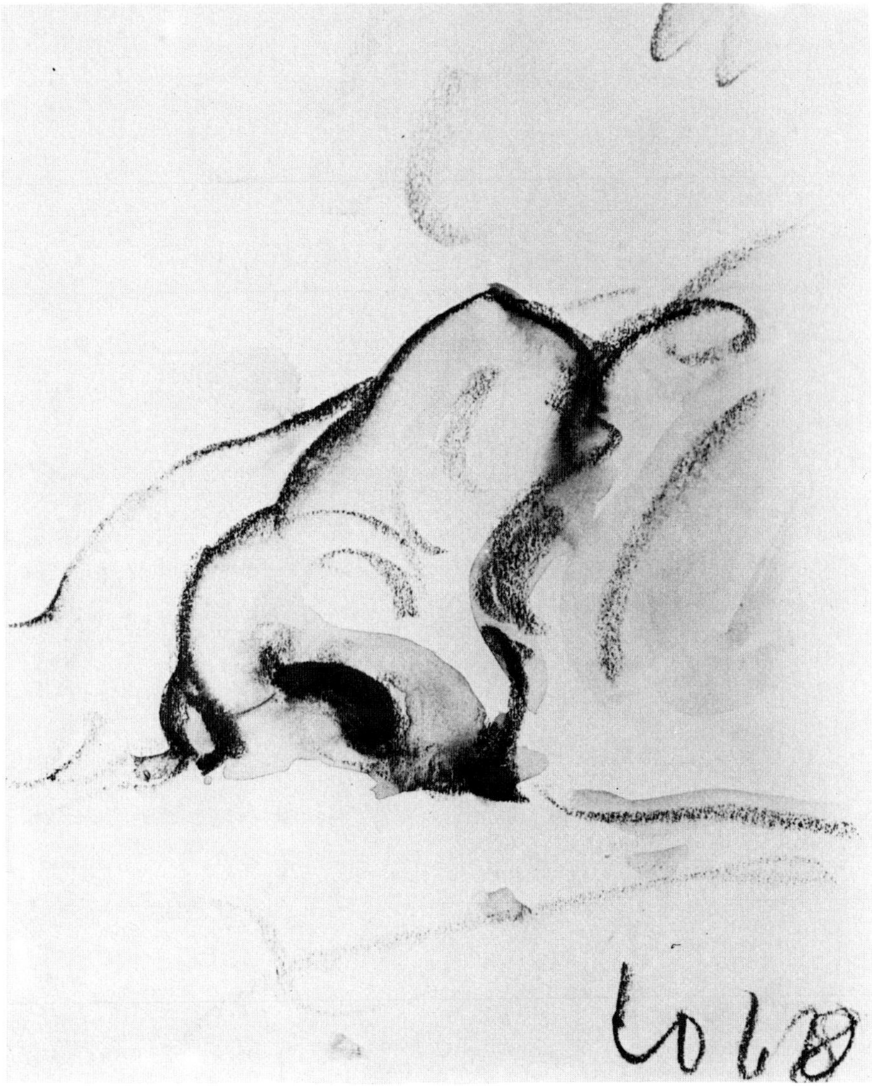

303. Design for a Tunnel Entrance in the Form of a Nose.

Diner in the Form of a Knee—1968
Location: Los Angeles.
Status: Hypothetical proposal.

Design for a Tunnel Entrance in the Form of a Nose—1968
Location: California.
Status: Hypothetical proposal.
I was involved with the nose as an object or a detachable portion of the anatomy like the knees. The nose seemed to be a good object to use as a tunnel entrance; for example, on the freeway to Pasadena which goes through several little hills.

Claes Oldenburg, Object into Monument, 1971.

304. City as Alphabet.

City as Alphabet—1968
Location: Los Angeles.
Status: Hypothetical proposal.
Sitting in a car and watching letters silhouetted against the sky has always seemed the basic Los Angeles experience. Another source of the association of letters and landscape is the map of the area one has to consult. Imagine the coordinates, for example, constructed to cover the territory they fill on the map, or a colossal alphabet spilled haphazardly over the basin—an effect like an earthquake. The characters become landmarks of the community. One may say, "I live down by the L. You know, you can spot it from the freeway." It may ease the sense of loss at the removal of the verbal element from telephone exchanges. A city is all words—a newspaper, an alphabet.

Claes Oldenburg, Object into Monument, 1971.

Sketch for a Bridge Based on the Word Philadelphia—1972
Location: Philadelphia.
Status: Hypothetical proposal.

305. Design for a Bridge Over Delaware River.

Robert Owen (Great Britain 1771—Great Britain 1858)
Education: 1780, formal education terminated at age 9.
Among Major Writings: 1810, *The Philanthropist,* a periodical; 1813–1814, *New View of Society: or, Essays on the Foundation of Character;* 1857–1858, *The Life of Robert Owen.*

A textile worker from age 10, the Welshman Robert Owen achieved success in the Manchester area, and in 1799 purchased mills in New Lanark, Scotland, which he converted into a model industrial community. He became internationally famous and politically influential in Britain as an early socialist.

Thomas Stedman Whitwell (England—England 1840)
Among Major Works: 1819–1820, Independent Meeting House, Birmingham, England; 1820–1821, New Library (Italian Style), Birmingham, England; 1821–1822, Brampton Park (Gothic) for Lady Olivia Sparrow, England; 1827–1828, Brunswick Theatre, London, England—it remained in use for only two nights before the iron roof collapsed.

Whitwell was a London architect and social reformer who liked to spend his time writing verses and making drawings of elaborate community palaces. Noting with disgust the tendency in America to name one town after another 'Washington' or 'Springfield', Whitwell decided that this poverty of invention must be stopped. Each locality was to be given a distinctive name which would express in words the latitude and longitude of the place, thus enabling it to be located geographically once the cipher was known. Letters were substituted for numerals in a complex system of ciphers, to which were added rules for pronunciation of the names arrived at and advice for overcoming various technical difficulties. New York, had Whitwell had his way, would have become, Otke Notive and London, Lafa Vovutu. Lockwood tells us that the 'principal argument in favour of the new system presented by the author was that the name of a neighbouring Indian chief, "Occoneocoglecoco-cachecachecodungo", was even worse than some of the effects produced by this "rational system" of nomenclature'.
Mark Halloway, *Heaven on Earth,* 1951.

New Harmony—ca. 1825
Location: Indiana.
Status: Dissensions among the Owenites and economic difficulties led to its collapse without Owen's own architectural model ever being substituted for the existing dwellings in old Harmony.
In the mid-1820s, the town of New Harmony, Indiana, was purchased by Robert Owen and his followers from the Harmony Society which had decided to return to Pennsylvania. Owen planned to begin his transformation of modern industrial society in America, in New Harmony, along principles he had evolved for new town development. Owen brought to America not only a six foot square model of the ideal community edifice he had been talking about but also a live architect to explain it—Stedman Whitwell by name.

It [the model] was displayed at Owen's public meetings in New York and Philadelphia in the course of the month, and was exhibited briefly at Rembrandt Peale's museum in the former city. At the end of the month Whitwell and Captain Macdonald left Owen in Philadelphia, and took the model to Washington. It was unpacked at the Patent Office and installed in an anteroom of the White House, where the two deputies of Owen presented it to President John Quincy Adams on December 3, 1825. After a short trip to Monticello to visit Jefferson, Whitwell and Macdonald returned to the capital for ten days, during which time they felt free to conduct visitors to the White House for an examination of the model, even when the President was out.

Abridged from Arthur Eugene Bestor, Jr., Backwoods Utopias, 1950.

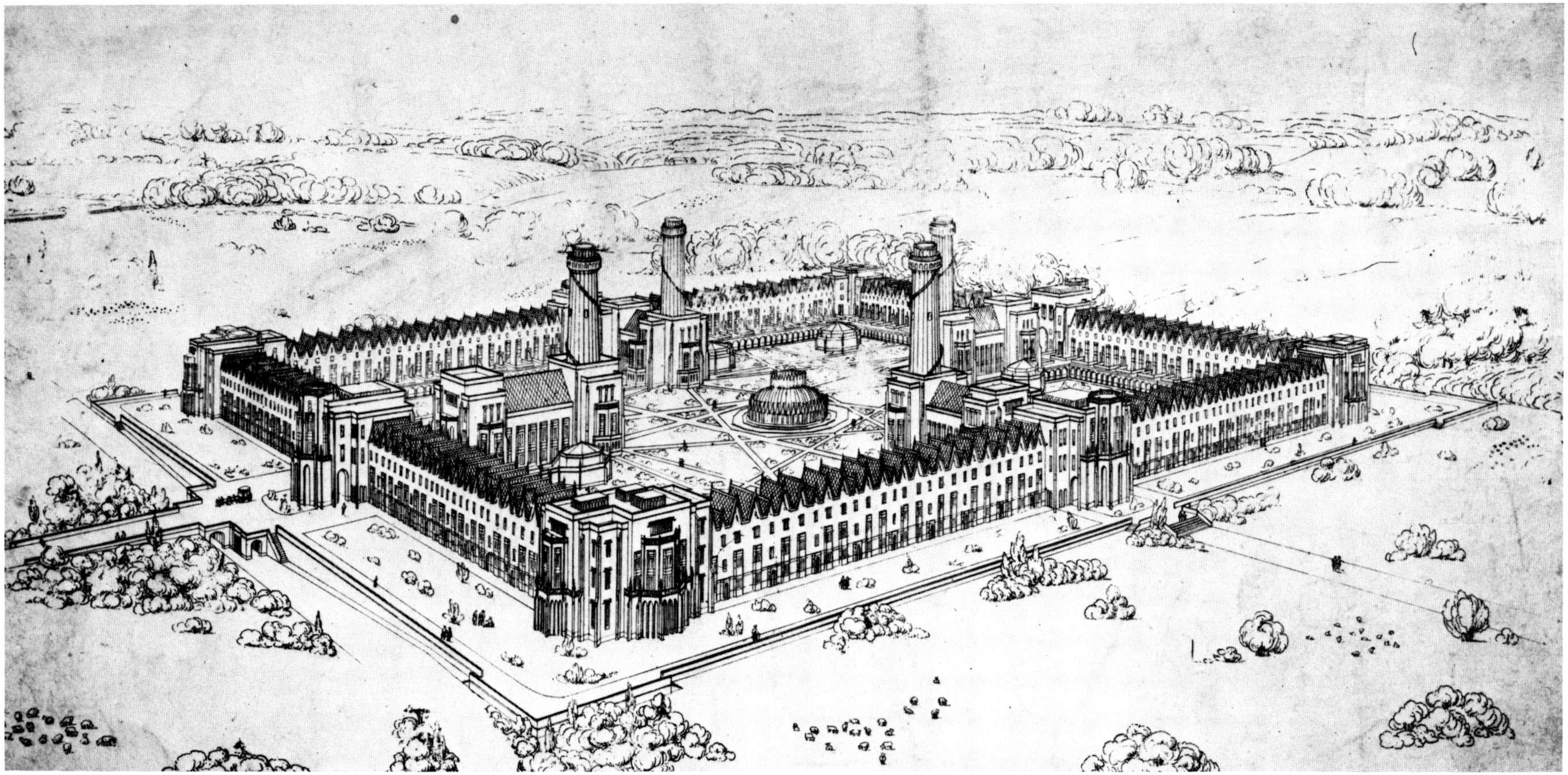

306. New Harmony. A Bird's Eye View of One of the New Communities at Harmony in the State of Indiana, North America. An Association of Two Thousand Persons Formed Upon the Principles Advocated by Robert Owen. Stedman Whitwell, Architect.

Written caption on drawing:
The site is nearly in the centre of an area of 2,000 acres possessed by the community, situated upon high land about three miles from the eastern shore of the great Wabash River and twelve miles from the town of Mount Vernon, on the River Ohio.

The general arrangement of the buildings is a square, each side of which is 1,000 feet. The centres & the extremities are occupied by the public buildings. The parts between them are the dwellings of the members. In the interior of the square are the botanical & other gardens, the exercise grounds &c. The whole is raised above the level of the natural surface, and surrounded by an esplanade. The descent to the offices is upon the outside of the whole—one of the diagonals of the square coincides with a meridian, and the disposition of every other part is so regulated by a careful attention to the most important discoveries & facts in science, as to form a new combination of circumstances, capable of producing permanently greater physical, moral, and intellectual advantages to every individual, than have ever yet been realized in any age or country.

307. Suggested Peristyle and Arch, San Francisco. Aerial View.

Suggested Peristyle and Arch—1897
Location: San Francisco.
Status: Unbuilt.

The colonnade was proposed to wrap around the front of the Ferry Building, which was designed by A. Page Brown. Construction on the building had begun in 1893, but Page died in 1896 before it was completed. Willis Polk, who evidently had some connection with the original design when he had worked for Brown, made the drawings of the peristyle in 1897. Whether he was asked to do the drawings or did them to focus attention on his ability to complete the building is not certain. In any case, he was hired to complete the Ferry Building, without the colonnade.

Kenneth Cardwell, University of California at Berkeley.

Willis Polk (Kentucky 1867— California 1924)
Education: No formal education—tutored at home.
Among Major Works: 1917, Hallidie Building, San Francisco; 1920, Restoration of the Mission Dolores, San Francisco.

In 1900, Polk entered the office of Daniel Burnham. There he participated in the design of several large structures including the First National Bank of Chicago, and the Merchant's Exchange in San Francisco. In 1903 Burnham accepted the commission to develop a new and comprehensive plan for San Francisco, and Polk went there with Burnham. In 1915 he co-directed the San Francisco Panama-Pacific Exposition.

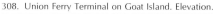

Union Ferry Terminal—ca. 1922
Location: Goat Island, San Francisco.
Status: Unbuilt.

As its name implied, it was intended to combine facilities of the Southern Pacific and Western Pacific Railroads (and perhaps the Key System . . . the local electric trams) into one facility that would extend much further out than the existing slips did. Polk had done several buildings for the Western Pacific (including their mole), and this may have been why he was chosen to draw up the proposed plans. The idea behind it was to cut the time taken for the ferry trips from San Francisco to Oakland, perhaps by as much as half. It was assumed at the time that constructing a bridge across the bay was in the far distant future. That, of course was not true, as the San Francisco-Oakland Bay Bridge was begun in the following decade.

Richard Longstreth, Rhode Island Historical Society.

308. Union Ferry Terminal on Goat Island. Elevation.

William G. Preston (Boston 1844—Boston 1910)
Education: Graduate, Harvard College; École des Beaux Arts, Paris.
Among Major Works: ca. 1863, New England Museum of Natural History; 1888, Exhibition Building (later known as Mechanics' Hall); Cadet Armory; Boston University School of Law; Mason Building, all in Boston.

New York International Exhibition Building—1880
Location: New York City, 1883.
Status: Unable to raise necessary funds.
The first gentleman to propose the holding of a World's Fair in this City was ex-Judge Henry Hilton. Associated with him were men of wealth and position, whose money and reputation would have been staked to make the Fair a success. Congress, however, refused to grant the legislation (declaration as a national exhibition, allocation of funds, etc.) which this body of representative men deemed necessary for the proper execution of their scheme, and the natural result was that they gave up the project. Congress had, instead, incorporated the Exhibition Company which engaged in months of debate concerning the proper site (twelve in all were considered), and determined to raise the necessary funds through private, national, state and city subscription. By 1881, after no final agreement could be reached concerning the actual location, and sharp public criticism, the necessary funding had not been raised and the whole idea was abandoned.

The site proposed, as shown by the diagram, is at the upper part of New York City, just above Central Park, between One Hundred and Tenth and One Hundred and Twenty-fifth Streets. The oval form of the 1867 Paris Exhibition building has been adopted, but enclosed within an oblong structure. The special advantages of the French system already recognized are that while all important departments are covered by one roof, they are so arranged as to be studied either by countries or by subjects as the visitor may prefer: in the first case walking from the outer edge to the centre, and so remaining in one country; and in the other case following the product, raw or manufactured, concentrically through all countries. The distance around the oblong building is one mile and three fifths; the total length of the concentric walks, about twelve miles. An internal railroad 7,200 feet long (nearly one and a half miles) is proposed, to be run by compressed air. Arrangements to be made for eight stations in the circuit, all connected by electricity, so that eight trains would follow one another, making a stop of a half minute at each station. Four spandrel-shaped spaces, of about three and a half acres each, are left at the interior angles of the oblong. It is proposed to utilize these for separate buildings, indicating Europe, Asia, Africa, and America, affording an opportunity for typifying the architecture of the four quarters of the globe, and for landscape gardening, decoration, and for pleasant light-and-fair spaces.

Abridged from *American Architect and Building News,* VII, March 1880.

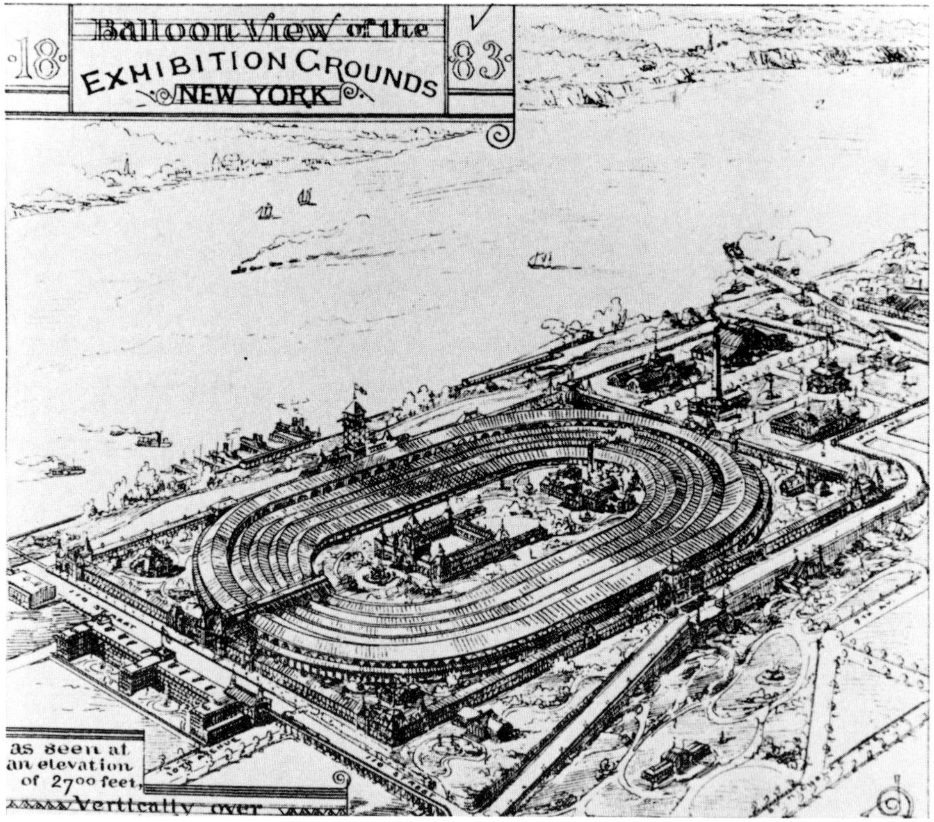

309. New York International Exhibition Building. Aerial View.

Bruce Price (Maryland 1845—Paris 1903)
Education: College of New Jersey (Princeton University). Price was forced to return home due to the death of his father. He then became a shipping clerk, and studied architecture with the established Baltimore firm of Niersée and Neilson.
Among Major Works: 1880, George's Inn, Coney Island, N.Y.; 1880, Hotel, 18 cottages, and 1,275 bathhouses, Long Beach, N.Y.; 1894, American Surety Company Building, N.Y.C.; 1897, Memorial to Richard Morris Hunt, N.Y.C.; 1899, International Banking and Trust Co. Building, N.Y.C.

Sun Building (second proposal?)—1891
Location: New York City.
Status: Unbuilt.
The building was to have a base 100 feet square. The tower, or main body of the structure, was to be eighty feet square and planted directly on a corner site. Wings of twenty feet were to be built on the remaining space on each street. These wings would be built up against the tower to the height of ten or twelve stories only, and were to serve the double purpose of connecting the tower with the buildings immediately adjoining, which were assumed to be structures of average height, and of providing an L shaped court on the inner corner of the lot for light and air. Some superficial area was lost to the total floor space, but this was more than compensated for by the absolutely free light gained for the upper stories, and as this particular building was to be thirty-four stories high the gain for this purpose was of practical utility. Aesthetically the advantage was very great, since it then became possible to treat the four sides exactly alike and of equal importance.

If the building is 300 feet high it should by law be compelled to have all its façades of equal import, and to do so the owner should be compelled to own or to control all the adjoining property to the extent of fifty or seventy-five feet, as the case may be, to be occupied by buildings of not more than ten or twelve stories in height. The skyscraper would then emerge above it as an architectural entity. It is true enough that the chances for building would, in this case, be few; and the expense would be great, but the inducement to make the high building beautiful would be everything, and the city would be the gainer in that it would have a few beautiful tower buildings instead of a number of dreadful ones with horrible back walls and façades that are mere fronts and not real expressions of the structure.

Abridged from Bruce Price in *Great American Architect,* V, 1899.

310. Sketch for a New York City Office Building. Believed to Be the Second Proposal for the Sun Building. Perspective.

Memorial—1898
Status: Unbuilt.
Study for a monument commemorative of the results of the conflict for the Union, the Federation of the States, and the Peace and Prosperity which followed.

Bruce Price in *American Architect,* LXV, September 1899.

311. Memorial. Elevation.

William Price (Pennsylvania 1861—Pennsylvania 1916)
Education: During the 1880s Price attended evening sessions at the School of Applied Arts Division, School of Industrial Arts, Philadelphia.
Among Major Works: 1898–1914, Traymore Hotel additions, Atlantic City, N.J.; 1901–1911, Rose Valley Planned Community, Pennsylvania; 1914–1919, Chicago Freight Terminal.

Overhanover—1909
Location: North Carolina.
Status: Unbuilt due to the inability to raise capital in view of the successful merchandising of competing resorts in Florida.
Additional Credit: Martin Hawley McLanahan.

In 1909, the firm of Will Price began designing half a dozen enormous buildings that were to serve as the core of a new resort community that would rival Atlantic City. Four hotels—two named after the beaches, the Hanover and the Onslow, and the others after North Carolina's

312. The Onslow Hotel. Elevation.

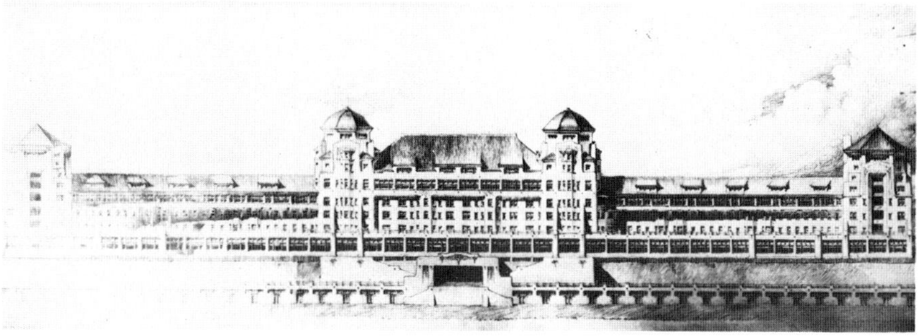

313. The Hanover Hotel. Elevation.

314. Overhanover. Water Towers and View Over Grand Boulevard Toward Atlantic Ocean.

principal cities, Wilmington and Raleigh, were to be built on one of the giant sand spits that formed along the North Carolina coast, just south of Cape Hatteras. The entire development, inclusive of a vast clubhouse, immense concrete water towers, sanatorium, golf club, automobile racetrack, paddock and stable, airport and two hundred house lots varying in size from a full to half acre, was to be called "Overhanover."

The mainland portion of the site was bordered to the east and west by large streams which emptied into a bay formed by the outer bank, a sandy strip several miles long and approximately half a mile wide. An island situated in the middle of the bay offered a means of access to the outer bank with a minimum of bridges. The plan for the community called for a long, straight highway running the length of the sand bar, paralleled by a trolley line serving a row of quarter acre cottage sites. In the middle of this road, a perpendicular causeway was to be constructed connecting the island and extending directly back into the mainland. This intersection was to be the site of the principal ocean front hotels, the Raleigh, the Wilmington, and the Onslow. These first two were to be placed on either side of the causeway, echoed by the positioning of the concrete water towers on either side of the highway where it joined the mainland.

Farther inland, the causeway crossed the racetrack and passed through a housing zone laid out in a standard developers' grid. This grid was broken only along the two bordering streams, where housing was planned four or five blocks deep. One novel touch was achieved by placing four golf courses in the housing tracts, assuring a considerable degree of open space.

Abridged from George Thomas,
William L. Price (1861–1916): Builder
of Men and of Buildings, 1975.

315. Atlantic City Pier. Theater. Elevation.

Below: 316. Seaward End of Pier. Elevation.

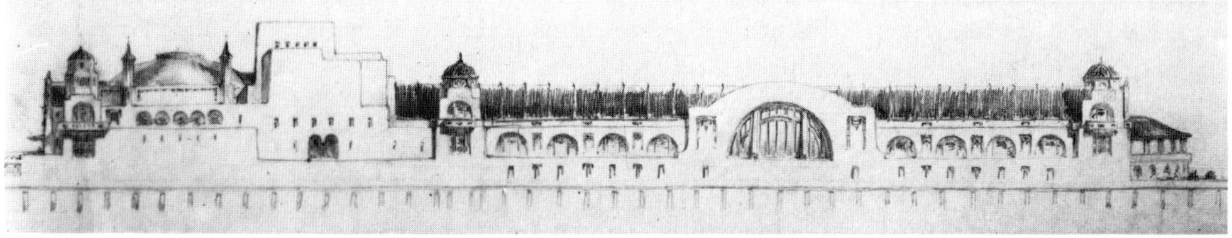

Atlantic City Pier—1912
Location: New Jersey.
Status: Unbuilt due to business recession and impending war.
Additional Credit: Martin Hawley McLanahan.
In early 1912 a group of New York and Atlantic City businessmen, aware of the rapid growth of Atlantic City, proposed that an ocean pier be constructed, extending out from the beach at Tennessee Avenue, to the north of the Traymore and the Marlborough-Blenheim hotels. Ocean piers were not particularly new, dating back to the early nineteenth century at English resorts and being common along the New Jersey shore after the 1870s. In the early 1890s, James H. Windrim had designed Atlantic City's Steel Pier and made various additions to it in the early years of this century. But the businessmen who hired Price and McLanahan in early 1912 had a grand vision—they proposed a pier which was to be nearly a mile long—a mile of reinforced concrete construction extending *out into* the Atlantic Ocean, on which were to be built a 3000-seat theater, an immense convention hall and numerous shops and stores. It was to be a Venetian dream— a city on a bridge with towers and dormers and slender minaret-like spheres—but built on a bridge out into the sea.

The architects were equal to their task, designing a ribbed and bony Art Nouveau and Exposition fantasy that contained numerous references to exotic structures from other cultures — minarets, Chinese roofs, etc. The pier commenced at the boardwalk where a giant arch, flanked by low, domed towers, signalled the entrance into a walkway. The principal auditoria stood one floor above the boardwalk and opened out onto porches and pavilions. Beyond the immense vaulted hall, was another tower, taller than those at the entrance, and including a balcony and window probably for observation, though it might also have held offices for the Pier Company.

Abridged from George Thomas,
William L. Price (1861–1916): Builder
of Men and of Buildings, 1975.

317. Atlantic City Pier. Perspective. Rendering by Jules Guerin.

Henry H. Richardson (Louisiana 1838—Massachusetts 1886)
Education: 1859, Harvard University; 1860, École des Beaux Arts, Paris.
Among Major Works: 1872, Trinity Church, Boston; 1880, Ames Gate Lodge, Mass.; 1884–1888, Allegheny County Courthouse, Pittsburgh; 1885–1887, Glessner House, Chicago; 1885–1887, Marshall Field Wholesale Store, Chicago.

Richardson is important for the expression of stalwart masonry design and in the development of the shingled style in American domestic architecture. His were rambling, spacious houses characterized by a free flowing asymmetrical plan with a keen appreciation of the colors and textures of local materials. He illustrated how an indigenous architecture could develop out of a historical style like the Romanesque. Richardson was the first important American architect to take an interest in functional buildings such as railroad stations and warehouses.

Castle Hill Light House—1885–1886
Location: Newport Rhode Island.
Status: Unbuilt.
Hitchcock calls this the Agassiz Lighthouse. In 1874 the naturalist Alexander Agassiz (1835–1910) purchased the thirty-acre peninsula called Castle Hill on the eastern side of the entrance to Narragansett Bay at Newport. In the winter of 1874–1875 he built a summer house there, adding his famous laboratory in 1877.

Congress first appropriated money for a lighthouse on Castle Hill in 1875, and on August 4, 1886, again appropriated $10,000 for light and foghorn if a site could be obtained at no expense. The land was deeded by Agassiz to the government on June 10, 1887, provided that the "Light House and fog signal station shall be constructed upon plans and specifications agreed upon . . . and annexed hereto."

James F. O'Gorman, H. H. Richardson and His Office—Selected Drawings [exhibit catalogue], Harvard College Library, 1974.

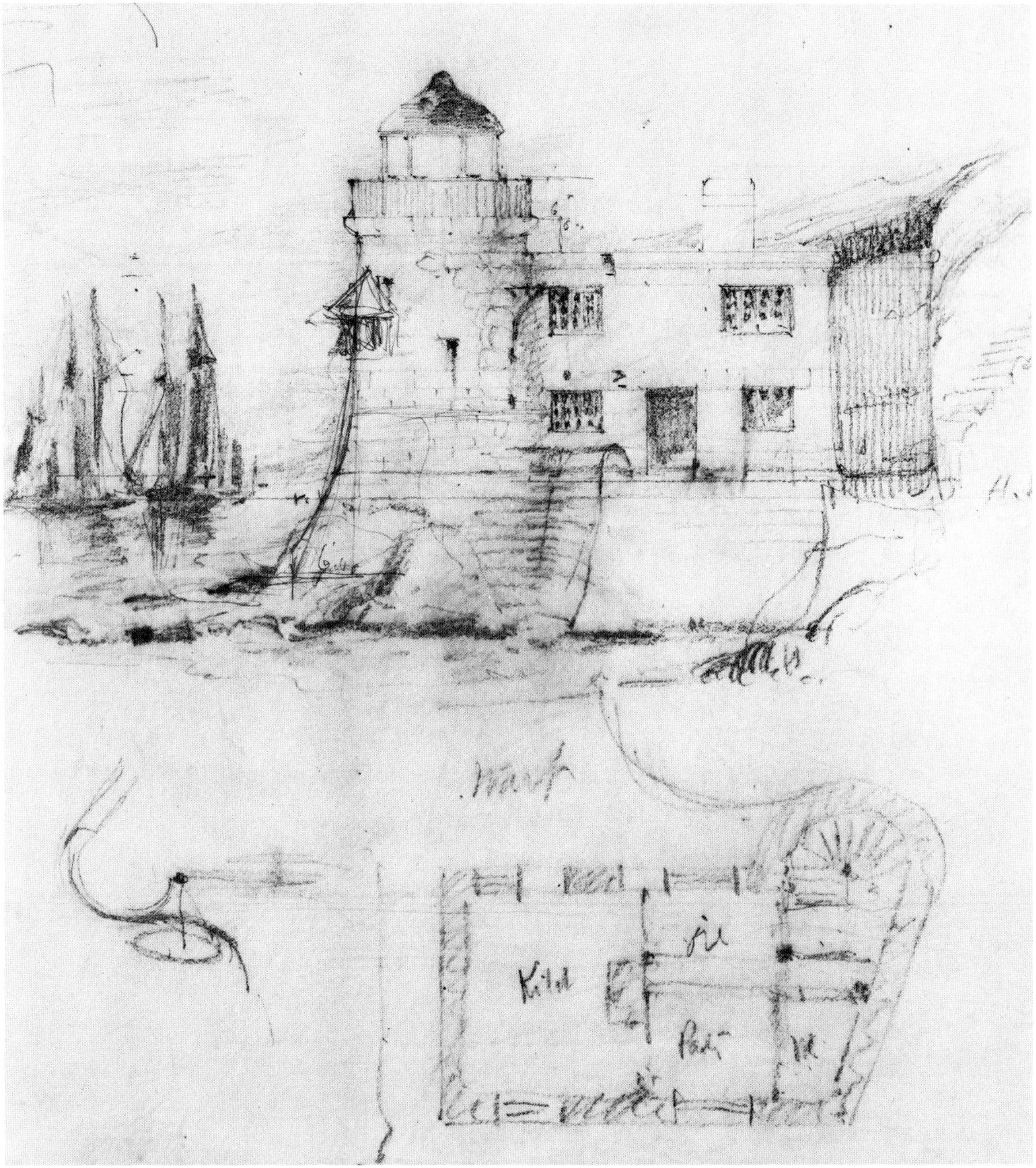

318. Castle Hill Lighthouse. Sketch.

Brookline Town Hall—1870
Location: Massachusetts.
Status: Unsuccessful competition entry.
The design is most Richardsonian in the indication of rugged masonry and simple dark and light polychromy. But the breadth of treatment and the lack of dependence on carved detail for interest are also characteristic. Significant, too, is the essential unimportance in the total effect of the documents from which he casually drew. This total effect is not Romanesque, except in feeling, and the elements borrowed from the High Gothic and the Late are so stylized as to be barely recognizable. This Town Hall, if executed, would undoubtedly have been worthy of Richardson's canon as his earlier works are not.

The massing is picturesque and even asymmetrical in detail. The late mediaeval silhouette is really the outline of the whole building and not merely of an attached tower, as at Worcester. The central part of the façade has a low loggia of pointed arches above which are the mullioned windows of the principal hall. This arrangement follows a conventional French scheme and is obviously suited to the function of the building. Over this broad central section of the façade, a curved saddle-back hip roof rises from a heavy corbelled cornice to the belfry crowning the ridge. A great stone-mullioned dormer breaks the front of this roof. The side sections of the façade have plainer cornices at a lower level and flatter roofs. A large corbelled chimney on one side balances a corbelled turret above a stone balcony on the other. High pointed gables rise from the middle of each of the end façades.

Van Rensselaer, H. H. Richardson and His Works, 1888.

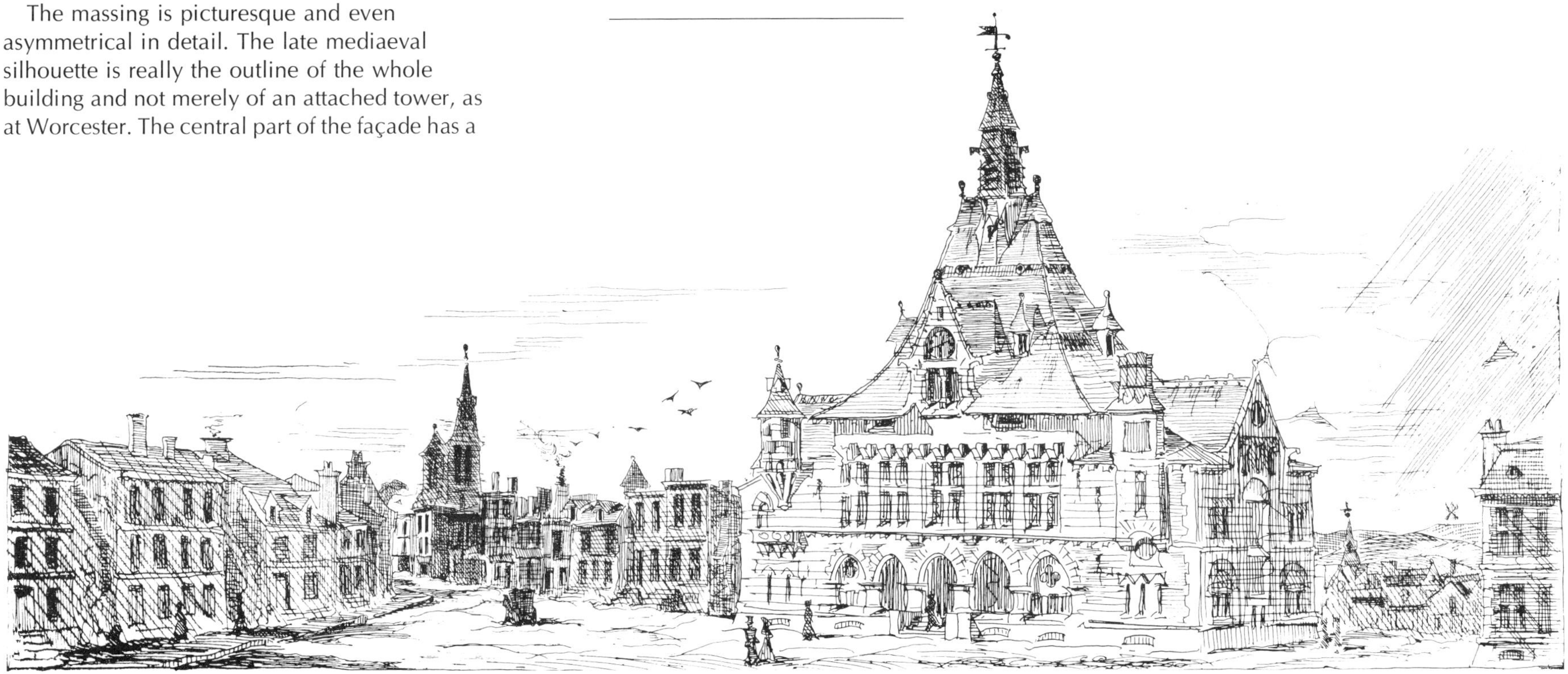

319. Brookline Town Hall. Sketch.

John Wellborn Root (Georgia 1850—Chicago 1891)
Education: 1869, BS, Civil Engineering, New York University.
Among Major Works: 1881–1882, Montauk Building, Chicago (utilized significant improvements in foundation and fireproofing design of skyscrapers); 1885–1888, The Rookery, Chicago; 1889–1892, Monadnock Building, Chicago (one of the last great masonry skyscrapers); 1889–1894, Reliance Building, Chicago (one of the earliest glass and steel skyscrapers); 1891, at the time of Root's death, the firm was at work on plans for the Chicago World's Columbian Exposition of 1893.

From 1866 to 1869, worked as unpaid apprentice in the office of James Renwick, Jr., N.Y.C.; 1872, became chief draftsman in the office of Peter B. Wight (Carter, Drake & White), Chicago; 1873, joined with Daniel Burnham to establish the firm of Burnham & Root, Chicago; 1873–1891, the firm of Burnham & Root was responsible for some 250 structures during the great period of Chicago commercial architecture.

Root was one of the first to discern clearly in the skyscraper type, the manifold challenges of engineering, human scale and amenities, and appropriate architectural expression.
Donald Hoffman, *The Architecture of John Wellborn Root,* 1973.

When Chicago was finally settled upon as the location for the World's Columbian Exposition, it was natural that Root, as the foremost Chicago architect, should be appointed consulting architect (August 1890); on Sept. 4, 1890, at his request, this appointment was changed to include his partner [Daniel Burnham]. While to the latter belongs the credit for the formation of the board of architects and the generalship of the whole, to Root must go much of the credit for the final choice of a lakeside site and the settlement of the basic plan. The World's Fair activity was the climax of his life. It was after a dinner to the architects that he caught a cold which rapidly developed into the pneumonia from which he died.

John Garraty and Edward James,
Dictionary of American Biography, 1974.

World's Columbian Exposition—1890
Location: Washington Park, Chicago.
Status: Too costly, and site was changed to nearby Jackson Park on the waterfront.
Among all the sketches and drawings which remain to show us Root's first tentative ideas of Fair architecture, perhaps the one for the main building at Washington Park is the most characteristic and suggestive. It was this building which was dubbed the Kremlin. The design was made in hot haste at the behest of directors. Root laughed at it as a *tour de force,* knowing it too costly to carry out as it stands, the great central tower being five or six hundred feet high. But it was a superb dream, a magnificent outburst of poetic energy. The building surrounds three sides of an oblong court. The two wings and the corners are low—two stories high, under a succession of low hipped roofs. From the centre, at the end of the court, rises an immense octagonal tower, sweeping straight upward for more than half its height, the tiled roof thence sloping straight to a point.

Abridged from Harriet Monroe, **John Wellborn Root**, 1966.

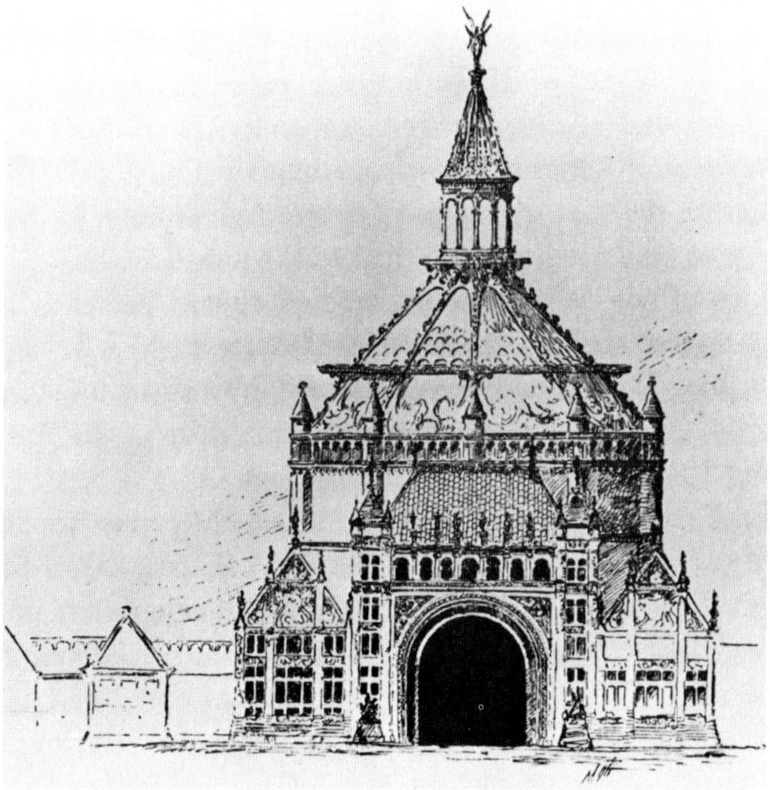

320. World's Columbian Exposition. Washington Park Site. Study for Central Pavilion of Main Building Dubbed "The Kremlin."

World's Columbian Exposition—1890
Location: Lake Front Site.
Status: Study sketch.
Root made many rapid sketches of Fair buildings for his own amusement; Burnham said they tended toward variety in style and color. The building springs over one of the canals, and, as a "lighter and more ornamental" structure, its Romanesque elements quickly dissolve into the spirit of the early Renaissance in France. Much of the interior appears to be given to observation decks: the building looks outward. The color probably is red, and certainly not white.

Abridged from Donald Hoffman, **The Architecture of John Wellborn Root,** 1973.

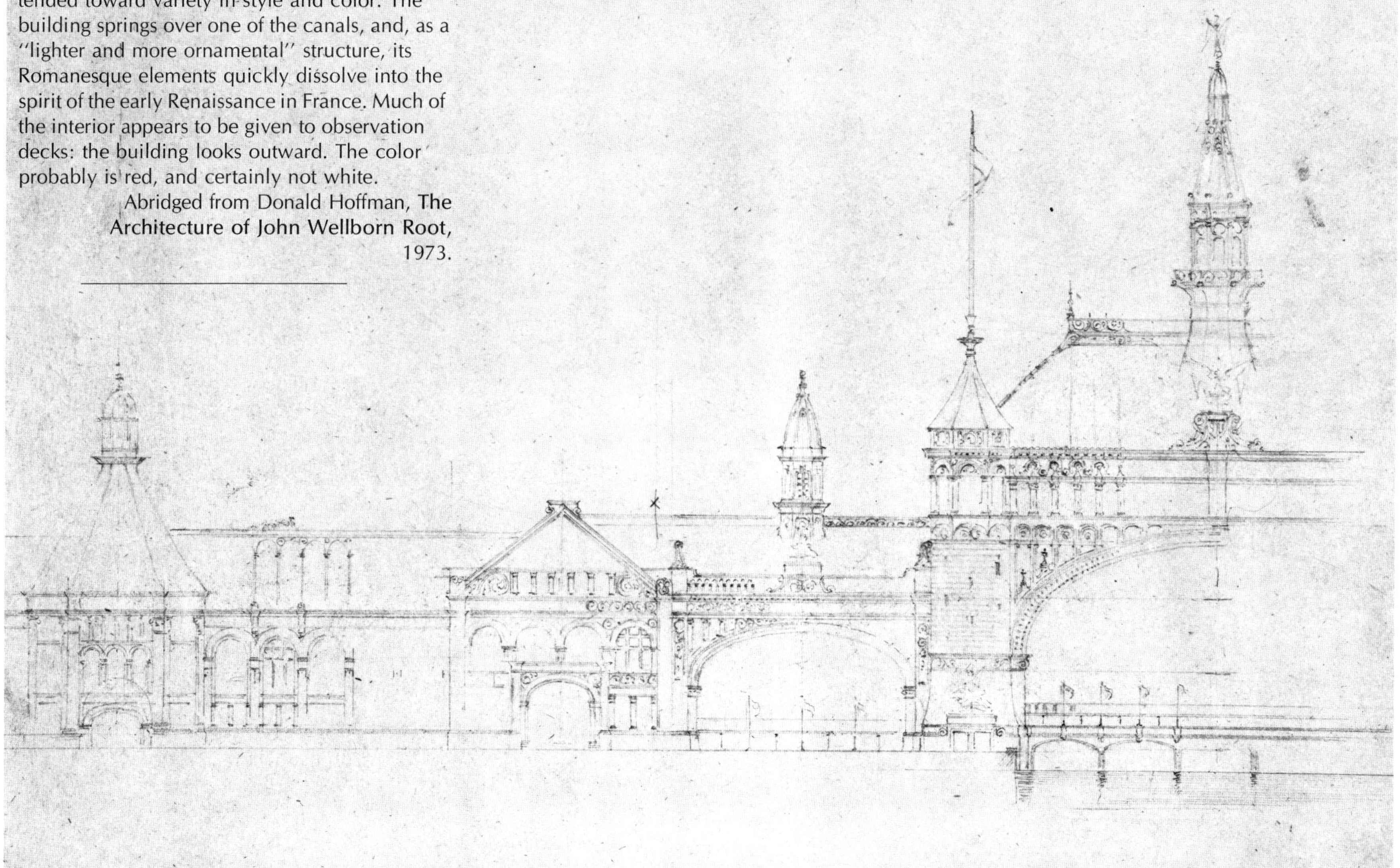

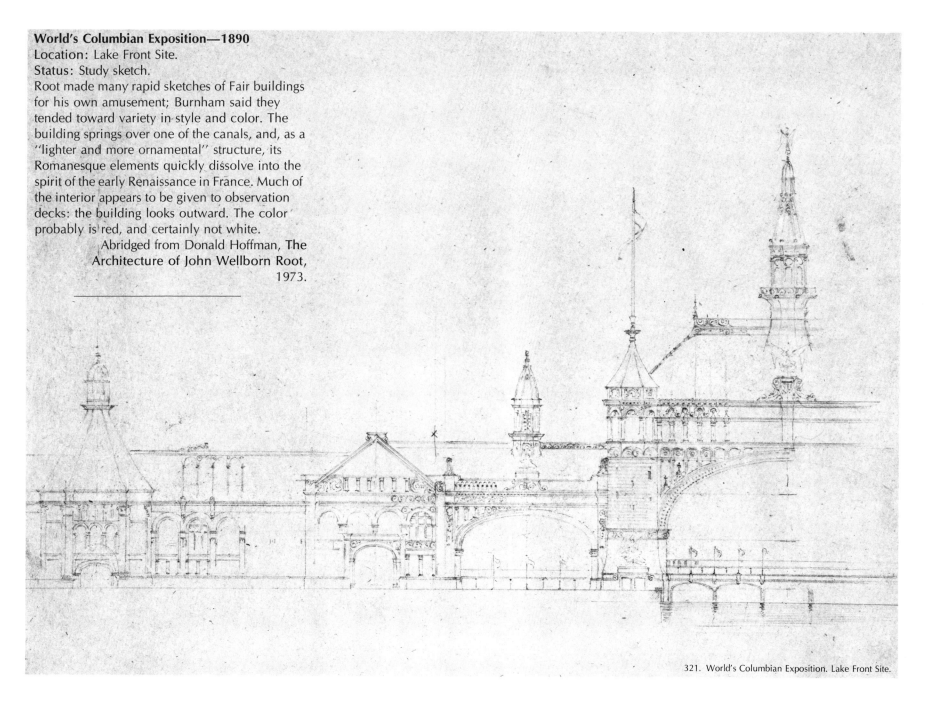

321. World's Columbian Exposition. Lake Front Site.

Fine Arts Museum—1890
Location: Lake Front site.
Status: Root died, and the concept was abandoned by the Art Institute as it required too much modification.
In August 1890 Root began to make studies for an Art Museum which would remain on the Lake Front site as a permanent civic institution after the Fair had ended. [This project was to be Root's last important work].

In a letter to his wife dated August 10, 1890, he wrote: "I have just finished a very satisfactory day on the design for the World's Fair Art Building. I really think I've got a good thing of it. I've been keeping it in my mind for some time till I could get a long quiet day to get it out; and a long quiet beautiful day this has been." Two days later he wrote again: "I have spent the day on the Art Building, which I solemnly promise to make a joy. The only thing I dread about it is that, like some other things; it may be too good to be true."

The building was to be of pink granite, with a basement of reddish brown. The lower part of the sloping roof was to be of brown Spanish tiles, and the upper two fifths of glass, for lighting purposes, vertically paned and crested with an ornamental ridge. The first study which remains shows a dome over the central section of the building, rising behind the low roof above the entrance.

[Root experimented with numerous variations until establishing the final design.] The most notable thing about this monumental design in the Romanesque is the grace, the lightness of it. It attains the dignity, the majesty which is recognizably within the scope of this style, but it attains as well an exquisite lyric beauty. The word "massive," which is descriptive of much of the most successful work in the Romanesque, would scarcely be applied to this building. It has great strength, but it has also a delicacy which is expressed, as a rule, only by the most successful designs in the classic.

[In December the final drawings were presented.] The design was never carried out; the officers of the Art Institute found that, owing to the need of more light and other causes, they could not use it without such serious modifications as might be injurious, so they abandoned it altogether. If Root had lived, doubtless he would have re-studied his idea many times before pronouncing it complete; but it is probable that he would have clung to the main lines of it.

Abridged from Harriet Monroe, **John Wellborn Root**, 1966.

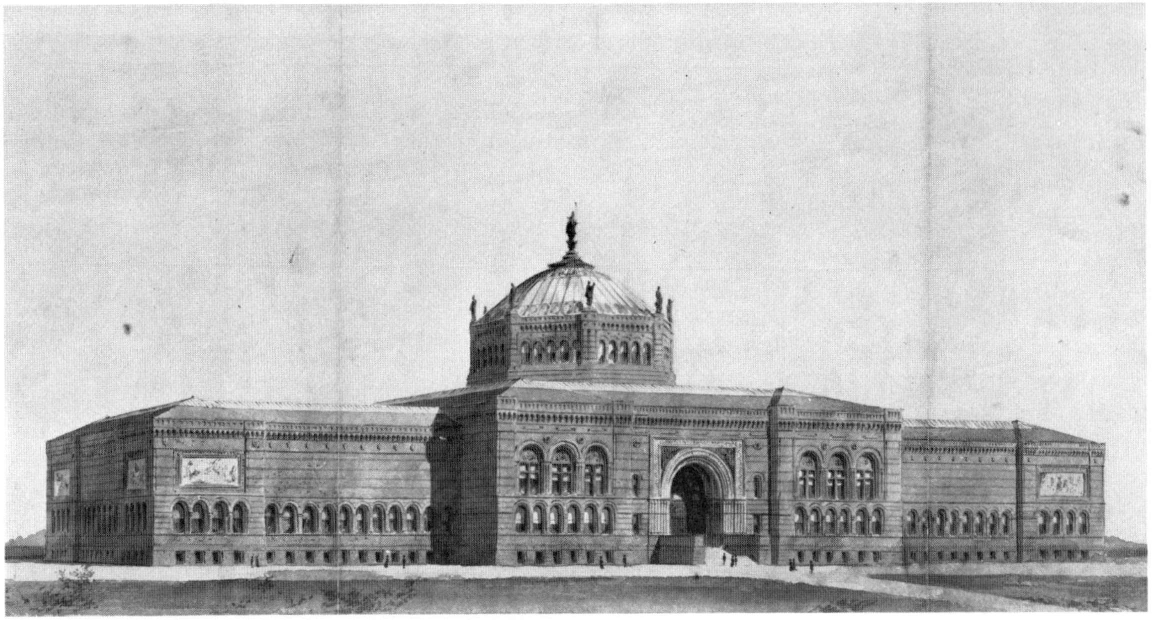

322. Fine Arts Museum, Chicago. Perspective of the First Design. Rendering by Paul C. Lautrup.

323. Fine Arts Museum, Chicago. Front Façade of the Final Design.

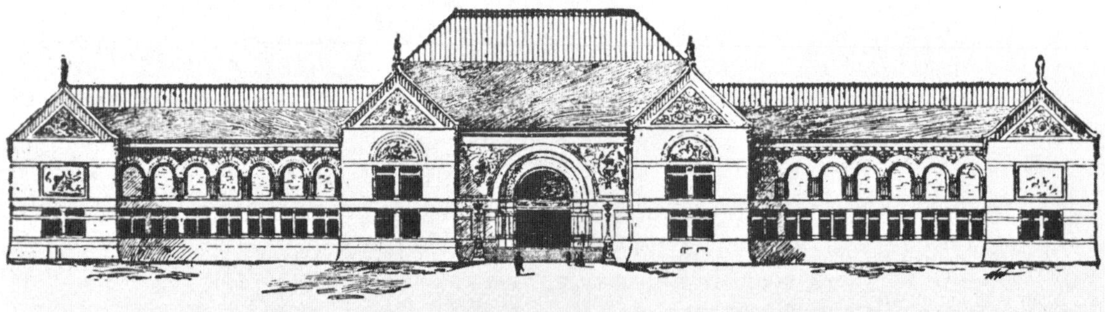

324. Graphic Arts Center. Aerial View of Model.

Paul Rudolph (Kentucky 1918—)
Residence: New York City.
Education: 1940, B Arch., Alabama Polytechnic Institute; 1947, M Arch., Harvard University.
Among Major Works: 1957, Riverview Junior-Senior High School, Sarasota, Fla.; 1957, Office Headquarters Building for the Blue Cross-Blue Shield, Boston; 1958, Art and Architecture Building for Yale University, New Haven; 1959, parking garage for 1500 automobiles for New Haven; 1968, Government Center including new City Hall, Library, Plaza, Police Station, New Haven.

Graphic Arts Center—1967

Location: New York City.
Status: Unbuilt.

In this proposal for a Graphic Arts Center, the West Side Drive would be lowered and bridged over by pedestrian walkways connecting the inner commercial areas with the residential towers located about the pier deck which extends 820 feet into the Hudson River. The complex includes high quality industrial spaces for legal and financial printers and color lithographers. This space is arranged to create a man-made hill forming a series of terraces for residential and commercial uses. At the base of this man-made hill, one level below grade, is the 520,000-square-foot trucking service floor. The second level is allocated for parking, as are three levels under the pier deck. The main pedestrian concourse is on the third level. Here one will be able to walk through a series of plazas and traffic-free streets onto the pier deck which will have an elementary school, a community center, a swimming pool, marina, and a series of restaurants and shops. Industrial space for the color lithographers is also contained on this and the next four floors. The space is constructed in such a way that every other floor is moveable or removeable. Five different ceiling heights are possible—a 9-foot ceiling suitable for office space; and 11-, 15-, 16- and 28-foot ceilings where appropriate. Above the lithography floors are seven floors for the legal and financial printers, and on top of these are two office towers. To complete the community concept are the 4,050 dwelling capsules gathered in clusters around their service cores.

Rudolph's dwelling unit is 60 feet long and 12 feet wide folded, but it tips out to 28 feet. The units themselves are arranged in a pinwheel and connected to the service core. "One of the good things about a pinwheel," says Rudolph, "is that it hides the repetitive nature of the building."

Apartments overlap so that the roof of a lower unit forms a terrace for the one above. Unlike other designers of dwelling capsules, Rudolph prefers to "hang," rather than "cage" his plug-ins. Steel trusses cantilevered from a central core carry 10 stories each by means of steel cables encased in concrete. The mobile units arrive on flat bed trucks, and "tip-outs" (added space within the standard 12 foot towing width) are unfolded and locked into place. The units are hoisted by hydraulic lifts attached to the main truss and are joined to adjacent sections and to the central core tower.

Abridged from "The Mobile Home is the 20th Century Brick," *Architectural Record,* CLVIII, April 1968.

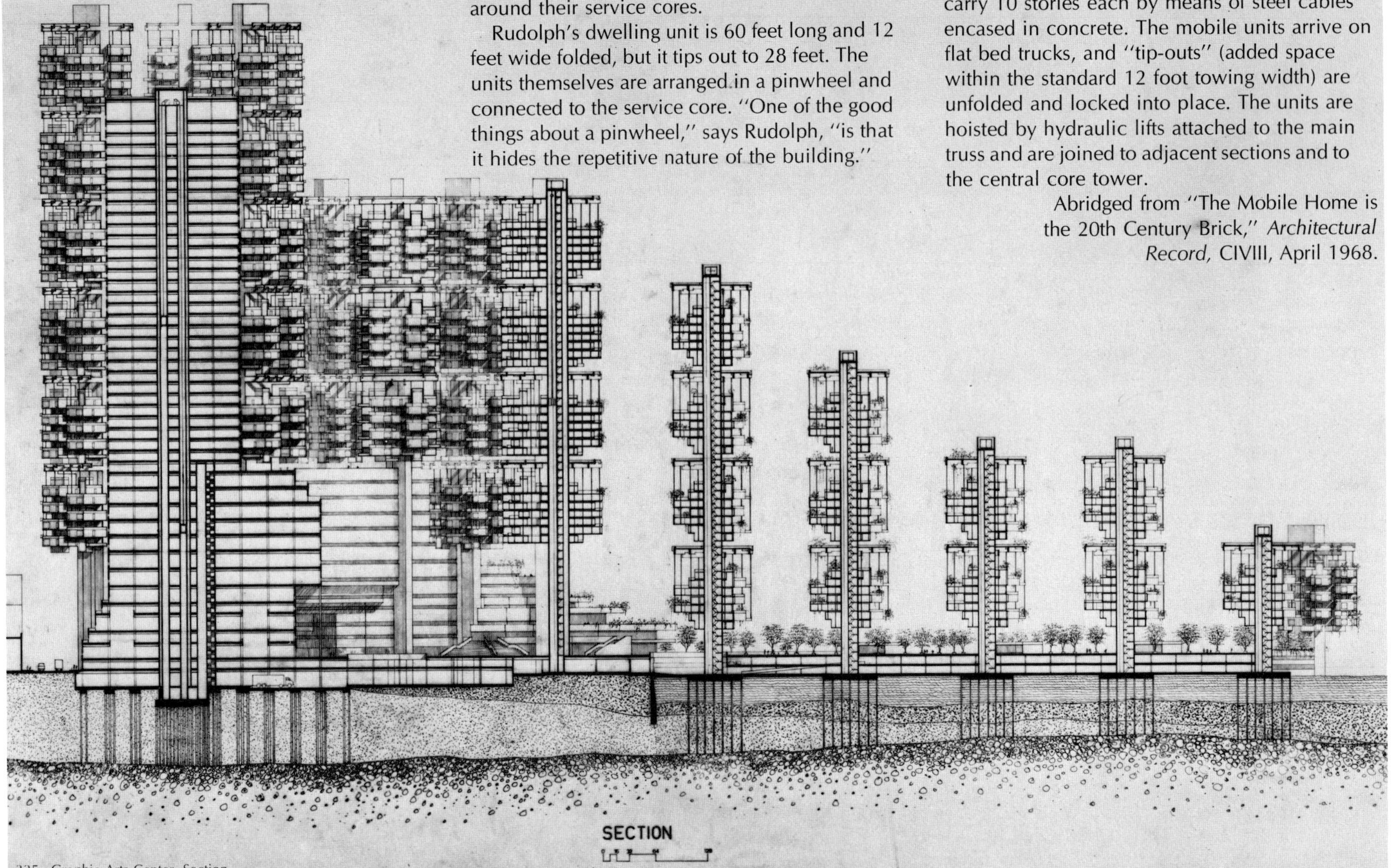

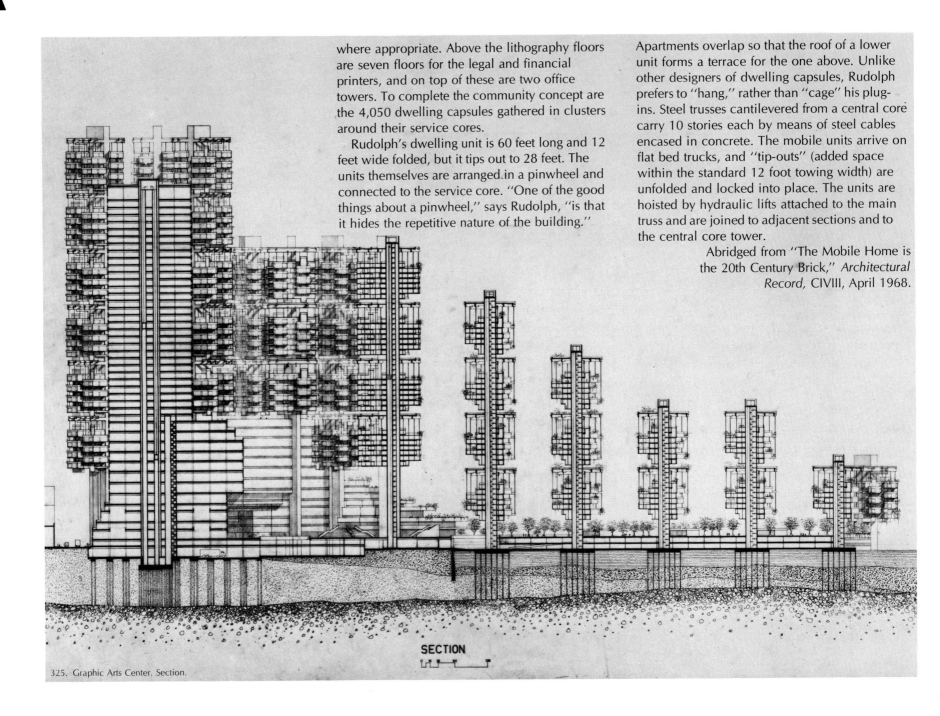

325. Graphic Arts Center. Section.

Moshe Safdie (Israel 1938—)
Residence: Montreal, Canada.
Education: 1955–1961, McGill University, Montreal.
Among Major Works: 1964–1967, Habitat '67, Montreal; 1970, Yeshivat Porat Joseph, Jerusalem; 1971, Coldspring, a "New-Town-in-Town," Baltimore, Md.; 1973, Master Plan, center of Stamford, Conn.; 1973, Hebrew Union College, Jerusalem.

San Francisco State College Student Union—1967
Location: San Francisco.
Status: Unbuilt because of opposition from the Trustees of the California State College System.
The location of the college union within the campus generated the building's organization; it was to be located at the crossroads of all paths of pedestrian movement on campus. Rather than divert pedestrian circulation around it, the massing and the organization of the building attempts to capture this movement, and direct it through the archlike structure.

The existing buildings around the campus green are primarily painted boxlike concrete frame structures, forming a hard edge to its pinestudded lawn. The Union was to be integrated with the campus green and not the surrounding structures. By extending up over the structure, making the building glass and grass, it would have been possible for students to climb and sit on the walls of the building, and for the park and structure to become one.

A method of construction was developed in which a small number of repetitive elements that could be mass produced and easily assembled on the site would be grouped in a variety of ways to form a hierarchy of spaces from the smallest to the largest required. We chose a single repetitive module with auxiliary floor slab elements.

Moshe Safdie.

326. San Francisco State College Student Union. Superimposed on Site.

327. San Francisco State College Student Union. Plan.

Rudolph M. Schindler (Vienna 1887—Los Angeles 1953)
Education: 1911, Diploma, Imperial Technical Institute, Vienna; 1914, Diploma, Academy of Arts, Vienna.
Among Major Works: 1926, beach house for Dr. Phillip Lovell, Newport Beach, Calif.; 1933, Oliver House, Los Angeles; 1934, Buck House, Los Angeles; 1935, Walker House, Los Angeles; Rodakiewicz House, Los Angeles.
Schindler had great interest in the possibilities of new materials and techniques, and a sensitive response to climate and site conditions.

Log House—1916

Location: Summer vacation spot.
Status: Prototype.

The scheme of a symmetrical pavilion with interlocking smaller volumes was of course Wrightian in flavour. But the way in which Schindler related his volumes was much more sculptural than most of Wright's designs of the Prairie years. By suspending the log-enclosed volume on recessed or projecting stone piers, Schindler makes the building float above the ground in a manner that is non-Wrightian (although it foreshadows Wright's Kaufmann house of 1936). Also non-Wrightian in its intensity is the self-conscious declaration of the log structure. Schindler not only thrusts the ends of the logs far out beyond the corners, he makes the floor joists and ceiling rafters plainly visible. His narrow horizontal windows are simply open spaces where the logs have been removed. Shortly after coming to Chicago, Schindler had become intrigued with modular planning: the design of the log house is the outgrowth of his horizontal and vertical use of a four foot module, which he was to employ, with minor refinements, in most of his later work.

David Gebhard, **Schindler**, 1972.

328. Plan for a Log House.

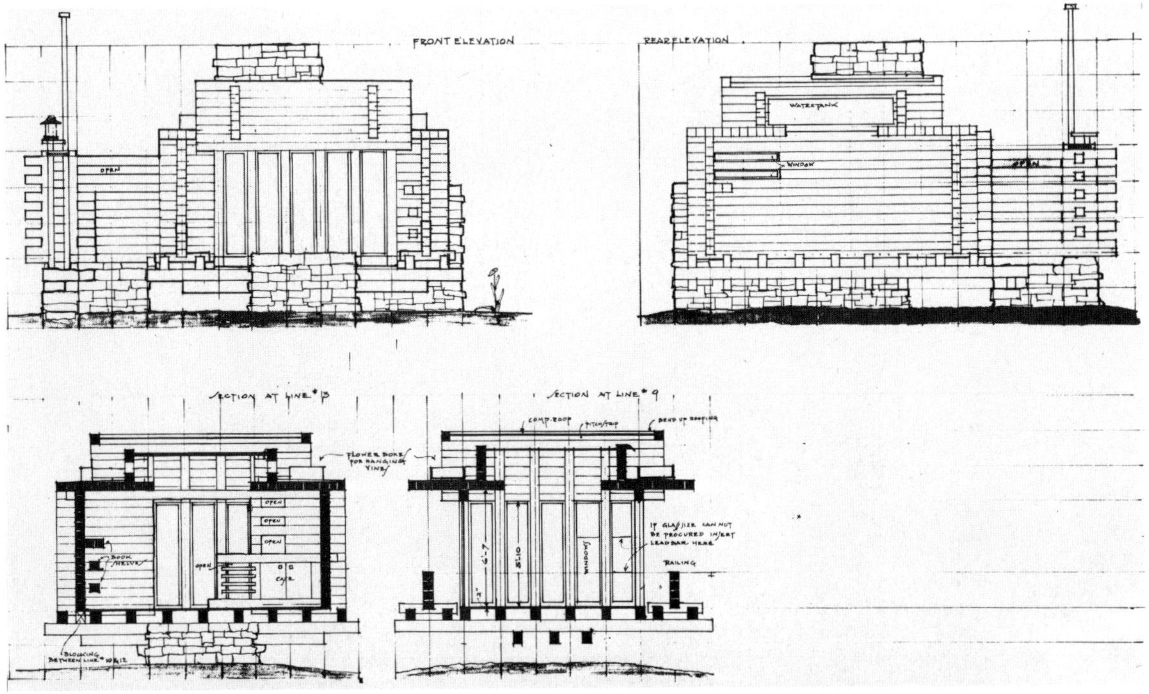

Translucent House—1927
Location: California.
Status: Unbuilt.
The Palos Verdes area enjoys a year-round cool climate; it is often enshrouded by fog and mist, and the winds from the ocean can be strong, continual and cold. The two elements needed to counter the adverse features of the climate are seclusion from the winds and the introduction of a maximum amount of light into the interior. Schindler easily solved the first problem by orienting the U-shaped courtyard so that its back was to the prevailing winds, and then by introducing sheltered spaces protected by partial walls and roofs. His solution to the light problem was to clothe the upper zone of the battened walls of the house with translucent glass, panels of which fold over and form the first eighteen inches of the flat roof, giving the impression of a horizontal roof plane floating over a glass area. While the metal, glass and wood walls and roof units were extremely advanced in design, the working drawings indicate that the house would nevertheless have been easily built with existing technology.

David Gebhard, Schindler, 1972.

329. Translucent House. Aerial View.

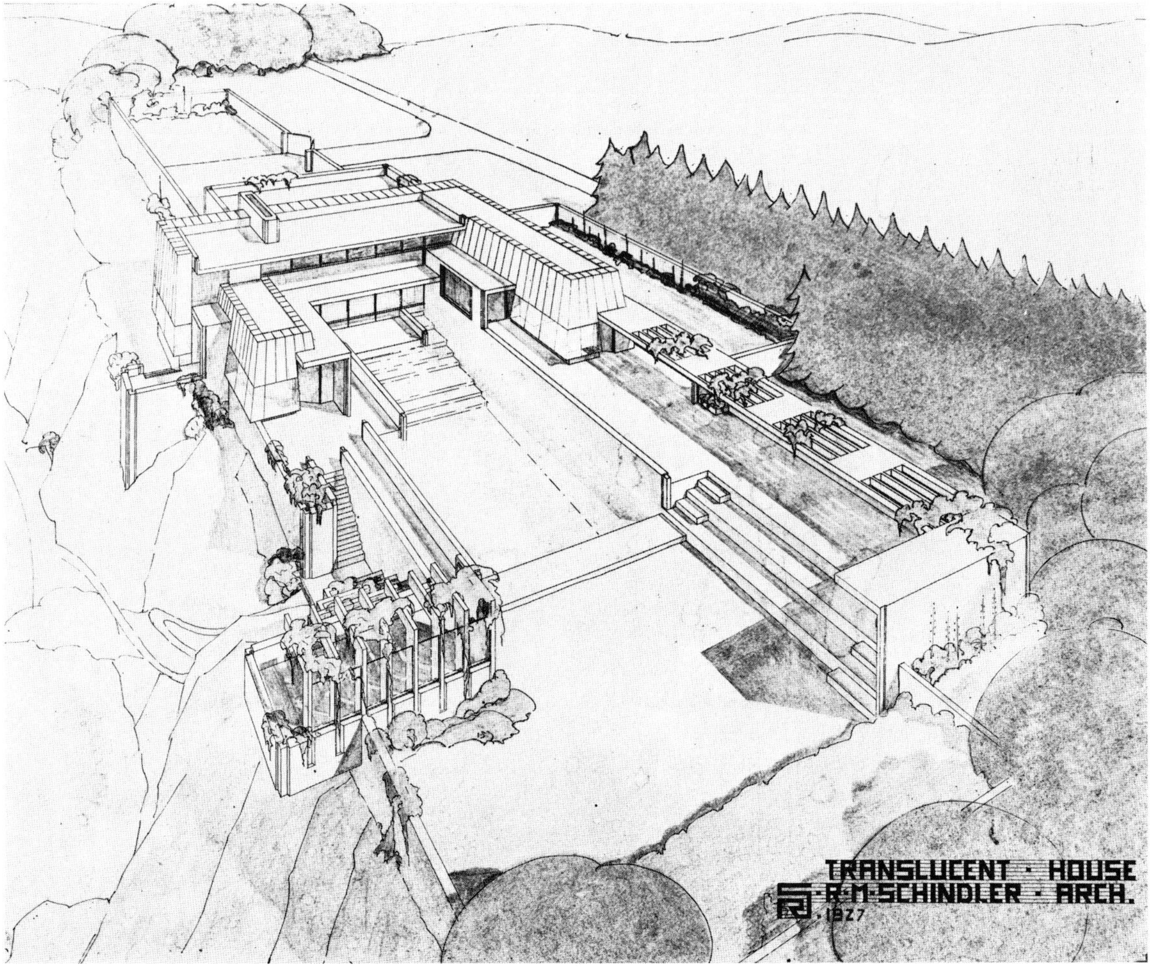

Charles Simonds (New York City 1945—)
Residence: New York City.
Education: 1967, BA, University of California, Berkeley; 1969, MFA, Rutgers University.
Among Major Works: 1970–1976, miniature clay "Dwellings" for an imaginary civilization of "little people" migrating through N.Y.C.; 1974, "Excavated and Reinhabited Tunnel Remains and Cairns," Art Park, Niagara Gorge, N.Y.; 1975, park-playlot-sculpture, East Second St., N.Y.C. (in cooperation with the Lower East Side Coalition for Human Housing).

The primary focus of my activities has been working in the streets of New York City.
Charles Simonds.

A Series of Living Structures
Life Architecture—1970
Status: Studies.

People Who Live in a Line

Their dwellings make a pattern on the earth as of a great tree laid flat, branching and forking according to their loves and hates, forming an ancestral record of life lived as an odyssey, its roots in a dark and distant past. . . .

When moved from one dwelling to the next, they left everything behind untouched, as a museum of personal effects. As dwelling followed dwelling, traces of a diminishingly distinct personal history remained.

Webs and thickets of old and new dwellings emerged creating strange cities that combined houses with ruins, gardens with parks, that exposed personal histories to everyone's view. The past was a temptation and a threat, the begettor of insanities. Periodically messengers returned from journeys into the past with maps documenting some large meeting place of dwellings that had occurred long ago, and this discovery would be used to explain why certain families had maintained their beliefs, shared genetic traits, where feuds had originated.

330. People Who Live in a Line.

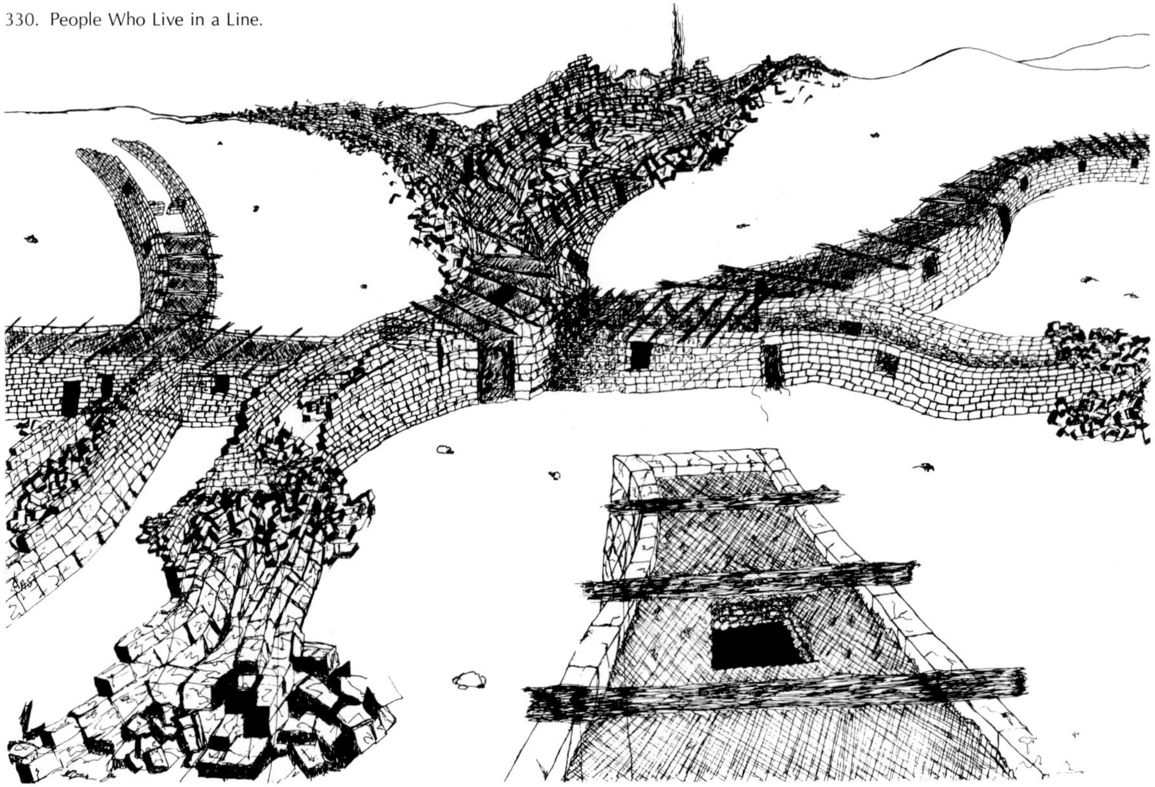

People Who Live in a Circle

There is a warning tale—a troubling memory—repeated every year among of a child who was born unhappily spinning toward the future instead of turning clockwise toward his past. For some time his confusion went unnoticed. But when he came of age, he joined in the rebirth and was caught in the whirling dance. Suddenly he was spun, wrenched and twisted out of the circle—dying horribly alone.

lives had two aspects: the first was the daily keeping of time, placing events in space and history, merging past and present; the second was the yearly concentration of birth and growth energy into one ritual at the winter solstice. The first aspect governed the daily task of reconstructing the new dwelling from the remains of the old. This effort was a recapitulation and re-working of personal memories into myth and history. The second, ritual aspect re-enacted original creation in a dizzying celebration of sexual possibility.

This gathering took place in the dome-womb, at the center of the earth-dwelling universe that could be entered through the top. The cyclical

331. People Who Live in a Circle.

dwellings were built around it in two concentric rings. As portions of the structure were abandoned, they were sealed up and left to deteriorate; after one revolution was completed they were dug up and rebuilt. The dwelling functioned palpably as a personal and cosmological clock, its encircling architecture operating as an elaborate sundial.

The continual sifting and sorting of the rubble from the previous dwellings formed an uroborus in which the present devoured the past. Some things recovered were collected and reused; some were reminisced over and became artifacts or keepsakes.

People Who Live in an Ascending Spiral ◎

◎ believed in a world entirely created by their own wills, in which nature's realities were of little concern. Their dwelling formed an ascending spiral—with the past, constantly buried, serving as a building material for the future.

◎ aspired towards an ecstatic death. Their goal was to achieve both the greatest possible height and to predict the very moment of collapse, the moment when the last of their resources would be consumed and their death inevitable.

The monument relentlessly consumed all material goods. Property had importance only as it related to the construction. Life was merely a function of shelter and height. As the highest elevations were reached, and fewer laborers were needed to continue, large groups jumped voluntarily from the forward edge of the structure, giving their bodies to the task of pushing the edifice higher.

The dwelling's past was reconstructed by a mathematical model to be used in dynamic relationship to its future. The slightest error might mean failure, which was, in fact, inevitable, so that the work process itself was punctuated by pangs of doubt that led to depression, and finally to extinction.

Abridged from Charles Simonds, Three Peoples, 1975.

332. People Who Live in an Ascending Spiral.

The Growth Brick and Growth House—1975
Status: Prototype.

The Growth Brick: A building unit of earth with seeds inside.

The Growth House: As the seeds sprout growth transforms the built structure; the dwelling is converted from shelter to food and is harvested and eaten.

Charles Simonds.

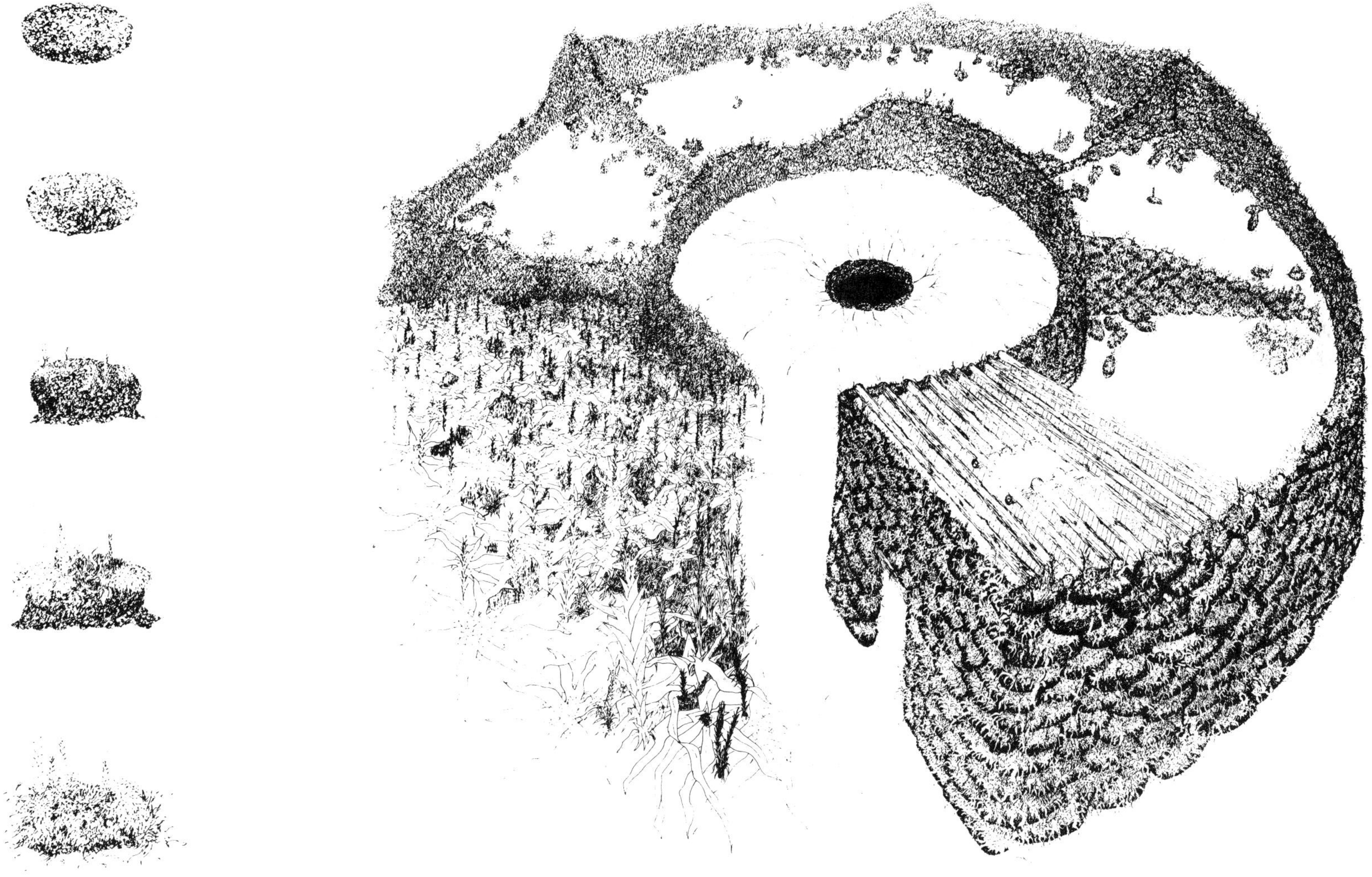

333. The Growth Brick and Growth House.

Franklin Webster Smith (Boston 1825–1911)
Education: No formal architectural training.
Among Major Works: 1888–1889, Pompeia or House of Pansa, Florida, a full scale completely furnished reconstruction of one of the villas described in Bulwer-Lytton's *The Last Days of Pompeii;* 1898, Halls of the Ancients, in an old skating rink in Washington, D.C.

Franklin Smith was interested in concrete mixtures, and experimented with the use of crushed coquina shell to strengthen the compound. Smith had been an early abolitionist, a founder of the Republican Party in Massachusetts, and a founder of the Y.M.C.A. in America.

The Aggrandisement of Washington—1891
Location: Washington, D.C.
Status: Unbuilt.
Additional Credit: James Renwick of Renwick, Aspinwall and Russell.

On the threshold of a new century it was time for Americans to "pass onward toward nobler aims than mere financial and material aggregation."

To remedy the nation's cultural and intellectual inferiority Mr. Smith, a former hardware merchant, proposed one of the most grandiose schemes that has ever been seriously suggested. His intention was to transform Washington, D.C., into a capital of such beauty and cultural advantage that never again would an American be tempted to go abroad for artistic or intellectual reasons. To the contrary, all Europe would flock from its shattered monuments and art treasures to a new Athens on the Potomac whose Periclean glory would symbolize a second and better great age of democracy.

"Washington must become a glory of the Republic," he said, "beyond its possession of national force, in its resources for knowledge, its grandeur of art and architecture."

Nor was this only the idle dream of a crackpot. Smith's Petition to Congress relative to his proposal for National Galleries of History and Art was presented to the Senate on February 12, 1900, by Senator Hoar of Massachusetts. It was ordered printed in 5,000 copies as Senate Document No. 209, 56th Congress, First Session. It was supported, as letters to Smith indicate, by a number of prominent men from all over the country.

On the hill at the head of Twenty-fourth Street, where once stood the Naval Observatory and now stands the United States Naval Hospital, Smith proposed to build an American Acropolis. At the summit, answering with its lofty pediment the grand dome of the Capitol, was to stand a great Memorial Temple of the Presidents of the United States, an exact replica of the Parthenon but one-half larger. On either side of this central temple were to stand smaller reproductions of the Theseion at Athens for the Army and Navy or for the Sons and Daughters of the American Revolution.

Behind the three main temples, with an 800-foot colonnade (imitated from the Forum at Pompeii) stretching along the Potomac, would rise a Gallery of American History displaying paintings and models and relics of the glorious development of the country and of its peaceful crafts. From the magnificent portal of the Parthenonic memorial temple would extend toward the Capitol a *via sacra* of American democracy bordered with statues of the great and good.

Terraced down the slope in front of the Acropolis, four on each side of the *via sacra,* were to stand eight galleries, each one representing in its architecture and contents one of the eight great civilizations of the past: Egyptian, Assyrian, Greek, Roman, Byzantine, Medieval, Saracenic, and East Indian. Each of the eight galleries was to be 500 feet square, covering six acres, and each would be built around a central court.

Since walking through so many miles of gallery would be hard on the feet (especially on concrete floors), Mr. Smith charitably suggested the installation of slowly moving seats, some facing each way, on which the visitor would be effortlessly drawn along the main corridors.

In the side corridors were to be casts and models illustrating the statuary and architecture and domestic furnishings of past ages. But unlike the museums of Europe, the National Galleries were to have no broken or imperfect objects. Everything was to be restored to its original state. Smith thus planned to ransack the galleries of Europe for objects for reproduction. Whereas each of them had only a few great works, his galleries would have all.

Adjacent to the galleries, on the land near the river, there would be a Park Istoria or historical park. Here the lofty castle of Rheinstein would look down on the Potomac as once on the Rhine. A Roman *castrum* or fort would guard the reproduction of the Pompeian forum. The Washington Monument (an obelisk) would be embellished by an avenue of sphinxes at its bottom, and nearby would rise the Great Sphinx and the Pyramids of Cheops (they could be hollow and used for auditoriums or storehouses). Adjacent to these would rise a new National Museum and a glass and steel National Pavilion.

Not far away a series of houses of all nations, modeled on those built by Viollet le Duc for the Paris Exposition of 1867, would be (as Smith phrased it) "the utmost compensation for the great majority of people, who in the limits of economy cannot range the earth for either study or pastime." The little island of Analostan in the Potomac was to be transformed into an Isola Bella ornamented with a Chaldean Tower at the summit, the Hanging Gardens of Babylon, a Roman bath, an Italian palace around a columned court, and "full sized concrete models of Stonehenge, Etrurian tombs, Tiryns and Mycenae, the primitive architecture of Greece, the Catacombs."

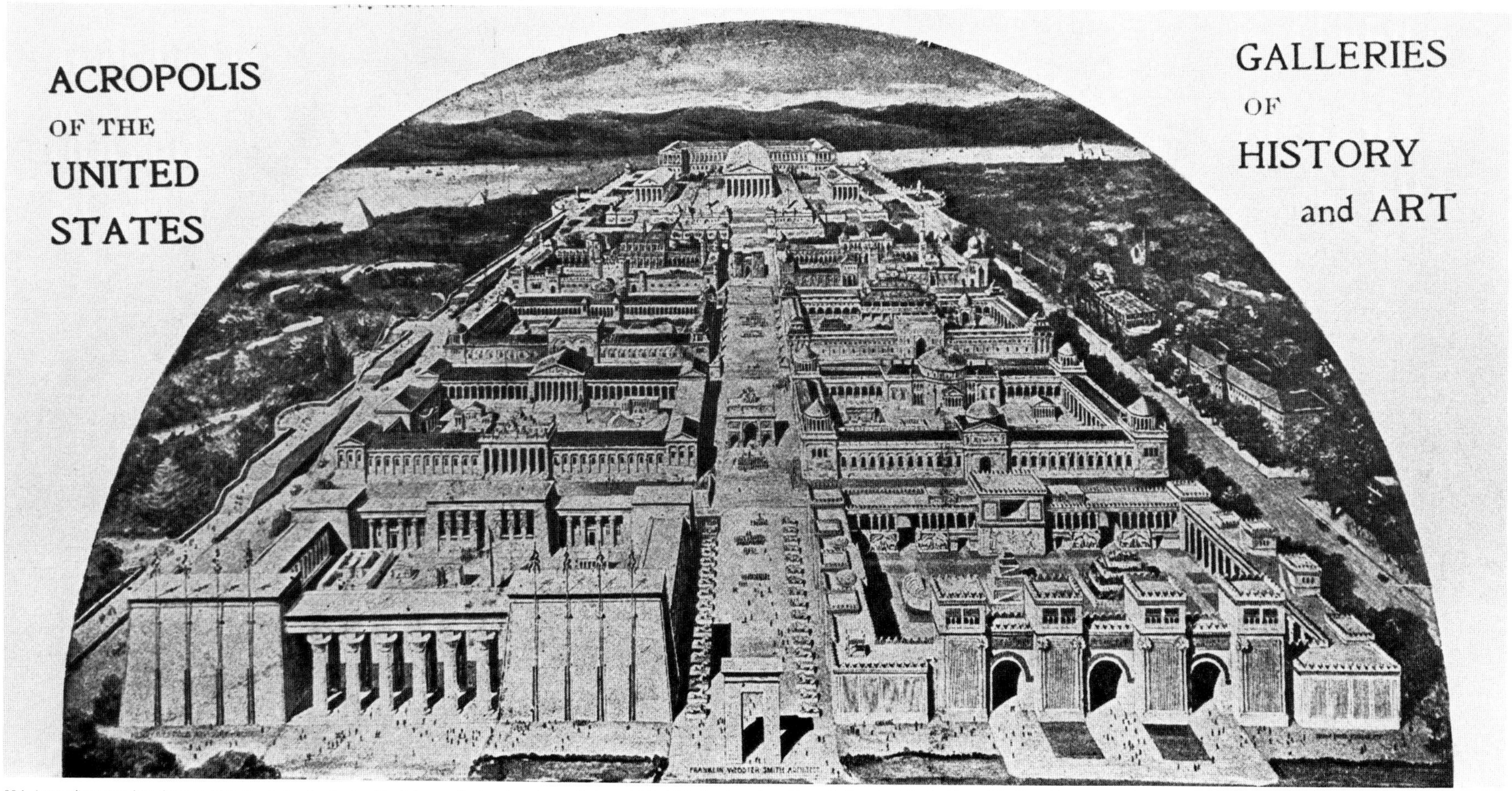

334. Aggrandisement of Washington, D.C. Situated on the Banks of the Potomac, the American Acropolis (at rear) Would Be Dominated by a Memorial Temple of the President of the United States. On Each Side of the Via Sacra (center) Were to Stand Immense Galleries and Courts Representing the Eight Great Civilizations of the Past.

Pennsylvania Avenue was to be improved. The ramshackle buildings along it were to be condemned; new classical buildings were to be erected; and colonnades twenty feet wide were to be built along much of it to protect pedestrians from rain and sun. Just in front of the Capitol the avenue was to be spanned by a copy of the Brandenburg Gate as a memorial to Abraham Lincoln. The Pennsylvania Railroad Station (since removed) was to be reconstructed on a new site on the plan of the Forum of Trajan with a Column of Peace (Trajan's Column) in a central plaza.

Sixteenth Street was to be broadened and ennobled into Executive Avenue. Though the old White House was to be retained as a national shrine, a new one, on much more impressive classical lines but with more than a hint of the Palace of Versailles, would be built arching over the new Executive Avenue. Within its confines would be extensive gardens and a mansion for visiting celebrities.

Mr. Smith labored over this project for fifty years, until 1906 when all of his projects—in Washington, Saratoga Springs, and St. Augustine—were foreclosed.

Abridged from Curtis Dahl in *American Heritage,* VII, June 1956.

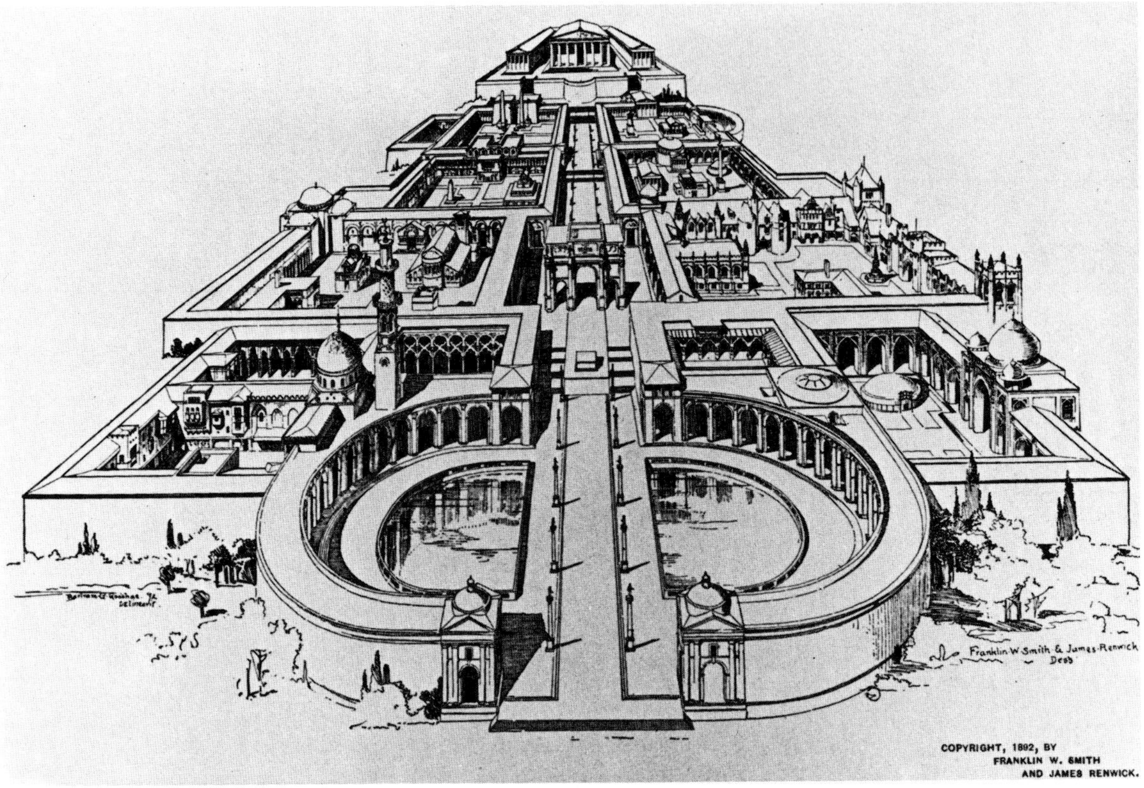

335. Aggrandisement of Washington, D.C. Rendering "gratuitously made by Mr. Bertram G. Goodhue of Boston, architect."

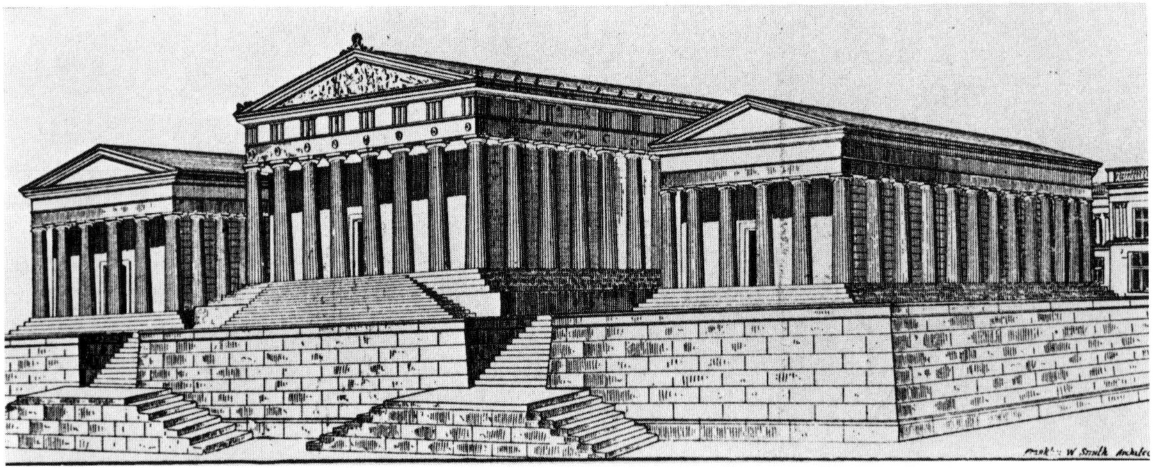

336. Aggrandisement of Washington, D.C. A Full Scale Replica of the Parthenon in Athens was planned as a Memorial Hall of Presidents of the United States.

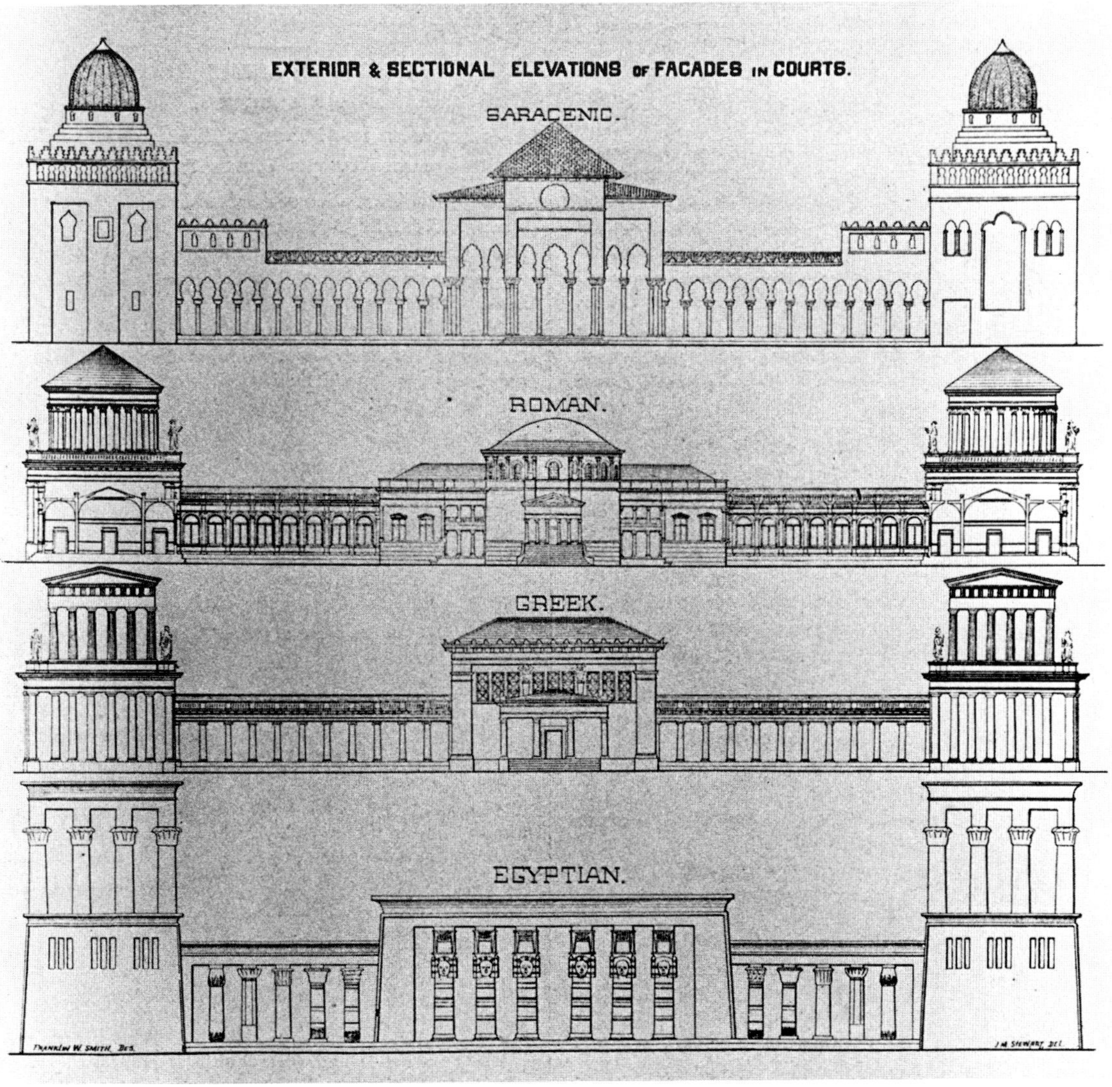

337. The Aggrandisement of Washington, D.C. Exterior and Sectional Elevations of Facades in Courts.

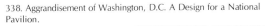

338. Aggrandisement of Washington, D.C. A Design for a National Pavilion.

339. Aggrandisement of Washington, D.C. Rossini's Restoration of the Villa of Cassius, with Additions by Franklin W. Smith.

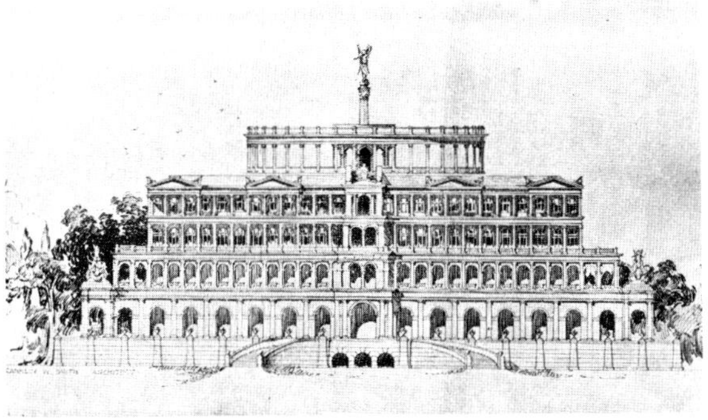

Robert Smithson (New Jersey 1938—Texas 1973)
Education: Art Students League; Brooklyn Museum School.
Among Major Works: 1969, "Asphalt Rundown", in a quarry near Rome, Italy; 1970, "Partially Buried Woodshed", Kent State University, Ohio; 1970, "The Spiral Jetty", Great Salt Lake, Utah; 1971, "Spiral Hill", Emmen, Holland; 1973, "Amarillo Ramp", Amarillo, Texas (died in a plane crash while working on this project).

Dallas-Fort Worth Regional Airport—1967
Location: Texas.
Status: The firm which hired Smithson lost the contract and the projects he planned were not built.
[In 1966 Robert Smithson was hired as artist consultant by Tippetts-Abbett-McCarthy-Stratton (Engineers and Architects), the firm which was designing the Dallas–Fort Worth Regional Airport. Smithson planned a series of earthworks on the fringes of the airfield which would have incorporated projects by Robert Morris, Sol LeWitt, and other artists, in addition to himself.]

The future air terminal exists both in terms of mind and thing. It suggests the infinite in a finite way. The straight lines of landing fields and runways bring into existence a perception of "perspective" that evades all our conceptions of nature. The naturalism of seventeenth-, eighteenth- and nineteenth-century art is replaced by non-objective sense of site. The landscape begins to look more like a three dimensional map rather than a rustic garden. Aerial photography and air transportation bring into view the surface features of this shifting world of perspectives. The rational structures of buildings disappear into irrational disguises and are pitched into optical illusions. The world seen from the air is abstract and illusive. From the window of an airplane one can see drastic changes of scale, as one ascends and descends. The effect takes one from the dazzling to the monotonous in a short space of time—from the shrinking terminal to the obstructing clouds.

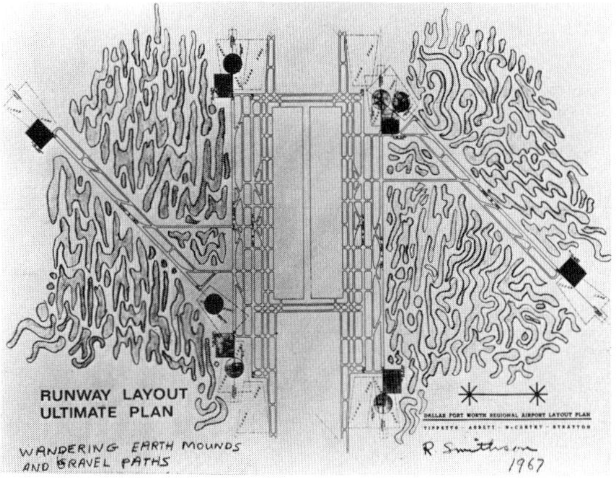

340. Dallas-Fort Worth Regional Airport. Runway Layout. Ultimate Plan. Wandering Earth Mounds and Gravel Paths.

Below this concatenation of aerial perceptions is the conception of the air terminal itself, firmly rooted in the earth. The principal runways and series of terminals will extend from 11,000 ft. to 14,000 ft., or about the length of Central Park. The outer limits of the terminal could be brought into consciousness by a type of art, which I will call *aerial art,* that could be seen from aircraft on takeoff and landing, or not seen at all.

On the boundaries of the taxiways, runways or approach "clear zones" we might construct "earthworks" or grid type frameworks close to the ground level. These aerial sites would not only be visible from arriving and departing aircraft, but they would also define the terminal's man-made perimeters in terms of landscaping.

The terminal complex might include a gallery (or aerial museum) that would provide visual information about where these aerial sites are situated. Diagrams, maps, photographs, and movies of the projects under construction could be exhibited—thus the terminal complex and its entire airfield site would expand its meaning from the central spaces of the terminal itself to the edges of the airfields.

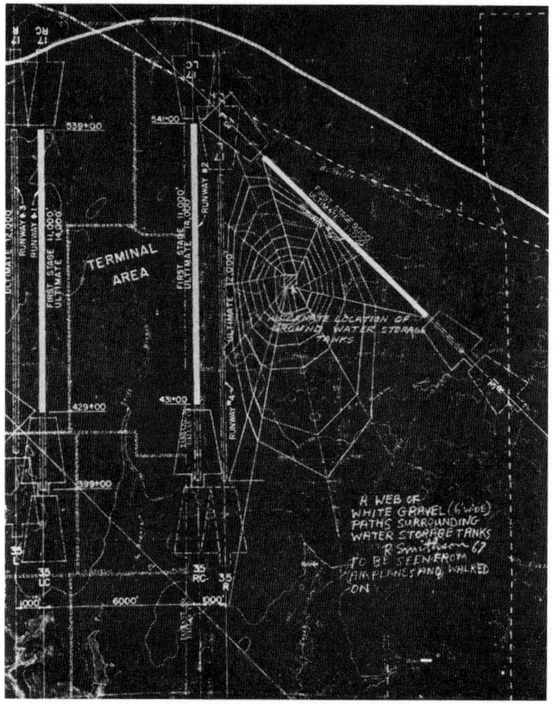

341. Dallas-Fort Worth Regional Airport. A Web of White Gravel Paths Surrounding Water Storage Tanks. To Be Seen from Airplanes and Walked on.

Excerpted from Robert Smithson in "Aerial Art," *Studio International,* CLXXVII, April 1969.

Art today is no longer an architectural afterthought, or an object to attach to a building after it is finished, but rather a total engagement with the building process from the ground up and from the sky down.

Robert Smithson.

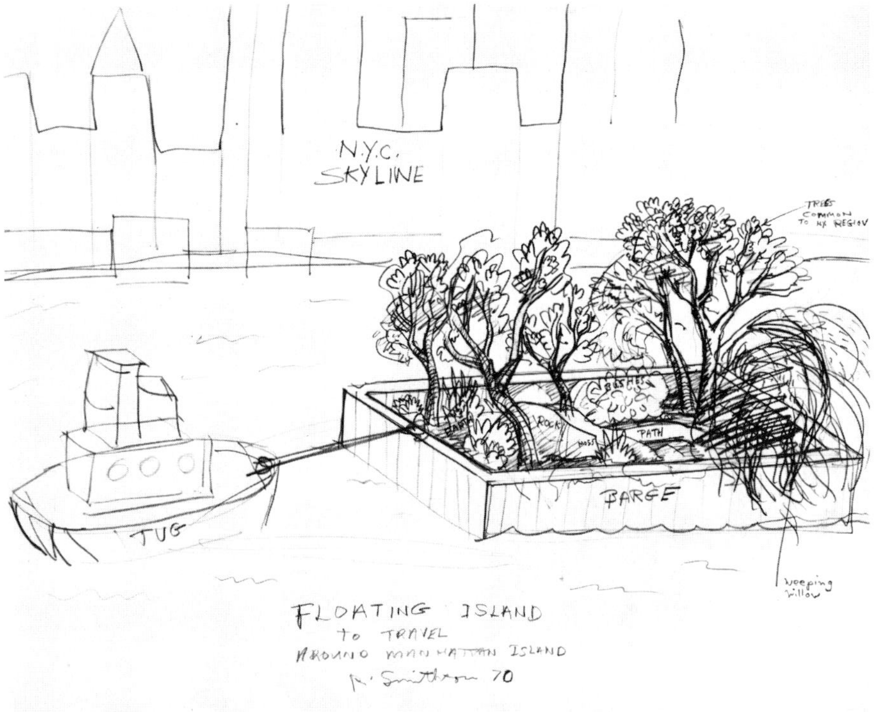

342. Floating Island to Travel Around Manhattan Island.

Floating Island—1970
Location: New York City.
Status: Rejected by the Parks Department in 1970.
Floating Island to Travel Around Manhattan Island.

343. Forking Island.

Forking Island—1971
Status: Study sketch.

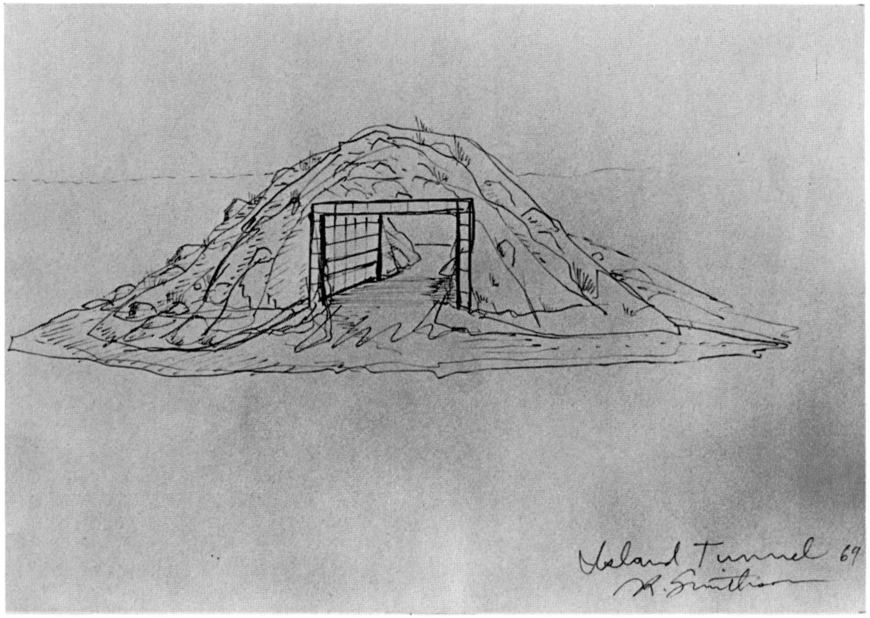

344. Island Tunnel.

Island Tunnel—1969
Status: Study sketch.

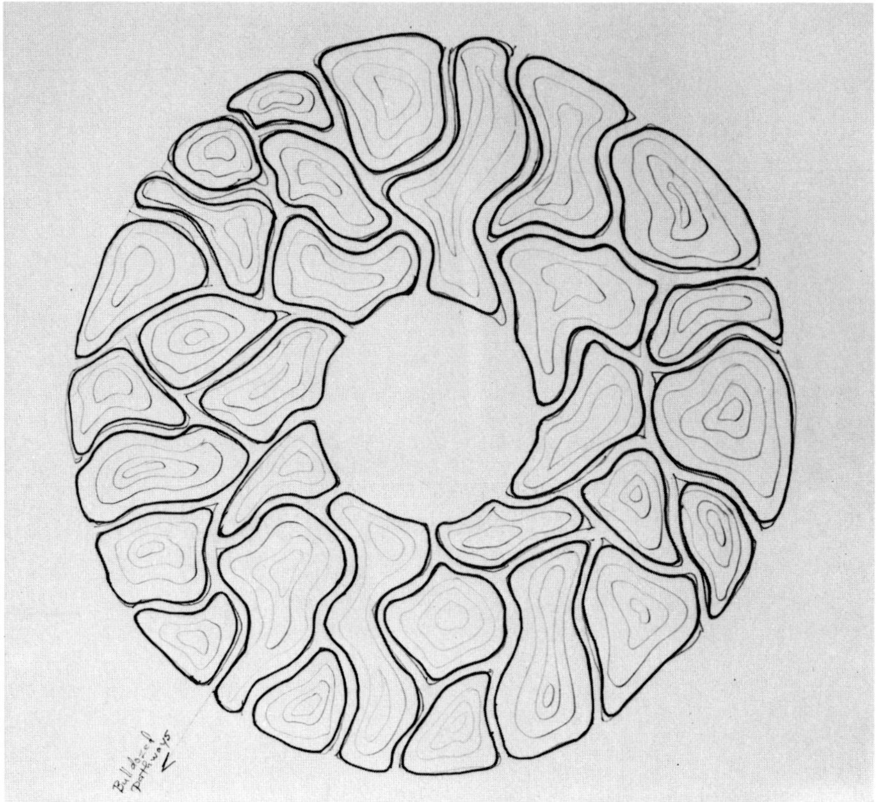

345. Meandering Ring Project for Tailings.

Meandering Ring
Project for Tailings—1973
Location: Creede, Colorado.
Status: Study sketch for Minerals Engineering. Project was delayed.
Across the country there are mining areas, disused quarries, and polluted lakes and rivers. One practical solution for the utilization of such devastated places would be land and water recycling in terms of Earth Art. . . . Economics, when abstracted from the world, is blind to natural processes.

Robert Smithson, Typescript, 1972.

[Robert Smithson became increasingly interested in working with industry and the possibilities of transforming the waste products of industrial sites into earthworks. In 1972 he made numerous proposals to strip mining companies and in 1973 developed a reclamation project for the Bingham Copper Mining Pit in Utah and several projects for tailings (the refuse left in various processes of mining). Minerals Engineering in Creede, Colorado, expressed interest in his project for a tailings pond. However in 1973 the project was delayed and Smithson left for Amarillo, Texas, where he died while working on a commissioned work, "Amarillo Ramp."]

Richard Snibbe (Baltimore 1916—)
Residence: New York City.
Education: 1939, St. John's College; 1940, Harvard School of Design.
Among Major Works: 1961, Storm King School, N.Y.C.; 1962, Tennis Pavilion for Princeton University, N.J.; Stapelton Houses, Staten Island, N.Y.; Hudson Paper Company Plant, Conn.; P.S. 615 experimental school and early childhood center, N.Y.C.

The Handloser Project—1973
Location: A Mountainous Region.
Status: Prototype.
Additional Credit: Thomas Handloser, sponsor; Lev Zetlin, structural engineer; Francis Ferguson, urban planner.
The Handloser Project, a two year study of a satellite town of 60,000 people to be built in a mountainous region.

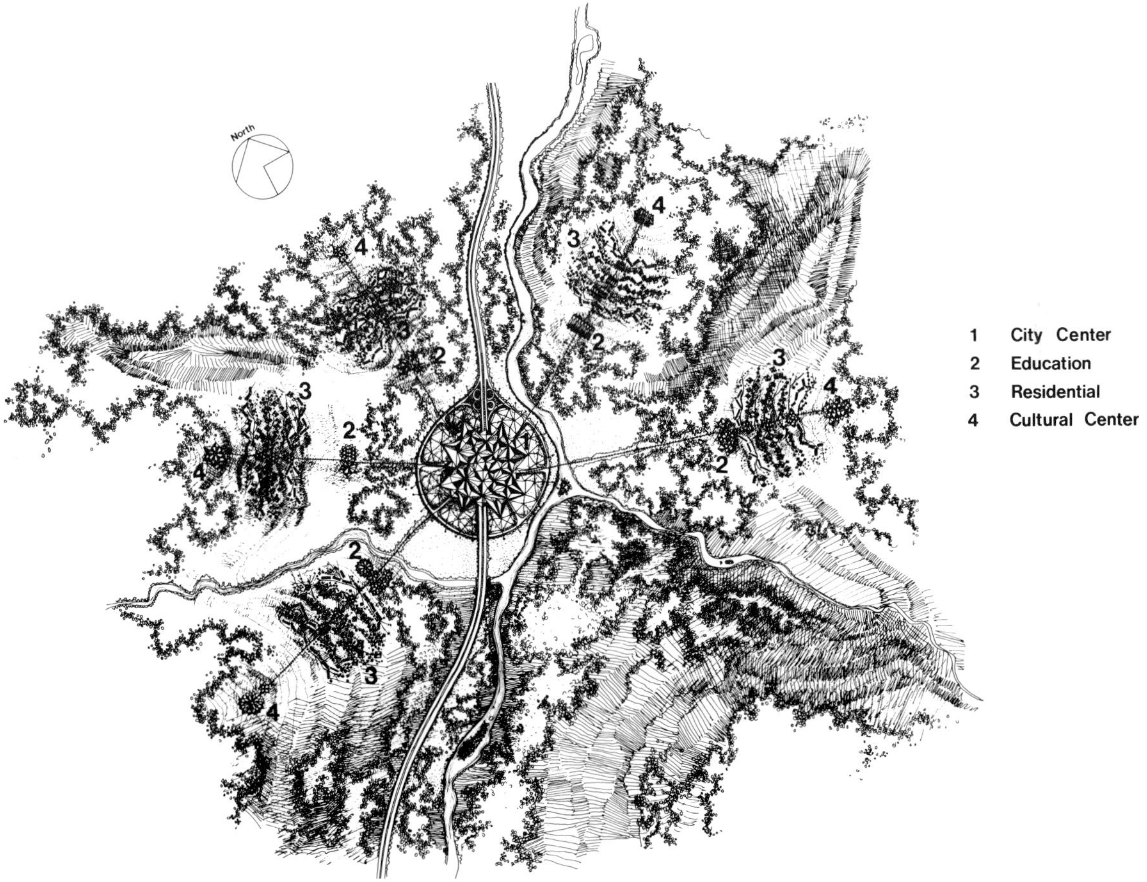

346. The Handloser Project. Site Plan.

347. Front Elevation.

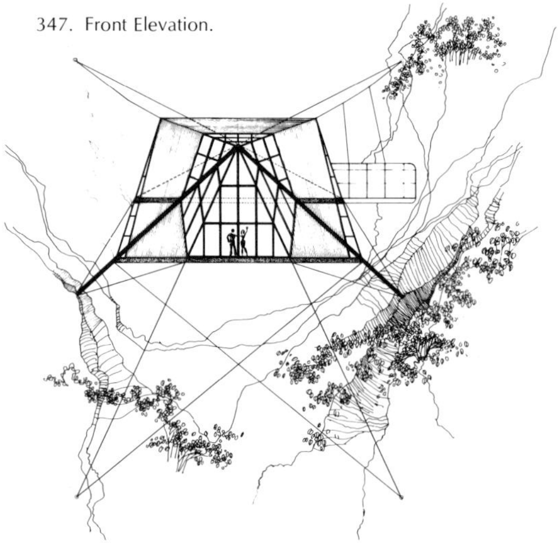

348. Side Elevation.

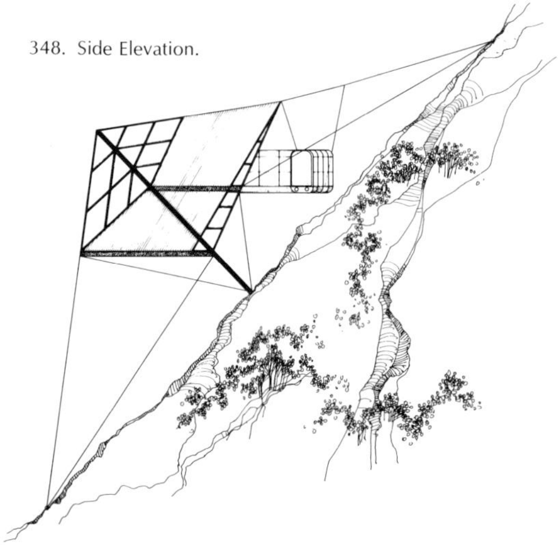

349. The Handloser Project. A Segment of the Mountainside Neighborhood. Cultural Center Above.

Housing in suspended structures supported by steel pipe and cable tied to the mountain by rock anchors, leaves the surface virtually untouched. Access by funicular and elevated covered passageways protect the terrain. These and the carrying of utilities in the floor of the passageways and on the funicular supports to central plants prevent the damage of cutting roads and burying utilities, causing erosion and rock fall. Of the 10,000-acre area studied, total construction "coverage" is 1350 acres. The town center itself is concentrated in a 150-acre circle leaving the valley floor open for community crops and recreation. One major highway leads through the valley, and carries tracks for the commuter train—a cable car with wheels. The possibilities of the use of our space-age technology in transportation, communications, and computer control of all the operations of the town challenges the imagination. The new life style is a combination of all the best elements of the country and the city, the convenience of Manhattan in the beauty of the Alps.

Richard Snibbe.

Paolo Soleri (Torino 1919—)
Residence: Scottsdale, Arizona.
Education: 1946, PhD, Torino Politecnico, Italy; 1947–1949, apprenticeship under Frank Lloyd Wright.
Among Major Works: 1951–1952, Artistica Ceramica Solimene (a large ceramics factory), Italy; 1956, Earth House, Cosanti Foundation, Arizona; 1969–1976, Arcosanti, Cordes Junction, Mayer, Arizona.
Among Major Writings: 1969, *Arcology: The City in the Image of Man;* 1971, *The Sketchbooks of Paolo Soleri;* 1973, *Matter Becoming Spirit.*

Soleri is best known for his archologies. Archology is the word he coined as a fusion of two words: Architecture and Ecology. Arcosanti, is an experimental archology for 3,000 people using only 10 acres within an 860 acre land sanctuary. When completed, the town will rise 15 stories, and will serve as a study center for the social, economic, and ecological implications of its architectural framework. From 1970 to date, over 2,500 students and professionals of all ages, races, and backgrounds have participated in experimental workshops and seminars.

3-D Jersey—1968–1970
Location: New Jersey.
Status: Theoretical proposal.
3-D Jersey was a project with a programmatic base designed as an urban transportation nucleus in the state of New Jersey, located in the New York–Philadelphia corridor. The study was conducted as a joint effort between Soleri, Rutgers University Environmental Science Department, and the Ford Motor Company. The main structure of the transportation center covers about one square mile and is about 1/2 mile high. The city is circular in plan, and designed to house a million people. Industrial and warehouse spaces including jet hangars radiate from the main structure and would be covered with parks and gardens. The entire site including park area covers less than 14 square miles. It was an attempt to answer the problem of connecting air travel with a new urban center in a direct manner; integrating the air facilities into the matrix of the system, not merely as an appendage as Kennedy International is to New York or Dulles is to Washington. This new arcology solution incorporates a circular jet runway ringing the entire 14 square mile site with long underground airtaxi corridors leading towards the central city structure.

Paolo Soleri.

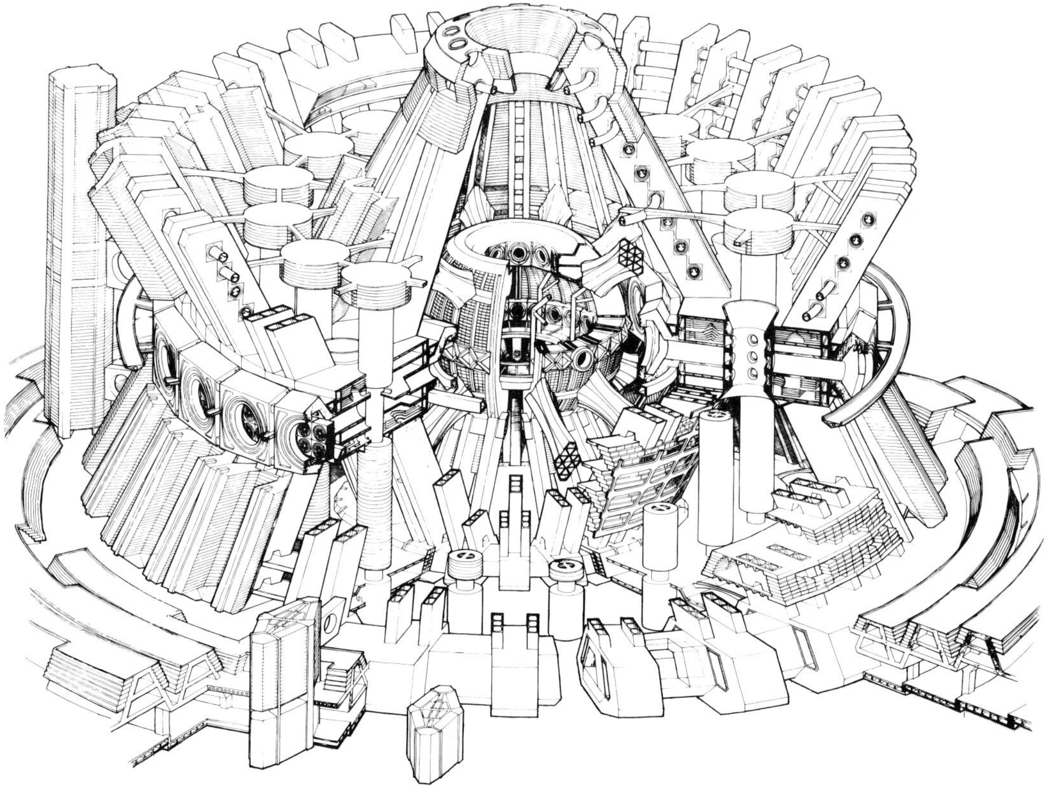

350. 3-D Jersey. Population One Million.
Isometric Drawing by Junji Shirai.

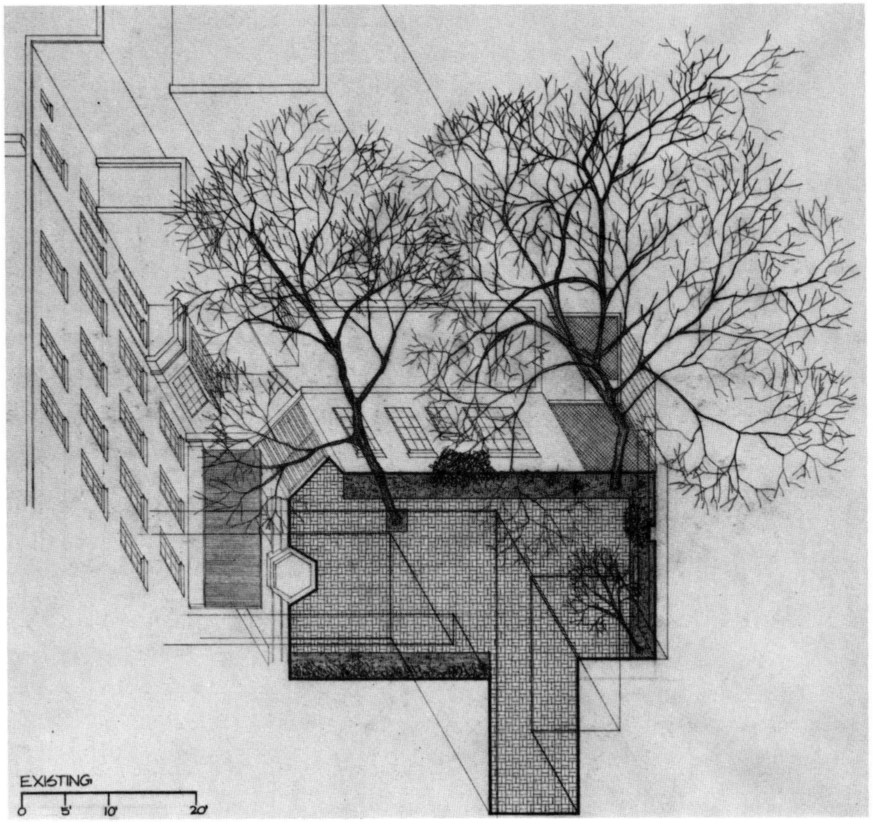

351. Time Landscape. Aerial View of Site.

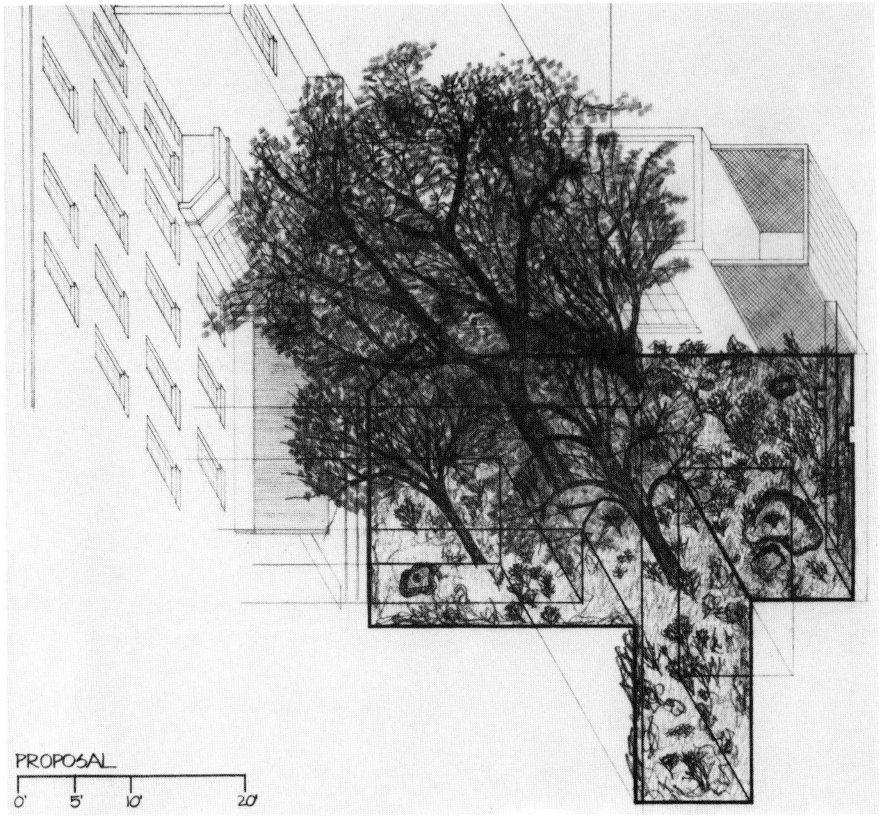

352. Time Landscape. Aerial View of Proposed Changes.

Alan Sonfist (Brooklyn, New York 1946—)
Residence: New York City.
Education: 1963, Art Students League, N.Y.C.; 1965–1966, Pratt Institute; 1967, BA Fine Arts, Western Illinois University; 1969, MFA, Hunter College.
Among Recent Major Exhibitions: 1972, (One-Artist) "Army Ants: Patterns and Structures", Automation House, N.Y.C.; 1974, (Group) "Materials and Manipulation" Whitney Museum of American Art, N.Y.C.; 1975, (One-Artist) "Running Dead Animal" Stefanotty Gallery, N.Y.C.; "Autobiography of Alan Sonfist," Cornell University, Ithaca, N.Y.; (Group) Biennale de Paris, France.

Time Landscape—1969
Location: New York City.
Status: Unbuilt due to bankruptcy of client.
The Time Landscape is a contemporary re-creation of the natural phenomena that once existed on a particular site. It is a public monument honoring the history of these elements in a city. Different periods of time can be selected for re-creation.

The project for New York City was developed in 1969 for an area adjacent to the Finch College Art Museum on 78th Street between Madison and Park Avenues. This Time Landscape would have re-created the pre-Colonial forest, beginning at the first succession and planning for natural evolution to a mature forest. Presently, the 2,000 square foot site is partially paved and partially landscaped with nonindigenous trees and shrubs.

Alan Sonfist.

Raphael Soriano (Island of Rhodes 1907—)
Residence: Tiburon, California.
Education: 1934, B Arch., University of Southern California.
Among Major Works: Site planning, apartments, hospitals, harbor facilities, office and medical buildings.

Raphael Soriano, who worked with Richard Neutra, is a pioneer in the development of steel construction in housing.

World Institute of International Business and Sociological Studies—1969

Location: Alcatraz Island, San Francisco.
Status: Unbuilt due to committee opposition.
Additional Credit: Ann Smith.

The City of San Francisco, which currently has the opportunity to purchase Alcatraz Island from the General Services Administration, must encourage this transaction. A development worthy of the dynamic environment and of the Island's central location, must have an ingenious and creative approach worthy of the cultural peoples of this City.

This development is designed to create a complete reformulation of the present reputation of the Island. It is desired to change it from a symbol of despair—from impotence and idleness to strength and energy, from ignorance and evil to education and understanding, from destructiveness and immorality to the full meaning of creativity.

The purpose is the establishment of an Institute of International Business and Sociological Studies. The program will lend itself to both large and small businesses on all levels of middle and executive management in the fields of international commerce. It will become a center for institutions, corporations and individuals, both domestic and foreign, to gain bilaterally complete knowledge and understanding of each other's goals and skills.

A Symphony Hall will be erected having a total capacity of 2,000 persons. It will be designed with flexibility to also accommodate seminars, conferences and conventions and will be equipped with a simultaneous translation system. With this system, its uses for civic and cultural affairs as well as Institute affairs will be a valuable asset.

The United Nations tower will be a reminder to all that San Francisco was the birthplace of the United Nations. It will also act as the economic fountainhead for the Institute and Symphony Hall. This structure of 110 stories can be built only of aluminum; no other material can perform as well, nor be as free from upkeep. A part of the revenue obtained from this tower will be returned

354. View of Alcatraz Island.

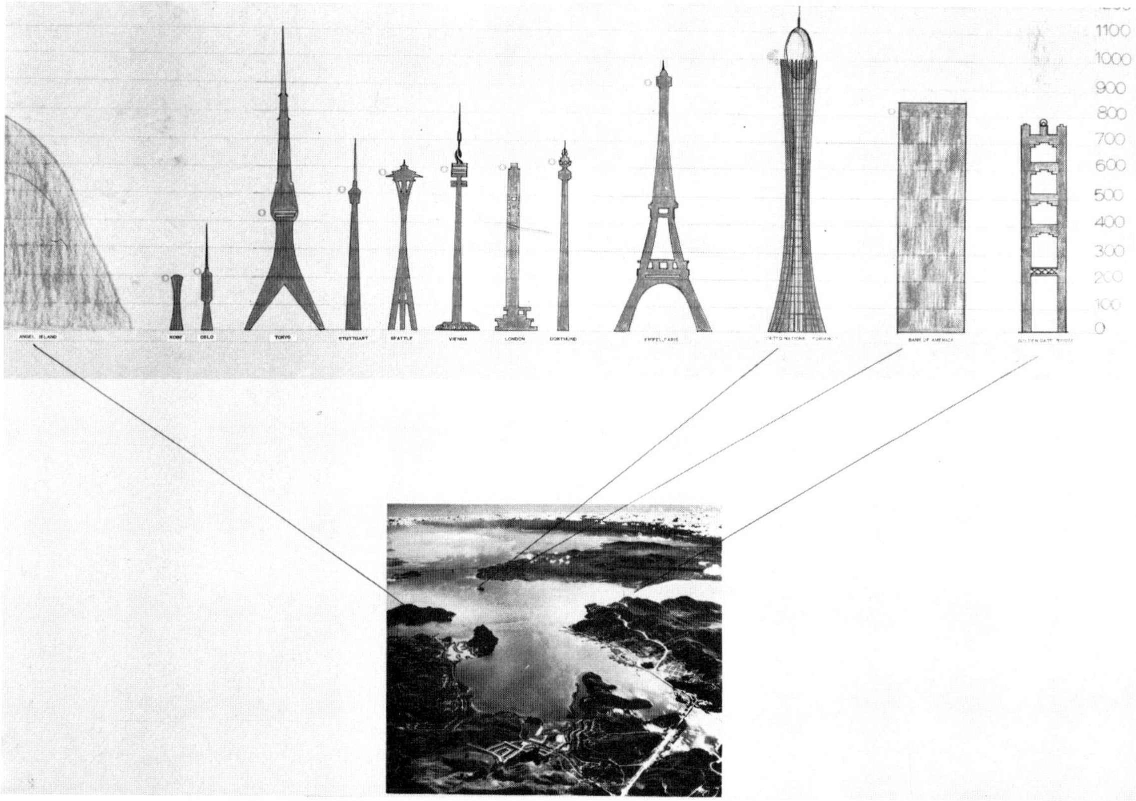

353. World Institute of International Business and Sociological Studies. Comparison of United Nations Tower to Other Monuments.

to the Institute to expand its facilities and to conduct research programs in the fields of International business and sociological studies. The structure will have a World Executive Club. This will be a meeting place for executives from all nations to further their understanding of each other's needs and problems in the World market and the sociological effects upon their respective areas. Other features of the tower include: a television studio, an observation level, and a revolving restaurant.

All in all, the World Institute of International Business and Sociological Studies will occupy only 12 percent of the land. This would leave the remainder free for parks, piazzas, and wildlife.

Raphael Soriano.

[According to Raphael Soriano, a proposal to turn Alcatraz Island into a tourist attraction submitted by Lamar Hunt, a Texas millionaire, so strongly won the Mayor's favor, that neither Soriano's nor any other development for the island, was given consideration. Scholars supported the Soriano proposal, however, and the Hunt proposal won a considerable amount of disfavor among the San Francisco community. The area is currently being reevaluated as to what the proper development should be.]

355. United Nations Tower. Detail.

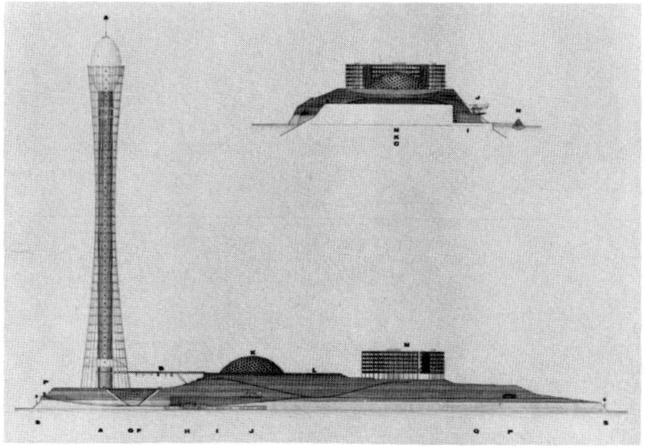

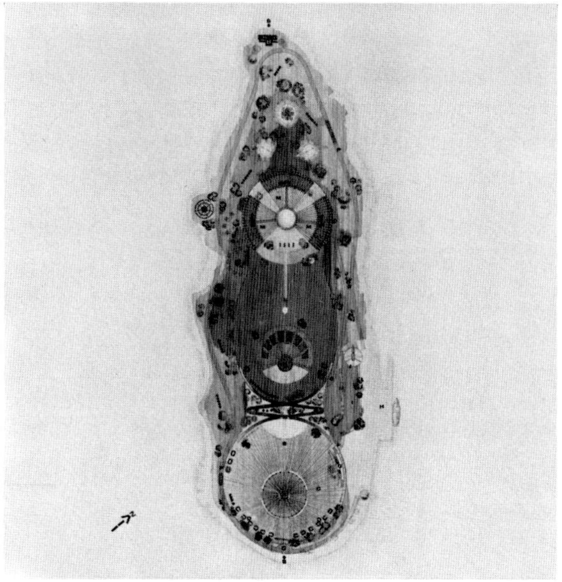

Above: 356,357. A. Aluminum Tower. B. Bridge. C. Piaza. D. Kiosk Shops. E. Garden Ramps. F. Shops. G. Escalators. H. Dock for Shuttle Boats. I. Historic Fort Restored. J. Heliport. K. Symphony Hall. L. Central Mall. M. Exhibition Gallery. N. Buildings for Business and Sociological Studies. O. Service Areas. P. Scenic Road for Electric Motor Cable Cars. Q. Faculty Housing. R. Restaurant. S. Coast Guard Navigation Beacon. T. Computer Communications Center.

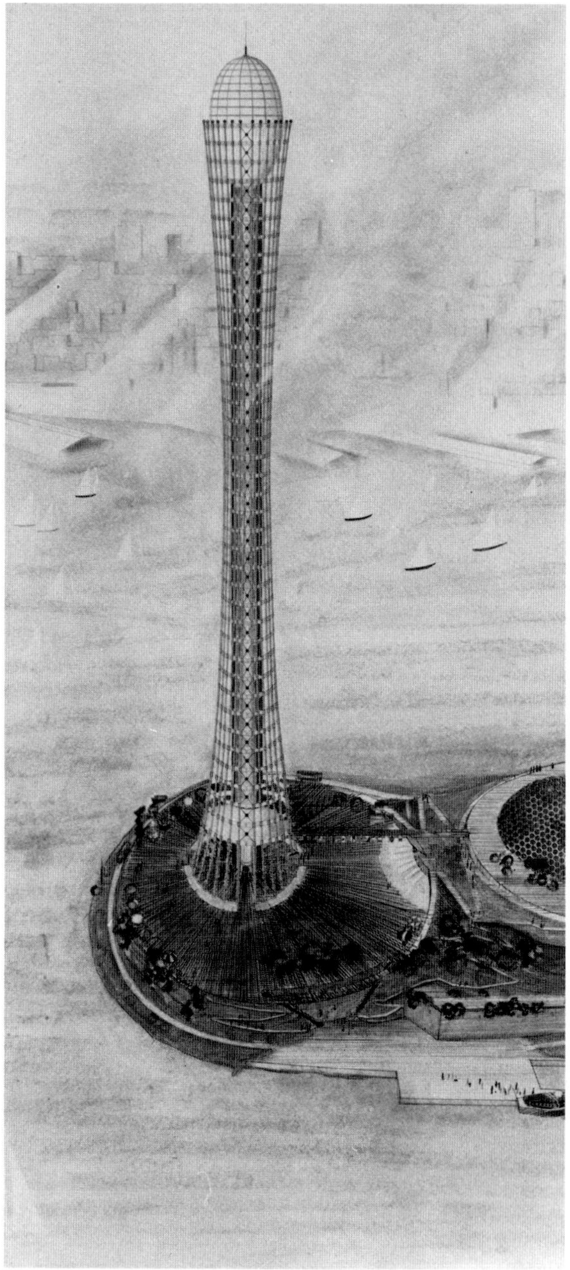

358. United Nations Tower. Perspective.

Robert B. Stacy-Judd (London 1884—Los Angeles 1975)
Education: Acton College, London; Regent's St. Polytechnic Institute, London; Southend Technical Institute, England; South Kensington Science and Art Institute, London.
Among Major Works: Aztec Hotel, Monrovia, Calif.; La Jolla Yacht and Beach Club, Calif.; First Baptist Church, Ventura, Calif.; Village of Krotona Institute of Theosophy, Ojai, Calif.; Zoological Gardens and Club House, Minot, North Dakota.

Wanted an All-American Architecture

America! World's most dominant factor, cynosure of lesser powers, leader in many branches of science, mechanics and "modernism." The foremost nation in claiming originality, yet the world's greatest imitator when it comes to architecture and its allied arts.

A national art style is indicative of cultural eminence. America *must* possess her own art.

At America's back door, buried beneath a vast carpet of almost impenetrable jungle, lies a great culture. Pathetic to relate, it remained undiscovered until recent times. The country is the great peninsula of Yucatan and adjacent areas. The masters are known as the ancient Mayas. Therefore it is to be hoped that in the Maya art we will visualise the opportunity to create and establish an All-American Architectural Style.

That the Mayas came from a land much larger and more generous in natural resources than Yucatan is very evident. That they came from the lost continent of Atlantis, that they are the remnant of what I term the Mother of Civilization, that they were one of the greatest of all races of mankind, are statements no less momentous than the two above mentioned theories, but they differ, insomuch as they are supported by an abundance of corroborative evidence far beyond mere coincidence.

Environment plays an important part in national character building and the quality of its art. There was certainly nothing to inspire one in Yucatan when the Mayas arrived. The country is flat, without rivers or scenery. It is a limestone peninsula a little above sea level. The quarries produced plenty of stone but the principal objection is the smallness of the pieces. A nation which produces stupendous works on a prolific scale, as did the Mayas, is a big people mentally.

Because of so many parallel traits, because of the romance, antiquity and mystery surrounding these great people, because of their magnificent arts and sciences, perhaps also because they may be termed the First Americans, the Mayas qualify more than any other race as masters to whom we should turn.

Excerpted from **Robert Stacy-Judd** in *The Architect and Engineer*, CXV, October–December 1933.

359. House Utilizing Ancient Maya Art Motifs. Perspective.

Building Utilizing Ancient Maya Art—1927
Status: Hypothetical study.

360. National Hall Project. (Two City Blocks) Vine & Sunset Blvd., Hollywood, California. Hotel, Office Building, Department Store, Convention Hall (Seat 23000) and Theater. Maya Art Motifs Throughout. Perspective.

National Hall Project—1931
Location: Los Angeles.
Status: Prototype.
The project includes an enormous auditorium capable of seating 23,000 people, a thirteen-story department store, an office block, a hotel, and a 2,500 seat theatre. The last is not seen in the perspective. The group covers two city blocks and the intervening street. Among the interesting features are the tower top of the office block, which shows the so-called Maya "arch" as the motif for the silhouette; the general façade of the office block and the entrances to the department store. The two exposed façades of the latter are comprised of V-shaped plate glass windows in continuous bays eleven stories high.

Robert Stacy-Judd in *The Architect and Engineer,* CXVI, February 1934.

Streets of All Nations—1955
Status: Unbuilt.
Millions of Americans who yearn to travel in other countries will never realize their dreams, because of lack of the necessary finances, or due to business, or family reasons. Even those fortunate enough to travel very seldom learn much in the lands they visit. Either they did not allow sufficient time, failed to prepare a rational itinerary, lacked comprehension of the language, or all three conditions combined, creating a barrier to conversation and mutual understanding.

The "Streets of All Nations" Project is intended to bring into a permanent center the most beautiful and representative example of a community from each of the approximately fifty countries invited to participate. Each "Street" and "Village" will be either an exact reproduction of the original or a combination of beauty spots selected from within the country in question. Natives are to be imported from each country represented—to live in the "Street" or "Village" and to make, by hand, the most attractive items for which their people are famous. An International Temple is suggested as the major attraction. It will be dedicated to the use of all Faiths, having a Revolving Rostrum.

Robert Stacy-Judd.

361. Streets of All Nations. Enchanted Boundary. Aerial View.

Louis Henri Sullivan (Boston 1856—Chicago 1924)
Education: 1872, Massachusetts Institute of Technology; 1874–1876, L'École des Beaux Arts, Paris.
Among Major Works: 1886–1889, Auditorium Building, Chicago; 1890–1891, Wainwright Building, St. Louis; 1893, Transportation Building, Chicago World's Fair; 1894–1895, Guaranty Building, Buffalo, N.Y.; 1899, Schlesinger and Mayer Department Store, Chicago.

Sullivan is noted for the refinements he introduced in the design of large metal-frame commercial buildings and for the development of an organic theory of architecture and design.

Setback Skyscraper City—1891
Location: Chicago (?).
Status: Prototype.

The High Building Question

To elaborate in all its details and ramifications, its varied selfish and unselfish interests, its phases of public and individual equity, its bearings present and future, its larger and narrower values, to attempt indeed but a sketch of its general outline would carry the discussion of the high-building question far beyond the limits of space that a journal such as this could afford. I desire, therefore, to pass by untouched the broad sociological aspects of this very elaborate discussion, and to confine myself to a phase of it which, so far as I am aware, has not yet been touched upon, but which may prove a factor in the final solution. It must seem a hardship to the individual owner of land that he should be debarred from erecting upon it such building as he deems fit. It will seem, however, to the remaining stubborn majority of the community—non-owners of land—a distinct impudence that the individual should build otherwise than as they themselves see fit. It is between these extremes that my suggestion lies, for I believe it is possible to preserve in a building of high altitude the equities both of the individual and of the public.

Briefly, then, the individual owner seeks rentable space, the public wish light and air; it follows, then, that up to a certain limit of height the individual owner manifestly should be free to regulate his rentable space as he chooses, but beyond this limit a sense of public welfare should control him either with or without his consent. What more simple solution can there be than this—that the individual be allowed to continue the further erection of his building above the prescribed limit, provided that, in so continuing, the area of his building as it emerges from the limit shall occupy not more than, say, fifty percent of the area of his land? Let him so continue until he has reached, say, twice the height of the original limit. If the area of his land is sufficient he may profitably continue, let him be allowed to do so, provided, however, that in so doing he occupy, not to exceed, say, twenty-five percent of the area of his ground; and so on indefinitely, restricting the area as he progresses upward.

This is, so far, a very pretty theory. But we well know, after a moment's reflection, that with his customary go-ahead proclivities, the average American citizen, desiring, as usual, to be right up in the front row, would translate this to mean a thirty-story building on the street line with a great big hole behind. We would, therefore, have to teach him the manners he does not possess, and would gently inform him that after the first limit is passed the fifty percent restriction will apply not only to area but to frontage. He will scowl at this condition, but if there is "money in it" he will accept it just the same. When the second limit is reached we will push him back unceremoniously from the street line to the middle of his ground, and if he can see a dollar in it he will accept this condition also.

It seems to me a subject not at all debatable that here in Chicago the freedom of thought and action of the individual should be not only maintained, but held sacred. By this I surely do not mean the license of the individual to trample on his neighbor and disregard the public welfare, but I do just as surely mean that our city has acquired and maintained its greatness by virtue of its brainy men, who have made it what it is and who guarantee its future. These men may be selfish enough to need regulation, but it is monstrous to suppose that they must be suppressed, for they have in themselves qualities as noble, daring, and inspired as ever quickened knights of old to deeds of chivalry.

Abridged from Louis Sullivan in *The Graphic,* V, December 1891.

Setback Skyscraper as defined by Donald Hoffman: that type of high building characterized by pronounced and progressive diminishments of plan in the upper stories, with corresponding "steps" in the profile of the building-mass.

Donald Hoffman, *Journal of the Society of Architectural Historians,* May 1970.

362. Setback Skyscraper City. Street View Showing Full Development of the Idea.

363. New New York. The Continuous Monument. Aerial View.

Superstudio (Florence, Italy 1966—)
Location: Florence, Italy.
Principals: Adolfo Natalini (founder), Cristiano Toraldo di Francia (founder), Roberto Magris, Piero Frassinelli, Alessandro Magris.
Among Major Works: Publications—1968, *A Journey Into the Realms of Reason* (architecture as a means of changing the world); 1969, *Istogrammi D'Architettura* (transitions and metamorphosis); 1970, *The Continuous Monument* (total urbanization); *Didactic Architectural Projects*—1971, "Reflected Architecture," "Interplanetary Architecture," "The 12 Ideal Cities"; Films—1973, *Life, Education, Ceremony, Love, Death* (five films about fundamental acts—the relationship between architecture and human life.)

An Architectural Model for Total Urbanization—1969
Location: New York City.
Status: Hypothetical proposal.

For those who, like ourselves, are convinced that architecture is one of the few ways to realize cosmic order on earth, to put things to order and above all to affirm humanity's capacity for acting according to reason, it is a "moderate utopia" to imagine a near future in which all architecture will be created with a single act, from a single design capable of clarifying once and for all the motives which have induced man to build dolmens, menhirs, pyramids, and lastly to trace (ultima ratio) a white line in the desert.

Between the terms *natura naturans* and *natura naturata,* we choose the latter. We move towards the "continuous monument": a form of architecture all equally emerging from a single continuous environment: the world rendered uniform by technology and culture.

New New York

New York for example. A superstructure passes over the Hudson and the point of the peninsula joining Brooklyn and New Jersey. And a second perpendicular structure for expansion. All the rest is Central Park. This is sufficient to hold the entire built-up volume of Manhattan. A bunch of ancient skyscrapers, preserved in memory of a time when cities were built with no single plan. . . . And from the Bay, we see New New York arranged by the Continuous Monument into a great plain of ice, clouds or sky.

Abridged from **Superstudio, The Continuous Monument**, 1970.

Stanislaw Szukalski (Poland 1895—?)
Education: Studied art at the Krakow Academy, Poland.

In 1913 at the age of eighteen, Szukalski came to Chicago, where he remained for ten years. He published his first book here in 1923. Szukalski had long been distressed by American skyscrapers, as well as by other architecture of the past three or four centuries. The skyscraper architect especially, he felt had neglected his opportunities. Architecture had been dominated by the engineer, interested only in scientific aspects. . . . The artist was at last beginning to take his rightful place beside the engineer. . . . The architect was still hesitant and uncertain of his mastery of modern materials, steel and concrete, and their possibilities. Roger A. Crane, Introduction, *Projects in Design,* 1929.

What makes an architect in my conception of the term is the aesthetic element in his work, not the constructional or utilitarian. The technical part of an architectural project can be taken care of by engineer or contractor, for theirs is a learnable science. The function of the so-called architects for the last four hundred years has been largely parasitic; it has consisted of rehashing the ancient "motifs." Within that long space of time there has been invented not one decorative motif, not one new ornament. The more productive seasons, like the neo-Classic, the Empire, or the American Colonial were beautiful, but with the beauty that was Greek; there was no new element to testify their creative productivity. All other fashions, like the Barocco, the Rococo, the Biedemayer, the Vienna Secession, and the modern insipid constructionist styles, are only pitiable examples of what has been done by aesthetic impotents who in the absence of the rightful masters, have entered the orphaned craft and shamelessly appropriated the title of architect. The bad taste of architects is as proverbial as that of opera singers and economists. The recent addition of the "architect–interior decorator" has added nothing to the glory of the cult; they are no more architects than the others, but they come boldly and brazenly, with rouged lips and magenta manners. The good taste they sometimes display proves rather the senility of our culture than its virility.

Stanislaw Szukalski, Projects in Design, 1929.

Projects for a Solo Structure—1929
Status: Prototype.

365. Project for a Solo Structure. Perspective.

364. Project for a Solo Structure. Perspective.

Athena Tacha (Greece 1936—)
Residence: Ohio.
Education: MA, National Academy of Fine Arts, Athens, Greece; 1961, MA, Oberlin College; 1963, PhD, University of Paris (Sorbonne), France.
Among Major Exhibitions: One Artist—1973, Webster College, St. Louis; 1974, Project Inc. Gallery, Cambridge, Massachusetts. Group—1971, Outdoor Sculpture, Blossom Music Center, Ohio; 1973, Six Artists, Akron Art Institute; 1973–1974, "Ca. 7,500," traveling show.

Step Sculptures for the Banks of the Charles River—1974

Location: Cambridge, Massachusetts.
Status: Unbuilt.

Due to the proximity of the river, natural forms and rhythms become an important source of inspiration for this work. The double nature of water—flowing liquid and brittle solid—emerged in my awareness as the river had started freezing when I arrived in Cambridge, and sharp sheets of ice were wedged along the banks while the deeper water in the middle continued moving. Each of the two sculptures, the curvilinear and the rectilinear, starts with a basic element: the arc of the circle on the west area and the right angle on the east. But neither is used in a way encountered in normal architectural spaces of step-formations; there are never any parallel lines (or concentric circles). Centers and curvatures of arcs, as well as inclinations of straight lines—therefore width of steps—constantly change, pursuing the creation of a shifting, unstable space. Towards the outer ends (the main entrances for each sculpture being at the highest point of the adjacent roadway over the dividing trainline), the arcs gradually turn into segments of ellipses or other irregular curves, and the angles become overwhelmingly obtuse and acute. The rolling terraces of twisting cascades evolve into quieter, more uniform wave-rhythms.

Athena Tacha.

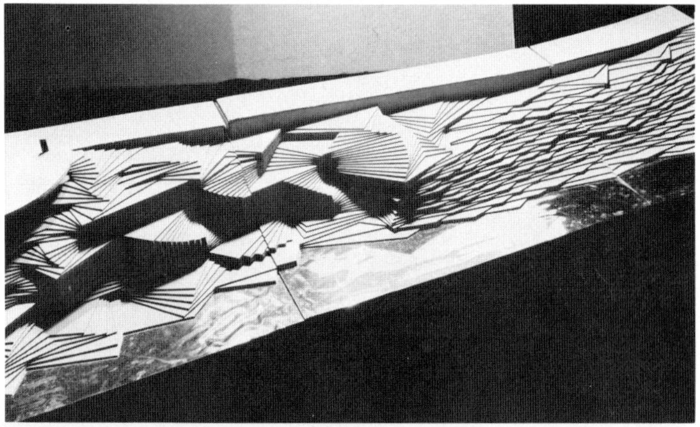

367. Step Sculptures for the Banks of the Charles River, Cambridge. Model. Detail.

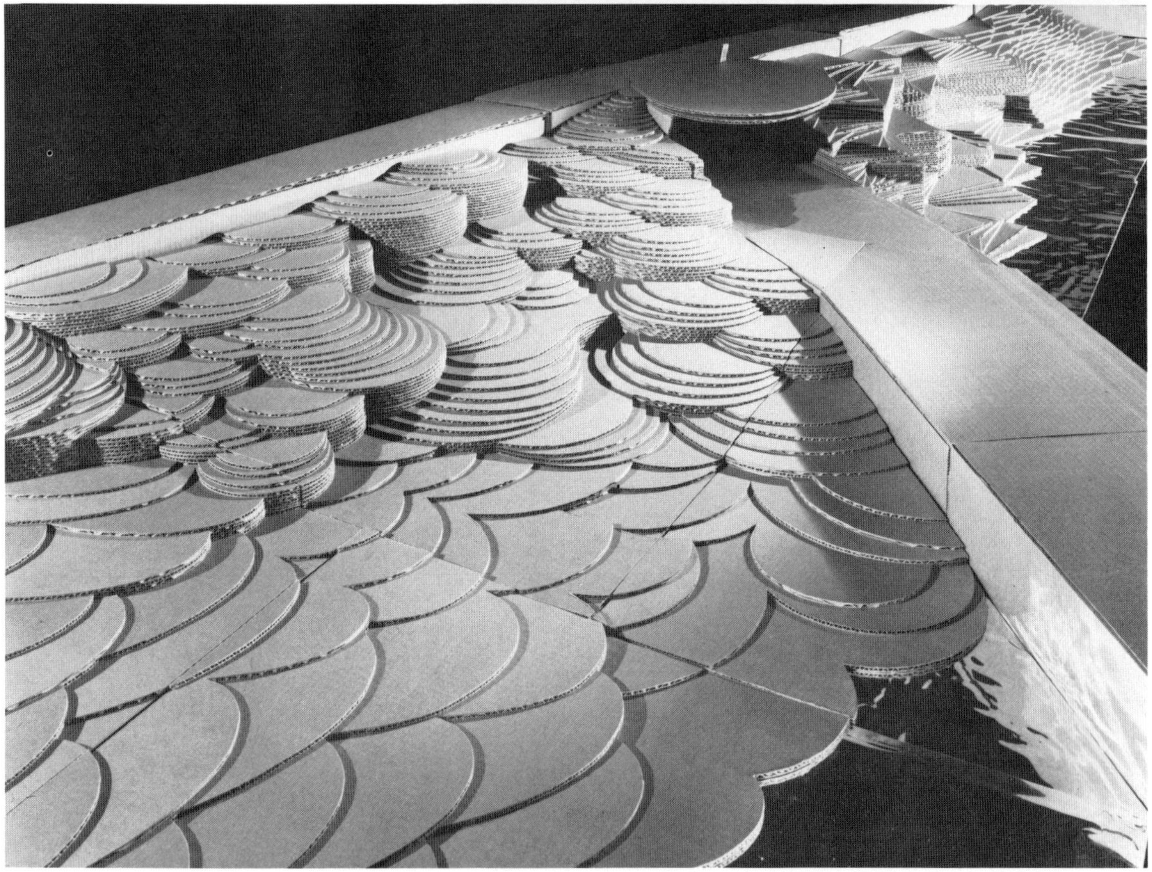

366. Step Sculptures for the Banks of the Charles River, Cambridge. Model.

368. Instant Football. Superimposed on Site.

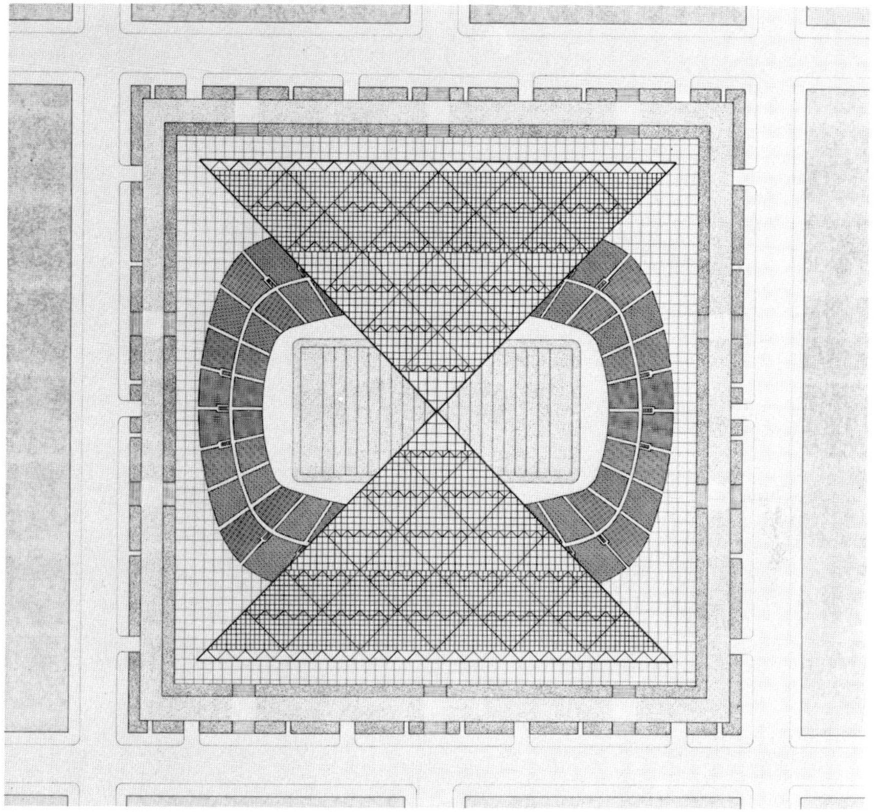

369. Instant Football. Plan.

Stanley Tigerman (Chicago 1930—)
Residence: Chicago.
Education: 1948–1949, Massachusetts Institute of Technology; B and M Arch., Yale University.

Stanley Tigerman's architectural career is characterized by three aspects: his widely known concepts of megastructures, floating cities, airports, and studies into the formal nature of structures; his moderate income housing projects and work with community organizations in planning rehabilitation, and new construction; and his projects in the Canadian New Town "Nun's Island" and in the emerging country of Bangladesh.

Instant Football—1968
Location: Above a football stadium.
Status: Prototype.

"Instant Football" has been planned as an integrated complex of stadium, hotels, and office facilities. These facilities are coordinated to work independently, yet their integration is complimentary. The project consists of two parts—a base structure containing stadium seating, parking, pedestrian and vehicular access tunnels, locker rooms, etc., and a semi-pyramidal superstructure, open on two sides, containing the hotels, press and T.V. facilities, office space, and mechanical rooms. The complex is situated on a ten-acre urban site, centrally located, thereby encouraging maximum use on a year around basis.

The project as presented herein accommodates approximately 55,000 spectators for a football game. This number can be greatly increased or reduced to meet specific project requirements. The base is a relatively inexpensive concrete structure built on, or somewhat below, grade. The superstructure, sloping inward over the base, consists of one hundred foot by one hundred foot tetrahedronal megastructures, framed in steel. Multicored slabs span the horizontal geometric vector of 50 feet creating a series of levels for varying activities.

Stanley Tigerman.

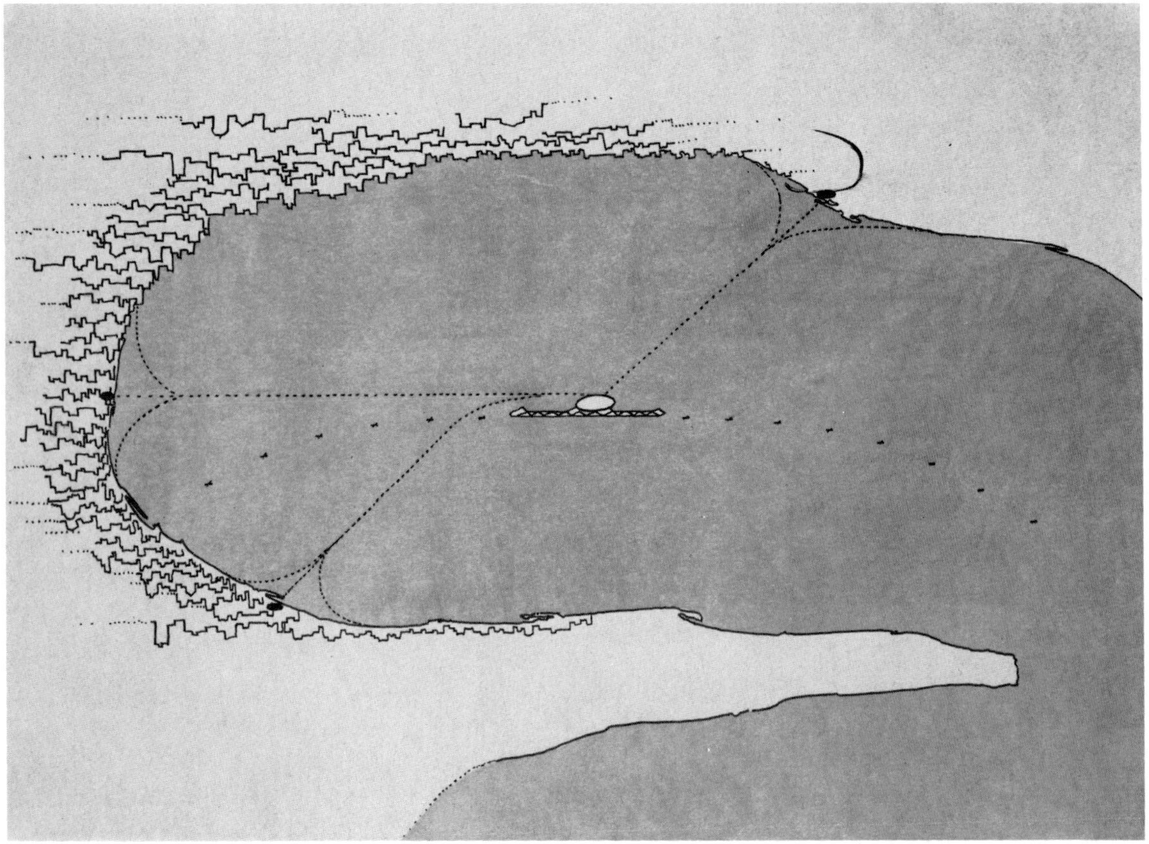

370. Floating Airport. Points of Access to the City.

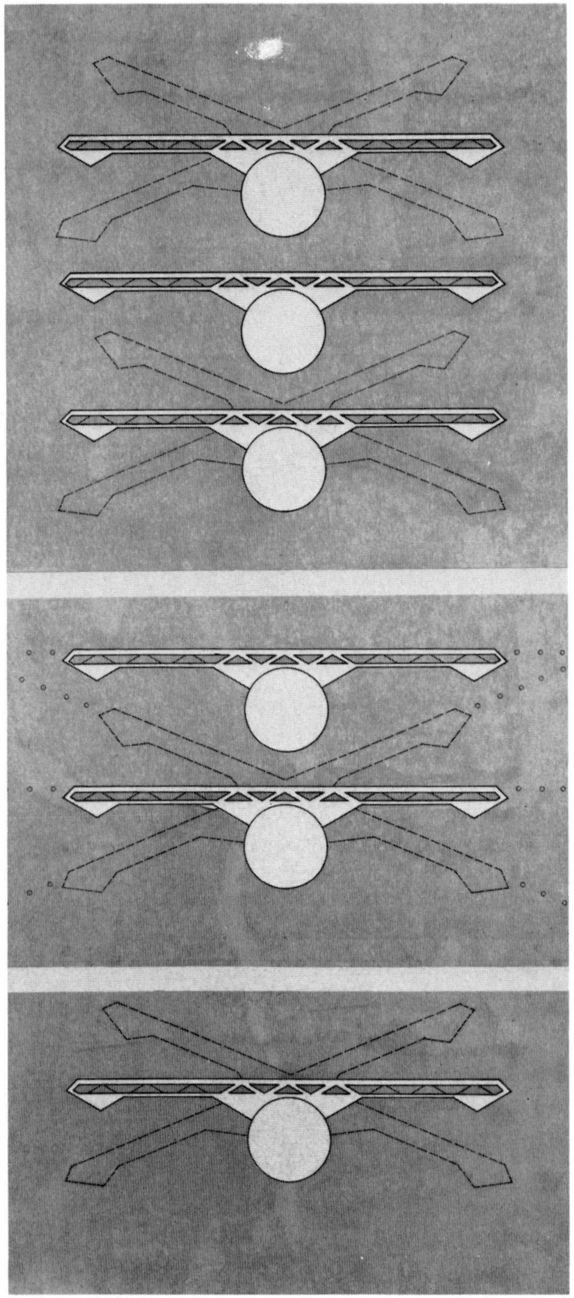

Floating Airport—1972
Location: Offshore from major city.
Status: Prototype.
Projected growth of air travel requires that facilities at all major airports be expanded. Most existing municipal airports are physically restricted for adequate expansion so that new major terminals are being planned. New inland airports require large areas of land at close proximity to city centers. This can pose serious problems in terms of: conflicts with existing land uses, inadequacy of existing roadway systems, noise level, etc.

Many cities have large areas of water available near their centers. Location of new airports on water avoids the problems described and permits easy access from the shoreline, thus servicing the most densely populated urban areas in the most direct manner. Constructed of lightweight alloys, these floating structures would support heavy loads and rotate into various positions with respect to wind. To construct them, cities would lease water rights in lieu of purchasing land.

Stanley Tigerman.

371. Floating Airport. Floating Structure. Detail.

William Turnbull, Jr. (New York City 1935—)
Residence: San Francisco.
Education: 1956, BA, Princeton University; 1956, École des Beaux Arts de Fontainbleau; 1959, MFA Arch., Princeton University.
Among Major Works: 1961, South Coast Master Plan, Big Sur, Calif.; 1963, Design group for President Kennedy's Advisory Council; 1970, author, *The Sea Ranch/MLTW Moore Turnbull*, from the Global Architecture Series; 1974, illustrator, *The Place of Houses.*

Ellis Island—1959
Location: New York City.
Status: Developed for Master's Thesis, Princeton University.

Ellis Island represents a unique and special place in America's cultural history. For the crowds of European immigrants, it was the landing point in New York Harbor for well over one hundred years. The Statue of Liberty, a scant half mile to the south, symbolically represented the opportunities of the new land, and Ellis Island, the first intensive memories of arrival.

To commemorate its role in American history, I proposed a landmark combination of monument and public park. The design solution evolved from the recognition that the Statue of Liberty, so powerful in its presence, could never be competed with successfully in the traditional sense, nor would it be appropriate to do so. Therefore, instead of building up from the Island's skyline, I elected to "sink" it and make a subsurface plaza defined by sea walls. What was historically is no longer, and what was physically is emptied in a symbolic gesture.

The massive walls are buttressed to restrain the water and their placement varies in response to differing depths. Spaces between the buttresses can be used as display areas for Fairs or Shows. An assembly building for performances was included as part of the Park and the cribbed walls of the towers were to be filled with seasonal flowers. Boat landings were provided along the upper promenade for tourist and recreational access.

Ellis Island becomes then a special place; symbolic and poetic as a monument, but alive and vital as an active urban plaza.

William Turnbull.

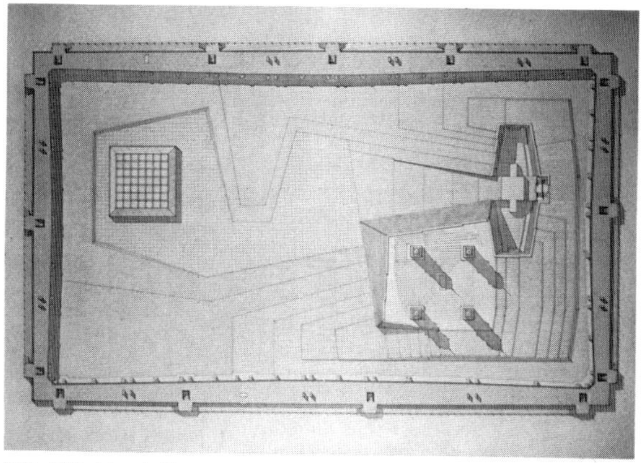

373. Ellis Island. Plan.

372. Ellis Island. Detail.

Anne Griswold Tyng (China 1920—)
Residence: Philadelphia.
Education: 1942, BA, Radcliffe College; 1944, M Arch., Harvard Graduate School of Design; 1975, PhD Arch., Graduate School of Arts and Sciences, University of Pennsylvania.
Among Major Works: 1952–1953, Associate Consultant Architect to Philadelphia City Planning Commission and Redevelopment Authority; 1954, Associate Consultant Architect on Mill Creek Redevelopment Plan, Penna.
Among Major Exhibitions: 1964, The Divine Proportion in the Platonic Solids, University of Pennsylvania Graduate School of Fine Arts; 1971, Metamorphology—New Sources of Form Making, Philadelphia Chapter American Institute of Architects; 1974, Women in the Design of the Environment, Philadelphia Chapter AIA.

From 1947 to 1973, Anne Tyng worked in the office of, and in association with, Louis Kahn.

Spiral Urban Hierarchies—1970
Status: Prototype.
Hierarchical design is an essential tool for the architect who is continuously concerned with transformation of scale which quite frequently results in a literal "blowing up" of a small drawing ill-conceived for its full-size realization. This scaleless "blown-up" effect is particularly evident in many large developments where endlessly repetitive modules of window divisions give no sense of *progression* of scale between the window module and the total form, so that the sheer collectivity of such numbers of similar modules becomes overwhelming. Hierarchical forming principles provide for the reaffirmation of human scale and values and for the humanization of forms at the largest scales of built environment.

In creating forms for an urban hierarchy, geometry is the means of extending individual creativity from the design of a single architectural unit through progressive increments of scale and symmetry to an interlacing hierarchy in a total "field." Beginning with the familiar orientation of bilateral form for bilateral man, geometry provides principles of relationship which operate in transformations to more and more dynamic stages of symmetry. I have developed a proposal for an urban hierarchical structure which attempts to illustrate one possibility of such forming principles.

Bilateral Symmetry is the basis of a court block of 40 dwelling units arranged in rectangular form. Pedestrian-park crossovers within the rectangle provide a central neighborhood meeting place. The principle of street access to and parking under

374. Spiral Urban Hierarchies. Model.

each house diffuses traffic so that the street once more becomes a friendly place.

Rotational Symmetry or symmetry around a point expresses the pattern of vehicular movement in the form of pentagonal ramps. A double helix is formed by two interlocking pentagonal ramps, one up and one down, which provide access to the units, so that a car need go only half the apparent number of levels to get to a house. Vehicular cross overs also connect the up and down ramp system.

Helical Symmetry forms the "hill villages" which contain day care, Head Start, and incidental shopping facilities. Clusters of six or more helices with more random connective patterns comprise an elementary school community with supermarket shopping and other community facilities. These connections also provide alternate horizontal access to units (as well as the ramp access). The structure of the helix may be a compression system with prebuilt party walls as support. These would allow the flexibility of "plug-in" prefab units or individually designed houses. Helical forms may also be supported in a tower structure with an internal compression mast and with the streets acting in tension on the perimeter. In this type of structure the units may be used for offices, apartments, motel units, or other commercial uses.

Spiral Symmetry connects the elementary school communities around two Junior High schools and one Senior High, with additional shopping, offices, motels, amusements or recreational facilities, community services, and institutions. The top level of the spiral form may be planted and used as a park-promenade and for outdoor exhibits and festivities, providing another social link at the larger collective scale of the development.

Bilateral Symmetry at a Larger Scale includes four spiral forms which act as collectors and diffusers of the expressway system with multilevel roadways forming the exits and entrances to a high speed system. The spiral forms offer further growth possibilities for population expansion. In this way both density and open space can be maintained and be related to the overall hierarchical ordering of forms and scale. The spaces formed at the denser "joints" between the spiral forms may become commercial shopping malls.

In hierarchical forming principles, each hierarchy offers more "random" possibilities of form, with emphasis shifting from the design of the *solid* to the design of the *void*.

Anne Griswold Tyng.

375. Spiral Urban Hierarchies. Model.

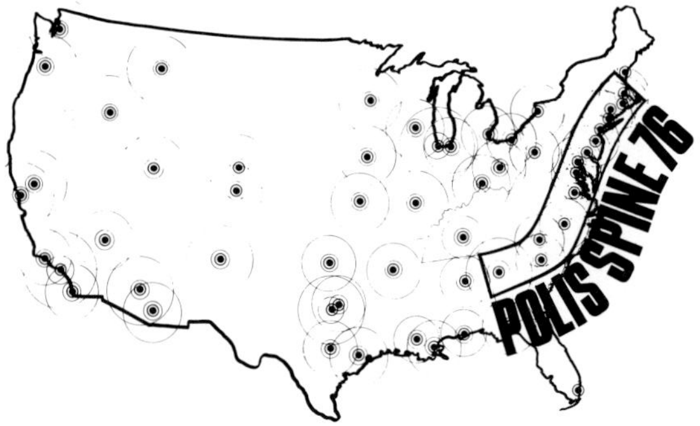

376. Polis '76. Transportation Spine Linking Thirteen Original Colonies.

Bicentennial—Cambridge Seven Associates, Inc.

Cambridge Seven Associates, Inc. (Boston 1962—)
Location: Cambridge, Massachusetts and New York City (associated with Chermayeff & Geismar).
Principals: Cambridge—Louis J. Bakanowsky, Peter Chermayeff, Paul E. Dietrich, Terry Rankine, Charles Redmon; New York City—Ivan Chermayeff, Thomas Geismar.
Among Major Works: Interior and exhibits of U.S. Pavilion at Expo '67; New England Aquarium; Columbia Schools, Rochester, N.Y.; recycling an existing brewery into an Art Museum, San Antonio, Texas.

Polis '76—1967

Status: Unsuccessful Bicentennial proposal.
Additional Credit: Robert Hollister, James Chard, WORKS.
This was to be a multi-city celebration involving coordinated festivities in all of the major cities of the original thirteen colonies, linked by a high-speed train and an extensive telecommunications information network. The train itself was to be designed so that the visitor would feel that he was inside the exhibition. Lounge and pavilion cars would provide information and entertainment while in transit. Films or exhibits could be synchronized at certain points en route, as the theater would open up to show the real action on the outside. The entire trip would be a super-montage of real and electronic audio-visual elements.

Channelling the excitement and public spirit kindled by the nation's Bicentennial, the planners of Polis hoped it would be possible to reallocate energies and funds to address nationwide problems; the high-speed train would be a very tangible example of this. Polis would reflect new concepts of community and movement which a single city could not express and demonstrate that man would increasingly live on a regional scale—which would demand different types of social structures and modified means of communication. Polis emphasized information flow as opposed to monument building, and at the conclusion of the bicentennial celebration, the nation would be left not with useless, scattered fair pavilions, but with improved cultural and recreational facilities, new transportation centers, and an integrated transportation system which would promote more rational urban growth and reduce pollution and traffic congestion.

Cambridge Seven.

377. Polis '76. Rendering by WORKS.

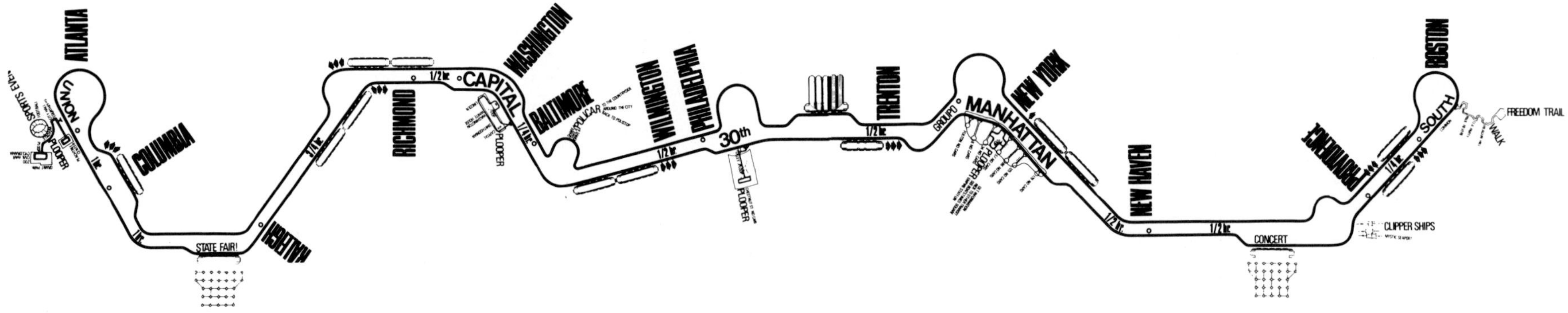

378. World Environmental Laboratory. Detail.

Bicentennial—Davis, Brody and Associates

Davis, Brody and Associates (established N.Y.C. 1956—)
Principals: Lewis Davis, Samuel M. Brody, Alan Schwartzman.
Among Major Works: U.S. Pavilion, Japan World Exposition 1970 (Geiger-Berger, structural engineers for roof system), Osaka, Japan; Ruppert Housing, N.Y.C.; Waterside Housing, N.Y.C.; East Midtown Plaza, N.Y.C.; River Park Towers, Bronx, N.Y.

World Environmental Laboratory—1971
Location: Central United States.
Status: Bicentennial proposal (required too much research to realize in time).
Additional Credit: Geiger-Berger, structural-mechanical engineers for the roof system.
The World Environmental Laboratory is an encapsulated, inflated structure enclosing an 8,000-foot-diameter space, containing recreational and educational facilities and festive events. Visitors would leave their cars at some distant location and travel to the structure by means of nonpolluting mass transit systems. Since the interior would be protected from hostile environments, nonconventional building materials could be used, such as high-strength cardboards, fabrics, plastics, etc. Within this space a microcosm-complex of environments, ranging from arctic to tropical, would house botanical gardens, zoos, and aquariums containing living species from all over the world.

Data and Characteristics:

Roof—Height: 40 stories at zenith (height of the United Nations Secretariat Building); volume enclosed: 20 billion cubic feet (volume is equivalent to 300 Houston Astrodomes); Diameter: 8,000 feet or 1½ miles (length of Lincoln Tunnel); shape: circular in plan, low shallow dome in elevation.

Roof Membrane System—A clear, inert film combined with stainless steel strips (the effect would be that of a transparent structural screen which allows an unobstructed view of the sky).

Cable System—The roof membrane would be attached to high strength bridge strand cables strung from one side of a funicular concrete compression ring to the other (the span between cables is 40 feet to 160 feet).

Pressurization System—The roof membrane and adjoining cables would be supported by a combination of natural forces caused by thermal buoyancy (the warm air that collects at the top of the roof) and air currents (exerting forces that help to keep the roof up), plus an auxiliary blower system which pumps air into the enclosure. The air-supported roof can sustain an opening of 50,000 square feet (an acre of 80 feet wide by 600 feet long—almost large enough to accommodate three 747 airplanes) without deflating. For this type of structure, the larger the span, the less the pressure required for inflation. Once the membrane is inflated, very little mechanical output is needed.

Climate Control System—The specially designed film membrane would control solar radiation, thereby providing year around comfortable temperatures plus the coexistence of a range of artificial and diverse climates.

Water System—The condensation which collects at the underside of the film membrane could handle all water requirements, including drinking water and the irrigation of the interior space.

Davis, Brody and Associates.

379. Drawing of a House Inhabited by Kitty Ewens in Her Twenties, as Remembered by Her at Age 100.

AREAS NOT REMEMBERED
WOULD NOT BE CONSTRUCTED

380. Interview with Kitty Ewens.

Bicentennial—Roger Welch

Roger Welch (New Jersey 1946—)
Residence: New York City.
Education: 1969, BFA, Miami University, Ohio; 1971, MFA, The School of the Chicago Art Institute.
Among Recent One-Artist Exhibitions: 1973, John Gibson Gallery, N.Y.C.; 1974, Milwaukee Art Center, Wisconsin; 1975, Galleria Forma, Genoa, Italy; Galerie Gerald Piltzer, Paris; Stefanotty Gallery, N.Y.C.

Proposal for a Bicentennial Project—1975
Status: Hypothetical Bicentennial proposal.
A proposal to reconstruct the earliest house inhabited by the oldest living person in the United States, as it exists in his memory. Plans are derived from interviews with this person.

[Charlie Smith who claims to have been born in Liberia in 1842, brought to the U.S. on a slave ship in 1854, then reared on a Texas ranch as a family member rather than a slave, is recognized by the Social Security Administration as the oldest living American. *Newsweek,* Feb. 9, 1976.]

Although the proposal is actually to reconstruct a house as it exists in the memory of the oldest living person in the United States, the following interview with Kitty Ewens, age 100, and drawing of a house she inhabited in her twenties, is exemplary of how the Bicentennial proposal would be implemented.

Excerpts from a conversation recorded on August 28, 1974, with Kitty Ewens, interviewed by Roger Welch:
K.E.: "Oh, yes, well when I was married. See, my husband was an architect and we were married in 1898. We moved right into our own duplex. He built a duplex-up and down, and we moved downstairs and we had a tenant upstairs. When we were first married, well, the apartment was small—only one bedroom, and then we had one baby after another and we sold that and then he built another one right next door with two bedrooms. We lived there a couple of years and then we had some more babies and then that was too small. He always did like to remodel old places. He enjoyed doing that. Then he bought a regular old farmhouse a little more than a block away from where we lived. It was a regular old farmhouse with a barn and he remodeled that. We had one, two, three, four bedrooms and a sitting room on the second floor and a dining room and a living room, a reception room, a kitchen, and a little washroom downstairs. It was very nice. We lived there nineteen years while the children went to grade school. They all went to the same grade school and then we moved to the east side after that. Then he bought this house. This was a rundown rooming house and this little house next door had a barn. He made a house out of that barn and remodeled this house. Didn't he do a good job? He was seventy years old then."
R.W.: "He remodeled it when he was seventy?"
K.E.: "Yes, and I just love it. I'd like to stay here until they carry me out."

Roger Welch.

Boston—Friedrich St. Florian

Friedrich St. Florian (Austria 1932—)
Residence: Cambridge, Massachusetts.
Education: 1958, Diploma, Institute of Technology, Graz, Austria; 1961–1962, Fulbright Fellow; 1962, MS Arch., Columbia University, N.Y.C.
Among Major Works: 1959–1960, House Dr. Dapra, with R. Abraham, Austria; 1959–1962, House Pless, with R. Abraham, Austria; 1962–1967, Elements of the City (projects), N.Y.C., Providence, R. I., and Rome; 1970–1976, Imaginary Spaces (projects), Providence and Rome; 1974, Park Lovell, Lovell Island, Boston Harbor.

Proposal for a New Harvard Bridge—1972
Location: Boston.
Status: Unsuccessful Bicentennial proposal.
Additional Credit: Jeffrey Owen Brosk.
This bridge is intended as a replacement for the existing Harvard Bridge, a structure which is particularly dominant in the context of our investigation. Crossing the Charles River between Boston and Cambridge, it is a key element in the fabric of this metropolitan arena. As a symbolic gesture it nevertheless reaches beyond its local geographical limitations: every metropolis has a Harvard Bridge.

Our proposal establishes this as a place of encounter not unlike the Ponte Vecchio in Florence, where cultural, social, political, educational, and recreational activities can be held. The bridge is scaled for both pedestrians and automobiles. To the person in a car, driving along the river by night, it will be a ribbon of rainbows. A light steel sculpture covers the entire length. On this structure are long strips of one-way mirror diffraction gratings. During the day they reflect the river itself, and at night reflect the light from vehicles onto the water. The motorist, therefore, sees the bridge as a prismatic fantasy form: the pedestrian on his walkway is conscious of an imaginary ceiling and of the light reflecting up and down—it would be rather like crossing on the promenade deck of an ocean liner.

The main deck of the bridge has been transformed into a pedestrian mall. Various facilities such as shops, galleries, cafes, restaurants, theaters, day care centers, playgrounds, public open space areas, and marinas will be incorporated. There could be other activities and smaller cafes on floats in the river. A monorail service would run free of charge in a continuous loop around the center of the pedestrian level. Motor traffic would be directed along the elevated level, and a parking area for approximately 250 cars could be constructed under the river—and linked directly to the pedestrian mall.

Friedrich St. Florian.

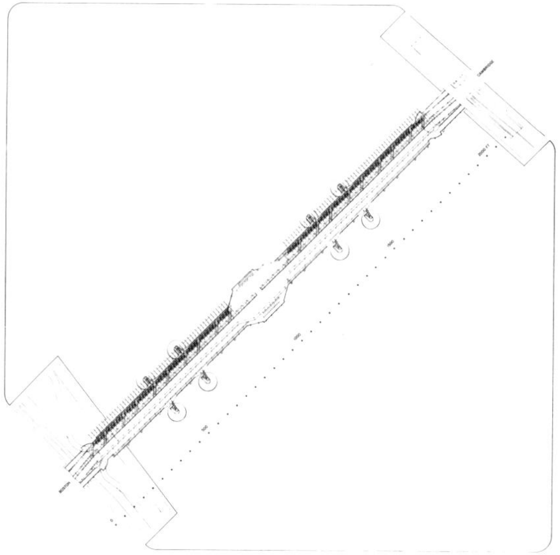
381. New Harvard Bridge. Axonometric.

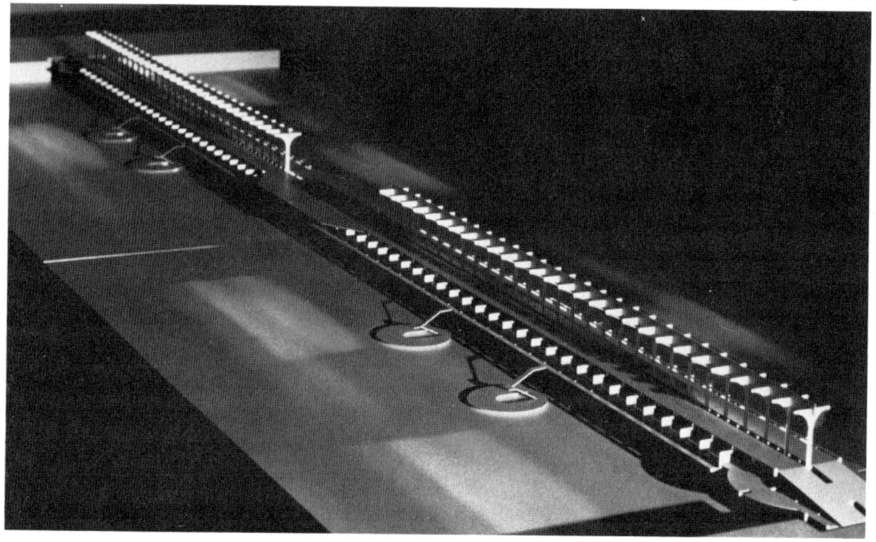
382. Proposal for a New Harvard Bridge. Model.

383. United States Bicentennial World Exposition Site.

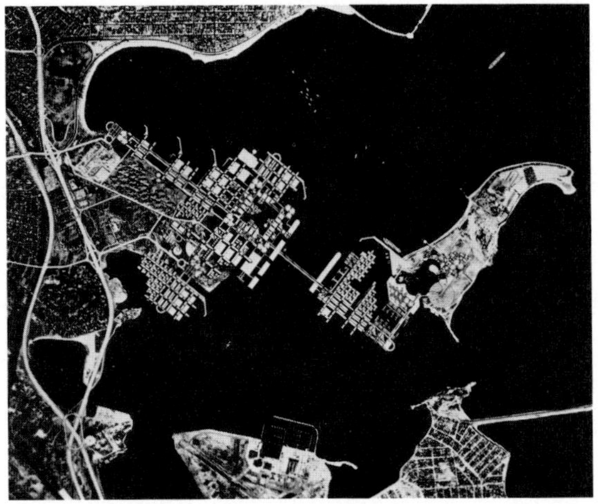

384. The Exposition/New Community Prototype.

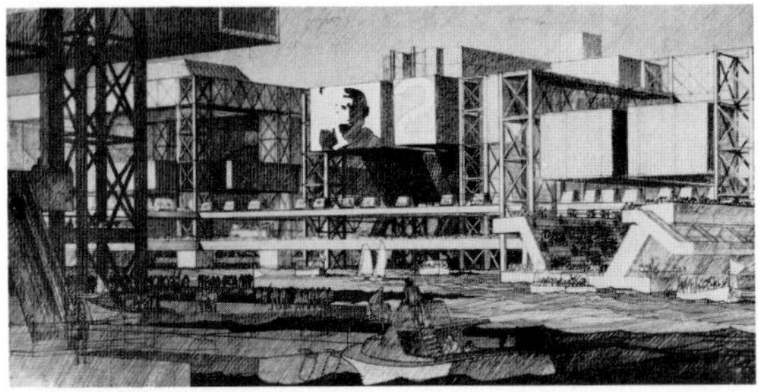

385. The Water Plaza. Perspective.

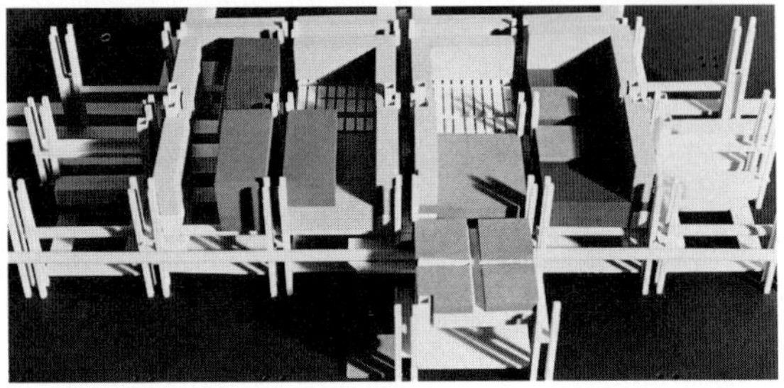

386. The Framework Concept. Model.

Boston—Jan Wampler

Jan Wampler (Ohio 1939—)
Residence: Jamaica Plain, Massachusetts.
Education: 1963, BS Arch., Rhode Island School of Design; 1964, M Arch. in Urban Design, Harvard Graduate School of Design.
Among Major Works: 1960, Master Plan for Cape Cod new town; 1968, study for air rights over Massachusetts turnpike; 1969, housing for migratory workers, Harvard, Mass.; 1969, Warehouse Cooperative School, Watertown, Mass.; 1970, Park for Martha Elliot Health Center, Jamaica Plain, Mass.

Boston Bicentennial—Expo '76
Proposal Developed: 1969.
Location: Boston.
Status: Unsuccessful Bicentennial proposal.
The greatest opportunity today lies in communication systems, organizational ability, and our tremendous technological ability—particularly in the systems approach to problem solving. This approach combines the efforts of many different producers into one great product.

The theme we have chosen for a Boston exposition—The Interdependence of Man—provides a framework to organize these resources in three ways. They are: the theme itself which will coordinate the research of urban problems; the testing of innovative solutions through a working urban laboratory; and the creation of a new community to demonstrate potential quality of urban life.

One of the primary purposes of the exposition will be its role as a working laboratory testing and evaluating solutions to urban problems. The exposition can experiment in housing, communication, recreation, and other physical, social, or economic problems of urbanization. These experiments will be constructed at full scale so they can be walked through, ridden on, and lived in to be properly evaluated by laymen and experts alike. As part of the exposition there will be 20,000 housing units where visitors may stay from one- to three-day periods and experience all aspects of a New Community.

As a final extension of the theme and the urban laboratory concept, the exposition organization—program and physical structure—has been designed to become a New Community. This New Community will provide a real alternative to existing urban, suburban, and rural life, as we have known it over the past century.

The Water Plaza is the exposition's Crystal Palace, Harvard Square, and Boston Common all in one. Here, surrounding an open expanse of water, are concentrated the highest intensity and diversity of activities of the exposition. As the Crystal Palace did in 1851, the Water Plaza will offer an opportunity to show the potential of the technology of our time to create a totally new environment.

The physical plan of the Exposition is a framework designed to provide order, to accept diversity and finally to accept changes of activities. This is highly applicable to the theme of the exposition and its reuse in a New Community.

Jan Wampler.

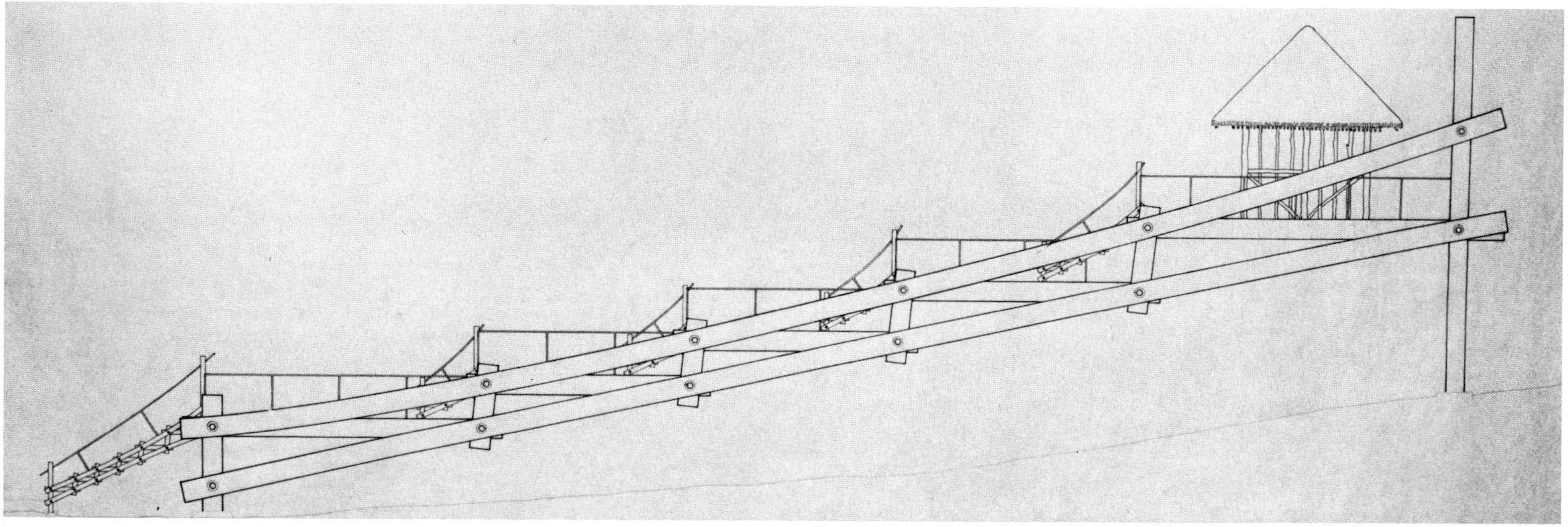

387. The Nebraska Stair. Elevation.

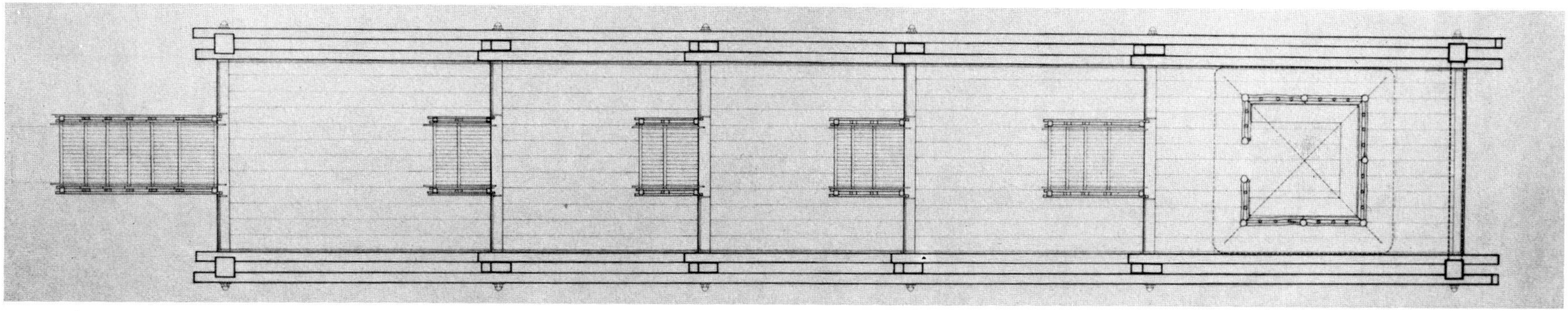

388. The Nebraska Stair. Plan.

Nebraska—Alan Saret

Alan Daniel Saret (New York City 1944—)
Residence: New York City.
Education: 1966, BA Arch., Cornell University; 1967, Hunter College.
Among Major Works: 1971, the India Ramp, New Delhi, India; 1974, the Water Arrangement Temple, the Theater of the Sun, the Universal Replicating Theater, N.Y.C.; 1974, the Ghosthouse of Alael, Art Park, Lewiston, N.Y.

The Nebraska Stair—1975

Location: Route 80, Sidney, Nebraska.
Status: Unsuccessful competition entry.
The Nebraska Stair is an idea involving elevation and shelter in a low-rolling area where a slight change in height greatly increases the extent to which we can see around us. The gradually rising arc of the stair can be perceived in turn from a substantial distance along the highway by the approaching vehicles. The stair is a bridge spanning 80 feet, and constructed from timber (8 × 16 inches), and a specially designed hardware truss. The shelter at the top, including benches to sit on, is to be built with people from the area, using local materials. The opposing arcs of the truss give the impression that the structure has been thrust into space, and the discontinuity of the stair at the top suggests an invisible ascent beyond.

Alan Saret.

Nebraska—SITE, Inc.

SITE, Inc. (New York City 1969—)
Location: New York City.
Principals: Alison Sky, Emilio Sousa, Michelle Stone, James Wines.
Among Major Works: 1972, Peeling Facade, BEST Products Co., Inc., Richmond, Va.; 1974, Intermediate School 25—Courtyard, (Building Architect, David Todd, Associates), N.Y.C.; 1975, Indeterminate Facade, BEST Products Co., Inc., Houston, Texas.
Among Major Publications: Since 1972 SITE has produced a series of books entitled *ON SITE* dealing with architecture and the environmental arts. *ON ENERGY (ON SITE 5/6)* and *UNBUILT AMERICA (ON SITE 7)* are the most recent in this series.

SITE, Inc. is an organization composed of artists, architects, writers, and technicians chartered in 1970 for the purpose of exploring new concepts relative to the urban visual environment.

Interstate 80—1975

Location: Nebraska-Platte River rest stop.
Status: Department of Highways in Nebraska rejected any project involving use of highway surface and median area.
Concept: James Wines.

As a part of the Bicentennial celebration the State of Nebraska plans to place a series of works by American sculptors in the various rest stop areas branching off Interstate 80. Based upon the assumption that the greater number of sculptures will be object art for the pedestrian, SITE's concept explores an alternative for the moving traveler in an automobile. The proposal utilizes the grass-covered gore area separating the shoulder of the road from the rest stop. The grass plots are to be elevated into a series of gradually diminishing corrugations (achieved by an inner construction of precast concrete shells). The effect is intended to suggest both a ritual environment and an ambiguous inversion of the standard roadway terrain.

James Wines.

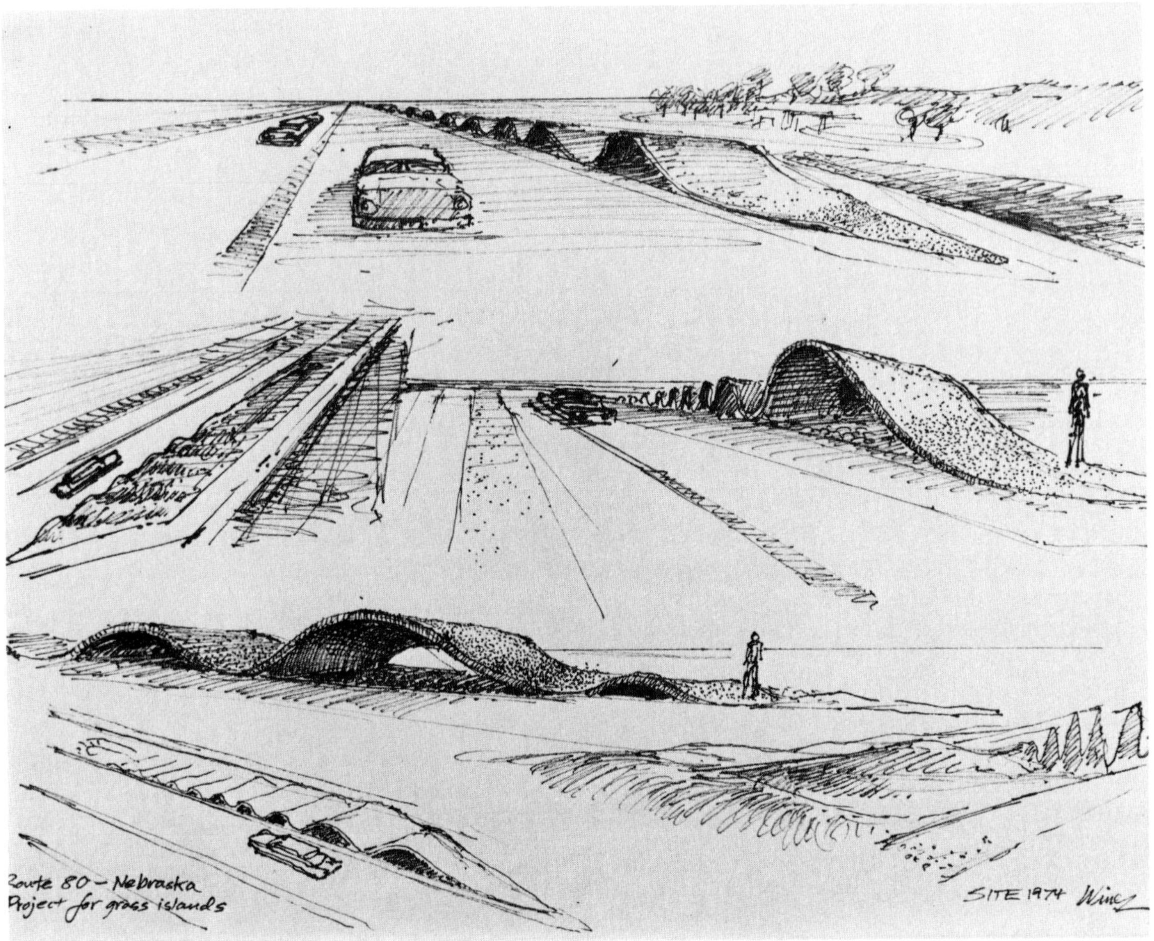

389. Interstate 80. Nebraska-Platte River Rest Stop. Project for Grass Islands.

390. Interstate 80. Nebraska-Platte River Rest Stop Model. Aerial View.

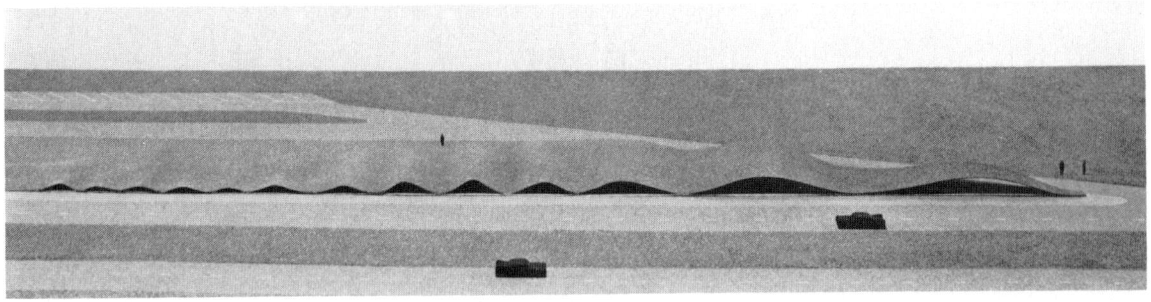

391–393. Interstate 80. REST STOP. Model.

Nebraska—SITE, Inc.

Interstate 80—1975
Location: Any rest stop area.
Status: Department of Highways in Nebraska rejected any project involving use of highway surface and median area.
Concept: Alison Sky.
This proposal is developed for the motorist travelling at high speed. The stenciled words REST STOP begin to appear as though metamorphosized from the dotted highway divider lines approximately one mile before the actual rest stop site. The letters grow slowly until the words REST STOP are completely formed (about one quarter mile from the area). Upon reaching the grass gore, the letters become three dimensional—beginning with the letter 'R' and continuing in both two and three dimensional form. At the center of the rest area, the concrete letters begin to drop away until they disappear at the exit tip of the gore. The stenciled letters, as well, reverse and return slowly into the paving division. These reversed letters can be read through the rear-view mirror of the passing automobile.

Alison Sky.

394. Nebraska State Entrance Proposal.

Nebraska—Jeff Vandeberg

Jeff J. Vandeberg (The Netherlands 1936—)
Residence: New York City.
Education: 1960, B Arch., University of Nebraska; graduate work at University of Oregon and University of Michigan.
Among Major Projects: Houses in Amsterdam and Long Island; design consultant on a variety of planning and design projects; mural in Hewlett Resource Center, Long Island, N.Y.; the Solar Year Fotogrid.

Nebraska State Entrance Proposal—1975
Location: Interstate 80, Omaha-Lincoln, Nebraska.
Status: Both of the local sponsors fell out of favor, and there are plans for resubmission.

This was developed in response to a local "Nebraska Gateway to the West" proposal spanning the Omaha-Lincoln Interstate 80. The project consists of a one minute 3/4-mile-long high speed entrance experience. The black steel "welcome" fragments range from 20 to 60 feet and are outlined with blue reflectors. They are discernible at 1,000 feet, readable at 250 feet, and at 175 feet the fragments align to complete a nonperspective "welcome" sign, followed by disintegration and scale reversal. A sequential arch is placed 1,000 feet ahead, its triangular steel arc sections are 75 feet in radius and spaced at 100 foot intervals, tracing a 180 degree arc in 15 degree segments. The members are held in tension by a steel cable on which lights are attached. At night this traces a half rotation of a double helix over a distance of 2,400 feet to welcome the visitor.

Jeff Vandeberg.

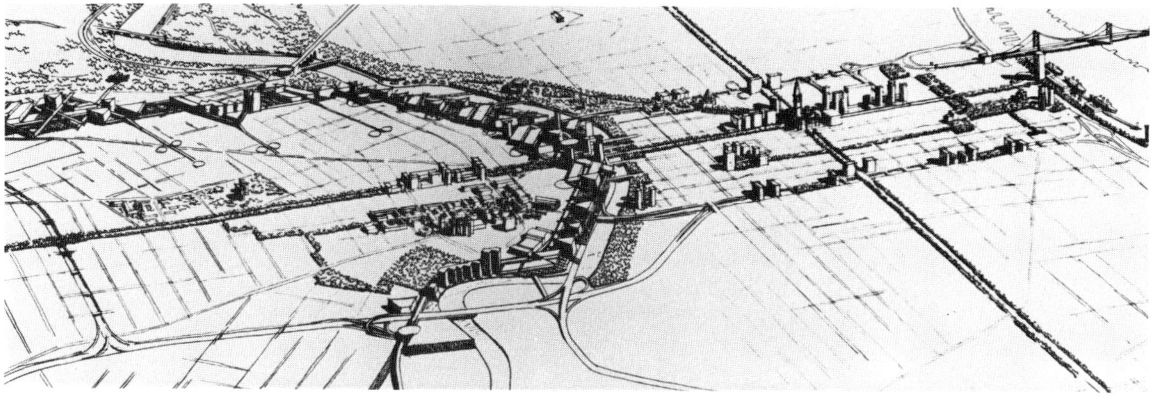

395. Proposal for a Megastructure Over the Tracks of the Penn Central Railroad.

396. Detail of Megastructure and Transportation System.

Philadelphia Bicentennial Proposals

In total Philadelphia spent about $4 million planning an international exposition. The city was officially selected by the President in 1970, and the exposition was internationally authorized by the official body, the Bureau of International Expositions in Paris. The U.S. is the second nation in the 40-year history of the Bureau to have received designation and defaulted.

John Andrew Gallery.

John Andrew Gallery (Boston 1940—)
Residence: Austin, Texas.
Education: 1961, BA, Harvard College; 1964, M Arch., Harvard University.
Among Major Works: Bicentennial Planning Group (the creation of a Bicentennial program); Planning and Design for International Exposition in Philadelphia; Design Supervision, Skidmore Owings Merrill Market East Urban Renewal, Philadelphia; Design Supervision, Master Plan, University of Pennsylvania and Temple University, Philadelphia.
Among Publications: 1972, *Man-Made Philadelphia* (with Richard Saul Wurman).

Wurman, Richard Saul (Philadelphia 1935—)
Residence: Philadelphia.
Education: 1959, B Arch., and M Arch., University of Pennsylvania.
Firm: Murphy Levy Wurman.
Among Major Publications: *City: Form and Intent; Urban Atlas; Making the City Observable; The Architecture of Information;* 1964, *The Notebooks and Drawings of Louis I. Kahn* (with Eugene Feldman), 1972, *Man-Made Philadelphia* (with John Andrew Gallery).

Committee for an International Exposition in Philadelphia

Proposal for a Megastructure—1967

Location: Over the Pennsylvania Railroad, Philadelphia.
Status: This was a conceptual idea, developed to encourage the city to undertake an ambitious program for 1976.
Developed by: Committee for an International Exposition in Philadelphia (Richard Wurman, Thomas Todd, John Andrew Gallery).
The site: the west bank of the Schuylkill River over the right of way of the Pennsylvania Railroad.

The physical structure: a megastructure—a continuous architectural environment—designed by an international interdisciplinary team, extending for about four-and-a-half miles in the air rights over the railroad tracks.

The form of the megastructure will be generated by the international exhibition areas and the linear transportation systems that run throughout its entire length. The transportation spine will consist of a series of unique minirails and moving platforms of varying speeds.

The flexibility of the structure allows for the development of different kinds of spaces in proximity to one another, including revolutionary housing forms. It will provide a unifying organization incorporating all exhibition areas into a single environment.

The megastructure's adaptability for large and varied spaces for the exposition makes it equally adaptable to its future use in providing expansion of the residential, institutional, and commercial space around it. Its prototypical form allows it to continue to grow over similar sites both during and after the Bicentennial celebration as part of the process of rebuilding the city.

Committee for an International Exposition in Philadelphia.

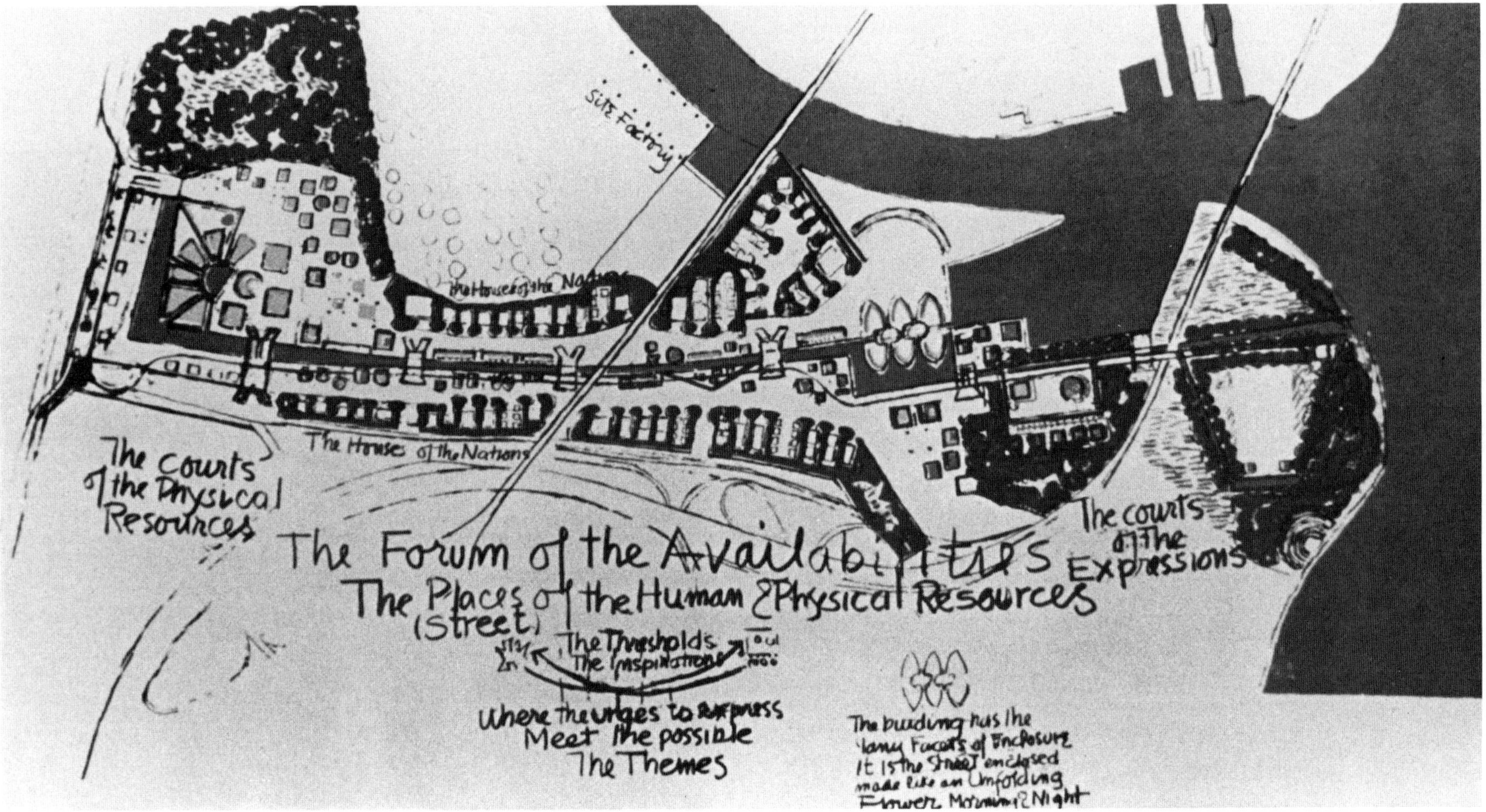

397. United States International Exposition in Philadelphia.

Philadelphia—Louis I. Kahn

Louis I. Kahn (see Kahn for biographical information).

Philadelphia Bicentennial—1972
Status: Unsuccessful Bicentennial proposal.
Developed by: Louis I. Kahn.
This scheme moves beyond the city's concept of a single boulevard, flanked by National and Theme Buildings, and connected by overhead and surface transportation.

What is the city but the seat of Availabilities? They are connected in the city, and that connection is the city's value. Today, dissension is out in the open. It stems from the desire for what is not yet made, not yet expressed. Bare needs come from the known, and supplying only what is lacking can bring no lasting joy. Did the world need the Fifth Symphony? Did Beethoven need it? He desired it; now the world needs it. Such desires bring about the new need. My feeling for the Threshold is part of this realization, where the will to be, the will to express, meets the possible. Those points are the points of Availability.

Louis Kahn in *Architectural Forum* CXXXVII, July-August 1972.

Philadelphia—Mitchell/Giurgola Associates

Mitchell/Giurgola Associates (see Mitchell for biographical information).

30th Street Station—1969
Location: Air rights over the Pennsylvania Railroad, Philadelphia.
Status: Abandoned in December 1970 due to insufficient commitment of Federal funds and local community opposition.
Developed by: Philadelphia 1976 Bicentennial Corporation, John Andrew Gallery, Director; David A. Crane Associates and Mitchell/Giurgola Associates, Principal Consultants.
This proposal was related to the megastructure plan of 1967, and developed the idea of building over 100 acres of railroad yards for an exposition, with later conversion to commercial and residential use.

John Andrew Gallery.

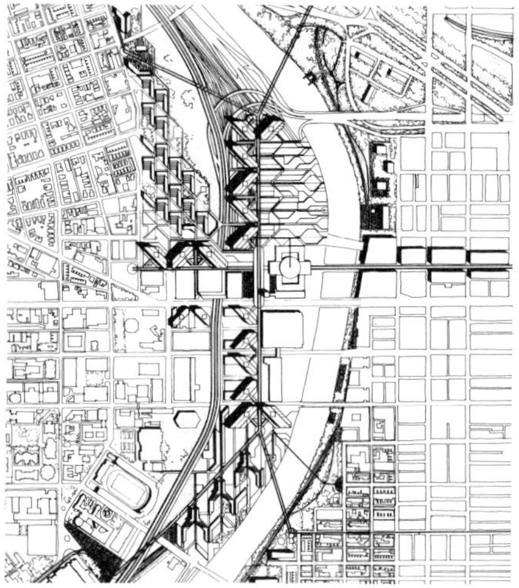

398. 30th Street Station Plan. Schematic Study.

399. 30th Street Station International Exposition Plan. Sketch.

Philadelphia Bicentennial—1972
Location: Eastwick.
Status: Federal government rejected the idea of having only one major exposition.
Developed by: Mitchell/Giurgola Associates.
This scheme, located on a site adjacent to the International Airport, is organized along a transportation spine which has a water canal for slow moving boats as well as high capacity transit systems. All activities are related to the spine making the public area the dominant form of the fair. At either end, there are two major thematic pavilions dealing with public performance and participation.

Mitchell/Giurgola Associates.

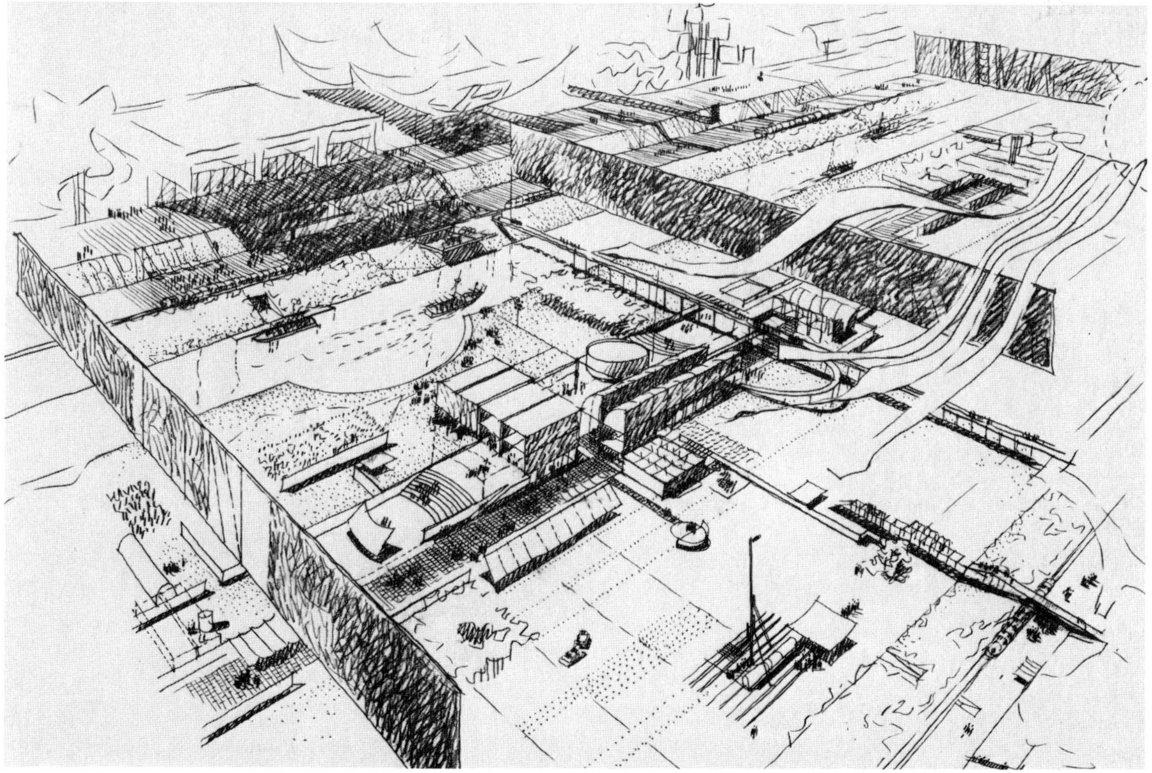

400. Eastwick Site. Aerial View.

401. Petty's Island Exposition Plan. Bridge Structure. Model.

Philadelphia—Kevin Roche John Dinkeloo

Kevin Roche John Dinkeloo and Associates (established Connecticut 1966—)
Among Major Works of Firm: 1966, Aetna Life Insurance Company Computer Building, Hartford, Conn.; 1967, College Life Insurance Company Headquarters, Indianapolis, Ind.; 1967, the Ford Foundation Building, N.Y.C.; 1969, Oakland Museum, Calif.

Kevin Roche John Dinkeloo and Associates is the successor firm to Eero Saarinen and Associates.

Petty's Island—1971
Location: Over the Delaware River.
Status: Site was abandoned and plan was never officially presented.
Developed by: Kevin Roche John Dinkeloo and Associates.

The design for the Bicentennial celebration in Philadelphia proposed a bridge structure connecting Philadelphia and Camden, New Jersey, which was 8,000 feet long, 1,250 feet wide, containing a total of 40,000,000 square feet on four levels. The bridge spans were 1,000 feet clear, the height of the central pavilion 300 feet, and the height of the bridge off the river 175 feet.

The exhibition space was to have been housed in a series of glass barrel-vaulted spaces, each 250 feet wide by as long as required by the exhibit program, and arranged in a manner which would best serve the overall plan. These barrel vaults would have sprung from the primary trussing system. On the level immediately below the main exhibition level were motels, restaurants, and service facilities. The lower two levels contained space for 50,000 cars flanking an interstate highway connecting I-95 and I-84 and the primary means of access to the structure.

It was envisioned that after the Exposition, the structure could be used as ground on which to build a whole community containing parking and manufacturing on the lower levels, housing, commercial and office space on the upper levels, with ample park space in between.

Kevin Roche John Dinkeloo and Associates.

Philadelphia—Venturi and Rauch

Venturi and Rauch (see Venturi for biographical information).

Benjamin Franklin Parkway—1972

Status: Unbuilt due to lack of funding.
Developed by: Venturi and Rauch.
Additional Credit: Denise Scott Brown, Steven Izenour.

The Benjamin Franklin Parkway is the context for much of Philadelphia's rich cultural heritage as well as a fabulous piece of nineteenth century design.

In preliminary planning for the Parkway Celebration, we concluded that by *day* the Parkway can hardly be improved on architecturally. Therefore, we recommended maintaining this traditional element of our city as it is, as a valued part of our heritage, adding to its architecture only some modest facilities to enhance the pedestrian vitality and amenity of the area. Thus the premise of our plan: achievement of activity by day, and through lighting, not architecture, spectacle by night.

By *night* we can enhance and dramatize the classic forms of this monumental boulevard through the additional dimension of moving light not available when the Parkway was designed. A *new* symbolism and lighting sympathetically imposed on a *traditional* form or urbanism can make a memorable setting for a national celebration.

Plans were formulated to activate the Parkway as an arena for performance, the visual arts, and the sciences through "front yard" areas linking institutions, their programs, and the people.

Venturi and Rauch.

402. Benjamin Franklin Parkway Celebration for '76. Illuminated Night View.

United States Capitol Competition

James Diamond (?–?)
We know little beyond what is told us by Diamond's competitive drawings. The legends of these state that he was of Somerset County, Md., at the very end of the Eastern Shore. The census records of 1790 are missing for Somerset County, so we do not know even what was the size of his household or whether he owned slaves. Fiske Kimball and Wells Bennett, *AIA Journal,* VII, August 1919.

Stephen Hallet (Paris 1775—New York 1825)
Education: Received architectural training in France. Emigrated to America ca.1788.

Philip Hart (?–?)
The work of Philip Hart is as little known as his personal life, and his status as a designer can be judged only from the drawings submitted in the Federal Competitions. Inspection of these designs reveals the hand of the carpenter-builder, with little knowledge of the principles of design or of draftsmanship. Fiske Kimball and Wells Bennett, *AIA Journal,* VII, August 1919.

Samuel McIntire (Massachusetts 1757—1811)
The most celebrated among American craftsman, Samuel McIntire, is still far from being really known. In all the flood of recent notices and studies, of photographs and drawings of buildings ascribed to him, the necessary foundations for an authentic knowledge of his works and his style have not yet been laid. Fiske Kimball and Wells Bennett, *AIA Journal,* VII, August 1919.

403. Entry by Samuel McIntire. Plan and Elevation.

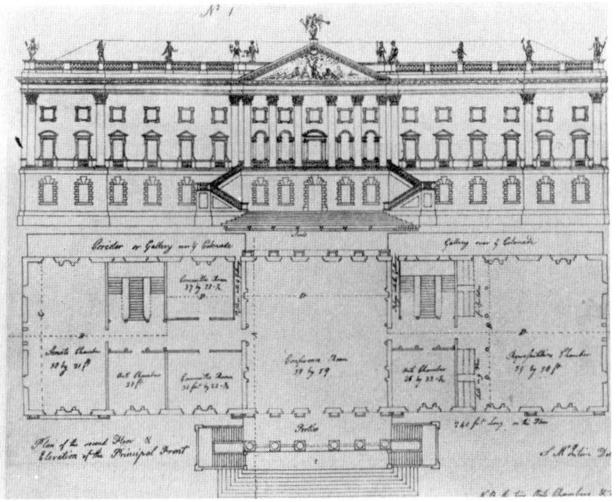

404. Entry by Stephen Hallet. Elevation.

William Thornton (Virgin Islands 1759—Washington, D.C. 1828)
Education: 1781–1784, University of Edinburgh (studied medicine), Scotland.
Among Major Works: 1789, won competition for the Library Company, Philadelphia. Of this competition Thornton said: "When I travelled I never thought of architecture. But I got some books and worked a few days, then gave a plan in the ancient Ionic order which carried the day." John Garraty and Edward James, *Dictionary of American Biography,* 1974.

William Thornton served as head of the U.S. Patent Office from 1802 to 1828.

U.S. Capitol Competition—1792-1793

Location: Washington, D.C.
Status: Unsuccessful competition entries.
The competition for the National Capitol in Washington in 1792–1793 was the first important architectural competition in the United States. Before that time, indeed, there had been but few competitions here for buildings of any sort. In general, the difficulty had been, not to choose an architect or a design from among many, but to secure any competent designer or adequate design in advance at all. These modest forerunners were insignificant compared with the competition now instituted by the new Federal Government for the Capitol, a competition in which the best talent of the entire country took part.

The competition holds an interest for us in a number of quite distinct ways. One interest is through the light it throws on our competitions in general; the origins of our methods of conducting them; the misunderstanding by public authorities; the occasional breaches of professional etiquette, and the wasted efforts and charges of plagiarism. We gain an insight into the different conditions of work at the outset of our national life and at the same time see how modern conditions have grown out of them. There is interest of a different sort in the supreme effort made by the competitors to solve the then novel problems created by the adoption of a republican form of government for a great modern nation. Finally there is the interest which the competitive drawings and related documents have in revealing to us, freshly or in greater fullness, the personalities of a great number of early designers from all classes and from every part of the country. Some of these men are already honered as the founders of our national architecture; others, now really studied for the first time, prove to have been of unsuspected importance. Even the minor men were influential in their own local spheres, and the data furnished by their appearance on the national stage leads to the establishment of new reputations.

The first suggestion of holding a competition came from Thomas Jefferson, then Secretary of State, in a memorandum of September 8, 1791. He was influenced doubtless by his knowledge of the practice of securing designs for public buildings by competition in France. His original "sketch or specimen of advertisement" of the Capitol competition, which accompanied the suggestion, reveals the tentative state of the plans for the new capital city, which had not yet received its name. It was this very draught, sent back to the President and which was then once more, on March 6, 1792, sent to the Commissioners with some corrections. These corrections, interlined by Jefferson in the draught, introduce the name of the city "Washington in the territory of Columbia," and suggest July 20, 1792 as the time limit.

At the close of the competition the Commissioners, in a letter to Stephen Hallet, invited him—as author of the design "approaching nearest to the leading ideas of the President [Washington] and the Commissioners"—to come to Georgetown and study the matter further under their direction, with a liberal guarantee of expenses and the possibility that his design might be "improved into approbation." Revised designs by Hallet were considered but again, "none appeared so complete on the whole as to fix a decided opinion."

Meanwhile a new competitor had appeared, Dr. William Thornton. He had written from Tortola in the West Indies on July 12, 1792, stating that he had drawings ready and that he would bring them with him to America. [Although arriving after the competition deadline, the drawings] so impressed the President and others that Washington then practically decided the matter in Thornton's favor. In Washington's letter of that day to the Commissioners, after recognizing that Hallet's plans "undoubtedly have a great deal of merit," he says the qualities of Thornton's design "will, I doubt not, give it a preference in your eyes as it

406. Entry by Philip Hart. Elevation.

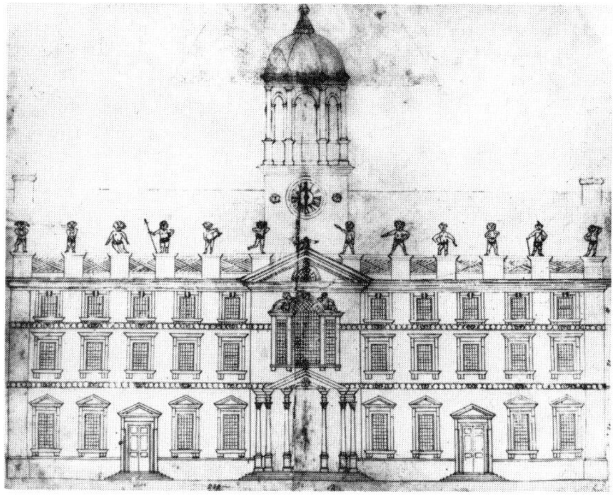

405. Entry by James Diamond. Elevation.

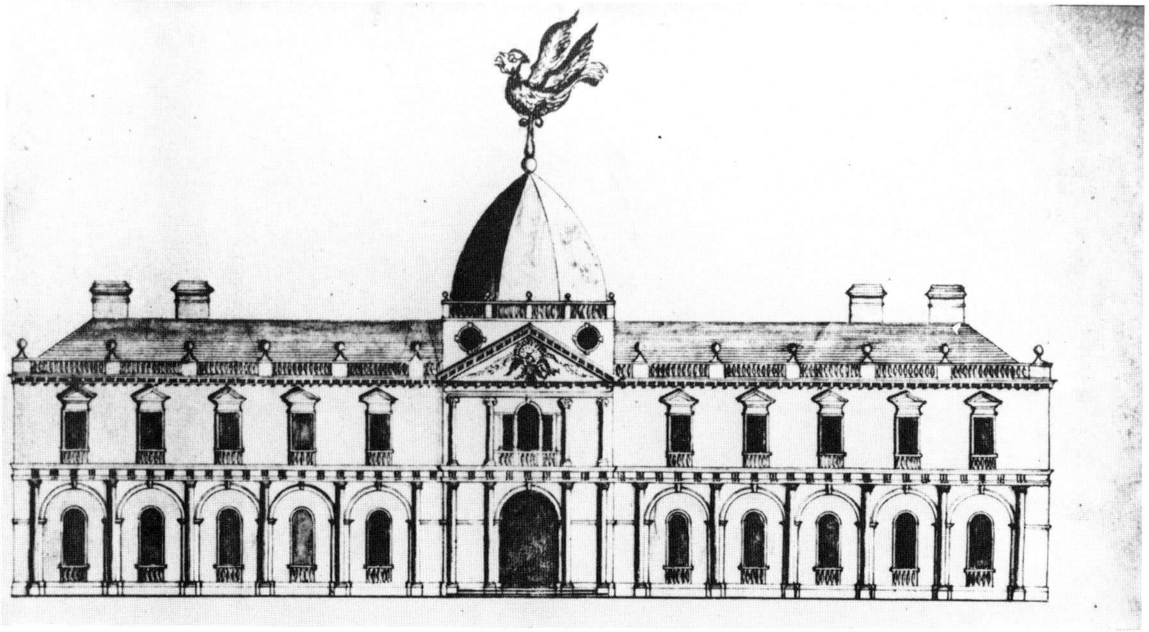

has done in mine." Appreciating that his design was not wholly satisfactory, but not realizing that the issue had already been decided, over the heads of the Commissioners, by Washington and Jefferson, Hallet, after his return to Georgetown prepared and submitted to the Commissioners one more design. [It was to no avail.] On April 5 the Commissioners notified Thornton: "The President has given his formal approbation of your plan."

In their conduct of the competition there can be no question that the public authorities were actuated by a sincere desire to act fairly to all parties, to the best of their understanding of such an unfamiliar matter. Hallet himself acknowledged that he had been honestly treated by the Commissioners, and only complained that the competition should be closed to the first design which was really his own.

That it was so closed was hardly the fault of the Commissioners, for the final decision had really been taken out of their hands. Moreover they were again urged to haste by the long delay which had already ensued, and the positive necessity of getting the Capitol under way in order to establish confidence in the whole Federal city project. That they were thus led to make their decision in favor of an unfinished design, which the Commissioners had not even seen, was a misfortune, however, quite irrespective of the merits or demerits of Thornton's original plan. The Building of the Capitol was thereby burdened with a legacy of controversy, which has descended even to modern partisans of the various contestants.

Abridged from Fiske Kimball and Wells Bennett in *AIA Journal,* VII, August 1919.

Thornton never had clear sailing in the execution of his design. He declined to supervise its construction; he lacked the technical experience to carry through the work on a major public building in a day when the architect was obliged to provide truly "comprehensive services." The short-tempered doctor thereupon had a succession of difficulties with Hallet, who was retained as supervising architect, and George Hadfield who later succeeded to the job. Both had sought to alter his design, and the even-tempered James Hoban assumed the responsibility for construction from the year 1798, until the appointment of Benjamin Latrobe in March 1803.

Latrobe brought to the position an already established reputation as an architect of great talent and skill. He was much respected by President Jefferson and managed to impose his own ideas upon the interior design and in plans for the central portion of the building which were carried out, after his retirement in 1817, by Charles Bulfinch who completed the original building in 1829.

Francis D. Lethbridge in *AIA Journal,* XLV, April 1966.

[The present Capitol is quite different from the building of 1829. Additional prominent figures have contributed to the building as we now know it. They include Robert Mills, Thomas U. Walter, and Frederick Law Olmsted. The controversy still continues, and to this day changes and additions to the building are being considered.]

407. Entry by William Thornton. Elevation.

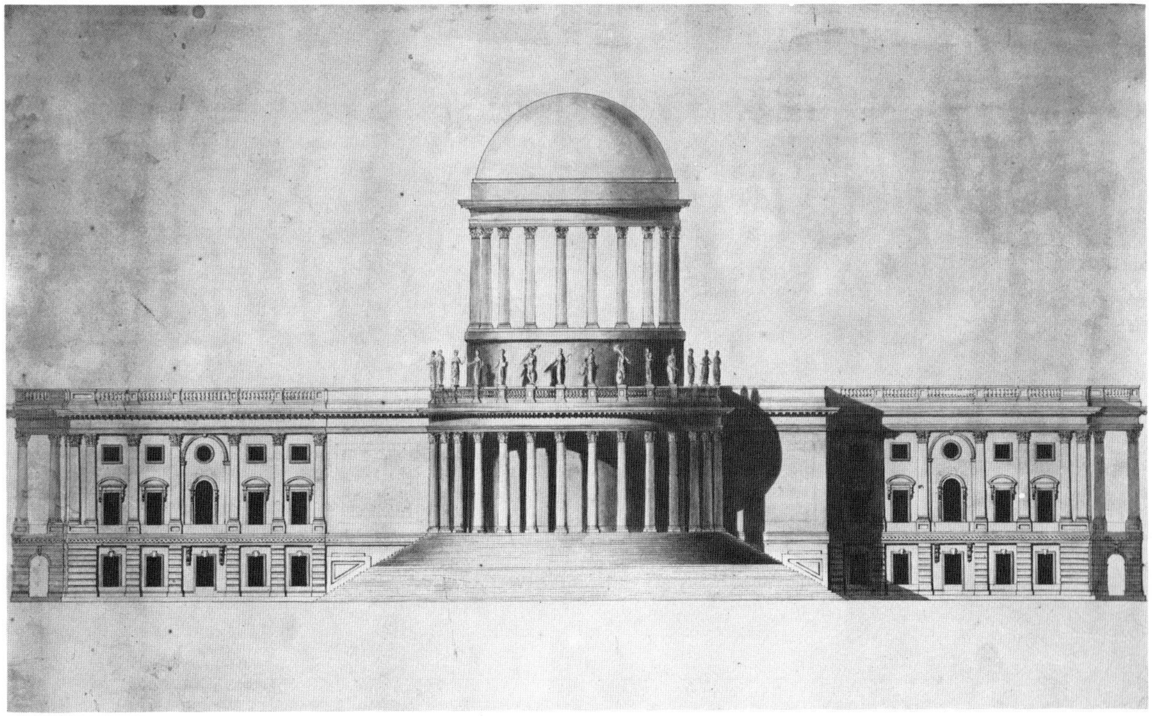

United States Centennial Competition

John McArthur, Jr. (Scotland 1823—Philadelphia 1890)
Education: ca.1883, apprenticed to an uncle, a carpenter, Philadelphia; studied evenings at the Franklin Institute, Philadelphia; attended course of lectures by Thomas U. Walter.
Among Major Works: City Hall; Girard Hotel; La Pierra Hotel; Public Ledger Building; George W. Child Mansion; all in Philadelphia.

Vaux and Radford
Calvert Vaux (London 1824—New York City 1895)
Education: Merchant Tailor's School, London.
Among Major Works: (with Frederick Law Olmsted) 1858, Central Park, New York City; 1866, Prospect Park, Brooklyn, New York (with Jacob Wrey Mould); 1874, Museum of Natural History, New York City; 1880, Metropolitan Museum of Art, New York City.

In 1857, Calvert Vaux published *Villas and Cottages,* a summary of his work in residential architecture. In the 1870s through 1890s, Vaux was a partner of George K. Radford.

Joseph Wilson (Pennsylvania 1838—Philadelphia 1902)
Education: 1858, Civil Engineering degree, Rensselaer Polytechnic Institute.
Among Major Works: Susquehanna Bridge; Schuylkill Bridge; Old Broadstreet Station; 1891, Drexel Institute; all in Philadelphia.

U.S. Centennial Exhibition—1876

Developed: 1873.
Location: Philadelphia.
Status: Unsuccessful competition entries.

Architects, Engineers, and others are hereby invited to offer preliminary sketches or designs for the buildings to be erected in Fairmount Park, Philadelphia, for the International Exhibition in 1876.

The entire buildings connected with the Exhibition will cover at least 50 acres of ground. The main building will be complete within itself. It must be of such a character, and constructed of such substantial materials, as that it shall remain after the close of the Exhibition for a *permanent* Art Museum. The Memorial Building will not exceed five acres of floor space. The remaining portion of the main building will be removed after the close of the Exhibition, and must be planned accordingly.

Report of the Committee on Plans and Architecture to the U.S. Centennial Commission, 1873.

Entry by Collins and Suteurieth

The fact that the Memorial Hall is intended to be a permanent and therefore a prominent building, suggests almost naturally that, during the time of the exposition, it should not be hidden from view by being completely encircled by the temporary buildings. Of equal importance with the *location* is the *shape* of this permanent structure. The shape of the available ground being oblong, it seemed the easiest and most natural to give a corresponding outline to the building, the more so since it adapted itself fully to the outline of the Memorial Hall on one side and to the natural formation of the ground, the grouping of trees, etc., on the other. By this combination we were enabled to set the buildings so far back from the street line of Elm Avenue as to afford at one time a full view over the whole extent of the front.

408. Entry by Collins and Suteurieth. South Elevation.

409. Entry by Francis Gatchell and Stephen Rush. Main Building.

410. Entry by Francis Gatchell and Stephen Rush. Plan.

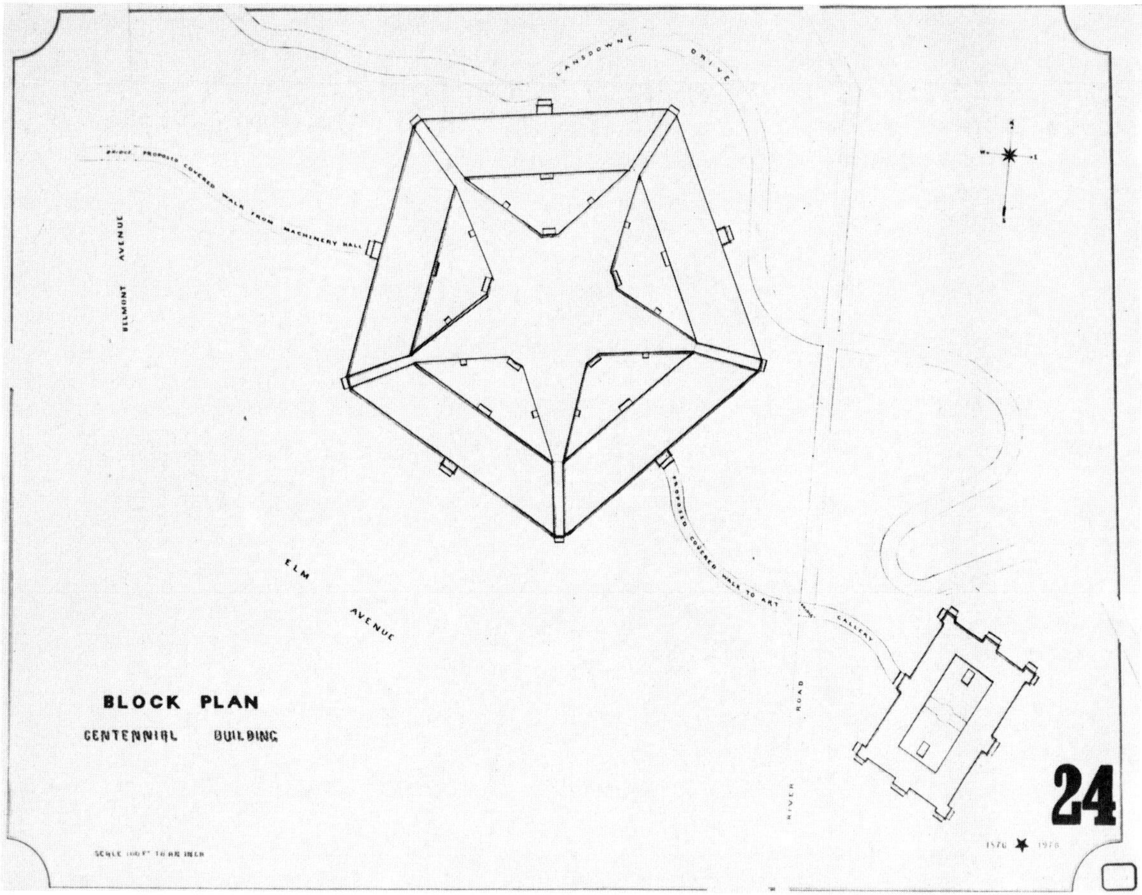

The Exposition Building proper is faced on the South by a 40 ft. Main Avenue, and flanked on East and West ends with octagonal pavilions of 100 ft. diameter, which will serve as resting places, rendezvous, etc. These, as well as the large centre dome, we propose to decorate with grass-plots, flower-beds, and flower-stands, fountains, aquariums, etc., while the 40 ft. Main Avenue is to be treated in a more ornamental style than the rest, and to be used only for the exposition of select objects of industrial arts, including the use of windows in these avenues, in the pavilions, and over main centre entrance, for exposition of stained, embossed, and otherwise decorated glass. On the North the exposition floor will be enclosed by a centre building 540 ft. long by an average width of about 55 ft., and by East and West one-story wings, terminating at the corner pavilions, and intended for restaurants.

Collins and Suteurieth.

Entry by Francis Gatchell and Stephen Rush
Previous to the meeting of the Commission in March, 1872, we conceived the plan for an Exhibition Building in the form of a star surmounted by a dome; this shape was selected for various reasons, one of which was, the star being one of the proud emblems of our nationality, it seemed peculiarly appropriate, and was in keeping with the desire subsequently expressed by some of the Honorable Commissioners, that we should have a building unlike any of its predecessors, yet combining all of their advantages and at the same time be significant of our country. The star plan with its five court yards in the angles, gave the opportunity of locating the United States in the most prominent position, the centre of the star, while the five grand divisions of the earth were

accommodated in the points in their true geographical position, relative to this country.

In this Memorial Hall, we have one room, the floor space of which is five acres, unobstructed, save by the columns, the points of the star forming magnificent vistas, the perspective being heightened by their shape; standing in the centre beneath the lofty dome, the tout-ensemble presented to the view of the beholder, would no doubt be grand in the extreme.

Francis Gatchell and Stephen Rush.

Entry by John McArthur and Joseph Wilson

The requirement of permanency in the Memorial Hall of our buildings, should lead us to profit by the experience of previous exhibitions, and erect something superior in architectural effect, to anything that has ever been done before in this species of building. An opportunity is afforded us in the design and construction of our great Centennial Exhibition structure, to demonstrate to the world that our country, which is now making rapid strides in everything else, is capable of taking a position in architecture far higher than she has ever yet done and that before the next Centennial period of her history arrives, she is destined to occupy a place in this respect equal to that of nations who claim the prestige of by-gone ages. The Memorial Hall especially should be a monument of the constructive capabilities of the Age; and should be fully up to the latest efforts of the Engineering world. It consists of two Main Spans crossing each other at right angles, each being covered with a braced wrought iron arch of 200 feet in the clear, and having a rise or height from the floor to the ridge of the roof of 128 feet. At the intersection an iron tower rises to the height of 500 feet above the ground. When the temporary buildings are removed there will

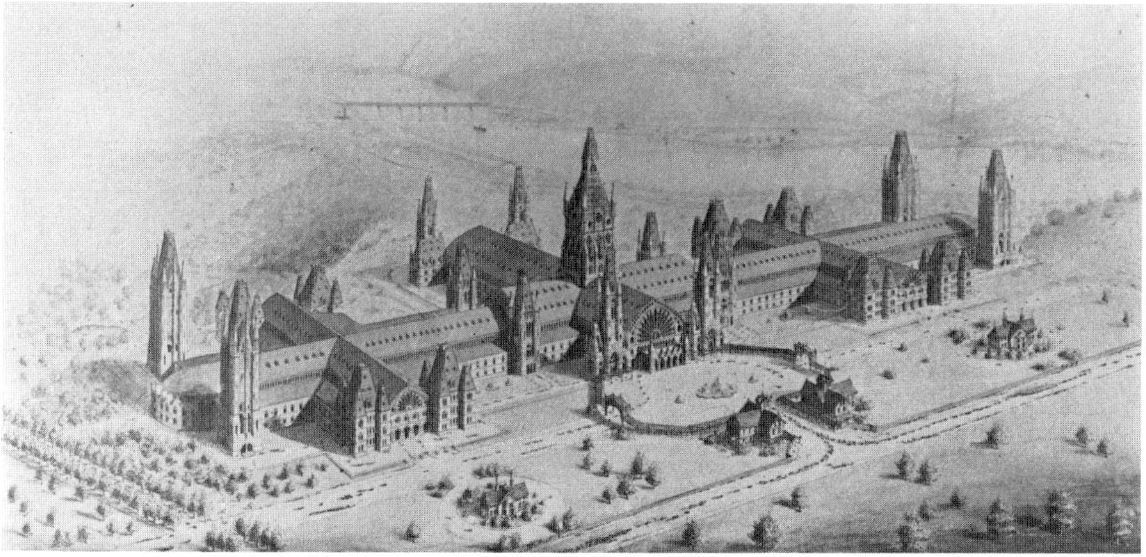

411. Entry by John McArthur, Jr. and Joseph M. Wilson.

412. Entry by Samuel Sloan. Permanent and Temporary Buildings.

be four grand fronts, each protected by towers, and presenting an imposing and complete appearance in themselves.

John McArthur and Joseph Wilson.

Entry by Jas C. Sidney

I have placed the permanent building, or Memorial building, in the centre in such a position that the grounds surrounding it can be used to the best advantage temporarily, as well as after the close of the Exhibition, and so as to form, in itself, an attractive feature of the Park. This building would have a front of 385 feet, and a depth through the centre of 500 feet. To be generally two stories in height, with three stories in the projection and corners, affording five acres of floor space, independently of the basement, which would give one and a half acres more.

The projections on each front are intended for offices, reception, and committee rooms. The Rotunda is octagonal at the base, oval in the second story, and circular on the top. This Memorial building I should propose to build of stone or marble, as being the most satisfactory and economical in the end. A building of iron and glass in our climate would be difficult to keep water-tight, would require constant repairs, would be very hot in summer, and would not be in keeping with the Park.

The Art building is 275 feet wide on the front by 225 feet deep, affording two acres of floor space as required by your instructions. The large Rotunda would give an unequalled room for the display on its floors of statuary and other works of art, with all the hanging space that can possibly be required on the sides and in its courts.

Jas C. Sidney.

Entry by Samuel Sloan

The main building will occupy the centre of the whole structure, and will be built with a view to complete permanence. The materials proposed to be used will be *iron, stone and brick,* so combined as to facilitate its construction, as well as to ensure its durability and safety from fire. Its dimensions will be 600 by 350 feet, and its centre will be covered by a dome 100 feet in diameter, 310 feet high from the ground line to the top of the statue of "America," which will crown it. Within this permanent building, and underneath the dome, will be the Memorial Hall, which is 350 ft. long from north to south, and 200 feet wide in the centre, and 85 ft. high to the crown of the arch ceiling. It is surrounded by a colonnade of richly ornamented columns, rising from a stylobate 25 feet high. This stylobate forms a continuous arcade to the four sides of the hall, with a gallery above it. The walls and ceilings it is proposed to enrich within the panels with appropriate emblematic designs. Around the Memorial Hall and connected with it at the four vestibules, are buildings two stories in height, the second story being on a level with the gallery of the hall. These are intended in future for the Art Museum, and will form part of the main structure. The dome of this centre building will be the impressive feature of the whole design, as it will also be of the permanent building, when it is isolated. In the interior it will be 250 feet in height from the floor to the eye of the dome.

Samuel Sloan.

413. Entry by Jas. C. Sidney. East Elevation.

Entry by Calvert Vaux and G. K. Radford
Although several large structures are to be erected in connection with the proposed scheme for the International Exhibition in 1876, it is evident that the problem to be first solved is the plan for the main building. In the present study the aim has been to make the building itself furnish the elements of a spacious and impressive design, that shall be equal in desirability for exhibition purposes in every part. Instead of one detached dome with a span of three hundred and thirty-three feet, the present design is made up of twenty-one domed or vaulted pavilions, each two hundred and forty feet in diameter, clustered together and connected by arches of one hundred and fifty feet opening, and fountain courts sixty feet in diameter.

The various parts of the building are thus included in one grand whole, and the result becomes a spacious hall, adequate to the emergencies of the occasion, with long vistas, central and intermediate points of emphasis, direct lines of transit throughout its length and breadth, diagonal lines of communication where really needed, and an entire relief from any appearance of contraction anywhere, for the visitor is always in an apartment over two hundred feet wide, that opens without any intermediate corridor into other apartments, also over two hundred feet wide.

It is proposed that a branch from the existing railroad, arranged for passenger traffic, should pass at a level of about twenty feet above the side-walk, inside the boundary line of the exhibition ground, and parellel to Elm Avenue, with high and low level entrances to the building. This will bring all visitors who may arrive by railroad, to the main entrance, without interfering with pedestrians or those who come in carriages or street cars.

Calvert Vaux and G. K. Radford.

414. Entry by Calvert Vaux and George K. Radford. Main Pavilion. Interior View.

415. Entry by Calvert Vaux and George K. Radford. Main Pavilion. Perspective.

Clarke, Reeves and Company (Civil Engineers)
Firm: Phoenixville Bridge Works, Phoenixville, Pennsylvania.

Centennial Tower One Thousand Feet High—1874
Location: Fairmount Park (?), Pennsylvania.
Status: Abandoned due to lack of financial support.
How high, comparatively speaking, will this thousand foot structure appear? In the illustration are grouped the highest structures in the world; and in the center, springing far above them all, is the airy network of the great tower.

The designers of this tower are Messrs. Clarke, Reeves and Co., a firm represented by its productions throughout the whole country. The plan is to be circular, and the material, American wrought iron. Four elevators, in a central tube extending the entire length, are to ascend in three and descend in five minutes, so as to be capable of transporting about 500 persons per hour. There are also spiral staircases winding around the central tube.

The tower could be constructed in one year at an estimated cost of one million dollars. By calcium and electric lights from the tower, the buildings of the Centennial Exposition, with their adjoining grounds, might be brilliantly illuminated at night. The summit of the spire would also form a magnificent observatory, while the view of the surrounding country would be unparalleled.

Abridged from "Centennial Tower One Thousand Feet High," *Scientific American,* XXX, January 1874.

416. Centennial Tower One Thousand Feet High.

Joseph Urban (Vienna 1872—New York City 1933)
Education: Art Academy, Vienna; Polytechnicum, Vienna; Studio of Karl von Hasenauer, where in 1891 Hasenauer gave Urban the opportunity to decorate the Abdin Palace for the Khedive of Egypt.
Among Major Works: 1926, Ziegfeld Theatre, N.Y.C.; 1930, New School for Social Research, N.Y.C.; 1933, Lighting and color consultant for the Chicago Century of Progress Exposition of 1933.

From 1911 to 1931, Joseph Urban was responsible for stage designs for the Boston Opera Company, Metropolitan Opera Company, Interstate Opera Company, and Ziegfeld Theatre—totalling over 160 productions.

The Reinhardt Theatre—1928

Location: New York City.
Status: Unbuilt.

Wedding Theatre Beauty to Ballyhoo

In designing the theatre Max Reinhardt is expected to occupy in New York, I have brought the fire escape out of the alleyways and tried to make it a base for the electric signs as well as a decorative feature of the façade. The face of the house is to be of vitrolite, a gleaming black glass. At various levels across the front stretch the horizontal lines of the fire escape balconies in golden metal work. Down the centre runs a grilled tower containing the emergency stairways, and this tower is continued high in the air as a kind of pinnacle. Thus I have tried to apply the fire escapes as a golden arabesque against the shining black of the façade itself.

To accommodate the advertising signs to this design, I have inserted long panels of interchangeable letters across the front of the various levels of the fire escape balconies. And I have also, of course, provided a frame for the name of the theatre running up one corner of the building.

Joseph Urban, *The American Architect,* CXXXIV, September 1928.

417. The Reinhardt Theatre. Perspective.

Venturi and Rauch (Philadelphia 1964—)
Location: Philadelphia, Pennsylvania.
Principals: Robert Venturi, John Rauch, Denise Scott Brown, Steven Izenour, David M. Vaughan, Robert T. Renfro, Jeffrey D. Ryan, Stanley F. Taraila.
Among Major Works: 1960–1963, Guild House, Friends' Housing for the Elderly, Philadelphia; 1965, Fire Station No. 4, Columbus, Indiana; 1968, Renovation of St. Francis de Sales Church, Philadelphia; 1970, the Trubek and Wislocki Houses, Nantucket Island, Mass.; 1972–1976, Franklin Court, Philadelphia.

The partnership of Robert Venturi and John Rauch was organized in 1964. In 1969, Denise Scott Brown joined the partnership and the firm's services were expanded to include urban planning. Subsequently, exhibition and graphic design were added under the direction of Steven Izenour.

Wissahickon Housing—1972
Location: Wissahickon Avenue, Philadelphia.
Status: Developers could not be secured.

This was a large, old, five acre estate in West Mount Airy, Philadelphia. It was to be subdivided—the rear portion sold with the original Art Nouveau house, and the driveway leading up to this to be sawed off in six lots. We produced a recommendation for West Mount Airy neighbors and the civic association, to show them that this could be done well. We developed a series of little manor houses "manorettes" designed to go with the style of the house at the end of the driveway, and in a way to lead up to it. At the same time they would have their own very definite character, and yet be in keeping with the much larger houses in the neighborhood. We felt we could achieve this through the way in which they related to each other, rather than through size, as we didn't have this alternative.

In the end there were no developers interested. The neighbors who had hoped to acquire the property found they couldn't, and the developer who originally did acquire the property did the houses very differently.

Venturi and Rauch.

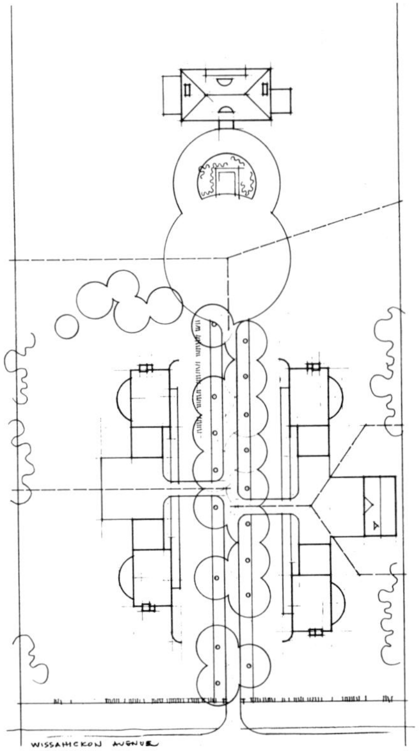

418. Site Plan.

419. Variation with Square Windows.

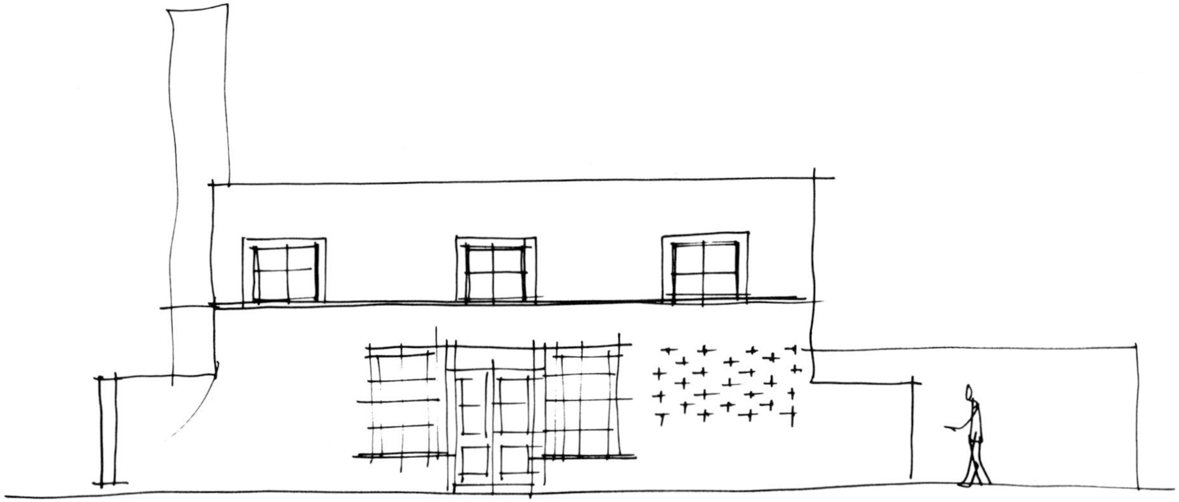

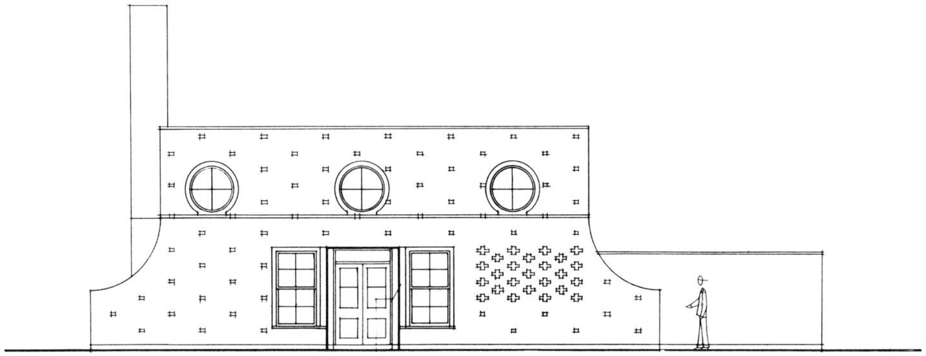

420. Front Elevation.

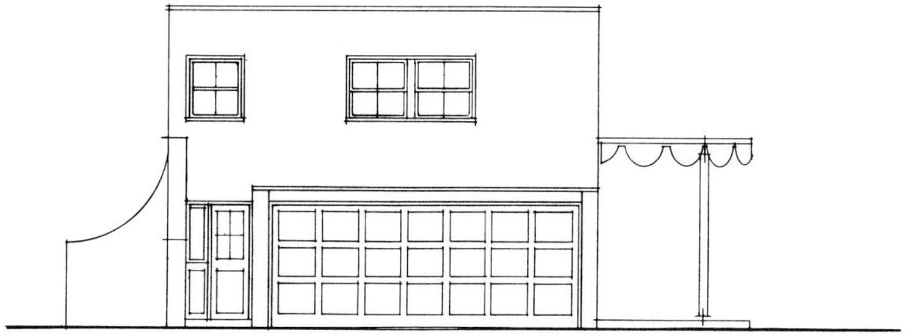

421. Side Elevation Towards Garage Court.

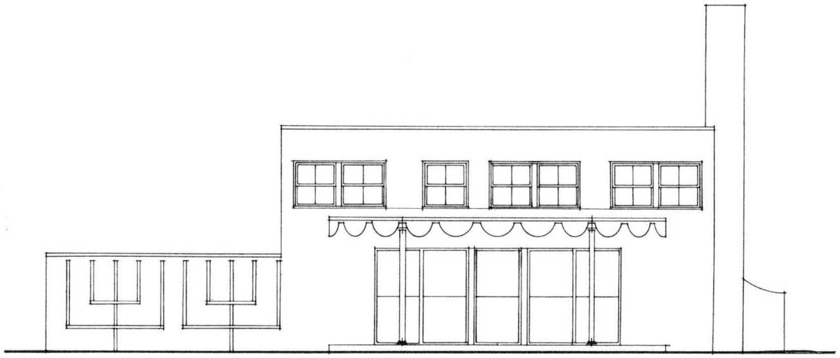

422. Back Elevation Towards Garden.

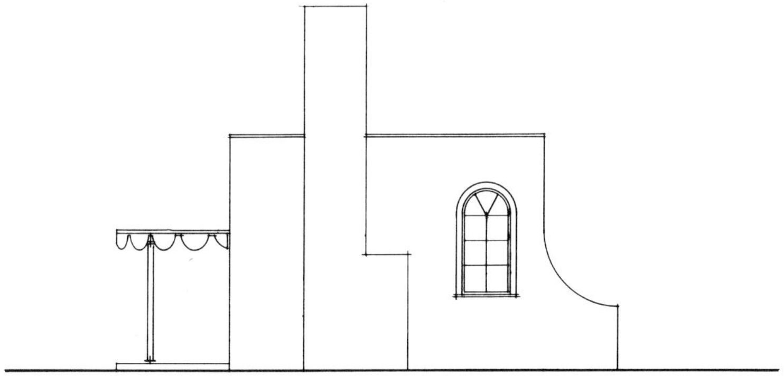

423. Side Elevation Towards Wissahickon Avenue.

424. Cross Section of Site.

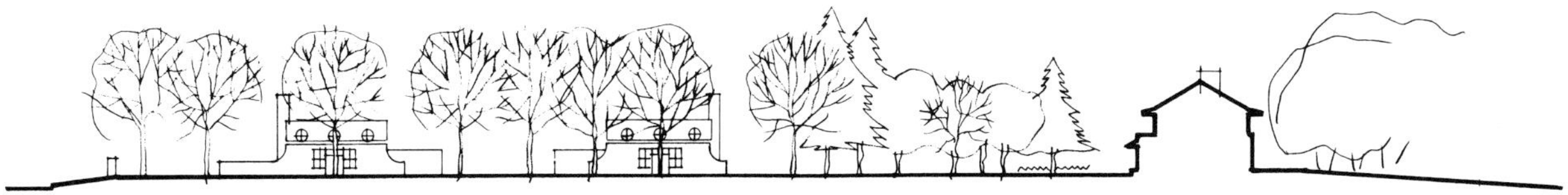

425. Longitudinal Section of Site.

426. A Bill-Ding-Board for the National Football Hall of Fame Competition. Structure.

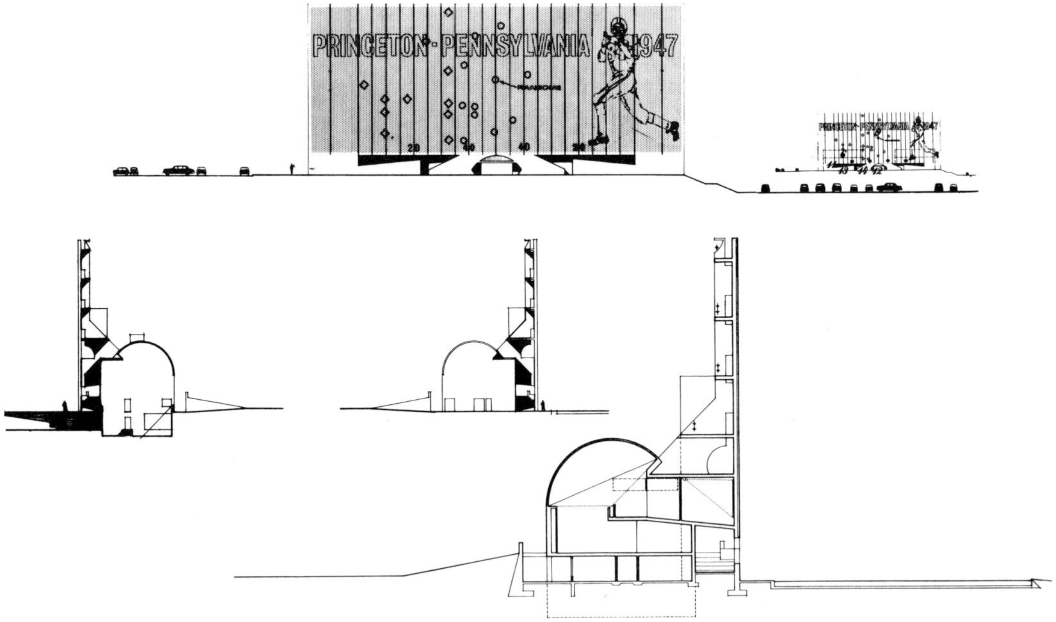

427. A Bill-Ding-Board. Model.

A Bill-Ding-Board for the National Football Hall of Fame—1967
Location: New Brunswick, New Jersey.
Status: Unsuccessful competition entry.
Our submission for the National Football Hall of Fame Competition is a building *and* a billboard.

Our original idea was to make the building in the shape of a football. But we made a sign instead of a sculpture: an essentially two-dimensional billboard, big in size but economical in cubage, which is also a building: a "bill-ding-board."

The front of our building, which is a billboard, inflects toward the big parking spaces and the stadium. The back, which is a building, relates to the exhibition field in the rear and, in fact, turns, into a quasi-grandstand. The enormous billboard, 100 feet high and 210 feet long, needs buttressing in the back. These buttresses integrate the building with the sign. The giant screen has the approximate proportions of a football field. On it, 200,000 electronically programmed lights produce moving sequences of naturalistic images, words and phrases, and diagrammatic choreographies of famous football plays. These displays can be viewed from the parking lots, the picnic green in front, and the Rutgers stadium, which is beyond.

From nearby, the billboard corresponds to the largely false west façade of a Gothic cathedral, especially an Italian one like Orvieto, teeming with glittering mosaics and niched statues, whose main function is to communicate information toward the piazza. From a distance the analogy with the billboard on the highway is obvious. Immediately in front of the screen, where the seats are bad at a movie, is a moat. Below the screen are various ways to enter the building. The ceiling of the interior gallery is vaulted to act as a screen for continuous and huge movie projections from the parapet of the balcony. [Movies] spill over the surfaces, essentially independent of the architectural forms they smother. The message dominates the space.

Robert Venturi, Denise Scott Brown, Steven Izenour, Learning from Las Vegas, 1972.

Twenty Mule Team Parkway—1970
Location: California City.
Status: Project was abandoned when ownership of California City changed.
Additional Credit: Denise Scott Brown, Paul Hirshorn.
Twenty Mule Team Parkway parallels a historical dirt track over which mule teams transported borax. We were asked to design stopping places along the parkway that would act as cue stops for the salesmen and revivers for the customers. Each place was to have a sign alluding to some aspect of the city that the salesman could describe: its history, fauna, or amenities: and several should have picnic tables, shelters, shade trees, and parking space.

We knew that to hold people's attention these signs must look "beautiful" and therefore must not resemble billboards since people do not find billboards beautiful. Their shape and content must be "uncommercial." We chose desert flowers as our theme, partly because flowers are regarded as beautiful (they are also uncontroversial), partly to reinforce our own aim to push desert gardening to save the ecology. We felt also that these flowers should be painted realistically and nonabstractly to make them appealing to the eyes of their beholders.

We tried to choose locations for the stopping places where the original twenty-mule-team track was visible from the new road so that, like the intertwining Via Appia Antica and Via Appia Nuova, the history of the former could be demonstrated in passing on the latter. The Via Appia used inconography on the tombs and monuments of its great men to mark history; California City iconography will mark the activities of Borax Bill and other real or legendary heroes.

Venturi, Brown, Izenour, Learning from Las Vegas, 1972.

428. Detail of Sign.

429. Detail of Sign.

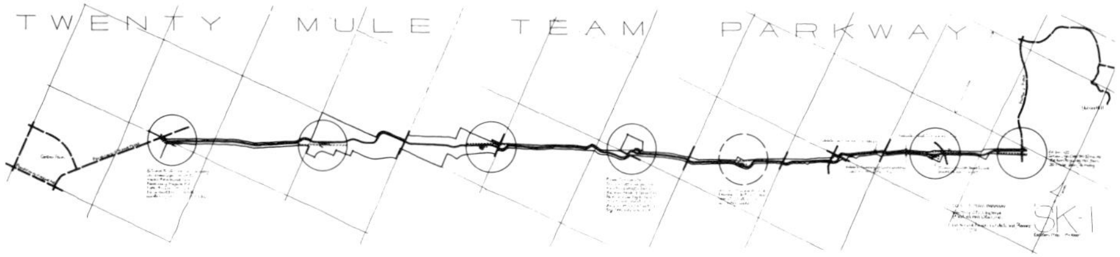

430. Twenty Mule Team Parkway. Location Plan.

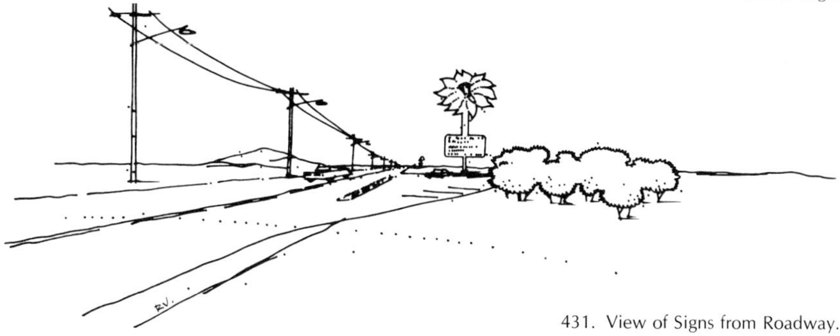
431. View of Signs from Roadway.

Konrad Wachsmann (Frankfurt, Germany 1901—)
Residence: Los Angeles, California.
Among Projects: 1941–1949, the General Panel System—with Walter Gropius (stressed-skin plywood panel system of construction utilizing interchangeable components); 1942, Mobilar Structure (to construct free-standing, self-sustaining wall units); 1961–1963, city and harbor developments, Genoa, Italy (utilizing standard prefabricated elements); 1969–1971, the Locomotion Orientation Manipulator (a physical tool for the control, measurement and display of the kinematics of production and assembly design).

In the first 200 years of its history — after a formidable start—the United States made very little progress in the application of electrical energy in industrialized processes to create the artificial, man-made environment. This is particularly remarkable, since the influence of industrialization in all other human endeavors resulted in a new social organism which we today recognize as the most technically advanced society with the highest standard of living, the United States of America of 1976.

Here are two projects which strangely enough appear to be unusual to many people. These two random applications of available technologies in the field of building are actually nothing more than the result of what man knows today and are therefore only natural *conservative solutions* to contemporary problems.

If we agree that science and technology are here to stay and that "the machine is the tool of our time," then every *conventional* method of construction should actually appear *unusual* and should not really belong anymore to the ideology and thinking of modern man.

Konrad Wachsmann.

Air Force Hangar—1951
Status: Research funds were discontinued.
A prefabricated tubular-space-frame building system for airplane hangars or any kind of wide-span structure, e.g., bridges, towers, was commissioned by the U.S. Air Force at the Institute of Design, Illinois Institute of Technology. One standard joint and two tube sizes, 3½ and 6 inches, are assembled three-dimensionally creating a space-frame construction. Up to 20 structural members can be connected around the centroid of each joint.

Robertson Ward, Jr., *AIA Journal,* LVII, March 1972.

The pipes of the space framework and the parts of the multiple joint are, however, already premounted and welded to such an extent that at the site only one socket has to be used to assemble them, and finally three simple steel wedges will lock them indissolubly in place. The module of this system is 10 feet; the distance between the multiple joints is always 10 feet in any direction. The basic spatial element is the tetrahedron. These spatial elements can be joined together in any number and thus can cover vast areas. The whole structure is carried by special supporting pyramids which are the only parts with different dimensions.

Conrads, Sperlich & Collins, The Architecture of Fantasy, 1962.

432. Air Force Hangar. Model. Detail.

433. Air Force Hangar. Model. Detail of Tubular Space Frame.

California City Civic Center—1966-1971
Location: California.
Status: Contrary to prediction, the city's population began decreasing, and programs for expansion were abandoned.
The project involves a high-tension cable structure for a California city civic center. A straight-line system of 1¼ inch outside-diameter cables, each tensioned at 94,000 pounds, (2 feet on center horizontally and 18 inches vertically), form the 80-foot wide "floating" roof structure between abutments and vertical tie-downs that are 192 feet apart. Stressed-skin fiberglass panels 16 feet wide and 80 feet long, connected with an accordian-type neoprene expansion joint, form the surface of the roof.

Robertson Ward, Jr., *AIA Journal,* LVII, March 1972.

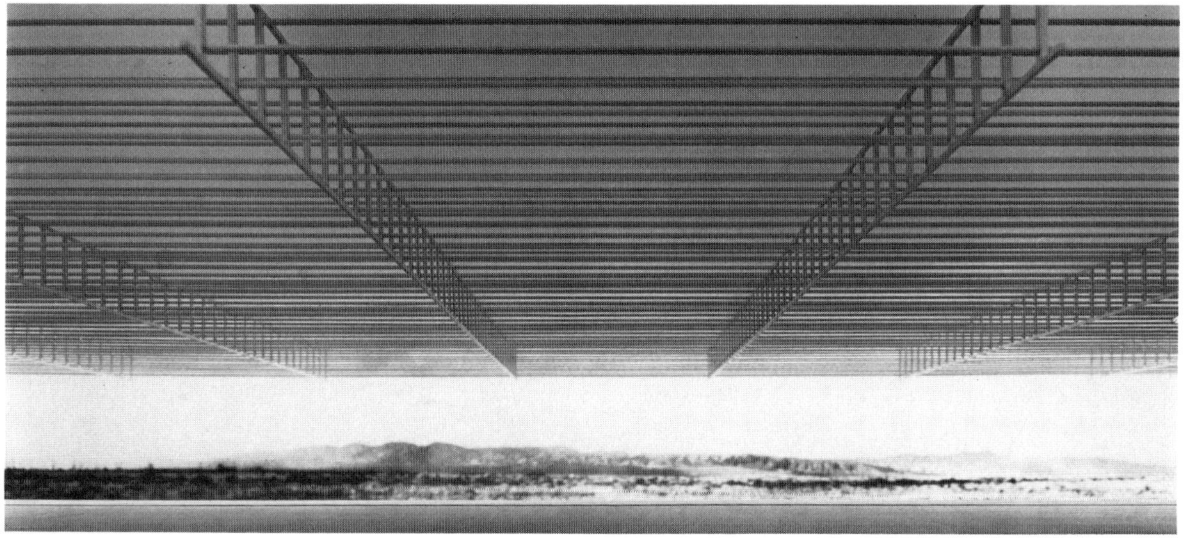

435. Civic Center. Detail.

434. California City Civic Center. Model. Aerial View.

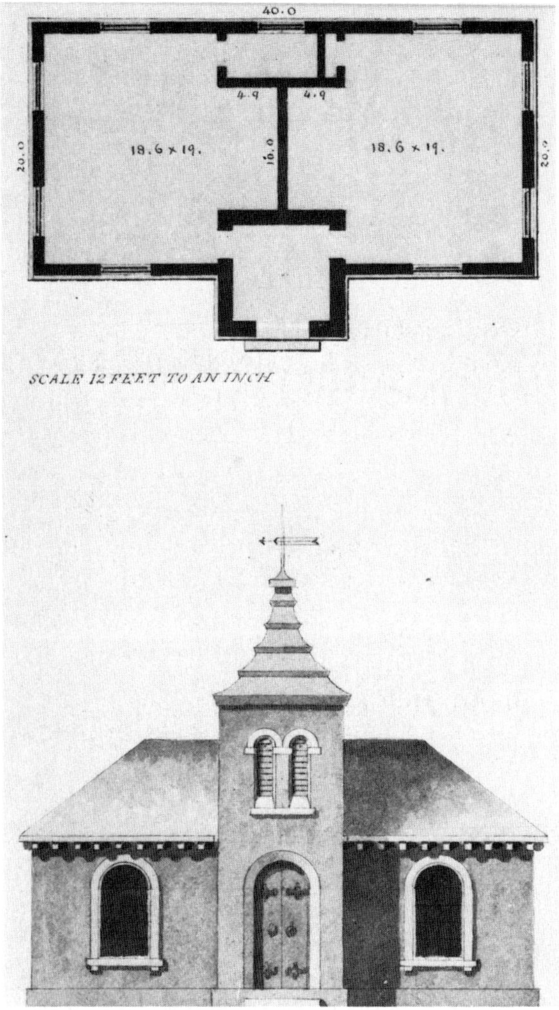

436. Schoolhouse. Plan and Elevation.

Thomas Ustick Walter (Philadelphia 1804—Philadelphia 1887)
Education: 1819, entered the office of William Strickland, where he learned the art of drawing. At Strickland's urging he studied physical science and methods of construction.
Among Major Works: 1833–1847, Girard College, Philadelphia; 1851–1865, Capitol Building wings and dome, Washington, D.C.

Schoolhouses—1850

Status: Prototypes.

The schoolhouses were designed at the request of Cortland Van Rensselaer, who subsequently published them in *The House, the School, and the Church, The Presbyterian Education Repository* (Cortland Van Rensselaer, ed.), in 1850 in Philadelphia.

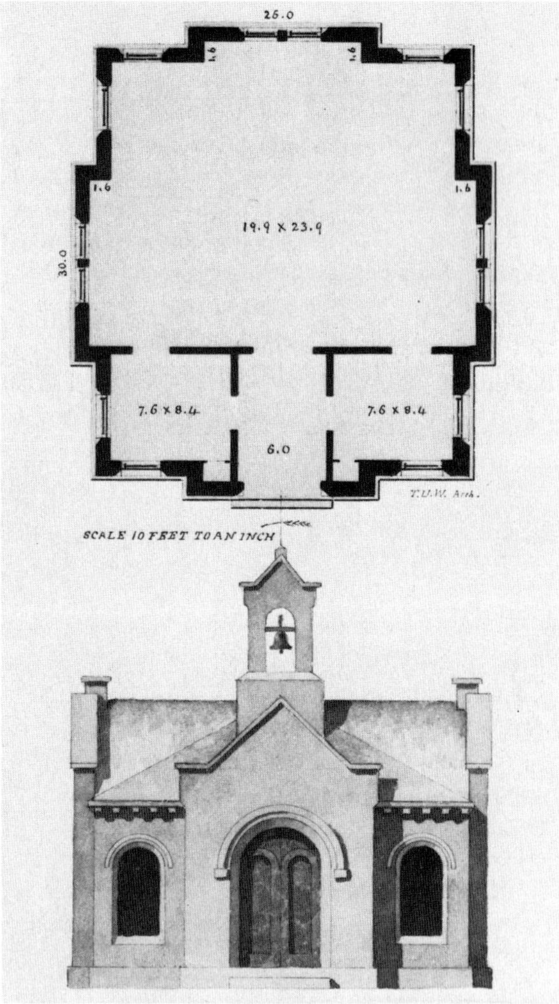

437. Schoolhouse. Plan and Elevation.

438. Big Four Bridge. Superimposition of Apartment Complex to Be Incorporated into Bridge Structure. Developed by Arthur Foran.

Jasper D. Ward (New Jersey 1921—)
Residence: Louisville, Kentucky.
Education: 1943, B Arch., Massachusetts Institute of Technology.
Among Major Works: 1963, Neighborhood House (settlement house), Louisville, Ky.; 1964, University of Louisville Radiation Center, Ky.; 1968, Portland Elementary School, Louisville; 1971, Doctors Office Building, Louisville; 1971, Alice Lloyd College Science Building, Pippa Passes, Ky.

Big Four Bridge—1968
Location: Crosses the Ohio River between Louisville, Ky., and Jeffersonville, Ind.
Status: The bridge approaches on both sides of the river have been torn down, and the span now stands alone over the river with no access.
Additional Credit: Arthur J. Foran III, Ronald Gascoyne, Day Johnston, Fred DeSanto, Robert Kingsley.
The Big Four Bridge was constructed in 1893 under a franchise granted to the Louisville and Jefferson Bridge Company. It was taken over by the Cleveland, Cincinnati, Chicago and St. Louis Railway Company, the "Big-Four," and eventually acquired by the New York Central. When the New York Central and the Pennsylvania Railroads merged it was decided that the Pennsylvania Railroad Bridge would be used, and the Big Four Bridge was abandoned. The bridge is a historical tribute to Louisville's importance as a rail center and the role this has played in the commercial development of the city.

Early in 1968 theatrical producer Richard Block suggested that the Big Four Bridge should be "turned into a Ponte Vecchio type structure and bring fame and fortune to Louisville," and the firm then proceeded to develop a number of possibilities.

A proposal evolved by Arthur Foran incorporated 160 apartment units, a restaurant, shops, cafes and a small marina into the bridge structure. The multi-level apartments (one, two,

439. Interior of Converted Bridge. Illus. V. Bartoli.

440. Ballard Mills. Preliminary Sketch of Proposed Apartment Buildings.

three bedroom and efficiencies) would be brought in on flatcars, raised up and secured between the spans, and reached via elevators and walkways. Small rubber-wheel commuter vehicles running at shop level (below the pedestrian way), would transport people to and from the downtown and riverfront area.

The director of Building and Housing Inspection in Louisville decided that he wanted the bridge and its approaches removed, describing it as an eyesore and safety hazard under the then new "eyesore" law passed in 1970 by the Kentucky General Assembly.

Under the present city administration the approaches were allowed to be torn down without the central span being removed. Thus the center of the bridge alone remains, spanning the river, with no access. It has survived (unlike the approaches) because it will cost more to demolish than the scrap metal of the structure is worth.

Jasper D. Ward.

Ballard Mills—1970
Location: Louisville, Kentucky.
Status: Were unable to obtain a mortgage, and silos have subsequently been demolished.
Additional Credit: Gill Hardwick.
In 1968, three Louisville real estate developers purchased a big milling plant on the fringe of the downtown area from Pillsbury Co. for $550,000. Milling operations at the plant had ceased in 1961, and included in the deal were 24 huge (98 feet high) interconnected silos which once stored a million bushels of wheat and a grain elevator.

The silos were to be transformed into twelve-story apartment buildings at a cost of $2,000,000. Floors would be installed by pouring concrete into suspended forms starting at the top floor, dropping floor to floor. Holes cut through the 8-inch-thick walls would become windows. A total of 132 circular apartments (including 84 split-levels, each 23 feet in diameter) would be incorporated into the silos, and 24 rectangular apartments in the grain elevator. The top floor of the silos would contain a restaurant and bar. A swimming pool at roof level under a dome would be sunk into the center of the bar with port holes to view the swimmers or drinkers. The entire complex would include storage buildings on the property converted into office space.

Construction on the project was to be completed in 1971. Rents, including utilities and furnishings (even the beds in the circular apartments were to be circular), were to range from $150 to $175 a month. In 1969, cash

441. Ballard Mills. Silos Prior to Being Demolished.

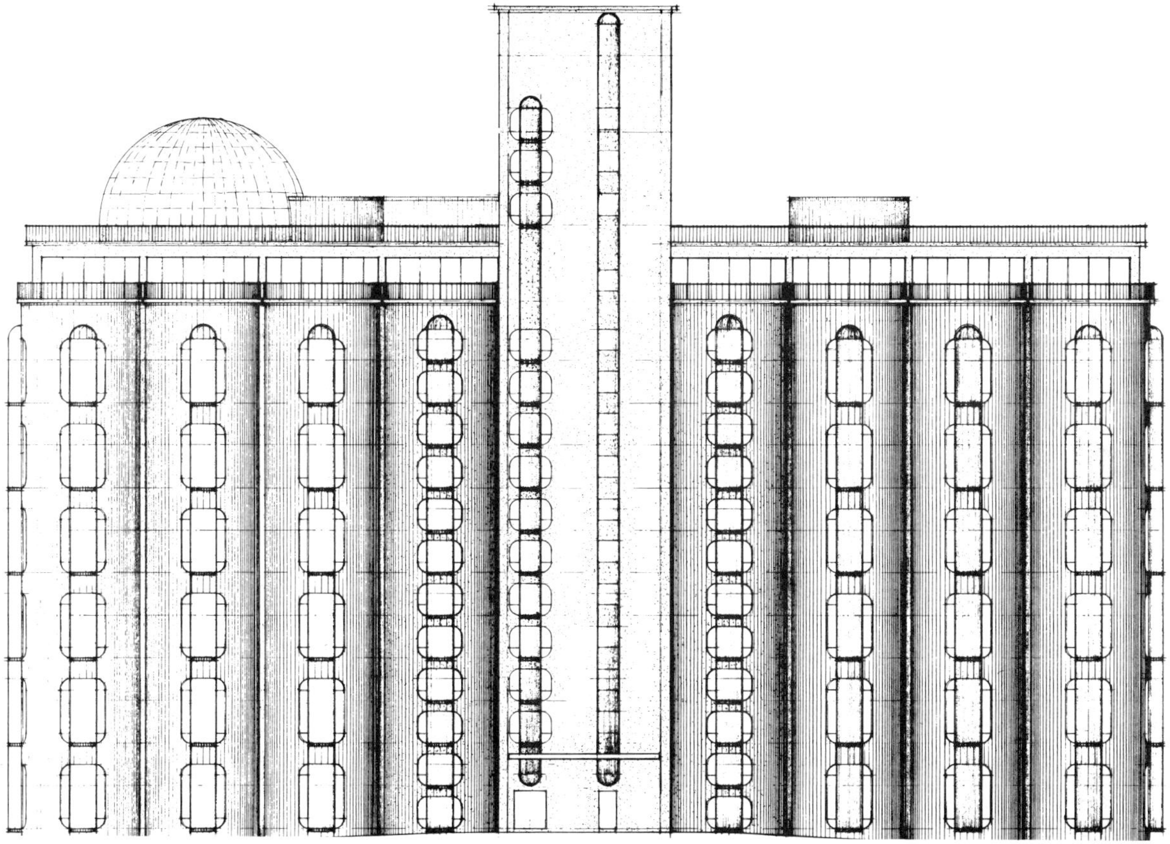

442. Ballard Mills. Apartment Buildings. East Elevation.

deposits for the apartments were already coming in, and the local newspapers had titled the prospective tenants "flour children."

It will look like a bunch of silos with bay windows. We will do as little as possible not to destroy the natural form of the silos.

Jasper D. Ward.

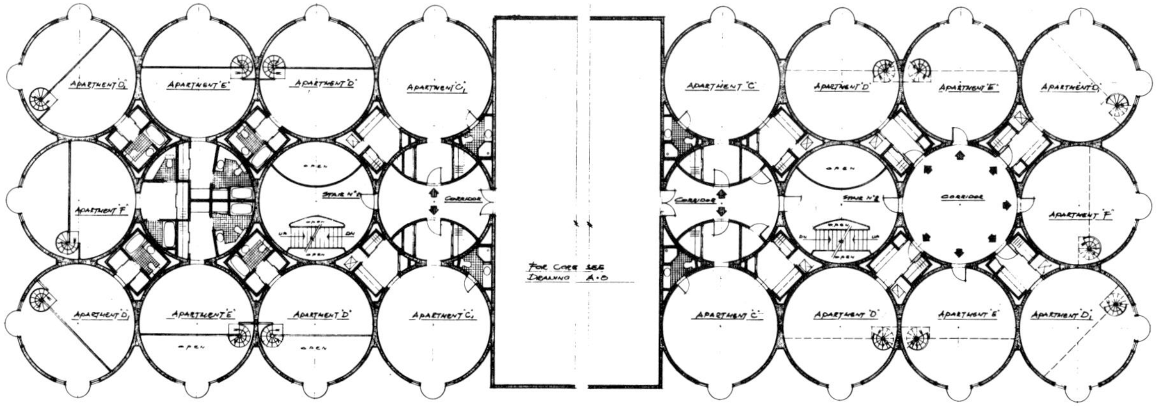

443. Apartment Buildings. Plan.

The Washington Monument Project in Washington, D.C.—1836–1884

Peter Force (New Jersey 1790—1868)
Education: Learned the printer's trade in New York City.
Among Major Published Works: 1823–1931, the *National Journal* (A semi-weekly newspaper devoted to the candidacy of John Quincy Adams. In 1824 it became a daily newspaper); 1820–1836, the *National Calendar and Annals of the United States* (an annual of historical and statistical information); 1836–1846, *Tracts and Other Papers, Relating Principally to the Origin, Settlement, and Progress of the Colonies in North America* (reprints of rare pamphlets bearing on the early history of the colonies); 1837–1853, the *American Archives* (his greatest work—twenty or more folio volumes of important original materials of American history from the seventeenth century through 1789).

Robert Mills (South Carolina 1781—Washington, D.C. 1855)
Education: College of Charleston, South Carolina.
Among Major Works: 1812, Upper Ferry Bridge, Philadelphia (a single span of 360 feet, the longest in the world at that time); 1822, State Hospital for the Insane, Columbia, South Carolina (Mills was an early advocate of social and hygienic planning); 1836–1839, Treasury Building, Washington, D.C.; 1836–1840, Patent Office, Washington, D.C.; 1839, Post Office, Washington, D.C.

Robert Mills was the first native-born American to be trained as an architect in this country. In 1800 he worked in the office of James Hoban, the architect of the White House; 1803, he was taken into Jefferson's family at Monticello; 1804–1808, worked in the office of Benjamin H. Latrobe, Washington, D.C.; 1836–1851, appointed "Architect of Public Buildings," Washington, D.C.

Claes Oldenburg (1929—) (see Oldenburg for biographical information).

William Wetmore Story (Salem 1819—Italy 1895)
Education: 1838, BA, Harvard; 1840, LLB, Harvard.
Among Major Sculptures: "Cleopatra" (a replica is in the Metropolitan Museum, New York City); "Libyan Sibyl," National Gallery of Art, Washington, D.C.; 1864, "Medea," Metropolitan Museum of Art, New York City; 1870, "Salome," Pennsylvania Academy of Fine Arts, Philadelphia.

In 1836, advertisements were published by order of the Washington National Monument Society inviting designs from American artists, but no limitation was placed upon the form of the design. It was determined by the Society and so recommended, that any plans submitted should "Harmoniously blend durability, simplicity and grandeur." The estimated cost for the proposed monument was not less than one million dollars.

A great many designs were submitted, but the one selected among the number was that of Mr. Robert Mills, an eminent architect of the times.

Frederick L. Harvey, **History of the Washington Monument**, 1903.

In 1848, sixty-four years after Congress had made the first proposal for a memorial to the first President, it granted a 37-acre site for it to the Washington National Monument Society.

On July 4, 1848 the cornerstone was laid. Shortly after construction had begun, the original height as proposed by Mills was reduced from 600 to 500 feet, and the pantheon was deferred to some future date (and finally abandoned in 1874).

The funds of the Society were soon exhausted. In the years which followed, appeals and efforts to raise the amount necessary to complete the monument were largely unsuccessful. At the outbreak of the Civil War, the monument still stood at its 176-foot height, and in the words of Mark Twain "looked like a hollow, over-sized chimney." Construction was thus halted in 1861 when the shaft was barely one-third completed. It was not to be taken up again until 15 years later when public shame swept the Nation and the Congress over the failure to complete this memorial to its outstanding hero.

As the centennial year of the establishment of the United States neared, Congress was stirred to complete the Washington Monument by a wave of patriotism that swept the Nation.

Abridged from George J. Olszewski, A **History of The Washington Monument**, 1971.

Original Proposal by Robert Mills—ca.1837
Location: Washington, D.C.
Status: This was the winning entry, but it was severely altered during construction.
[Robert Mills was twenty-nine and had recently been appointed as the Nation's first Federal architect by President Andrew Jackson, when his design was chosen by the Washington National Monument Society. During the thirty-six years it took to complete the construction of this monument, the Society severely altered its original concept by reducing the intended height of the shaft, and entirely eliminating the colonnade and all of the ornamentation.]

Robert Mills referred to his design as the "National Pantheon":

This design embraces the idea of a grand circular colonnaded building, 250 feet in diameter and 100 feet high, from which springs an obelisk shaft 70 feet at the base and 500 feet high, making a total elevation of 600 feet.

This vast rotunda, forming the grand base of the Monument, is surrounded by 30 columns of massive proportions, being 12 feet in diameter and 45 feet high. The statues surrounding the rotunda outside, under the colonnade, are all elevated upon pedestals, and will be those of the glorious signers of the Declaration of Independence. Niches in the sides of the gallery contain the statues of the fathers of the Revolution, contemporary with the immortal Washington.

Robert Mills in Frederick L. Harvey's **History of the Washington National Monument**, 1903.

444. Winning Competition Entry by Robert Mills for the Washington Monument. Engraving by A. C. Warren.

In 1876 Congress decided to complete the Washington Monument begun in 1848. "'For twenty-four years the rotting crane upon its summit has been idle." Henry Van Brunt, "The Washington Monument," *The American Art Review,* I. 1880). The following are several of the many proposals submitted offering alternative designs for completing the structure.

445. Competition Entry by Peter Force for the Washington Monument.

Proposal by Peter Force—1837
Location: Washington, D.C.
Status: Unsuccessful competition entry (?).
No description could be found for this entry.

446. Proposal by Albert Noerr.

447. Proposal by William Wetmore Story.

448. Proposal Submitted Anonymously from California.

Proposal by Albert Noerr—ca. 1879
Location: Washington, D.C.
Status: Design for completion of the Washington Monument.
This design by Albert Noerr of Washington, D.C. was published in *The American Architect and Building News,* January 1880. No description accompanied the illustration.

Proposal by William Wetmore Story—1878
Location: Washington, D.C.
Status: Design for completion of the Washington Monument.
The monument, as it stands, I took as the core of my structure, encasing it with the colored marbles, in which America is so rich, and changing its character into a tower with a portico at its base. In front of this porch, or rather, enniched beneath it, I placed a colossal statue of Washington within reach of the eye. On the opposite side, I proposed a statue of Liberty,—achieved by Washington for our country,—and on the two sides, two great bronze doors figured over with the principal events of the Revolution, and the portraits of the distinguished men of the period,

the coadjutors of Washington. Fame on the top of the tower in gilt bronze,—the spiritual essence of his life,—he himself at the base, the corporeal presence.

William Wetmore Story in *The American Architect and Building News,* V, January 1879.

Anonymous proposal—1879
Location: Washington, D.C.
Status: Design for completion of the Washington Monument.
This is the substance of the description which accompanies the design [from California]—The panels on the face of the first terrace are stones presented by the various States of the Union; those presented by foreign states find a place in the battering plinth of the monument. The statue of Washington is seated in front of a niche, and the pedestal of the statue is supported by figures of Truth and Industry. The niche is flanked on either hand by groups representing Peace and War. Against the die of the pedestal of the monument are placed busts of the Revolutionary worthies, and under the corner of the pedestal is a frieze enriched with a procession of Industry; above, on the four angles of the cornice of the pedestal, are figures of Liberty, Justice, Education, and Suffrage. Against the next stage are the emblematical statues of the original States, and the gables which decorate the centres of the third stage bear statues typifying the North, the South, the East, and the West. The frieze under the main cornice is filled with a warlike procession, and the figure of America surmounts the whole, at a height of three hundred and thirty feet.

Abridged from Henry Van Brunt, "The Washington Monument," *The American Art Review,* I, 1880.

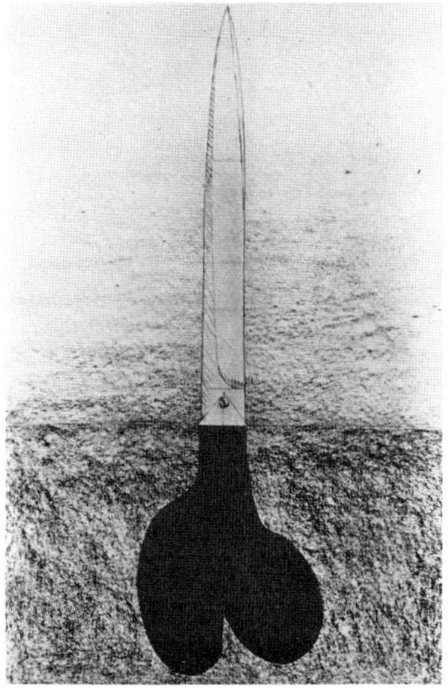
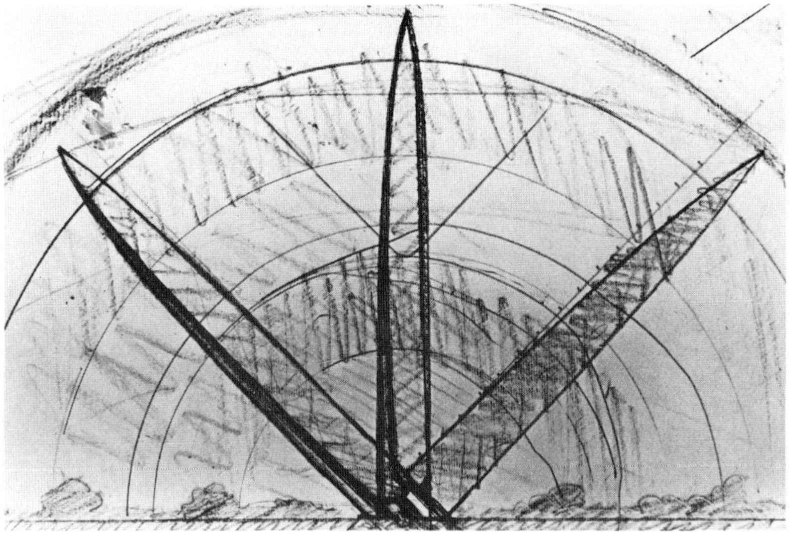

449, 450. Proposal by Claes Oldenburg. Scissors Closed (left). Scissors in Motion (right).

Proposal by Claes Oldenburg
Proposed Colossal Monument
to Replace the Washington Obelisk—1967
Location: Washington, D.C.
Status: Suggested replacement for existing structure.
In the New Washington Monument there is an interest in national symbolism, particularly the Great Seal, which was the starting point. It was a matter of translating the seal into a familiar and simple object for my purposes. Both sides of the seal are planned on an X pattern, the eagle and the pyramid (the upper part of the X invisible). The seal has an eye, the eagle has a beak, and the United States' obsession with division ("united we stand . . . ," etc.) all suggested a scissors. A strange intolerance of division, separation, in the U.S.A. is expressed by the cruelty of the scissors in obtaining union: as the scissors close—unifying—they separate the material they close about.

Like the scissors, the U.S.A. is screwed together—two violent parts destined in their arc to meet as one. The scissors have played as important a part in the U.S.A. history as the neoclassic inheritance from the French architects around the revolution (the last brilliant symbolist architects). Betsy Ross cut her flag from a dress, didn't she? The capacity to separate material is as great an invention as fire and the mirror.

The scissors are an obvious morphological equivalent to the obelisk, with interesting differences—metal for stone, humble and modern for ancient, movement for monumentality.

The handles of the monument are underground, balanced in great troughs which may be looked into. The blades part in the course of a day. At the evening, the colossal red handles rise above the ground; they sink out of sight again when the sun sets. The closing continues slowly all night until dawn when the colossal blades are joined, forming a structure like the obelisk, catching the sun's light at the tips.

Claes Oldenburg, Object into Monument, 1971.

The Washington Monument Project in New York—1842–1856

There had been perennial demand, since 1802, for a memorial to Washington in New York. In 1833, "The New York Washington Monument Association" was incorporated to erect a memorial. Although a committee was formed, and a considerable sum of money collected, no action was taken until 1842, when there was a renewed interest in the project. In 1844 the association accepted the design submitted by Calvin Pollard, a New York architect. Public protest followed, demanding an open competition, and many unsolicited designs were submitted to the association. In 1847 the charter of the "late" Washington Monument Association was revived, and architects were invited to submit plans in an open competition. Dissatisfied with the results of its competition, the Association decided not to adopt any of the projects. From this point on the situation became increasingly chaotic. The association went back to Pollard's design, objections continued to appear in the press, and the association again began to accept projects for the monument by other architects. By the end of 1848 an obelisk design by Minard Lafever was chosen by vote by the citizens of New York. The monument was to be erected in granite on Murray hill, but it was never executed for lack of sufficient funds. It was not until 1856 that a Washington Monument (a bronze equestrian statue by Henry Kirke Brown and John Q. A. Ward) was unveiled in Union Square, New York City.

Abridged from Jacob Landy in "The Washington Monument Project in New York," *Journal of the Society of Architectural Historians,* XXVIII, December 1969.

451. Proposal by Calvin Pollard for the Washington Monument, New York City.

Calvin Pollard (Massachusetts 1797—New York City 1850)
Calvin Pollard was a prominent architect and builder in New York City from 1818 to 1850.

Proposal by Calvin Pollard—1843

Location: Union Square, New York City.
Status: Unbuilt due to public protest.
The style of Pollard's projected tower was Gothic. It was to be built of granite, at an estimated cost of $400,000, and was to rise 425 feet on Union Square, giving promise of being "the noblest monument in the known world." Pollard conceived of the design as a sequence of three pentagonal sections, each with its own rotunda.

Abridged from Jacob Landy in "The Washington Monument Project in New York," *Journal of the Society of Architectural Historians,* XXVIII, December 1969.

Weidlinger Associates (Consulting Engineers) (established Washington, D.C. 1949—)
Location: New York City.
Principals: Paul Weidlinger, Mario G. Salvadori, Melvin L. Baron, Matthys P. Levy.
Among Major Works of Firm: 1958, air supported roof and tent construction, MEBAC Theater, Boston; 1964, St. Francis de Sales Church, Michigan; 1965, Banque Lambert, Belgium; 1971, One Liberty Plaza Office Building, N.Y.C.; 1972, sculpture of 4 Trees by Jean Dubuffet, N.Y.C.

Pipeline for Autos—1965

Location: A cold windy climate.
Status: Prototype.
The two unique but interdependent features are a cylindrical prestressed shell that acts as the stiffening girder and a self-anchoring cable system. The girder is, in effect, a suspended tunnel affording complete protection from severe weather conditions and reducing maintenance factors to a minimum. The girder is made up of precast modular units incorporating the shell, a stiffener ring and a transverse girder that carries the traffic decks. These units are prefabricated on shore and then towed to their positions after the foundations, towers, and cables are erected. They are then hoisted into place. This system eliminates the need for falsework so that the navigation channel is left open throughout construction.

Excerpted from Phyllis Birkby in *Design and Environment,* Spring, 1970.

452. Pipeline for Autos.

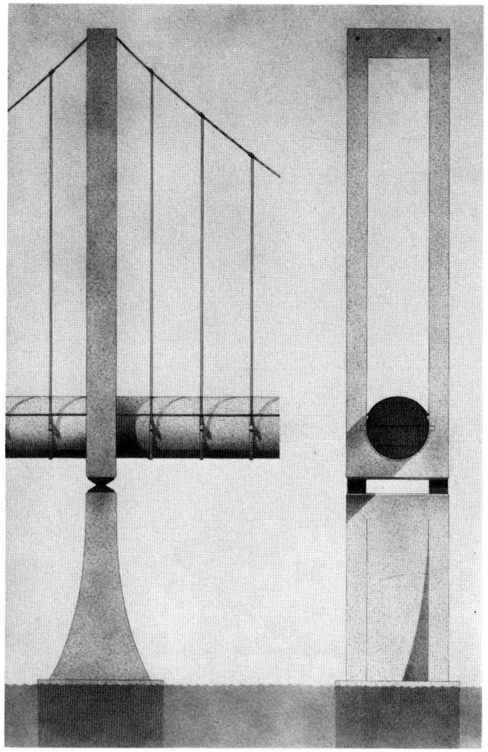

453. Pipeline for Autos. Section.

Floating Airport (FLAIR)—1969
Location: New York City.
Status: Feasibility study.
The FLAIR concept is of a platform positioned high enough so that the deck will not be awash under the most severe sea conditions and connected by vertical columns to buoyancy chambers below the wave base. The buoyancy of the deck/buoyancy-chamber combination will raise the platform and will elevate the chambers to the surface.

FLAIR's deck structure is made up of 200 ft by 200 ft steel and concrete flotation chambers. These chambers are anchored to the ocean floor by means of taut mooring cables continuously under tension. This provides a tensile foundation which stabilizes the units both horizontally and vertically and eliminates the need for a power source, making it possible to place the FLAIR platform in water 200 ft or more deep. A conventional pile or caisson foundation could not be used at such depth.

The airport is designed to be operational in severe sea conditions and to survive winds of 130 mph and waves 40 ft high. The design can be adapted to even higher waves by increasing the depth of the buoyancy chambers and the height of the platform above sea level. The anchoring system is designed to withstand currents and tides encountered in offshore locations.

Abridged from Phyllis Birkby in *Design and Environment,* Spring, 1970; Paul Weidlinger in *Ocean Industry,* V, May 1970.

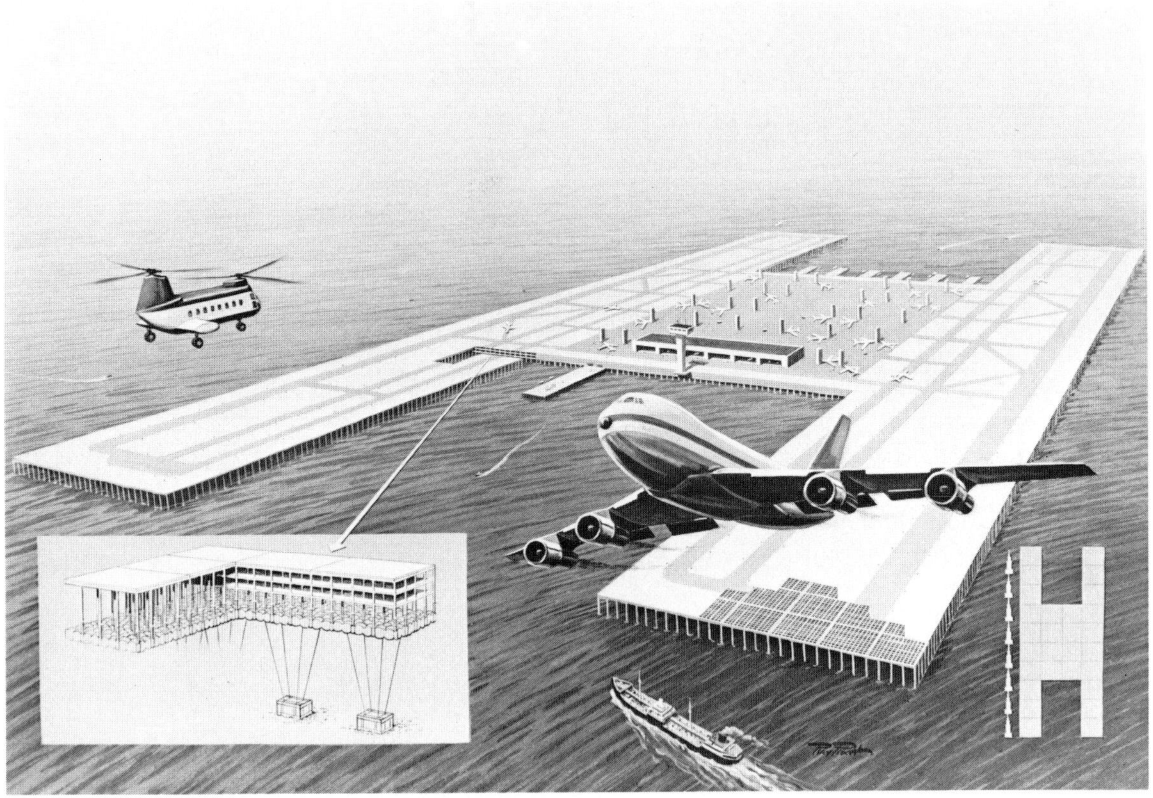

454. Floating Airport (FLAIR). Aerial View and Detail Section of Anchorage System.

455. Underground Suburbia. Aerial View.

456. Underground House. Section and Perspective.

Malcolm Wells (New Jersey 1926—)
Residence: Cherry Hill, New Jersey.
Education: 1943–1945, Civil Engineering, Georgia Tech.
Among Major Works: Underground Office (his own), Cherry Hill, N.J.; Cherry Hill Library; RCA Color TV Pavilion, N.Y. World's Fair (1964); The True-year calendar (solar), and the 15-point wilderness-values graph for use in rating man-works against the constants found in natural systems (recently made into a magnetized demonstration-board by the National Park Service and hung in park headquarters).

Underground Suburbia—1965
Location: Suburbia.
Status: Prototype.
Suburbia, Ten feet under, warm, green, and *private*.

Except for exhausting the roadway fumes there's no problem here. And even with the roads exposed the advantages, both to man and to nature, would be impressive.

Underground House—1964
Location: Cherry Hill, N.J.
Status: Clients for concept have not materialized.
The house was to have been formed of bent reinforcing bars, covered with metal lath, plaster, spray concrete, insulation, and water proofing; it is, of course, inherently strong.

Still, in spite of all the other underground designs I've done over the years, this one remains the most requested design of all—not for construction, so far, but at least for dreaming. It seems to tug at something in a lot of people.

Have we ever, for a minute, stopped to realize that what we do each day in the name of architecture is just as ruthless, just as destructive, as the work the buffalo-hunters did? Until we've seen ourselves in that light, we'll go on missing the point, always feeling that our work is somehow different, important. After all, we're registered professionals. We plan. We create. . . . The simple fact remains, though, that there just isn't any building as beautiful, or as appropriate, or as important, as the bit of forest it replaces. We are so preoccupied with our own problems that we forget the only reality in this world: Nature.

Malcolm Wells.

457. Proposal for Manhattan Skyline. Sequence.

Allan Wexler (Connecticut 1949—)
Residence: New York City.
Education: 1971, BFA Fine Arts, Rhode Island School of Design; 1972, BA Arch., Rhode Island School of Design.
Among Major Projects: Proposal to utilize outdoor advertising for the purpose of stimulating community involvement and awareness to neighborhoods; 1969–1972, as part of team designed renovation of 6 mill buildings, Providence, R.I.; 1973–1975, proposal for a pedestrian space underneath and adjacent to the approach ramps of the Brooklyn Bridge, N.Y.; designed a playground for Lawrence Halprin Associates.

Manhattan Skyline World Trade Center—1973
Location: New York City.
Status: Feasibility study.
Each office in the World Trade Center Towers would be provided with a marked calendar. At the end of each day, the participating employees would consult their calendars, leaving the lights in their respective offices on or off as indicated.

This study was developed with a grant from the Architectural League of New York. It was presented to the Port Authority, and rejected due to the current energy crises, and their lack of willingness to draw further attention to the Trade Center Towers.

Allan Wexler.

458. Proposal for Manhattan Skyline.

Frank Lloyd Wright (Wisconsin ca. 1869—Arizona 1959)
Education: Studied engineering, University of Wisconsin.
Among Major Works: 1909, Robie House, Oak Park, Illinois (one of the most notable in his series of Prairie Houses, which revolutionized house design in America and then internationally); 1904, Larkin office building, Buffalo, New York (one of a series of early reinforced concrete structures, highly influential internationally); 1916–1922, Imperial Hotel, Tokyo; 1923, Millard House, Pasadena (one of a group of concrete-block houses); 1911, Taliesin, Spring Green, Wisconsin (his own house, rebuilt in 1914 and 1925 after fires); 1936, "Falling Water," the Kaufman house, Bear Run, Pennsylvania (cantilevered structure integrated with its surroundings); 1930s, "Usonian" houses; 1938, Taliesin West, Scottsdale, Arizona (his own house utilizing "desert concrete").
Among Major Writings: 1931, *Modern Architecture;* 1932, *Autobiography;* 1954, *The Natural House and Disappearing City;* 1957, *A Testament.*

Frank Lloyd Wright, America's outstanding architect, worked in the offices of the minor "Shingle Style" architect J. L. Silsbee, in Chicago, and in 1888 entered the employ of Louis Sullivan, later establishing his own practice in 1893.

Broadacre City—1930s-1950s
Location: United States:
Status: Prototype.
The three major inventions already at work building Broadacres, are:

1. The motor car: general mobilization of the human being.
2. Radio, telephone and telegraph: electrical intercommunication becoming complete.
3. Standardized machine-shop production: machine invention plus scientific discovery.

The three inherent rights of any man are:

1. His social right to a direct medium of exchange in place of gold as a commodity: some form of social credit.
2. His social right to his place on the ground as he has had it in the sun and air: land to be held only by use and improvements.
3. His social right to the ideas by which and for which he lives: public ownership of invention and scientific discoveries that concern the life of the people.

The only assumption made by Broadacres as ideal is that these three rights will be the citizen's. So I have called it a new freedom for living in America.

In Broadacres, by elimination of cities and towns the present curse of petty and minor officialdom, government, has been reduced to one minor government for each county. In the hands of the state, but by way of the county, is all redistribution of land—a minimum of one acre going to the childless family and more to the larger family. All public utilities are concentrated in the hands of the state and country government.

Here now may be seen the elemental units of our social structure: The correlated farm, the factory—its smoke and gases eliminated by burning coal at places of origin, the decentralized school, the various conditions of residence, the home offices, safe traffic, simplified government. All common interests take place in a simple coordination wherein all are employed: *little* farms, *little* homes for industry, *little* factories, *little* schools, a *little* university going to the people mostly by way of their interest in the ground, *little* laboratories on their own ground for professional men. And the farm itself, notwithstanding its animals, becomes the most attractive unit of the city.

To build Broadacres as conceived would automatically end unemployment and all its evils forever. In an organic architecture the ground itself predetermines all features; the climate modifies them; available means limit them; function shapes them. Form and function are one in Broadacres.

The traffic problem has been given special attention, as the more mobilization is made a comfort and a facility the sooner will Broadacres arrive. Every Broadacre citizen has his own car. Multiple-lane highways make travel safe and enjoyable.

In the affair of air transport Broadacres rejects the present airplane and substitutes the self-contained mechanical unit that is sure to come: an aerotor capable of rising straight up and by reversible rotors able to travel in any given direction under radio control at a maximum speed of, say, 200 miles an hour, and able to descend safely into the hexacomb from which it arose or anywhere else. By a doorstep if desired.

The only fixed transport trains kept on the arterial are the long-distance-monorail cars traveling at a speed (already established in Germany) of 220 miles per hour. All other traffic is by motor car on the twelve lane levels or on the triple truck lanes on the lower levels.

Houses in the new city are varied: make much of fireproof synthetic materials, factory-fabricated units adapted to free assembly and varied arrangement, but do not neglect the older nature-materials wherever they are desired and available. There is the professional's house with its laboratory, the minimum house with its workshop, the medium house ditto, the larger house and the house of machine-age-luxury. We might speak of them as a one-car house, a two-car house, a three-car house and a five-car house. Glass is extensively used as are roofless rooms. The roof is used often as a trellis or a garden.

Individuality established on such terms must thrive. Unwholesome life would get no encouragement and the ghastly heritage left by overcrowding in overdone ultra-capitalistic centers would be likely to disappear in three or four generations. The old success ideals having no chance at all, new ones more natural to the best in man would be given a fresh opportunity to develop naturally.

Abridged from **Frank Lloyd Wright**, "Broadacre City," *The Architectural Record,* LXXCII, April 1935.

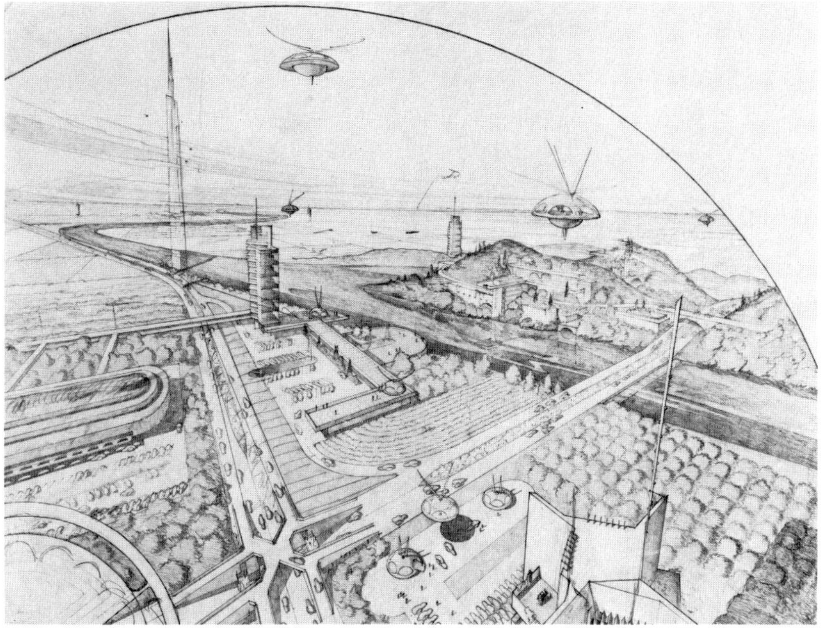

459. Broadacre City—1930s–1950s. The Landscape of Broadacre City Included an Example of Every Building Type Designed by Frank Lloyd Wright During His Career.

460. Broadacre City. Aerial View of Countryside and Detail of "Aerotors."

Mile High Skyscraper "The Illinois"—1956
Location: Chicago.
Status: Were unable to interest an investor.
[The Illinois is an outgrowth of Frank Lloyd Wright's proposal of a half-mile high building for the Century of Progress Exhibition, 1933. Plans for the Mile-High Building were unveiled by Frank Lloyd Wright on October 17 at a testimonial dinner, "Frank Lloyd Wright Day."]

Most stable of all forms of structure is the tripod. For general stability at great height this form is combined with new principles of cantilever-steel in suspension in my proposed mile-high office tower for Chicago, the "Illinois."

The exterior is entirely metal-faced, carried by steel wires suspended from a rigid steel core buried in lightweight concrete. The building is thus designed from inside out instead of the usual construction from outside inward. Floor slabs are extended across the central core and balanced. This is the same type of construction used in the airplane, the ocean liner, and the Imperial Hotel in Tokyo (built in 1915 and proved earthquake-proof in 1922), and in several of my other buildings. The same system of taproot foundation, extending the main core down into bedrock, also proven in the Imperial Hotel, would be employed here.

The framework of the Illinois is like a tree; the horizontal floor slabs (branches) are integral with the vertical core (trunk), making the total structure light and rigid. The balance of the structural members would be such that there would be no sway at the peak of the Illinois.

The light floor slabs are tapered hollow from the core to carry air conditioning and lighting systems. All outer glass surfaces are set 4 feet back under the metal parapets to give the building emphasis as an all metal structure, avoid glare, and to afford a human sense of protection at such enormous heights as characterize the

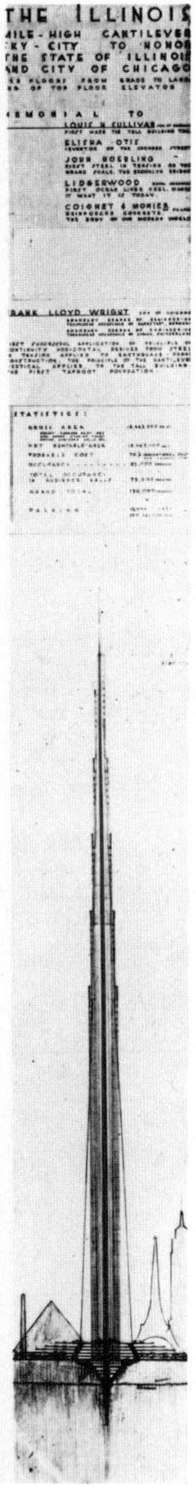

Illinois Sky-city.

The Illinois is entered at four points and is reached by four, four-lane approaches. Covered parking for about 15,000 cars is reached by ramps and there are also two decks for 50 helicopters each. A combination of escalators and 56 elevators run by atomic power engines should fill or empty the entire building within the hour. Population in spacious comfort: 130,000.

All this done well, the building will be centuries more permanent than the Pyramids.

Abridged from **Frank Lloyd Wright** in "Frank Lloyd Wright's Mile High Office Tower," *The Architectural Record,* CV, November 1956.

Left 461. Frank Lloyd Wright with the Mile-High Skyscraper, "The Illinois." "A rapier with a handle the breadth of the hand set firmly into the ground, blade upright, the Illinois will be five times the highest structure existing in the world." Frank Lloyd Wright.

462. Mile-High Skyscraper, "The Illinois." Detail.

Lloyd Wright (Illinois 1890—)
Residence: Los Angeles, California.
Education: University of Wisconsin; Harvard University.
Among Major Works: Together with Associates brought the first slum clearance, Federal Housing and Urban Renewal to Los Angeles; chief architect for Aliso Village Housing Administration Center; designed the prototype for the Hollywood Bowl Shell.

Lloyd Wright is the eldest son of Frank Lloyd Wright. He is currently engaged in preparing schematic regional planning material for the Los Angeles area.

A Design for a Twentieth Century Metropolitan Catholic Cathedral—1931
Location: Central Los Angeles.
Status: Unbuilt due to the death of the Bishop of the Los Angeles Diocese of that time.
The Cathedral was developed by Lloyd Wright, in conjunction with Margaret Brunswig, whose concept it was that the central theme and symbol be expressed in the total structure as a cross in plan, elevation and details, and be executed with twentieth century building techniques.

A precast unit construction of lightweight concrete reinforced with steel in precast modular units 16 feet × 16 feet square is locked together with steel and concrete grout and assembled on site by elevators and cranes. These units interlock to make vertical and horizontal box beams thereby creating room cells, vertical transportation shafts, ducts, and corridors. The flexibility and simplicity of assembly of these standardized units utilized for the fabrication of the structure reduce construction costs to a minimum and expedite operations in every phase of the construction. By reducing the structural elements to their most economical service a structure of lace-like delicacy, but with great strength, is produced. This technique makes it possible to reproduce the cross theme throughout the building, illuminated with colored glass and plastics, all combined to produce a monumental shaft of glowing light, articulate with color and variety of expression, yet all correlated and totally integrated with the purpose and concept of the building and its symbol. The unity and integration of this structure is uniquely complete and monumentally expressive.

The enclosed space provides a nave and crossing, soaring 950 feet to roof level above the structure's central crossing from which is hung a cable pendulum supporting a canopy adjacent to the high altar. The pendulum and canopy swing in continual movement centered on the nave, and narthex symbolizing the path of the earth and other planets in the universe.

Banks of rapid transit elevators, electrically operated at four inner corners of the structure, provide transportation to all floors (rooms, service, basement, below grade parking placed under garden areas), from six stories below to 50 stories (800 feet) above grade. Glass-faced crosses on each of the four facades (which lock over the crown of the building and to the structure) and the perforated cross, are electrically illuminated at night. Luminous cross unit panels, produce a column of light 800 feet high by 160 feet wide. The entire face of the cathedral becomes a multiple monument day and night of the symbol of the cross.

Sunken gardens, ambulatories, and colonnades adjacent to diocesan offices and school accommodations, are placed at the four corners of the property. Buttressing the base of the central building, each opening to its own garden and ambulatory are: (a) the three-story episcopal residence and study building; (b) the three-story diocesan library; (c) the three-story chancery, synod hall, and offices; (d) the school. The floor area contained in the building totals more than 716,800 square feet. The cathedral's main floor encloses the following areas: the narthex, nave, side aisles, and the four corner chapels. The nave opens to the central high altar terrace. Behind the high altar is placed the sanctuary, the bishop's throne, and stalls. The Stations of the Cross along the aisles lead to the altar and chapels. The total complex would provide the cathedral's multiple services for the community and congregation.

Lloyd Wright.

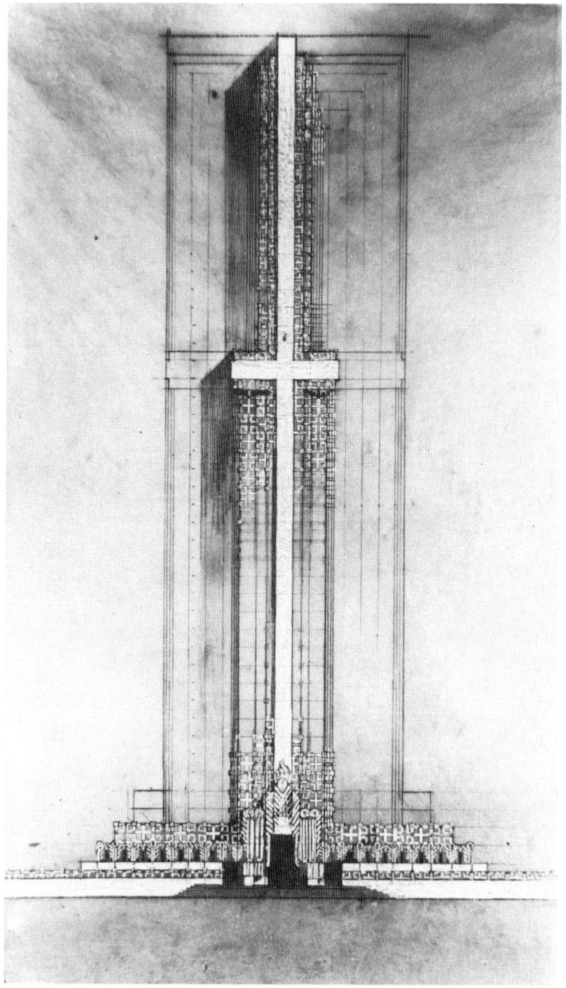

463. Cathedral Complex. Elevation.

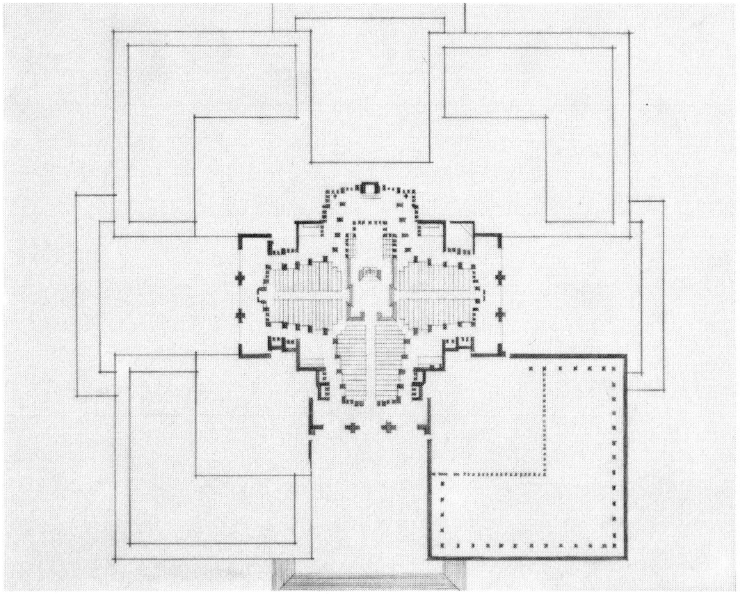

464. Cathedral Complex. Plan.

465. Cathedral Complex. Aerial View of Section. Model.

466. Cathedral Complex. Three Quarter View of Model Showing Interior Lighting of Facades and Crosses.

Joseph Wythe (California 1920—)
Residence: Monterey, California.
Education: University of California at Berkeley; University of Oklahoma, School of Architecture, where he studied with Bruce Goff, and was so influenced by "the wonderfully imaginative and sensitive architect," that to this date he is passing on the inspiration that he received.

Joseph Wythe has worked in the offices of Conner and Pojezny; Bryan Miller, Reynolds and Morrison; and Robert Stanton — all small offices doing "interesting" work. In addition to this, he has done engineering on the Oklahoma Turnpike. Mr. Wythe presently teaches architecture at the Monterey Peninsula College, he has previously taught at the School of Architecture, Oklahoma University.

Eagle Nest—1948

Status: Hypothetical drawing.

While the project was conceived in pure fantasy, it is completely functional in all respects and can be built. The upper level, which is approached by a bridge from each side, includes the living-dining space, kitchen and studio which are enclosed by curved, sliding glass doors that can be stacked in one quadrant so that on warm days, the whole upper level can become an almost completely open deck. Where the structural ribs come too close to the deck for proper headroom, planters have been placed, and below the planters are ballast tanks for water which can be pumped from one tank to another as the need arises to compensate for unbalanced loading conditions. In addition to the skylight above, there is a window below so that a person descending the stairs can look down to the stream flowing by. The lower level contains three bedrooms and bathrooms. The windows curve down to meet the floor deck in such a way that a person can look downward to the water and the vistas beyond. The building is designed to sway gently in the wind, and the effect might be likened to that of life aboard a yacht. The utilities are brought in under the floor of the bridge, and the waste flows down the "imbecilic tube" to the septic tank downstream. The structure is of aluminum in various colors, fabricated in the shop and assembled at the site.

Joseph Wythe.

467. Eagle Nest. A Fantasy for California.

Zion and Breen

Robert Zion (New York 1921—)
Residence: Imlaystown, New Jersey.
Education: BA, MBA, MLA, Harvard University.
Among Major Works of Firm: 1961, Sculpture Garden, Museum of Modern Art, N.Y.C.; 1965, Paley Park, N.Y.C.; 1965, Co-op City, Bronx, N.Y.; 1966, Weybosset Hill Public Open Spaces, Providence, R.I.; 1973, Cincinnati Riverfront Park, Ohio.

Pennsylvania Station/Galleria—1963
Location: New York City.
Status: Theoretical proposal, submitted as a protest.
Pennsylvania Station is now being demolished but its loss can help us in the fight ahead to save other such landmarks. Ignorance of the true greatness of Penn. Station was, more than any other factor, responsible for its destruction. Those who knew said too little about the architectural quality of the building, the spaces it created, the materials and workmanship that went into it. The public was asked to save Penn. Station, but was never convincingly told *why*.

It would not have been difficult to conceive of uses for Penn. Station. For instance, it could have housed the greatest transportation museum in the world, with spaces large enough to exhibit complete locomotives and airplanes. The glass and steel roofed concourse, converted into a great palm garden, might have been lined with shops and cafes to give us a *galleria* of our own, a great indoor square in midtown Manhattan. The bitter lesson for New York and for all communities is that the public is the most vital factor in preservation. Imaginative use of landmark buildings must be communicated, and interest and enthusiasm aroused, if we are not to lose our heritage to indifference.

Robert Zion.

468. Pennsylvania Station/Galleria. Detail of Interior.

THE SPACE AGE

Gerard O'Neill
Brian O'Leary

469. Large Space-Community. Illus. Frank Guidice.

Gerard O'Neill (New York City 1927—)
Residence: Princeton, New Jersey.
Education: 1950, BA Physics, Swarthmore College; 1954, PhD Physics, Cornell University.
Among Major Works: 1956–1965, designed and developed the "Storage Ring," a devise used in high-energy particle physics; 1965–1976, fundamental work in the area of space colonization and manufacturing.

Gerard O'Neill has been on the faculty of Princeton University since 1954, where he is Professor of Physics.

Brian O'Leary (Boston 1940—)
Residence: Lumberville, Pennsylvania.
Education: 1961, BA Physics, Williams College; 1964, MA Astronomy, Georgetown University; 1967, PhD Astronomy, University of California, Berkeley.

Brian O'Leary, a former NASA scientist-astronaut, is a colleague of Gerard O'Neill on the physics faculty at Princeton University. His interest lies in Planetary Science, and within this area he has been for the past year, advisor and speech writer to Morris Udall.

Living in Space—1976
Location: Outer Space.
Status: Prototype.

The idea first broached by my Princeton colleague Dr. Gerard O'Neill, would be to build aesthetically pleasing space habitats which are manufactured from material mined and launched from the moon and asteroids. Much to the initial surprise of those physicists, engineers, and economists who have studied the matter, it was discovered that such a program could be started, in principle, with an investment similar to that for Apollo and could in time become earth-independent, using today's technology.

The first step would be to make use of the space shuttle, a rocket-plane NASA has under development for launching and returning large cargoes to-and-from orbits close to the earth. Derivatives of the shuttle could be used to launch materials for the first lunar mining base and high orbital manufacturing facility. The factory would then replicate itself and new space habitats in a geometrically growing pattern. The colonies and manufacturing facilities would be located in orbit around the earth near a point called L5, a point in space equidistant from the earth and moon. The French mathematician Legrange found that objects in orbit around the earth near this point would not drift astray because of the varying gravitational pull of the sun and other planets.

One aim of colonizing space would be the construction of large space solar power stations which would beam microwaves to receivers on earth, for use as electricity. Dr. O'Neill has estimated that the total U.S. electrical energy capacity could be provided in this way twenty years after the start of the program.

Dr. O'Neill envisions the first space habitat to be rather Spartan compared to what could follow. It would house about 10,000 highly motivated workers. One arrangement of their first space community would be inside a slowly spinning sphere about 500 meters in diameter—making a walk along the circumference about one mile. The two spins per minute would give residents along the equator the effect of one-earth gravity. Their light would be provided by mirrors which would reflect sunlight through windows; mirror movements would allow the sun to move around the "sky" and to create day and night. Climates can be varied according to the tastes of the residents, and vegetation planted to go along with the climate.

Brian O'Leary.

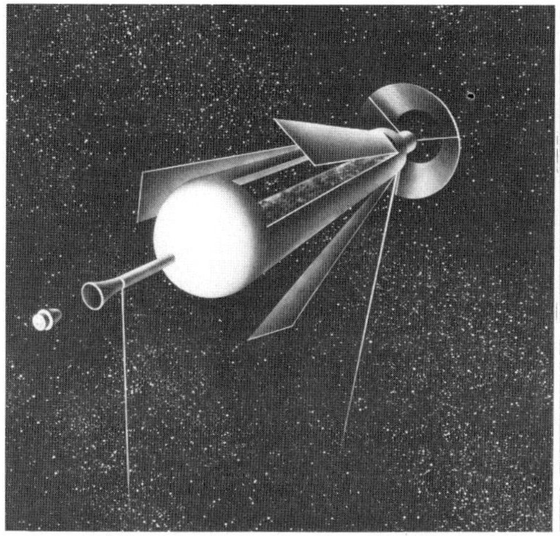

470. Space Habitat. Illus. Walter Zawoijski.

471. Model Four Colony. Interior. Illus. F. Guidice.

472. Spherical Concept of First Space Habitat.

TEXT CREDITS

This listing includes material quoted from previously published sources. It is arranged according to the name of the designer or competition appearing in the book. This is not a complete listing of everyone included in UNBUILT AMERICA, as in many instances the descriptions have not been previously published.

From *Invisible Cities* by Italo Calvino. Copyright © 1972 by Giulio Einaudi editore s.p.a.; English Translation © 1974 by Harcourt Brace Jovanovich, Inc. and reprinted with their permission. **Jefferson, Thomas.** Desmond Guinness and Julius Trousdale Sadler, Jr., *Mr. Jefferson, Architect* (New York:The Viking Press, 1973), pp.37,40. © 1973 The Viking Press, Inc. Thomas Jefferson, *Papers of Thomas Jefferson,* ed. Julian P. Boyd (Princeton: Princeton University Press, 1950-), VIII. Fiske Kimball, *Thomas Jefferson Architect* (New York:Da Capo Press, 1968), pp.129–135. Buford Pickens, "Mr. Jefferson as Revolutionary Architect," *JSAH,* XXXIV (December 1975): pp.266–271. Copyright © 1975 by the Society of Architectural Historians (all rights reserved). **Barber, Donn.** "A Selection of Drawings of Works by the Late Donn Barber," *Pencil Points,* VI (December 1925):77–78. **Barnard, George Grey.** Harold E. Dickson, *George Grey Barnard: Centenary Exhibition 1863–1963* (University Park,PA.:Pennsylvania State University Press, 1964), pp.8–9. **Bayley, John Barrington.** John Barrington Bayley, "The Dinsha House," *Classical America,* I, no. 1 (1971):45–50. **Beard, William H.** J. R. G. Hassard, "An American Museum of Art," *Scribner's Journal* (August 1871):409–415. **Bel Geddes, Norman.** Norman Bel Geddes, *Horizons* (Boston: Little, Brown and Company, 1932), pp.100–108, 191–199, 293. © 1932 by Norman Bel Geddes. By permission of Edith Lutyens Bel Geddes executrix of the Norman Bel Geddes Estate. **Benedict, Jacques.** Robert H. Moulton, "A Mountain Palace for our Presidents," *The Craftsman,* XXVII (February 1915) :494–497. **Bonestell, Chesley.** "The Most Amazing Construction Job in History," *New York Sunday Mirror Magazine,* 19 June 1949. **Burnham, Daniel H.** Daniel Burnham and Edward Bennet, *Plan of Chicago* (Chicago:The Commercial Club, 1906; reprint ed., New York:Da Capo Press, Inc., 1970), pp. 115–118. John Garraty and Edward James, eds., *Dictionary of American Biography* (New York:Charles Scribner's Sons, 1974), p.305. **Carrère and Hastings.** "A New Versailles," *The American Architect,* CIX (June 1916):412–413. *New Versailles* (New York:National Academy of Design, 1916). **Cathedral of St. John the Divine Competition 1889.** Ralph Adams Cram, *My Life in Architecture* (Boston:Little, Brown and Company, 1936), pp.167–171. Copyright © 1936 by Ralph Adams Cram. All Rights Reserved. **Century of Progress Exposition 1933.** From *Raymond Hood, Architect of Ideas,* Copyright © '73 by Walter H. Kilham, Jr., permission by Architectural Book Publishing Co., N.Y., p.108. "Preliminary Studies for the Chicago World's Fair," *Pencil Points,* X (April 1929): pp. 218–228. Ralph T. Walker, *Ralph Walker, Architect* (New York:Henahan House, 1957), pp.84–85. **Chambless, Edgar.** Edgar Chambless, *Roadtown* (New York: Roadtown Press, 1910). Edgar Chambless, *Roundtown to Roadtown* (New York:Harry Singer, 1931). **Chicago Tribune Tower Competition 1922.** Claes Oldenburg in Barbara Haskell, *Claes Oldenburg Object into Monument* (Los Angeles:The Ward Ritchie Press, 1971),p.66. © Pasadena Art Museum, 1971. *Tribute Tower Competition* (Chicago:The Tribune Company, 1923). **Cole, Thomas.** Rev. Louis Legrand Noble, *The Life and Work of Thomas Cole* (New York:Sheldon, Blakeman and Company, 1856), pp.214–215. **Corbett, Harvey Wiley.** Harvey Wiley Corbett, "The Problem of Traffic Congestion and a Solution," *The Architectural Forum,* XLVI (March 1927): pp.201–208. **Cram, Ralph Adams.** Ralph Adams Cram, *My Life in Architecture* (Boston:Little, Brown and Company, 1936), pp.167–171. Copyright © 1936 by Ralph Adams Cram. All Rights Reserved. "Report of the Sub-Committee to the Mayor of Boston," 1921, Collection Boston Public Library. **Crystal Palace Competition 1852.** H. Allen Brooks, Jr., "Leopold Eidlitz, 1823–1903" (PhD. diss., Yale University, 1955), pp.20–21. Professor B. Silliman, Jr., and C. R. Goodrich, Esq., eds., *The World of Art and Industry* (New York:Putnam and Company, 1854), pp.3–7. **Davis, Alexander Jackson.** "Alexander Jackson Davis, Architect," *The American Architect and Building News,* XXXV (February 1852). Alexander Jackson Davis, *Rural Residences* (New York, 1837). Talbot Hamlin, "The Rise of Eclecticism in New York," *Journal of the Society of Architectural Historians,* XI (May 1952):p.4. **Delano, William Adams.** William Adams Delano in Robert L. Anderson, "A Reply to Mr. Howe," *Pencil Points,* XIII (July 1932): p.507. **Despradelle, Constant Desiré.** Desiré Despradelle, "The Beacon of Progress," *The Technology Review,* II (October 1900): pp.305–307. **Ferriss, Hugh.** Hugh Ferriss, *The Metropolis of Tomorrow* (New York:Ives Washburn, 1929), pp.62,64,70,109,111,136–140. **Field, Erastus Salisbury.** Mary Black, "Rediscovery: Erastus Salisbury Field," *Art in America,* LIV (January–February 1966): pp.49–55. **Friedman, Yona.** Oscar Newman, "Countdown for Small Towns," *Esquire,* LXXIII (December 1969): pp.182–187. **Fuller, R. Buckminster.** R. Buckminster Fuller, "Why Not Roofs Over Our Cities," *Think,* XXXIV (January–February, 1968): pp.8–11. © 1968 R. Buckminster Fuller. **Gilbert, Cass.** "War Memorials, Impressions of an Interview with Cass Gilbert," *The American Architect,* CXIX (January 1921): pp. 33–36. **General Grant Memorial Competition 1885.** "Suggestions as to a Competition for a Monument to General Grant," *The American Architect and Building News,* XVIII (September 1885): p.138. **Greenough, Horatio.** John Garraty and Edward James, eds., *Dictionary of American Biography* (New York:Charles Scribner's Sons, 1974) p.588. G. W. Warren, *History of the Bunker Hill Monument* (Boston:James R. Osgood and Company, 1877), pp.159–160. **Guastavino, Rafael.** U.S. Patent No. 915,026, *The Official Gazette of the U.S. Patent Office,* CXL (March 1909). **Gugler, Eric.** "The Hall of Our History," *National Sculpture Review,* II, no. 4 (1953):pp.9,11. **Helmle and Corbett.** Eugene Clute, "The Restoration of King Solomon's Temple and Citadel," *Pencil Points,* VI (November 1925): pp.69–86. **Hood, Raymond.** From *Raymond Hood, Architect of Ideas,* Copyright © '73 by Walter H. Kilham, Jr., permission by Architectural Book Publishing Co. **Howe and Lescaze.** Robert Stern, *George Howe: Toward a Modern American Architecture* (New Haven, CT.:Yale University Press, 1975), pp.104–106. **Kahn, Louis I.** Romaldo Giurgola and Jaimini Mehta, *Louis I. Kahn* (Boulder, CO.:Westview Press, 1975), p.44. **Katavolos, William.** William Katavolos, *Organics* (The Netherlands:Steendruikkerij de Jong & Co., 1961). © William Katavolos. **Kiesler, Frederick.** Frederick Kiesler, "The Future: Notes on Architecture as Sculpture," *Art in America,* LIV (May–June 1966):pp.57–68. Frederick Kiesler, "The Grotto for Meditation," *Craft Horizons,* XXVI (July/August 1966): pp.22–27. "Frederick J. Kiesler," *Lotus,* III (1966–1967), p.9. **Lamb, Charles.** Charles Lamb, "City Plan," *The Craftsman,* VI (April 1904): pp.3–7. **Larkin, Edward.** Francisco Mujica, *History of the Skyscraper* (New York:Archaeology and Architecture Press, 1929), pp.20,65–66. **Latrobe, Benjamin Henry.** Talbot Hamlin, *Benjamin Henry Latrobe* (New York:Oxford University Press, Inc., 1955), p.218. **Loewy, Raymond.** "Mid-town Airport," *Architectural Forum,* LXXV (November 1941): p.14. **Mahoney, Marion.** Marion Mahoney (Griffin), "The Magic of America," Manuscript Collection, The New York Historical Society, New York, N.Y. **Malcolmson, Reginald.** Reginald Malcolmson, *Visionary Projects for Buildings and Cities* (Baltimore:International Exhibitions Foundation, 1974). **Mies van der Rohe, Ludwig.** Peter Carter, *Mies van der Rohe at Work* (New York:Praeger Publishers, Inc., 1974), pp.79–81. © 1974 by the Pall Mall Press, London, England. Quote from L. Hilberseimer, *Mies van der Rohe* (Chicago:Paul Theobald Company, 1956), pp. 176–179. **Morgan, Julia.** Robert Clements, "Santa Maria de Ovila," *American Heritage* (forthcoming). **Mujica, Francisco.** Francisco Mujica, *History of the Skyscraper* (New York:Archaeology and Architecture Press, 1929), pp.20,65–66. **Mullgardt, Louis Christian.** Robert Judson Clark, *Louis Christian Mullgardt* (Santa Barbara, CA.:University of California, 1966), pp.7,12–13. **Neutra, Richard.** "Rush City Reformed," *Shelter,* III (March 1938): pp.23–35. **Newman, Oscar.** Oscar Newman, "Countdown for Small Towns," *Esquire,* LXXIII (December 1969): pp.182–187. **Niagara Ship Canal.** *The Niagara Ship Canal: Its Military and Commercial Necessity* (New York, 1863), pp.1–15. **Noguchi, Isamu.** Isamu Noguchi, *A Sculptor's World* (New York:Harper & Row, Publishers, Inc., 1968), pp.21–22,160, 176. **Oldenburg, Claes.** Claes Oldenburg in Barbara Haskell, *Claes Oldenburg Object into Monument* (Los Angeles:The Ward Ritchie Press, 1971), pp.81,83. © Pasadena Art Museum.

Owen, Robert. Arthur Eugene Bestor, Jr., *Backwoods Utopias* (Philadelphia:University of Pennsylvania Press, 1950), pp.128–129. Mark Holloway, *Heavens on Earth* (New York:Dover Publications, 1951), p.108. **Preston, William G.** "Sketch for the New York International Exhibition Building, 1883," *The American Architect and Building News,* VII (March 1880): p.106. **Price, Bruce,** Bruce Price in *American Architect,* LXV (September 1899). "Interview with Bruce Price," *Great American Architect,* V (1899). **Price, William.** George E. Thomas, "William L. Price (1861–1916): Builder of Men and Buildings," (PhD. diss., University of Pennsylvania, 1975), pp.189–198,224–228. **Richardson, Henry H.** James F. O'Gorman, *H. H. Richardson and His Office—Selected Drawings* (Cambridge, MA.:Harvard College, 1974), p. 198. Van Rensselaer, *H. H. Richardson and His Works* (Boston:Houghton Mifflin and Van Rensselaer, 1888),pp.87–89. **Root, John Wellborn.** John Garraty and Edward James, eds., *Dictionary of American Biography* (New York:Charles Scribner's Sons, 1974), p.150. Donald Hoffman, *The Architecture of John Wellborn Root* (Baltimore:The Johns Hopkins University Press, 1973), pp.232–233. Harriet Monroe, *John Wellborn Root, A Study of His Life and Work* (Park Forest, IL.:The Prairie School Press, 1966), pp.150,250–255. **Rudolph, Paul.** "The Mobile Home is the 20th Century Brick," *Architectural Record,* CXLIII (April 1968): pp.137–146. **Schindler, Rudolph M.** David Gebhard, *Schindler* (New York:The Viking Press, Inc., 1972), pp.30,34,103–104. © Thames and Hudson Limited, London. **Simonds, Charles.** Charles Simonds, *Three Peoples* (Italy:Samanedizioni, 1975), © Charles Simonds. **Smith, Franklin Webster.** Curtis Dahl, "Mr. Smith's American Acropolis." © 1956 American Heritage Publishing Co., Inc. Reprinted by permission from *American Heritage* (June, 1956): pp.38–43,104–105. **Smithson, Robert.** Robert Smithson, "Aerial Art," *Studio International,* CLXXV (February/April 1969): pp.180–181. Robert Smithson, "Typescript," Collection Nancy Holt Smithson, New York. **Stacy-Judd, Robert.** Robert Stacy-Judd, "Wanted an All-American Architecture," *The Architect and Engineer,* CXV (October–December 1933). Robert Stacy-Judd, "Some Local Examples of Mayan Adaptations," *The Architect and Engineer,* CXVI (February 1934): pp.21–30. **Sullivan, Louis.** Louis Sullivan, "The High Building Question," *The Graphic,* 1891 published in Donald Hoffman, "The Setback Skyscraper City of 1891," *JSAH,* XXIX (May 1970):pp.181–186. "Copyright © 1970 by the Society of Architectural Historians (all rights reserved)." **Superstudio.** Superstudio, *The Continuous Monument* (Florence, Italy:Superstudio, 1970). **Szukalski, Stanislaw,** *Projects in Design* (Chicago:The University of Chicago Press, 1929), pp.7–53. © 1929 The University of Chicago. **Tyng, Anne Griswold.** Anne Griswold Tyng, "Simultaneous Randomness and Order, The Fibonacci-Divine Proportion as a Universal Forming Principle," (PhD. diss., University of Pennsylvania, 1975). **United States Bicentennial Proposals 1976.** Louis I. Kahn in *Architectural Forum,* CXXVII (July–August 1972):p. 84. **United States Capitol Competition 1792.** Fiske Kimball and Wells Bennett, "The Competition for the Federal Buildings, 1792–1793," *AIA Journal,* VII, VIII (January, March, August, 1919, February 1920). Francis D. Lethbridge, "More Capitol Punishment," *AIA Journal,* XLV (April 1966): pp.41–47. **United States Centennial Competition 1876.** *Report of the Committee on Plans and Architecture to the U.S. Centennial Commission* (Philadelphia:J. B. Lippincott & Co., 1873). "Centennial Tower One Thousand Feet High," *Scientific American,* XXX (January, 1874): p. 50. **Urban, Joseph.** Joseph Urban, "Wedding Theatre Beauty to Ballyhoo," *The American Architect,* CXXXIV (September 1928): p.361. **Venturi and Rauch.** Robert Venturi, Denise Scott Brown, Steven Izenour, *Learning from Las Vegas* (Cambridge, MA.:The MIT Press, 1972), pp.116–119, 181–182. **Wachsmann, Konrad.** Ulrich Conrads and Hans Sperlich, *The Architecture of Fantasy,* trans.,ed., expand. Christiane C. Collins and George R. Collins (New York:Praeger Publishers, Inc. 1962), p.180. © 1960 by Verlag Gerd Hatje, Stuttgart. Robertson Ward, Jr., "Konrad Wachsmann," *AIA Journal,* LVII (March 1972). **Washington Monument Project.** *The American Architect and Building News,* V (January 1879): pp.13–14. Frederick L. Harvey, *History of the Washington Monument and Washington National Monument Society* (Washington:Senate Document No. 224, 57th Cong., 2d Sess., 1903), pp.18–22. Jacob Landy, "The Washington Monument Project in New York," *JSAH,* XXVIII (December 1969): pp.291–297. Copyright © 1969 by the Society of Architectural Historians (all rights reserved). Claes Oldenburg in Barbara Haskell, *Claes Oldenburg Object into Monument* (Los Angeles:The Ward Ritchie Press, 1971), pp.57,59. © Pasadena Art Museum. George J. Olszewski, "A History of the Washington Monument, 1844–1968," (Washington, D.C.:National Park Service, 1971), pp.4–10,15–16,21–22. Henry Van Brunt, "The Washington Monument," *American Art Review,* I (1880): pp.7–12,57–65. **Weidlinger Associates.** Phyllis Birkby, "Over, On and Under Water: Three Astounding Structural Systems," *Design and Environment,* I (Spring 1970): pp.52–57. Paul Weidlinger, "Floating Airport," *Ocean Industry,* V (May 1970): pp. 47–49. **Wright, Frank Lloyd.** Frank Lloyd Wright, "Broadacre City," *Architectural Record,* LXXVII (April 1935): pp.244–254. Frank Lloyd Wright, "Frank Lloyd Wright's Mile High Office Tower," *Architectural Record,* CV (November 1956): p.106.

ILLUSTRATION CREDITS

The authors are indebted to all those persons and organizations listed for permission to publish the respective photographs.

1–3. The Thomas Jefferson Coolidge, Jr. Collection. Courtesy The Massachusetts Historical Society, Boston. **4,5.** Courtesy The Maryland Historical Society, Baltimore. **6–15.** Raimund Abraham. **16.** Alley Friends. **17–19.** Siah Armajani. **20,21.** Alice Aycock. **22.** *Pencil Points,* VI, Dec. 1925, p.78. **23.** Courtesy Anthony Barnard. **24,25.** Edward Larrabee Barnes. **26.** Photo:Javan Bayer, Courtesy Herbert Bayer. **27–33.** John Barrington Bayley. **34–41.** From the Bel Geddes Collection at the University of Texas by permission of Edith Lutyens Bel Geddes executrix of the Norman Bel Geddes Estate. **42.** *The Craftsman,* Feb. 1915, p.494. **43.** International Space Museum and Gallery, Washington, D.C. Courtesy Chesley Bonestell. **44.** Painting © 1964 by Chesley Bonestell. Reproduced by permission of Harcourt Brace Jovanovich, Inc. from *MARS* by Robert S. Richardson and Chesley Bonestell. **45–47.** Leroy Buffington Collection, Northwest Architectural Archives, University of Minnesota, MN. **48,49.** Daniel H. Burnham and Edward H Bennett, *Plan of Chicago,* The Commercial Club, Chicago, 1909. Reprinted Da Capo Press, N.Y., 1970. **50,51.** *The American Architect,* CIX, June 1916, pp.412–413. **52–57.** *Competitive Drawings for the Cathedral of St. John the Divine, New York City,* Heliotype Printing Co., Boston, 189-?. **58.** *Pencil Points,* X, April 1929, pp.218–228. **59.** Photo: Brown Brothers. Courtesy John F. Harbeson, Philadelphia. **60–62.** *Pencil Points,* X, April 1929. **63,64.** Photos: Ira Wright Martin. Courtesy Haines Lundberg and Waehler, N.Y. **65–68.** Photos:Brown Brothers. Courtesy John F. Harbeson, Philadelphia. **69,70.** Haines Lundberg and Waehler, N.Y. **71–73.** Harry Singer, Tamarac, Fla. **74–86.** *Tribune Tower Competition,* The Tribune Company, Chicago, 1923. **87.** Collection Charles Cowles, N.Y. Courtesy Claes Oldenburg. **88,89.** Christo. **90,91.** Mario J. Ciampi. **92.** Munson-Williams-Proctor Institute, Utica, N.Y. **93,94.** Conklin and Rossant. **95.** James Rossant. **96–99.** *The Architectural Forum,* XLVI, March 1927, pp.202–203. **100.** *Scientific American,* July 1913, Cover. **101,102.** Jack R. Cosner. **103.** Avery Library, Columbia University, N.Y. **104,105.** Ralph Adams Cram Collection, Boston Public Library, Boston. **106,107.** *The American Architect,* CXLVII, Oct. 1935, p.32. **108–110.** Professor B. Silliman, Jr. and C. R. Goodrich, Esq., ed., *The World of Art and Industry,* C. P. Putnam and Co., N.Y., 1854, pp.1,4. **111,112.** Daniel, Mann, Johnson, and Mendenhall. **113.** Alexander Jackson Davis, *Rural Residences,* N.Y., 1837. **114,115.** The Metropolitan Museum of Art, Harris Brisbane Dick Fund, 1924, N.Y. **116,117.** *Pencil Points,* July 1932, p.507. **118,119.** The Historical Collections, MIT, Cambridge, MA. **120,121.** Juan Downey. **122–125.** Eggers and Higgins. **126, 127.** Hugh Ferriss, *The Metropolis of Tomorrow,* Ives Washburn, N.Y., 1929, pp.65,71. **128.** Avery Library,

Columbia University, N.Y. **129.** "Historical Monument of the American Republic" by Erastus Salisbury Field, The Morgan Wesson Memorial Collection, Museum of Fine Arts, Springfield, MA. **130.** Giuliano Fiorenzoli. **131.** Roger Hane, N.Y. **132,133.** R. Buckminster Fuller Archives, Philadelphia. **134.** General Electric Company, Re-Entry Systems, Philadelphia. **135–139.** Harlan Georgesco. **140.** *Pencil Points,* VIII, Oct. 1927, p.590. **141–144.** Bruce Goff. **145–147.** Bertrand Goldberg. **148.** *The American Architect and Building News,* XVIII, Sept. 1885. **149.** Avery Library, Columbia University, N.Y. **150–154.** *The American Architect and Building News,* XVIII, Sept. 1885. **155–161.** Michael Graves. **162.** G. W. Warren, *History of the Bunker Hill Monument,* R. Osgood and Co., Boston, 1877. **163.** Professor Nathalia Wright, The University of Tennessee, Knoxville. **164.** Robert Grosvenor. **165,166.** Gruen Associates, N.Y. **167.** *The Official Gazette of the U.S. Patent Office,* CXL, March 9, 1909. No. 915,026. **168.** Rafael Guastavino, Rock Hall, MD. **169–172.** Ferdinand Eiseman, Walker O. Cain Associates, N.Y. **173,174.** Richard Haas. **175,176.** Marcel Breuer. **177–184.** Lawrence Halprin and Associates. **185–188.** *Pencil Points,* VI, Nov. 1927, pp.69–86. **189–191.** Hans Hollein. **192.** Doloris Holmes. **193.** McGraw-Hill Co., N.Y. **194.** Mrs. Jean F. Leich, Cornwall Bridge, CT. **195–198.** Robert A. M. Stern, *George Howe: Toward A Modern American Architecture,* Yale University Press, New Haven, London, 1975, Figs. 75–78. Courtesy The Museum of Modern Art, N.Y. **199–203.** Photos: George Roos. Courtesy Will Insley. **204.** Burnham Library, University of Illinois Microfilming Project, Chicago. Courtesy Jensen and Halstead, Chicago. **205–209.** John Johansen. **210.** Philip Johnson & John Burgee, Architects. **211,212.** Photos:Louis Checkman, Jersey City. Courtesy Philip Johnson & John Burgee, Architects. **213.** Philip Johnson & John Burgee, Architects. **214.** The Museum of Modern Art, N.Y. **215.** Photo:George Pohl. Courtesy The Museum of Modern Art, N.Y. **216.** William Katavolos. **217,218.** Ed Kienholz. **219–225.** Courtesy Mrs. Frederick Kiesler, N.Y. **226,227.** Alison Knowles. **228–230.** Paul Laffoley. **231,232.** *The Craftsman,* VI, April 1904, pp.4–5. **233,234.** James Lambeth. **235.** Morris Lapidus Associates. **236.** Francisco Mujica, *History of the Skyscraper,* Archaeology and Architecture Press, N.Y., 1929, Plate 73. **237,238.** Paul Laszlo. **239–242.** The Library of Congress, Washington, D.C. **243,244.** John Lautner. **245–252.** Robert Le Ricolais and Alexander Messinger. **253–255.** Mimi Lobell. **256–258.** *Architectural Forum,* LXXV, Nov. 1941, p.14. **259.** Burnham Library Archive, The Art Institute of Chicago, Chicago. **260–265.** Reginald Malcolmson. **266–268.** Collection Karl Gruppe, Southold, N.Y. Courtesy Mrs. Reginald Marsh, N.Y. **269–277.** MIT Historical Collections, Cambridge, MA. **278.** Documents Collection, College of Environmental Design, University of California, Berkeley. **279.** Photo: Hedrich-Blessing, Chicago. **280,281.** Photos: Williams & Meyer Co., Chicago. **282.** Photo: Rollin R. La France. Courtesy Mitchell/Giurgola Associates. **283.** Courtesy Mitchell/Giurgola Associates. **284.** Photo: Robert M. Clements, Berkeley, **285.** Documents Collection, College of Environmental Design, University of California, Berkeley. **286.** Photo: Robert M. Clements, Berkeley, CA. **287.** Francisco Mujica, *History of the Skyscraper,* Archaeology and Architecture Press, N.Y., 1929, plates XVIII, LXXIII. **288.** *Architect and Engineer,* March 1914, p.75. **289.** Theo. H. Davies & Co., Ltd., Honolulu, Hawaii. **290,291.** *Architect and Engineer,* March 1927, pp.64,67. **292,293.** C. F. Murphy Associates. **294–296.** Photographs Courtesy Office of Richard and Dion Neutra, Los Angeles. **297.** Jean Lagarrigue, Paris. **298.** Smithsonian Institution, Washington, D.C. **299–301.** Isamu Noguchi. **302.** Claes Oldenburg. **303.** Collection Mr. and Mrs. Robert J. Woods, Jr., Rolling Hills, CA. Courtesy Claes Oldenburg. **304,305.** Claes Oldenburg. **306.** The New York Historical Society, N.Y. **307,308.** Documents Collection, College of Environmental Design, University of California, Berkeley. **309.** *American Architect and Building News,* VII, March 1880, plate 220. **310.** *American Architect and Building News,* VIII, August 1903. **311.** American Architect, LXV, Sept. 1899. **312–317.** Photos: George E. Thomas, Philadelphia. **318,319.** Harvard College Library, Department of Printing and Graphic Arts, Cambridge, MA. **320.** Harriet Monroe, *John Wellborn Root,* The Prairie School Press, Park Forest, IL., 1966, p.217.**321,322.** Burnham Library Archive, The Art Institute of Chicago, Chicago. **323.** Harriet Monroe, *John Wellborn Root,* The Prairie School Press, Park Forest, IL., 1966, p.254. **324.** Photo: Ezra Stoller, ESTO, Mamaroneck, N.Y. **325.** Paul Rudolph. **326,327.** Moshe Safdie. **328,329.** R. M. Schindler Collection, Univ. Art Galleries, Univ. of Calif., Santa Barbara. **330–333.** Charles Simonds. **334.** Franklin Webster Smith, *The Halls of the Ancients,* ca. 1897. Collection Avery Library, Columbia University. **335.** In Franklin Webster Smith, *Designs, Plans and Suggestions for the Aggrandisement of Washington,* Govt. Printing Office, Washington, D.C., 1900. **336,337.** Franklin Webster Smith, *The Halls of the Ancients,* ca. 1897. **338,339.** Franklin Webster Smith, *Design, Plans and Suggestions for the Aggrandisement of Washington,* Govt. Printing Office, Washington, D.C., 1900, plates 90, 142. **340–345.** John Weber Gallery, N.Y. **346–349.** Richard W. Snibbe. **350.** Photo:Ivan Pintar. Courtesy Paolo Soleri. **351,352.** Alan Sonfist. **353–358.** Raphael Soriano. **359–361.** Robert Stacy-Judd Collection, Univ. Art Galleries, Univ. of Calif., Santa Barbara. **362.** *The Graphic,* Dec. 19, 1891, p.405. Courtesy Chicago Historical Society, Chicago. **363.** Superstudio. **364,365.** In Stanislaw Szukalski, *Projects in Design,* The University of Chicago Press, Chicago, 1929. © 1929 The University of Chicago. **366,367.** Zabriskie Gallery, N.Y. **368–371.** Stanley Tigerman. **372,373.** William Turnbull, Jr. **374,375.** Photos: Rick Madler. Courtesy Anne Griswold Tyng. **376.** Cambridge Seven Associates, Inc. **377.** Robert Mangurian, WORKS, N.Y. **378.** Davis, Brody & Associates. **379,380.** Roger Welch. **381,382.** Friedrich St. Florian. **383–386.** Jan Wampler. **387,388.** Alan Daniel Saret. **389–393.** SITE, Inc. **394.** Jeff J. Vandeberg. **395–396.** Richard Saul Wurman. **397.** John Andrew Gallery. **398–400.** Mitchell/Giurgola Associates. **401.** Kevin Roche John Dinkeloo and Associates. **402.** Venturi and Rauch. **403,404.** Glenn Brown, *History of the United States Capitol,* U.S. Govt. Printing Office, Washington, D.C., 1900. **405,406.** Fine Arts Commission, The National Archives, Washington, D.C. **407.** The Library of Congress, Washington, D.C. **408–416.** *Report of the Committee on Plans and Architecture to the U.S. Centennial Commission,* J. B. Lippincott & Co., Philadelphia, 1873. Courtesy Archive, City of Philadelphia. **414.** Courtesy John Maass, Philadelphia. **417.** *The American Architect,* CXXXIV, Sept. 1928, p.362. **418–426.** Venturi and Rauch. **427.** Photo: George Pohl. Courtesy Venturi and Rauch. **428–431.** Venturi and Rauch. **432–435.** Konrad Wachsmann. **436,437.** Cortland Van Rensselaer, ed. *The House, the School, and the Church, The Presbyterian Education Repository,* I, Philadelphia, 1850, pp.204–208. Courtesy Presbyterian Historical Society, Philadelphia. **438.** Jasper D. Ward. **439.** Arthur F. Foran III, Philadelphia. **440–443.** Jasper D. Ward. **444,445.** The Library of Congress, Washington, D.C. **446.** *American Architect and Building News,* VII, Jan. 1880, plate 211. **447.** *American Architect and Building News,* V, Feb. 1879. **448.** *American Architect and Building News,* VI, Nov. 1879, plate 202. **449.** Claes Oldenburg. **450.** Collection Philip Johnson, New Canaan, CT. Courtesy Claes Oldenburg. **451.** The Library of Congress, Washington, D.C. **452–454.** Weidlinger Associates. **455,456.** Malcolm B. Wells. **457,458.** Allan Wexler. **459,460.** From the Collection, The Frank Lloyd Wright Foundation. Courtesy The Museum of Modern Art, N.Y. **461.** Chicago Historical Society, Chicago. **462.** Photo: Barrows. From the Collection, The Frank Lloyd Wright Foundation. Courtesy The Museum of Modern Art, N.Y. **463–466.** Lloyd Wright. **467.** Joseph Wythe. **468.** Zion & Breen Associates. **469.** NASA. Courtesy Brian O'Leary. **470.** Brian O'Leary. **471.** NASA. Courtesy Brian O'Leary. **472.** Brian O'Leary.

SELECTED BIBLIOGRAPHY

American Competitions. v. I–III. Philadelphia: T Square Club, 1907–1913.
Bell Geddes, Norman. *Horizons*. Boston: Little, Brown, and Co., 1932.
Brown, Glenn. *History of the United States Capitol*. Washington, D.C.: Government Printing Office, 1903.
Chambless, Edgar. *Roadtown*. New York: Roadtown Press, 1910.
Competitive Designs for the Cathedral of St. John the Divine. New York: Boston Heliotype Printing Co., 189-?
Conrads, Ulrich, and Sperlich, Hans G. *The Architecture of Fantasy: Utopian Building and Planning in Modern Times*. Translated, edited, and expanded by Christiane Crasemann Collins and George R. Collins. New York: Praeger Publishers, Inc., 1962.
Dahinden, Justus. *Urban Structures for the Future*. Translated by Gerald Onn. New York: Praeger Publishers, Inc., 1972.
Ferriss, Hugh. *The Metropolis of Tomorrow*. New York: Ives Washburn, Publisher, 1929.
Higgins, Richard Carter, and Vostell, Wolf. *Fantastic Architecture*. New York: Something Else Press, 1971.
Kemper, Alfred M. *Drawings by American Architects*. Associates: Sam Mori and Jacqueline Thompson. New York: Wiley, 1973.
Mujica, Francisco. *History of the Skyscraper*. New York: Archaeology and Architecture Press, 1930.
Ponten, Joseph. *Architektur die nicht gebaut wurde* (Architecture that was not Built). Stuttgart: Deutsche verlags-anstalt, 1925.
Smith, Franklin Webster. *A Design and Prospectus for a National Gallery of History and Art at Washington*. Washington, D.C.: Gibson Brothers, Printers, 1891.
Smith, Franklin Webster. *Designs, Plans, and Suggestions for the Aggrandizement of Washington*. Washington, D.C.: Government Printing Office, 1900.
Smith, Franklin Webster. *The Halls of the Ancients, 1312, 1314, 1316 and 1813 New York Avenue, Washington. Constructed by the National Galleries Company, for Promotion of National Galleries of History and Art*. Washington, D.C., 1902.
Tribune Tower Competition. Chicago: The Chicago Tribune Co., 1923.
Wright, Frank Lloyd. *The Drawings of Frank Lloyd Wright* by Arthur Drexler. New York: Published for the Museum of Modern Art by Horizon Press, 1962.

The American Architect and Building News. v. I–CLII (Jan. 1896/Feb. 1938).
Craftsman. v. I–XXXI (1901–1916).
National Institute for Architectural Education. Bulletin. v. I–XXXIX (Oct. 1924–Sept. 1963).
Pencil Points. v. I–XXVII (1920–1946).
Ragon, Michel. "Retrospective de la prospective architecturale." *Architecture: formes; functions*. v. XIV (1968).
Society of Architectural Historians. Journal. v. I (1941–).

INDEX